"Culture is everything."

— Aime Cesair

Discover the best of literary culture with Longman's Literature and Culture Series.

*T*he Longman Literature and Culture Series presents thoughtful and diverse approaches to the teaching of literature. Each of the five volumes in the series is devoted to a special topic and designed for classes ranging from composition courses with a literature emphasis to introductory courses in literature to literature courses that focus on special topics. Teaching critical analysis and critical thinking, the selections induce students to read, re-read, think, sort out ideas, and connect personal views to the explicit and implicit values expressed in the literary works.

Culture is...*Defining.*

Literature, Race, and Ethnicity
Contesting American Identities
Joseph T. Skerrett, Jr.

ISBN 0-321-01162-7

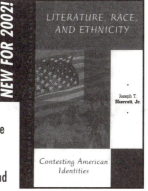

*L*iterature, Race, and Ethnicity is a text-anthology of American literature organized around problems posed for the democratic ideals of the nation by issues of race and ethnicity. Providing a broad cross-section of writers from many racial and ethnic communities, this text presents racial and ethnic identities in the context of group struggles for political and economic rights and personal, social and psychological development.

Culture is...*Representational.*

Literature, Class, and Culture: *An Anthology*
Paul Lauter and Ann Fitzgerald
ISBN 0-321-01163-5

*L*iterature, Class, and Culture is a thematic l[i]
on the consideration of class in "classless"
interdisciplinary focus, this anthology includes di[v]
selections, which call attention to the unique the[r]

Culture is... *Interactive.*

Literature and Gender: *Thinking Critically Through Fiction, Poetry, and Drama*

Robyn Wiegman and Elena Glasberg

ISBN 0-321-01260-7

*T*his innovative anthology of fiction, poetry, and drama explores the links between cultural beliefs, social institutions, sexual roles, and personal identity. Arranged around three themes of Learning, Living, and Resisting, *Literature and Gender* introduces students to current issues in literary and gender studies.

Culture is... *Controversial.*

Literature and the Environment: *A Reader on Nature and Culture*

Lorraine Anderson, Scott Slovic, and John P. O'Grady

ISBN 0-321-01149-X

*T*his thematic, multi-genre anthology explores our relationship to nature and the role literature can play in shaping a culture responsive to environmental realities. Drawing from both early writers and contemporary voices, this text deals with some of the most important and controversial issues of our historical moment.

Culture is... *Pervasive.*

Popular Fiction: *An Anthology*

Gary Hoppenstand

ISBN 0-321-01164-3

*T*his ground-breaking anthology brings together an expansive collection of historical and contemporary works of prose fiction. The text presents selections from detective, romance, adventure, horror, and science fiction, along with essays on the craft and nature of popular fiction. Additional features include an Appendix entitled "Critical Perspectives on Popular Fiction," critical biographies, and a Filmography.

To order an examination copy of any of the texts in this brochure:

- Contact your local Allyn & Bacon/Longman sales representative
- Email your request to exam.copies@ablongman.com
- Fax your request to (617) 848-7490
- Visit us on the Web at http://www.ablongman.com
- Phone us at (800) 852-8024

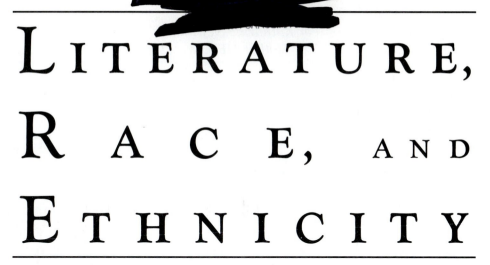

LITERATURE, RACE, AND ETHNICITY

CONTESTING AMERICAN

IDENTITIES

Joseph T. Skerrett, Jr.
University of Massachusetts at Amherst

THE LONGMAN LITERATURE AND CULTURE SERIES
General Editor: Charles I. Schuster, University of Wisconsin at Milwaukee

New York   San Francisco   Boston
London   Toronto   Sydney   Tokyo   Singapore   Madrid
Mexico City   Munich   Paris   Cape Town   Hong Kong   Montreal

For Katharine Newman,
Mother MELUS

Acquisitions Editor: Erika Berg
Associate Editor: Barbara Santoro
Supplements Editor: Donna Campion
Marketing Manager: Melanie Craig
Project Manager/Electronic Page Makeup: Dianne Hall
Cover Design Manager: Nancy Danahy
Cover Image: "America" © Diana Ong/Superstock, Inc.
Senior Manufacturing Buyer: Dennis J. Para
Printer and Binder: Maple Press
Cover Printer: The Lehigh Press, Inc.

For permission to use copyrighted material, grateful acknowledgment is made to the copyright holders on pages 559–562, which are hereby made part of this copyright page.

Library of Congress Cataloging-in-Publication Data

Literature, race, and ethnicity: contesting American identities / [edited by] Joseph T. Skerrett, Jr.
    p. cm.—(The Longman literature and culture series)
  Includes bibliographical references and index.
  ISBN 0-321-01162-7 (softcover)
    1. United States—Race relations—Sources. 2. United States—Ethnic relations—Sources. 3. Ethnicity—United States—History—Sources. 4. Pluralism (Social sciences)—United States—History—Sources. 5. United States—Race relations—Literary collections. 6. United States—Ethnic relations—Literary collections. 7. Ethnicity—United States—Literary collections. 8. Puralism (Social sciences)—United States—Literary collections. 9. American literature. I. Skerrett, Joseph T. II. Series.

E184.A1 L57 2002
305.8'00973--dc21   2001038066

Please visit our website at http://www.ablongman.com.

ISBN 0-321-01162-7

12345678910—MA—04030201

305.8
Lit

CONTENTS

PART III. RECONSTITUT(ION)ING THE NATION: PROBLEMS AND SOLUTIONS 377

FOREWORD

*If an answer does not give rise
to a new question from itself,
it falls out of the dialogue.*
—Mikhail Bakhtin

The Longman Literature and Culture Series, of which this volume is a part, presents thoughtful and diverse approaches to the teaching of literature. Each is devoted to a special topic and designed for classes ranging from composition courses with a literature emphasis to introductory courses in literature to literature courses that focus on special topics, American studies, and cultural studies. Although the selections in each volume can be considered in terms of their formal literary properties, the power of these works also derives from their ability to induce students to read, re-read, think, sort out ideas, and connect personal views to the explicit and implicit values expressed in the literary works. In this way, the Longman Literature and Culture Series teaches critical analysis and critical thinking, abilities that will serve all students well, regardless of their majors.

Popular Fiction focuses on prose fiction through the exploration of many types of fiction not ordinarily studied in the college classroom. *Literature and the Environment; Literature, Class, and Culture; Literature, Race, and Ethnicity;* and *Literature and Gender* are all multigenre, with thematic clusters of readings exploring the central topic of the individual anthologies. These thematic clusters create series of links, allusions, and inflections among a wide variety of texts, and in this way, invite students to read actively and think critically. Meaningful contexts for the readings are provided by an introduction to each volume as well as chapter introductions and headnotes for every selection. An Instructor's Manual is also available for each anthology. These anthologies can be used in combination with each other, individually, and with other texts to suit the focus of the course.

- *Popular Fiction: An Anthology*, by Gary Hoppenstand (Michigan State University), is a collection of historical and contemporary works of prose fiction, including such authors as Edgar Allan Poe, Janet Dailey, Tony Hillerman, Walter Mosely, Stephen King, and Octavia Butler, representing five popular genres: detective, romance, adventure, horror, and science fiction.

- *Literature and the Environment: A Reader on Nature and Culture*, by Lorraine Anderson, Scott Slovic (University of Nevada, Reno), and John P. O'Grady (Boise State University), is a thematic multigenre anthology that explores our relationship to nature and the role literature can play in shaping a culture responsive to environmental realities. It includes early writers such as John Muir, Henry David Thoreau, and Mary Austin, alongside contemporary voices such as Gary Snyder and Terry Tempest Williams.

- *Literature, Class, and Culture: An Anthology*, by Paul Lauter (Trinity College) and Ann Fitzgerald (American Museum of Natural History), is a consideration of class in "classless" America, including such authors as Edith Wharton, F. Scott Fitzgerald, Woody Guthrie, Alice Childress, Jimmy Santiago Baca, and Dorothy Allison. The selections allow students to better understand their own economic, political, and psychological contexts through learning about the ways in which social class and "class consciousness" have been experienced and changed over time in America.

- *Literature, Race, and Ethnicity: Contesting American Identities*, by Joseph T. Skerrett, Jr. (University of Massachusetts at Amherst), invites students to examine the history, depth, and persistence of the complex cultural attitudes toward race and ethnicity in America. The selections span from the late 1700s to the present, including a variety of genres—poems, letters, fiction, autobiography, essays, speeches, advertisements, and historical documents—with works by such writers as Thomas Jefferson, Frederick Douglass, Jacob Riis, Henry James, Langston Hughes, Maxine Hong Kingston, Constantine Panunzio, Lorna Dee Cervantes, Lawson Inada, and Louise Erdrich.

- *Literature and Gender: Thinking Critically Through Fiction, Poetry, and Drama*, by Robyn Wiegman (University of California, Irvine) and Elena Glasberg (California State University, Los Angeles), assembles a provocative array of literary texts by such writers as Charlotte Perkins Gilman, Ernest Hemingway, Adrienne Rich, Tobias Wolff, Sherman Alexie, and Rita Dove, which explore the links between cultural beliefs, social institutions, sexual roles, and personal identity.

Although no single anthology, or series for that matter, can address the full complexity of literary expression, these anthologies do hope to engage students in the critical process of analysis by connecting literary texts to current social and cultural debates. In addition, these anthologies frame literature in pedagogically innovative ways, ways that will enable those students who find literature difficult to read, who think meaning is somehow locked inside a text, to critically engage with issues of interpretation, biography, and context. In this way, students begin to see that literature is a cultural expression that emerges from a complex consideration of and response to the world they share with the writers they read.

Very often, literary texts invite discussion in the classroom of explosive issues, provoking students to argue about the sexism of a short story or the racism expressed by a character. These anthologies, however, encourage students to take a step backward so that they can interrogate the cultural contexts of diverse works of literature. This shift away from the personal and toward the cultural should invite thoughtful and considered classroom discussion. Once students perceive this cultural frame, they will be better able to engage with texts, to see them as both profound expressions of the ordinary and eloquent achievements written by real people living in real time.

In addition, no set of anthologies can hope to resolve completely what is intended by the two central terms that anchor this discussion: "literature" and "culture." One of the most exciting contemporary discussions in English departments today centers on the very definition of literature: what it is, what it excludes, and what makes it work. If figuring out what we mean by "the literary" is difficult, determining the definition of "culture" is probably impossible. Like "nature," a term that John Stuart Mill analyzed over a hundred years ago, "culture" seems to designate everything or nothing at all. Is it something we make or does it make us? Is culture a neutral term designating human social activity, or something akin to class and status, a quality that marks you as either refined or vulgar, well-bred or common?

Not that we presume to have the correct answers or even all the appropriate questions. We realize that both the questions and the answers will be tentative and exploratory. Literature, it seems to all of us involved in this series, demands a willingness to maintain uncertainty, to probe multiple possibilities. It invites analysis and demands interpretation. It provokes conversations. This is the intention of the Longman Literature and Culture Series: to invite readings and rereadings of texts and contexts, of literature within the cultural and culture within the literary. Rather than answers, these anthologies pose questions and invitations.

Crafted to the vision of the individual editors, *Popular Fiction; Literature and the Environment; Literature, Class, and Culture; Literature, Race, and Ethnicity;* and *Literature and Gender* present an extraordinary range of material in such a way as to unsettle previous readings and provoke new ones. We hope the Longman Literature and Culture Series provides a welcoming invitation to all students to see that literature is deeply reflective of the fabric of everyday life.

CHARLES I. SCHUSTER
General Editor
University of Wisconsin at Milwaukee

ACKNOWLEDGMENTS

This project could not have been completed without the help of many friends, students, and colleagues. Many thanks to Charles Moran for guiding me through the mysteries of word processing; to Gretchen Papazian at the University of Wisconsin at Milwaukee, and to Robert Hayashi and Angelo Robinson at the University of Massachusetts at Amherst, for research on the headnotes for individual entries; and to Arlene Rodriguez for providing key texts and sound advice. I am also indebted to Wendy Bergoffen and Chris Vails at the University of Massachusetts at Amherst for help with a difficult case. Thanks to Karen Rubin at the University of Massachusetts at Amherst and to Todd Gernes at Providence College for helping me to pin down permissions. Thanks also to the anonymous readers who made many useful suggestions for changes to the original plans. Thanks to my friends and colleagues at the University of Massachusetts at Amherst—Jules Chametzky, Arlyn Diamond, Ron Welburn, Randall Knoper, Margo Culley, and Mason Lowance—for support and suggestions. I am grateful for similar support and suggestions from my colleagues in MELUS, the Society for the Study of the Multi-Ethnic Literature of the United States, in particular my friends John Lowe at Louisiana State University, James R. Payne at New Mexico State University, and Amritjit Singh at Rhode Island College. Thanks are due to the series editor, Charles Schuster, for his encouragement and hands-on help. I thank my succession of editors—Kathryn Glynn, Lisa Moore, Ruth Halikman, Liza Rudneva, and Erika Berg—for the patience and prodding that were needed to bring this project to a satisfactory conclusion. Thanks also to Chrysta Meadowbrooke for her brilliant copyediting.

The editors would like to thank the reviewers of the manuscript and a number of other colleagues who contributed substantially to creating this book. They include: Hester Blum, University of Pennsylvania; Janelle Collins, Arkansas State University; Kathleen Dixon, University of North Dakota; Mark Eaton, Oklahoma City University; Vince Grotera, University of Northern Iowa; Sandra Gunning, University of Michigan, Ann Arbor; William R. Handley, University of California, Los Angeles; Wilma H. Hasse, Mitchell College; Katherine Kinney, University of California, Riverside; Peggy J. Oliver, San Jacinto College South; Gretchen Ronnow, Wayne State University; Bruce Simon, Princeton University; Michael Shapiro, University of Illinois; and Gladys J. Willis, Lincoln University.

INTRODUCTION

Why is identity—the feeling of relatedness, membership, and acceptance—so problematic in these United States? As one citizen famously asked, "Why can't we all get along?" While struggles for national unity and identity do also take place in other countries—China, Brazil, Mexico, and, lately, the United Kingdom offer depressing examples—issues of identity revolving around questions of race and ethnicity seem particularly powerful in the United States. In recent years conflicts over affirmative action, immigration, and bilingual education have aroused loud and often angry debate. Because these issues are often perceived as challenging national values like liberty and equality, they are politically and culturally potent. Large portions of the populations are uncomfortable because they see the question of "American identity" as a question already answered. In effect, they see American values like racial and social equity as achieved. Others acknowledge the unfinished nature of American democracy, viewing such values as goals rather than achievements. Wishing race and ethnicity not to matter, as both groups do, these citizens often deny the reports of immigrants and citizens who experience the sometimes painful ways in which both matter considerably.

Most white Americans do not experience race or ethnicity as defining elements of their lives. They assume that "whiteness" is normal and synonymous with "American" and that members of other racial groups are abnormal exceptions. Nor do they remember the interactions with Native Americans, Africans, and Asians that have shaped national values and styles, defining the American food, American music, and American English that they take for granted. As generation succeeds generation, the ethnic component of white identity—Frenchness, Irishness, Germanness—slips steadily away, reduced, in many cases, to a few scraps of language, items of cuisine, and family stories. Further, as individuals marry outside their own ethnic groups, they come to see their ethnicity (and that of others) as a matter of choice, celebrating multiple ethnic identities by attending symbolic events like St. Patrick's Day and

Columbus Day parades. This weakening of ethnic commitment and identification in the white majority renders it less able to understand either the commitment to ethnicity on the part of some new immigrant groups or the resentment of people of color at their entrapment in a definition—"race"—that they never made.

These kinds of conflicts raise significant questions about our society. What, in fact, do we have in common with one another? If race and ethnicity are complex and powerful forces in the American imagination, how have they shaped "the common culture"? What does it mean to consider American identity from the point of view of a Cherokee housewife, a Japanese immigrant farmer, a Jewish-American soldier? How will we be changed by hearing these voices? How will new voices in the American chorus—Arab restauranteurs, computer scientists from India and Russia, African and Caribbean filmmakers—change the tune? The struggle among these various groups of citizens is a struggle to define the reality of what it means to be an American. An effort to understand the tangle of ideas involved in this contestation requires us to look back at the origins of the terms of dispute.

Race and Ethnicity in the New World

Race and ethnicity have always been important components of the American experience. From the moment Columbus landed in the Caribbean, the encounter between the New World and the Old was an encounter between and among peoples who were acutely aware of their physical, linguistic, and religious differences. The interaction of European settlers, enslaved Africans, and the more than 500 nations of pre-Columbian America during the Spanish expansion and conquest shaped all of the nations of the New World. Like the Spanish, British colonists came to North America with a sense of themselves—an identity—that would be profoundly changed by their interactions with the indigenous Americans, the slaves the colonists imported from Africa, and other immigrants from Europe. Later, with increasingly intense impact, new shaping influences would arrive in the form of immigrants from other parts of the world—Asia, the Caribbean, and South America.

The New World had been a site—in fact, many sites—of contestation long before the colonists of British North America declared their independence. The native population struggled among themselves over land and resources even before the Spanish conquistadores arrived in Mexico and the Caribbean islands early in the sixteenth century. And these same Spanish (and Portuguese) conquerors very early on introduced Africans into the lands they had "discovered" and claimed for their homelands; at least one of Columbus's sailors was an African. When their efforts to convert the Native populations into a colonial workforce failed because the Native Americans had no immunities to infectious diseases carried by the Europeans, they imported Africans to serve as slave labor. Decades later, when colonies were established in the new territory claimed by England, the British settlers quickly adopted the practice of importing Africans as workers. Although they at first resisted the idea of the Africans as a permanent hereditary slave population, this pattern was established in the laws of most of the colonies before the turn of the eighteenth century. Equally well established by then was the pattern of resistance and self-assertion on the part of Natives and slaves, who both fought and fled for their freedom. The struggle of the Native peoples and the African slaves for human equality within the societies of colonial America is thus the first story of contested American identity.

British colonial settlers came to Virginia and Massachusetts in the early seventeenth century with a secure identity that was primarily religious and national. They were English Christians gathered in communities for "commonweal": the communal good or welfare. In the case of the Massachusetts Bay colonists, the common good extended back across the ocean to their English countrymen, for whom they wished to provide in their "city upon a hill" an example of a godly Protestant community. Others were defined in terms of language and nationality—French, Dutch, Italian—and whether they were within or outside the Christian community. Their vision of the world divided humans into two significant groups: Christians and infidels. They carried with them to the New World a sense of superiority that they shared with other European Christians, but not a sense of European "racial" superiority. They did not believe their bodies were inherently superior; they believed the conditions of their baptized souls to be superior to that of the unredeemed "savages" they encountered in Africa and America.

While the peoples of the earth have always distinguished Us from Them, they have only rather lately used "race"—a set of physical characteristics presumed to be shared and inherited by a human group—to describe and categorize communities. The American colonists reinforced the Christian/infidel differences between themselves and the Africans and Native Americans by developing sets of attitudes toward the non-European body. Europeans, who in earlier times had acknowledged the "civilization" of non-Europeans such as the Moors who ruled most of Spain from the seventh through the thirteenth centuries, denied the humanity of the indigenous American population and the imported African population on the grounds that they were not white people, and thus were inferior. Europeans in the New World, who had thought of themselves as English, French, or Spanish Christians, became "white" people as a response to their encounter with and domination of unfamiliar peoples of color. Inventing a hierarchy of peoples helped them to justify their oppressive treatment of both Natives and slaves. The association of darker skin with evil, stupidity, and incapacity became a frame of reference for relations among these groups, defining "whiteness" as a quality of the settlers that clearly implied a metaphysical superiority. Physical difference was thus constructed as an unchangeable barrier between hierarchically arranged "racial" communities. Race further served as a means for the leadership class to divide working-class Europeans from the Africans and Natives: "whiteness" served as a status gift that prevented the poor and the successive waves of immigrants from uniting with the Africans and Indians against their common oppressors.

The conflicts among Europeans in America were not racial but political. Europeans came from Spain, France, England, the Netherlands, and Sweden to found the colonies in the New World during the seventeenth and eighteenth centuries. As English political power grew through the same periods, many of these colonies—like Dutch New Amsterdam, annexed in 1664, and French Quebec, conquered in 1759—were absorbed into British North America. The differences between the English settlers and the other Euro-Americans were ethnic differences, differences of language, customs, sometimes religion, and national history. Not marked by bodily features like skin color, these ethnic differences were from early on considered either circumstantial and mutable or irrelevant. As Crèvecoeur noted in the 1780s, the colonist in New Sweden or New Amsterdam could change his political allegiance, change his name, adopt a new language, and become a British American in short order.

Defining Race and Identity

After the United Colonies became the United States of America and won its freedom from England, the problem of defining who was an American continued to involve questions of race and ethnicity. Common notions of racial distinction, based on presumedly obvious differences in nose and eye shape, skin color, and hair texture, circulated then as they do today. Among the common people, these were the terms that defined the most significant difference among human groups.

The denial of human equality to African slaves was at first justified on religious grounds. Africans were considered descendants of Ham, the son of Noah in the book of Genesis, who sinfully looked on his father's drunken nakedness and was condemned to be "a servant of servants . . . unto his brethren." The interpreters of Genesis 9:25 decided that the Africans were marked by God with their dark color as a sign of divine disapproval. It was but a small step from this to excluding the "sons of Ham" from the human family. They were not only unredeemed heathens, they were accursed of God, fit only for bondage and servitude.

Beginning in the late eighteenth century, scientists, theologians, and philosophers in Europe and America speculated upon whether the physical differences marked between the races separated them into different species. These speculators are divisible into two groups: The monogenists viewed all of humankind as having a single origin and thus the same human qualities; the polygenists saw each of the races as having separate origins and thus different and distinctive qualities. Some among the polygenists saw non-Europeans as not only inferior in their skills and abilities but also as not actually fully human. If red Indians and black Africans were not fully human, it was easier to justify the oppressive treatment meted out to them by white Europeans and Americans. The monogenists, including theologians (who objected to the polygenists' disregard of the monogenetic Biblical story of human origin) and scientists like Charles Darwin (whose studies rejected the significance of racial differences in biology) won this debate, but not before decades of pseudo-scientific and pseudo-anthropological disputation had permanently clouded American discourse about the races.

Another important element in the ongoing discussion of race and ethnicity in America throughout the nineteenth century was both biological and historical. The theory of national traits proposed that every identifiable group (often referred to as "races" in this discourse) exhibited specific and identifying characteristics. In this frame of thinking, British and American democratic political institutions can be traced back to the Anglo-Saxon election of kings. Political freedom and a spirit of independence was thus seen as an imperative of the Anglo-Saxon "race." Similarly, the Spanish and Italians, the "Latin races," were seen as passive or impotent in politics as a result of the shaping influence of a hierarchical Roman Catholicism long since cast off by the British descendants of the Anglo-Saxons. The theory of national traits became part of American thinking about both race and ethnicity. Many of the stereotypes of race and ethnicity familiar to us today were codified in the nineteenth century by theorists of national traits. Images of thrifty Scots, amorous French, drunken Irish, feckless Negroes, and devious Chinese derive in part from the idea that people manifest different virtues or vices as a product of descent or heredity.

During the early twentieth century a new approach to race and ethnicity, based on the developing science of anthropology led by scholars like Franz Boas, focused on culture, the expression of group identity in observable social and human attitudes, values, and experiences. Avoiding speculation as to origins, Boas and his disciples considered human groups scientifically, by close observation of the group as a cultural system. They rejected the idea that the physical differences used to define the races marked any significant or distinctive qualities, abilities, or handicaps, and they called for scientific evidence from those who insisted that race markers were indicators of intelligence or imagination. In their view, the Irish or Navahos were who they were because of the interactions of language, religion, customs, communal history, and social organization. Under the influence of this new cultural anthropology, the study of race and ethnicity considered issues such as the survival in America of African languages, values and religion among Native Americans, and the differences between generations of Italian-American immigrants.

In recent years, the understanding of race has turned on the concept of power relations. Peoples and nations with military, technological, and political power, the colonizers in the expanding empires of "white" Europe, got to define the colonized and did so in terms that they then installed in law and custom, which was thereafter disseminated and enforced.

From the perspective of the twenty-first century, we can see that racial difference was—and remains—a social construction, an idea manipulated by various forces and institutions to maintain the hierarchy established by conquest, enslavement, and colonization. The emphasis placed upon physical differences between peoples was always to the benefit of the dominant white European (or American) no matter what theory of racial difference was employed. To be perceived as standing outside the defining circle of "whiteness" was to be discriminated against, considered a second-class human being, or not human at all. In the United States, political, religious, and social institutions, ranging from employment to education, were all shaped around ideas of race superiority and inferiority that privileged whiteness and oppressed non-whites. Further, the analysis of power relations illuminates the impact of racial and ethnic minorities of the relentless argument for white superiority that dominates American culture. Over the course of American history non-white people were so relentlessly battered with images and arguments of white superiority and their own inferiority that they came to believe it (or some portions of it) to be true. Having internalized this pervasive sense of their own inadequacy, physical and intellectual, they became complicitous with their oppression, self-censoring and limiting themselves to conform with the majority's idea of them.

Of course, not all members of minority groups succumbed to this hegemonic relationship to their own oppression, nor did those who did succumb accept the projected images of their dependence, incapacity, or inferiority completely or uniformly.

Nation/Self/Identity

The United States of America is a nation founded not upon a shared ethnic identity, but upon a set of political and social principles. Despite the fact that eight out of ten white citizens in 1790 were of British descent, the new nation was not oriented around some reconstruction of the Britain/colony relationship. The documents that initiated the United States's sense of itself—the Declaration of Independence, the Constitution, and the Bill of Rights—conceived of the new nation in terms of ideology. The new United States defined itself by its commitment to "life, liberty, and the pursuit of happiness," equality of citizens before the law, and government at the consent of the governed. The interaction between these ideas and citizens' common experiences, including ideas, events, and realities such as the denial of citizenship to Native Americans and African slaves that negated or compromised those ideals, determines the "American identity." The psychoanalyst Erik Erikson describes the impact of this interaction: "A nation's identity is derived from the ways in which history has, as it were, counterpointed certain opposite potentialities, the ways in which it lifts this counterpoint to a unique style of civilization, or lets it disintegrate into mere contradiction" (*Identity: Youth and Crisis*, 19). The struggle to live up to the ideals expressed in or implied by our foundation documents, the struggle to avoid "mere contradiction" in public and private life, thus structures American national identity.

In William James's formulation, individuals recognize their identity in the moment when they most clearly understand who they are in relation to their memory of the personal past and potential personal future. "A man's character is discernible in the mental or moral attitude in which, when it came upon him, he felt himself most deeply and intensely alive. At such moments there is a voice inside which speaks and says 'This is the real me'" (*Correspondence*, Volume One, 199). The American ideal of "citizen" is the person who recognizes in a moment of public or personal crisis his or her true self and then acts to advance the national ideas of liberty, equality, and the right to human happiness and to defeat contradictory practices. Examples can be found in every human arena and in every period of United States history, from abolitionists to Civil War soldiers, from politicians who supported civil rights legislation to baseball players who welcomed non-white players like Jackie Robinson and Roberto Clemente, from the women who organized unions of immigrant seamstresses and housekeepers to students who supported the organization of Chicano farm labor by boycotting produce. Whether through actions political or personal, the pitfalls of "mere contradiction" are eliminated by the involvement of citizens who most deeply "identify" with democratic values, who feel most intensely alive in connecting themselves to the best the United States has been or may become.

Ethnicity and Identity

For members of ethnic and racial communities, identity in America is doubly determined. Like all Americans, members of these groups measure themselves against the national ideals and define themselves as citizens both desirous of and worthy of the blessings of American liberty. Members of ethnic groups have always been quick to respond to challenges to American democratic ideals. But at the same time, they must also measure themselves against the yardsticks provided by their ethnic communities. Issues of conformity with and assimilation into American customs with regard to food, language, marriage, and so forth vary from group to group but concern all. Every ethnic community has a sense of itself borne across the oceans or borders from the old countries to the new situation. Ceasing to be Irish or Jewish or Syrian or Japanese is never completely possible for the immigrant, even as he or she wholeheartedly embraces the ideals of American democracy. For both ethnic and racialized Americans, citizenship can be a complex psychological position. Ethnic and racialized identities are double identities and subject to strain, division, and confusion from within.

At the same time that the ethnic and racialized citizen must manage the double pressures to maintain an acceptable community identity and to be or become a satisfactory American, he or she also must cope with the judgments of fellow citizens who consider him or her "a problem of democracy." This is especially true for African Americans, as the African-American philosopher Alain Locke noted in *The New Negro* in 1925:

> For generations in the mind of America, the Negro himself has been more of a formula than a human being—a something to be argued about, condemned or defended, to be "kept down," or "in his place," or "helped up," to be worried with or worried over, harassed or patronized, a social bogey or a social burden.

As W. E. B. Du Bois remarked in *The Souls of Black Folk* in 1903, "Being a problem is a strange experience." But being a problem is part of the historical experience of American racial and ethnic groups, whether they are Norwegian immigrants, Mexican braceros, or newly freed Africans. The discourse of American social life is filled with documents and expressions of racial and ethnic definition drawn by the majority. The experience of being thus both subject and object in the struggle for American identity is a special burden of the minority citizen.

Literature and Racial Identity

The struggles for self-definition are both embodied and recorded in literature, art, music, and other forms of cultural expression. The pictures we make (or take); the novels and poems we read; the songs, jokes, and stories we hear; and the movies we see draw from and add to the stock of images of Americans engaged in expressing the national character or identity. Literature and the arts are the records of our feelings about experience: the artist is engaged in putting experience into an order that is personal but not private, an order or form that can be shared with others—viewers, readers, audiences. This personal, artistic order may engage public experience or draw from public history, using historical events, persons, and documents to frame or flavor the work. A tension exists here for the artist who is, as noted earlier, charged with maintaining allegiance to the truths of his or her ethnic community. For artists who are members of racial or ethnic communities, public sources and artistic traditions are often absent, distorted, or actively devoted to demonizing their communities. They must also cope with writing or art or music purportedly about their ethnic communities by ignorant or hostile majority artists, which further distorts and demonizes the community. For this reason much of what they write draws rather from the pool of communal memory, the ethnic community's alternative history and interpretation of events, recorded in folktales, ballads, fugitive documents, and oral performances.

Writers and scholars of American literature have variously noted the importance of the ethnic subject. In *Beyond Ethnicity: Consent and Descent in American Culture*, Werner Sollors revised the marginalization of ethnic writing: "Though it is often regarded a very minor adjunct to great American mainstream writing, ethnic literature is, as several readers pointed out in the past, prototypically American literature". William Boelhower (*Through a Glass Darkly*) and others have explored the concept of "ethnogenesis"—the development of ethnic consciousness—as a defining aspect of the development of American culture. Novelist Toni Morrison, in her essay "Unspeakable Things Unspoken: The Afro-American Presence in American Literature," asserted that to recognize and study African-American literature—and I would include all ethnic literature—"is to examine centers of the self and to have the opportunity to compare these centers with the 'raceless' one with which we are, all of us, most familiar". Turning the critical tables, she also called for scholarly attention to be given to the implications of the absence or avoidance of African-American experience in mainstream writing, to the way that American literature has been shaped by fear of confronting the full and equal humanity of people of color.

"Ethnic literature"—writing by members of racial and ethnic groups—like its authors, exists in a complex and often turbulent relationship with writing by majority writers. Ethnic writers feel compelled to revise the negative, distorted, or merely inaccurate images of their communities composed by generations of outsiders. Aware that their audience is a double one, consisting of both members and nonmembers of the group, they find themselves in the position of interpreter, not only telling a tale but also pointing out the meaning of gestures, manners, verbal expressions, and so forth for the often clueless majority reader or reader from another ethnic group.

The artist's conception of the ethnic self or community is very likely to differ from the stereotypes and cliches of the majority discourse, but it may also differ from the group's preferred self-image. The ethnic artist struggles, frequently, between majority and community definitions of the "essential" African-American, or Ojibway, or Puerto Rican self to establish his or her own vision of a human response to particular experiences. Communities invested in essentialist views of their unchanging nature, for example, resist the work of authors who focus on alternative views. Communities that resist assimilation, seeing in it a source of disintegration and loss of ethnic values, may similarly reject the work of writers who focus on subjects like ethnically mixed marriages or criticisms of group attitudes and mores.

THE CONCEPT
OF THIS BOOK

Literature, Race, and Ethnicity: Contesting American Identities aims to make visible in literature, art, popular culture, political documents, and journalism some of the ways in which the definition of who is an American has been struggled over and is still being struggled over. Rather than papering over and repressing differences between groups and histories of oppression, this book will attempt to put some of them into a context for reading, discussion, and writing. Toward achieving that goal, it assembles a wide range of materials, covering a historical spectrum from the late eighteenth century, when our foundation documents were written, to the late twentieth century, when we were becoming aware that the future is likely to radically change the relations between and among citizens of color, immigrant citizens, and the white majority.

There is much to be gained by examining the tensions and conflicts in the discourse about American identity as it is expressed in texts—fiction, poetry, essays, drama, treaties, presidential executive orders, letters, public laws, song lyrics, cartoons, art, advertisements, and journalism—by and/or about members of racial and ethnic groups. Bringing these tensions and conflicts into more legible relief may help us as a society to move more deliberately toward their resolution. This book presents visual and verbal texts that connect to one another, developing a commentary on themes and currents within the issues of race and ethnicity. *Literature, Race, and Ethnicity: Contesting American Identities* will help students to see and understand the history, depth, and persistence of the complex cultural attitudes toward race and ethnicity in America. It is intended to make the reader draw further connections between his or her own experiences and the conflicts illuminated by the chosen texts. Studying from this book will enable students not only to appreciate strong and beautiful works of visual and verbal art but also to participate in the ongoing contestations of American identity: President Clinton's commission on racial reconciliation, "English only" debates and legislation, immigration reform,

mixed race categories for the U.S. Census, and debates over interracial and intereth-
nic dating and marriage.

Some problems are inherent to the construction of a book like this. While one
would like to be comprehensive and include representation of every American ethnic group, space does not permit that. Only a very few of the hundreds of Native
American communities are represented here, and only a half dozen or so of the
European immigrant communities that have become an equally essential element of
American culture. The flow of the text is roughly historical, but this is not a history
of ethnic literature. Within the historical frame, the book focuses on selected issues
and themes of ethnic relations. The selection of the issues has been made in part
with the intention of demonstrating that progress in racial and ethnic relations is
neither impossible nor inevitable, but rather advances or retards according to the
involvement of committed citizens interacting with large economic and social
forces. Nor is this book a celebration of "ethnic diversity," allowing the majority
reader to explore the quaint and colorful ways of life of people unlike himself or
herself. Indeed, locating the majority in this text is a final problem. "White" America, of course, plays a very significant role in defining racial and ethnic groups, often
oppressively. While that history is acknowledged here, this book intends to compli-
cate the reader's view of the white majority not only by considering white ethnicities but also by considering some views of the ostensibly "raceless" assimilated
Euro-American population.

The items selected for inclusion in this book all meet three general criteria. First,
the works of literature and art are generally accepted as reflecting superior talent
and craftsmanship. While the writers presented here may not all be well known,
their work is of the highest quality. Second, the text presents works that are easily
accessible, avoiding texts with specialized or technical vocabularies. Wherever possible, works are presented in their entirety, avoiding especially excerpts from novels. Third, all of the items, visual or verbal, literary or documentary, connect clearly
to the theme of the unit in which they appear.

I

FRAMING THE PEOPLE: DEFINITIONS AND CONTESTATIONS

The new nation, the United States of America, promised an open society, a community where the individual could create a life not dependent on the status or occupation or wealth of ancestors. From early on in the existence of the republic, its citizens believed that they could achieve personal, financial, and spiritual freedom by the strength of their own efforts. But this possibility was not without cost. It depended considerably upon Native land and African labor, for example. The incorporation of former French, Spanish, and Mexican territories through the Louisiana Purchase of 1804, the annexation of Florida in 1819, and the Mexican War of 1846; the assimilation of formerly French, German, Swedish, and Dutch inhabitants of British North America; and the absorption of later arrivals from Germany, Ireland, and elsewhere in Europe prior to the Civil War expanded the scope of the struggle for an American identity. These new citizens and immigrant citizens-to-be had to find a place for themselves, and they usually struck an implicit bargain in which they traded elements of their ethnic identity, such as language, for social mobility and status. The struggle for social mobility brought them into conflict not only with the mass of formerly British Americans but also with one another. The struggle for status brought them into conflict with the Natives and the Africans, who occupied the lowest status ranks in the society, a position against which the immigrant ethnic might measure his or her own standing.

The three sections of Part I map some of these conflicts between American values and American realities through public documents, imaginative literature, oratory, and graphic art.

1

VALUES:
INVITATIONS AND
EXCLUSIONS

Values: Invitations and Exclusions sets statements of national values, like the Declaration of Independence, against items that fill out their generalizations, like the Immigration Act of 1790. It demonstrates how "the American people" are defined not only by acts of inclusion and invitation to Europeans but also by acts of rejection and exclusion of Natives, Asians, and Africans.

The Declaration of Independence, signed by the members of the Continental Congress on July 4, 1776, is a bold statement of the values underlying the colonists' break with the mother country. It stands in contrast to the ideas of human inequality expressed by its principal author, Thomas Jefferson, in his *Notes on the State of Virginia*. It is useful to measure the values presented in the Declaration also with laws established within twenty years to restrict immigration to the new country to whites only. In Benjamin Franklin's essay addressed to "such as would remove to America" we can hear the voice of capitalism as a basic American value. Franklin's cautions contrast with the famous optimism of the third of Hector St. John de Crèvecoeur's *Letters from an American Farmer*, which addresses itself directly to who and what the new "Americans" thought themselves to be. The former Europeans, native or immigrant, increasingly defined themselves against their sense of the others, the outsiders, *Them*. Both Natives—who they had but recently termed "Americans" in contrast to the Englishmen they had now ceased to be—and Africans were generally excluded from conceptions of the new nation. Works by Frances Harper and Frederick Douglass represent the efforts of African Americans—whose ancestors had been removed to America—to write themselves into the nation. The Natives were repeatedly driven off land the United States had agreed was theirs as white settlers and entrepreneurs coveted its natural resources. Native writers and orators, like Red Jacket, addressed the hypocrisy of American Christianity and egalitarianism in the face of these oppressive tactics. All of the texts in this first section provide insights into how the newly post-colonial nation conceived of itself and how it behaved toward outsiders and newcomers.

The Declaration
of Independence

The first document of the new nation is an explanation of the conflict in values that led to the break with Great Britain. It was created by a committee of the Continental Congress that included Thomas Jefferson and John Adams, but it seems most clearly indebted to the ideas of Jefferson, who was well read in British and Continental philosophy. In explaining why the colonists were breaking their political connection to the mother country, the Declaration affirms the idea of a social contract—the idea that governments derive their authority from the consent of the governed—rather than absolute monarchical power or social-class organization as the organizing principle of civil society, a concept drawn largely from British philosopher John Locke. Aware that their actions would be considered treasonous, the signers were eager to portray themselves as the rational victims of a rapacious and irrational government. They wished to find a middle way between the violence and regicide of the English Civil War of the 1640s and the Bloodless Revolution of 1688, which merely substituted one monarch for another. Revisions to the committee's draft led to the exclusion of arguments against slavery, thus further blunting the edge of the document's contemporary radicalism. The Declaration's assertion that "all men are created equal" is undercut by its silence on the issue of slavery, which was at the moment under attack by many British and American clergy and politicians. Throughout the nineteenth century many citizens worked to eliminate the contradiction between these political and social ideas and the practices of American society, abolishing slavery and extending the vote to women. The struggle to square the reality of American political and social life with the principles of the Declaration continues in the twenty-first century, as immigrants, the handicapped, and homosexuals argue for their inclusion in the national identity.

In the long run, many would argue, it is the substitution of "the pursuit of happiness" for "property" as a key term of the social contract that makes the Declaration a defining document of our society.

The Unanimous Declaration of the
Thirteen United States of America

July 4, 1776

When, in the course of human events, it becomes necessary for one people to dissolve the political bonds which have connected them with another, and to assume among the powers of the earth, the separate and equal station to which the laws of nature and of nature's God entitle them, a decent respect to the opinions of mankind requires that they should declare the causes which impel them to the separation.

We hold these truths to be self-evident, that all men are created equal, that they are endowed by their Creator with certain unalienable rights, that among these are life, liberty and the pursuit of happiness. That to secure these rights, governments are instituted among men, deriving their just powers from the consent of the governed. That whenever any form of government becomes destructive to these ends, it is the right of the people to alter or to abolish it, and to institute new government, laying its foundation on such principles and organizing its powers in such form, as to them shall seem most likely to effect their safety and happiness. Prudence, indeed, will dictate that governments long established should not be changed for light and transient causes; and accordingly all experience hath shown that mankind are more disposed to suffer, while evils are sufferable, than to right themselves by abolishing the forms to which they are accustomed. But when a long train of abuses and usurpations, pursuing invariably the same object evinces a design to reduce them under absolute despotism, it is their right, it is their duty, to throw off such government, and to provide new guards for their future security.—

Such has been the patient sufferance of these colonies; and such is now the necessity which constrains them to alter their former systems of government. The history of the present King of Great Britain is a history of repeated injuries and usurpations, all having in direct object the establishment of an absolute tyranny over these states. To prove this, let facts be submitted to a candid world.

He has refused his assent to laws, the most wholesome and necessary for the public good.

He has forbidden his governors to pass laws of immediate and pressing importance, unless suspended in their operation till his assent should be obtained; and when so suspended, he has utterly neglected to attend to them.

He has refused to pass other laws for the accommodation of large districts of people, unless those people would relinquish the right of representation in the legislature, a right inestimable to them and formidable to tyrants only.

He has called together legislative bodies at places unusual, uncomfortable, and distant from the depository of their public records, for the sole purpose of fatiguing them into compliance with his measures.

He has dissolved representative houses repeatedly, for opposing with manly firmness his invasions on the rights of the people.

He has refused for a long time, after such dissolutions, to cause others to be elected; whereby the legislative powers, incapable of annihilation, have returned to the people at large for their exercise; the state remaining in the meantime exposed to all the dangers of invasion from without, and convulsions within.

He has endeavored to prevent the population of these states; for that purpose obstructing the laws for naturalization of foreigners; refusing to pass others to encourage their migration hither, and raising the conditions of new appropriations of lands.

He has obstructed the administration of justice, by refusing his assent to laws for establishing judiciary powers.

He has made judges dependent on his will alone, for the tenure of their offices, and the amount and payment of their salaries.

He has erected a multitude of new offices, and sent hither swarms of officers to harass our people, and eat out their substance.

He has kept among us, in times of peace, standing armies without the consent of our legislature.

He has affected to render the military independent of and superior to civil power.

He has combined with others to subject us to a jurisdiction foreign to our constitution, and unacknowledged by our laws; giving his assent to their acts of pretended legislation:

- For quartering large bodies of armed troops among us:
- For protecting them, by mock trial, from punishment for any murders which they should commit on the inhabitants of these states:
- For cutting off our trade with all parts of the world:
- For imposing taxes on us without our consent:
- For depriving us in many cases, of the benefits of trial by jury:
- For transporting us beyond seas to be tried for pretended offenses:
- For abolishing the free system of English laws in a neighboring province, establishing therein an arbitrary government, and enlarging its boundaries so as to render it at once an example and fit instrument for introducing the same absolute rule in these colonies:
- For taking away our charters, abolishing our most valuable laws, and altering fundamentally the forms of our governments:
- For suspending our own legislatures, and declaring themselves invested with power to legislate for us in all cases whatsoever.

He has abdicated government here, by declaring us out of his protection and waging war against us.

He has plundered our seas, ravaged our coasts, burned our towns, and destroyed the lives of our people.

He is at this time transporting large armies of foreign mercenaries to complete the works of death, desolation and tyranny, already begun with circumstances of cruelty and perfidy scarcely paralleled in the most barbarous ages, and totally unworthy the head of a civilized nation.

He has constrained our fellow citizens taken captive on the high seas to bear arms against their country, to become the executioners of their friends and brethren, or to fall themselves by their hands.

He has excited domestic insurrections amongst us, and has endeavored to bring on the inhabitants of our frontiers, the merciless Indian savages, whose known rule of warfare, is undistinguished destruction of all ages, sexes and conditions.

[In Jefferson's draft there is a part on slavery here.]

In every stage of these oppressions we have petitioned for redress in the most humble terms: our repeated petitions have been answered only by repeated injury. A prince, whose character is thus marked by every act which may define a tyrant, is unfit to be the ruler of a free people.

Nor have we been wanting in attention to our British brethren. We have warned them from time to time of attempts by their legislature to extend an unwarrantable jurisdiction over us. We have reminded them of the circumstances of our emigration and settlement here. We have appealed to their native justice and magnanimity, and we have conjured them by the ties of our common kindred to disavow these usurpations, which, would inevitably interrupt our connections and correspondence. We must, therefore, acquiesce in the necessity, which denounces our separation, and hold them, as we hold the rest of mankind, enemies in war, in peace friends.

We, therefore, the representatives of the United States of America, in General Congress, assembled, appealing to the Supreme Judge of the world for the rectitude of our intentions, do, in the name, and by the authority of the good people of these colonies, solemnly publish and declare, that these united colonies are, and of right ought to be free and independent states; that they are absolved from all allegiance to the British Crown, and that all political connection between them and the state of Great Britain, is and ought to be totally dissolved; and that as free and independent states, they have full power to levy war, conclude peace, contract alliances, establish commerce, and to do all other acts and things which independent states may of right do. And for the support of this declaration, with a firm reliance on the protection of Divine Providence, we mutually pledge to each other our lives, our fortunes and our sacred honor.

JOHN HANCOCK, President

Attested, CHARLES THOMSON, Secretary

New Hampshire
    JOSIAH BARTLETT
    WILLIAM WHIPPLE
    MATTHEW THORNTON

Massachusetts-Bay
    SAMUEL ADAMS
    JOHN ADAMS
    ROBERT TREAT PAINE
    ELBRIDGE GERRY

Rhode Island
    STEPHEN HOPKINS
    WILLIAM ELLERY

Connecticut
    ROGER SHERMAN
    SAMUEL HUNTINGTON
    WILLIAM WILLIAMS
    OLIVER WOLCOTT

Georgia
    BUTTON GWINNETT
    LYMAN HALL
    GEO. WALTON

Maryland
    SAMUEL CHASE
    WILLIAM PACA
    THOMAS STONE
    CHARLES CARROLL OF CARROLLTON

Virginia
    GEORGE WYTHE
    RICHARD HENRY LEE
    THOMAS JEFFERSON
    BENJAMIN HARRISON
    THOMAS NELSON, JR.
    FRANCIS LIGHTFOOT LEE

Virginia *continued*
    CARTER BRAXTON

New York
    WILLIAM FLOYD
    PHILIP LIVINGSTON
    FRANCIS LEWIS
    LEWIS MORRIS

Pennsylvania
    ROBERT MORRIS
    BENJAMIN RUSH
    BENJAMIN FRANKLIN
    JOHN MORTON
    GEORGE CLYMER
    JAMES SMITH
    GEORGE TAYLOR
    JAMES WILSON
    GEORGE ROSS

Delaware
    CAESAR RODNEY
    GEORGE READ
    THOMAS M'KEAN

North Carolina
    WILLIAM HOOPER
    JOSEPH HEWES
    JOHN PENN

South Carolina
    EDWARD RUTLEDGE
    THOMAS HEYWARD, JR.
    THOMAS LYNCH, JR.
    ARTHUR MIDDLETON

New Jersey
    RICHARD STOCKTON
    JOHN WITHERSPOON
    FRANCIS HOPKINS
    JOHN HART
    ABRAHAM CLARK

THOMAS JEFFERSON
(1743-1826)

Thomas Jefferson, third president of the United States of America and the writer of the American Declaration of Independence, was born April 13, 1743, in Shadwell, Virginia. His father died when Jefferson was fourteen, leaving him an estate of over 2,700 acres and numerous slaves. He attended the College of William and Mary and was admitted to the bar in 1767. He served in Virginia's House of Burgesses from 1769 until the start of the Revolution. During this time, he wrote what was to become one of his most influential political pieces: "A Summary View of the Rights of British America." In it he argued for an end to British taxation and a commercial agreement between England and the colonies based on trade. Many have suggested that the other representatives at the Second Continental Congress asked Jefferson to write the Declaration of Independence based on the rhetorical strengths of this earlier piece. Jefferson also drafted several versions of a constitution for the state of Virginia and served as Governor of Virginia from 1779 to 1781.

In 1781, he retired to his self-designed home, Monticello, where he worked on Notes on the State of Virginia. *This book, which was written in response to a set of questions asked by a French diplomat about Virginia and America generally, provides a view into eighteenth-century modes of scientific observation and factual details about life in colonial America (religion, race, politics, geography, manners, industry, commerce, and culture), as well as the distortion and prejudice that were an essential part of American life.*

In 1783, Jefferson was elected to Congress and his voluntary retirement ended. He served as minister to France, Secretary of State (under Washington), and eventually President (1800–1808). He retired again to Monticello in 1809, and died there on July 4, 1826.

FROM NOTES ON THE
STATE OF VIRGINIA

Many of the laws which were in force during the monarchy being relative merely to that form of government, or inculcating principles inconsistent with republicanism, the first assembly which met after the establishment of the commonwealth appointed a committee to revise the whole code, to reduce it into proper form and volume, and report it to the assembly. This work has been executed by three gentlemen, and reported; but probably will not be taken up till a restoration of peace shall leave to the legislature leisure to go through such a work.

The plan of the revisal was this. The common law of England, by which is meant, that part of the English law which was anterior to the date of the oldest statutes extant, is made the basis of the work. It was thought dangerous to attempt to reduce it to a text: it was therefore left to be collected from the usual monuments of it. Necessary alterations in that, and so much of the whole body of the British statutes, and of acts of assembly, as were thought proper to be retained, were digested into 126 new acts, in which simplicity of stile was aimed at, as far as was safe. The following are the most remarkable alterations proposed:

To change the rules of descent, so as that the lands of any person dying intestate shall be divisible equally among all his children, or other representatives, in equal degree.

To make slaves distributable among the next of kin, as other moveables.

To have all public expences, whether of the general treasury, or of a parish or county, (as for the maintenance of the poor, building bridges, court-houses, &c.) supplied by assessments on the citizens, in proportion to their property.

To hire undertakers for keeping the public roads in repair, and indemnify individuals through whose lands new roads shall be opened.

To define with precision the rules whereby aliens should become citizens, and citizens make themselves aliens.

To establish religious freedom on the broadest bottom.

To emancipate all slaves born after passing the act. The bill reported by the revisors does not itself contain this proposition; but an amendment containing it was prepared, to be offered to the legislature whenever the bill should be taken up, and further directing, that they should continue with their parents to a certain age, then be brought up, at the public expence, to tillage, arts or sciences, according to their geniusses, till the females should be eighteen, and the males twenty-one years of age, when they should be colonized to such place as the circumstances of the time should render most proper, sending them out with arms, implements of houshold and of the handicraft arts, feeds, pairs of the useful domestic animals, &c. to declare them a free and independent people, and extend to them our alliance and protection, till they shall have acquired strength; and to send vessels at the same time to other parts of the world for an equal number of white inhabitants; to induce whom to migrate hither, proper encouragements were to be proposed. It will probably be asked, Why not retain and incorporate the blacks into the state, and thus save the expence of supplying, by importation of white settlers, the vacancies they will leave? Deep rooted prejudices entertained by the whites; ten thousand recollections, by the blacks, of the injuries they have sustained; new provocations; the real distinctions which nature has made; and many other circumstances, will divide us into parties, and produce convulsions which will probably never end but in the extermination of the one or the other race.—To these objections, which are political, may be added others, which are physical and moral. The first difference which strikes us is that of colour. Whether the black of the negro resides in the reticular membrane between the skin and scarf-skin, or in the scarf-skin itself; whether it proceeds from the colour of the blood, the colour of the bile, or from that of some other secretion, the difference is fixed in nature, and is as real as if its seat and cause were better known to us. And is this difference of no importance? Is it not the foundation of a greater or less share of beauty in the two races? Are not the fine mixtures of red and white, the expressions of every passion by greater or less suffusions of colour in the one, preferable to that eternal monotony, which reigns in the countenances, that immoveable veil of black which covers all the emotions of the other race? Add to these, flowing hair, a more elegant symmetry of form, their own judgment in favour of the whites, declared by their preference of them, as uniformly as is the preference of the Oranootan for the black women over those of his own species. The circumstance of superior beauty, is thought worthy attention in the propagation of our horses, dogs, and other domestic animals; why not in that of man? Besides those of colour, figure, and hair, there are other physical distinctions proving a difference of race. They have less hair on the face and body. They secrete less by the kidnies, and more by the glands of the skin, which gives them a very strong and disagreeable odour. This greater degree of transpiration renders them more tolerant of heat, and less so of cold, than the whites. Perhaps too a difference of structure in the pulmonary apparatus, which a late ingenious experimentalist* has discovered to be the principal regulator of animal heat, may have disabled them from extricating, in the act of inspiration, so much of that fluid from the outer air, or obliged them in expiration, to part with more of it. They seem to require less sleep. A black, after hard labour through the day, will be induced by the slightest amusements to sit up till midnight, or later, though knowing he must be out with the first dawn of the morning. They are at least as brave, and more adventuresome. But this may perhaps proceed from a want of forethought, which prevents their seeing a danger till it be present. When present, they do not go through it with more coolness or steadiness than the whites. They are more ardent after their female: but love seems with them to be more an eager desire, than a tender delicate mixture of sentiment and sensation. Their griefs are transient. Those numberless afflictions, which render it doubtful whether heaven has given life to us in mercy or in wrath, are less felt, and sooner forgotten with them. In general, their existence appears to participate more of sensation than reflection. To this must be ascribed their disposition to sleep when abstracted from their diversions, and unemployed in labour. An animal whose body is at rest, and who does not reflect, must be disposed to sleep of course. Comparing them by their faculties of memory, reason, and imagination, it appears to me, that in memory they are equal to the whites; in reason much inferior, as I think one could scarcely be found capable of tracing and comprehending the investigations of Euclid; and that in imagination they are dull, tasteless, and anomalous. It would be unfair to follow them to Africa for this investigation. We will consider them here, on the same stage with the whites, and where the facts are not apocryphal on which a judgment is to be formed. It will be right to make great allowances for the difference of condition, of education, of conversation, of the sphere in which they move. Many millions of them have been brought to, and born in America. Most of them indeed have been confined to tillage, to their own homes, and their own society: yet many have been so situated, that they might have availed themselves of the conversation of their masters; many have been brought up to the handicraft arts, and from that circumstance have always been associated with the whites. Some have been liberally educated, and all have lived in countries where the arts and sciences are cultivated to a considerable degree, and have had before their eyes samples of the best works from abroad. The Indians, with no advantages of this kind, will often carve figures on their pipes not destitute of design and merit. They will crayon out an animal, a plant, or a country, so as to prove the existence of a germ in their minds which only wants cultivation. They astonish you with strokes of the most sublime oratory; such as prove their reason and sentiment strong, their imagination glowing and elevated. But never yet could I find that a black had uttered a thought above the level of plain narration; never see even an elementary trait of painting or sculpture. In music they are more generally gifted than the whites with accurate ears for tune

---

*Crawford

and time, and they have been found capable of imagining a small catch.* Whether they will be equal to the composition of a more extensive run of melody, or of complicated harmony, is yet to be proved. Misery is often the parent of the most affecting touches in poetry.—Among the blacks is misery enough, God knows, but no poetry. Love is the peculiar œstrum of the poet. Their love is ardent, but it kindles the senses only, not the imagination. Religion indeed has produced a Phyllis Whately; but it could not produce a poet. The compositions published under her name are below the dignity of criticism. The heroes of the Dunciad are to her, as Hercules to the author of that poem. Ignatius Sancho has approached nearer to merit in composition; yet his letters do more honour to the heart than the head. They breathe the purest effusions of friendship and general philanthropy, and shew how great a degree of the latter may be compounded with strong religious zeal. He is often happy in the turn of his compliments, and his stile is easy and familiar, except when he affects a Shandean fabrication of words. But his imagination is wild and extravagant, escapes incessantly from every restraint of reason and taste, and, in the course of its vagaries, leaves a tract of thought as incoherent and eccentric, as is the course of a meteor through the sky. His subjects should often have led him to a process of sober reasoning: yet we find him always substituting sentiment for demonstration. Upon the whole, though we admit him to the first place among those of his own colour who have presented themselves to the public judgment, yet when we compare him with the writers of the race among whom he lived, and particularly with the epistolary class, in which he has taken his own stand, we are compelled to enroll him at the bottom of the column. This criticism supposes the letters published under his name to be genuine, and to have received amendment from no other hand; points which would not be of easy investigation. The improvement of the blacks in body and mind, in the first instance of their mixture with the whites, has been observed by every one, and proves that their inferiority is not the effect merely of their condition of life. We know that among the Romans, about the Augustan age especially, the condition of their slaves was much more deplorable than that of the blacks on the continent of America. The two sexes were confined in separate apartments, because to raise a child cost the master more than to buy one. Cato, for a very restricted indulgence to his slaves in this particular, †took from them a certain price. But in this country the slaves multiply as fast as the free inhabitants. Their situation and manners place the commerce between the two sexes almost without restraint.—The same Cato, on a principle of œconomy, always sold his sick and superannuated slaves. He gives it as a standing precept to a master visiting his farm, to sell his old oxen, old waggons, old tools, old and diseased servants, and every thing else become useless. 'Vendat boves vetulos, plaustrum vetus, ferramenta vetera, servum senem, servum morbosum, & si quid aliud supersit vendat.' Cato de re rusticâ. c. 2. The American slaves cannot enumerate this among the injuries and insults they receive. It was the common practice to expose in the island of Æsculapius, in the Tyber, diseased slaves, whose cure was like to become tedious. The Emperor Claudius, by an edict, gave freedom to such of them as should recover, and first declared, that if any person chose to kill rather than to expose them, it

---

*The instrument proper to them is the Banjar, which they brought hither from Africa, and which is the original of the guitar, its chords being precisely the four lower chords of the guitar.

†Τὂς δὂλὂς εταξεν ὡρισμενὂ νομισματος ὁμιλειν ταις θεραπαινισιν.

should be deemed homicide. The exposing them is a crime of which no instance has existed with us; and were it to be followed by death, it would be punished capitally. We are told of a certain Vedius Pollio, who, in the presence of Augustus, would have given a slave as food to his fish, for having broken a glass. With the Romans, the regular method of taking the evidence of their slaves was under torture. Here it has been thought better never to resort to their evidence. When a master was murdered, all his slaves, in the same house, or within hearing, were condemned to death. Here punishment falls on the guilty only, and as precise proof is required against him as against a freeman. Yet notwithstanding these and other discouraging circumstances among the Romans, their slaves were often their rarest artists. They excelled too in science, insomuch as to be usually employed as tutors to their master's children. Epictetus, Terence, and Phædrus, were slaves. But they were of the race of whites. It is not their condition then, but nature, which has produced the distinction.— Whether further observation will or will not verify the conjecture, that nature has been less bountiful to them in the endowments of the head, I believe that in those of the heart she will be found to have done them justice. That disposition to theft with which they have been branded, must be ascribed to their situation, and not to any depravity of the moral sense. The man, in whose favour no laws of property exist, probably feels himself less bound to respect those made in favour of others. When arguing for ourselves, we lay it down as a fundamental, that laws, to be just, must give a reciprocation of right: that, without this, they are mere arbitrary rules of conduct, founded in force, and not in conscience: and it is a problem which I give to the master to solve, whether the religious precepts against the violation of property were not framed for him as well as his slave? And whether the slave may not as justifiably take a little from one, who has taken all from him, as he may slay one who would slay him? That a change in the relations in which a man is placed should change his ideas of moral right and wrong, is neither new, nor peculiar to the colour of the blacks. Homer tells us it was so 2600 years ago.

Ἥμιου, γαζ τ᾽ ἀρετῆς ἀποαίνυ]αι εὐρύθπα Ζεὺς
Ἀνερος, ευτ᾽ ἄν μιν κατὰ δδλιον ἥμαζ ἕλησιν.

Od. 17. 323.

Jove fix'd it certain, that whatever day
Makes man a slave, takes half his worth away.

But the slaves of which Homer speaks were whites. Notwithstanding these considerations which must weaken their respect for the laws of property, we find among them numerous instances of the most rigid integrity, and as many as among their better instructed masters, of benevolence, gratitude, and unshaken fidelity.— The opinion, that they are inferior in the faculties of reason and imagination, must be hazarded with great diffidence. To justify a general conclusion, requires many observations, even where the subject may be submitted to the Anatomical knife, to Optical glasses, to analysis by fire, or by solvents. How much more then where it is a faculty, not a substance, we are examining; where it eludes the research of all the senses; where the conditions of its existence are various and variously combined; where the effects of those which are present or absent bid defiance to calculation; let me add too, as a circumstance of great tenderness, where our conclusion would degrade a whole race of men from the rank in the scale of beings which their Creator may perhaps have given them. To our reproach it must be said, that though for a century and a half we have had under our eyes the races of black and of red men, they have never yet been viewed by us as subjects of natural history. I advance it therefore as a suspicion only, that the blacks, whether originally a distinct race, or made distinct by time and circumstances, are inferior to the whites in the endowments both of body and mind. It is not against experience to suppose, that different species of the same genus, or varieties of the same species, may possess different qualifications. Will not a lover of natural history then, one who views the gradations in all the races of animals with the eye of philosophy, excuse an effort to keep those in the department of man as distinct as nature has formed them? This unfortunate difference of colour, and perhaps of faculty, is a powerful obstacle to the emancipation of these people. Many of their advocates, while they wish to vindicate the liberty of human nature, are anxious also to preserve its dignity and beauty. Some of these, embarrassed by the question 'What further is to be done with them?' join themselves in opposition with those who are actuated by sordid avarice only. Among the Romans emancipation required but one effort. The slave, when made free, might mix with, without staining the blood of his master. But with us a second is necessary, unknown to history. When freed, he is to be removed beyond the reach of mixture.

HECTOR ST. JOHN
DE CRÈVECOEUR
(1735-1813)

Michel Guillaume Jean de Crèvecoeur was born into a landholding but not wealthy family in Caen, France, in 1735. After finishing his education at the age of nineteen he enlisted in the French army, first going to England and later to Canada, where he served as a surveyor and cartographer during the French and Indian War. After his discharge in 1759, Crèvecoeur worked as a trader and surveyor, traveling extensively from Maine to Virginia, then westward to Detroit, St. Louis, and Chicago. In 1765 he became a naturalized citizen, taking the name James Hector St. John de Crèvecoeur, and buying land to farm in New York.

In 1778, in the midst of uncertainties generated by the American Revolutionary War, he returned to France. Detained in New York City by British forces, he finally arrived in England in 1781. While there, he sold to a publisher a collection of short pieces in the form of letters. These twelve essays, published as Letters from an American Farmer *in 1782, celebrate the everyday experiences of an American farmer and the opportunities offered by the American colonies to immigrants like himself.*

Crèvecoeur published the Letters *in France as* Lettres d'un Cultivateur Américain *in 1784, to great acclaim, and returned to America in 1783 as a French consul, friend to Thomas Jefferson and Benjamin Franklin. After his retirement, he published a second volume of essays,* Voyage dans la Haute

Pennsylvania et dans l'état de New-York (Journey into Northern Pennsylvania and the State of New York).

Over 100 years after his death, a series of unpublished essays were found among the Crèvecoeur family papers; they were published in 1925 as Sketches of Eighteenth Century America.

LETTERS FROM AN AMERICAN FARMER

LETTER III
WHAT IS AN AMERICAN?

I wish I could be acquainted with the feelings and thoughts which must agitate the heart and present themselves to the mind of an enlightened Englishman, when he first lands on this continent. He must greatly rejoice that he lived at a time to see this fair country discovered and settled. He must necessarily feel a share of national pride when he views the chain of settlements which embellish these extended shores. When he says to himself, this is the work of my countrymen, who, when convulsed by factions, afflicted by a variety of miseries and wants, restless and impatient, took refuge here. They brought along with them their national genius, to which they principally owe what liberty they enjoy and what substance they possess. Here he sees the industry of his native country displayed in a new manner, and traces, in their works, the embryos of all the arts, sciences, and ingenuity, which flourish in Europe. Here he beholds fair cities, substantial villages, extensive fields, an immense country filled with decent houses, good roads, orchards, meadows, and bridges, where, a hundred years ago, all was wild, woody, and uncultivated! What a train of pleasing ideas this fair spectacle must suggest! It is a prospect which must inspire a good citizen with the most heartfelt pleasure! The difficulty consists in the manner of viewing so extensive a scene. He is arrived on a new continent: a modern society offers itself to his contemplation, different from what he had hitherto seen. It is not composed, as in Europe, of great lords who possess every thing, and of a herd of people who have nothing. Here are no aristocratical families, no courts, no kings, no bishops, no ecclesiastical dominion, no invisible power giving to a few a very visible one, no great manufactures employing thousands, no great refinements of luxury. The rich and the poor are not so far removed from each other as they are in Europe. Some few towns excepted, we are all tillers of the earth, from Nova Scotia to West Florida. We are a people of cultivators, scattered over an immense territory, communicating with each other by means of good roads and navigable rivers, united by the silken bands of mild government, all respecting the laws, without dreading their power, because they are equitable. We are all animated with the spirit of an industry which is unfettered and unrestrained, because each person works for himself. If he travels through our rural districts, he views not the hostile castle and the haughty mansion contrasted with the clay-built hut and miserable cabin, where cattle and men help to keep each other warm, and dwell in meanness, smoke, and indigence. A pleasing uniformity of decent competence appears throughout our habitations. The meanest of our log-houses is a dry and comfortable habitation.

Lawyer or merchant are the fairest titles our towns afford: that of a farmer is the only appellation of the rural inhabitants of our country. It must take some time ere he can reconcile himself to our dictionary, which is but short in words of dignity and names of honour. There, on a Sunday, he sees a congregation of respectable farmers and their wives, all clad in neat homespun, well mounted, or riding in their own humble waggons. There is not among them an esquire, saving the unlettered magistrate. There he sees a parson as simple as his flock, a farmer who does not riot on the labour of others. We have no princes, for whom we toil, starve, and bleed. We are the most perfect society now existing in the world. Here man is free as he ought to be; nor is this pleasing equality so transitory as many others are. Many ages will not see the shores of our great lakes replenished with inland nations, nor the unknown bounds of North America entirely peopled. Who can tell how far it extends? Who can tell the millions of men whom it will feed and contain? for no European foot has, as yet, travelled half the extent of this mighty continent.

The next wish of this traveller will be, to know whence came all these people? They are a mixture of English, Scotch, Irish, French, Dutch, Germans, and Swedes. From this promiscuous breed, that race, now called Americans, have arisen. The Eastern provinces must indeed be excepted, as being the unmixed descendents of Englishmen. I have heard many wish that they had been more intermixed also: for my part, I am no wisher, and think it much better as it has happened. They exhibit a most conspicuous figure in this great and variegated picture. They too enter for a great share in the pleasing perspective displayed in these thirteen provinces. I know it is fashionable to reflect on them, but I respect them for what they have done; for the accuracy and wisdom with which they have settled their territory; for the decency of their manners; for their early love of letters; their antient college, the first in this hemisphere; for their industry; which to me, who am but a farmer, is the criterion of every thing. There never was a people, situated as they are, who, with so ungrateful a soil, have done more in so short a time. Do you think that the monarchical ingredients, which are more prevalent in other governments, have purged them from all foul stains? Their histories assert the contrary.

In this great American asylum, the poor of Europe have by some means met together, and in consequence of various causes. To what purpose should they ask one another what countrymen they are? Alas, two thirds of them had no country. Can a wretch, who wanders about, who works and starves, whose life is a continual scene of sore affliction or pinching penury; can that man call England or any other kingdom his country? A country that had no bread for him; whose fields procured him no harvest; who met with nothing but the frowns of the rich, the severity of the laws, with jails and punishments; who owned not a single foot of the extensive surface of this planet. No! Urged by a variety of motives here they came. Every thing has tended to regenerate them. New laws, a new mode of living, a new social system. Here they are become men. In Europe they were as so many useless plants, wanting vegetative mould and refreshing showers. They withered; and were mowed down by want, hunger, and war; but now, by the power of transplantation, like all other plants, they have taken root and flourished! Formerly they were not numbered in any civil lists of their country, except in those of the poor: here they rank as citizens. By what invisible power hath this surprising metamorphosis been performed? By that of the laws and that of their industry. The laws, the indulgent laws, protect them as they arrive, stamping on them the symbol of adoption: they receive ample rewards for their labours: these accumulated rewards procure them lands: those lands confer on them the title of freemen, and to that title every benefit is affixed which men can possibly require. This is the great operation daily performed by our laws. Whence proceed these laws? From our government. Whence that government? It is derived from the original genius and strong desire of the people ratified and confirmed by the crown. This is the great chain which links us all; this is the picture which every province exhibits, Nova Scotia excepted. There the crown has done all. Either there were no people who had genius, or it was not much attended to. The consequence is, that the province is very thinly inhabited indeed. The power of the crown, in conjunction with the musketoes, has prevented men from settling there. Yet some parts of it flourished once, and it contained a mild harmless set of people. But, for the fault of a few leaders, the whole was banished. The greatest political error, the crown ever committed in America, was, to cut off men from a country which wanted nothing but men.

What attachment can a poor European emigrant have for a country where he had nothing? The knowledge of the language, the love of a few kindred as poor as himself, were the only cords that tied him. His country is now that which gives him his land, bread, protection, and consequence. *Ubi panis ibi patria* is the motto of all emigrants. What then is the American, this new man? He is neither an European, nor the descendent of an European: hence that strange mixture of blood, which you will find in no other country. I could point out to you a family, whose grandfather was an Englishman, whose wife was Dutch, whose son married a French woman, and whose present four sons have now four wives of different nations. He is an American, who, leaving behind him all his antient prejudices and manners, receives new ones from the new mode of life he has embraced, the new government he obeys, and the new rank he holds, He becomes an American by being received in the broad lap of our great *alma mater.* Here individuals of all nations are melted into a new race of men, whose labours and posterity will one day cause great changes in the world. Americans are the western pilgrims, who are carrying along with them that great mass of arts, sciences, vigour, and industry, which began long since in the east. They will finish the great circle. The Americans were once scattered all over Europe. Here they are incorporated into one of the finest systems of population which has ever appeared, and which will hereafter become distinct by the power of the different climates they inhabit. The American ought therefore to love this country much better than that wherein either he or his forefathers were born. Here the rewards of his industry follow, with equal steps, the progress of his labour. His labour is founded on the basis of nature, *self-interest:* can it want a stronger allurement? Wives and children, who before in vain demanded of him a morsel of bread, now, fat and frolicksome, gladly help their father to clear those fields whence exuberant crops are to arise, to feed and to clothe them all, without any part being claimed, either by a despotic prince, a rich abbot, or a mighty lord. Here religion demands but little of him; a small voluntary salary to the minister, and gratitude to God: can he refuse these? The American is a new man, who acts upon new principles; he must therefore entertain new ideas and form new opinions. From involuntary idleness, servile dependence, penury, and useless labour, he has passed to toils of a very different nature, rewarded by ample subsistence.—This is an American.

British America is divided into many provinces, forming a large association, scattered along a coast of 1500 miles extent and about 200 wide. This society I would fain examine, at least such as it appears in the middle provinces; if it does not afford that variety of tinges and gradations which may be observed in Europe, we have colours peculiar to ourselves. For instance, it is natural to conceive that those who live near the sea must be very different from those who live in the woods: the intermediate space will afford a separate and distinct class.

Men are like plants. The goodness and flavour of the fruit proceeds from the peculiar soil and exposition in which they grow. We are nothing but what we derive from the air we breathe, the climate we inhabit, the government we obey, the system of religion we profess, and the nature of our employment. Here you will find but few crimes; these have acquired as yet no root among us. I wish I were able to trace all my ideas. If my ignorance prevents me from describing them properly, I hope I shall be able to delineate a few of the outlines, which is all I propose.

Those, who live near the sea, feed more on fish than on flesh, and often encounter that boisterous element. This renders them more bold and enterprising: this leads them to neglect the confined occupations of the land. They see and converse with a variety of people. Their intercourse with mankind becomes extensive. The sea inspires them with a love of traffic, a desire of transporting produce from one place to another; and leads them to a variety of resources, which supply the place of labour. Those who inhabit the middle settlements, by far the most numerous, must be very different. The simple cultivation of the earth purifies them; but the indulgences of the government, the soft remonstrances of religion, the rank of independent freeholders, must necessarily inspire them with sentiments very little known in Europe among a people of the same class. What do I say? Europe has no such class of men. The early knowledge they acquire, the early bargains they make, give them a great degree of sagacity. As freemen they will be litigious. Pride and obstinacy are often the cause of law-suits; the nature of our laws and governments may be another. As citizens, it is easy to imagine that they will carefully read the newspapers, enter into every political disquisition, freely blame, or censure, governors and others. As farmers, they will be careful and anxious to get as much as they can, because what they get is their own. As northern men, they will love the cheerful cup. As Christians, religion curbs them not in their opinions: the general indulgence leaves every one to think for themselves in spiritual matters. The law inspects our actions; our thoughts are left to God. Industry, good living, selfishness, litigiousness, country politics, the pride of freemen, religious indifference, are their characteristics. If you recede still farther from the sea, you will come into more modern settlements: they exhibit the same strong lineaments in a ruder appearance. Religion seems to have still less influence, and their manners are less improved.

Now we arrive near the great woods, near the last inhabited districts. These men seem to be placed still farther beyond the reach of government, which, in some measure, leaves them to themselves. How can it pervade every corner, as they were driven there by misfortunes, necessity of beginnings, desire of acquiring large tracks of land, idleness, frequent want of œconomy, antient debts. The reunion of such people does not afford a very pleasing spectacle. When discord, want of unity and friendship, when either drunkenness or idleness, prevail in such remote districts, contention, inactivity, and wretchedness, must ensue. There are not the same remedies to these evils as in a long-established community. The few magistrates they have are, in general, little better than the rest. They are often in a perfect state of war; that of man against man; sometimes decided by blows, sometimes by means of the law: that of man against every wild inhabitant of these venerable woods, of which they are come to dispossess them. There men appear to be no better than carnivorous animals, of a superior rank, living on the flesh of wild animals when they can catch them, and, when they are not able, they subsist on grain. He, who would wish to see America in its proper light, and to have a true idea of its feeble beginnings and barbarous rudiments, must visit our extended line of frontiers, where the last settlers dwell, and where he may see the first labours of settlement, the mode of clearing the earth, in all their different appearances. Where men are wholly left dependent on their native tempers and on the spur of uncertain industry, which often fails when not sanctified by the efficacy of a few moral rules. There, remote from the power of example and check of shame, many families exhibit the most hideous parts of our society. They are a kind of forlorn hope, preceding, by ten or twelve years, the most respectable army of veterans which come after them. In that space, prosperity will polish some, vice and the law will drive off the rest, who, uniting again with others like themselves, will recede still farther, making room for more industrious people, who will finish their improvements, convert the log-house into a convenient habitation, and, rejoicing that the first heavy labours are finished, will change, in a few years, that hitherto-barbarous country into a fine, fertile, well-regulated, district. Such is our progress, such is the march of the Europeans toward the interior parts of this continent. In all societies there are off-casts. This impure part serves as our precursors or pioneers. My father himself was one of that class; but he came upon honest principles, and was therefore one of the few who held fast. By good conduct and temperance he transmitted to me his fair inheritance, when not above one in fourteen of his contemporaries had the same good fortune.

Forty years ago this smiling country was thus inhabited. It is now purged. A general decency of manners prevails throughout, and such has been the fate of our best countries.

Exclusive of those general characteristics, each province has its own, founded on the government, climate, mode of husbandry, customs, and peculiarity of circumstances. Europeans submit insensibly to these great powers, and become, in the course of a few generations, not only Americans in general, but either Pennsylvanians, Virginians, or provincials, under some other name. Whoever traverses the continent must easily observe those strong differences which will grow more evident in time. The inhabitants of Canada, Massachuset, the middle provinces, the southern ones, will be as different as their climates. Their only points of unity will be those of religion and language.

As I have endeavoured to shew you how Europeans became Americans, it may not be disagreeable to shew you likewise how the various Christian sects introduced wear out, and how religious indifference becomes prevalent. When any considerable number of a particular sect happen to dwell contiguous to each other, they immediately erect a temple, and there worship the Divinity agreeably to their own peculiar ideas. Nobody disturbs them. If any new sect springs up in Europe, it may happen that many of its professors will come and settle in America. As they bring their zeal with them, they are at liberty to make proselytes if they can, and to build a meeting, and to follow the dictates of their consciences; for neither the government nor any other power interferes. If they are peaceable subjects, and are industrious, what is it to their neighbours how and in what manner they think fit to address their prayers to the Supreme Being? But, if the sectaries are not settled close together, if they are mixed with other denominations, their zeal will cool for want of fuel, and will be extinguished in a little time. Then the Americans become, as to religion what they are as to country, allied to all. In them the name of Englishman, Frenchman, and European, is lost, and, in like manner, the strict modes of Christianity, as practised in Europe, are lost also. This effect will extend itself still farther hereafter, and, though this may appear to you as a strange idea, yet it is a very true one. I shall be able perhaps hereafter to explain myself better; in the mean while, let the following example serve as my first justification.

Let us suppose you and I to be travelling. We observe that in this house, to the right, lives a Catholic, who prays to God as he has been taught, and believes in transubstantiation. He works and raises wheat, he has a large family of children, all hale and robust. His belief, his prayers, offend nobody. About one mile farther, on the same road, his next neighbour may be a good honest plodding German Lutheran, who addresses himself to the same God, the God of all, agreeably to the modes he has been educated in, and believes in consubstantiation; by so doing he scandalizes nobody. He also works in his fields, embellishes the earth, clears swamps, &c. What has the world to do with his Lutheran principles? He persecutes nobody, and nobody persecutes him; he visits his neighbours, and his neighbours visit him. Next to him lives a Seceder, the most enthusiastic of all sectaries; his zeal is hot and fiery; but, separated as he is from others of the same complexion, he has no congregation of his own to resort to, where he might cabal and mingle religious pride with worldly obstinacy. He likewise raises good crops, his house is handsomely painted, his orchard is one of the fairest in the neighbourhood. How does it concern the welfare of the country, or of the province at large, what this man's religious sentiments are, or really whether he has any at all? He is a good farmer, he is a sober, peaceable, good, citizen. William Penn himself would not wish for more. This is the visible character; the invisible one is only guessed at, and is nobody's business. Next again lives a Low Dutchman, who implicitly believes the rules laid down by the synod of Dort. He conceives no other idea of a clergyman than that of a hired man. If he does his work well he will pay him the stipulated sum; if not, he will dismiss him, and do without his sermons, and let his church be shut up for years. But, notwithstanding this coarse idea, you will find his house and farm to be the neatest in all the country; and you will judge, by his waggon and fat horses, that he thinks more of the affairs of this world than of those of the next. He is sober and laborious, therefore he is all he ought to be as to the affairs of this life; as for those of the next, he must trust to the great Creator. Each of these people instruct their children as well as they can, but these instructions are feeble compared to those which are given to the youth of the poorest class in Europe. Their children will therefore grow up less zealous and more indifferent in matters of religion than their parents. The foolish vanity, or rather the fury of making proselytes, is unknown here: they have no time: the seasons call for all their attention; and thus, in a few years, this mixed neighbourhood will exhibit a strange religious medley, that will be neither pure Catholicism nor pure Calvinism. A very perceptible indifference, even in the first generation, will become apparent; and it may happen that the daughter of the Catholic will marry the son of the Seceder, and settle by themselves at a distance from their parents. What religious education will they give their children? A very imperfect one. If there happens to be in the neighbourhood any place of worship, we will suppose a Quaker's meeting, rather than not shew their fine clothes, they will go to it, and some of them may perhaps attach themselves to that society. Others will remain in a perfect state of indifference. The children of these zealous parents will not be able to tell what their religious principles are, and their grandchildren still less. The neighbourhood of a place of worship generally leads them to it, and the action of going thither is the strongest evidence they can give of their attachment to any sect. The Quakers are the only people who retain a fondness for their own mode of worship; for, be they ever so far separated from each other, they hold a sort of communion with the society, and seldom depart from its rules, at least in this country. Thus all sects are mixed as well as all nations. Thus religious indifference is imperceptibly disseminated from one end of the continent to the other, which is at present one of the strongest characteristics of the Americans. Where this will reach no one can tell: perhaps it may leave a vacuum fit to receive other systems. Persecution, religious pride, the love of contradiction, are the food of what the world commonly calls religion. These motives have ceased here: zeal, in Europe, is confined; here, it evaporates in the great distance it has to travel; there, it is a grain of powder inclosed; here, it burns away in the open air, and consumes without effect.

But to return to our back settlers. I must tell you, that there is something in the proximity of the woods which is very singular. It is with men as it is with the plants and animals that grow and live in the forests. They are entirely different from those that live in the plains. I will candidly tell you all my thoughts, but you are not to expect that I shall advance any reasons. By living in or near the woods, their actions are regulated by the wildness of the neighbourhood. The deer often come to eat their grain, the wolves to destroy their sheep, the bears to kill their hogs, the foxes to catch their poultry. This surrounding hostility immediately puts the gun into their hands: they watch these animals; they kill some; and thus, by defending their property, they soon become professed hunters. This is the progress. Once hunters, farewel to the plough. The chase renders them ferocious, gloomy, and unsocial. A hunter wants no neighbour; he rather hates them, because he dreads the competition. In a little time their success in the woods makes them neglect their tillage. They trust to the natural fecundity of the earth, and therefore do little. Carelessness in fencing often exposes what little they sow to destruction: they are not at home to watch: in order therefore to make up the deficiency, they go oftener to the woods. That new mode of life brings along with it a new set of manners, which I cannot easily describe. These new manners, being grafted on the old stock, produce a strange sort of lawless profligacy, the impressions of which are indelible. The manners of the Indian natives are respectable compared with this European medley. Their wives and children live in sloth and inactivity, and, having no proper pursuits, you may judge what education the latter receive. Their tender minds have nothing else to contemplate but the example of their parents; like them they grow up a mongrel breed, half civilized, half savage, except nature stamps on them some constitutional propensities. That rich, that voluptuous, sentiment is gone, which struck them so forcibly. The possession of their freeholds no longer conveys to their minds the same pleasure and pride. To all these reasons you must add their lonely situation, and you cannot imagine what an effect on manners the great distances they live from each other has! Consider one of the last settlements in its first view: of what is it composed? Europeans, who have not that sufficient share of knowledge they ought to have, in order to prosper: people, who have suddenly passed from oppression, dread of government, and fear of laws, into the unlimited freedom of the woods. This sudden change must have a very great effect on most men, and on that class particularly. Eating of wild meat, whatever you may think, tends to alter their temper, though all the proof I can adduce is, that I have seen it; and, having no place of worship to resort to, what little society this might afford is denied them. The Sunday meetings, exclusive of religious benefits, were the only social bonds that might have inspired them with some degree of emulation in neatness. Is it then surprising to see men, thus situated, immersed in great and heavy labours, degenerate a little? It is rather a wonder the effect is not more diffusive. The Moravians and the Quakers are the only instances in exception to what I have advanced. The first never settle singly; it is a colony of the society which emigrates: they carry with them their forms, worship, rules, and decency. The others never begin so hard; they are always able to buy improvements in which there is a great advantage, for, by that time, the country is recovered from its first barbarity. Thus our bad people are those who are half cultivators and half hunters; and the worst of them are those who have degenerated altogether into the hunting state. As old ploughmen and new men of the woods, as Europeans and new-made Indians, they contract the vices of both. They adopt the moroseness and ferocity of a native, without his mildness, or even his industry at home. If manners are not refined, at least they are rendered simple and inoffensive by tilling the earth: all our wants are supplied by it: our time is divided between labour and rest, and leaves none for the commission of great misdeeds. As hunters, it is divided between the toil of the chase, the idleness of repose, or the indulgence of inebriation. Hunting is but a licentious idle life, and, if it does not alway pervert good dispositions, yet, when it is united with bad luck, it leads to want: want stimulates that propensity to rapacity and injustice, too natural to needy men, which is the fatal gradation. After this explanation of the effects which follow by living in the woods, shall we yet vainly flatter ourselves with the hope of converting the Indians? We should rather begin with converting our back-settlers; and now, if I dare mention the name of religion, its sweet accents would be lost in the immensity of these woods. Men, thus placed, are not fit either to receive or remember its mild instructions; they want temples and ministers; but, as soon as men cease to remain at home and begin to lead an erratic life, let them be either tawny or white, they cease to be its disciples.

Thus have I faintly and imperfectly endeavoured to trace our society from the sea to our woods; yet you must not imagine that every person, who moves back, acts upon the game principles, or falls into the same degeneracy. Many families carry with them all their decency of conduct, purity of morals, and respect of religion; but these are scarce, the power of example is sometimes irresistible. Even among these back-settlers, their depravity is greater or less, according to what nation or province they belong. Were I to adduce proofs of this, I might be accused of partiality. If there happens to be some rich intervals, some fertile bottoms in those remote districts, the people will there prefer tilling the land to hunting, and will attach themselves to it; but, even on these fertile spots, you may plainly perceive the inhabitants to acquire a great degree of rusticity and selfishness.

It is in consequence of this straggling situation, and the astonishing power it has on manners, that the back-settlers of both the Carolinas, Virginia, and many other parts, have been long a set of lawless people; it has been even dangerous to travel among them. Government can do nothing in so extensive a country; better it should wink at these irregularities than that it should use means inconsistent with its usual mildness. Time will efface those stains: in proportion as the great body of population approaches them, they will reform, and become polished and subordinate. Whatever has been said of the four New-England provinces, no such degeneracy of manners has ever tarnished their annals: their back-settlers have been kept within the bounds of decency and government, by means of wise laws, and by the influence of religion. What a detestable idea such people must have given to the natives of the Europeans! They trade with them; the worst of people are permitted to do that which none but persons of the best characters should be employed in. They get drunk with them, and often defraud the Indians. Their avarice, removed from the eyes of their superiors, knows no bounds; and, aided by a little superiority of knowledge, these traders deceive them, and even sometimes shed blood. Hence those shocking violations, those sudden devastations which have so often stained our frontiers, when hundreds of innocent people have been sacrificed for the crimes of a few. It was in consequence of such behaviour that the Indians took the hatchet against the Virginians in 1774. Thus are our first steps trodden, thus are our first trees felled, in general, by the most vicious of our people; and thus the path is opened for the arrival of a second and better class, the true American freeholders; the most respectable set of people in this part of the world: respectable for their industry, their happy independence, the great share of freedom they possess, the good regulation of their families, and for extending the trace and the dominion of our mother-country.

Europe contains hardly any other distinctions but lords and tenants; this fair country alone is settled by freeholders, the possessors of the soil they cultivate, members of the government they obey, and the framers of their own laws, by means of their representatives. This is a thought which you have taught me to cherish; our distance from Europe, far from diminishing, rather adds to, our usefulness and consequence as men and subjects. Had our forefathers remained there, they would only have crouded it, and perhaps prolonged those convulsions which had shaken it so long. Every industrious European, who transports himself here, may be compared to a sprout growing at the foot of a great tree; it enjoys and draws but a little portion of sap; wrench it from the parent roots, transplant it, and it will become a tree bearing fruit also. Colonists are therefore entitled to the consideration due to the most useful subjects; a hundred families, barely existing in some parts of Scotland, will here, in six years, cause an annual exportation of 10,000 bushels of wheat: 100 bushels being but a common quantity for an industrious family to fell, if they cultivate good land. It is here then that the idle may be employed, the useless become useful, and the poor become rich; but by riches I do not mean gold and silver, we have but little of those metals: I mean a better sort of wealth; cleared lands, cattle, good houses, good clothes, and an increase of people to enjoy them.

There is no wonder that this country has so many charms, and presents to Europeans so many temptations to remain in it. A traveller in Europe becomes a stranger as soon as he quits his own kingdom; but it is otherwise here. We know, properly speaking, no strangers; this is every person's country; the variety of our soils, situations, climates, governments, and produce, hath something which must please every body. No sooner does an European arrive, no matter of what condition, than his eyes are opened upon the fair prospect; he hears his language spoken, he retraces many of his own country manners, he perpetually hears the names of families and towns with which he is acquainted; he sees happiness and prosperity in all places disseminated; he meets with hospitality, kindness, and plenty, every where: he beholds hardly any poor, he seldom hears of punishments and executions; and he wonders at the elegance of our towns, those miracles of industry and freedom. He cannot admire enough our rural districts, our convenient roads, good taverns, and our many accommodations; he involuntarily loves a country where every thing is so lovely. When in England, he was a mere Englishman; here he stands on a larger portion of the globe, not less than its fourth part, and may see the productions of the north, in iron and naval stores; the provisions of Ireland, the grain of Egypt, the indigo, the rice, of China. He does not find, as in Europe, a crouded society, where every place is over-stocked; he does not feel that perpetual collision of parties, that difficulty of beginning, that contention which oversets so many. There is room for every body in America; has he any particular talent or industry? he exerts it in order to procure a livelihood, and it succeeds. Is he a merchant? the avenues of trade are infinite. Is he eminent in any respect? he will be employed and respected. Does he love a country life? pleasant farms present themselves; he may purchase what he wants, and thereby become an American farmer. Is he a labourer, sober and industrious? he need not go many miles, nor receive many informations before he will be hired, well fed at the table of his employer, and paid four or five times more than he can get in Europe. Does he want uncultivated lands? thousands of acres present themselves, which he may purchase cheap. Whatever be his talents or inclinations, if they are moderate, he may satisfy them. I do not mean that every one who comes will grow rich in a little time; no, but he may procure an easy decent maintenance by his industry. Instead of starving he will be fed, instead of being idle he will have employment; and these are riches enough for such men as come over here. The rich stay in Europe; it is only the middling and poor that emigrate. Would you wish to travel in independent idleness, from north to south, you will find easy access, and the most cheerful reception, at every house; society without ostentation, good cheer without pride, and every decent diversion which the country affords, with little expence. It is no wonder that the European, who has lived here a few years, is desirous to remain; Europe, with all its pomp, is not to be compared to this continent, for men of middle stations or labourers.

An European, when he first arrives, seems limited in his intentions as well as in his views; but he very suddenly alters his scale; two hundred miles formerly appeared a very great distance, it is now but a trifle; he no sooner breathes our air than he forms schemes, and embarks in designs, he never would have thought of in his own country. There the plenitude of society confines many useful ideas, and often extinguishes the most laudable schemes which here ripen into maturity. Thus Europeans become Americans.

But how is this accomplished in that croud of low indigent people, who flock here every year from all parts of Europe? I will tell you; they no sooner arrive than they immediately feel the good effects of that plenty of provisions we possess: they fare on our best food, and are kindly entertained; their talents, character, and peculiar industry, are immediately inquired into; they find countrymen every where disseminated, let them come from whatever part of Europe. Let me select one as an epitome of the rest; he is hired, he goes to work, and works moderately; instead of being employed by a haughty person, he finds himself with his equal, placed at the substantial table of the farmer, or else at an inferior one as good; his wages are high, his bed is not like that bed of sorrow on which he used to lie: if he behaves with propriety, and is faithful, he is caressed, and becomes as it were a member of the family. He begins to feel the effects of a sort of resurrection; hitherto he had not lived, but simply vegetated; he now feels himself a man, because he is treated as such; the laws of his own country had overlooked him in his insignificancy; the laws of this cover him with their mantle. Judge what an alteration there must arise in the mind and the thoughts of this man; he begins to forget his former servitude and dependence, his heart involuntarily swells and glows; this first swell inspires him with those new thoughts which constitute an American. What love can he entertain for a country where his existence was a burthen to him? if he is a generous good man, the love of this new adoptive parent will sink deep into his heart. He looks around, and sees many a prosperous person, who, but a few years before, was as poor as himself. This encourages him much; he begins to form some little scheme, the first, alas! he ever formed in his life. If he is wise, he thus spends two or three years, in which time he acquires knowledge, the use of tools, the modes of working the lands, felling trees, &c. This prepares the foundation of a good name, the most useful acquisition he can make. He is encouraged, he has gained friends; he is advised and directed, he feels bold, he purchases some land; he gives all the money he has brought over, as well as what he has earned, and trusts to the God of harvests to the discharge of the rest. His good name procures him credit; he is now possessed of the deed, conveying to him and his posterity the fee simple and absolute property of two hundred acres of land, situated on such a river. What an epocha in this man's life! He is become a freeholder, from perhaps a German boor; he is now an American, a Pennsylvanian, an English subject. He is naturalized, his name is enrolled with those of the other citizens of the province. Instead of being a vagrant, he has a place of residence; he is called the inhabitant of such a country, or of such a district, and, for the first time in his life, counts for something; for hitherto he had been a cipher. I only repeat what I have heard many say; and no wonder their hearts should glow, and be agitated with a multitude of feelings, not easy to describe. From nothing, to start into being; from a servant, to the rank of a master; from being the slave of some despotic prince, to become a free man, invested with lands, to which every municipal blessing is annexed! What a change indeed! It is in consequence of that change that he becomes an American. This great metamorphosis has a double effect; it extinguishes all his European prejudices, he forgets that mechanism of subordination, that servility of disposition, which poverty had taught him; and sometimes he is apt to forget it too much, often passing from one extreme to the other. If he is a good man, he forms schemes of future prosperity, he proposes to educate his children better than he has been educated himself; he thinks of future modes of conduct, feels an ardour to labour he never felt before. Pride steps in, and leads him to every thing that the laws do not forbid: he respects them; with a heart-felt gratitude he looks toward the east, toward that insular government from whose wisdom all his new felicity is derived, and under whose wings and protection he now lives. These reflections constitute him the good man and the good subject. Ye poor Europeans, ye, who sweat, and work for the great; ye, who are obliged to give so many sheaves to the church, so many to your lords, so many to your government, and have hardly any left for yourselves, ye who are held in less estimation than favourite hunters or useless lap-dogs; ye, who only breathe the air of nature, because it cannot be withholden from you; it is here that ye can conceive the possibility of those feelings I have been describing; it is here the laws of naturalization invite every one to partake of our great labours and felicity, to till unrented, untaxed, lands! Many, corrupted beyond the power of amendment, have brought with them all their vices, and, disregarding the advantages held to them, have gone on in their former career of iniquity, until they have been overtaken and punished by our laws, It is not every emigrant who succeeds; no, it is only the sober, the honest, and industrious: happy those to whom this transition has served as a powerful spur to labour, to prosperity, and to the good establishment of children, born in the days of their poverty! and who had no other portion to expect but the rags of their parents, had it not been for their happy emigration. Others, again, have been led astray by this enchanting scene; their new pride, instead of leading them to the fields, has kept them in idleness; the idea of possessing lands is all that satisfies them; though surrounded with fertility, they have mouldered away their time in inactivity, misinformed husbandry, and ineffectual endeavours. . . .

After a foreigner from any part of Europe is arrived, and become a citizen, let him devoutly listen to the voice of our great parent, which says to him, "Welcome to my shores, distressed European; bless the hour in which thou didst see my verdant fields, my fair navigable rivers, and my green mountains!—If thou wilt work, I have bread for thee; if thou wilt be honest, sober, and industrious, I have greater rewards to confer on thee—ease and independence. I will give thee fields to feed and clothe thee; a comfortable fireside to sit by, and tell thy children by what means thou hast prospered; and a decent bed to repose on. I shall endow thee beside with the immunities of a freeman, if thou wilt carefully educate thy children, teach them gratitude to God, and reverence to that government, that philanthropic government, which has collected here so many men and made them happy. I will also provide for thy progeny; and to every good man this ought to be the most holy, the most powerful, the most earnest, wish we can possibly form, as well as the most consolatory prospect when he dies. Go thou, and work, and till; thou shalt prosper, provided thou be just, grateful, and industrious."

THE IMMIGRATION ACT OF 1790

In their constitution of the new nation, the first few federal Congresses were preoccupied with solidifying the rights of citizens and setting up relations among the former colonies and relations with foreign states. When they turned their thinking to the matter of who would be welcome to immigrate to and become citizens of the United States, the atmosphere was charged with the debates about race and slavery that had been so central to the construction and ratification of the Constitution. As the Constitution agreed to put an end to the importation of further African slaves after 1808, so this Act made clear that only persons of European heritage would be welcomed as potential citizens. Using the term "white" to describe these desirable immigrants, the Act excluded possible immigrants from Arab North Africa and the Middle East as well as from Asia, Africa, and the Caribbean.

AN ACT TO ESTABLISH AN UNIFORM
RULE OF NATURALIZATION

SECTION 1. *Be it enacted by the Senate and House of Representatives of the United States of America in Congress assembled,* That any alien, being a free white person, who shall have resided within the limits and under the jurisdiction of the United States for the term of two years, may be admitted to become a citizen thereof, on application to any common law court of record, in any one of the states wherein he shall have resided for the term of one year at least, and making proof to the satisfaction of such court, that he is a person of good character, and taking the oath or affirmation prescribed by law, to support the constitution of the United States, which oath or affirmation such court shall administer; and the clerk of such court shall record such application, and the proceedings thereon; and thereupon such person shall be considered as a citizen of the United States. And the children of such persons so naturalized, dwelling within the United States, being under the age of twenty-one years at the time of such naturalization, shall also be considered as citizens of the United States. And the children of citizens of the United States, that may be born beyond sea, or out of the limits of the United States, shall be considered as natural born citizens: *Provided,* That the right of citizenship shall not descend to persons whose fathers have never been resident in the United States: *Provided also,* That no person heretofore proscribed by any state, shall be admitted a citizen as aforesaid, except by an act of the legislature of the state in which such person was proscribed.

APPROVED, March 26, 1790.

BENJAMIN FRANKLIN
(1706–1790)

Franklin, the youngest son of a Boston candle and soap maker, was born July 17, 1706. After two years of formal schooling, at the age of ten he began to work for his father. At the age of twelve, he became an apprentice at his brother's printing shop. He became a published writer at the age of sixteen, when he anonymously submitted a manuscript to his brother's paper. In 1723, following increasing friction between Franklin and his family, Franklin abandoned his apprentice duties and set out for Philadelphia. His skills as a printer helped him find work quickly, and after a few setbacks Franklin established his own printing business in 1728. Well on his way to financial security, and having proven himself as an upstanding member of the Philadelphia community, Franklin married Deborah Reed in 1730. In 1732, Franklin began publishing Poor Richard's Almanac—*an annual publication of aphorisms pilfered from world literature ("Fish and visitors smell in three days," "He that lies with dogs, shall rise with fleas," "Have you somewhat to do to-morrow; do it today").*

At the age of forty-two, Franklin retired from the printing business, feeling wealthy enough to be able to devote his entire attention to his other interests—science, public works, and politics. Franklin's experiments with electricity remain his most significant scientific work, but he is also remembered for a number of inventions: the Franklin stove, the lightning rod, and bifocal glasses. In addition to city improvement projects such as paving and cleaning streets, he helped establish the first public library in America, a police force and fire company, the American Philosophical Society, a volunteer militia, a hospital, and an academy that would later become the University of Pennsylvania. His political interests, however, soon eclipsed his scientific and public works endeavors. He became a member of the Pennsylvania Assembly and in 1757 went to England to represent the colony's interests at Parliament. It was as a member of the Continental Congress and later as American Ambassador to France that Franklin gained his greatest political fame.

Franklin is most frequently remembered as a writer for his Autobiography *(begun in 1771 and never completed), which in many ways serves as a model of what was to become the paradigm of American-ness—the self-made man. The way of understanding the world that informs the* Autobiography *is also central to many of Franklin's other works, including "Advice to Such As Would Remove to America" in which he portrays America as a place of opportunity for the virtuous and hardworking.*

ADVICE TO SUCH AS WOULD
REMOVE TO AMERICA

Many persons in Europe, having directly or by letters, expressed to the writer of this, who is well acquainted with North America, their desire of transporting and establishing themselves in that country; but who appear to have formed, through ignorance, mistaken ideas and expectations of what is to be obtained there; he thinks it may be useful, and prevent inconvenient, expensive, and fruitless removals and voyages of improper persons, if he gives some clearer and truer notions of that part of the world, then appear to have hitherto prevailed.

He finds it is imagined by numbers, that the inhabitants of North America are rich, capable of rewarding, and disposed to reward, all sorts of ingenuity; that they are at the same time ignorant of all the sciences, and consequently, that strangers, possessing talents in the belles-lettres, fine arts, &c., must be highly esteemed, and so well paid, as to become easily rich themselves; that there are also abundance of profitable offices to be disposed of, which the natives are not qualified to fill; and that, having few persons of family among them, strangers of birth must be greatly respected, and of course easily obtain the best of those offices, which will make all their fortunes; that the governments too, to encourage emigrations from Europe, not only pay the expense of personal transportation, but give lands gratis to strangers, with Negroes to work for them, utensils of husbandry, and stocks of cattle. These are all wild imaginations; and those who go to America with expectations founded upon them will surely find themselves disappointed.

The truth is, that though there are in that country few people so miserable as the poor of Europe, there are also very few that in Europe would be called rich; it is rather a general happy mediocrity that prevails. There are few great proprietors of the soil, and few tenants; most people cultivate their own lands, or follow some handicraft or merchandise; very few rich enough to live idly upon their rents or incomes, or to pay the high prices given in Europe for paintings, statues, architecture, and the other works of art, that are more curious than useful. Hence the natural geniuses, that have arisen in America with such talents, have uniformly quitted that country for Europe, where they can be more suitably rewarded. It is true, that letters and mathematical knowledge are in esteem there, but they are at the same time more common than is apprehended; there being already existing nine colleges or universities, viz., four in New England, and one in each of the provinces of New York, New Jersey, Pennsylvania, Maryland, and Virginia, all furnished with learned professors; besides a number of smaller academies; these educate many of their youth in the languages, and those sciences that qualify men for the professions of divinity, law, or physic.* Strangers indeed are by no means excluded from exercising those professions; and the quick increase of inhabitants everywhere gives them a chance of employ, which they have in common with the natives. Of civil offices, or employments, there are few; no superfluous ones, as in Europe; and it is a rule established in some of the states, that no office should be so profitable as to make it desirable. The 36th Article of the Constitution of Pennsylvania, runs expressly in these words: "As every freeman, to preserve his independence, (if he has not a sufficient estate) ought to have some profession, calling, trade, or farm, whereby he may honestly subsist, there can be no necessity for, nor use in, establishing offices of profit; the usual effects of which are dependance and servility, unbecoming freemen, in the possessors and expectants; faction, contention, corruption, and disorder among the people. Wherefore, whenever an office, through increase of fees or otherwise, becomes so profitable, as to occasion many to apply for it, the profits ought to be lessened by the legislature."

These ideas prevailing more or less in all the United States, it cannot be worth any man's while, who has a means of living at home, to expatriate himself, in hopes of obtaining a profitable civil office in America; and, as to military offices, they are at an end with the war,† the armies being disbanded. Much less is it advisable for a person to go thither, who has no other quality to recommend him but his birth. In Europe it has indeed its value; but it is a commodity that cannot be carried to a worse market than that of America, where people do not inquire concerning a stranger, *what is he?* but, *what can he do?* If he has any useful art, he is welcome; and if he exercises it, and behaves well, he will be respected by all that know him; but a mere man of quality, who, on that account, wants to live upon the public, by some office or salary, will be despised and disregarded. The husbandman‡ is in honor there, and even the mechanic,§ because their employments are useful. The people have a saying, that God Almighty is Himself a mechanic, the greatest in the universe; and he is respected and admired more for the variety, ingenuity, and utility of his handyworks, than for the antiquity of his family. They are pleased with the observation of a Negro, and frequently mention it, that *Boccarorra* (meaning the white men) *make de black man workee, make de horse workee, make de ox workee, make eberyting workee; only de hog. He, de hog, no workee; he eat, he drink, he walk about, he go to sleep when he please; he libb like a gentleman.* According to these opinions of the Americans, one of them would think himself more obliged to a genealogist, who could prove for him that his ancestors and relations for ten generations had been plowmen, smiths, carpenters, turners, weavers, tanners,¶ or even shoemakers, and consequently that they were useful members of society; than if he could only prove that they were gentlemen, doing nothing of value, but living idly on the labor of others, mere *fruges consumere nati,#* and otherwise *good for nothing,* till by their death their estates, like the carcass of the negro's gentleman hog, come to be *cut up.*

With regard to encouragements for strangers from government, they are really only what are derived from good laws and liberty. Strangers are welcome, because there is room enough for them all, and therefore the old inhabitants are not jealous of them; the laws protect them sufficiently, so that they have no need for the patron-

---

*Medicine   †The Revolutionary War   ‡Farmer   §Manual laborer   ¶Those who convert hides into leather   #"'. . . born / Merely to eat up the corn.'—Watts" [Franklin's note]

age of great men; and every one will enjoy securely the profits of his industry. But, if he does not bring a fortune with him, he must work and be industrious to live. One or two years' residence gives him all the rights of a citizen; but the government does not at present, whatever it may have done in former times, hire people to become settlers, by paying their passages, giving land, negroes, utensils, stock, or any other kind of emolument whatsoever. In short, American is the land of labor, and by no means what the English call *Lubberland,* and the French Pays de Cocagne, where the streets are said to be paved with half-peck loaves, the houses tiled with pancakes, and where the fowls fly about ready roasted, crying *come eat me!*

Who then are the kind of persons to whom an emigration to America may be advantageous? And what are the advantages they may reasonably expect?

Land being cheap in that country, from the vast forests still void of inhabitants, and not likely to be occupied in an age to come, insomuch that the propriety of an hundred acres of fertile soil full of wood may be obtained near the frontiers, in many places, for eight or ten guineas, hearty young laboring men, who understand the husbandry of corn and cattle, which is nearly the same in that country as in Europe, may easily establish themselves there. A little money saved of the good wages they receive there, while they work for others, enables them to buy the land and begin their plantation, in which they are assisted by the good will of their neighbors, and some credit. Multitudes of poor people from England, Ireland, Scotland, and Germany, have by this means in a few years become wealthy farmers, who, in their own countries, where all the lands are fully occupied, and the wages of labor low, could never have emerged from the poor condition wherein they were born.

From the salubrity of the air, the healthiness of the climate, the plenty of good provisions, and the encouragement to early marriages by the certainty of subsistence in cultivating the earth, the increase of inhabitants by natural generation is very rapid in America, and becomes still more so by the accession of strangers; hence there is a continual demand for more artisans of all the necessary and useful kinds, to supply those cultivators of the earth with houses, and with furniture and utensils of the grosser sorts, which cannot so well be brought from Europe. Tolerably good workmen in any of those mechanic arts are sure to find employ, and to be well paid for their work, there being no restraints preventing strangers from exercising any art they understand, nor any permission necessary. If they are poor, they begin first as servants or journeymen;* and if they are sober, industrious, and frugal, they soon become masters, establish themselves in business, marry, raise families, and become respectable citizens.

Also, persons of moderate fortunes and capitals, who, having a number of children to provide for, are desirous of bringing them up to industry,† and to secure estates for their posterity, have opportunities of doing it in America, which Europe does not afford. There they may be taught and practice profitable mechanic arts, without incurring disgrace on that account, but on the contrary acquiring respect by such abilities. There small capitals laid out in lands, which daily become more valuable by the increase of people, afford a solid prospect of ample fortunes thereafter for those children. The writer of this has known several instances of large tracts of land, bought, on what was then the frontier of Pennsylvania, for ten pounds per hundred acres, which after 20 years, when the settlements had been extended far beyond

---

*Those who have served their apprenticeship and are paid by the day   †To be skillful in whatever they undertake in the way of a vocation

them, sold readily, without any improvement made upon them, for three pounds per acre. The acre in America is the same with the English acre, or the acre of Normandy.

Those, who desire to understand the state of government in America, would do well to read the constitutions of the several states, and the Articles of Confederation that bind the whole together for general purposes, under the direction of one assembly, called the Congress. These constitutions have been printed, by order of Congress, in America; two editions of them have also been printed in London; and a good translation of them into French has lately been published at Paris.

Several of the princes of Europe having of late years, from an opinion of advantage to arise by producing all commodities and manufactures within their own dominions, so as to diminish or render useless their importations, have endeavored to entice workmen from other countries by high salaries, privileges, &c. Many persons, pretending to be skilled in various great manufactures, imagining that America must be in want of them, and that the Congress would probably be disposed to imitate the prince above mentioned, have proposed to go over, on condition of having their passages paid, lands given, salaries appointed, exclusive privileges for terms of years, &c. Such persons, on reading the Articles of Confederation, will find, that the Congress have no power committed to them, or money out into their hands, for such purposes; and that if any such encouragement is given, it must be by the government of some separate state. This, however, has rarely been done in America; and, when it has been done, it has rarely succeeded, so as to establish a manufacture, which the country was not yet so ripe for as to encourage private persons to set it up; labor being generally too dear there, and hands difficult to be kept together, every one desiring to be a master, and the cheapness of lands inclining many to leave trades for agriculture. Some indeed have met with success, and are carried on to advantage; but they are generally such as require only a few hands, or wherein great part of the work is performed by machines. Things that are bulky, and of so small value as not well to bear the expense of freight, may often be made cheaper in the country, than they can be imported; and the manufacture of such things will be profitable wherever there is a sufficient demand. The farmers in America produce indeed a good deal of wool and flax; and none is exported, it is all worked up; but it is in the way of domestic manufacture, for the use of the family. The buying up quantities of wool and flax, with the design to employ spinners, weavers, &c., and form great establishments, producing quantities of linen and woollen goods for sale, has been several times attempted in different provinces; but those projects have generally failed, goods of equal value being imported cheaper. And when the governments have been solicited to support such schemes by encouragements, in money, or by imposing duties on importation of such goods, it has been generally refused, on this principle, that, if the country is ripe for the manufacture, it may be carried on by private persons to advantage; and if not, it is a folly to think of forcing Nature. Great establishments of manufacture require great numbers of poor to do the work for small wages; these poor are to be found in Europe, but will not be found in America, till the lands are all taken up and cultivated, and the excess of people, who cannot get land, want employment. The manufacture of silk, they say, is natural in France, as that of cloth in England, because each country produces in plenty the first material; but if England will have a manufacture of silk as well as that of cloth, and France one of cloth as well as that of silk, these unnatural operations must be supported by mutual prohibitions, or high duties on the importation of each other's goods; by which means the workmen are enabled to tax the home consumer by greater prices, while the higher wages they receive makes them neither happier nor richer, since they only drink more and work less. Therefore the governments in America do nothing to encourage such projects. The people, by this means, are not imposed on, either by the merchant or mechanic. If the merchant demands too much profit on imported shoes, they buy of the shoemaker; and if he asks too high a price, they take them of the merchant; thus the two professions are checks on each other. The shoemaker, however, has, on the whole, considerable profit upon his labor in America, beyond what he had in Europe, as he can add to his price a sum nearly equal to all the expenses of freight and commission, risk or insurance, &c., necessarily charged by the merchant. And the case is the same with the workmen in every other mechanic art. Hence it is, that artisans generally live better and more easily in America than in Europe; and such as are good economists[*] make a comfortable provision for age, and for their children. Such may, therefore, remove with advantage to America.

In the long-settled countries of Europe, all arts, trades, professions, farms, &c., are so full, that it is difficult for a poor man, who has children, to place them where they may gain, or learn to gain, a decent livelihood. The artisans, who fear creating future rivals in business, refuse to take apprentices, but upon conditions of money, maintenance, or the like, which the parents are unable to comply with. Hence the youth are dragged up in ignorance of every gainful art, and obliged to become soldiers, or servants, or thieves, for a subsistence. In America, the rapid increase of inhabitants takes away that fear of rivalship, and artisans willingly receive apprentices from the hope of profit by their labor, during the remainder of the time stipulated, after they shall be instructed. Hence it is easy for poor families to get their children instructed; for the artisans are so desirous of apprentices, that many of them will even give money to the parents, to have boys from ten to fifteen years of age bound apprentices to them till the age of twenty-one; and many poor parents have, by that means, on their arrival in the country, raised money enough to buy land sufficient to establish themselves, and to subsist the rest of their family by agriculture. These contracts for apprentices are made before a magistrate, who regulates the agreement according to reason and justice, and, having in view the formation of a future useful citizen, obliges the master to engage by a written indenture, not only that, during the time of service stipulated, the apprentice shall be duly provided with meat, drink, apparel, washing, and lodging, and, at its expiration, with a complete new suit of clothes, but also that he shall be taught to read, write, and cast accounts, and that he shall be well instructed in the art or profession of his master, or some other, by which he may afterwards gain a livelihood, and be able in his turn to raise a family. A copy of this indenture is given to the apprentice or his friends, and the magistrate keeps a record of it, to which recourse may be had, in case of failure by the master in any point of performance. This desire among the masters, to have more hands employed in working for them, induces them to pay the passages of young persons, of both sexes, who, on their arrival, agree to serve them one, two, three, or four years; those, who have already learned a trade, agreeing for a shorter term, in proportion to their skill, and the consequent immediate value of their service; and those, who have none, agreeing for a longer term, in consideration of being taught an art their poverty would not permit them to acquire in their own country.

The almost general mediocrity of fortune that prevails in America obliging its people to follow some business for subsistence, those vices, that arise usually from idleness, are in a great measure prevented. Industry and constant employment are great

---

*Providers.

preservatives of the morals and virtue of a nation. Hence bad examples to youth are more rare in America, which must be a comfortable consideration to parents. To this may be truly added, that serious religion, under its various denominations, is not only tolerated, but respected and practiced. Atheism is unknown there; infidelity rare and secret; so that persons may live to a great age in that country, without having their piety shocked by meeting with either an atheist or an infidel. And the Divine Being seems to have manifested His approbation of the mutual forbearance and kindness with which the different sects treat each other, by the remarkable prosperity with which He has been pleased to favour the whole country.

SLAVE AUCTION NOTICE

Slavery was an institution, an interlocking set of ideas, businesses, attitudes, and prejudices. The most ardent antislavery American could hardly spend a day without engaging some aspect of this many-headed hydra. Even though slave labor was most densely organized around large farms or plantations, slaves also worked in towns and cities at nonagricultural labor, as carpenters, ironworkers, potters, and so forth. And in many cities, North and South, the arrival of slave traders by land and sea was followed by the spectacle of the slave auction. The auctions were periodic, but often as frequent as weekly. They were attended not only by slave owners seeking to purchase new workers or to sell excess (or troublesome) ones but also by local people interested in the spectacle, which also, of course, served to mark their superior status in relation to the slaves.

PUBLIC SALE
OF SLAVES!!

FRANKLIN CIRCUIT COURT.

JAMES HARLAN'S Administrators, Plaintiffs.
        vs.   } In Equity.
JAMES HARLAN'S Heirs, Defendants.

The undersigned, as COMMISSIONER of said Court, will, on

Monday, November 16, 1863,

(County Court day,) sell at public auction, the following Slaves, viz:

THREE NEGRO MEN;

ONE NEGRO WOMAN AND A SMALL CHILD, ADOPTED;

ONE NEGRO WOMAN AND TWO CHILDREN.

TERMS—Six months credit, with interest from date, the purchasers giving bond with security, to have the force and effect of replevin bond.

GEORGE W. GWIN,

OCTOBER 30, 1863.   Master Commissioner.

COMMISSIONER'S SALE IN 1863

FRANCES E. W. HARPER

(1825-1911)

Frances Ellen Watkins was born in Baltimore, Maryland, in 1825. Her parents were free blacks, but growing up in Maryland she witnessed slavery first-hand. After her parents died in 1828, she was adopted by an aunt and uncle who ran a school, which she attended until the age of fourteen. At the age of sixteen, while working as a servant for a Baltimore family, she published her first volume of poetry, Forest Leaves *(there are no extant copies of this book).*

In 1850 she found a job as a teacher at the Union Seminary near Columbus, Ohio (this school later became Wilberforce University). In 1853, when Maryland began to refuse to recognize free blacks (making it possible to enslave free African Americans traveling there), she became intensely involved with the Underground Railroad. Here her political and artistic passions fused as she embarked on what was to become a long and brilliant career as a public speaker. Harper served as spokesperson for a range of causes (such as the establishment of Sunday schools) and organizations (such as the American Association of Educated and Colored Youth and the National Council of Women). She briefly retired from the lecture circuit in 1860, when she married Fenton Harper. However, after his death in 1864, she resumed her career, most notably touring the post–Civil War South, speaking to racially mixed audiences about issues of African-American education, civil rights, temperance, domestic reform, and an end to lynching. Unfortunately, few of her speeches survive; attesting to her skill as an orator, eyewitness accounts frequently comment that Harper often spoke without a written text or notes.

Nonetheless, Harper proved herself to be a very gifted writer. She published three books of poetry, a number of short stories, and a novel, Iola Leroy, or Shadows Uplifted *(1892). Like much of her poetry, "The Slave Auction" exhibits elements of both popular and "high culture" traditions, while it explores an experience of African Americans that was largely unfamiliar to most of her white readers.*

THE SLAVE AUCTION

The sale began—young girls were there,
    Defenceless in their wretchedness,
Whose stifled sobs of deep despair
    Revealed their anguish and distress.

And mothers stood with streaming eyes,
    And saw their dearest children sold;
Unheeded rose their bitter cries,
    While tyrants bartered them for gold.

And woman, with her love and truth—
    For these in sable forms may dwell—

Gaz'd on the husband of her youth,
　　With anguish none may paint or tell.

And men, whose sole crime was their hue,
　　The impress of their Maker's hand,
And frail and shrieking children, too,
　　Were gathered in that mournful band.

Ye who have laid your love to rest,
　　And wept above their lifeless clay,
Know not the anguish of that breast,
　　Whose lov'd are rudely torn away.

Ye may not know how desolate
　　Are bosoms rudely forced to part,
And how a dull and heavy weight
　　Will press the life-drops from the heart.

FREDERICK DOUGLASS
(1818-1895)

Frederick Augustus Washington Bailey was born a slave in Talbot County, Virginia, in February 1818. His mother was a slave who died when he was eight. His father was a white man—possibly the overseer of the plantation where Douglass was born. As a young boy, Douglass was sent to Baltimore to work in the home of a relative of his master. There, he learned to read and write, in part by trading poor white boys food for lessons. It was during this time that Douglass came to understand what it meant to be a slave. In 1838, at the age of twenty-one, he escaped slavery, eventually settling in New Bedford, Massachusetts, and marrying Anne Murray (a free black woman he'd known in Baltimore and who was instrumental in his escape). Like many former slaves, Douglass renamed himself once he settled in the North. Douglass became involved with the Massachusetts Anti-Slavery Society, eventually being hired to speak on the organization's lecture tour.

　　A skillful and popular speaker, Douglass soon decided to put his story down on paper, and in 1845 published the first of his three autobiographies, Narrative of the Life of Frederick Douglass, an American Slave: Written by Himself. *His* Narrative *is a powerful, complex rendering of an individual's struggle for education, identity, and freedom. In addition to two other autobiographies,* My Bondage and My Freedom *(1855) and* Life and Times of Frederick Douglass *(1881), Douglass also wrote a fictional narrative,* The Heroic Slave *(1851). The Independence Day or Fourth of July Oration is an example of Douglass's mastery of public speaking in the service of liberty. It reflects the thinking not only of this remarkably successful citizen but also that of many African Americans of the period.*

INDEPENDENCE DAY SPEECH

Fellow citizens, pardon me, allow me to ask, why am I called upon to speak here today? What have I, or those I represent, to do with your national independence? Are the great principles of political freedom and of natural justice, embodied in that Declaration of Independence, extended to us? and am I, therefore, called upon to bring our humble offering to the national altar, and to confess the benefits and express devout gratitude for the blessings resulting from your independence to us?

Would to God, both for your sakes and ours, that an affirmative answer could be truthfully returned to these questions! Then would my task be light, and my burden easy and delightful. For who is there so cold that a nation's sympathy could not warm him? Who so obdurate and dead to the claims of gratitude that would not thankfully acknowledge such priceless benefits? Who so stolid and selfish that would not give his voice to swell the hallelujahs of a nation's jubilee, when the chains of servitude had been torn from his limbs? I am not that man. In a case like that the dumb might eloquently speak and the "lame man leap as an hart."

But such is not the state of the case. I say it with a sad sense of the disparity between us. I am not included within the pale of this glorious anniversary! Your high independence only reveals the immeasurable distance between us. The blessings in which you, this day, rejoice are not enjoyed in common. The rich inheritance of justice, liberty, prosperity, and independence bequeathed by your fathers is shared by you, not by me. The sunlight that brought light and healing to you has brought stripes and death to me. This Fourth of July is yours, not mine. You may rejoice, I must mourn. To drag a man in fetters into the grand illuminated temple of liberty, and call upon him to join you in joyous anthems, were inhuman mockery and sacrilegious irony. Do you mean, citizens, to mock me by asking me to speak today? If so, there is a parallel to your conduct. And let me warn you that it is dangerous to copy the example of a nation whose crimes, towering up to heaven, were thrown down by the breath of the Almighty, burying that nation in irrevocable ruin! I can today take up the plaintive lament of a peeled and woe-smitten people!

> By the rivers of Babylon, there we sat down. Yea! we wept when we remembered Zion. We hanged our harps upon the willows in the midst thereof. For there, they that carried us away captive, required of us a song; and they who wasted us required of us mirth, saying, Sing us one of the songs of Zion. How can we sing the Lord's song in a strange land? If I forget thee, O Jerusalem, let my right hand forget her cunning. If I do not remember thee, let my tongue cleave to the roof of my mouth.

Fellow citizens, above your national, tumultuous joy, I hear the mournful wail of millions! whose chains, heavy and grievous yesterday, are, today, rendered more intolerable by the jubilee shouts that reach them. If I do forget, if I do not faithfully remember those bleeding children of sorrow this day, "may my right hand forget her cunning, and may my tongue cleave to the roof of my mouth"! To forget them, to pass lightly over their wrongs, and to chime in with the popular theme would be treason most scandalous and shocking, and would make me a reproach before God and the world. My subject, then, fellow citizens, is *American slavery.* I shall see this day and its popular characteristics from the slave's point of view. Standing there identified with the American bondman, making his wrongs mine. I do not hesitate to declare with all my soul that the character and conduct of this nation never looked blacker to me than on this Fourth of July! Whether we turn to the declarations of the past or to the professions of the present, the conduct of the nation seems equally hideous and revolting. America is false to the past, false to the present, and solemnly binds herself to be false to the future. Standing with God and the crushed and bleeding slave on this occasion, I will, in the name of humanity which is outraged, in the name of liberty which is fettered, in the name of the Constitution and the Bible which are disregarded and trampled upon, dare to call in question and to denounce, with all the emphasis I can command, everything that serves to perpetuate slavery—the great sin and shame of America! "I will not equivocate, I will not excuse"; I will use the severest language I can command; and yet not one word shall escape me that any man, whose judgment is not blinded by prejudice, or who is not at heart a slaveholder, shall not confess to be right and just.

But I fancy I hear someone of my audience say, "It is just in this circumstance that you and your brother abolitionists fail to make a favorable impression on the public mind. Would you argue more and denounce less, would you persuade more and rebuke less, your cause would be much more likely to succeed." But, I submit, where all is plain, there is nothing to be argued. What point in the antislavery creed would you have me argue? On what branch of the subject do the people of this country need light? Must I undertake to prove that the slave is a man? That point is conceded already. Nobody doubts it. The slaveholders themselves acknowledge it when they punish disobedience on the part of the slave. There are seventy-two crimes in the state of Virginia which, if committed by a black man (no matter how ignorant he be), subject him to the punishment of death; while only two of the same crimes will subject a white man to the like punishment. What is this but the acknowledgment that the slave is a moral, intellectual, and responsible being? The manhood of the slave is conceded. It is admitted in the fact that the Southern statute books are covered with enactments forbidding, under severe fines and penalties, the teaching of the slave to read or to write. When you can point to any such laws in reference to the beasts of the field, then I may consent to argue the manhood of the slave. When the dogs in your streets, when the fowls of the air, when the cattle on your hills, when the fish of the sea and the reptiles that crawl shall be unable to distinguish the slave from a brute, then will I argue with you that the slave is a man!

For the present, it is enough to affirm the equal manhood of the Negro race. Is it not astonishing that, while we are plowing, planting, and reaping, using all kinds of mechanical tools, erecting houses, constructing bridges, building ships, working in metals of brass, iron, copper, silver, and gold: that, while we are reading, writing, and ciphering, acting as clerks, merchants, and secretaries, having among us lawyers, doctors, ministers, poets, authors, editors, orators, and teachers; that, while we are engaged in all manner of enterprises common to other men, digging gold in California, capturing the whale in the Pacific, feeding sheep and cattle on the hillside, living, moving, acting, thinking, planning, living in families as husbands, wives, and children, and, above all, confessing and worshipping the Christian's God, and looking hopefully for life and immortality beyond the grave, we are called upon to prove that we are men!

Would you have me argue that man is entitled to liberty? That he is the rightful owner of his own body? You have already declared it. Must I argue the wrongfulness of slavery? Is that a question for republicans? Is it to be settled by the rules of logic and argumentation, as a matter beset with great difficulty, involving a doubtful application of the principle of justice, hard to be understood? How should I look today, in the presence of Americans, dividing and subdividing a discourse, to show that men have a natural right to freedom? speaking of it relatively and positively, negatively and affirmatively? To do so would be to make myself ridiculous and to offer an insult to your understanding. There is not a man beneath the canopy of heaven that does not know that slavery is wrong for him.

What, am I to argue that it is wrong to make men brutes, to rob them of their liberty, to work them without wages, to keep them ignorant of their relations to their fellow men, to beat them with sticks, to flay their flesh with the lash, to load their limbs with irons, to hunt them with dogs, to sell them at auction, to sunder their families, to knock out their teeth, to burn their flesh, to starve them into obedience and submission to their masters? Must I argue that a system thus marked with blood, and stained with pollution, is wrong? No! I will not. I have better employment for my time and strength than such arguments would imply.

What, then, remains to be argued? Is it that slavery is not divine: that God did not establish it; that our doctors of divinity are mistaken? There is blasphemy in the thought. That which is inhuman cannot be divine! Who can reason on such a proposition? They that can may: I cannot. The time for such argument is past.

At a time like this, scorching iron, not convincing argument, is needed. O! had I the ability, and could I reach the nation's ear, I would today pour out a fiery stream of biting ridicule, blasing reproach, withering sarcasm, and stern rebuke. For it is not light that is needed, but fire; it is not the gentle shower, but thunder. We need the storm, the whirlwind, and the earthquake. The feeling of the nation must be quickened; the conscience of the nation must be roused; the propriety of the nation must be startled; the hypocrisy of the nation must be exposed; and its crimes against God and man must be proclaimed and denounced.

What, to the American slave, is your Fourth of July? I answer: a day that reveals to him, more than all other days in the year, the gross injustice and cruelty to which he is the constant victim. To him, your celebration is a sham; your boasted liberty, an unholy license; your national greatness, swelling vanity; your sounds of rejoicing are empty and heartless; your denunciation of tyrants, brass-fronted impudence; your shouts of liberty and equality, hollow mockery; your prayers and hymns, your sermons and thanksgivings, with all your religious parade and solemnity, are, to Him, mere bombast, fraud, deception, impiety, and hypocrisy—a thin veil to cover up crimes which would disgrace a nation of savages. There is not a nation on the earth guilty of practices more shocking and bloody than are the people of the United States at this very hour.

Go where you may, search where you will, roam through all the monarchies and despotisms of the Old World, travel through South America, search out every abuse, and when you have found the last, lay your facts by the side of the everyday practices of this nation, and you will say with me that, for revolting barbarity and shameless hypocrisy, American reigns without a rival.

ABRAHAM LINCOLN

(1809-1865)

Abraham Lincoln, the sixteenth President of the United States and one of the best known (and perhaps most mythologized) figures of American history, was born in 1809 in Hardin County, Kentucky. The son of a pioneer farmer, Lincoln was mostly self-educated. His childhood interests in story-telling, drama, and rhetoric later served him well during his career as both a lawyer and a politician.

Lincoln was elected to the Illinois State Legislature in 1834 and served four four-year terms. In 1836 he was admitted to the bar, and in 1837 he moved to Springfield, Illinois, where he met and eventually married Mary Todd and where he set up his law practice. His vocal resistance to slavery led to his nomination for the United States Senate in 1858. Although he lost the race to incumbent Stephen Douglas, Lincoln received the Republican nomination for President of the United States. In the election of 1860, he carried every Northern state except New Jersey and lost every Southern state, but he won a majority of electoral votes. As soon as the election results were known, Southern states began to secede.

Still, Lincoln was not exactly the antislavery advocate that the abolitionists had wanted. His position was more moderate and conciliatory. This can be seen in his 1861 Inaugural Address, which made plain that his first concern was to save the union—even if that meant slavery would continue. By the time of his Second Inaugural Address (1865), his position had shifted somewhat. These addresses, like the familiar Gettysburg Address, showcase Lincoln's rhetorical skills. He was a masterful speaker. Not only could he shape public opinion but he also was skilled at balancing competing considerations and extraordinarily adept at getting rival groups to work together towards a common goal. The Emancipation Proclamation is both a legal document and an example of Lincoln's forceful writing.

BY THE PRESIDENT OF THE UNITED STATES OF AMERICA:

A PROCLAMATION.

Whereas on the 22d day of September, A.D. 1862, a proclamation was issued by the President of the United States, containing, among other things, the following, to wit:

"That on the 1st day of January, A.D. 1863, all persons held as slaves within any State or designated part of a State the people whereof shall then be in rebellion against the United States shall be then, thenceforward, and forever free; and the executive government of the United States, including the military and naval authority thereof, will recognize and maintain the freedom of such persons and will do no act or acts to repress such persons, or any of them, in any efforts they may make for their actual freedom.

"That the executive will on the 1st day of January aforesaid, by proclamation, designate the States and parts of States, if any, in which the people thereof, respectively, shall then be in rebellion against the United States; and the fact that any State or the people thereof shall on that day be in good faith represented in the Congress of the United States by members chosen thereto at elections wherein a majority of the qualified voters of such States shall have participated shall, in the absence of strong countervailing testimony, be deemed conclusive evidence that such State and the people thereof are not then in rebellion against the United States."

Now, therefore, I, Abraham Lincoln, President of the United States, by virtue of the power in me vested as Commander-in-Chief of the Army and Navy of the United States in time of actual armed rebellion against the authority and government of the United States, and as a fit and necessary war measure for suppressing said rebellion, do, on this 1st day of January, A.D. 1863, and in accordance with my purpose so to do, publicly proclaimed for the full period of one hundred days from the first day above mentioned, order and designate as the States and parts of States wherein the people thereof, respectively, are this day in rebellion against the United States the following, to wit:

Arkansas, Texas, Louisiana (except the parishes of St. Bernard, Plaquemines, Jefferson, St. John, St. Charles, St. James, Ascension, Assumption, Terrebonne, Lafourche, St. Mary, St. Martin, and Orleans, including the city of New Orleans), Mississippi, Alabama, Florida, Georgia, South Carolina, North Carolina, and Virginia (except the forty-eight counties designated as West Virginia, and also the counties of Berkeley, Accomac, Northhampton, Elizabeth City, York, Princess Anne, and Norfolk, including the cities of Norfolk and Portsmouth), and which excepted parts are for the present left precisely as if this proclamation were not issued.

And by virtue of the power and for the purpose aforesaid, I do order and declare that all persons held as slaves within said designated States and parts of States are, and henceforward shall be, free; and that the Executive Government of the United States, including the military and naval authorities thereof, will recognize and maintain the freedom of said persons.

And I hereby enjoin upon the people so declared to be free to abstain from all violence, unless in necessary self-defense; and I recommend to them that, in all cases when allowed, they labor faithfully for reasonable wages.

And I further declare and make known that such persons of suitable condition will be received into the armed service of the United States to garrison forts, positions, stations, and other places, and to man vessels of all sorts in said service.

And upon this act, sincerely believed to be an act of justice, warranted by the Constitution upon military necessity, I invoke the considerate judgment of mankind and the gracious favor of Almighty God.

INDIAN REMOVAL ACT OF 1837

While the federal government established treaties with the various Native communities as sovereign nations, many citizens viewed the Natives as threats and obstructions to the possession of rich farm land and potentially valuable mineral rights. As the white populations moved inland from established coastal cities and towns in states like Georgia, Florida, and the Carolinas, conflicts with the Native Americans grew. During the administration of Andrew Jackson, a politician who understood and supported the desire for land of the landless white masses, treaties were forced upon the Native groups of the Southeast. These treaties essentially traded ancestral homelands for land in the Indian Territory, west of the Mississippi. Thousands of Cherokee and other Natives were literally marched across the continent from Georgia, Tennessee, Florida, and Alabama to their new homes in what we now call Oklahoma. Hundreds died en route; those who survived suffered for generations the alienation of their displacement to this very different environment.

CHAP. CXLVIII

AN ACT TO PROVIDE FOR AN EXCHANGE OF LANDS WITH THE INDIANS RESIDING IN ANY OF THE STATES OR TERRITORIES, AND FOR THEIR REMOVAL WEST OF THE RIVER MISSISSIPPI.

*B*e it enacted by the Senate and House of Representatives of the United States of America, in Congress assembled, That it shall and may be lawful for the President of the United States to cause so much of any territory belonging to the United States, west of the river Mississippi, not included in any state or organized territory, and to which the Indian title has been extinguished, as he may judge necessary, to be divided into a suitable number of districts, for the reception of such tribes or nations of Indians as may choose to exchange the lands where they now reside, and remove there; and to cause each of said districts to be so described by natural or artificial marks, as to be easily distinguished from every other.

SEC. 2. *And be it further enacted,* That it shall and may be lawful for the President to exchange any or all of such districts, so to be laid off and described, with any tribe or nation of Indians now residing within the limits of any of the states or territories, and with which the United States have existing treaties, for the whole or any part or portion of the territory claimed and occupied by such tribe or nation, within the bounds of any one or more of the states or territories, where the land claimed and occupied by the Indians, is owned by the United States, or the United States are bound to the state within which it lies to extinguish the Indian claim thereto.

SEC. 3. *And be it further enacted,* That in the making of any such exchange or exchanges, it shall and may be lawful for the President solemnly to assure the tribe or nation with which the exchange is made, that the United States will forever secure and guaranty to them, and their heirs or successors, the country so exchanged with them; and if they prefer it, that the United States will cause a patent or grant to be made and executed to them for the same: *Provided always,* That such lands shall revert to the United States, if the Indians become extinct, or abandon the same.

SEC. 4. *And be it further enacted,* That if, upon any of the lands now occupied by the Indians, and to be exchanged for, there should be such improvements as add value to the land claimed by any individual or individuals of such tribes or nations, it shall and may be lawful for the President to cause such value to be ascertained by appraisement or otherwise, and to cause such ascertained value to be paid to the person or persons rightfully claiming such improvements. And upon the payment of such valuation, the improvements so valued and paid for, shall pass to the United States, and possession shall not afterwards be permitted to any of the same tribe.

SEC. 5. *And be it further enacted,* That upon the making of any such exchange as is contemplated by this act, it shall and may be lawful for the President to cause such aid and assistance to be furnished to the emigrants as may be necessary and proper to enable them to remove to, and settle in, the country for which they may have exchanged; and also, to give them such aid and assistance as may be necessary for their support and subsistence for the first year after their removal.

SEC. 6. *And be it further enacted,* That it shall and may be lawful for the President to cause such tribe or nation to be protected, at their new residence, against all interruption or disturbance from any other tribe or nation of Indians, or from any other person or persons whatever.

SEC. 7. *And be it further enacted,* That it shall and may be lawful for the President to have the same superintendence and care over any tribe or nation in the country to which they may remove, as contemplated by this act, that he is now authorized to have over them at their present places of residence: *Provided,* That nothing in this act contained shall be construed as authorizing or directing the violation of any existing treaty between the United States and any of the Indian tribes.

SEC. 8. *And be it further enacted,* That for the purpose of giving effect to the provisions of this act, the sum of five hundred thousand dollars is hereby appropriated, to be paid out of any money in the treasury, not otherwise appropriated.

APPROVED, May 28, 1830.

RED JACKET
(SA-GO-YE-WAT-HA)
(1756?-1830)

Born near Lake Geneva, New York, in approximately 1756 as O-Te-Ti-Ani (Always Ready), he took the name Sa-Go-Ye-Wat-Ha (He That Keeps Them Awake) upon his election to Sachem (tribal chief). His people, the Seneca, were the westernmost nation of the Iroquois alliance. The Iroquois confederacy, which spanned much of present-day New York State and southeastern Ontario and which had an unwritten constitution and representative government, included the Seneca, Mohawk, Cayuga, Onondaga, and Oneida. These five nations (later joined by the Tuscaroras and called the Six Nations) united forces against the English during the colonial period; however, during the Revolutionary War they joined the British against the colonists. Red Jacket acquired his English name during the latter war; as payment for services rendered, he was given a British military dress jacket. It became such a notable feature of his dress that the English referred to him by it.

According to his biographer, William L. Stone, who published The Life and Times of Red Jacket, or Sa-Go-Ye-Wat-Ha; Being the Sequel to the History of the Six Nations *in 1841, Red Jacket was not born to a distinguished family but became a chief in his tribe through the force of his own accomplishments. He served as the principal spokesperson for the Seneca, as well as for the Iroquois as a whole, in numerous treaty negotiations with the U.S. government. He addressed the Senate on the importance of negotiating with the Native American tribes. He was very vocal in his opposition to assimilation. As he does in this excerpt from Stone's biography, Red Jacket urged the Iroquois to be particularly cautious of Christianity and to preserve their own beliefs and traditions before it was too late. He was one of the greatest Native American orators, claiming, when asked about his accomplishments, "I am an orator! I was born an orator!"*

1805 ORATION OF RED JACKET

"FRIEND AND BROTHER: It was the will of the Great Spirit that we should meet together this day. HE orders all things, and has given us a fine day for our Council. HE has taken his garment from before the sun, and caused it to shine with brightness upon us. Our eyes are opened, that we see clearly; our ears are unstopped, that we have been able to hear distinctly the words you have spoken. For all these favors we thank the Great Spirit; and HIM *only*.

"BROTHER: This council fire was kindled by you. It was at your request that we came together at this time. We have listened with attention to what you have said. You requested us to speak our minds freely. This gives us great joy; for we now consider that we stand upright before you, and can speak what we think. All have heard your voice, and all speak to you now as one man. Our minds are agreed.

"BROTHER: You say you want an answer to your talk before you leave this place. It is right you should have one, as you are a great distance from home, and we do not wish to detain you. But we will first look back a little, and tell you what our fathers have told us, and what we have heard from the white people.

"BROTHER: Listen to what we say. There was a time when our forefathers owned this great island. Their seats extended from the rising to the setting sun. The Great Spirit had made it for the use of Indians. HE had created the buffalo, the deer, and other animals for food. HE had made the bear and the beaver. Their skins served us for clothing. HE had scattered them over the country, and taught us how to take them. HE had caused the earth to produce corn for bread. All this HE had done for his red children, because HE loved them. If we had some disputes about our hunting ground, they were generally settled without the shedding of much blood. But an evil day came upon us. Your forefathers crossed the great water and landed on this island. Their numbers were small. They found friends and not enemies. They told us they had fled from their own country for fear of wicked men, and had come here to enjoy their religion. They asked for a small seat. We took pity on them, granted their request; and they sat down amongst us. We gave them corn and meat; they gave us poison* in return.

"The white people, BROTHER, had now found our country. Tidings were carried back, and more came amongst us. Yet we did not fear them. We took them to be friends. They called us brothers. We believed them and gave them a larger seat. At length their numbers had greatly increased. They wanted more land; they wanted our country. Our eyes were opened, and our minds became uneasy. Wars took place. Indians were hired to fight against Indians, and many of our people were destroyed. They also brought strong liquor amongst us. It was strong and powerful, and has slain thousands.

"BROTHER: Our seats were once large and yours were small. You have now become a great people, and we have scarcely a place left to spread our blankets. You have got our country, but are not satisfied; you want to force your religion upon us.

"BROTHER: Continue to listen. You say that you are sent to instruct us how to worship the Great Spirit agreeably to his mind, and, if we do not take hold of the religion which you white people teach, we shall be unhappy hereafter. You say that you are right and we are lost. How do we know this to be true? We understand that your religion is written in a book. If it was intended for us as well as you, why has not the Great Spirit given to us, and not only to us, but why did he not give to our forefathers, the knowledge of that book, with the means of understanding it rightly? We only know what you tell us about it. How shall we know when to believe, being so often deceived by the white people?

"BROTHER: You say there is but one way to worship and serve the Great Spirit. If there is but one religion, why do you white people differ so much about it? Why not all agreed, as you can all read the book?

"BROTHER: We do not understand these things. We are told that your religion was given to your forefathers, and has been handed down from father to son. We also have a religion, which was given to our forefathers, and has been handed down to us their children. We worship in that way. It teaches us to be thankful for all the favors we receive; to love each other, and to be united. We never quarrel about religion.

"BROTHER: The Great Spirit has made us all, but HE has made a great difference between his white and red children. HE has given us different complexions and different customs. To you HE has given the arts. To these HE has not opened our eyes. We know these things to be true. Since HE has made so great a difference between us in other things, why may we not conclude that he has given us a different religion according to our understanding? The Great Spirit does right. HE knows what is best for his children; we are satisfied.

"BROTHER: We do not wish to destroy your religion, or take it from you. We only want to enjoy our own.

"BROTHER: We are told that you have been preaching to the white people in this place. These people are our neighbors. We are acquainted with them. We will wait a little while, and see what effect your preaching has upon them. If we find it does them good, makes them honest and less disposed to cheat Indians, we will then consider again of what you have said.

"BROTHER: You have now heard our answer to your talk, and this is all we have to say at present. As we are going to part, we will come and take you by the hand, and hope the Great Spirit will protect you on your journey, and return you safe to your friends."

_____

*Rum

GERTRUDE BONNIN/ZITKALA-SA*

(1876-1938)

Born February 22, 1876, on the Pine Ridge Reservation in South Dakota, Gertrude Simmons didn't learn to speak English until the age of eight, when she left the reservation to attend a Quaker school in Wabash, Indiana. Later she studied at Earlham College in Indiana, where she won awards for oratory. After graduating in 1897, she worked as a teacher at a well-known school for Native American children in Pennsylvania (the Carlisle Indian School). However, troubled by the school's assimilationist political stance, in 1899 she resigned to pursue her interests in music at the New England Conservatory of Music in Boston. Freer to focus on her creative and intellectual interests, she became increasingly concerned with how Native Americans were understood and treated by the dominant American culture.

She began her writing career around 1900, first publishing autobiographical essays and short stories in popular magazines, such as The Atlantic Monthly *and* Harper's Magazine, *under her Sioux name, Zitkala-Sa, or Red Bird. These writings, which often reveal her indignation over the treatment of Native Americans by the state, the church, and the population at large, were later collected and republished in 1921 as* American Indian Stories. *She also translated and published* Old Indian Legends, *a collection of traditional Sioux stories, in 1901.*

She returned to South Dakota around 1902, where she met and married Raymond T. Bonnin. While the remainder of her life was filled with political and social work on the behalf of her fellow Sioux and other Native people, Bonnin never continued the autobiographical record she began at the turn of the century.

"The School Days of an Indian Girl" indicates both the expectations and disappointments involved in the attempts of Native Americans to "fit in" with the culture of the Europeans who by the nineteenth century had completely overrun their territories.

FROM THE SCHOOL DAYS

OF AN INDIAN GIRL

I The Land of Red Apples

There were eight in our party of bronzed children who were going East with the missionaries. Among us were three young braves, two tall girls, and we three little ones, Judéwin, Thowin, and I.

We had been very impatient to start on our journey to the Red Apple Country, which, we were told, lay a little beyond the great circular horizon of the Western prairie. Under a sky of rosy apples we dreamt of roaming as freely and happily as we had chased the cloud shadows on the Dakota plains. We had anticipated much

---

*Her name has also been transcribed as Zitkala Sa and Zitkala-Sä.

pleasure from a ride on the iron horse, but the throngs of staring palefaces disturbed and troubled us.

On the train, fair women, with tottering babies on each arm, stopped their haste and scrutinized the children of absent mothers. Large men, with heavy bundles in their hands, halted near by, and riveted their glassy blue eyes upon us.

I sank deep into the corner of my seat, for I resented being watched. Directly in front of me, children who were no larger than I hung themselves upon the backs of their seats, with their bold white faces toward me. Sometimes they took their forefingers out of their mouths and pointed at my moccasined feet. Their mothers, instead of reproving such rude curiosity, looked closely at me, and attracted their children's further notice to my blanket. This embarrassed me, and kept me constantly on the verge of tears.

I sat perfectly still, with my eyes downcast, daring only now and then to shoot long glances around me. Chancing to turn to the window at my side, I was quite breathless upon seeing one familiar object. It was the telegraph pole which strode by at short paces. Very near my mother's dwelling, along the edge of a road thickly bordered with wild sunflowers, some poles like these had been planted by white men. Often I had stopped, on my way down the road, to hold my ear against the pole, and, hearing its low moaning, I used to wonder what the paleface had done to hurt it. Now I sat watching for each pole that glided by to be the last one.

In this way I had forgotten my uncomfortable surroundings, when I heard one of my comrades call out my name. I saw the missionary standing very near, tossing candies and gums into our midst. This amused us all, and we tried to see who could catch the most of the sweet-meats. The missionary's generous distribution of candies was impressed upon my memory by a disastrous result which followed. I had caught more than my share of candies and gums, and soon after our arrival at the school I had a chance to disgrace myself, which, I am ashamed to say, I did.

Though we rode several days inside of the iron horse, I do not recall a single thing about our luncheons.

It was night when we reached the school grounds. The lights from the windows of the large buildings fell upon some of the icicled trees that stood beneath them. We were led toward an open door, where the brightness of the lights within flooded out over the heads of the excited palefaces who blocked the way. My body trembled more from fear than from the snow I trod upon.

Entering the house, I stood close against the wall. The strong glaring light in the large whitewashed room dazzled my eyes. The noisy hurrying of hard shoes upon a bare wooden floor increased the whirring in my ears. My only safety seemed to be in keeping next to the wall. As I was wondering in which direction to escape from all this confusion, two warm hands grasped me firmly, and in the same moment I was tossed high in midair. A rosy-cheeked paleface woman caught me in her arms. I was both frightened and insulted by such trifling. I stared into her eyes, wishing her to let me stand on my own feet, but she jumped me up and down with increasing enthusiasm. My mother had never made a plaything of her wee daughter. Remembering this I began to cry aloud.

They misunderstood the cause of my tears, and placed me at a white table loaded with food. There our party were united again. As I did not hush my crying, one of the older ones whispered to me, "Wait until you are alone in the night."

It was very little I could swallow besides my sobs, that evening.

"Oh, I want my mother and my brother Dawée! I want to go to my aunt!" I pleaded; but the ears of the palefaces could not hear me.

From the table we were taken along an upward incline of wooden boxes, which I learned afterward to call a stairway. At the top was a quiet hall, dimly lighted. Many narrow beds were in one straight line down the entire length of the wall. In them lay sleeping brown faces, which peeped just out of the coverings. I was tucked into bed with one of the tall girls, because she talked to me in my mother tongue and seemed to soothe me.

I had arrived in the wonderful land of rosy skies, but I was not happy, as I had thought I should be. My long travel and the bewildering sights had exhausted me. I fell asleep, heaving deep, tired sobs. My tears were left to dry themselves in streaks, because neither my aunt nor my mother was near to wipe them away.

II The Cutting of My Long Hair

The first day in the land of apples was a bitter-cold one; for the snow still covered the ground, and the trees were bare. A large bell rang for breakfast, its loud metallic voice crashing through the belfry overhead and into our sensitive ears. The annoying clatter of shoes on bare floors gave us no peace. The constant clash of harsh noises, with an undercurrent of many voices murmuring an unknown tongue, made a bedlam within which I was securely tied. And though my spirit tore itself in struggling for its lost freedom, all was useless.

A paleface woman, with white hair, came up after us. We were placed in a line of girls who were marching into the dining room. These were Indian girls, in stiff shoes and closely clinging dresses. The small girls wore sleeved aprons and shingled hair. As I walked noiselessly in my soft moccasins, I felt like sinking to the floor, for my blanket had been stripped from my shoulders. I looked hard at the Indian girls, who seemed not to care that they were even more immodestly dressed than I, in their tightly fitting clothes. While we marched in, the boys entered at an opposite door. I watched for the three young braves who came in our party. I spied them in the rear ranks, looking as uncomfortable as I felt.

A small bell was tapped, and each of the pupils drew a chair from under the table. Supposing this act meant they were to be seated, I pulled out mine and at once slipped into it from one side. But when I turned my head, I saw that I was the only one seated, and all the rest at our table remained standing. Just as I began to rise, looking shyly around to see how chairs were to be used, a second bell was sounded. All were seated at last, and I had to crawl back into my chair again. I heard a man's voice at one end of the hall, and I looked around to see him. But all the others hung their heads over their plates. As I glanced at the long chain of tables, I caught the eyes of a paleface woman upon me. Immediately I dropped my eyes, wondering why I was so keenly watched by the strange woman. The man ceased his mutterings, and then a third bell was tapped. Every one picked up his knife and fork and began eating. I began crying instead, for by this time I was afraid to venture anything more.

But this eating by formula was not the hardest trial in that first day. Late in the morning, my friend Judéwin gave me a terrible warning. Judéwin knew a few words of English; and she had overheard the paleface woman talk about cutting our long, heavy hair. Our mothers had taught us that only unskilled warriors who were captured had their hair shingled by the enemy. Among our people, short hair was worn by mourners, and shingled hair by cowards!

We discussed our fate some moments, and when Judéwin said, "We have to submit, because they are strong," I rebelled.

"No, I will not submit! I will struggle first!" I answered.

I watched my chance, and when no one noticed I disappeared. I crept up the stairs as quietly as I could in my squeaking shoes,—my moccasins had been exchanged for shoes. Along the hall I passed, without knowing whither I was going. Turning aside to an open door, I found a large room with three white beds in it. The windows were covered with dark green curtains, which made the room very dim. Thankful that no one was there, I directed my steps toward the corner farthest from the door. On my hands and knees I crawled under the bed, and cuddled myself in the dark corner.

From my hiding place I peered out, shuddering with fear whenever I heard footsteps near by. Though in the hall loud voices were calling my name, and I knew that even Judéwin was searching for me, I did not open my mouth to answer. Then the steps were quickened and the voices became excited. The sounds came nearer and nearer. Women and girls entered the room. I held my breath, and watched them open closet doors and peep behind large trunks. Some one threw up the curtains, and the room was filled with sudden light. What caused them to stoop and look under the bed I do not know. I remember being dragged out, though I resisted by kicking and scratching wildly. In spite of myself, I was carried downstairs and tied fast in a chair.

I cried aloud, shaking my head all the while until I felt the cold blades of the scissors against my neck, and heard them gnaw off one of my thick braids. Then I lost my spirit. Since the day I was taken from my mother I had suffered extreme indignities. People had stared at me. I had been tossed about in the air like a wooden puppet. And now my long hair was shingled like a coward's! In my anguish I moaned for my mother, but no one came to comfort me. Not a soul reasoned quietly with me, as my own mother used to do: for now I was only one of many little animals driven by a herder.

III The Snow Episode

A short time after our arrival we three Dakotas were playing in the snowdrifts. We were all still deaf to the English language, excepting Judéwin, who always heard such puzzling things. One morning we learned through her ears that we were forbidden to fall lengthwise in the snow, as we had been doing, to see our own impressions. However, before many hours we had forgotten the order, and were having great sport in the snow, when a shrill voice called us. Looking up, we saw an imperative hand beckoning us into the house. We shook the snow off ourselves, and started toward the woman as slowly as we dared.

Judéwin said: "Now the paleface is angry with us. She is going to punish us for falling into the snow. If she looks straight into your eyes and talks loudly, you must wait until she stops. Then, after a tiny pause, say, 'No.'" The rest of the way we practiced upon the little word "no."

As it happened, Thowin was summoned to judgment first. The door shut behind her with a click.

Judéwin and I stood silently listening at the keyhole. The paleface woman talked in very severe tones. Her words fell from her lips like crackling embers, and her inflection ran up like the small end of a switch. I understood her voice better than the things she was saying. I was certain we had made her very impatient with us. Judéwin heard enough of the words to realize all too late she had taught us the wrong reply.

"Oh, poor Thowin!" she gasped, as she put both hands over her ears.

Just then I heard Thowin's tremulous answer, "No."

With an angry exclamation, the woman gave her a hard spanking. Then she stopped to say something. Judéwin said it was this: "Are you going to obey my word the next time?"

Thowin answered again with the only word at her command, "No."

This time the woman meant her blows to smart, for the poor frightened girl shrieked at the top of her voice. In the midst of the whipping the blows ceased abruptly, and the woman asked another question: "Are you going to fall in the snow again?"

Thowin gave her bad password another trial. We heard her say feebly, "No! No!"

With this the woman hid away her half-worn slipper, and led the child out, stroking her black shorn head. Perhaps it occurred to her that brute force is not the solution for such a problem. She did nothing to Judéwin nor to me. She only returned to us our unhappy comrade, and left us alone in the room.

During the first two or three seasons misunderstandings as ridiculous as this one of the snow episode frequently took place, bringing unjustifiable frights and punishments into our little lives.

Within a year I was able to express myself somewhat in broken English. As soon as I comprehended a part of what was said and done, a mischievous spirit of revenge possessed me. One day I was called in from my play for some misconduct. I had disregarded a rule which seemed to me very needlessly binding. I was sent into the kitchen to mash the turnips for dinner. It was noon, and steaming dishes were hastily carried into the dining room. I hated turnips, and their odor which came from the brown jar was offensive to me. With fire in my heart, I took the wooden tool that the paleface woman held out to me. I stood upon a step, and, grasping the handle with both hands, I bent in hot rage over the turnips. I worked my vengeance upon them. All were so busily occupied that no one noticed me. I saw that the turnips were in a pulp, and that further beating could not improve them; but the order was, "Mash these turnips," and mash them I would! I renewed my energy; and as I sent the masher into the bottom of the jar, I felt a satisfying sensation that the weight of my body had gone into it.

Just here a paleface woman came up to my table. As she looked into the jar, she shoved my hands roughly aside. I stood fearless and angry. She placed her red hands upon the rim of the jar. Then she gave one lift and a stride away from the table. But lo! the pulpy contents fell through the crumbled bottom to the floor! She spared me no scolding phrases that I had earned. I did not heed them. I felt triumphant in my revenge, though deep within me I was a wee bit sorry to have broken the jar.

As I sat eating my dinner, and saw that no turnips were served, I whooped in my heart for having once asserted the rebellion within me. . . .

VI Four Strange Summers

After my first three years of school, I roamed again in the Western country through four strange summers.

During this time I seemed to hang in the heart of chaos, beyond the touch or voice of human aid. My brother, being almost ten years my senior, did not quite understand my feelings. My mother had never gone inside of a schoolhouse, and so she was not capable of comforting her daughter who could read and write. Even nature seemed to have no place for me. I was neither a wee girl nor a tall one; neither a wild Indian nor a tame one. This deplorable situation was the effect of my brief course in the East, and the unsatisfactory "teenth" in a girl's years.

It was under these trying conditions that, one bright afternoon, as I sat restless and unhappy in my mother's cabin, I caught the sound of the spirited step of my brother's pony on the road which passed by our dwelling. Soon I heard the wheels of a light buckboard, and Dawée's familiar "Ho!" to his pony. He alighted upon the bare ground in front of our house. Tying his pony to one of the projecting corner logs of the low-roofed cottage, he stepped upon the wooden doorstep.

I met him there with a hurried greeting, and, as I passed by, he looked a quiet "What?" into my eyes.

When he began talking with my mother, I slipped the rope from the pony's bridle. Seizing the reins and bracing my feet against the dashboard, I wheeled around in an instant. The pony was ever ready to try his speed. Looking backward, I saw Dawée waving his hand to me. I turned with the curve in the road and disappeared. I followed the winding road which crawled upward between the bases of little hillocks. Deep water-worn ditches ran parallel on either side. A strong wind blew against my cheeks and fluttered my sleeves. The pony reached the top of the highest hill, and began an even race on the level lands. There was nothing moving within that great circular horizon of the Dakota prairies save the tall grasses, over which the wind blew and rolled off in long, shadowy waves.

Within this vast wigwam of blue and green I rode reckless and insignificant. It satisfied my small consciousness to see the white foam fly from the pony's mouth.

Suddenly, out of the earth a coyote came forth at a swinging trot that was taking the cunning thief toward the hills and the village beyond. Upon the moment's impulse, I gave him a long chase and a wholesome fright. As I turned away to go back to the village, the wolf sank down upon his haunches for rest, for it was a hot summer day; and as I drove slowly homeward, I saw his sharp nose still pointed at me, until I vanished below the margin of the hilltops.

In a little while I came in sight of my mother's house. Dawée stood in the yard, laughing at an old warrior who was pointing his forefinger, and again waving his whole hand, toward the hills. With his blanket drawn over one shoulder, he talked and motioned excitedly. Dawée turned the old man by the shoulder and pointed me out to him.

"Oh, han!" (Oh, yes) the warrior muttered, and went his way. He had climbed the top of his favorite barren hill to survey the surrounding prairies, when he spied my chase after the coyote. His keen eyes recognized the pony and driver. At once uneasy for my safety, he had come running to my mother's cabin to give her warning. I did not appreciate his kindly interest, for there was an unrest gnawing at my heart.

As soon as he went away, I asked Dawée about something else.

"No, my baby sister. I cannot take you with me to the party to-night," he replied. Though I was not far from fifteen, and I felt that before long I should enjoy all the privileges of my tall cousin, Dawée persisted in calling me his baby sister.

That moonlight night, I cried in my mother's presence when I heard the jolly young people pass by our cottage. They were no more young braves in blankets and eagle plumes, nor Indian maids with prettily painted cheeks. They had gone three years to school in the East, and had become civilized. The young men wore the white man's coat and trousers, with bright neckties. The girls wore tight muslin dresses, with ribbons at neck and waist. At these gatherings they talked

English. I could speak English almost as well as my brother, but I was not properly dressed to be taken along. I had no hat, no ribbons, and no close-fitting gown. Since my return from school I had thrown away my shoes, and wore again the soft moccasins.

While Dawée was busily preparing to go I controlled my tears. But when I heard him bounding away on his pony, I buried my face in my arms and cried hot tears.

My mother was troubled by my unhappiness. Coming to my side, she offered me the only printed matter we had in our home. It was an Indian Bible, given her some years ago by a missionary. She tried to console me. "Here, my child, are the white man's papers. Read a little from them," she said most piously.

I took it from her hand, for her sake; but my enraged spirit felt more like burning the book, which afforded me no help, and was a perfect delusion to my mother. I did not read it, but laid it unopened on the floor, where I sat on my feet. The dim yellow light of the braided muslin burning in a small vessel of oil flickered and sizzled in the awful silent storm which followed my rejection of the Bible.

Now my wrath against the fates consumed my tears before they reached my eyes. I sat stony, with a bowed head. My mother threw a shawl over her head and shoulders, and stepped out into the night.

After an uncertain solitude, I was suddenly aroused by a loud cry piercing the night. It was my mother's voice wailing among the barren hills which held the bones of buried warriors. She called aloud for her brothers' spirits to support her in her helpless misery. My fingers grew icy cold, as I realized that my unrestrained tears had betrayed my suffering to her, and she was grieving for me.

Before she returned, though I knew she was on her way, for she had ceased her weeping, I extinguished the light, and leaned my head on the window sill.

Many schemes of running away from my surroundings hovered about in my mind. A few more moons of such a turmoil drove me away to the Eastern school. I rode on the white man's iron steed, thinking it would bring me back to my mother in a few winters, when I should be grown tall, and there would be congenial friends awaiting me.

VII Incurring My Mother's Displeasure

In the second journey to the East I had not come without some precautions. I had a secret interview with one of our best medicine men, and when I left his wigwam I carried securely in my sleeve a tiny bunch of magic roots. This possession assured me of friends wherever I should go. So absolutely did I believe in its charms that I wore it through all the school routine for more than a year. Then, before I lost my faith in the dead roots, I lost the little buckskin bag containing all my good luck.

At the close of this second term of three years I was the proud owner of my first diploma. The following autumn I ventured upon a college career against my mother's will.

I had written for her approval, but in her reply I found no encouragement. She called my notice to her neighbors' children, who had completed their education in three years. They had returned to their homes, and were then talking English with the frontier settlers. Her few words hinted that I had better give up my slow attempt to learn the white man's ways, and be content to roam over the prairies and find my living upon wild roots. I silenced her by deliberate disobedience.

Thus, homeless and heavy-hearted, I began anew my life among strangers.

As I hid myself in my little room in the college dormitory, away from the scornful and yet curious eyes of the students, I pined for sympathy. Often I wept in secret, wishing I had gone West, to be nourished by my mother's love, instead of remaining among a cold race whose hearts were frozen hard with prejudice.

During the fall and winter seasons I scarcely had a real friend, though by that time several of my classmates were courteous to me at a safe distance.

My mother had not yet forgiven my rudeness to her, and I had no moment for letterwriting. By daylight and lamplight, I spun with reeds and thistles, until my hands were tired from their weaving, the magic design which promised me the white man's respect.

At length, in the spring term, I entered an oratorical contest among the various classes. As the day of competition approached, it did not seem possible that the event was so near at hand, but it came. In the chapel the classes assembled together, with their invited guests. The high platform was carpeted, and gayly festooned with college colors. A bright white light illumined the room, and outlined clearly the great polished beams that arched the domed ceiling. The assembled crowds filled the air with pulsating murmurs. When the hour for speaking arrived all were hushed. But on the wall the old clock which pointed out the trying moment ticked calmly on.

One after another I saw and heard the orators. Still, I could not realize that they longed for the favorable decision of the judges as much as I did. Each contestant received a loud burst of applause, and some were cheered heartily. Too soon my turn came, and I paused a moment behind the curtains for a deep breath. After my concluding words, I heard the same applause that the others had called out.

Upon my retreating steps, I was astounded to receive from my fellow-students a large bouquet of roses tied with flowing ribbons. With the lovely flowers I fled from the stage. This friendly token was a rebuke to me for the hard feelings I had borne them.

Later, the decision of the judges awarded me the first place. Then there was a mad uproar in the hall, where my classmates sang and shouted my name at the top of their lungs; and the disappointed students howled and brayed in fearfully dissonant tin trumpets. In this excitement, happy students rushed forward to offer their congratulations. And I could not conceal a smile when they wished to escort me in a procession to the students' parlor, where all were going to calm themselves. Thanking them for the kind spirit which prompted them to make such a proposition, I walked alone with the night to my own little room.

A few weeks afterward, I appeared as the college representative in another contest. This time the competition was among orators from different colleges in our State. It was held at the State capital, in one of the largest opera houses.

Here again was a strong prejudice against my people. In the evening, as the great audience filled the house, the student bodies began warring among themselves. Fortunately, I was spared witnessing any of the noisy wrangling before the contest began. The slurs against the Indian that stained the lips of our opponents were already burning like a dry fever within my breast.

But after the orations were delivered a deeper burn awaited me. There, before that vast ocean of eyes, some college rowdies threw out a large white flag, with a drawing of a most forlorn Indian girl on it. Under this they had printed in bold black letters words that ridiculed the college which was represented by a "squaw." Such worse than barbarian rudeness embittered me. While we waited for the verdict of the judges, I gleamed fiercely upon the throngs of palefaces. My teeth were hard set, as I saw the white flag still floating insolently in the air.

Then anxiously we watched the man carry toward the stage the envelope containing the final decision.

There were two prizes given, that night, and one of them was mine!

The evil spirit laughed within me when the white flag dropped out of sight, and the hands which hurled it hung limp in defeat.

Leaving the crowd as quickly as possible, I was soon in my room. The rest of the night I sat in an armchair and gazed into the crackling fire. I laughed no more in triumph when thus alone. The little taste of victory did not satisfy a hunger in my heart. In my mind I saw my mother far away on the Western plains, and she was holding a charge against me.

2

IMMIGRANTS AND ATTITUDES

Immigrants and Attitudes looks at the lives and attitudes of immigrant Americans from the mid-nineteenth century to the late twentieth century. The experience of Jewish, Chinese, Italian, and Irish newcomers to the labor market is the focus. Narratives and graphics provide both external views—such as journalism by Jacob Riis that documents the conditions of immigrant life—and internal views, such as the poetry of early Chinese immigrants to California. Henry James's observation of immigrant workers in the New York of 1907 tells us what a sophisticated American thought about the changes that had and would be wrought in the States by these new citizens, while Constantine Panunzio, one of those workers, details his experience of America, showing us aspects of the situation that James could not see. Eva Hoffman and Chitra Divakaruni write of the alienation and resistance to assimilation of recent immigrants from Poland and India, respectively. Other selections expose contestations between and among racialized and ethnic Americans.

JAMES M. MCPHERSON
(1936-)

Historian James McPherson has written extensively on the American Civil War and has received widespread acclaim for his research. He was born in Valley City, South Dakota, and obtained a B.A. from Gustavus Adolphus College. He received his Ph.D. in 1963 from The Johns Hopkins University and has taught at Princeton University since 1962, where he is currently the George Henry Davis Professor of American History. He has produced several books on the history of the Civil War, and in 1989 his history of the war, Battle Cry of Freedom, *was a national bestseller and was awarded the Pulitzer Prize. He has received fellowships from the National Endowment for the Humanities and the John Simon Guggenheim Memorial Foundation. His most recent work is a collection of essays,* Drawn with the Sword: Reflections on the American Civil War.*

In this chapter from his study The Negro's Civil War: How American Negroes Felt and Acted During the War for the Union *(1965) McPherson focuses on reactions to the "Draft Riots" and other resentful mob actions against African Americans as the "cause" of the war.*

ANTI-NEGRO MOB VIOLENCE IN THE NORTH, 1862-63

*W*hatever the change in the spirit of Southern dreams may have been, the Negro had to overcome a great deal of hostility in the North before he could begin to exploit the potential opportunities for his race opened up by the Civil War. In an editorial on March 29, 1862, the Anglo-African *declared that a "strong impediment" to Negro advancement was "the prejudice of the North."*

We may as well look this prejudice in the face as a disturbing element in the way of emancipation. Its manifest expression is, that setting black men free to be the equals of white men in the slave States is something more dreadful than rebellion or secession, or even a dismembered union. . . . The other form in which this prejudice is pronounced, is, in the fear expressed that the retaining of colored free laborers in the South will interfere with the domain of white laborers. . . . Poor, chicken-hearted, semi-barbarous Caucasians, when will you learn that "the earth was made for MAN"? You have arts and arms, and culture, and an overwhelming majority in numbers. . . . Must you die and give no sign that you have been able to surmount the prejudice of race, or your dread of the Negro?

The Anglo-African *had good reasons for its apprehensions, for the anti-Negro feeling in the North boiled over into several serious race riots in 1862-63. These riots were sparked by job competition between white and Negro laborers, by the white workingman's fear that emancipation would loose a flood of Negroes upon the labor market and drive down wages, and by the inflammatory statements of the Democratic press and Democratic politicians. In southern Illinois, Indiana, Ohio, and Penn-*

sylvania, a small influx of freedmen from the South seeking employment lent reality to white fears of Negro competition. In other areas where violence occurred during the war, there was a long tradition of racial friction—this was especially true in New York City, Brooklyn, Philadelphia, and Buffalo.

Lorillard and Watson's tobacco factory in Brooklyn employed twenty-five colored people, most of them women and children. In August 1862, a mob of Irish workers forced their way into the factory and set it afire, hoping to burn down the building with the Negroes in it. Fortunately the police arrived in time to extinguish the flames and rescue the employees, but the murderous mood of the mob betokened ill for the future. The Anglo-African *published the following editorial concerning the Brooklyn incident:*

Irishmen! the day will come that you will find out that you are making a sad mistake in assisting to crush out our liberties. Learn! O learn, that the protection of the feeblest of your fellow beings, is the only guarantee you have of the protection for your own liberty in this or any other land. We call upon the world to bear witness to the dreadful effects which the system of slavery has had upon the Irish people. In their own country they are kind and hospitable to our poor and constantly abused race; but here, so dreadfully corrupted do some of them become that they are prepared for the vilest deed of diabolism which it is possible for the brain of man to conceive, as is witnessed in their attempt to roast alive a number of people who never did them the least harm. Americans! we charge you before high Heaven and the whole civilized world with being the authors of this great wickedness. It was you who first taught them to hate us. . . . Why, our countrymen, will you not put away this great wickedness from among you?

On March 6, 1863, a mob of white men marched into the Negro section of Detroit, destroyed thirty-two houses, killed several Negroes, and left more than two hundred people homeless. The Christian Recorder, *official organ of the A.M.E. Church, declared in an editorial:*

We have to chronicle one of the most disgraceful, inhuman, and heathen-like riots, ever recorded upon the pages of history. It occurred in the city of Detroit, Mich. . . . What have the coloured people done that they should be thus treated? Even here, in the city of Philadelphia, in many places it is almost impossible for a respectable colored person to walk the streets without being insulted by a set of blackguards and cowards; and the very lowest and most vulgar language that ever any human being uttered, is addressed to our wives and daughters. How long shall this state of things continue? For we solemnly declare that there is not a more true and loyal people to the Union than the colored people, and we hope that our city papers will come down on such conduct.

On July 13, 1863, New York's lower-class white population erupted into four of the bloodiest days of mob violence ever witnessed by the metropolis. The immediate object of the mob's wrath was the draft enrollment office, but the city's helpless Negro population bore the brunt of the violence. Dozens of Negroes were lynched in the streets or murdered in their homes. The Colored Orphan Asylum was burned to the ground. Four years later a Negro author published the following account of the riots:

The mob was composed of the lowest and most degraded of the foreign population (mainly Irish), raked from the filthy cellars and dens of the city, steeped in crimes of the deepest dye, and ready for any act, no matter how dark and damnable; together with the worst type of our native criminals. . . . Breaking into stores, hotels, and saloons, and helping themselves to strong drink, *ad libitum,* they became inebriated, and marched through every part of the city. Calling at places where large bodies of men were at work, and pressing them in, their numbers rapidly increased to thousands, and their fiendish depredations had no bounds. Having been taught by the leaders of the Democratic party to hate the negro, and having but a few weeks previous seen regiments of colored volunteers pass through New York on their way south, this infuriated band of drunken men, women, and children paid special visits to all localities inhabited by the blacks, and murdered all they could lay their hands on, without regard to age or sex. Every place known to employ negroes was searched: steamboats leaving the city, and railroad depots, were watched, lest some should escape their vengeance.

Hundreds of the blacks, driven from their homes, and hunted and chased through the streets, presented themselves at the doors of jails, prisons, and police-stations, and begged admission. . . .

Blacks were chased to the docks, thrown into the river and drowned; while some, after being murdered, were hung to lamp-posts. Between forty and fifty colored persons were killed [probably an exaggerated estimate], and nearly as many maimed for life.

The Brooklyn correspondent of the Christian Recorder *wrote shortly after the riots that*

many men were killed and thrown into the rivers, a great number hung to trees and lamp-posts, numbers shot down; no black person could show their [sic] heads but what they were hunted like wolves. These scenes continued for four days. Hundreds of our people are in station houses, in the woods, and on Blackwell's island. Over three thousand are to-day homeless and destitute, without means of support for their families. It is truly a day of distress to our race in this section. In Brooklyn we have not had any great trouble, but many of our people have been compelled to leave their houses and flee for refuge. The Irish have become so brutish, that it is unsafe for families to live near them, and while I write, there are many now in the stations and country hiding from violence. . . .

In Weeksville and Flatbush, the colored men who had manhood in them armed themselves, and threw out their pickets every day and night, determined to die defending their homes. Hundreds fled there from New York. . . . The mob spirit seemed to have run in every direction, and every little village catches the rebellious spirit. One instance is worthy of note. In the village of Flushing, the colored people went to the Catholic priest and told him that they were peaceable men doing no harm to any one, and that the Irish had threatened to mob them, but if they did, they would burn two Irish houses for every one of theirs, and would kill two Irish men for every colored man killed by them. They were not mobbed, and so in every place where they were prepared they escaped being mobbed. Most of the colored men in Brooklyn who remained in the city were armed daily for self-defence.

William P. Powell, a Negro physician, barely managed to save himself and his family from the mob. He published the following account:

On the afternoon of [July 13] my house . . . was invaded by a mob of half grown boys. . . . [They] were soon replaced by men and women. From 2 P.M. to 8 P.M. myself and family were prisoners in my own house to king mob, from which there was no way to excape but over the roofs of adjoining houses. About 4 P.M. . . . the mob commenced throwing stones at the lower windows, until they had succeeded in making an opening. I was determined not to leave until driven from the premises. My family including my invalid daughter . . . took refuge on the roof of the next house. I remained till the mob broke in, and then narrowly escaped the same way. . . . We remained on the roof for an hour; still I hoped that relief would come. The neighbors, anticipating the mob would fire my house, were removing their effects on the roof—all was excitement. But as the object of the mob was plunder, they were too busily engaged in carrying off all my effects to apply the torch. . . .

How to escape from the roof of a five story building, with four females—and one a cripple—besides eight men, without a ladder, or any assistance from outside, was beyond my not excited imagination. But the God that succored Hagar in her flight, came to my relief in the person of a little deformed, despised Israelite—who, Samaritan-like, took my poor helpless daughter under his protection in his house, where I presume she now is, until friends send her to me. He also supplied me with a long rope. I then took a survey of the premises, and fortunately found a way to escape, and though pitchy dark, I took soundings with the rope to see if it would touch the next roof, after which I took a clove-hitch around the clothes line which was fastened to the wall by pulleys, and which led from one roof to the other over a space of about one hundred feet. In this manner I managed to lower my family down on to the next roof, and from one roof to another, until I landed them in a neighbor's yard. We were secreted in our friend's cellar till 11 P.M., when we were taken in charge by the Police and locked up in the Station house for safety. In this dismal place we found upwards of seventy men, women and children—some with broken limbs—bruised and beaten from head to foot. . . .

All my personal property, to the amount of $3,000, has been destroyed and scattered to the four winds. . . . As a devoted loyal Unionist, I have done all I could to perpetuate and uphold the integrity of this free government. As an evidence of this devotedness, my oldest son is now serving my country as a surgeon in the U.S. army, and myself had just received a commission in the naval service. What more could I do? What further evidence was wanting to prove my allegiance in the exigencies of our unfortunate country? I am now an old man, stripped of everything, . . . but I thank God that He has yet spared my life, which I am ready to yield in defence of my country.

"Great God! what is this nation coming to?" asked the Christian Recorder *in an editorial on "The Riots in New York":*
These rioters of New York could not be satisfied with the resistance of the draft and doing all the damage they could against the government and those of the white citizens who are friends to the administration, but must wheel upon the colored people, killing and beating every one whom they could see and catch, and destroying their property. . . . A gloom of infamy and shame will hang over New York for centuries. . . . Our citizens are expecting every day that a mob will break out here, in Philadelphia. . . . If so, we have only to say this to our colored citizens of Philadelphia and vicinity: Have plenty of powder and ball in your houses, and use it with effect, if necessary, in the protection of your wives and children; and even [boiling] water, if need be; for any and every person has a perfect right to protect their [sic] homes.

Dr. J. W. C. Pennington discussed the lessons of the Draft Riots in a speech at Poughkeepsie on August 24, 1863, which deserves quotation at length:
The elements of this mob have been centering and gathering strength in New York, for more than two years. And, as soon as the rebellion broke out, prominent

colored men in passing the streets, were often hailed as "Old Abe," or "Jeff. Davis," evidently to feel their loyal pulse, and as it became evident that our sympathies were with the Federal government, we became objects of more marked abuse and insult. From many of the grocery corners, stones, potatoes, and pieces of coal, would often be hurled, by idle young loafers, standing about. . . . The language addressed to colored men, not seemly to record on paper, became the common language of the street, and even of some of the fashionable avenues. . . . In no other country in the world would the streets of refined cities be allowed to be polluted, as those of New York have been, with foul and indecent language, without rebuke from the press, the pulpit, or the authorities. . . . What has been the result? Why, just what we might have expected,—the engendering of a public feeling unfriendly toward colored people. This feeling, once created, might at any moment be intensified into an outbreak against its unoffending objects. . . .

The opposition to the draft comes largely from that class of men of foreign birth who had declared their intention to become citizens, but who have not done so. They have been duly notified that they could leave the country within sixty days, or submit to the draft. . . . They do not wish to leave the country, and they do not wish to fight. . . . Dishonest politicians aim to make these men believe that the war has been undertaken to abolish slavery; and so far as they believe so, their feelings are against colored people. . . .

Let the greedy foreigner know that a part of this country BELONGS TO US; and that we assert the right to live and labor here: That in New York and other cities, we claim the right to buy, hire, occupy and use houses and tenements, for legal considerations; to pass and repass on the streets, lanes, avenues, and all public ways. Our fathers have fought for this country, and helped to free it from the British yoke. We are now fighting to help to free it from the British yoke. We are now fighting to help to free it from the combined conspiracy of Jeff. Davis and Co.; we are doing so with the distinct understanding, that WE ARE TO HAVE ALL OUR RIGHTS AS MEN AND AS CITIZENS, and, that there are to be no side issues, no RESERVATIONS, either political, civil, or religious. In this struggle we know nothing but God, Manhood, and American Nationality, full and unimpaired. . . .

How does the matter sum up? It sums up thus; for more than a year, the riot spirit had been culminating, before it burst forth. . . . The loss of life and property make only a small part of the damage. The breaking up of families; and business relations just beginning to prosper; the blasting of hopes just dawning; the loss of precious harvest time which will never again return; the feeling of insecurity engendered; the confidence destroyed; the reaction; and lastly, the gross insult offered to our character as a people, sum up a weight of injury which can be realized by the most enlightened and sensitive minds among us. . . .

For all the purposes, therefore, of social, civil, and religious enjoyment, and right, we hold New York solemnly bound to insure us, as citizens, permanent security in our homes. Relief, and damage money, is well enough. But it cannot atone, fully, for evils done by riots. It cannot bring back our murdered dead. It cannot remove the insults we feel; and finally, it gives no proof that the people have really changed their minds, for the better towards us.

In the end, the sympathy aroused for the colored victims of the Draft Riots helped to better the status of Negroes not only in New York but all over the North. But the black man still had to face many decisions and trials before his position improved.

G. F. STRECKFUSS

A small number of early nineteenth-century immigrants returned to Europe after a period of adventure and money making in America.. G. F. Streck-fuss, about whom little is known, recorded his adventure in America in his book, Der Auswanderer nach America, *published in his native Germany in 1836. This excerpt from his book reveals the nature of prejudice against Jews in the United States in the period of Jacksonian expansion.*

EXCERPT FROM

DER AUSWANDERER NACH AMERICA

I continued my peddling until January 1835, when one evening, in deep snow and quite frozen, I came to Easton, a pretty little town in Delaware, and entered an inn. A number of guests sat around the glowering stoves; and as they saw me enter, a pale and snow-covered merchant, a feeling of compassion must have come over them, for nearly everyone bought something of me; and thus even in the evening, I did some good business, after I had run about the whole day in terrible winter weather, earning scarcely enough for a drink. While preoccupied with my business, I was watched by an oldish-looking, occasionally smiling but apparently uncon-cerned man behind the stove. He allowed me to finish the business in peace but then he got up, tapped me on the shoulder, and bade me follow him. Out of doors, his first question was whether I had a trade-license for peddling. I still felt so strange in America, and he spoke in so low a voice, that I did not understand him and, there-fore, looked at him in astonishment. My long, ten-days-old beard struck him, and he asked me further whether I was a Jew. He did not want to believe me when I denied it. Fortunately, I had with me the passport of my homeland, which I presented to him. Now he grew somewhat better disposed, looking at me sympathetically, and said, "Since I see that you are an honest Protestant Christian I shall let you go, although I am losing twenty-five dollars through it. I have no kind feelings for the Jews, and were you one of them, I would not treat you so gently. If I wanted to arrest you, you would have to pay fifty dollars' fine or, until you were able to raise it, you would have to go to jail, and half the fine would be mine. Still, I shall forego that; but you better give up your trade and look for another one. Sooner or later you will be caught and then you'll be out of luck."

After having said this he shook my hand and went away. . . .

When I stepped again into the room, the friendly innkeeper was able to observe my embarrassment and guess what had taken place. He praised the humane con-stable, laughed at his Jew-hatred, but he, too, advised me to quit my trade.

NO IRISH NEED APPLY

The Irish immigrants who came to the United States during and after the Potato Famine of the mid-1840s encountered prejudices aimed at their religion and their ethnicity. The Protestant majority was suspicious of Catholic allegiance to the Pope, who was then still a significant force in European politics, and British propaganda treated the Irish as a virtually subhuman species, little better than the "uncivilized" black and brown subjects of their empire in Asia, Africa, and the Caribbean. While Irish women found work as domestics and mill hands, Irish men, particularly those with skills, were faced by postings indicating that their applications for work were not welcome.

> # HELP WANTED
> ## NO IRISH NEED APPLY

Like the oppressed everywhere, these Irish-Americans made fun of such bigoted employers in story and song. The following nineteenth-century ballad is called simply "No Irish Need Apply."

> I'm a decent lad just landed from the town of Ballyfad;
> I want a situation and I want it very bad.
> I've seen employment advertised. "It's just the thing," says I,
> But the dirty spalpeen [rascal] ended with "No Irish Need Apply."
> "Whoo," says I, "that is an insult, but to get the place I'll try."
> So I went there to see the blackguard with his "No Irish Need Apply."
>
> *Chorus:*
> Some do think it is a misfortune to be christened Pat or Dan,
> But to me it is an honor to be born an Irishman.
>
> I started out to find the house, I got there mighty soon;
> I found the old chap seated—he was reading the *Tribune.*
> I told him what I came for, when he in a rage did fly;
> "No!" he says. "You are a Paddy, and no Irish need apply."
> Then I gets my dander rising, and I'd like to black his eye
> For to tell an Irish gentleman "No Irish Need Apply."
>
> I couldn't stand it longer so a-hold of him I took,
> And I gave him such a welting as he'd get at Donnybrook.
> He hollered "Milia Murther," and to get away did try,
> And swore he'd never write again "No Irish Need Apply."
> Well, he made a big apology; I told him then goodbye,
> Saying, "When next you want a beating, write 'No Irish Need Apply.'"

SONGS FROM GOLD MOUNTAIN

Most of the Chinese who immigrated to the United States in the late 1800s were former residents of Canton Province in southeast China. Many of these immigrants eventually settled in San Francisco's Chinatown, where a vibrant literary community developed. Chinese-language newspapers regularly published poetry, poetry writing groups were established, and writing contests were regularly held. These poems represent one form of vernacular poetry referred to as "Gold Mountain Songs." Two anthologies of these rhymes, containing over 1,600 poems, were published in the early 1900s by a Chinatown publisher. A selection of 220 of these poems was later published by Marlon K. Hom, and the poems included here are from that anthology. Since these poems were vernacular rhymes using colloquial language, the authors, as was tradition, did not identify themselves.

THREE GOLD MOUNTAIN POEMS

In search of a pin-head gain,
I was idle in an impoverished village.
I've risked a perilous journey to come to the Flowery Flag Nation.
Immigration officers interrogated me:
And, just for a slight lapse of memory,
I am deported, and imprisoned in this barren mountain.
A brave man cannot use his might here,
And he can't take one step beyond the confines.

At home I was in poverty,
    constantly worried about firewood and rice.
I borrowed money
    to come to Gold Mountain.
Immigration officers cross-examined me;
    no way could I get through.
Deported to this island,
    like a convicted criminal.
Here—
Mournful sighs fill the gloomy room.
A nation weak; her people often humiliated
Like animals, tortured and destroyed at others' whim.

So, liberty is your national principle;
Why do you practice autocracy?
You don't uphold justice, you Americans,

You detain me in prison, guard me closely.
Your officials are wolves and tigers,
All ruthless, all wanting to bite me.
An innocent man implicated, such an injustice!
When can I get out of the prison and free my mind?

MAXINE HONG KINGSTON
(1940-)

Maxine Hong Kingston is the child of Chinese immigrants and was raised in Stockton, California. She studied English and American literature at the University of California, Berkeley, where she received her B.A. in 1962. She earned a teaching certificate from the state of California in 1965 and taught English and mathematics in Hayward, California, for two years. She moved to Hawaii in 1967, where she continued her teaching career, and in 1976 her first book, The Woman Warrior, Memoirs of a Girlhood Among Ghosts, *was published. In the book, Kingston used a unique blending of personal history, myth, and autobiography to tell the various stories of the women in her family. The book was an immediate success, becoming a bestseller and winning the National Book Critic's Circle Award for nonfiction. Her innovative style continued with her second book,* China Men, *which brought her further acclaim. It was also a national bestseller and received the American Book Award for nonfiction in 1981. She has since written a more straightforward fiction novel,* Tripmaster Monkey: His Fake Book *(1989), and contributed stories and articles to numerous publications. She lives in Oakland, California.*

The following excerpt from China Men *summarizes the sequence of anti-Chinese immigration laws and other legislation that oppressed Kingston's ancestors.*

THE LAWS

The United States of America and the Emperor of China cordially recognize the inherent and inalienable right of man to change his home and allegiance, and also the mutual advantage of the free migration and emigration of their citizens and subjects respectively from the one country to the other for purposes of curiosity, of trade, or as permanent residents. ARTICLE V OF THE BURLINGAME TREATY, SIGNED IN WASHINGTON, D.C., JULY 28, 1868, AND IN PEKING, NOVEMBER 23, 1869

The First Years: 1868, the year of the Burlingame Treaty, was the year 40,000 miners of Chinese ancestry were Driven Out. The Fourteenth Amendment, adopted in that same year, said that naturalized Americans have the same rights as native-born

Americans, but in 1870 the Nationality Act specified that only "free whites" and "African aliens" were allowed to apply for naturalization. Chinese were not white; this had been established legally in 1854 when Chan Young unsuccessfully applied for citizenship in Federal District Court in San Francisco and was turned down on grounds of race. (He would have been illegal one way or another anyway; the Emperor of China did not give permission for any of his subjects to leave China until 1859.) Debating the Nationality Act, Congressmen declared that America would be a nation of "Nordic fiber."

1878: California held a Constitutional Convention to settle "the Chinese problem." Of the 152 delegates, 35 were not American citizens but Europeans. The resulting constitution, voted into existence by a majority party of Working Men and Grangers, prohibited Chinese from entering California. New state laws empowered cities and counties to confine them within specified areas or to throw them out completely. Shipowners and captains were to be fined and jailed for hiring or transporting them. (This provision was so little respected that the American merchant marine relied heavily on Chinese seamen from the Civil War years to World War I.) "Mongolians, Indians, and Negroes" were barred from attending public schools. The only California fishermen forced to pay fishing and shellfish taxes were the Chinese, who had brought shrimp nets from China and started the shrimp, abalone, and lobster industries. (The taxes were payable monthly.) Those Chinese over eighteen who were not already paying a miner's tax had to pay a "police tax," to cover the extra policing their presence required. Though the Chinese were filling and leveeing the San Joaquin Delta for thirteen cents a square yard, building the richest agricultural land in the world, they were prohibited from owning land or real estate. They could not apply for business licenses. Employers could be fined and jailed for hiring them. No Chinese could be hired by state, county, or municipal governments for public works. No "Chinese or Mongolian or Indian" could testify in court "either for or against a white man."

At this time San Francisco supplemented the anti-Chinese state laws with some of its own: a queue tax, a "cubic air ordinance" requiring that every residence have so many cubic feet of air per inhabitant, a pole law prohibiting the use of carrying baskets on poles, cigar taxes, shoe taxes, and laundry taxes.

Federal courts declared some of the state and city laws unconstitutional, and occasionally citizens of a county or city repealed an especially punitive ordinance on the grounds that it was wrong to invite the Chinese to come to the United States and then deny them a livelihood. The repealed laws were often reenacted in another form.

1880: The Burlingame Treaty was modified. Instead of being free, the immigration of Chinese laborers to the United States would be "reasonably limited." In return (so as not to bring about limits on American entry into China), the American government promised to protect Chinese from lynchings.

1881: The Burlingame Treaty was suspended for a period of twenty years. (Since 1881 there has been no freedom of travel between China and the United States.) In protest against this suspension and against the refusal to admit Chinese boys to U.S. Army and Naval academies, China ordered scholars studying in the United States to return home. The act suspending the treaty did have two favorable provisions: all Chinese already resident in the United States in 1882 could stay; and they were permitted to leave and reenter with a Certificate of Return.

1882: Encouraged by fanatical lobbying from California, the U.S. Congress passed the first Chinese Exclusion Act. It banned the entrance of Chinese laborers, both skilled and unskilled, for ten years. Anyone unqualified for citizenship could not come in—and by the terms of the Nationality Act of 1870, Chinese were not qualified for citizenship. Some merchants and scholars were granted temporary visas.

1884: Congress refined the Exclusion Act with An Act to Amend an Act. This raised fines and sentences and further defined "merchants" to exclude "hucksters, peddlers, or those engaged in taking, draying, or otherwise preserving shell or other fish for home consumption or exportation."

1888: The Scott Act, passed by Congress, again forbade the entry of Chinese laborers. It also declared that Certificates of Return were void. Twenty thousand Chinese were trapped outside the United States with now-useless re-entry permits. Six hundred returning travelers were turned back at American ports. A Chinese ambassador, humiliated by immigration officers, killed himself. The law decreed that Certificates of Residence had to be shown on demand; any Chinese caught without one was deported.

1889: Chinese pooled money to fight the various Exclusion Acts in the courts. They rarely won. In *Chae Chan Ping* v. *The United States,* Chae Chan Ping argued for the validity of his Certificate of Return. The Supreme Court ruled against him, saying that "regardless of the existence of a prior treaty," a race "that will not assimilate with us" could be excluded when deemed "dangerous to . . . peace and security. . . . It matters not in what form aggression and encroachment come, whether from the foreign nation acting in its national character or from vast hordes of its people crowding in upon us." Moreover, said the Court, "sojourners" should not "claim surprise" that any Certificates of Return obtained prior to 1882 were "held at the will of the government, revocable at any time, at its pleasure."

1892: The Geary Act extended the 1882 Exclusion Act for another ten years. It also decreed that Chinese caught illegally in the United States be deported after one year of hard labor.

Chinese Americans formed the Equal Rights League and the Native Sons of the Golden State in order to fight disenfranchisement bills. Chinese Americans demanded the right to have their citizenship confirmed before traveling abroad.

1893: In *Yue Ting* v. *The United States,* the U.S. Supreme Court ruled that Congress had the right to expel members of a race who "continue to be aliens, having taken no steps toward becoming citizens, and incapable of becoming such under the naturalization laws." This applied only to Chinese; no other race or nationality was excluded from applying for citizenship.

1896: A victory. In *Yick Wo* v. *Hopkins,* the U.S. Supreme Court overturned San Francisco safety ordinances, saying that they were indeed designed to harass laundrymen of Chinese ancestry.

1898: Another victory. The Supreme Court decision in *The United States* v. *Wong Kim Ark* stated that a person born in the United States to Chinese parents is an American. This decision has never been reversed or changed, and it is the law on which most Americans of Chinese ancestry base their citizenship today.

1900: Deciding *The United States* v. *Mrs. Cue Lim,* the Supreme Court ruled that wives and children of treaty merchants—citizens of China, aliens traveling on visas—were allowed to come to the United States.

1904: The Chinese Exclusion Acts were extended indefinitely, and made to cover Hawai'i and the Philippines as well as the continental United States. The question of exclusion was not debated in Congress; instead, the measure passed as a rider on a routine appropriations bill. China boycotted American goods in protest.

1906: The San Francisco Board of Education ordered that all Chinese, Japanese, and Korean children be segregated in an Oriental school. President Roosevelt, responding to a protest from the Japanese government, persuaded the Board of Education to allow Japanese to attend white schools.

1917: Congress voted that immigrants over sixteen years of age be required to pass an English reading test.

1924: An Immigration Act passed by Congress specifically excluded "Chinese women, wives, and prostitutes." Any American who married a Chinese woman lost his citizenship; any Chinese man who married an American woman caused her to lose her citizenship. Many states had also instituted antimiscegenation laws. A Supreme Court case called *Chang Chan et al.* v. *John D. Nagle* tested the law against wives; Chang Chan et al. lost. For the first time, the 1924 Immigration Act distinguished between two kinds of "aliens": "immigrants" were admitted as permanent residents with the opportunity to become citizens eventually; the rest—scholars, merchants, ministers, and tourists—were admitted on a temporary basis and were not eligible for citizenship. The number of persons allowed in the category of immigrant was set by law at one-sixth of one percent of the total population of that ancestry in the United States as of the 1920 census. The 1920 census had the lowest count of ethnic Chinese in this country since 1860. As a result, only 105 Chinese immigrants were permitted each year.

In *Cheuno Sumchee* v. *Nagle,* the Supreme Court once again confirmed the right of treaty merchants to bring their wives to the United States. This was a right that continued to be denied to Chinese Americans.

1938: A Presidential proclamation lifted restriction on immigration for Chinese and nationals of a few other Asian countries. The Chinese were still ineligible for citizenship, and the quota was "100."

1943: The United States and China signed a treaty of alliance against the Japanese, and Congress repealed the Exclusion Act of 1882. Immigration continued to be limited to the 1924 quota of 105, however, and the Immigration and Nationalization Service claimed to be unable to find even that many qualified Chinese. A "Chinese" was defined as anyone with more than 50 percent Chinese blood, regardless of citizenship or country of residence. At this time Japanese invaders were killing Chinese civilians in vast numbers; it is estimated that more than 10 million died. Chinese immigration into the United States did not rise.

1946: Congress passed the War Bride Act, enabling soldiers to bring Japanese and European wives home, then enacted a separate law allowing the wives and children of Chinese Americans to apply for entry as "non-quota immigrants." Only now did the ethnic Chinese population in the United States begin to approach the level of seventy years previous. (When the first Exclusion Act was passed in 1882, there were some 107,000 Chinese here; the Acts and the Driving Out steadily reduced the number to fewer than 70,000 in the 1920s.)

1948: The Refugee Act passed by Congress this year applied only to Europeans. A separate Displaced Persons Act provided that for a limited time—1948 to 1954—ethnic Chinese already living in the United States could apply for citizenship. During the post-war period, about 10,000 Chinese were permitted to enter the country under individual private bills passed by Congress. Confidence men, like the Citizenship Judges of old, defrauded hopeful Chinese by promising to acquire one of these bills for $1,500.

1950: After the Chinese Communist government took over in 1949, the United States passed a series of Refugee Relief Acts and a Refugee Escapee Act expanding the number of "non-quota immigrants" allowed in. As a condition of entry, the Internal Security Act provided that these refugees swear they were not Communists. (Several hundred "subversives or anarchists" of various races were subsequently deported; some were naturalized citizens who were "denaturalized" beforehand.)

1952: The Immigration and Nationality Act denied admission to "subversive and undesirable aliens" and made it simpler to deport "those already in the country." Another provision of this act was that for the first time Chinese women were allowed to immigrate under the same conditions as men.

1954: Ruling on *Mao* v. *Brownell,* the Supreme Court upheld laws forbidding Chinese Americans to send money to relatives in China. Before the Communist Revolution, there were no such restrictions in effect; Chinese Americans sent $70 million during World War II. Nor could they send money or gifts through CARE, UNESCO, or church organizations, which provided only for non-Communist countries.

1957: The Refugee Relief Act of 1953 expired in 1956 and was followed by the Act of 1957, which provided for the distribution of 18,000 visas that had remained unused.

1959: Close relatives, including parents, were allowed to enter.

1960: A "Fair Share Refugee Act" allowed certain refugees from Communist and Middle Eastern countries to enter. Close to 20,000 people who were "persecuted because of race, religion, or political beliefs" immigrated before this act was repealed in 1965, when a new act allowed the conditional entry of 10,200 refugees annually.

1962: A Presidential directive allowed several thousand "parolees" to enter the United States from Hong Kong. Relatives of citizens and resident aliens were eligible. President Kennedy gave Congress a special message on immigration, saying, "It is time to correct the mistakes of the past."

1965: A new Immigration and Nationality Act changed the old quota system so that "national origin" no longer means "race" but "country of birth." Instead of being based on a percentage of existing ethnic populations in the United States, quotas were reallocated to countries—20,000 each. But this did not mean that 20,000 Chinese immediately could or did come to the United States. Most prospective immigrants were in Hong Kong, a British colony. Colonies received 1 percent of the mother country's allotment: only 200. "Immediate relatives," the children, spouses, and parents of citizens, however, could enter without numerical limitations. Also not reckoned within the quota limitations were legal residents returning from a visit abroad.

1968: Amendments to the Immigration and Nationality Act provided that immigrants not be allocated by race or nation but by hemispheres, with 120,000 permitted to enter from the Western Hemisphere and 170,000 from the Eastern Hemisphere. This act limits immigration from the Western Hemisphere for the first time in history. The 20,000-per-country quota remained in effect for the Eastern Hemisphere, no per-country limitation for the Western Hemisphere.

1976: The Immigration and Nationality Act Amendments, also called the Western Hemisphere Bill, equalized the provisions of law regulating immigration from the two hemispheres. The House Committee on the Judiciary in its report on this legislation stated, "This constitutes an essential first step in a projected long-term reform of U.S. Immigration law." The 20,000-per-country limit was extended to the Western Hemisphere. The limitation on colonies was raised from 200 to 600.

1978: The separate quotas for the two hemispheres were replaced by a worldwide numerical limitation on immigration of 290,000 annually. On the basis of the "immediate relatives" clause, about 22,000 Chinese enter legally each year, and the rate is increasing. There are also special quotas in effect for Southeast Asian refugees, most of whom are of Chinese ancestry. In the last decade, the ethnic Chinese population of the United States has doubled. The 1980 census may show a million or more.

EDITH MAUDE EATON
(SUI SIN FAR)
(1865–1914)

Edith Eaton was the first professional writer of Asian descent to have her work published in the United States by the English language press. Born in Macclesfield, England, she immigrated to Canada in 1872 with her English father, Chinese mother, and several siblings. She was educated in both British and Canadian grade schools and worked as a stenographer in Montreal before moving to the United States. While in the United States, she lived mainly in San Francisco and Seattle. Although her Chinese heritage was often missed by whites whom she encountered socially, Eaton decided not to "pass" but rather to assert her Chineseness whenever possible. Under her pen name, Sui Sin Far, she contributed essays and short stories to such popular magazines as Good Housekeeping *and* Ladies' Home Journal. *Much of her writing recounts the experiences of Chinese immigrants in San Francisco's Chinatown. Her collection of stories,* Mrs. Spring Fragrance, *was published in 1912.*

"In the Land of the Free" brought to Sui Sin Far's readers insight into the human impact of the Chinese Exclusion legislation. It couches the politics of the situation in the strong emotion of mother love in conflict with societal hostility.

IN THE LAND OF THE FREE

I

"See, Little One—the hills in the morning sun. There is thy home for years to come. It is very beautiful and thou wilt be very happy there."

The Little One looked up into his mother's face in perfect faith. He was engaged in the pleasant occupation of sucking a sweetmeat; but that did not prevent him from gurgling responsively.

"Yes, my olive bud; there is where thy father is making a fortune for thee. Thy father! Oh, wilt thou not be glad to behold his dear face. 'Twas for thee I left him."

The Little One ducked his chin sympathetically against his mother's knee. She lifted him on to her lap. He was two years old, a round, dimple-cheeked boy with bright brown eyes and a sturdy little frame.

"Ah! Ah! Ah! Ooh! Ooh! Ooh!" puffed he, mocking a tugboat steaming by.

San Francisco's waterfront was lined with ships and steamers, while other craft, large and small, including a couple of white transports from the Philippines, lay at anchor here and there off shore. It was some time before the *Eastern Queen* could get docked, and even after that was accomplished, a lone Chinaman who had been waiting on the wharf for an hour was detained that much longer by men with the initials U.S.C. on their caps, before he could board the steamer and welcome his wife and child.

"This is thy son," announced the happy Lae Choo.

Hom Hing lifted the child, felt of his little body and limbs, gazed into his face with proud and joyous eyes; then turned inquiringly to a customs officer at his elbow.

"That's a fine boy you have there," said the man. "Where was he born?"

"In China," answered Hom Hing, swinging the Little One on his right shoulder, preparatory to leading his wife off the steamer.

"Ever been to America before?"

"No, not he," answered the father with a happy laugh.

The customs officer beckoned to another.

"This little fellow," said he, "is visiting America for the first time."

The other customs officer stroked his chin reflectively.

"Good day," said Hom Hing.

"Wait!" commanded one of the officers. "You cannot go just yet."

"What more now?" asked Hom Hing.

"I'm afraid," said the customs officer, "that we cannot allow the boy to go ashore. There is nothing in the papers that you have shown us—your wife's papers and your own—having any bearing upon the child."

"There was no child when the papers were made out," returned Hom Hing. He spoke calmly; but there was apprehension in his eyes and in his tightening grip on his son.

"What is it? What is it?" quavered Lae Choo, who understood a little English.

The second customs officer regarded her pityingly.

"I don't like this part of the business," he muttered.

The first officer turned to Hom Hing and in an official tone of voice, said:

"Seeing that the boy has no certificate entitling him to admission to this country you will have to leave him with us."

"Leave my boy!" exclaimed Hom Hing.

"Yes; he will be well taken care of, and just as soon as we can hear from Washington, he will be handed over to you."

"But," protested Hom Hing, "he is my son."

"We have no proof," answered the man with a shrug of his shoulders; "and even if so we cannot let him pass without orders from the Government."

"He is my son," reiterated Hom Hing, slowly and solemnly. "I am a Chinese merchant and have been in business in San Francisco for many years. When my wife told to me one morning that she dreamed of a green tree with spreading branches and one beautiful red flower growing thereon, I answered her that I wished my son to be born in our country, and for her to prepare to go to China. My wife complied with my wish. After my son was born my mother fell sick and my wife nursed and cared for her; then my father, too, fell sick, and my wife also nursed and cared for him. For twenty moons my wife care for and nurse the old people, and when they died they bless her and my son, and I send for her to return to me. I had no fear of trouble. I was a Chinese merchant and my son was my son."

"Very good, Hom Hing," replied the first officer. "Nevertheless, we take your son."

"No, you not take him; he my son too."

It was Lae Choo. Snatching the child from his father's arms she held and covered him with her own.

The officers conferred together for a few moments; then one drew Hom Hing aside and spoke in his ear.

Resignedly Hom Hing bowed his head, then approached his wife. "'Tis the law," said he, speaking in Chinese, "and 'twill be but for a little while—until tomorrow's sun arises."

"You, too," reproached Lae Choo in a voice eloquent with pain. But accustomed to obedience she yielded the boy to her husband, who in turn delivered him to the first officer. The Little One protested lustily against the transfer; but his mother covered her face with her sleeve and his father silently led her away. Thus was the law of the land complied with.

II

Day was breaking. Lae Choo, who had been awake all night, dressed herself, then awoke her husband.

"'Tis the morn," she cried. "Go, bring our son."

The man rubbed his eyes and arose upon his elbow so that he could see out of the window. A pale star was visible in the sky. The petals of a lily in a bowl on the windowsill were unfurled.

"'Tis not yet time," said he, laying his head down again.

"Not yet time. Ah, all the time that I lived before yesterday is no so much as the time that has been since my Little One was taken from me."

The mother threw herself down beside the bed and covered her face.

Hom Hing turned on the light, and touching his wife's bowed head with a sympathetic hand inquired if she had slept.

"Slept!" she echoed, weepingly. "Ah, how could I close my eyes with my arms empty of the little body that has filled them every night for more than twenty moons! You do not know—man—what it is to miss the feel of the little fingers and the little toes and the soft round limbs of your little one. Even in the darkness his darling eyes used to shine up to mine, and often have I fallen into slumber with his pretty babble at my ear. And now, I see him not; I touch him not; I hear him not. My baby, my little fat one!"

"Now! Now! Now!" consoled Hom Hing, patting his wife's shoulder reassuringly; "there is no need to grieve so; he will soon gladden you again. There cannot be any law that would keep a child from its mother!"

Lae Choo dried her tears.

"You are right, my husband," she meekly murmured. She arose and stepped about the apartment, setting things to rights. The box of presents she had brought for her California friends had been opened the evening before; and silks, embroideries, carved ivories, ornamental lacquer-ware, brasses, camphor-wood boxes, fans, and chinaware were scattered around in confused heaps. In the midst of unpacking the thought of her child in the hands of strangers had overpowered her, and she had left everything to crawl into bed and weep.

Having arranged her gifts in order she stepped out on to the deep balcony.

The star had faded from view and there were bright streaks in the western sky. Lae Choo looked down the street and around. Beneath the flat occupied by her and her husband were quarters for a number of bachelor Chinamen, and she could hear them from where she stood, taking their early morning breakfast. Below their dining-room was her husband's grocery store. Across the way was a large restaurant. Last night it had been resplendent with gay colored lanterns and the sound of music. The rejoicings over "the completion of the moon," by Quong Sum's firstborn, had been long and loud, and had caused her to tie a handkerchief over her ears. She, a bereaved mother, had it not in her heart to rejoice with other parents. This morning the place was more in accord with her mood. It was still and quiet. The revellers had dispersed or were asleep.

A roly-poly woman in black sateen, with long pendant earrings in her ears, looked up from the street below and waved her a smiling greeting. It was her old neighbor, Kuie Hoe, the wife of the gold embosser, Mark Sing. With her was a little boy in yellow jacket and lavender pantaloons. Lae Choo remembered him as a baby. She used to like to play with him in those days when she had no child of her own. What a long time ago that seemed! She caught her breath in a sigh, and laughed instead.

"Why are you so merry?" called her husband from within.

"Because my Little One is coming home," answered Lae Choo. "I am a happy mother—a happy mother."

She pattered into the room with a smile on her face.

The noon hour had arrived. The rice was steaming in the bowls and a fragrant dish of chicken and bamboo shoots was awaiting Hom Hing. Not for one moment had Lae Choo paused to rest during the morning hours; her activity had been ceaseless. Every now and again, however, she had raised her eyes to the gilded clock on the curiously carved mantlepiece. Once, she had exclaimed:

"Why so long, oh! why so long?" Then, apostrophizing herself: "Lae Choo, be happy. The Little One is coming! The Little One is coming!" Several times she burst into tears, and several times she laughed aloud.

Hom Hing entered the room; his arms hung down by his side.

"The Little One!" shrieked Lae Choo.

"They bid me call tomorrow."

With a moan the mother sank to the floor.

The noon hour passed. The dinner remained on the table.

III

The winter rains were over: the spring had come to California, flushing the hills with green and causing an ever-changing pageant of flowers to pass over them. But there was no spring in Lae Choo's heart, for the Little One remained away from her arms. He was being kept in a mission. White women were caring for him, and though for one full moon he had pined for his mother and refused to be comforted he was now apparently happy and contented. Five moons or five months had gone by since the day he had passed with Lae Choo through the Golden Gate; but the great Government at Washington still delayed sending the answer which would return him to his parents.

Hom Hing was disconsolately rolling up and down the balls in his abacus box when a keen-faced young man stepped into his store.

"What news?" asked the Chinese merchant.

"This!" The young man brought forth a typewritten letter. Hom Hing read the words:

"Re Chinese child, alleged to be the son of Hom Hing, Chinese merchant, doing business at 425 Clay Street, San Francisco.

"Same will have attention as soon as possible."

Hom Hing returned the letter, and without a word continued his manipulation of the counting machine.

"Have you anything to say?" asked the young man.

"Nothing. They have sent the same letter fifteen times before. Have you not yourself showed it to me?"

"True!" The young man eyed the Chinese merchant furtively. He had a proposition to make and was pondering whether or not the time was opportune.

"How is your wife?" he inquired solicitously—and diplomatically.

Hom Hing shook his head mournfully.

"She seems less every day," he replied. "Her food she takes only when I bid her and her tears fall continuously. She finds no pleasure in dress or flowers and cares not to see her friends. Her eyes stare all night. I think before another moon she will pass into the land of spirits."

"No!" exclaimed the young man, genuinely startled.

"If the boy not come home I lose my wife sure," continued Hom Hing with bitter sadness.

"It's not right," cried the young man indignantly. Then he made his proposition.

The Chinese father's eyes brightened exceedingly.

"Will I like you to go to Washington and make them give you the paper to restore my son?" cried he. "How can you ask when you know my heart's desire?"

"Then," said the young fellow, "I will start next week. I am anxious to see this thing through if only for the sake of your wife's peace of mind."

"I will call her. To hear what you think to do will make her glad," said Hom Hing.

He called a message to Lae Choo upstairs through a tube in the wall.

In a few moments she appeared, listless, wan, and hollow-eyed; but when her husband told her the young lawyer's suggestion she became electrified; her form straightened, her eyes glistened; the color flushed to her cheeks.

"Oh," she cried, turning to James Clancy. "You are a hundred man good!"

The young man felt somewhat embarrassed; his eyes shifted a little under the intense gaze of the Chinese mother.

"Well, we must get your boy for you," he responded. "Of course"—turning to Hom Hing—"it will cost a little money. You can't get fellows to hurry the Government for you without gold in your pocket."

Hom Hing stared blankly for a moment. Then: "How much do you want, Mr. Clancy?" he asked quietly.

"Well, I will need at least five hundred to start with."

Hom Hing cleared his throat.

"I think I told to you the time I last paid you for writing letters for me and see-ing the Custom boss here that nearly all I had was gone!"

"Oh, well then we won't talk about it, old fellow. It won't harm the boy to stay where he is, and your wife may get over it all right."

"What that you say?" quavered Lae Choo.

James Clancy looked out of the window.

"He says," explained Hom Hing in English, "that to get our boy we have to have much money."

"Money! Oh, yes."

Lae Choo nodded her head.

"I have not got the money to give him."

For a moment Lae Choo gazed wonderingly from one face to the other; then, comprehension dawning upon her, with swift anger, pointing to the lawyer, she cried: "You not one hundred man good; you just common white man."

"Yes, ma'am," returned James Clancy, bowing and smiling ironically.

Hom Hing pushed his wife behind him and addressed the lawyer again: "I might try," said he, "to raise something; but five hundred—it is not possible."

"What about four?"

"I tell you I have next to nothing left and my friends are not rich."

"Very well!"

The lawyer moved leisurely toward the door, pausing on its threshold to light a cigarette.

"Stop, white man; white man, stop!"

Lae Choo, panting and terrified, had started forward and now stood beside him, clutching his sleeve excitedly.

"You say you can go to get paper to bring my Little One to me if Hom Hing give you five hundred dollars?"

The lawyer nodded carelessly; his eyes were intent upon the cigarette which would not take the fire from the match.

"Then you go get paper. If Hom Hing not can give you five hundred dollars—I give you perhaps what more that much."

She slipped a heavy gold bracelet from her wrist and held it out to the man. Mechanically he took it.

"I go get more!"

She scurried away, disappearing behind the door through which she had come.

"Oh, look here, I can't accept this," said James Clancy, walking back to Hom Hing and laying down the bracelet before him.

"It's all right," said Hom Hing, seriously, "pure China gold. My wife's parent give it to her when we married."

"But I can't take it anyway," protested the young man.

"It is all same as money. And you want money to go to Washington," replied Hom Hing in a matter-of-fact manner.

"See, my jade earrings—my gold buttons—my hairpins—my comb of pearl and my rings—one, two, three, four, five rings; very good—very good—all same much money. I give them all to you. You take and bring me paper for my Little One."

Lae Choo piled up her jewels before the lawyer.

Hom Hing laid a restraining hand upon her shoulder. "Not all, my wife," he said in Chinese. He selected a ring—his gift to Lae Choo when she dreamed of the tree with the red flower. The rest of the jewels he pushed toward the white man.

"Take them and sell them," said he. "They will pay your fare to Washington and bring you back with the paper."

For one moment James Clancy hesitated. He was not a sentimental man; but something within him arose against accepting such payment for his services.

"They are good, good," pleadingly asserted Lae Choo, seeing his hesitation.

Whereupon he seized the jewels, thrust them into his coat pocket, and walked rapidly away from the store.

IV

Lae Choo followed after the missionary woman through the mission nursery school. Her heart was beating so high with happiness that she could scarcely breathe. The paper had come at last—the precious paper which gave Hom Hing and his wife the right to the possession of their own child. It was ten months now since he had been taken from them—ten months since the sun had ceased to shine for Lae Choo.

The room was filled with children—most of them wee tots, but none so wee as her own. The mission woman talked as she walked. She told Lae Choo that little Kim, as he had been named by the school, was the pet of the place, and that his little tricks and ways amused and delighted every one. He had been rather difficult to manage at first and had cried much for his mother; "but children so soon forget, and after a month he seemed quite at home and played around as bright and happy as a bird."

"Yes," responded Lae Choo. "Oh, yes, yes!"

But she did not hear what was said to her. She was walking in a maze of anticipatory joy.

"Wait here, please," said the mission woman, placing Lae Choo in a chair. "The very youngest ones are having their breakfast."

She withdrew for a moment—it seemed like an hour to the mother—then she reappeared leading by the hand a little boy dressed in blue cotton overalls and white-soled shoes. The little boy's face was round and dimpled and his eyes were very bright.

"Little One, ah, my Little One!" cried Lae Choo.

She fell on her knees and stretched her hungry arms toward her son.

But the Little One shrunk from her and tried to hide himself in the folds of the white woman's skirt.

"Go 'way, go 'way!" he bade his mother.

JACOB RIIS
(1849–1914)

Jacob August Riis was born in Ribe, Denmark, and came to the United States in 1870. He settled in New York City, where he worked as a police reporter for the New York Tribune, *until he later joined the* New York Evening Sun. *A social reformer, Riis was distressed by the squalid and dangerous living and working conditions of New York City's poor and worked to change them. He was associated with and supported in this work by*

Theodore Roosevelt, who had been a police commissioner in New York when Riis was a reporter. Riis's exposé with photographs, How the Other Half Lives *(1890), influenced authorities to address the conditions of New York City's urban poor. He also wrote four other books about the urban poor and an autobiography,* The Making of an American *(1901).*

In this chapter, "The Mixed Crowd," from How the Other Half Lives, *Riis explores ethnic interactions in the New York slums.*

THE MIXED CROWD

When once I asked the agent of a notorious Fourth Ward alley how many people might be living in it I was told: One hundred and forty families, one hundred Irish, thirty-eight Italian, and two that spoke the German tongue. Barring the agent herself, there was not a native-born individual in the court. The answer was characteristic of the cosmopolitan character of lower New York, very nearly so of the whole of it, wherever it runs to alleys and courts. One may find for the asking an Italian, a German, a French, African, Spanish, Bohemian, Russian, Scandinavian, Jewish, and Chinese colony. Even the Arab, who peddles "holy earth" from the Battery as a direct importation from Jerusalem, has his exclusive preserves at the lower end of Washington Street. The one thing you shall vainly ask for in the chief city of America is a distinctively American community. There is none; certainly not among the tenements. Where have they gone to, the old inhabitants? I put the question to one who might fairly be presumed to be of the number, since I had found him sighing for the "good old days" when the legend "no Irish need apply" was familiar in the advertising columns of the newspapers. He looked at me with a puzzled air. "I don't know," he said. "I wish I did. Some went to California in '49, some to the war and never came back. The rest, I expect, have gone to heaven, or somewhere. I don't see them 'round here."

Whatever the merit of the good man's conjectures, his eyes did not deceive him. They are not here. In their place has come this queer conglomerate mass of heterogeneous elements, ever striving and working like whiskey and water in one glass, and with the like result: final union and a prevailing taint of whiskey. The once unwelcome Irishman has been followed in his turn by the Italian, the Russian Jew, and the Chinaman, and has himself taken a hand at opposition, quite as bitter and quite as ineffectual, against these later hordes. Wherever these have gone they have crowded him out, possessing the block, the street, the ward with their denser swarms. But the Irishman's revenge is complete. Victorious in defeat over his recent as over his more ancient foe, the one who opposed his coming no less than the one who drove him out, he dictates to both their politics, and, secure in possession of the offices, returns the native his greeting with interest, while collecting the rents of the Italian whose house he has bought with the profits of his saloon. As a landlord he is picturesquely autocratic. An amusing instance of his methods came under my notice while writing these lines. An inspector of the Health Department found an Italian family paying a man with a Celtic name twenty-five dollars a month for three small rooms in a ramshackle rear tenement—more than twice what they were worth—and expressed his astonishment to the tenant, an ignorant Sicilian laborer. He replied that he had once asked the landlord to reduce the rent, but he would not do it.

"Well! What did he say?" asked the inspector.

"'Damma, man!' he said; 'if you speaka thata way to me, I fira you and your things in the streeta.'" And the frightened Italian paid the rent.

In justice to the Irish landlord it must be said that like an apt pupil he was merely showing forth the result of the schooling he had received, re-enacting, in his own way, the scheme of the tenements. It is only his frankness that shocks. The Irishman does not naturally take kindly to tenement life, though with characteristic versatility he adapts himself to its conditions at once. It does violence, nevertheless, to the best that is in him, and for that very reason of all who come within its sphere soonest corrupts him. The result is a sediment, the product of more than a generation in the city's slums, that, as distinguished from the larger body of his class, justly ranks at the foot of tenement dwellers, the so-called "low Irish."

It is not to be assumed, of course, that the whole body of the population living in the tenements, of which New Yorkers are in the habit of speaking vaguely as "the poor," or even the larger part of it, is to be classed as vicious or as poor in the sense of verging on beggary.

New York's wage-earners have no other place to live, more is the pity. They are truly poor for having no better homes; waxing poorer in purse as the exorbitant rents to which they are tied, as ever was serf to soil, keep rising. The wonder is that they are not all corrupted, and speedily, by their surroundings. If, on the contrary, there be a steady working up, if not out of the slough, the fact is a powerful argument for the optimist's belief that the world is, after all, growing better, not worse, and would go far toward disarming apprehension, were it not for the steadier growth of the sediment of the slums and its constant menace. Such an impulse toward better things there certainly is. The German rag-picker of thirty years ago, quite as low in the scale of his Italian successor, is the thrifty tradesman or prosperous farmer of to-day.[*]

The Italian scavenger of our time is fast graduating into exclusive control of the corner fruit-stands, while his black-eyed boy monopolizes the boot-blacking industry in which a few years ago he was an intruder. The Irish hod-carrier in the second generation has become a brick-layer, if not the Alderman of his ward, while the Chinese coolie is in almost exclusive possession of the laundry business. The reason is obvious. The poorest immigrant comes here with the purpose and ambition to better himself and, given half a chance, might be reasonably expected to make the most of it. To the false plea that he prefers the squalid homes in which his kind are housed there could be no better answer. The truth is, his half chance has too long been wanting, and for the bad result he has been unjustly blamed.

As emigration from east to west follows the latitude, so does the foreign influx in New York distribute itself along certain well-defined lines that waver and break only under the stronger pressure of a more gregarious race or the encroachments of inexorable business. A feeling of dependence upon mutual effort, natural to strangers in a strange land, unacquainted with its language and customs, sufficiently accounts for this.

The Irishman is the true cosmopolitan immigrant. All-pervading, he shares his lodging with perfect impartiality with the Italian, the Greek, and the "Dutchman,"

---

[*]The Sheriff Street Colony of rag-pickers, long since gone, is an instance in point. The thrifty Germans saved up money during years of hard work in squalor and apparently wretched poverty to buy a township in a Western State, and the whole colony moved out there in a body. There need be no doubt about their thriving there.

yielding only to sheer force of numbers, and objects equally to them all. A map of the city, colored to designate nationalities, would show more stripes than on the skin of a zebra, and more colors than any rainbow. The city on such a map would fall into two great halves, green for the Irish prevailing in the West Side tenement districts, and blue for the Germans on the East Side. But intermingled with these ground colors would be an odd variety of tints that would give the whole the appearance of an extraordinary crazy-quilt. From down in the Sixth Ward, upon the site of the old Collect Pond that in the days of the fathers drained the hills which are no more, the red of the Italian would be seen forcing its way northward along the line of Mulberry Street to the quarter of the French purple on Bleecker Street and South Fifth Avenue, to lose itself and reappear, after a lapse of miles, in the "Little Italy" of Harlem, east of Second Avenue. Dashes of red, sharply defined, would be seen strung through the Annexed District, northward to the city line. On the West Side the red would be seen overrunning the old Africa of Thompson Street, pushing the black of the negro rapidly uptown, against querulous but unavailing protests, occupying his home, his church, his trade and all, with merciless impartiality. There is a church in Mulberry Street that has stood for two generations as a sort of milestone of these migrations. Built originally for the worship of staid New Yorkers of the "old stock," it was engulfed by the colored tide, when the draft-riots drove the negroes out of reach of Cherry Street and the Five Points. Within the past decade the advance wave of the Italian onset reached it, and to-day the arms of United Italy adorn its front. The negroes have made a stand at several points along Seventh and Eighth Avenues; but their main body, still pursued by the Italian foe, is on the march yet, and the black mark will be found overshadowing to-day many blocks on the East Side, with One Hundredth Street as the centre, where colonies of them have settled recently.

Hardly less aggressive than the Italian, the Russian and Polish Jew, having overrun the district between Rivington and Division Streets, east of the Bowery, to the point of suffocation, is filling the tenements of the old Seventh Ward to the river front, and disputing with the Italian every foot of available space in the back alleys of Mulberry Street. The two races, differing hopelessly in much, have this in common: they carry their slums with them wherever they go, if allowed to do it. Little Italy already rivals its parent, the "Bend," in foulness. Other nationalities that begin at the bottom make a fresh start when crowded up the ladder. Happily both are manageable, the one by rabbinical, the other by the civil law. Between the dull gray of the Jew, his favorite color, and the Italian red, would be seen squeezed in on the map of sharp streak of yellow, marking the narrow boundaries of Chinatown. Dovetailed in with the German population, the poor but thrifty Bohemian might be picked out by the sombre hue of his life as of his philosophy, struggling against heavy odds in the big human bee-hives of the East Side. Colonies of his people extend northward, with long lapses of space, from below the Cooper Institute more than three miles. The Bohemian is the only foreigner with any considerable representation in the city who counts no wealthy man of his race, none who has not to work hard for a living, or has got beyond the reach of the tenement.

Down near the Battery the West Side emerald would be soiled by a dirty stain, spreading rapidly like a splash of ink on a sheet of blotting paper, headquarters of the Arab tribe, that in a single year has swelled from the original dozen to twelve hundred, intent, every mother's son, on trade and barter. Dots and dashes of color here and there would show where the Finnish sailors worship their djumala (God), the Greek pedlars the ancient name of their race, and the Swiss the goddess of thrift. And so on to the end of the long register, all toiling together in the galling fetters of the tenement. Were the question raised who makes the most of life thus mortgaged, who resists most stubbornly its levelling tendency—knows how to drag even the barracks upward a part of the way at least toward the ideal plane of the home—the palm must be unhesitatingly awarded the Teuton. The Italian and the poor Jew rise only by compulsion. The Chinaman does not rise at all; here, as at home, he simply remains stationary. The Irishman's genius runs to public affairs rather than domestic life; wherever he is mustered in force the saloon is the gorgeous centre of political activity. The German struggles vainly to learn his trick; his Teutonic wit is too heavy, and the political ladder he raises from his saloon usually too short or too clumsy to reach the desired goal. The best part of his life is lived at home, and he makes himself a home independent of the surroundings, giving the lie to the saying, unhappily become a maxim of social truth, that pauperism and drunkenness naturally grow in the tenements. He makes the most of his tenement, and it should be added that whenever and as soon as he can save up money enough, he gets out and never crosses the threshold of one again.

ABRAHAM CAHAN
(1860-1951)

Abraham Cahan was born in Podberezy, Lithuania, and immigrated to the United States in 1882. In Lithuania, he attended Vilna Teachers' Institute and worked as a teacher until his political activities made him a target of investigation by Russian authorities. Cahan arrived in Philadelphia but soon moved to New York, where he settled in Manhattan's Lower East Side and soon established himself as an influential labor organizer, journalist, editor, and fiction writer. After a failed attempt at editing a radical newspaper, Cahan began contributing to other political newspapers and to the Yiddish labor newspapers. In 1897 he cofounded the highly successful Jewish Daily Forward, *which he edited almost continuously until his death in 1951. In 1895, his first story in English, "Providential Match," was published and subsequent works of fiction, including the novel* The Rise of David Levinsky *(1917) followed.*

Cahan's fiction focuses upon the alienation from family and culture experienced by Jewish immigrants to America during the process of assimilation. "A Ghetto Wedding" comments on the mixed blessing of establishing home and family in a new and hostile land.

A GHETTO WEDDING

Had you chanced to be in Grand Street on that starry February night, it would scarcely have occurred to you that the Ghetto was groaning under the culmination of a long season of enforced idleness and distress. The air was exhilaratingly crisp, and the glare of the cafés and millinery shops flooded it with contentment and kindly good will. The sidewalks were alive with shoppers and promenaders, and lined with peddlers.

Yet the dazzling, deafening chaos had many a tale of woe to tell. The greater part of the surging crowd was out on an errand of self-torture. Straying forlornly by inexorable window displays, men and women would pause here and there to indulge in a hypothetical selection, to feast a hungry eye upon the object of an imaginary purchase, only forthwith to pay for the momentary joy with all the pangs of awakening to an empty purse.

Many of the peddlers, too, bore piteous testimony to the calamity which was then preying upon the quarter. Some of them performed their task of yelling and gesticulating with the desperation of imminent ruin; others implored the passers-by for custom with the abject effect of begging alms; while in still others this feverish urgency was disguised by an air of martyrdom or of shamefaced unwontedness, as if peddling were beneath the dignity of their habitual occupations, and they had been driven to it by sheer famine—by the hopeless dearth of employment at their own trades.

One of these was a thick-set fellow of twenty-five or twenty-six, with honest, clever blue eyes. It might be due to the genial, inviting quality of his face that the Passover dishes whose praises he was sounding had greater attraction for some of the women with an "effectual demand" than those of his competitors. Still, his comparative success had not as yet reconciled him to his new calling. He was constantly gazing about for a possible passer-by of his acquaintance, and when one came in sight he would seek refuge from identification in closer communion with the crockery on his push-cart.

"Buy nice dishes for the holidays! Cheap and strong! Buy dishes for Passover!" When business was brisk, he sang with a bashful relish; when the interval between a customer and her successor was growing too long, his singsong would acquire a mournful ring that was suggestive of the psalm-chanting at an orthodox Jewish funeral.

He was a cap-blocker, and in the busy season his earnings ranged from ten to fifteen dollars a week. But he had not worked full time for over two years, and during the last three months he had not been able to procure a single day's employment.

Goldy, his sweetheart, too, who was employed in making knee breeches, had hardly work enough to pay her humble board and rent. Nathan, after much hesitation, was ultimately compelled to take to peddling; and the longed-for day of their wedding was put off from month to month.

They had become engaged nearly two years before; the wedding ceremony having been originally fixed for a date some three months later. Their joint savings then amounted to one hundred and twenty dollars—a sum quite adequate, in Nathan's judgment, for a modest, quiet celebration and the humble beginnings of a household establishment. Goldy, however, summarily and indignantly overruled him.

"One does not marry every day," she argued, "and when I have at last lived to stand under the bridal canopy with my predestined one, I will not do so like a beggar maid. Give me a respectable wedding, or none at all, Nathan, do you hear?"

It is to be noted that a "respectable wedding" was not merely a casual expression with Goldy. Like its antithesis, a "slipshod wedding," it played in her vocabulary the part of something like a well-established scientific term, with a meaning as clearly defined as that of "centrifugal force" or "geometrical progression." Now, a slipshod wedding was anything short of a gown of white satin and slippers to match; two carriages to bring the bride and the bridegroom to the ceremony, and one to take them to their bridal apartments; a wedding bard and a band of at least five musicians; a spacious ball-room crowded with dancers, and a feast of a hundred and fifty covers. As to furniture, she refused to consider any which did not include a pier-glass and a Brussels carpet.

Nathan contended that the items upon which she insisted would cost a sum far beyond their joint accumulations. This she met by the declaration that he had all along been bent upon making her the target of universal ridicule, and that she would rather descend into an untimely grave than be married in a slipshod manner. Here she burst out crying; and whether her tears referred to the untimely grave or to the slipshod wedding, they certainly seemed to strengthen the cogency of her argument; for Nathan at once proceeded to signify his surrender by a kiss, and when ignominiously repulsed he protested his determination to earn the necessary money to bring things to the standard which she held up so uncompromisingly.

Hard times set in. Nathan and Goldy pinched and scrimped; but all their heroic economies were powerless to keep their capital from dribbling down to less than one hundred dollars. The wedding was postponed again and again. Finally the curse of utter idleness fell upon Nathan's careworn head. Their savings dwindled space. In dismay they beheld the foundation of their happiness melt gradually away. Both were tired of boarding. Both longed for the bliss and economy of married life. They grew more impatient and restless every day, and Goldy made concession after concession. First the wedding supper was sacrificed; then the pier-mirror and the bard were stricken from the program; and these were eventually succeeded by the hired hall and the Brussels carpet.

After Nathan went into peddling, a few days before we first find him hawking chinaware on Grand Street, matters began to look brighter, and the spirits of our betrothed couple rose. Their capital, which had sunk to forty dollars, was increasing again, and Goldy advised waiting long enough for it to reach the sum necessary for a slipshod wedding and establishment.

It was nearly ten o'clock. Nathan was absently drawling his "Buy nice dishes for the holidays!" His mind was engrossed with the question of making peddling his permanent occupation.

Presently he was startled by a merry soprano mocking him: "Buy nice di-i-shes! Mind that you don't fall asleep murmuring like this. A big lot you can make!"

Nathan turned a smile of affectionate surprise upon a compact little figure, small to drollness, but sweet in the amusing grace of its diminutive outlines—an epitome of exquisite femininity. Her tiny face was as comically lovely as her form; her applelike cheeks were firm as marble, and her inadequate nose protruded between them like the result of a hasty tweak; a pair of large, round black eyes and a thick-lipped little mouth inundating it all with passion and restless, good-natured shrewdness.

"Goldy! What brings *you* here?" Nathan demanded, with a fond look which instantly gave way to an air of discomfort. "You know I hate you to see me peddling."

"Are you really angry? Bite the feather bed, then. Where is the disgrace? As if you were the only peddler in America! I wish you were. Wouldn't you make heaps of money then! But you had better hear what *does* bring me here. Nathan, darling-dearest little heart, dearest little crown that you are, guess what a plan I have hit upon!" she exploded all at once. "Well, if you hear me out, and you don't say that

Goldy has the head of a cabinet minister, then—well, then you will be a big hog, and nothing else."

And without giving him time to put in as much as an interjection, she rattled on, puffing for breath and smacking her lips for ecstasy. Was it not stupid of them to be racking their brains about the wedding while there was such a plain way of having both a "respectable" celebration and fine furniture—Brussels carpet, pier-glass, and all—with the money they now had on hand?

"Come, out with it, then," he said morosely.

But his disguised curiosity only whetted her appetite for tormenting him, and she declared her determination not to disclose her great scheme before they had reached her lodgings.

"You have been yelling long enough today, anyhow," she said, with abrupt sympathy. "Do you suppose it does not go to my very heart to think of the way you stand out in the cold screaming yourself hoarse?"

Half an hour later, when they were alone in Mrs. Volpiansky's parlor, which was also Goldy's bedroom, she set about emptying his pockets of the gross results of the day's business, and counting the money. This she did with a preoccupied, matter-of-fact air, Nathan submitting to the operation with fond and amused willingness; and the sum being satisfactory, she went on to unfold her plan.

"You see," she began, almost in a whisper, and with the mien of a care-worn, experience-laden old matron, "in a week or two we shall have about seventy-five dollars, shan't we? Well, what is seventy-five dollars? Nothing! We could just have the plainest furniture, and no wedding worth speaking of. Now, if we have no wedding, we shall get no presents, shall we?"

Nathan shook his head thoughtfully.

"Well, why shouldn't we be up to snuff and do this way? Let us spend all our money on a grand, respectable wedding, and send out a big lot of invitations, and then—well, won't uncle Leiser send us a carpet or a parlor set? And aunt Beile, and cousin Shapiro, and Charley, and Meyerke, and Wolfke, and Bennie, and Sore-Gitke— won't each present something or other, as is the custom among respectable people? May God give us a lump of good luck as big as the wedding present each of them is sure to send us! Why, did not Beilke get a fine carpet from uncle when she got married? And am I not a nearer relative than she?"

She paused to search his face for a sign of approval, and, fondly smoothing a tuft of his dark hair into place, she went on to enumerate the friends to be invited and the gifts to be expected from them.

"So you see," she pursued, "we will have both a respectable wedding that we shan't have to be ashamed of in after years and the nicest things we could get if we spent two hundred dollars. What do you say?"

"What *shall* I say?" he returned dubiously.

The project appeared reasonable enough, but the investment struck him as rather hazardous. He pleaded for caution, for delay; but as he had no tangible argument to produce, while she stood her ground with the firmness of conviction, her victory was an easy one.

"It will all come right, depend upon it," she said coaxingly. "You just leave everything to me. Don't be uneasy, Nathan," she added. "You and I are orphans, and you know the Uppermost does not forsake a bride and bridegroom who have nobody to take care of them. If my father were alive, it would be different," she concluded, with a disconsolate gesture.

There was a pathetic pause. Tears glistened in Goldy's eyes.

"May your father rest in a bright paradise," Nathan said feelingly. "But what is the use of crying? Can you bring him back to life? I will be a father to you."

"If God be pleased," she assented. "Would that mamma, at least—may she be healthy a hundred and twenty years—would that she, at least, were here to attend our wedding! Poor mother! it will break her heart to think that she has not been foreordained by the Uppermost to lead me under the canopy."

There was another desolate pause, but it was presently broken by Goldy, who exclaimed with unexpected buoyancy, "By the way, Nathan, guess what I did! I am afraid you will call me braggart and make fun of me, but I don't care," she pursued, with a playful pout, as she produced a strip of carpet from her pocketbook. "I went into a furniture store, and they gave me a sample three times as big as this. I explained in my letter to mother that this is the kind of stuff that will cover my floor when I am married. Then I enclosed the sample in the letter, and sent it all to Russia."

Nathan clapped his hands and burst out laughing. "But how do you know that is just the kind of carpet you will get for your wedding present?" he demanded, amazed as much as amused.

"How do I know? As if it mattered what sort of carpet! I can just see mamma going the rounds of the neighbors, and showing off the 'costly tablecloth' her daughter will trample upon. Won't she be happy!"

Over a hundred invitations, printed in as luxurious a black and gold as ever came out of an Essex Street hand press, were sent out for an early date in April. Goldy and Nathan paid a month's rent in advance for three rooms on the second floor of a Cherry Street tenement house. Goldy regarded the rent as unusually low, and the apartments as the finest on the East Side.

"Oh, haven't I got lovely rooms!" she would ejaculate, beaming with the consciousness of the pronoun. Or, "You ought to see *my* rooms! How much do you pay for yours?" Or again, "I have made up my mind to have my parlor in the rear room. It is as light as the front one, anyhow, and I want that for a kitchen, you know. What do you say?" For hours together she would go on talking nothing but rooms, rent, and furniture; every married couple who had recently moved into new quarters, or were about to do so, seemed bound to her by the ties of a common cause; in her imagination, humanity was divided into those who were interested in the question of rooms, rent and furniture and those who were not—the former, of whom she was one, constituting the superior category; and whenever her eye fell upon a bill announcing rooms to let, she would experience something akin to the feeling with which an artist, in passing, views some accessory of his art.

It is customary to send the bulkier wedding presents to a young couple's apartments a few days before they become man and wife, the closer relatives and friends of the betrothed usually settling among themselves what piece of furniture each is to contribute. Accordingly, Goldy gave up her work a week in advance of the day set for the great event, in order that she might be on hand to receive the things when they arrived.

She went to the empty little rooms, with her lunch, early in the morning, and kept anxious watch till after nightfall, when Nathan came to take her home.

A day passed, another, and a third, but no expressman called out her name. She sat waiting and listening for the rough voice, but in vain.

"Oh, it is too early, anyhow. I am a fool to be expecting anything so soon at all," she tried to console herself. And she waited another hour, and still another; but no wedding gift made its appearance.

"Well, there is plenty of time, after all; wedding presents do come a day or two before the ceremony," she argued; and again she waited, and again strained her ears, and again her heart rose in her throat.

The vacuity of the rooms, freshly cleaned, scrubbed, and smelling of whitewash, began to frighten her. Her overwrought mind was filled with sounds which her over-strained ears did not hear. Yet there she sat on the window sill, listening and listening for an expressman's voice.

"Hush, hush-sh, hush-sh-sh!" whispered the walls; the corners muttered awful threats; her heart was ever and anon contracted with fear; she often thought herself on the brink of insanity; yet she stayed on, waiting, waiting, waiting.

At the slightest noise in the hall she would spring to her feet, her heart beating wildly, only presently to sink in her bosom at finding it to be some neighbor or a peddler; and so frequent were these violent throbbings that Goldy grew to imagine herself a prey to heart disease. Nevertheless the fifth day came, and she was again at her post, waiting, waiting, waiting for her wedding gifts. And what is more, when Nathan came from business, and his countenance fell as he surveyed the undisturbed emptiness of the rooms, she set a merry face against his rueful inquiries, and took to bantering him as a woman quick to lose heart, and to painting their prospects in roseate hues, until she argued herself, if not him, into a more cheerful view of the situation.

On the sixth day an expressman did pull up in front of the Cherry Street tenement house, but he had only a cheap huge rocking chair for Goldy and Nathan; and as it proved to be the gift of a family who had been set down for nothing less than a carpet or a parlor set, the joy and hope which its advent had called forth turned to dire disappointment and despair. For nearly an hour Goldy sat mournfully rocking and striving to picture how delightful it would have been if all her anticipations had come true.

Presently there arrived a flimsy plush-covered little corner table. It could not have cost more than a dollar. Yet it was the gift of a near friend, who had been relied upon for a pier-glass or a bedroom set. A little later a cheap alarm clock and an icebox were brought in. That was all.

Occasionally Goldy went to the door to take in the entire effect; but the more she tried to view the parlor as half finished, the more cruelly did the few lonely and mismated things emphasize the remaining emptiness of the apartments: whereupon she would sink into her rocker and sit motionless, with a drooping head, and then desperately fall to swaying to and fro, as though bent upon swinging herself out of her woebegone, wretched self.

Still, when Nathan came, there was a triumphant twinkle in her eye, as she said, pointing to the gifts, "Well, mister, who was right? It is not very bad for a start, is it? You know most people do send their wedding presents after the ceremony—why, of course!" she added, in a sort of confidential way. "Well, we have invited a big crowd, and all people of no mean sort, thank God; and who ever heard of a lady or a gentleman attending a respectable wedding and having a grand wedding supper, and then cheating the bride and the bridegroom out of their presents?"

The evening was well advanced; yet there were only a score of people in a hall that was used to hundreds.

Everybody felt ill at ease, and ever and anon looked about for the possible arrival of more guests. At ten o'clock the dancing preliminary to the ceremony had not yet ceased, although the few waltzers looked as if they were scared by the ringing echoes of their own footsteps amid the austere solemnity of the surrounding void and the depressing sheen of the dim expanse of floor.

The two fiddles, the cornet, and the clarinet were shrieking as though for pain, and the malicious superabundance of gaslight was fiendishly sneering at their tortures. Weddings and entertainments being scarce in the Ghetto, its musicians caught the contagion of misery: hence the greedy, desperate gusto with which the band plied their instruments.

At last it became evident that the assemblage was not destined to be larger than it was, and that it was no use delaying the ceremony. It was, in fact, an open secret among those present that by far the greater number of the invited friends were kept away by lack of employment: some having their presentable clothes in the pawn shop; others avoiding the expense of a wedding present, or simply being too cruelly borne down by their cares to have a mind for the excitement of a wedding; indeed, some even thought it wrong of Nathan to have the celebration during such a period of hard times, when everybody was out of work.

It was a little after ten when the bard—a tall, gaunt man, with a grizzly beard and a melancholy face—donned his skullcap, and, advancing toward the dancers, called out in a synagogue intonation, "Come, ladies, let us veil the bride!"

An odd dozen of daughters of Israel followed him and the musicians into a little side room where Goldy was seated between her two brideswomen (the wives of two men who were to attend upon the groom). According to the orthodox custom she had fasted the whole day, and as a result of this and of her gnawing grief, added to the awe-inspiring scene she had been awaiting, she was pale as death; the effect being heightened by the wreath and white gown she wore. As the procession came filing in, she sat blinking her round dark eyes in dismay, as if the bard were an executioner come to lead her to the scaffold.

The song or address to the bride usually partakes of the qualities of prayer and harangue, and includes a melancholy meditation upon life and death; lamenting the deceased members of the young woman's family, bemoaning her own woes, and exhorting her to discharge her sacred duties as a wife, mother, and servant of God. Composed in verse and declaimed in a solemn, plaintive recitative, often broken by the band's mournful refrain, it is sure to fulfill its mission of eliciting tears even when hearts are brimful of glee. Imagine, then, the funeral effect which it produced at Goldy's wedding ceremony.

The bard, half starved himself, sang the anguish of his own heart; the violins wept, the clarinet moaned, the cornet and the double-bass groaned, each reciting the sad tale of its poverty-stricken master. He began:

Silence, good women, give heed to *my* verses!
Tonight, bride, thou dost stand before the
    Uppermost.
Pray to him to bless thy union,
To let thee and thy mate live a hundred and
    twenty peaceful years,
To give you your daily bread,
To keep hunger from your door.

Several women, including Goldy, burst into tears, the others sadly lowering their gaze. The band sounded a wailing chord, and the whole audience broke into loud, heartrending weeping.

The bard went on sternly:

Wail, bride, wail!
This is a time of tears.
Think of thy past days:
Alas! they are gone to return nevermore.

Heedless of the convulsive sobbing with which the room resounded, he continued to declaim, and at last, his eye flashing fire and his voice tremulous with emotion, he sang out in a dismal, uncanny high key:

And thy good mother beyond the seas,
And thy father in his grave
Near where thy cradle was rocked,
Weep, bride, weep!
Though his soul is better off
Than we are here underneath
In dearth and cares and ceaseless pangs,
Weep, sweet bride, weep!

Then, in the general outburst that followed the extemporaneous verse, there was a cry—"The bride is fainting! Water! quick!"

"Murderer that you are!" flamed out an elderly matron, with an air of admiration for the bard's talent as much as of wrath for the far-fetched results it achieved.

Goldy was brought to, and the rest of the ceremony passed without accident. She submitted to everything as in a dream. When the bridegroom, escorted by two attendants, each carrying a candelabrum holding lighted candles came to place the veil over her face, she stared about as though she failed to realize the situation or to recognize Nathan. When, keeping time to the plaintive strains of a time-honored tune, she was led, blindfolded, into the large hall and stationed beside the bridegroom under the red canopy, and then marched around him seven times, she obeyed instructions and moved about with the passivity of a hypnotic. After the Seven Blessings had been recited, when the cantor, gently lifting the end of her veil, presented the wineglass to her lips, she tasted its contents with the air of an invalid taking medicine. Then she felt the ring slip down her finger, and heard Nathan say, "Be thou dedicated to me by this ring, according to the laws of Moses and Israel."

Whereupon she said to herself, "Now I am a married woman!" But somehow, at this moment the words were meaningless sounds to her. She knew she was married, but could not realize what it implied. As Nathan crushed the wineglass underfoot, and the band struck up a cheerful melody, and the gathering shouted, "Good luck! Good luck!" and clapped their hands while the older women broke into a wild hop, Goldy felt the relief of having gone through a great ordeal. But still she was not distinctly aware of any change in her position.

Not until fifteen minutes later, when she found herself in the basement, at the head of one of three long tables, did the realization of her new self strike her consciousness full in the face, as it were.

The dining room was nearly as large as the dancing hall on the floor above. It was as brightly illuminated, and the three tables, which ran almost its entire length, were set for a hundred and fifty guests. Yet there were barely twenty to occupy them. The effect was still more depressing than in the dancing room. The vacant benches and the untouched covers still more agonizingly exaggerated the emptiness of the room, in which the sorry handful of a company lost themselves.

Goldy looked at the rows of plates, spoons, forks, knives, and they weighed her down with the cold dazzle of their solemn, pompous array.

"I am not the Goldy I used to be," she said to herself. "I am a married woman, like mamma, or auntie, or Mrs. Volpiansky. And we have spent every cent we had on this grand wedding, and now we are left without money for furniture, and there are no guests to send us any, and the supper will be thrown out, and everything is lost, and I am to blame for it all!"

The glittering plates seemed to hold whispered converse and to exchange winks and grins at her expense. She transferred her glance to the company, and it appeared as if they were vainly forcing themselves to partake of the food—as though they, too, were looked out of countenance by that ruthless sparkle of the unused plates.

Nervous silence hung over the room, and the reluctant jingle of the score of knives and forks made it more awkward, more enervating, every second. Even the bard had not the heart to break the stillness by the merry rhymes he had composed for the occasion.

Goldy was overpowered. She thought she was on the verge of another fainting spell, and, shutting her eyes and setting her teeth, she tried to imagine herself dead. Nathan, who was by her side, noticed it. He took her hand under the table, and, pressing it gently, whispered, "Don't take it to heart. There is a God in heaven."

She could not make out his words, but she felt their meaning. As she was about to utter some phrase of endearment, her heart swelled in her throat, and a piteous, dovelike, tearful look was all the response she could make.

By-and-by, however, when the foaming lager was served, tongues were loosened, and the bard, although distressed by the meager collection in store for him, but stirred by an ardent desire to relieve the insupportable wretchedness of the evening, outdid himself in offhand acrostics and witticisms. Needless to say that his efforts were thankfully rewarded with unstinted laughter; and as the room rang with merriment, the gleaming rows of indisturbed plates also seemed to join in the general hubbub of mirth, and to be laughing a hearty, kindly laugh.

Presently, amid a fresh outbreak of deafening hilarity, Goldy bent close to Nathan's ear and exclaimed with sobbing vehemence, "My husband! My husband! My husband!"

"My wife!" he returned in her ear.

"Do you know what you are to me now?" she resumed. "A husband! And I am your wife! Do you know what it means—*do* you, *do* you, Nathan?" she insisted, with frantic emphasis.

"I do, my little sparrow; only don't worry over the wedding presents."

It was after midnight, and even the Ghetto was immersed in repose. Goldy and Nathan were silently wending their way to the three empty little rooms where they were destined to have their first joint home. They wore the wedding attire which they had rented for the evening: he a swallowtail coat and high hat, and she a white satin gown and slippers, her head uncovered—the wreath and veil done up in a newspaper, in Nathan's hand.

They had gone to the wedding in carriages, which had attracted large crowds both at the point of departure, and in front of the hall; and of course they had expected to make their way to their new home in a similar "respectable" manner. Toward the close of the last dance, after supper, they found, however, that some small change was all they possessed in the world.

The last strains of music were dying away. The guests, in their hats and bonnets, were taking leave. Everybody seemed in a hurry to get away to his own world, and to abandon the young couple to their fate.

Nathan would have borrowed a dollar or two of some friend. "Let us go home as behooves a bride and bridegroom," he said. "There is a God in heaven: he will not forsake us."

But Goldy would not hear of betraying the full measure of their poverty to their friends. "No! no!" she retorted testily. "I am not going to let you pay a dollar and a half for a few blocks' drive, like a Fifth Avenue nobleman. We can walk," she pursued, with the grim determination of one bent upon self-chastisement. "A poor woman who dares spend every cent on a wedding must be ready to walk after the wedding."

When they found themselves alone in the deserted street, they were so overcome by a sense of loneliness, of a kind of portentous, haunting emptiness, that they could not speak. So on they trudged in dismal silence; she leaning upon his arm, and he tenderly pressing her to his side.

Their way lay through the gloomiest and roughest part of the Seventh Ward. The neighborhood frightened her, and she clung closer to her escort. At one corner they passed some men in front of a liquor saloon.

"Look at dem! Look at dem! A sheeny fellar an' his bride, I'll betch ye!" shouted a husky voice. "Jes' comin' from de weddin'."

"She ain't no bigger 'n a peanut, is she?" The simile was greeted with a horse-laugh.

"Look a here, young fellar, what's de madder wid carryin' dat lady of yourn in your vest pocket?"

When Nathan and Goldy were a block away, something like a potato or a carrot struck her in the back. At the same time the gang of loafers on the corner broke into boisterous merriment. Nathan tried to face about, but she restrained him.

"Don't! They might kill you!" she whispered, and relapsed into silence.

He made another attempt to disengage himself, as if for a desperate attack upon her assailants, but she nestled close to his side and held him fast, her every fiber tingling with the consciousness of the shelter she had in him.

"Don't mind them, Nathan," she said.

And as they proceeded on their dreary way through a somber, impoverished street, with here and there a rustling tree—a melancholy witness of its better days—they felt a stream of happiness uniting them, as it coursed through the veins of both, and they were filled with a blissful sense of oneness the like of which they had never tasted before. So happy were they that the gang behind them, and the bare rooms toward which they were directing their steps, and the miserable failure of the wedding, all suddenly appeared too insignificant to engage their attention—paltry matters alien to their new life, remote from the enchanted world in which they now dwelt.

The very notion of a relentless void abruptly turned to a beatific sense of their own seclusion, of there being only themselves in the universe, to live and delight in each other.

"Don't mind them, Nathan darling," she repeated mechanically, conscious of nothing but the tremor of happiness in her voice.

"I should give it to them!" he responded, gathering her still closer to him. "I should show them how to touch my Goldy, my pearl, my birdie!"

They dived into the denser gloom of a sidestreet.

A gentle breeze ran past and ahead of them, proclaiming the bride and the bridegroom. An old tree whispered overhead its tender felicitations.

HENRY JAMES
(1843-1916)

Henry James was born in New York City and received his education mainly in Europe, where he traveled extensively as a youth. From 1862 to 1863, he studied law at Harvard Law School. James eventually returned to Europe permanently in 1875, where he worked as a newspaper correspondent in Paris before settling in London. Among his major works are the novels Daisy Miller *(1878),* The Portrait of a Lady *(1881),* The Bostonians *(1885), and* The Ambassadors *(1903), almost all of which deal with "the international theme"—naive Americans living abroad and interacting with sophisticated Europeans—that was his major subject from the start. During his long career, James wrote book reviews and literary criticism, short stories, plays, novels, and travel books. Although many of his novels were regularly serialized in widely read British and American magazines, he received little critical acclaim during his lifetime. Today his fiction, with its psychological depth and its controlled narrative posture, is viewed as innovative and influential.*

In 1904 James returned to America for a visit. His observations resulted in a travel book, The American Scene, *published in 1907. In this work James applied to his homeland and his countrymen his acute powers of observation and interpretation, mingling the perspectives of an "inquiring stranger" with those of an "initiated native." In this excerpt, James comments on his visit to New York City and his observation of immigrant Europeans very different from the aristocrats who people his novels.*

FROM THE AMERICAN SCENE

I

It was a concomitant, always, of the down-town hour that it could be felt as *most* playing into the surrendered consciousness and making the sharpest impression; yet, since the up-town hour was apt, in its turn, to claim the same distinction, I could only let each of them take its way with me as it would. The oddity was that they seemed not at all to speak of different things—by so quick a process does any one aspect, in the United States, in general, I was to note, connect itself with the rest; so little does any link in the huge looseness of New York, in especial, appear to come as a whole, or as final, out of the fusion. The fusion, as of elements in solution in a vast hot pot, is always going on, and one stage of the process is as typical or as vivid as another. Whatever I might be looking at, or be struck with, the object or the phase was an item in the pressing conditions of the place, and as such had more in common with its sister items than it had in difference from them. It mattered little, moreover, whether this might be a proof that New York, among cities, most deeply languishes and palpitates, or vibrates and flourishes (whichever way one may put it) under the breath of her conditions, or whether, simply, this habit of finding a little of *all* my impressions reflected in any one of them testified to the enjoyment of a real relation with the subject. I like indeed to think of my relation to New York as, in that manner, almost inexpressibly intimate, and as hence making, for daily sensation, a keyboard as continuous, and as free from hard transitions, as if swept by the fingers of a master-pianist. You cannot, surely, say more for your sense of the underlying unity of an occasion than that the taste of each dish in the banquet recalls the taste of most of the others; which is what I mean by the "continuity," not to say the affinity, on the island of Manhattan, between the fish and the sweets, between the soup and the game. The whole feast affects one as eaten—that is the point—with the general queer sauce of New York; a preparation as freely diffused, somehow, on the East side as on the West, in the quarter of Grand Street as in the quarter of Murray Hill. No fact, I hasten to add, would appear to make the place more amenable to delineations of the order that may be spoken of as hanging together.

I must confess, notwithstanding, to not being quite ready to point directly to the common element in the dense Italian neighbourhoods of the lower East side, and in the upper reaches of Fifth and of Madison Avenues; though indeed I wonder at this inability in recollecting two or three of those charming afternoons of early summer, in Central Park, which showed the fruit of the foreign tree as shaken down there with a force that smothered everything else. The long residential vistas I have named were within a quarter of an hour's walk, but the alien was as truly in possession, under the high "aristocratic" nose, as if he had had but three steps to come. If it be asked why, the alien still striking you so as an alien, the singleness of impression, throughout the place, should still be so marked, the answer, close at hand, would seem to be that the alien himself fairly *makes* the singleness of impression. Is not the universal sauce essentially *his* sauce, and do we not feel ourselves feeding, half the time, from the ladle, as greasy as he chooses to leave it for us, that he holds out? Such questions were in my ears, at all events, with the cheerful hum of that babel of tongues established in the vernal Park, and they supplied, beyond doubt, the livelier interest of any hour of contemplation there. I hate to drift into dealing with them at the expense of a proper tribute, kept distinct and vivid, to the charming bosky precinct itself, the great field of recreation with which they swarmed; but it could not be the fault of the brooding visitor, and still less that of the restored absentee, if he was conscious of the need of mental adjustment to phenomena absolutely fresh. He could remember still how, months before, a day or two after his restoration, a noted element of one of his first impressions had been this particular revealed anomaly. He had been, on the Jersey shore, walking with a couple of friends through the grounds of a large new rural residence, where groups of diggers and ditchers were working, on those lines of breathless haste which seem always, in the United States, of the essence of any question, toward an expensive effect of landscape gardening. To pause before them, for interest in their labour, was, and would have been everywhere, instinctive; but what came home to me on the spot was that whatever *more* would have been anywhere else involved had here inevitably to lapse.

What lapsed, on the spot, was the element of communication with the workers, as I may call it for want of a better name; that element which, in a European country, would have operated, from side to side, as the play of mutual recognition, founded on old familiarities and heredities, and involving, for the moment, some impalpable exchange. The men, in the case I speak of, were Italians, of superlatively southern type, and any impalpable exchange struck me as absent from the air to positive intensity, to mere unthinkability. It was as if contact were out of the question and the sterility of the passage between us recorded, with due dryness, in our staring silence. This impression was for one of the party a shock—a member of the party for whom, on the other side of the world, the imagination of the main furniture, as it might be called, of any rural excursion, of *the* rural in particular, had been, during years, the easy sense, for the excursionist, of a social relation with any encountered type, from whichever end of the scale proceeding. Had that not ever been, exactly, a part of the vague warmth, the intrinsic colour, of any honest man's rural walk in his England or his Italy, his Germany or his France, and was not the effect of its so suddenly dropping out, in the land of universal brotherhood—for I was to find it drop out again and again—rather a chill, straightway, for the heart, and rather a puzzle, not less, for the head? Shortly after the spring of this question was first touched for me I found it ring out again with a sharper stroke. Happening to have lost my way, during a long ramble among the New Hampshire hills, I appealed, for information, at a parting of the roads, to a young man whom, at the moment of my need, I happily saw emerge from a neighboring wood. But his stare was blank, in answer to my inquiry, and, seeing that he failed to understand me and that he had a dark-eyed "Latin" look, I jumped to the inference of his being a French Canadian. My repetition of my query in French, however, forwarded the case as little, and my trying him with Italian had no better effect. "What *are* you then?" I wonderingly asked—on which my accent loosened in him the faculty of speech. "I'm an Armenian," he replied, as if it were the most natural thing in the world for a wage-earning youth in the heart of New England to be—so that all I could do was to try and make my profit of the lesson. I could have made it better, for the occasion, if, even on the Armenian basis, he had appeared to expect brotherhood; but this had been as little his seeming as it had been that of the diggers by the Jersey shore.

To inquire of these things on the spot, to betray, that is, one's sense of the "chill" of which I have spoken, is of course to hear it admitted, promptly enough, that there is no claim to brotherhood with aliens in the first grossness of their alienism. The material of which they consist is being dressed and prepared, at this stage, for brotherhood, and the consummation, in respect to many of them, will not be, can not from the nature of the case be, in any lifetime of their own. Their children are another matter—as in fact the children throughout the United States, are an immense matter, are almost the greatest matter of all; it is the younger generation who will fully profit, rise to the occasion and enter into the privilege. The machinery is colossal—nothing is more characteristic of the country than the development of this machinery, in the form of the political and social habit, the common school and the newspaper; so that there are always millions of little transformed strangers growing up in regard to whom the idea of intimacy of relation may be as freely cherished as you like. *They* are the stuff of whom brothers and sisters are made, and the making proceeds on a scale that really need leave nothing to desire. All this you take in, with a wondering mind, and in the light of it the great "ethnic" question rises before you on a corresponding scale and with a corresponding majesty. Once it has set your observation, to say nothing of your imagination, working, it becomes for you, as you go and come, the wonderment to which everything ministers and that is quickened well-nigh to madness, in some places and on some occasions, by every face and every accent that meet your eyes and ears. The sense of the elements in the cauldron—the cauldron of the "American" character—becomes thus about as vivid a thing as you can at all quietly manage, and the question settles into a form which makes the intelligible answer further and further recede. "What meaning, in the presence of such impressions, can continue to attach to such a term as the 'American' character?—what type, as the result of such a prodigious amalgam, such a hotchpotch of racial ingredients, is to be conceived as shaping itself?" The challenge to speculation, fed thus by a thousand sources, is so intense as to be, as I say, irritating; but practically, beyond doubt, I should also say, you take refuge from it— since your case would otherwise be hard; and you find your relief not in the least in any direct satisfaction or solution, but absolutely in that blest general drop of the immediate need of conclusions, or rather in that blest general feeling for the impossibility of them, to which the philosophy of any really fine observation of the American spectacle must reduce itself, and the large intellectual, quite even the large æsthetic, margin supplied by which accompanies the spectator as his one positively complete comfort. . . .

II

The process of the mitigation and, still more, of the conversion of the alien goes on, meanwhile, obviously, not by leaps and bounds or any form of easy magic, but under its own mystic laws and with an outward air of quite declining to be unduly precipitated. How little it may be thought of in New York as a quick business we readily perceive as the effect of merely remembering the vast numbers of their kind that the arriving reinforcements, from whatever ends of the earth, find already in possession of the field. There awaits the disembarked Armenian, for instance, so warm and furnished an Armenian corner that the need of hurrying to get rid of the sense of it must become less and less a pressing preliminary. The corner growing warmer and warmer, it is to be supposed, by rich accretions, he may take his time, more and more, for becoming absorbed in the surrounding element, and he may in fact feel more and more that he can do so on his own conditions. I seem to find indeed in this latter truth a hint for the best expression of a whole side of New York—the best expression of much of the medium in which one consciously moves. It is formed by this fact that the alien is taking his time, and that you go about with him meanwhile, sharing, all respectfully, in his deliberation, waiting on his convenience, watching him at his interesting work. The vast foreign quarters of the city present him as thus engaged in it, and they are curious and portentous and "picturesque" just by reason of their doing so. You recognize in them, freely, those elements that are not elements of swift convertibility, and you lose yourself in the wonder of what becomes, as it were, of the obstinate, the unconverted residuum. The country at large, as you cross it in different senses, keeps up its character for you as the hugest thinkable organism for successful "assimilation"; but the assimilative force itself has the residuum still to count with. The operation of the immense machine, identical after all with the total of American life, trembles away into mysteries that are beyond our present notation and that reduce us in many a mood to renouncing analysis.

Who and what is an alien, when it comes to that, in a country peopled from the first under the jealous eye of history?—peopled, that is, by migrations at once extremely recent, perfectly traceable and urgently required. They are still, it would appear, urgently required—if we look about far enough for the urgency; though of that truth such a scene as New York may well make one doubt. Which is the American, by these scant measures?—which is *not* the alien, over a large part of the country at least, and where does one put a finger on the dividing line, or, for that matter, "spot" and identify any particular phase of the conversion, any one of its successive moments? The sense of the interest of so doing is doubtless half the interest of the general question—the possibility of our seeing lucidly presented some such phenomenon, in a given group of persons, or even in a felicitous individual, as the dawn of the American spirit while the declining rays of the Croatian, say, or of the Calabrian, or of the Lusitanian, still linger more or less pensively in the sky. Fifty doubts and queries come up, in regard to any such possibility, as one circulates in New York, with the so ambiguous element in the *launched* foreign personality always in one's eyes; the wonder, above all, of whether there be, comparatively, in the vastly greater number of the representatives of the fresh contingent, any spirit that the American does not find an easy prey. Repeatedly, in the electric cars, one seemed invited to take that for granted—there being occasions, days and weeks together, when the electric cars offer you nothing else to think of. The carful, again and again, is a foreign carful; a row of faces, up and down, testifying, without exception, to alienism unmistakable, alienism undisguised and unashamed. You do here, in a manner perhaps, discriminate; the launched condition, as I have called it, is more developed in some types than in others; but I remember observing how, in the Broadway and the Bowery conveyances in especial, they tended, almost alike, to make the observer gasp with the sense of isolation. It was not for this that the observer on whose behalf I more particularly write had sought to take up again the sweet sense of the natal air.

The great fact about his companions was that, foreign as they might be, newly inducted as they might be, there were *at home*, really more at home, at the end of their few weeks or months or their year or two, than they had ever in their lives been before; and that *he* was at home too, quite with the same intensity: and yet that it was this very equality of condition that, from side to side, made the whole medium so strange. Here again, however, relief may be sought and found—and I say this at the risk of perhaps picturing the restored absentee as too constantly requiring it; for there is fascination in the study of the innumerable ways in which this sense of being at home, on the part of all the types, may show forth. New York offers to such a study a well-nigh unlimited field, but I seem to recall winter days, harsh, dusky, sloshy winter afternoons, in the densely-packed East-side street-cars, as an especially intimate surrender to it. It took its place thus, I think, under the general American law of *all* relief from the great equalizing pressure: it took on that last disinterestedness which consists of one's getting away from one's subject by plunging into it, for sweet truth's sake, still deeper. If I speak, moreover, of this general first gross-ness of alienism as presented in "types," I use that word for easy convenience and not in respect to its indicating marked variety. There are many different ways, cer-tainly, in which obscure fighters of the battle of life may look, under new high lights, queer and crude and unwrought; but the striking thing, precisely, in the crepuscu-lar, tunnel-like avenues that the "Elevated" overarches—yet without quenching, either, that constant power of any American exhibition rather luridly to light itself—the striking thing, and the beguiling, was always the manner in which figure after figure and face after face already betrayed the common consequence and action of their whereabouts. Face after face, unmistakably, was "low"—particularly in the men, squared all solidly in their new security and portability, their vague but grow-ing sense of many unprecedented things; and as signs of the reinforcing of a large local conception of manners and relations it was difficult to say if they most affected one as promising or as portentous.

The great thing, at any rate, was that they were all together so visibly on the new, the lifted level—that of consciously not being what they *had* been, and that this immediately glazed them over as with some mixture, of indescribable hue and con-sistency, the wholesale varnish of consecration, that might have been applied, out of a bottomless receptacle, by a huge white-washing brush. Here, perhaps, was the nearest approach to a seizable step in the evolution of the oncoming citizen, the stage of his no longer being for you—for any complacency of the romantic, or even verily of the fraternizing, sense in you—the foreigner of the quality, of the kind, that he might have been *chez lui.* Whatever he might see himself becoming, he was never to see himself that again, any more than you were ever to see him. He became then, to my vision (which I have called fascinated for want of a better description of it), a creature promptly despoiled of those "manners" which were the grace (as I am again reduced to calling it) by which one had best known and, on opportunity, best liked him. He presents himself thus, most of all, to be plain—and not only in New York, but throughout the country—as wonderingly conscious that his manners of the other world, that everything you have there known and praised him for, have been a huge mistake: to that degree that the sense of this luminous discovery is what we mainly imagine his weighted communications to those he has left behind charged with; those rich letters home as to the number and content of which the Post Office gives us so remarkable a statistic. If there are several lights in which the great assim-ilative organism itself may be looked at, does it not still perhaps loom largest as an agent for revealing to the citizen-to-be the error in question? He hears it, under this ægis, proclaimed in a thousand voices, and it is as listening to these and as, accord-ing to the individual, more or less swiftly, but always infallibly, penetrated and con-vinced by them, that I felt myself see him go about his business, see him above all, for some odd reason, sit there in the street-car, and with a slow, brooding gravity, a dim calculation of bearings, which yet never takes a backward step, expand to the full measure of it.

So, in New York, largely, the "American" value of the immigrant who arrives at all mature is restricted to the enjoyment (all prepared to increase) of that impor-tant preliminary truth; which makes him for us, we must own, till more comes of it, a tolerably neutral and colourless image. He resembles for the time the dog who sniffs round the freshly-acquired bone, giving it a push and a lick, betraying a sense of its possibilities, but not—and quite as from a positive deep tremor of con-sciousness—directly attacking it. There are categories of foreigners, truly, meanwhile, of whom we are moved to say that only a mechanism working with scientific force could have performed this feat of making them colourless. The Italians, who, over the whole land, strike us, I am afraid, as, after the Negro and the Chinaman, the human value most easily produced, the Italians meet us, at every turn, only to make us ask what has become of that element of the agreeable address in *them* which has, from far back, so enhanced for the stranger the interest and pleasure of a visit to their beautiful country. They shed it utterly, I couldn't but observe, on their advent, after a deep inhalation or two of the clear native air; shed it with a conscientious completeness which leaves one looking for any faint trace of it. "Colour," of that pleasant sort, was what they had appeared, among the races of the European family, most to have; so that the effect I speak of, the rapid action of the ambient air, is like that of the tub of hot water that reduces a piece of bright-hued stuff, on immersion, to the proved state of not "washing": the only fault of my image indeed being that if the stuff loses its brightness the water of the tub at least is more or less agreeably dyed with it. That is doubtless not the case for the ambient air operating after the fashion I here note—since we surely fail to observe that the property washed out of the new subject begins to tint with its pink or its azure his fellow-soakers in the terrible tank. If this property that has quitted him—the general amenity of attitude in the absence of provocation to its opposite—could be accounted for by its having rubbed off on any number of surrounding persons, the whole process would be easier and perhaps more comforting to follow. It will not have been his first occasion of taking leave of short-sighted comfort in the United States, however, if the patient inquirer postpones that ideal to the real solicitation of the question I here touch on.

What *does* become of the various positive properties, on the part of certain of the installed tribes, the good manners, say, among them, as to which the process of shedding and the fact of eclipse come so promptly into play? It has taken long ages of history, in the other world, to produce them, and you ask yourself, with independent curiosity, if they may really be thus extinguished in an hour. And if they are not extinguished, into what pathless tracts of the native atmosphere do they virtually, do they provisionally, and so all undiscoverably, melt? Do they burrow underground, to await their day again?—or in what strange secret places are they held in deposit and in trust? The "American" identity that has profited by their sacrifice has meanwhile acquired (in the happiest cases) all apparent confidence and consistency; but may not the doubt remain of whether the extinction of qualities ingrained in generations is to be taken for quite complete? Isn't it conceivable that, for something like a final efflorescence, the business of slow comminglings and makings-over at last ended, they may rise again to the surface, affirming their vitality and value and playing their part? It would be for them, of course, in this event, to attest that they had been worth waiting so long for; but the speculation, at any rate, irresistibly forced upon us, is a sign of the interest, in the American world, of what I have called the "ethnic" outlook. The cauldron, for the great stew, has such circumference and such depth that we can only deal here with ultimate syntheses, ultimate combinations and possibilities. Yet I am well aware that if these vague evocations of them, in their nebulous remoteness, may charm the ingenuity of the student of the scene, there are matters of the foreground that they have no call to supplant. Any temptation to let them do so is meanwhile, no doubt, but a proof of that impulse irresponsibly to escape from the formidable foreground which so often, in the American world, lies in wait for the spirit of intellectual dalliance.

III

New York really, I think, is all formidable foreground; or, if it be not, there is more than enough of this pressure of the present and the immediate to cut out the close sketcher's work for him. These things are a thick growth all round him, and when I recall the intensity of the material picture in the dense Yiddish quarter, for instance, I wonder at its not having forestalled, on my page, mere musings and, as they will doubtless be called, moonings. There abides with me, ineffaceably, the memory of a summer evening spent there by invitation of a high public functionary domiciled on the spot—to the extreme enhancement of the romantic interest his visitor found him foredoomed to inspire—who was to prove one of the most liberal of hosts and most luminous of guides. I can scarce help it if this brilliant personality, on that occasion the very medium itself through which the whole spectacle showed, so colours my impressions that if I speak, by intention, of the facts that played into them I may really but reflect the rich talk and the general privilege of the hour. That accident moreover must take its place simply as the highest value and the strongest note in the total show—so much did it testify to the quality of appealing, surrounding life. The sense of this quality was already strong in my drive, with a companion, through the long, warm June twilight, from a comparatively conventional neighbourhood; it was the sense, after all, of a great swarming, a swarming that had begun to thicken, infinitely, as soon as we had crossed to the East side and long before we had got to Rutgers Street. There is no swarming like that of Israel when once Israel has got a start, and the scene here bristled, at every step, with the signs and sounds, immitigable, unmistakable, of a Jewry that had burst all bounds. That it has burst all bounds in New York, almost any combination of figures or of objects taken at hazard sufficiently proclaims; but I remember how the rising waters, on this summer night, rose, to the imagination, even above the housetops and seemed to sound their murmur to the pale distant stars. It was as if we had been thus, in the crowded, hustled roadway, where multiplication, multiplication of everything, was the dominant note, at the bottom of some vast sallow aquarium in which innumerable fish, of overdeveloped proboscis, were to bump together, for ever, amid heaped spoils of the sea.

The children swarmed above all—here was multiplication with a vengeance; and the number of very old persons, of either sex, was almost equally remarkable; the very old persons being in equal vague occupation of the doorstep, pavement, curbstone, gutter, roadway, and every one alike using the street for overflow. As overflow, in the whole quarter, is the main fact of life—I was to learn later on that, with the exception of some shy corner of Asia, no district in the world known to the statistician has so many inhabitants to the yard—the scene hummed with the human presence beyond any I had ever faced in quest even of refreshment; producing part of the impression, moreover, no doubt, as a direct consequence of the intensity of the Jewish aspect. This, I think, makes the individual Jew more of a concentrated person, savingly possessed of everything that is in him, than any other human, noted at random—or is it simply, rather, that the unsurpassed strength of the race permits of the chopping into myriads of fine fragments without loss of race-quality? There are small strange animals, known to natural history, snakes or worms, I believe, who, when cut into pieces, wriggle away contentedly and live in the snippet as completely as in the whole. So the denizens of the New York Ghetto, heaped as thick as the splinters on the table of a glass-blower, had each, like the fine glass particle, his or her individual share of the whole hard glitter of Israel. This diffused intensity, as I have called it, causes any array of Jews to resemble (if I may be allowed another image) some long nocturnal street where every window in every house shows a maintained light. The advanced age of so many of the figures, the ubiquity of the children, carried out in fact this analogy; they were all there for race, and not, as it were, for reason: that excess of lurid meaning, in some of the old men's and old women's faces in particular, would have been absurd, in the conditions, as a really directed attention—it could only be the gathered past of Israel mechanically pushing through. The way, at the same time, this chapter of history did, all that evening, seem to push, was a matter that made the "ethnic" apparition again sit like a skeleton at the feast. It was fairly as if I could see the spectre grin while the talk of the hour gave me, across the board, facts and figures, chapter and verse, for the extent of the Hebrew conquest of New York. With a reverence for intellect, one should doubtless have drunk in tribute to an intellectual people; but I remember being at no time more conscious of that merely portentous element, in the aspects of American growth, which reduces to inanity any marked dismay quite as much as any high elation. The portent is one of too many—you always come back, as I have hinted, with your easier gasp, to *that*: it will be time enough to sigh or to shout when the relation of the particular appearance to all the other relations shall have cleared itself up. Phantasmagoric for me, accordingly, in a high degree, are the interesting hours I here glance at content to remain—setting in this respect, I recognize, an excellent example to all the rest of the New York phantasmagoria. Let me speak of the remainder only as phantasmagoric too, so that I may both the more kindly recall it and the sooner have done with it.

I have not done, however, with the impression of that large evening in the Ghetto; there was too much in the vision, and it has left too much the sense of a rare experience. For what did it all really come to but that one had seen with one's eyes the New Jerusalem on earth? What less than that could it all have been, in its far-spreading light and its celestial serenity of multiplication? There it was, there it is, and when I think of the dark, foul, stifling Ghettos of other remembered cities, I shall think by the same stroke of the city of redemption, and evoke in particular the rich Rutgers Street perspective—rich, so peculiarly, for the eye, in that complexity of fire-escapes with which each house-front bristles and which gives the whole vista so modernized and appointed a look. Omnipresent in the "poor" regions, this neat applied machinery has, for the stranger, a common side with the electric light and the telephone, suggests the distance achieved from the old Jerusalem. (These frontal iron ladders and platforms, by the way, so numerous throughout New York, strike more New York notes than can be parenthetically named—and among them perhaps most sharply the note of the ease with which, in the terrible town, on opportunity, "architecture" goes by the board; but the appearance to which they often most conduce is that of the spaciously organized cage for the nimbler class of animals in some great zoological garden. This general analogy is irresistible—it seems to offer, in each district, a little world of bars and perches and swings for human squirrels and monkeys. The very name of architecture perishes, for the fire-escapes look like abashed afterthoughts, staircases and communications forgotten in the construction; but the inhabitants lead, like the squirrels and monkeys, all the merrier life.) It was while I hung over the prospect from the windows of my friend, however, the presiding genius of the district, and it was while, at a later hour, I proceeded in his company, and in that of a trio of contributive fellow-pilgrims, from one "characteristic" place of public entertainment to another: it was during this rich climax, I say, that the city of redemption was least to be taken for anything less than it was. The windows, while we sat at meat, looked out on a swarming little square in which an ant-like population darted to and fro; the square consisted in part of a "district" public garden, or public lounge rather, one of those small backwaters or refuges, artfully economized for rest, here and there, in the very heart of the New York whirlpool, and which spoke louder than anything else of a Jerusalem disinfected. What spoke loudest, no doubt, was the great overtowering School which formed a main boundary and in the shadow of which we all comparatively crouched.

But the School must not lead me on just yet—so colossally has its presence still to loom for us; that presence which profits so, for predominance, in America, by the failure of concurrent and competitive presences, the failure of any others looming at all on the same scale save that of Business, those in particular of a visible Church, a visible State, a visible Society, a visible Past; those of the many visibilities, in short, that warmly cumber the ground in older countries. Yet it also spoke loud that my friend was quartered, for the interest of the thing (from his so interesting point of view), in a "tenement-house"; the New Jerusalem would so have triumphed, had it triumphed nowhere else, in the fact that this charming little structure *could* be ranged, on the wonderful little square, under that invidious head. On my asking to what latent vice it owed its stigma, I was asked in return if it didn't sufficiently pay for its name by harbouring some five-and-twenty families. But this, exactly, was the way it testified—this circumstance of the simultaneous enjoyment by five-and-twenty families, on "tenement" lines, of conditions so little sordid, so highly "evolved." I remember the evolved fireproof staircase, a thing of scientific surfaces, impenetrable to the microbe, and above all plated, against side friction, with white marble of a goodly grain. The white marble was surely the New Jerusalem note, and we followed that note, up and down the district, the rest of the evening, through more happy changes than I may take time to count. What struck me in the flaring streets (over and beyond the everywhere insistent, defiant, unhumorous, exotic face) was the blaze of the shops addressed to the New Jerusalem wants and the splendour with which these were taken for granted; the only thing indeed a little ambiguous was just this look of the trap too brilliantly, too candidly baited for the wary side of Israel itself. It is not *for* Israel, in general, that Israel so artfully shines—yet its being moved to do so, at last, in that luxurious style, might be precisely the grand side of the city of redemption. Who can ever tell, moreover, in any conditions and in presence of any apparent anomaly, what the genius of Israel may, or may not, really be "up to"?

The grateful way to take it all, at any rate, was with the sense of its coming back again to the inveterate rise, in the American air, of every value, and especially of the lower ones, those most subject to multiplication; such a wealth of meaning did this keep appearing to pour into the value and function of the country at large. Importances are all strikingly shifted and reconstituted, in the United States, for the visitor attuned, from far back, to "European" importances; but I think of no other moment of my total impression as so sharply working over my own benighted vision of them. The scale, in this light of the New Jerusalem, seemed completely rearranged; or, to put it more simply, the wants, the gratifications, the aspirations of the "poor," as expressed in the shops (which were the shops of the "poor"), denoted a new style of poverty; and this new style of poverty, from street to street, stuck out of the possible purchasers, one's jostling fellow-pedestrians, and made them, to every man and woman, individual throbs in the larger harmony. One can speak only of what one has seen, and there were grosser elements of the sordid and the squalid that I doubtless never saw. That, with a good deal of observation and of curiosity, I should have failed of this, the country over, affected me as by itself something of an indication. To miss that part of the spectacle, or to know it only by its having so unfamiliar a pitch, was an indication that made up for a great many others. It is when this one in particular is forced home to you—this immense, vivid *general* lift of poverty and general appreciation of the living unit's paying property in himself—that the picture seems most to clear and the way to jubilation most to open. For it meets you there, at every turn, as the result most definitely attested. You are as constantly reminded, no doubt, that these rises in enjoyed value shrink and dwindle under the icy breath of Trusts and the weight of the new remorseless monopolies that operate as no madnesses of ancient personal power thrilling us on the historic page ever operated; the living unit's property in himself becoming more and more merely such a property as may consist with a relation to properties over-whelmingly greater and that allow the asking of no questions and the making, for co-existence with them, of no conditions. But that, in the fortunate phrase, is another story, and will be altogether, evidently, a new and different drama. There is such a thing, in the United States, it is hence to be inferred, as freedom to grow up to be blighted, and it may be the only freedom in store for the smaller fry of future generations. If it is accordingly of the smaller fry I speak, and of how large they massed on that evening of endless admonitions, this will be because I caught them thus in their comparative humility and at an early stage of their American growth. The life-thread has, I suppose, to be of a certain thickness for the great shears of Fate to feel for it. Put it, at the worst, that the Ogres were to devour them, they were but the more certainly to fatten into food for the Ogres.

Their dream, at all events, as I noted it, was meanwhile sweet and undisguised— nowhere sweeter than in the half-dozen picked beer-houses and cafés in which our ingenuous *enquête*, that of my fellow-pilgrims and I, would up. These establish-ments had each been selected for its playing off some facet of the jewel, and they wondrously testified, by their range and their individual colour, to the spread of that lustre. It was a pious rosary of which I should like to tell each bead, but I must let the general sense of the adventure serve. Our successive stations were in no case of the "seamy" order, an inquiry into seaminess having been unanimously pro-nounced futile, but each had its separate social connotation, and it was for the num-ber and variety of these connotations, and their individual plenitude and prosperity, to set one thinking. Truly the Yiddish world was a vast world, with its own deeps and complexities, and what struck one above all was that it sat there at its cups (and in no instance vulgarly the worse for them) with a sublimity of good conscience that took away the breath, a protrusion of elbow never aggressive, but absolutely proof against jostling. It was the incurable man of letters under the skin of one of the party who gasped, I confess; for it was in the light of letters, that is in the light of our lan-guage as literature has hitherto known it, that one stared at this all-unconscious impudence of the agency of future ravage. The man of letters, in the United States, has his own difficulties to face and his own current to stem—for dealing with which his liveliest inspiration may be, I think, that they are still very much his own, even in an Americanized world, and that more than elsewhere they press him to intimate communion with his honour. For that honour, the honour that sits astride of the consecrated English tradition, to his mind, quite as old knighthood astride of its caparisoned charger, the dragon most rousing, over the land, the proper spirit of St. George, is just this immensity of the alien presence climbing higher and higher, climbing itself into the very light of publicity.

I scarce know why, but I saw it that evening as in some dim dawn of that promise to its own consciousness, and perhaps this was precisely what made it a little exasperating. Under the impression of the mere mob the question doesn't come up, but in these haunts of comparative civility we saw the mob sifted and strained, and the exasperation was the sharper, no doubt, because what the process had left most visible was just the various possibilities of the waiting spring of intelligence. Such elements constituted the germ of a "public," and it was impossible (possessed of a sensibility worth speaking of) to be exposed to them without feeling how new a thing under the sun the resulting public would be. That was where one's "lettered" anguish came in—in the turn of one's eye from face to face for some betrayal of a prehensile hook for the linguistic tradition as one had known it. Each warm lighted and supplied circle, each group of served tables and smoked pipes and fostered decencies and unprecedented accents, beneath the extravagant lamps, took on thus, for the brooding critic, a likeness to that terrible modernized and civilized room in the Tower of London, haunted by the shade of Guy Fawkes, which had more than once formed part of the scene of the critic's taking tea there. In this chamber of the present urbanities the wretched man had been stretched on the rack, and the critic's ear (how else should it have been a critic's?) could still always catch, in pauses of talk, the faint groan of his ghost. Just so the East side cafés—and increasingly as their place in the scale was higher—showed to my inner sense, beneath their bedizenment, as torture-rooms of the living idiom; the piteous gasp of which at the portent of lacerations to come could reach me in any drop of the surrounding Accent of the Future. The accent of the very ultimate future, in the States, may be destined to become the most beautiful on the globe and the very music of humanity (here the "ethnic" synthesis shrouds itself thicker than ever); but whatever we shall know it for, certainly, we shall not know it for English—in any sense for which there is an existing literary measure.

CONSTANTINE M. PANUNZIO

(1884–1964)

Constantine Panunzio was born in Molfetta, Italy, and immigrated to the United States in 1902. He attended Wesleyan University and pursued graduate study at Boston University, Harvard University, and Columbia University. In 1925, he obtained a Ph.D. from the Robert Brookings Graduate School of Economics and Government. Trained as a sociologist, Panunzio researched a wide range of subjects and produced nine books, including the autobiographical account of his youth, The Soul of an Immigrant *(1921). Many of his research projects focused on the social conditions of immigrants in America. He taught at several colleges and universities, and from*

1931 until 1952 he was a member of the sociology department at the University of California, Los Angeles. At the New York World's Fair in 1940, he was designated among those foreign-born who had made outstanding contributions to American culture.

This selection from Panunzio's autobiographical text presents his arrival in America as a seaman and his absorption into the labor pool that was managed by Italian-American padrones as middleman between the Yankee employers and the illiterate immigrants.

FROM THE SOUL OF AN IMMIGRANT

. . . Late in the evening of September 8, 1902, when the turmoil of the street traffic was subsiding, and the silence of the night was slowly creeping over the city, I took my sea chest, my sailor bag and all I had and set foot on American soil. I was in America. Of immigration laws I had not even a knowledge of their existence; of the English language I knew not a word; of friends I had none in Boston or elsewhere in America to whom I might turn for counsel or help. I had exactly fifty cents remaining out of a dollar which the captain had finally seen fit to give me. But as I was soon to earn money and return to Molfetta, I felt no concern. . . .

I roamed about the streets, not knowing where or to whom to turn. That day and the next four days I had one loaf of bread each day for food and at night, not having money with which to purchase shelter, I stayed on the recreation pier on Commercial Street. One night, very weary and lonely, I lay upon a bench and soon dozed off into a light sleep. The next thing I knew I cried out in bitter pain and fright. A policeman had stolen up to me very quietly and with his club had dealt me a heavy blow upon the soles of my feet. He drove me away, and I think I cried; I cried my first American cry. What became of me that night I cannot say. And the next day and the next. . . . I just roamed aimlessly about the streets, between the Public Garden with its flowers and the water-side, where I watched the children at play, even as I had played at the water's brink in old Molfetta.

Those first five days in America have left an impression upon my mind which can never be erased with the years, and which gives me a most profound sense of sympathy for immigrants as they arrive.

On the fifth day, by mere chance, I ran across a French sailor on the recreation pier. We immediately became friends. His name was Louis. Just to look at Louis would make you laugh. He was over six feet tall, lank, queer-shaped, freckle-faced, with small eyes and a crooked nose. I have sometimes thought that perhaps he was the "missing link" for which the scientist has been looking. Louis could not speak Italian; he had a smattering of what he called "italien," but I could not see it his way. On the other hand, I kept imposing upon his good nature by giving a nasal twang to Italian words and insisting on calling it "francese." We had much merriment. Two facts, however, made possible a mutual understanding. Both had been sailors and had traveled over very much the same world; this made a bond between us. Then too, we had an instinctive knowledge of "esperanto," a strange capacity for gesticulation and facial contortion, which was always our last "hope" in making each other understand.

Not far from the recreation pier on which we met is located the Italian colony of "North End," Boston. To this Louis and I made our way, and to an Italian boarding house. How we happened to find it and to get in I do not now recall. It was a "three-room apartment" and the landlady informed us that she was already "full," but since we had no place to go, she would take us in. Added to the host that was already gathered there, our coming made fourteen people. At night the floor of the kitchen and the dining table were turned into beds. Louis and I were put to sleep in one of the beds with two other men, two facing north and two south. As I had slept all my life in a bed or bunk by myself this quadrupling did not appeal to me especially. But we could not complain. We had been taken in on trust, and the filth, the smells and the crowding together were a part of the trust.

We began to make inquiries about jobs and were promptly informed that there was plenty of work at "pick and shovel." We were also given to understand by our fellow-boarders that "pick and shovel" was practically the only work available to Italians. Now these were the first two English words I had heard and they possessed great charm. Moreover, if I were to earn money to return home and this was the only work available for Italians, they were very weighty words for me, and I must master them as soon and as well as possible and then set out to find their hidden meaning. I practised for a day or two until I could say "peek" and "shuvle" to perfection. Then I asked a fellow-boarder to take me to see what the work was like. He did. He led me to Washington Street, not far from the colony, where some excavation work was going on, and there I did see, with my own eyes, what the "peek" and "shuvle" were about. My heart sank within me, for I had thought it some form of office work; but I was game and since this was the only work available for Italians, and since I must have money to return home, I would take it up. After all, it was only a means to an end, and would last but a few days.

It may be in place here to say a word relative to the reason why this idea was prevalent among Italians at the time, and why so many Italians on coming to America find their way to what I had called "peek and shuvle." It is a matter of common knowledge, at least among students of immigration, that a very large percentage of Italian immigrants were "contadini" or farm laborers in Italy. American people often ask the question, "Why do they not go to the farms in this country?" This query is based upon the idea that the "contadini" were farmers in the sense in which we apply that word to the American farmer. The facts in the case are that the "contadini" were not farmers in that sense at all, but simply farm-laborers, more nearly serfs, working on landed estates and seldom owning their own land. Moreover, they are not in any way acquainted with the implements of modern American farming. Their farming tools consisted generally of a "zappa," a sort of wide mattock; an ax and the wooden plow of biblical times. When they come to America, the work which comes nearest to that which they did in Italy is not farming, or even farm labor, but excavation work. This fact, together with the isolation which inevitably would be theirs on an American farm, explains, in a large measure, why so few Italians go to the farm and why so many go into excavation work. There is another factor to be considered, and that is that the "padrone" perhaps makes a greater per capita percentage in connection with securing and managing workers for construction purposes than in any other line, and therefore he becomes a walking delegate about the streets of Italian colonies spreading the word that only "peek and shuvle" is available.

Now, though Louis and I had never done such work, because we were Italians we must needs adapt ourselves to it and go to work with "peek and shuvle." (I should have stated that Louis, desiring to be like the Romans while living with them, for the time being passed for an Italian.)

So we went out to hunt our first job in America. For several mornings Louis and I went to North Square, where there were generally a large number of men loitering in groups discussing all kinds of subjects, particularly the labor market. One morning we were standing in front of one of those infernal institutions which in America are permitted to bear the name of "immigrant banks," when we saw a fat man coming toward us. "Buon giorno, padrone," said one of the men. "Padrone?" said I to myself. Now the word "padrone" in Italy is applied to a proprietor, generally a respectable man, at least one whose dress and appearance distinguish him as a man of means. This man not only showed no signs of good breeding in his face, but he was unshaven and dirty and his clothes were shabby. I could not quite understand how he could be called "padrone." However, I said nothing, first because I wanted to get back home, and second because I wanted to be polite when I was in American society!

The "padrone" came up to our group and began to wax eloquent and to gesticulate (both in Sicilian dialect) about the advantages of a certain job. I remember very clearly the points which he emphasized: "It is not very far, only twelve miles from Boston. For a few cents you can come back any time you wish, to see 'i parenti e gli amici,' your relatives and friends. The company has a 'shantee' in which you can sleep, and a 'storo' where you can buy your 'grosserie' all very cheap. 'Buona paga,'" he continued, "(Good pay), $1.25 per day, and you only have to pay me fifty cents a week for having gotten you this 'gooda jobba.' I only do it to help you and because you are my countrymen. If you come back here at six o'clock to-night with your bundles, I myself will take you out."

The magnanimity of this man impressed Louis and me very profoundly; we looked at each other and said, "Wonderful!" We decided we would go; so at the appointed hour we returned to the very spot. About twenty men finally gathered there and we were led to North Station. There we took a train to some suburban place, the name of which I have never been able to learn. On reaching our destination we were taken to the "shantee" where we were introduced to two long open bunks filled with straw. These were to be our beds. The "storo" of which we had been told was at one end of the shanty. The next morning we were taken out to work. It was a sultry autumn day. The "peek" seemed to grow heavier at every stroke and the "shuvle" wider and larger in its capacity to hold the gravel. The second day was no better than the first, and the third was worse than the second. The work was heavy and monotonous to Louis and myself especially, who had never been "contadini" like the rest. The "padrone" whose magnanimity had so stirred us was little better than a brute. We began to do some simple figuring and discovered that when we had paid for our groceries at the "storo," for the privilege of sleeping in the shanty, and the fifty cents to the "padrone" for having been so condescending as to employ us, we would have nothing left but sore arms and backs. So on the afternoon of the third day Louis and I held a solemn conclave and decided to part company with "peek and shuvle,"—for ever. We left, without receiving a cent of pay, of course.

Going across country on foot we came to a small manufacturing village. We decided to try our luck at the factory, which proved to be a woolen mill, and found employment. Our work was sorting old rags and carrying them in wheelbarrows into a hot oven, in which the air was almost suffocating. Every time a person went in it he was obliged to run out as quickly as possible, for the heat was unbearable. Unfortunately for us, the crew was composed almost entirely of Russians, who hated us from the first day, and called us "dagoes." I had never heard the word before; I asked Louis if he knew its meaning, but he did not. In going in and out of the oven the Russians would crowd against us and make it hard for us to pass. One morning as I was coming out, four of the men hedged me in. I thought I would suffocate. I finally succeeded in pushing out, my hand having been cut in the rush of the wheelbarrows.

The superintendent of the factory had observed the whole incident. He was a very kindly man. From his light complexion I think he was a Swede. He came to my rescue, reprimanded the Russians, and led me to his office, where he bandaged my hand. Then he called Louis and explained the situation to us. The Russians looked upon us as intruders and were determined not to work side by side with "the foreigners," but to drive them out of the factory. Therefore, as much as he regretted it, the superintendent was obliged to ask us to leave, since there were only two of us, as against the large number of Russians who made up his unskilled crew.

So we left. My bandaged hand hurt me, but my heart hurt more. This kind of work was hard and humiliating enough, but what went deeper than all else was the first realization that because of race I was being put on the road. And often since that day have I felt the cutting thrusts of race prejudice. They have been dealt by older immigrants, who are known as "Americans," as well as by more recent comers. All have been equally heart-rending and head-bending. I hold no grudge against any one; I realize that it is one of the attendant circumstances of our present nationalistic attitude the world over, and yet it is none the less saddening to the human heart. I have seen prejudice, like an evil shadow, everywhere. It lurks at every corner, on every street and in every mart. I have seen it in the tram and on the train; I have felt its dreaded power in school and college, in clubs and churches. It is an ever-present evil spirit, felt though unseen, wounding hearts, cutting souls. It passes on its poison like a serpent from generation to generation, and he who would see the fusion of the various elements into a truly American type must ever take into cognizance its presence in the hearts of some human beings. . . .

E V A   H O F F M A N
(1945-   )

Born in Cracow, Poland, Eva Hoffman immigrated to Canada in 1959 and then to the United States in 1963. She receive a B.A. degree from Rice University and in 1974 was awarded a Ph.D. degree by Harvard University. After obtaining her doctorate in literature, she taught briefly, at the University of New Hampshire and at Tufts University, before moving to New York City. For several years she worked as an editor for The New York Times *and* The New York Times Book Review. *Her autobiography,* Lost in Translation: Life in a New Language, *was published in 1989 to widespread acclaim. Work on this book was either supported or rewarded by fellowships from the Carnegie Mellon Foundation, the American Council of Learned Societies, and the Guggenheim Memorial Foundation. She has also written* Shtetl: The Life and Death of a Small Town and the World of Polish Jews.

Lost in Translation: Life in a New Language speaks for many of the cohort of late-twentieth-century immigrants. Coming from societies already permeated by idealized American commercial imagery, immigrants from these countries are often amazed or appalled by the real culture of the United States, which must necessarily fall short of the ideal.

FROM LOST IN TRANSLATION:
LIFE IN A NEW LANGUAGE

By the time we've reached Vancouver, there are very few people left on the train. My mother has dressed my sister and me in our best outfits—identical navy blue dresses with sailor collars and gray coats handmade of good gabardine. My parents' faces reflect anticipation and anxiety. "Get off the train on the right foot," my mother tells us. "For luck in the new life."

I look out of the train window with a heavy heart. Where have I been brought to? As the train approaches the station, I see what is indeed a bit of nowhere. It's a drizzly day, and the platform is nearly empty. Everything is the color of slate. From this bleakness, two figures approach us—a nondescript middle-aged man and woman—and after making sure that we are the right people, the arrivals from the other side of the world, they hug us; but I don't feel much warmth in their half-embarrassed embrace. "You should kneel down and kiss the ground," the man tells my parents. "You're lucky to be here." My parents' faces fill with a kind of naïve hope. Perhaps everything will be well after all. They need signs, portents, at this hour.

Then we all get into an enormous car—yes, this is America—and drive into the city that is to be our home.

The Rosenbergs' house is a matter of utter bafflement to me. This one-story structure surrounded by a large garden surely doesn't belong in a city—but neither can it be imagined in the country. The garden itself is of such pruned and trimmed neatness that I'm half afraid to walk in it. Its lawn is improbably smooth and velvety (Ah, the time and worry spent on the shaving of these lawns! But I will only learn of that later), and the rows of marigolds, the circles of geraniums seem almost artificial in their perfect symmetries, in their subordination to orderliness.

Still, I much prefer sitting out here in the sun to being inside. The house is larger than any apartment I have seen in Poland, with enormous "picture" windows, a separate room for every member of the family and soft pastel-colored rugs covering all the floors. These are all features that, I know, are intended to signify good taste and wealth—but there's an incongruity between the message I'm supposed to get and my secret perceptions of these surroundings. To me, these interiors seem oddly flat, devoid of imagination, ingenuous. The spaces are so plain, low-ceilinged, obvious; there are no curves, niches, odd angles, nooks or crannies—nothing that gathers a house into itself, giving it a sense of privacy, or of depth—of interiority. There's no solid wood here, no accretion either of age or dust. There is only the open sincerity of the simple spaces, open right out to the street. (No peering out the window here, to catch glimpses of exchanges on the street; the picture windows are designed to give everyone full view of everyone else, to declare there's no mystery, nothing to hide. Not true, of course, but that's the statement.) There is also the disingenuous-ness of the furniture, all of it whitish with gold trimming. The whole thing is too revealing of an aspiration to good taste, but the unintended effect is thin and insub-stantial—as if it was planned and put up just yesterday, and could just as well be dismantled tomorrow. The only rooms that really impress me are the bathroom and the kitchen—both of them so shiny, polished, and full of unfamiliar, fabulously functional appliances that they remind me of interiors which we occasionally glimpsed in French or American movies, and which, in our bedraggled Poland, we couldn't distinguish from fantasy. "Do you think people really live like this?" we would ask after one of these films, neglecting all the drama of the plot for the inter-est of these incidental features. Here is something worth describing to my friends in Cracow, down to such mind-boggling details as a shaggy rug in the bathroom and toilet paper that comes in different colors.

For the few days we stay at the Rosenbergs', we are relegated to the basement, where there's an extra apartment usually rented out to lodgers. My father looks up to Mr. Rosenberg with the respect, even a touch of awe due to someone who is a cer-tified millionaire. Mr. Rosenberg is a big man in the small Duddy Kravitz community of Polish Jews, most of whom have made good in junk peddling and real estate—but none as good as he. Mr. Rosenberg, who is now almost seventy, had the com-bined chutzpah and good luck to ride on Vancouver's real-estate boom—and now he's the richest of them all. This hardly makes him the most popular, but it auto-matically makes him the wisest. People from the community come to him for busi-ness advice, which he dispenses, in Yiddish, as if it were precious currency given away free only through his grandiose generosity.

In the uncompromising vehemence of adolescence and injured pride, I begin to see Mr. Rosenberg not as our benefactor but as a Dickensian figure of personal tyranny, and my feeling toward him quickly rises to something that can only be called hate. He has made stinginess into principle; I feel it as a nonhuman hardness, a conversion of flesh and feeling into stone. His face never lights up with humor or affection or wit. But then, he takes himself very seriously; to him too his wealth is the proof of his righteousness. In accordance with his principles, he demands money for our train tickets from Montreal as soon as we arrive. I never forgive him. We've brought gifts we thought handsome, but in addition, my father gives him all the dollars he accumulated in Poland—something that would start us off in Canada, we thought, but is now all gone. We'll have to scratch out our living somehow, start-ing from zero: my father begins to pinch the flesh of his arms nervously.

Mrs. Rosenberg, a worn-faced, nearly inarticulate, diffident woman, would prob-ably show us more generosity were she not so intimidated by her husband. As it is, she and her daughter, Diane, feed us white bread with sliced cheese and bologna for lunch, and laugh at our incredulity at the mushy textures, the plastic wrapping, the presliced convenience of the various items. Privately, we comment that this is not real food: it has no taste, it smells of plastic. The two women also give us clothing they can no longer use. I can't imagine a state of affairs in which one would want to discard the delicate, transparent bathrobes and the angora sweaters they pass on to us, but luscious though these items seem—beyond anything I ever hoped to own—the show of gratitude required from me on receiving them sours the pleasure of new ownership. "Say thank you," my mother prompts me in preparation for receiving a batch of clothing. "People like to be appreciated." I coo and murmur ingratiatingly;

I'm beginning to master the trick of saying thank you with just the right turn of the head, just the right balance between modesty and obsequiousness. In the next few years, this is a skill I'll have to use often. But in my heart I feel no gratitude at being the recipient of so much money.

On about the third night at the Rosenbergs' house, I have a nightmare in which I'm drowning in the ocean while my mother and father swim farther and farther away from me. I know, in this dream, what it is to be cast adrift in incomprehensible space; I know what it is to lose one's mooring. I wake up in the middle of a prolonged scream. The fear is stronger than anything I've ever known. My parents wake up and hush me up quickly; they don't want the Rosenbergs to hear this disturbing sound. I try to calm myself and go back to sleep, but I feel as though I've stepped through a door into a dark place. Psychoanalysts talk about "mutative insights," through which the patient gains an entirely new perspective and discards some part of a cherished neurosis. The primal scream of my birth into the New World is a mutative insight of a negative kind—and I know that I can never lose the knowledge it brings me. The black, bituminous terror of the dream solders itself to the chemical base of my being—and from then on, fragments of the fear lodge themselves in my consciousness, thorns and pinpricks of anxiety, loose electricity floating in a psyche that has been forcibly pried from its structures. Eventually, I become accustomed to it; I know that it comes, and that it also goes; but when it hits with full force, in its pure form, I call it the Big Fear.

After about a week of lodging us in his house, Mr. Rosenberg decides that he has done enough for us, and, using some acquired American wisdom, explains that it isn't good for us to be dependent on his charity: there is of course no question of kindness. There is no question, either, of Mrs. Rosenberg intervening on our behalf, as she might like to do. We have no place to go, no way to pay for a meal. And so we begin.

"Shut up, shuddup," the children around us are shouting, and it's the first word in English that I understand from its dramatic context. My sister and I stand in the schoolyard clutching each other, while kids all around us are running about, pummeling each other, and screaming like whirling dervishes. Both the boys and the girls look sharp and aggressive to me—the girls all have bright lipstick on, their hair sticks up and out like witches' fury, and their skirts are held up and out by stiff, wiry crinolines. I can't imagine wanting to talk their harsh-sounding language.

We've been brought to this school by Mr. Rosenberg, who, two days after our arrival, tells us he'll take us to classes that are provided by the government to teach English to newcomers. This morning, in the rinky-dink wooden barracks where the classes are held, we've acquired new names. All it takes is a brief conference between Mr. Rosenberg and the teacher, a kindly looking woman who tries to give us reassuring glances, but who has seen too many people come and go to get sentimental about a name. Mine—"Ewa"—is easy to change into its near equivalent in English, "Eva." My sister's name—"Alina"—poses more of a problem, but after a moment's thought, Mr. Rosenberg and the teacher decide that "Elaine" is close enough. My sister and I hang our heads wordlessly under this careless baptism. The teacher then introduces us to the class, mispronouncing our last name—"Wydra"— in a way we've never heard before. We make our way to a bench at the back of the room; nothing much has happened, except a small, seismic mental shift. The twist in our names takes them a tiny distance from us—but it's a gap into which the infinite hobgoblin of abstraction enters. Our Polish names didn't refer to us; they were as surely us as our eyes or hands. These new appellations, which we ourselves can't yet pronounce, are not us. They are identification tags, disembodied signs pointing to objects that happen to be my sister and myself. We walk to our seats, into a roomful of unknown faces, with names that make us strangers to ourselves.

When the school day is over, the teacher hands us a file card on which she has written, "I'm a newcomer. I'm lost. I live at 1785 Granville Street. Will you kindly show me how to get there? Thank you." We wander the streets for several hours, zigzagging back and forth through seemingly identical suburban avenues, showing this deaf-mute sign to the few people we see, until we eventually recognize the Rosenbergs' house. We're greeted by our quietly hysterical mother and Mrs. Rosenberg, who, in a ritual she has probably learned from television, puts out two glasses of milk on her red Formica counter. The milk, homogenized, and too cold from the fridge, bears little resemblance to the liquid we used to drink called by the same name.

Every day I learn new words, new expressions. I pick them up from school exercises, from conversations, from the books I take out of Vancouver's well-lit, cheerful public library. There are some turns of phrase to which I develop strange allergies. "You're welcome," for example, strikes me as a goucherie, and I can hardly bring myself to say it—I suppose because it implies that there's something to be thanked for, which in Polish would be impolite. The very places where language is at its most conventional, where it should be most taken for granted, are the places where I feel the prick of artifice.

Then there are words to which I take an equally irrational liking, for their sound, or just because I'm pleased to have deduced their meaning. Mainly they're words I learn from books, like "enigmatic" or "insolent"—words that have only a literary value, that exist only as signs on the page.

But mostly, the problem is that the signifier has become severed from the signified. The words I learn now don't stand for things in the same unquestioned way they did in my native tongue. "River" in Polish was a vital sound, energized with the essence of riverhood, of my rivers, of my being immersed in rivers. "River" in English is cold—a word without an aura. It has no accumulated associations for me, and it does not give off the radiating haze of connotation. It does not evoke.

The process, alas, works in reverse as well. When I see a river now, it is not shaped, assimilated by the word that accommodates it to the psyche—a word that makes a body of water a river rather than an uncontained element. The river before me remains a thing, absolutely other, absolutely unbending to the grasp of my mind.

When my friend Penny tells me that she's envious, or happy, or disappointed, I try laboriously to translate not from English to Polish but from the word back to its source, to the feeling from which it springs. Already, in that moment of strain, spontaneity of response is lost. And anyway, the translation doesn't work. I don't know how Penny feels when she talks about envy. The word hangs in a Platonic stratosphere, a vague prototype of all envy, so large, so all-encompassing that it might crush me—as might disappointment or happiness.

I am becoming a living avatar of structuralist wisdom; I cannot help knowing that words are just themselves. But it's a terrible knowledge, without any of the consolations that wisdom usually brings. It does not mean that I'm free to play with words at my wont; anyway, words in their naked state are surely among the least satisfactory play objects. No, this radical disjoining between word and thing is a desiccating alchemy, draining the world not only of significance but of its colors, striations, nuances—its very existence. It is the loss of a living connection.

The worst losses come at night. As I lie down in a strange bed in a strange house— my mother is a sort of housekeeper here, to the aging Jewish man who has taken us in in return for her services—I wait for that spontaneous flow of inner language which used to be my nighttime talk with myself, my way of informing the ego where the id had been. Nothing comes. Polish, in a short time, has atrophied, shriveled from sheer uselessness. Its words don't apply to my new experiences; they're not coeval with any of the objects, or faces, or the very air I breathe in the daytime. In English, words have not penetrated to those layers of my psyche from which a private conversation could proceed. This interval before sleep used to be the time when my mind became both receptive and alert, when images and words rose up to consciousness, reiterating what had happened during the day, adding the day's experiences to those already stored there, spinning out the thread of my personal story.

Now, this picture-and-word show is gone; the thread has been snapped. I have no interior language, and without it, interior images—those images through which we assimilate the external world, through which we take it in, love it, make it our own—become blurred too. My mother and I met a Canadian family who live down the block today. They were working in their garden and engaged us in a conversation of the "Nice weather we're having, isn't it?" variety, which culminated in their inviting us into their house. They sat stiffly on their couch, smiled in the long pauses between the conversation, and seemed at a loss for what to ask. Now my mind gropes for some description of them, but nothing fits. They're a different species from anyone I've met in Poland, and Polish words slip off of them without sticking. English words don't hook on to anything. I try, deliberately, to come up with a few. Are these people pleasant or dull? Kindly or silly? The words float in an uncertain space. They come up from a part of my brain in which labels may be manufactured but which has no connection to my instincts, quick reactions, knowledge. Even the simplest adjectives sow confusion in my mind; English kindness has a whole system of morality behind it, a system that makes "kindness" an entirely positive virtue. Polish kindness has the tiniest element of irony. Besides, I'm beginning to feel the tug of prohibition, in English, against uncharitable words. In Polish, you can call someone an idiot without particularly harsh feelings and with the zest of a strong judgment. Yes, in Polish these people might tend toward "silly" and "dull"— but I force myself toward "kindly" and "pleasant." The cultural unconscious is beginning to exercise its subliminal influence.

The verbal blur covers these people's faces, their gestures with a sort of fog. I can't translate them into my mind's eye. The small event, instead of being added to the mosaic of consciousness and memory, falls through some black hole, and I fall with it. What has happened to me in this new world? I don't know. I don't see what I've seen, don't comprehend what's in front of me. I'm not filled with language anymore, and I have only a memory of fullness to anguish me with the knowledge that, in this dark and empty state, I don't really exist. . . .

"The synonyms for 'strong' are mighty, vigorous, puissant, stout, hardy," I read. This string of words is followed by sentences from which I can infer the exact shading of these adjectives, and, on another form, different sentences with spaces left blank for the requisite mot juste. I fill them in quickly, and then turn to my history lesson. This requires more concentration, because of the strange names cropping up all the time—Lake Champlain, Frontenac, Diefenbaker—and because tableaux of frontier towns and of western explorations don't have the same pattern of conflict, war, rhetoric, and costume that I used to know as history. Where are the great personages, the grand battles, the patina of age? These tales of skirmishes in small townships, of people making their way across the inimical woods and the freezing northern expanses of the continent, move horizontally across space rather than vertically through time. They summon images of tiny dots on an enormous landscape, huddles of humanity clotting and then making barely visible ink lines across the map, and I find it hard to conceptualize them as events, with a beginning, a middle, and an end.

Right now, though, it is summer, and the sun rays cut right through the clear air down to the blanket in our narrow backyard, where I am doing the correspondence courses I've signed up for so I can get through high school in three years rather than four and catch up with students my own age after being placed a year behind because I am a newcomer.

I don't mind these form lessons or the games they ask me to play, as I don't mind anything that I know I can master easily. But there is another motive driving me as well, an extra edge to my ambition—an edge that wasn't there before, and that comes from a version of the Big Fear. I know how unprotected my family has become; I know I'd better do very well—or else. The "or else" takes many forms in my mind—vague images of helplessness and restriction and always being poor. "The Bowery," I come to call this congeries of anxieties. The Bowery is where I'll end up if I don't do everything exactly right. I have to make myself a steel breastplate of achievement and good grades, so that I'll be able to get out—and get in, so that I can gain entry into the social system from where I stand, on a precarious ledge. I am prevaded by a new knowledge that I have to fend for myself, and it pushes me on with something besides my old curiosity, or even simple competitiveness.

Immigrant energy, admirable name though it has gained for itself, does not seem a wholly joyful phenomenon to me. I understand the desperado drive that fuels it. But I also understand how it happens that so many immigrant Horatio Algers overshoot themselves so unexpectedly as they move on their sped-up trajectories through several strata of society all the way to the top. From the perspective outside, everything inside looks equally impenetrable, from below everything above equally forbidding. It takes the same bullish will to gain a foothold in some modest spot as to insist on entering some sacred inner sanctum, and that insistence, and ignorance, and obliviousness of the rules and social distinctions—not to speak of "your own place"—can land you anywhere at all. As a radically marginal person, you have two choices: to be intimidated by every situation, every social stratum, or to confront all of them with the same leveling vision, the same brash and stubborn spunk.

I too am goaded on by the forked whip of ambition and fear, and I derive a strange strength—a ferocity, a puissance—from the sense of my responsibility, the sense that survival is in my own hands. I don't feel much like a child anymore, and I am both weighted down and concentrated by the seriousness of my—our— situation. I know that I can do anything I have to do. I could jump out of that second-story window the way my father did, or escape out that door. The sense of necessity—that famously ambiguous master—relieves me from small trepidations, the Big Fear supplants small ones of adolescence. I harden myself for whatever battles await me, though it turns out that no battle will ever be as hard as this imaginary one I wage with the dangers in my head. I too suffer from the classic immigrant misconception, and I can't distinguish between the normal and the strenuous road in life, between moderate and high achievement. Becoming a lawyer seems as difficult to me as becoming a chief justice, a teacher of freshman English is as august a personage in my world as a college president. I don't envision that I can get to any of these exalted positions by an ordinary sequence of steps, by putting one foot in front of the other. I have to drive myself, to be constantly on the alert.

The only catch is that I have lost the sense of what, driven as I have become, I am driving toward. The patterns of my life have been so disrupted that I cannot find straight lines amid the disarray. Gradual change within one context, one diagram, is one thing; scrambling all the coordinates is another. "Being a pianist," for example, means something entirely different in my new cultural matrix. It is no longer the height of glamour or the heart of beauty. "What a nice tune," my friends say when I play a Beethoven sonata for them, but I see that they don't care. Moreover, Mrs. Steiner and others inform me, it's not a solid profession, and it will hardly assure my ability to support myself. "Where are you going to get the money for music lessons in New York?" somebody asks me. "A person in your position has to think practically." "You're too intelligent to become a musician," others tell me. But there is nothing in the world that takes a more incandescent intelligence, the intelligence of your whole being! I want to reply.

Still, I begin to see that my "destiny" is no longer going to pull me toward itself as if I were sitting in a chariot driven by the gods. Even the design and thrust of our passions is in large part written by where and when we happen to live, and mine are not yet molded so firmly that the shape of the wax can't be changed, though they are powerful enough so that the remolding will hurt. The unity, the seemingly organic growth of my desires is becoming fragmented, torn. That wholeness came from the simplicity—perhaps given to us only in childhood—of my wants. But now I don't know what to want, or how to want, any longer. Polish romanticism, in whatever naïve version it has infiltrated my imagination, doesn't superprint easily on the commonsensical pragmatism required of me here. During my solitary walks, I hold long debates with myself about how much I owe to God, and how much to Caesar. Is it right that I should neglect the demands of my emotions, which tell me that music is the medium of my self? No, a voice within me says—but it's a voice I try to silence. It may, by now, be a false siren; purely personal needs, it turns out, are a luxury affordable only by those who have some measure of security, of safety—at least of the internal kind. I'm beginning to respect the force of circumstance—though I am ornery enough that I won't give in to it completely. "Yet all experience is an arch wherethrough gleams that untraveled world . . ." I begin the valedictory speech I've been asked to deliver on graduating from Eric Hamber High School. Plunge into life, I tell my classmates with considerable passion, try to taste as much of it, to understand as much of human nature—experience—as you can. For this moment, I let my desires speak, and I feel a wild, clean urge to take flight.

But where to? I have no map of experience before me, not even the usual adolescent kind. Aside from the endless varieties of apparel, and swimming pools and cars, I don't know what goods this continent has to offer. I don't know what one can love here, what one can take into oneself as home—and later, when the dams of envy burst open again, I am most jealous of those who, in America, have had a sense of place.

I have an absurd fit of envy, for example, when I read *The Education of Henry Adams*—that idiosyncratic work so unlike anything else I've come across in American literature courses. So this is what it means to be a real American! All along, I've been taught about misfits and outsiders, about alienation and transcendence—which, I suspect, really come to the same thing. But for Henry Adams—and for a few others—America has been a fitting habitation for the mind rather than just a complex of ideas, a field for significant action rather than a launching pad for individual ambition, for making it. A fellow student at Harvard—for this is where this mini-epiphany takes place—is understandably incredulous. He points out that I might as well envy the king of Siam; he points out Henry Adams's horrendous sense of failure. It doesn't matter. In Henry Adams, for all the tortuous involutions of his psyche, I encounter a sense of belonging and of natural inheritance. And this, it turns out, from my displacement, is what I long for—the comfort that comes from being cradled by continuity, the freedom from insignificance. The more I come to know about America, the more I have the dizzying sensation that I'm a quantum particle trying to locate myself within a swirl of atoms. How much time and energy I'll have to spend just claiming an ordinary place for myself! And how much more figuring out what that place might be, where on earth I might find a stable spot that feels like it's mine, and from which I can calmly observe the world. "There are no such places anymore," my fellow student informs me. "This is a society in which you are who you think you are. Nobody gives you your identity here, you have to reinvent yourself every day." He is right, I suspect, but I can't figure out how this is done. You just say what you are and everyone believes you? That seems like a confidence trick to me, and not one I think I can pull off. Still, somehow, invent myself I must. But how do I choose from identity options available all around me? I feel, once again, as I did when facing those ten brands of toothpaste—faint from excess, paralyzed by choice.

And later still, when I see that it is through reading and writing that I'll have my adventures, I come to envy those New York Jewish intellectuals, like Alfred Kazin or Norman Podhoretz, who had the slight leg up of being born here, and who were therefore quicker to understand where they wanted to travel, the parabolas of their ambitions. Their journeys from the outer boroughs to Manhattan felt long and arduous to them, but at least they knew where the center was, they felt the compelling lure of its glittering lights. Their dreams were American dreams; their desires were inscribed in the American idiom. My desires, when freed from their protective covering, are forceful, and they are as unchanneled as an infant's id. I'll have to find new rivulets for them. For a long time, I'll thrash around like a fish thrown from sweet into salty ocean waters.

◆ ◆ ◆

We're driving to the airport and we are all made serious by the gravity of the occasion. I am going away to college, in Houston, Texas. "You've done so well, you must be so proud, your parents must be so proud of you"—I've heard this often in the last few months. After all, Rice University, which I'm going to attend, is reputed to have

very high academic standards—a phrase that at this point strikes awe into my heart—
and it has had the kindness to shower me with enough money to make my going there
possible. When I begin to receive a succession of letters informing me of the various
scholarships I've been awarded, I hold them delicately between my fingers as if they
might be pieces of air, or as if my good luck might break under the slightest pressure.

I've looked up Houston on the map, and I see that it's far. Such images of the
Wild West as I possess have been overlaid by photographs in *Time* magazine showing tall buildings, oil rigs, and other signs of an economic boom. I've been told it's
very hot there.

As I am about to go through the gate to board my first plane ever, my sister
embraces me with a fierceness that recalls her silent appeal when she was small and
very unhappy—and I feel again that perhaps, in this departure which might take me
much further away than the airplane, there is some betrayal. It is hard to pull myself
away from Alinka, hard to look at her suddenly pleading face. I try to remember
what Mrs. Steiner—who with her daughters has guided me toward this step—said
about living my own life. It is not so simple for me to accept this idea, to extricate
myself from the mesh of family need and love, to believe in the merits of a separate
life. I've hesitated, but there is no resisting this call. I think of vistas of knowledge,
steps ascending to the temple of intellect. In my application, I said I wanted to gain
genuine understanding of human nature, and I meant it.

On the plane, I strike up a conversation with a tall, tanned man beside me, and
an hour or so into the flight he suggests that I descend with him in San Francisco
and spend a few days in his house. Being a free woman now, I pretend to consider
this proposal carefully, but decide that I shouldn't miss the first days of classes. The
man tries to laugh this off and persuade me that a few days won't make any difference, and he could really show me around San Francisco. He is very handsome, but
I remain firm, and with a queenly graciousness decline the offer.

There is, of course, no real decision to make here, and after the man gets off, I
start thinking about what lies ahead. I hardly know, but I feel the tingling of anticipation. I am traveling toward Experience.

Among the many immigrant tales I've come across, there is one for which I feel a
particular affection. This story was written at the beginning of the century, by a
young woman named Mary Antin, and in certain details it so closely resembles my
own, that its author seems to be some amusing poltergeist, come to show me that
whatever belief in my own singularity I may possess is nothing more than a comical vanity. But this ancestress also makes me see how much, even in my apparent
maladaptations, I am a creature of my time—as she, in her adaptations, was a creature of hers.

Mary Antin was born in the 1880s, in a town within the Russian Pale, and came
to America with her mother and younger brother—her father had gone ahead some
years earlier—when she was fourteen, during one of those enormous movements
that washed whole Jewish populations across the ocean on crowded, typhoid-
infected ships. The family, once they remet in Boston (why they landed there, rather
than anywhere else, is never explained) went through about a decade of grinding,
hopeless, near-starvation poverty—poverty of a kind that immigrants in our own, in
some ways more benign, times almost never fall into. But Mary had several things
going for her—first and foremost, that she was a smart little girl. She had a bit of a
talent for language and a curious, lively mind—her writing has an unaffected, sweet

freshness, she is an irreverent observer, and her recollections of her childhood are suffused with lyrical detail. In America, she quickly became a star student. She wrote essays and poems, of an inspirational kind, about George Washington's heroism, and the virtues of the American Republic. And she had enough spunk to walk right into the editorial offices of her local newspaper to see if her poems could get published. Soon, she was being singled out and sought by important people; she was invited into their homes, treated kindly, and petted by them. Then, her success as a student took her to Boston Latin High School, and for a while her life was divided between trying to gather some pennies that would enable her family to pay the rent, and mingling with Boston's best.

Ah, how I recognize Mary Antin's youthful chutzpah, her desire to be happy and her troubles, her combination of adolescent shyness and a precocious maturity forced on her by her circumstances! But once she diverges from telling the tale and gives us her views of it, all similarities between us end. For, despite the hardships that leap out from the pages, Mary insists on seeing her life as a fable of pure success: success for herself, for the idea of assimilation, for the great American experiment. She ends her autobiography, entitled *The Promised Land,* as she is about to enter college and pursue her vocation as a natural scientist— and she gives us to understand that everything worked out wondrously well from then on.

There is only one hint that there is another side to the story, and it comes in the preface. "Happening when it did," Mary writes, "the emigration became of the most vital importance to me personally. All the processes of uprooting, transportation, replanting, acclimatization, and development took place in my own soul. I felt the pang, the fear, the wonder, and the joy of it. I can never forget, for I bear the scars. But I want to forget—sometimes I long to forget. . . . It is painful to be consciously of two worlds. The Wandering Jew in me seeks forgetfulness. I am not afraid to live on and on, if only I do not have to remember too much."

Being a close reader of such remarks, I can find volumes of implied meaning in them. But it is exactly the kind of meaning that Mary Antin was not encouraged to expand upon. And so there it is, a trace she never follows up on: a trace of the other story behind the story of triumphant progress.

Perhaps Mary Antin was more genetically predisposed toward optimism than I am, but I doubt it. It's just that she, like I, was affected by the sentiments of her time, and those sentiments made an inveterate positive thinker of her. The America of her time gave her certain categories within which to see herself—a belief in self-improvement, in perfectability of the species, in moral uplift—and those categories led her to foreground certain parts of her own experience, and to throw whole chunks of it into the barely visible background.

And what is the shape of my story, the story my time tells me to tell? Perhaps it is the avoidance of a single shape that tells the tale. A hundred years ago, I might have written a success story, without much self-doubt or equivocation. A hundred years ago, I might have felt the benefits of a steady, self-assured ego, the sturdy energy of forward movement, and the excitement of being swept up into a greater national purpose. But I have come to a different America, and instead of a central ethos, I have been given the blessings and the terrors of multiplicity. Once I step off that airplane in Houston, I step into a culture that splinters, fragments, and re-forms itself as if it were a jigsaw puzzle dancing in a quantum space. If I want to assimilate into my generation, my time, I have to assimilate the multiple perspectives and their constant shifting. Who, among my peers, is sure of what is success and what failure? Who would want to be sure? Who is sure of purposes, meanings, national goals? We slip between definitions with such acrobatic ease that straight narrative becomes impossible. I cannot conceive of my story as one of simple progress, or simple woe. Any confidently thrusting story line would be a sentimentality, an excess, an exaggeration, an untruth. Perhaps it is my intolerance of those, my cherishing of uncertainty as the only truth that is, after all, the best measure of my assimilation; perhaps it is in my misfittings that I fit. Perhaps a successful immigrant is an exaggerated version of the native. From now on, I'll be made, like a mosaic, of fragments—and my consciousness of them. It is only in that observing consciousness that I remain, after all, an immigrant.

◆ ◆ ◆

When I fall in love, I am seduced by language. When I get married, I am seduced by language. My husband too is a master of the riff, and when I listen to him improvise about Whitman's poetry, or his Jewish aunts and uncles, or a Wasp Connecticut wedding, I think, maybe this bebop speech can carry me right into the heart of America. . . . It's a tricky contract, and I get confused between my husband and his eloquence, distracted as by shadows and shimmers thrown on a white screen by a camera obscura, but I want to catch the wordplay, ride the energy of the nervy bounds and rebounds, give myself over to the insouciant leaps. . . .

All around me, the Babel of American voices, hardy midwestern voices, sassy New York voices, quick youthful voices, voices arching under the pressure of various crosscurrents. I've become a skilled diagnostician of voices, and of their neuroses. I know how people feel, how they are, not from what they say but from how they sound. I can hear the snags and broken rhythms of nervousness, the jumps of pitch that happen when someone is uncomfortable, the tensing of the vocal cords in disapproval. I can also hear the sounds of good health—the even tones of self-assurance, the deepening melodiousness in consent to deep feeling, the canter of clean enthusiasm.

Since I lack a voice of my own, the voices of others invade me as if I were a silent ventriloquist. They ricochet within me, carrying on conversations, lending me their modulations, intonations, rhythms. I do not yet possess them; they possess me. But some of them satisfy a need; some of them stick to my ribs. I could take on that stylish, ironic elongation which is X's mark of perpetual amusement; it fits something in my temperament, I could learn to speak a part of myself through it. And that curtailed, deliberate dryness that Y uses as an antidote to sentiment opens a door into a certain New England sensibility whose richness I would never otherwise understand. Eventually, the voices enter me; by assuming them, I gradually make them mine. I am being remade, fragment by fragment, like a patchwork quilt; there are more colors in the world than I ever knew.

Like a tourist in a new city, who has no particular neighborhood and who therefore is always confronting "the city" as a whole, I, an incompletely assimilated immigrant, am always confronting "the Culture." In this too it turns out that I am like my American friends, though perhaps a little more so. "The Culture," in America, has become a curious monster, a thing that throbs and vibrates out there and bellows. Everyone I know measures the Culture, gauges it, diagnoses it all the time, because, after all, the monster might enter the living room, and so it's important to be on the lookout. The Culture is becoming more conservative, more progressive, more celebrity obsessed, more materialistic, more sentimental. Each shift is carefully observed; the beast may, after all, lurch or bite, or co-opt us, make us more like itself, a graceless, lumpish, philistine thing. The Culture is a dangerous seducer; one must resist its pull.

I'm a vigilant Culture watcher, like everyone else. And undoubtedly, like everyone else, I've ingested parts of the Culture even while I've prudishly pulled my skirts around me. I see this paradox in my friends clearly enough, culture turning into counterculture and counterculture into culture despite everyone's best intentions, the organization man giving way to the dropout and the dropout to a new technocrat, loneliness to love-ins and then loneliness again, as if any set of cultural terms necessarily determines the terms of the subsequent rebellion, and the rejections carry in them the seeds of what is rejected. It is always difficult to know how a culture flows through our veins, and by now I've lost track of how much America flows through mine. Fragments of Janis Joplin songs and the Rolling Stones surface in my mind as I walk down the street; the landscape of Amagansett, where I've spent several summers, is just under my retina, to be retrieved whenever I think vacation, time off; films about New York are films about my hometown; "Gimme a break," I say, when a street vendor gets pushy, and the issues I debate—how to conduct one's career without losing one's sanity, what to eat without becoming contaminated, how to deal with passive-aggressive lovers—are American conversations, dictated by "the Culture" as much as this season's fashions. And I never, never say "It's only psychological" anymore. Maybe, behind my back and while I wasn't looking, I've acquired a second unconscious, an American one, made up of diverse cultural matter. Like any unconscious, this one is hard to pin down. I only know that the hybrid creature I've become is made up of two parts Americana, that the pastiche has lots of local color. Despite my resistance, or perhaps through its very act, I've become a partial American, a sort of resident alien.

CHITRA DIVAKARUNI
(1956–)

Born in Calcutta, India, Chitra Banerjee was educated at Calcutta University (B.A., 1976), Wright State University in Ohio (M.A., 1978), and the University of California, Berkeley (Ph.D., 1985). She married Murthy Divakaruni in 1979. She has regularly taught creative writing at the college level, at Foothill College in California and later at the University of Houston.

Divakaruni is a prolific writer of both poetry and fiction. Among her books of poetry are The Reason for Nasturtiums *(1990),* Black Candle *(1991), and* Leaving Yuba City: New and Selected Poems *(1997). Her stories are collected in* Arranged Marriage *(1995) and she has published two novels,* The Mistress of Spices *(1997) and* Sister of My Heart *(1999). In much of her narrative poetry and in her fiction, Divakaruni focuses on the expe-*

rience of immigrant women from India, Pakistan, and Bangladesh who must adjust to an American culture that causes them to question their gendered social roles.

"Indian Movie, New Jersey" is drawn from Leaving Yuba City, *which won her both a Pushcart Prize and an Allen Ginsberg Prize. Like many of the poems in that collection it joins her lyrical and personal expression to a social and cultural moment in which memory is charged with power.*

INDIAN MOVIE, NEW JERSEY

Not like the white filmstars, all rib
and gaunt cheekbone, the Indian sex-goddess
smiles plumply from behind a flowery
branch. Below her brief red skirt, her thighs
are satisfying-solid, redeeming
as tree trunks. She swings her hips
and the men-viewers whistle. The lover-hero
dances in to a song, his lip-sync
a little off, but no matter, we
know the words already and sing along.
It is safe here, the day
golden and cool so no one sweats,
roses on every bush and the Dal Lake
clean again.
                    The sex-goddess switches
to thickened English to emphasize
a joke. We laugh and clap. Here
we need not be embarrassed by words
dropping like lead pellets into foreign ears.
The flickering movie-light
wipes from our faces years of America, sons
who want mohawks and refuse to run
the family store, daughters who date
on the sly.
                    When at the end the hero
dies for his friend who also
loves the sex-goddess and now can marry her,
we weep, understanding. Even the men
clear their throats to say, "What *qurbani!*[*]
What *dosti!*"[†] After, we mill around
unwilling to leave, exchange greetings
and good news: a new gold chain, a trip
to India. We do not speak

---

[*]Sacrifice [†]Friendship

of motel raids, cancelled permits, stones
thrown through glass windows, daughters and sons
raped by Dotbusters.
                In this dim foyer,
we can pull around us the faint, comforting smell
of incense and *pakoras,*[*] can arrange
our children's marriages with hometown boys and girls,
open a franchise, win a million
in the mail. We can retire
in India, a yellow two-storeyed house
with wrought-iron gates, our own
Ambassador car. Or at least
move to a rich white suburb, Summerfield
or Fort Lee, with neighbors that will
talk to us. Here while the film-songs still echo
in the corridors and restrooms, we can trust
in movie truths: sacrifice, success, love and luck,
the America that was supposed to be.

---

[*]Fried dumplings

3

CITIZENS BY
CONQUEST

Citizens by Conquest explores the imperialist incorporation of Mexican territory
in 1846 and Spanish colonies in the Caribbean and the Pacific in 1898. John C. Calhoun's 1848 speech on the aftermath of the Mexican War tells us something about
the attitudes of many Americans toward the former Mexicans now being incorporated into the nation. María Amparo Ruiz de Burton gives fictional witness to how
the disposessed *Californios* related to the new American colonial order. Mark
Twain's essay on colonialism, religion, and capitalism, "To the Person Sitting in
Darkness," shows that imperialist adventurism was not without strong-voiced critics among the majority, while works such as "Immigrants" by Pat Mora and "Immigration Blues" by Bienvenido Nuqui Santos demonstrate in poetry and fiction the
complex identity engendered in communities folded into the United States without their consent. All of the readings help us to understand how one American
identity may broadly differ from another.

THE TREATY OF GUADALUPE HIDALGO

The 1848 treaty between Mexico and the United States that ended the Mexican War forced Mexico to cede almost half of its territory to the Americans. The states of California, Arizona, New Mexico, Nevada, and Colorado were all Mexican territories, as was Texas, which was not contested in the war but was "liberated" from Mexican rule by means of a revolt by the Americans who had been invited by the Mexican government to settle the vast but comparatively arid land. The Treaty of Guadalupe Hidalgo offered fairly reasonable terms to Mexican citizens who wished to remain on their land or in their businesses under the new American government, but these terms were soon undermined by local governments and the developing territorial and then state governments, which often aided and abetted the disenfranchisement of the new Mexican-American citizens. State and local governments, for example, voided the ancient Spanish and Mexican land grants and then taxed the owners into bankruptcy.

SIGNED, FEBRUARY 2, 1848; RATIFIED MAY 30, 1848

ART. I. There shall be firm and universal peace between the United States of America and the Mexican Republic, and between their respective countries, territories, cities, towns, and people, without exception of place or persons. . . .

ART. V. The boundary line between the two Republics shall commence in the Gulf of Mexico, three leagues from land, opposite the mouth of the Rio Grande, otherwise called Rio Bravo del Norte, or opposite the mouth of its deepest branch, if it should have more than one branch emptying directly into the sea; from thence up the middle of that river, following the deepest channel, where it has more than one, to the point where it strikes the southern boundary of New Mexico; thence, westwardly, along the whole southern boundary of New Mexico (which runs north of the town called *Paso*) to its western termination; thence, northward, along the western line of New Mexico, until it intersects the first branch of the River Gila; (or if it should not intersect any branch of that river, then to the point on the said line nearest to such branch, and thence in a direct line to the same;) thence down the middle of the said branch and of the said river, until it empties into the Rio Colorado; thence across the Rio Colorado, following the division line between Upper and Lower California, to the Pacific Ocean. . . .

ART. VII. The River Gila, and the part of the Rio Bravo del Norte lying below the southern boundary of New Mexico, being, agreeably to the fifth article, divided in the middle between the two republics, the navigation of the Gila and of the Bravo below said boundary shall be free and common to the vessels and citizens of both countries; and neither shall, without the consent of the other, construct any work that may impede or interrupt, in whole or in part, the exercise of this right; not even for the purpose of favoring new methods of navigation. . . .

ART. VIII. Mexicans now established in territories previously belonging to Mexico, and which remain for the future within the limits of the United States, as defined by the present treaty, shall be free to continue where they now reside, or to remove at any time to the Mexican republic, retaining the property which they possess in the said territories, or disposing thereof, and removing the proceeds wherever they please, without their being subjected, on this account, to any contribution, tax, or charge whatever. . . .

ART. XII. In consideration of the extension acquired by the boundaries of the United States, as defined in the fifth article of the present treaty, the Government of the United States engages to pay to that of the Mexican Republic the sum of fifteen millions of dollars. . . .

ART. XIII. The United States engage, moreover, to assume and pay to the claimants all the amounts now due them, and those hereafter to become due, by reason of the claims already liquidated and decided against the Mexican Republic, under the conventions between the two republics severally concluded on the eleventh day of April, eighteen hundred and thirty-nine, and on the thirtieth day of January, eighteen hundred and forty-three; so that the Mexican Republic shall be absolutely exempt, for the future, from all expense whatever on account of the said claims.

ART. XIV. The United States do furthermore discharge the Mexican Republic from all claims of citizens of the United States, not heretofore decided against the Mexican Government, which may have arisen previously to the date of the signature of this treaty; which discharge shall be final and perpetual, whether the said claims be rejected or be allowed by the board of commissioners provided for in the following article, and whatever shall be the total amount of those allowed. . . .

ART. XV. The United States, exonerating Mexico from all demands on account of the claims of their citizens mentioned in the preceding article, and considering them entirely and forever cancelled, whatever their amount may be, undertake to make satisfaction for the same, to an amount not exceeding three and one quarter millions of dollars. . . .

ART. XXI. If unhappily any disagreement should hereafter arise between the governments of the two republics, whether with respect to the interpretation of any stipulation in this treaty, or with respect to any other particular concerning the political or commercial relations of the two nations, the said governments, in the name of those nations, do promise to each other that they will endeavor, in the most sincere and earnest manner, to settle the differences so arising, and to preserve the state of peace and friendship in which the two countries are now placing themselves; using, for this end, mutual representations and pacific negotiations. And if, by these means, they should not be enabled to come to an agreement, a resort shall not, on this account, be had to reprisals, aggression, or hostility of any kind, by the one republic against the other, until the Government of that which deems itself aggrieved shall have maturely considered, in the spirit of peace and good neighborship, whether it would not be better that such difference should be settled by the arbitration of commissioners appointed on each side, or by that of a friendly nation. And should such course be proposed by either party, it shall be acceded to by the other, unless deemed by it altogether incompatible with the nature of the difference, or circumstances of the case.

JOHN CALDWELL CALHOUN
(1782-1850)

John Caldwell Calhoun, perhaps most frequently remembered as the seventh vice president of the United States, was born in March 1782 in South Carolina. His father, Patrick Calhoun, was one of the wealthiest landowners, as well as one of the largest slaveholders, in the area where Calhoun grew up. Calhoun received little formal education; he attended a local "field school" for a few months each year as a boy, and as a teenager he studied for a little over two years at a private academy in Georgia. Nonetheless, he maintained a diligent course of study on his own, and in 1802 he was admitted to Yale College. He studied to be a lawyer and passed the bar in 1807.

He became involved in local politics, and after serving two terms in the state legislature, he was elected to the United States House of Representatives in 1810. He was involved in Washington politics for the remainder of his life. In addition to serving in the Congress, he served as Secretary of War, as vice president (1824-1828 under John Quincy Adams, and 1828-1832 under Andrew Jackson), as Senator for South Carolina, and as Secretary of State. As a politician, he was adamantly in favor of state's rights and was one of the period's most prominent spokespersons for the slave-plantation system. He died of tuberculosis in 1850.

Calhoun spoke out against the Mexican War in his capacity as United States Senator from South Carolina in January 1848, as Congress and President Tyler considered what to make of the victory over Mexico.

FROM SPEECH

ON HIS RESOLUTIONS IN REFERENCE TO THE WAR WITH MEXICO, DELIVERED IN THE SENATE, JANUARY 4TH, 1848

"*Resolved,* That to conquer Mexico, and to hold it, either as a province or to incorporate it in the Union, would be inconsistent with the avowed object for which the war has been prosecuted; a departure from the settled policy of the Government; in conflict with its character and genius; and, in the end, subversive of our free and popular institutions.

"*Resolved,* That no line of policy in the further prosecution of the war should be adopted which may lead to consequences so disastrous."

MR. CALHOUN said: In offering, Senators, these resolutions for your consideration, I am governed by the reasons which induced me to oppose the war, and by which I have been governed since it was sanctioned by Congress. In alluding to my opposition to the war, I do not intend to touch on the reasons which governed me on that occasion further than is necessary to explain my motives on the present.

I, then, opposed the war, not only because it might have been easily avoided; not only because the President had no authority to order a part of the disputed territory in possession of the Mexicans to be occupied by our troops; not only because I believed the allegations upon which Congress sanctioned the war untrue; but from high considerations of policy—because I believed it would lead to many and serious evils to the country, and greatly endanger its free institutions. But, after the war was declared, by authority of the Government, I acquiesced in what I could not prevent, and which it was impossible for me to arrest; and I then felt it to be my duty to limit my efforts to give such direction to the war as would, as far as possible, prevent the evils and danger with which it threatened the country and its institutions. For this purpose, at the last session, I suggested to the Senate the policy of adopting a defensive line;—and for the same purpose I now offer these resolutions. This, and this only, is the motive which governs me on this occasion. I am moved by no personal or party considerations. My object is neither to sustain the Executive nor to strengthen the opposition;—but simply to discharge an important duty to the country. In doing so, I shall express my opinion on all points with the freedom and boldness which becomes an independent Senator, who has nothing to ask from the Government or from the People. But when I come to notice those points on which I differ from the President, I shall do it with all the decorum which is due to the Chief Magistrate of the Union.

I suggested a defensive line because, in the first place, I believed that the only certain mode of terminating the war successfully was to take indemnity into our own hands by occupying defensively, with our military force, a portion of the Mexican territory, which we might deem ample for indemnity; and, in the next, because I believed it would prevent a great sacrifice of life and property; but, above all, because I believed that it was the only way we could avoid the great danger to our institutions against which these resolutions are intended to guard. The President took a different view. He recommended a vigorous prosecution of the war—not for conquest—that was emphatically disavowed—but for the purpose of conquering peace—that is, to compel Mexico to sign a treaty ceding sufficient territory to indemnify the claims of our citizens and of the country for the expenses of the war. I could not approve of this policy. I opposed it, among other reasons, because I believed there was no certainty that the object intended to be effected would be accomplished let the war be ever so successful. Congress thought differently, and granted ample provisions, in men and money, for carrying out the policy recommended by the President. It has now been fully tested under the most favorable circumstances. It has been as successful as the most sanguine hope of the Executive could have anticipated. Victory after victory followed in rapid succession, without a single reverse. Santa Anna repelled and defeated with all his forces at Buena Vista—Vera Cruz, with its castle, captured—the heights of Cerro Gordo triumphantly carried—Jalapa, Perote, and Puebla occupied—and, after many triumphant victories under the walls of Mexico, its gates opened to us, and we put in possession of the capital. But what have all these splendid achievements accomplished? Has the avowed object of the war been attained? Have we conquered peace? Have we compelled Mexico to sign a treaty? Have we obtained indemnity? No. Not a single object contemplated by the campaign has been effected; and what is worse, our difficulties are greater now than they were at the commencement,—and the objects sought more difficult to be accomplished. To what is this complete failure to be attributed? Not to our army. It has done all that skill and gallantry could accomplish. It is to be attributed to the policy pursued. The Executive aimed at indemnity in a wrong way. Instead of taking it into our own hands, when we had territory in our possession ample to cover the claims of our citizens and the expenses of the war, he sought it indirectly through a treaty with Mexico. He thus put it out of our own power, and under the control of Mexico, to say whether we should have indemnity or not, and thereby enabled her to defeat the whole object of the campaign by simply refusing to treat with us. Owing to this mistaken policy, after a most successful and brilliant campaign, involving an expenditure of not less, probably, than $40,000,000, and the sacrifice, by the sword and by disease, of many valuable lives, probably not less than six or seven thousand, nothing is left but the glory which our army has acquired.

But, as an apology for this, it is insisted that the maintenance of a defensive line would have involved as great a sacrifice as the campaign itself. The President and the Secretary of War have assigned many reasons for entertaining this opinion. I have examined them with care. This is not the proper occasion to discuss them,—but I must say, with all due deference, they are, to my mind, utterly fallacious; and to satisfy your mind that such is the case, I will place the subject in a single point of view.

The line proposed by me, to which I suppose their reasons were intended to be applied, would be covered in its whole extent—from the Pacific Ocean to the Paso del Norte, on the Rio Grande—by the Gulf of California and the wilderness peopled by hostile tribes of Indians, through which no Mexican force could penetrate. For its entire occupancy and defence, nothing would be required but a few small vessels of war stationed in the gulf, and a single regiment to keep down any resistance from the few inhabitants within. From the Paso del Norte to the mouth of the river, a distance of a few hundred miles, a single fact will show what little force will be necessary to its defence. It was a frontier between Texas and Mexico, when the former had but an inconsiderable population—not more than an hundred and fifty thousand at the utmost, at any time—with no standing army, and but very few irregular troops; yet for several years she maintained this line without any, except slight occasional intrusion from Mexico, and this too when Mexico was far more consolidated in her power, and when revolutions were not so frequent, and her money resources were far greater than at present. If, then, Texas alone, under such circumstances, could defend that frontier for so long a period, can any man believe that now, when she is backed by the whole of the United States,—now that Mexico is exhausted, defeated, and prostrated—I repeat, can any man believe that it would involve as great a sacrifice to us of men and money, to defend that frontier, as did the last campaign? No. I hazard nothing in asserting, that, to defend it for an indefinite period would have required a less sum than the interest on the money spent in the campaign, and fewer men than were sacrificed in carrying it on.

So much for the past. We now come to the commencement of another campaign, and the question recurs, What shall be done? The President, in his message, recommends the same line of policy—a vigorous prosecution of the war—not for conquest, that is again emphatically disavowed; not to blot Mexico out of the list of nations; no, he desires to see her an independent and flourishing community—and assigns strong reasons for it—but to obtain an honorable peace. We hear no more of conquering peace, but I presume that he means by an honorable peace the same thing: that is, to compel Mexico to agree to a treaty, ceding a sufficient part of her territory, as an indemnity for the expenses of the war, and for the claims of our citizens. . . .

What is the object of a vigorous prosecution of the war? How can it be successful? I can see but one way of making it so, and that is,—by suppressing all resistance on the part of Mexico,—overpowering and dispersing her army, and utterly over-throwing her Government. But if this should be done; if a vigorous prosecution of the war should lead to this result, how are we to obtain an honorable peace? With whom shall we treat for indemnity for the past and security for the future? War may be made by one party, but it requires two to make peace. If all authority is over-thrown in Mexico, where will be the power to enter into negotiation and make peace? Our very success would defeat the possibility of making peace. In that case the war would not end in peace, but in conquest; not in negotiation, but in subju-gation; and defeat, I repeat, the very object you aim to accomplish,—and accomplish that which you disavow to be your intention, by destroying the separate existence of Mexico,—overthrowing her nationality, and blotting out her name from the list of nations,—instead of leaving her a free Republic, which the President has so earnestly expressed his desire to do.

If I understand his message correctly, I have his own authority for the conclu-sion to which I come. He takes very much the same view that I do, as to how a war ought to be prosecuted vigorously, and what would be its results,—with the dif-ference as to the latter resting on a single contingency, and that a remote one. He says that the great difficulty of obtaining peace results from this,—that the people of Mexico are divided under factious chieftains, and that the chief in power dare not make peace, because for doing so he would be displaced by a rival. He also says, that the only way to remedy this evil and to obtain a treaty, is to put down the whole of them, including the one in power, as well as the others. Well, what then? Are we to stop there? No. Our generals are, it seems, authorized to encour-age and to protect the well disposed inhabitants in establishing a republican gov-ernment. He says they are numerous, and are prevented from expressing their opinions and making an attempt to form such a government, only by fear of those military chieftains. He proposes, when they have thus formed a government, under the encouragement and protection of our army, to obtain peace by a treaty with the government thus formed, which shall give us ample indemnity for the past and security for the future. I must say I am at a loss to see how a free and independent republic can be established in Mexico under the protection and authority of its con-querors. I can readily understand how an aristocracy or a despotic government might be, but how a free republican government can be so established, under such circumstances, is to me incomprehensible. I had always supposed that such a gov-ernment must be the spontaneous wish of the people; that it must emanate from the hearts of the people, and be supported by their devotion to it, without support from abroad. But it seems that these are antiquated notions—obsolete ideas—and that free popular governments may be made under the authority and protection of a conqueror.

But suppose the difficulties surmounted, how can we make a free government in Mexico? Where are the materials? It is to be, I presume, a confederated government like their former. Where is the intelligence in Mexico for the construction and preservation of such a government? It is what she has been aiming at for more than twenty years, but so utterly incompetent are her people for the task, that it has been a complete failure from first to last. The great body of the intelligence and wealth of Mexico is concentrated in the priesthood, who are naturally disinclined to that form of government; the residue, for the most part, are the owners of the hacien-das, the larger planters of the country, but they are without concert and destitute of the means of forming such a government. But if it were possible to establish such a government, it could not stand without the protection of our army. It would fall as soon as it is withdrawn.

If it be determined to have a treaty, it would be a far preferable course, it appears to me, to abstain from attacking or destroying the government now existing in Mexico, and to treat with it, if indeed it be capable of forming a treaty which it could maintain and execute. Upon this point I do not profess to have any information beyond that derived from conversations with those who have been in Mexico; but from all that I can hear, it may be doubted, whether we have not already pushed what is called a vigorous prosecution of the war so far, as not to leave sufficient power and influence in the Government to enter into a treaty which would be respected, when our forces are withdrawn. Such I know to be the opinion of intelligent officers. They concur in thinking that the existing Government at Queretaro, if it should enter into a treaty in conformity with the views expressed by the Executive, would be overthrown, and that we should be compelled to defend that portion of Mexico which we require for indemnity defensively, or be compelled to return and renew the prosecution of the war. If such is its weakness, it may be apprehended that even now, without pushing the vigorous prosecution of the war further, we are greatly exposed to the danger which these resolutions are intended to guard against, and that it requires great discretion and prompt action on our part to avoid it.

But before leaving this part of the subject, I must enter my solemn protest, as one of the Representatives of a State of this Union, against pledging protection to any government established in Mexico under our countenance or encouragement. It would inevitably be overthrown as soon as our forces are withdrawn; and we would be compelled, in fulfillment of plighted faith, implied or expressed, to return and reinstate such Government in power, to be again overturned and again reinstated, until we should be compelled to take the government into our own hands, just as the English have been compelled again and again to do in Hindostan, under similar circumstances, until it has led to its entire conquest. Let us avoid following the example which we have been condemning, as far back as my recollection extends. . . .

We have heard much of the reputation which our country has acquired by this war. I acknowledge it to the full amount, as far as the military is concerned. The army has done its duty nobly, and conferred high honors on the country, for which I sincerely thank them; but I apprehend that the reputation acquired does not go beyond this,—and that, in other respects, we have lost instead of acquiring reputation by the war. It would seem certain, from all publications from abroad, that the Government itself has not gained reputation in the eyes of the world for justice, moderation, or wisdom. Whether this be deserved or not, it is not for me to inquire at present. I am now speaking merely of reputation; and in this view it appears that we have lost abroad, as much in civil and political reputation as we have acquired for our skill and valor in arms. But much as I regard military glory—much as I rejoice to witness the display of that indomitable energy and courage which surmounts all difficulties—I would be sorry indeed that our Government should lose any portion of that high character for justice, moderation, and discretion, which distinguished it in the early stages of our history.

The next reason assigned is, that either holding Mexico as a province, or incorporating her into the Union, would be unprecedented by any example in our history. We have conquered many of the neighboring tribes of Indians, but we have never thought of holding them in subjection, or of incorporating them into our Union. They have been left as an independent people in the midst of us, or been driven back into the forests. Nor have we ever incorporated into the Union any but the Caucasian race. To incorporate Mexico would be the first departure of the kind; for more than half of its population are pure Indians, and by far the larger portion of the residue mixed blood. I protest against the incorporation of such a people. Ours is the government of the white man. The great misfortune of what was formerly Spanish America, is to be traced to the fatal error of placing the colored race on an equality with the white. This error destroyed the social arrangement which formed the basis of their society. This error we have wholly escaped; the Brazilians, formerly a province of Portugal, have escaped also to a considerable extent, and they and we are the only people of this continent who made revolutions without anarchy. And yet, with this example before them, and our uniform practice, there are those among us who talk about erecting these Mexicans into territorial governments, and placing them on an equality with the people of these States. I utterly protest against the project.

It is a remarkable fact in this connection, that in the whole history of man, as far as my information extends, there is no instance whatever of any civilized colored race, of any shade, being found equal to the establishment and maintenance of free government, although by far the largest proportion of the human family is composed of them; and even in the savage state, we rarely find them any where with such governments, except it be our noble savages; for noble I will call them for their many high qualities. They, for the most part, had free institutions, but such institutions are much more easily sustained among a savage than a civilized people. Are we to overlook this great fact? Are we to associate with ourselves, as equals, companions, and fellow-citizens, the Indians and mixed races of Mexico? I would consider such association as degrading to ourselves, and fatal to our institutions.

The next remaining reasons assigned, that it would be in conflict with the genius and character of our Government, and, in the end, subversive of our free institutions, are intimately connected, and I shall consider them together.

That it would be contrary to the genius and character of our Government, and subversive of our free popular institutions, to hold Mexico as a subject province, is a proposition too clear for argument before a body so enlightened as the Senate. You know the American constitution too well,—you have looked into history, and are too well acquainted with the fatal effects which large provincial possessions have ever had on the institutions of free states,—to need any proof to satisfy you how hostile it would be to the institutions of this country, to hold Mexico as a subject province. There is not an example on record of any free state holding a province of the same extent and population, without disastrous consequences. The nations conquered and held as a province, have, in time, retaliated by destroying the liberty of their conquerors, through the corrupting effect of extended patronage and irresponsible power. Such, certainly, would be our case. The conquest of Mexico would add so vastly to the patronage of this Government, that it would absorb the whole powers of the States; the Union would become an imperial power, and the States reduced to mere subordinate corporations. But the evil would not end there; the process would go on, and the power transferred from the States to the Union, would be transferred from the Legislative Department to the Executive. All the immense patronage which holding it as a province would create,—the maintenance of a large army, to hold it in subjection, and the appointment of a multitude of civil officers necessary to govern it,—would be vested in him. The great influence which it would give the President, would be the means of controlling the Legislative Department, and subjecting it to his dictation, especially when combined with the principle of proscription which has now become the established practice of the Government. The struggle to obtain the Presidential chair would become proportionably great— so great as to destroy the freedom of elections. The end would be anarchy or despotism, as certain as I am now addressing the Senate.

Let it not be said that Great Britain is an example to the contrary; that she holds provinces of vast extent and population, without materially impairing the liberty of the subject, or exposing the Government to violence, anarchy, confusion, or corruption. It is so. But it must be attributed to the peculiar character of her government. Of all governments that ever existed, of a free character, the British far transcends all in one particular,—and that is, its capacity to bear patronage without the evils usually incident to it. She can bear more, in proportion to population and wealth, than any government of that character that ever existed:—I might even go further, and assert than despotism itself in its most absolute form. I will not undertake to explain why it is so. It will take me further from the course which I have prescribed for myself, than I desire; but I will say, in a few words, that it results from the fact that her Executive and the House of Lords (the conservative branches of her Government) are both hereditary, while the other House of Parliament has a popular character. The Roman Government exceeded the British in its capacity for conquest. No government ever did exist, and none probably ever will, which, in that particular, equalled it; but its capacity to hold conquered provinces in subjection, was as nothing compared to that of Great Britain; and hence, when the Roman power passed beyond the limits of Italy, crossed the Adriatic, the Mediterranean, and the Alps, liberty fell prostrate; the Roman people became a rabble; corruption penetrated every department of the Government; violence and anarchy ruled the day, and military despotism closed the scene. Now, on the contrary, we see England, with subject-provinces of vastly greater territorial extent, and probably of not inferior population (I have not compared them); we see her, I repeat, going on without the personal liberty of the subject being materially impaired, or the Government subject to violence or anarchy! Yet England has not wholly escaped the curse which must ever befall a free government which holds extensive provinces in subjection; for, although she has not lost her liberty, or fallen into anarchy, yet we behold the population of England crushed to the earth by the superincumbent weight of debt and taxation, which may one day terminate in revolution. The wealth derived from her conquests and provincial possessions may have contributed to swell the overgrown fortunes of the upper classes, but has done nothing to alleviate the pressure on the laboring masses below. On the contrary, the expenses incident to their conquest, and of governing and holding them in subjection, have been drawn mainly from their labor, and have increased instead of decreasing the weight of the pressure. It has placed a burden upon them which, with all their skill and industry,—with all the vast accumulation of capital and power of machinery with which they are aided,—they are scarce capable of bearing, without being reduced to the lowest depths of poverty. Take, for example, Ireland,— her earliest and nearest conquest,—and is it not to this day a cause of heavy expense, and a burden, instead of a source of revenue?

On the contrary, our Government, in this particular, is the very reverse of the British. Of all free governments, it has the least capacity, in proportion to the wealth and population of the country, to bear patronage. The genius of the two, in this particular, is precisely opposite, however, much alike in exterior forms and other particulars. The cause of this difference, I will not undertake to explain on the present occasion. It results from its federal character and elective chief magistrate; and so far from the example of Great Britain constituting a safe precedent for us to follow, the little she has gained from her numerous conquests and vast provincial possessions, and the heavy burdens which it has imposed upon her people to meet the consequent expenses, ought to be to us a warning never to be forgotten; especially when we reflect that, from the nature of our Government, we would be so liable to the other and greater evils from which she, from the nature of her Government, is, in a great measure, exempted. Such and so weighty are the objections to conquering Mexico, and holding it as a subject province.

Nor are the reasons less weighty against incorporating her into the Union. As far as law is concerned, this is easily done. All that is necessary is to establish a territorial government for the several States in Mexico,—of which there are upwards of twenty,—to appoint governors, judges, and magistrates,—and to give to the population a subordinate right of making laws—we defraying the cost of the government. So far as legislation goes, the work will be done; but there would be a great difference between these territorial governments, and those which we have heretofore established within our own limits. These are only the offsets of our own people, or foreigners from the same countries from which our ancestors came. The first settlers in the territories are too few in number to form and support a government of their own, and are under obligation to the Government of the United States for forming one for them, and defraying the expense of maintaining it; knowing, as they do, that when they have sufficient population, they will be permitted to form a constitution for themselves, and be admitted as members of the Union. During the period of their territorial government, no force is necessary to keep them in a state of subjection. The case will be entirely different with these Mexican territories; when you form them, you must have powerful armies to hold them in subjection, with all the expenses incident to supporting them. You may call them territories, but they would, in reality, be but provinces under another name, and would involve the country in all the difficulties and dangers which I have already shown would result from holding the country in that condition. How long this state of things would last, before they would be fitted to be incorporated into the Union as States, we may form some idea, from similar instances with which we are familiar. Ireland has been held in subjection by England for many centuries;—and yet remains hostile, although her people are of a kindred race with the conquerors. The French colony in Canada still entertain hostile feelings towards their conquerors, although living in the midst of them for nearly one hundred years. If we may judge from these examples, it would not be unsafe to conclude that the Mexicans never will be heartily reconciled to our authority. The better class have Castilian blood in their veins, and are of the old Gothic stock—quite equal to the Anglo-Saxons in many respects, and in some superior. Of all the people upon earth, they are the most pertinacious; they hold out longer, and often when there would seem to be no prospect of ever making effectual resistance. It is admitted, I believe, on all hands, that they are now universally hostile to us, and the probability is, will continue so.

But suppose this difficulty removed. Suppose their hostility should cease, and they should become desirous of being incorporated into our Union. Ought we to admit them? Are the Mexicans fit to be politically associated with us? Are they fit not only to govern themselves, but for governing us also? Are any of you, Senators, willing that your State should constitute a member of a Union, of which twenty odd Mexican States, more than one-third of the whole, would be a part, the far greater part of the inhabitants of which are pure Indians, not equal in intelligence and elevation of character to the Cherokees, Choctaws, or any of our Southern Indian tribes?

We make a great mistake in supposing all people are capable of self-government. Acting under that impression, many are anxious to force free governments on all the people of this continent, and over the world, if they had the power. It has been lately urged in a very respectable quarter, that it is the mission of this country to spread civil and religious liberty over all the globe, and especially over this continent—even by force, if necessary. It is a sad delusion. None but a people advanced to a high state of moral and intellectual excellence are capable in a civilized condition, of forming and maintaining free governments; and among those who are so far advanced, very few indeed have had the good fortune to form constitutions capable of endurance. It is a remarkable fact in the political history of man, that there is scarcely an instance of a free constitutional government, which has been the work exclusively of foresight and wisdom. They have all been the result of a fortunate combination of circumstances. It is a very difficult task to make a constitution worthy of being called so. This admirable federal constitution of ours, is the result of such a combination. It is superior to the wisdom of any or all of the men by whose agency it was made. The force of circumstances, and not foresight or wisdom, induced them to adopt many of its wisest provisions.

But of the few nations who have been so fortunate as to adopt a wise constitution, still fewer have had the wisdom long to preserve one. It is harder to preserve than to obtain liberty. After years of prosperity, the tenure by which it is held is but too often forgotten; and I fear, Senators, that such is the case with us. There is no solicitude now about liberty. It was not so in the early days of the republic. Then it was the first object of our solicitude. The maxim then was, that "Power is always stealing from the many to the few;" "The price of liberty is perpetual vigilance." Then no question of any magnitude came up, in which the first inquiry was not, "Is it constitutional?"—"Is it consistent with our free, popular institutions?"—"How is it to affect our liberty?" It is not so now. Questions of the greatest magnitude are now discussed without reference or allusion to these vital considerations. I have been often struck with the fact, that in the discussions of the great questions in which we are now engaged, relating to the origin and the conduct of this war, their effect on the free institutions and the liberty of the people have scarcely been alluded to, although their bearing in that respect is so direct and disastrous. They would, in former days, have been the great and leading topics of discussion; and would, above all others, have had the most powerful effect in arousing the attention of the country. But now, other topics occupy the attention of Congress and of the country—military glory, extension of the empire, and the aggrandizement of the country. To what is this great change to be attributed? Is it because there has been a decay of the spirit of liberty among the people? I think not. I believe that it was never more ardent. The true cause is, that we have ceased to remember the tenure by which liberty alone can be preserved. We have had so many years of prosperity— passed through so many difficulties and dangers without the loss of liberty—that we begin to think that we hold it by right divine from heaven itself. Under this impression, without thinking or reflecting, we plunge into war, contract heavy debts, increase vastly the patronage of the Executive, and indulge in every species of extravagance, without thinking that we expose our liberty to hazard. It is a great and fatal mistake. The day of retribution will come; and when it does, awful will be the reckoning, and heavy the responsibility somewhere.

María Amparo
Ruiz de Burton
(1832-1895)

*María Amparo Ruiz, the granddaughter of José Manuel Ruiz (the governor
of Baja California, 1822-1825), was born July 3, 1832, in Baja California.
When the United States forces took possession of Baja in 1847, she and her
family, along with almost 500 other refugees from the area, relocated to
the San Francisco area. In 1849, she married Henry Burton. After he died
in 1869, she began her writing career.*

After writing and producing a five-act play, she published her first novel,
Who Would Have Thought It? *in 1872 under the names "H. S. Burton" and
"Mrs. Henry S. Burton." In 1885, using the ironic pseudonym "C. Loyal"
(standing for* Ciudadano Leal—*loyal citizen—the standard closing for official
government correspondence in Mexico), she published* The Squatter and the
Don, *from which are here excerpted Chapters II and IV. Her novel, ostensibly a romance between an American man and a woman of Spanish-Mexican
heritage (a* California*), devotes considerable space to showing the clash of
cultures between the genteel and aristocratic* Californios *and the rough and
rugged Americans who flocked to the territory around the time of the acquisition of the area by the United States following the Mexican War.*

*Toward the end of her life, Ruiz de Burton tried to claim Mexican land
that had been granted to her grandfather. Her efforts included a series of
newspaper articles in which she attacked colonization companies. Her claim
was never recognized. She died in poverty in 1895.*

FROM THE SQUATTER AND THE DON

CHAPTER II

The Don's View of the Treaty of Guadalupe Hidalgo

If there had been such a thing as communicating by telephone in the days of '72,
and there had been those magic wires spanning the distance between William Darrell's house in Alameda County and that of Don Mariano Alamar in San Diego
County, with power to transmit the human voice for five hundred miles, a listener
at either end would have heard various discussions upon the same subject, differ-
entiated only by circumstances. No magic wires crossed San Francisco bay to bring
the sound of voices to San Diego, but the law of necessity made the Squatter and
the Don, distant as they were—distant in every way, without reckoning the miles
between them—talk quite warmly of the same matter. The point of view was of
course different, for how could it be otherwise? Darrell thought himself justified,
and *authorized,* to "take up lands," as he had done before. He had had more than
half of California's population on his side, and though the *"Squatter's Sovereignty"*

was now rather on the wane and the *"squatter vote"* was no longer the power, still the squatters would not abdicate, having yet much to say about election times.

But Darrell was no longer the active squatter that he had been. He controlled many votes yet, but in his heart he felt the weight which his wife's sad eyes invariably put there when the talk was of litigating against a Mexican land title.

This time, however, Darrell honestly meant to take no land but what belonged to the United States. His promise to his wife was sincere, yet his coming to Southern California had already brought trouble to the Alamar rancho.

Don Mariano Alamar was silently walking up and down the front piazza of his house at the rancho; his hands listlessly clasped behind and his head slightly bent forward in deep thought. He had pushed away to one side the many armchairs and wicker rockers with which the piazza was furnished. He wanted a long space to walk. That his meditations were far from agreeable could easily be seen by the compressed lips, slight frown, and sad gaze of his mild and beautiful blue eyes. Sounds of laughter, music and dancing came from the parlor, the young people were entertaining friends from town with their usual gay hospitality, and enjoying themselves heartily. Don Mariano, though already in his fiftieth year, was as fond of dancing as his sons and daughters, and not to see him come in and join the quadrille was so singular that his wife thought she must come out and inquire what could detain him. He was so absorbed in his thoughts that he did not hear her voice calling him— "What keeps you away? Lizzie has been looking for you; she wants you for a partner in the lancers," said Doña Josefa, putting her arm under that of her husband, bending her head forward and turning it up to look into his eyes.

"What is the matter?" she asked, stopping short, thus making her husband come to a sudden halt. "I am sure something has happened. Tell me."

"Nothing, dear wife. Nothing has happened. That is to say, nothing new."

"More squatters?" she asked. Señor Alamar bent his head slightly in affirmative reply.

"More coming, you mean?"

"Yes, wife; more. Those two friends of squatters Mathews and Hagar, who were here last year to locate claims and went away, did not abandon their claims, but only went away to bring proselytes and their families, and a large invoice of them will arrive on tomorrow's steamer. The worst of it all is, that among the new comers is that terrible and most dangerous squatter William Darrell, who some years ago gave so much trouble to the Spanish people in Napa and Sonoma Counties by locating claims there. John Gasbang wrote to Hogsden that besides Darrell, there will be six or seven other men bringing their families, so that there will be more rifles for my cattle."

"But, didn't we hear that Darrell was no longer a squatter, that he is rich and living quietly in Alameda?"

"Yes, we heard that, and it is true. He is quite well off, but Gasbang and Miller and Mathews went and told him that my rancho had been rejected, and that it is near enough to town to become valuable, as soon as we have a railroad. Darrell believed it, and is coming to locate here."

"Strange that Darrell should believe such men; I suppose he does not know how low they are."

"He ought to know them, for they were his teamsters when he crossed the plains in '48. That is, Miller, Mathews, Hughes and Hager were his teamsters, and Gasbang was their cook—the cook for the hired men. Mrs. Darrell had a colored woman who cooked for the Darrell family; she despised Gasbang's cooking as we despise his character, I suppose."

Doña Josefa was silent and, holding on to her husband's arm, took a turn with him up and down the piazza.

"Is it possible that there is no law to protect us; to protect our property; what does your lawyer say about obtaining redress or protection; is there no hope?" she asked, with a sigh.

"Protection for our land, or for our cattle, you mean?"

"For both, as we get it for neither," she said.

"In the matter of our land, we have to await for the attorney general, at Washington, to decide."

"Lizzie was telling Elvira, yesterday, that her uncle Lawrence is a friend of several influential people in Washington, and that George can get him to interest himself in having your title decided."

"But, as George is to marry my daughter, he would be the last man from whom I would ask a favor."

"What is that I hear about not asking a favor from me?" said George Mechlin, coming out on the piazza with Elvira on his arm, having just finished a waltz—"I am interested to know why you would not ask it."

"You know why, my dear boy. It isn't exactly the thing to bother you with my disagreeable business."

"And why not? And who has a better right? And why should it be a bother to me to help you in any way I can? My father spoke to me about a dismissal of an appeal, and I made a note of it. Let me see, I think I have it in my pocket now"—said George, feeling in his breast pocket for his memorandum book—"yes, here it is—'For uncle to write to the attorney general about dismissing the appeal taken by the squatters in the Alamar grant, against Don Mariano's title, which was approved.' Is that the correct idea? I only made this note to ask you for further particulars."

"You have it exactly. When I give you the number of the case, it is all that you need say to your uncle. What I want is to have the appeal dismissed, of course, but if the attorney general does not see fit to do so, he can, at least, remand back the case for a new trial. Anything rather than this killing suspense. Killing literally, for while we are waiting to have my title settled, the *settlers* (I don't mean to make puns) are killing my cattle by the hundred head, and I cannot stop them."

"But are there no laws to protect property in California?" George asked.

"Yes, some sort of laws, which in my case seem more intended to help the lawbreakers than to protect the law-abiding," Don Mariano replied.

"How so? Is there no law to punish the thieves who kill your cattle?"

"There are some enactments so obviously intended to favor one class of citizens against another class that to call them laws is an insult to law, but such as they are, we must submit to them. By those laws any man can come to my land, for instance, plant ten acres of grain, without any fence, and then catch my cattle which, seeing the green grass without a fence, will go to eat it. Then he puts them in a *'corral'* and makes me pay damages and so much per head for keeping them, and costs of legal proceedings and many other trumped up expenses, until for such little fields of grain I may be obliged to pay thousands of dollars. Or, if the grain fields are large enough to bring more money by keeping the cattle away, then the settler shoots the cattle at any time without the least hesitation, only taking care that no one sees him in the act of firing upon the cattle. He might stand behind a bush or tree and fire, but then he is not seen. No one can swear that they saw him actually kill the cattle, and no jury can convict him, for although the dead animals may be there, lying on the ground shot, still no one saw the settler kill them. And so it is all the time. I must pay damages and expenses of litigation, or my cattle get killed almost every day."

"But this is infamous. Haven't you—the cattle owners—tried to have some law enacted that will protect your property?" George asked. "It seems to me that could be done."

"It could be done, perhaps, if our positions were reversed, and the Spanish people—*'the natives'*—were the planters of the grain fields, and the Americans were the owners of the cattle. But as we, the Spaniards, are the owners of the Spanish—or Mexican—land grants and also the owners of the cattle ranchos, our State legislators will not make any law to protect cattle. They make laws *'to protect agriculture'* (they say proudly), which means to drive to the wall all owners of cattle ranchos. I am told that at this session of the legislature a law more strict yet will be passed, which will be ostensibly *'to protect agriculture'* but in reality to destroy cattle and ruin the native Californians. The agriculture of this State does not require legislative protection. Such pretext is absurd."

"I thought that the rights of the Spanish people were protected by our treaty with Mexico," George said.

"Mexico did not pay much attention to the future welfare of the children she left to their fate in the hands of a nation which had no sympathies for us," said Doña Josefa, feelingly.

"I remember," calmly said Don Mariano, "that when I first read the text of the treaty of Guadalupe Hidalgo, I felt a bitter resentment against my people; against Mexico, the mother country, who abandoned us—her children—with so slight a provision of obligatory stipulations for protection. But afterwards, upon mature reflection, I saw that Mexico did as much as could have been reasonably expected at the time. In the very preamble of the treaty the spirit of peace and friendship, which animated both nations, was carefully made manifest. That spirit was to be the *foundation* of the relations between the conqueror and conquered. How could Mexico have foreseen then that when scarcely half a dozen years should have elapsed the trusted conquerors would, *In Congress Assembled,* pass laws which were to be retroactive upon the defenseless, helpless, conquered people, in order to despoil them? The treaty said that our rights would be the same as those enjoyed by all other American citizens. But, you see, Congress takes very good care not to enact retroactive laws for Americans, laws to take away from American citizens the property which they hold now, already, with a recognized legal title. No, indeed. But they do so quickly enough with us—with us, the Spano-Americans, who were to enjoy equal rights, mind you, according to the treaty of peace. This is what seems to me a breach of faith, which Mexico could neither presuppose nor prevent."

"It is nothing else, I am sorry and ashamed to say," George said. "I never knew much about the treaty with Mexico, but I never imagined we had acted so badly."

"I think but few Americans know or believe to what extent we have been wronged by Congressional action. And truly, I believe that Congress itself did not anticipate the effect of its laws upon us and how we would be despoiled, we, the conquered people," said Don Mariano, sadly.

"It is the duty of law-givers to foresee the effect of the laws they impose upon people," said Doña Josefa.

"That I don't deny, but I fear that the conquered have always but a weak voice, which nobody hears," said Don Mariano.

"We have had no one to speak for us. By the treaty of Guadalupe Hidalgo the American nation pledged its honor to respect our land titles just the same as Mexico would have done. Unfortunately, however, the discovery of gold brought to California the riff-raff of the world, and with it a horde of land-sharks, all possessing the privilege of voting, and most of them coveting our lands, for which they very quickly began to clamor. There was, and still is, plenty of good government land, which anyone can take. But no. The forbidden fruit is the sweetest. They do not want government land. They want the land of the Spanish people, because we 'have too much,' they say. So, to win their votes, the votes of the squatters, our representatives in Congress helped to pass laws declaring all lands in California open to preemption, as in Louisiana, for instance. Then, as a coating of whitewash to the stain on the nation's honor, a 'land commission' was established to examine land titles. Because, having pledged the national word to respect our rights, it would be an act of despoliation, besides an open violation of pledged honor, to take the lands without some pretext of a legal process. So then, we became obliged to present our titles before the said land commission to be examined and approved or rejected. While these legal proceedings are going on, the squatters locate their claims and raise crops on our lands, which they convert into money to fight our titles. But don't let me, with my disagreeable subject, spoil your dance. Go back to your lancers, and tell Lizzie to excuse me," said Don Mariano.

Lizzie would not excuse him. With the privilege of a future daughter-in-law, she insisted that Don Mariano should be her partner in the lancers, which would be a far pleasanter occupation than to be walking up and down the porch thinking about squatters.

Don Mariano therefore followed Lizzie to their place in the dance. Mercedes sat at the piano to play for them. The other couples took their respective positions.

The well-balanced mind and kindly spirit of Don Mariano soon yielded to the genial influences surrounding him. He would not bring his trouble to mar the pleasure of others. He danced with his children as gaily as the gayest. He insisted that Mr. Mechlin, too, should dance, and this gentleman graciously yielded and led Elvira through a quadrille, protesting that he had not danced for twenty years.

"You have not danced because you were sick, but now you are well. Don't be lazy," said Mrs. Mechlin.

"You would be paying to San Diego climate a very poor compliment by refusing to dance now," George added.

"That is so, Papa. Show us how well you feel," Lizzie said.

"I shall have to dance a hornpipe to do that," Mr. Mechlin answered, laughing.

To understand this remark better, the reader must know that Mr. James Mechlin had come to San Diego, four years previously, a living skeleton, not expected to last another winter. He had lost his health by a too close application to business, and when he sought rest and relaxation his constitution seemed permanently undermined. He tried the climate of Florida. He spent several years in Italy and in the south of France, but he felt no better. At last, believing his malady incurable, he returned to his New York home to die. In New York a friend, who also had been an invalid, but whose health had been restored in Southern California, advised him to try the salubrious air of San Diego. With but little hope and only to please his family, Mr. Mechlin came to San Diego, and his health improved so rapidly that he made up his mind to buy a country place and make San Diego his home. William Mathews heard of this and offered to sell his place on what Mr. Mechlin thought very moderate terms. A lawyer was employed to pass upon the title, and on his recommendation the purchase was made. Mr. Mechlin had the Mathews house moved back near the barn and a new and much larger one built. Mr. Mechlin devoted himself to cultivating trees and flowers, and his health was bettered every day. This was the compensation to his wife and two daughters for exiling themselves from New York, for it was exile to Caroline and Lizzie to give up their fine house in New York City to come and live on a California rancho.

Soon, however, these two young ladies passed their time more pleasantly, after making the acquaintance of the Alamar family, and soon their acquaintance ripened into friendship, to be made closer by the intended marriage of Gabriel—Don Mariano's eldest son—to Lizzie. Shortly after, George—Mr. Mechlin's only son—came on a visit, and when he returned to New York he was already engaged to Elvira, third daughter of Señor Alamar.

Now, George Mechlin was making his second visit to his family. He had found New York so very dull and stupid on his return from California that when Christmas was approaching he told his uncle and aunt—with whom he lived—that he wanted to go and spend Christmas and New Year's Day with his family in California.

"Very well; I wish I could go with you. Give my love to James, and tell him I am delighted at his getting so well," Mr. Lawrence Mechlin said, and George had his leave of absence. Mr. Lawrence Mechlin was president of the bank of which George was cashier, so it was not difficult for him to get the assistant cashier to attend to his duties when he was away, particularly as the assistant cashier himself was George's most devoted friend. George could have only twelve days in California, but to see Elvira for even so short a time he would have traveled a much longer distance.

Mr. James Mechlin affirmed repeatedly that he owed his improved health to the genial society of the Alamar family as much as to the genial climate of San Diego County. Mr. Mechlin, however, was not the only one who had paid the same tribute to that most delightful family, the most charming of which—the majority vote said—was Don Mariano himself. His nobility of character and great kindness of heart were well known to everybody.

The Alamar family was quite patriarchal in size, if the collateral branches be taken into account, for there were many brothers, nephews and nieces. These, however, lived in the adjoining rancho, and yet another branch in Lower California, in Mexico. Don Mariano's own immediate family was composed of his wife and six children, two sons and four daughters.

All of these, as we have seen, were having a dance. The music was furnished by the young ladies themselves, taking their turn at the piano, assisted by Madame Halier (Mercedes' French governess), who was always ready to play for the girls to dance. Besides the Mechlins, there were three or four young gentlemen from town, but there were so many Alamares (brothers, nieces and nephews, besides) that the room seemed quite well filled. Such family gatherings were frequent, making the Alamar house very gay and pleasant.

George Mechlin would have liked to prolong his visit, but he could not. He consoled himself looking forward to the ninth of June, when he would come again to make a visit of two months' duration. On his return East, before renewing his duties at the bank, he went to Washington to see about the dismissal of the appeal. Unfortunately, the attorney general had to absent himself about that time, and the matter being left with the solicitor general, nothing was done. George explained to Don Mariano how the matter was delayed, and his case remained undecided yet for another year longer.

CHAPTER IV

Efforts to Right the Wrong

Darrell was not the man to make any delay in putting into practice a project, when once adopted. He therefore immediately wrote home saying that he "had located," and wished Clarence to come down as soon as home matter permitted it. All the crops must be in first, so that Everett and Webster could take care of the farm when Clarence left. They had two good farm hands and a man to take care of the dairy, but still, Darrell made his boys give their personal attention to all the work on the farm. He wrote to Clarence that he would build a small house quickly, which afterwards could be used for the hired men, and would wait until he came down to begin building their dwelling house. He would level the ground for the house, sink a couple of wells and put up two windmills, the running stream not being sufficient.

"I think I had better buy the lumber for the house up here and charter a schooner to send it down," Clarence said to his mother, after reading his father's letter.

"Did he say anything to you about the condition of the title?" Mrs. Darrell asked.

"Not a word. I suppose the land is vacant," Clarence replied. Mrs. Darrell shook her head, as if in doubt.

"I want you to see to that, before there is any house built in which I shall be expected to reside," she said. "The first thing you do when you get there is to inquire whether the land has been finally rejected and there is no litigation for it. If there is, I want you to pay for it to the owner. And if he will not or cannot sell, write to me at once."

"Very well, mother, I shall do as you say, and I assure you I do not wish Father to take up any land claimed by anyone under a Mexican title. I think those Spanish people ought to be allowed to keep the land that their government gave them. We ought not to have made any laws that would place their titles in a bad light and be questioned. We should have accepted the legality they had before their own Mexican government, without making some other legality requisite, to please ourselves," Clarence said.

"That has always been my opinion, but I have failed to convince your father. However, with our combined efforts, we might dissuade him from his present way of thinking," said Mrs. Darrell.

Clarence would not be able to leave home for a few weeks yet. In the meantime, his father had not been idle. He had lost no time in carrying out his plans, and shortly after making his *"location"* in the manner described, he had several men engaged in different employments at his place. When he had already begun building the small house, of which he spoke in his letter to Clarence, Don Mariano, accompanied by his two sons, rode up to the place where he was then superintending his workmen.

"Good morning, Mr. Darrell," said Don Mariano.

"Good morning," Darrell answered, laconically.

"Can I speak a few words with you?"

"Certainly," he said, going a few steps nearer.

"I see you have taken up some land here, and I suppose you think it is government land, but if so, you are misinformed. This land belongs to me," Don Mariano said.

"Why is it reported rejected then? I have seen the law report, stating that your title was rejected."

"Yes, I know that such is the case. For some mistake or other the entry was made placing my title in the list of those rejected, but I assure you that it is a mistake. My title is now before the attorney general in Washington, because, having been approved, the settlers took an appeal. If the attorney general sustains the appeal, I suppose he will remand the case for a new trial, but I have reasons to suppose he will dismiss the appeal and affirm the decision of the District Court in my favor."

"We will see about that," Darrell said.

"Undoubtedly we will; meantime I thought it was best to undeceive you, and give you warning that you are building on my land."

"Your land if you get it," was the answer.

"If you knew the condition of my title I don't think that you would doubt that this land is mind. However, all I wish to do is to prevent you from spending money here and then naturally get into litigation with me to defend your property," said Don Mariano.

Darrell thought of his wife, and her earnest injunctions. He wished to keep his promise to her. He said:

"If the courts say that this land rightfully belongs to you, I shall pay you for your land or vacate."

"But, Mr. Darrell, you will get me into litigation with you, and I wish to avoid that."

"No, I shall not get you into any lawsuit with me. I shall buy your land or leave."

"Very well, Mr. Darrell, I shall rely on your word. I shall remember what you say; please do the same."

"I am not in the habit of forgetting what I say."

Don Mariano and his two sons lifted their hats, bowed slightly, turned their horses' heads and moved off.

Darrell returned their bow, muttering to himself, "They take off their hats and bow like gentlemen, anyway."

While he was talking with Don Mariano, Mathews, Hughes, Gasbang, Miller and Pittikin had come. They heard all that was said and looked disappointed. They evidently had counted upon Darrell to help them to fight the rightful owner.

"Did I understand you to say to the Don that you will not maintain your claim, if the attorney general dismisses our appeal?" asked Gasbang.

"I don't know what you understood, or what you did not understand. What I said was that if the Don's title is decided to be right and legal, I shall not contest it. Why should I, if the land is his? I came here to take up government land, believing his title was rejected. He says it is not."

"He lies; it was rejected," Gasbang said.

"That is why we appealed," Mathews added.

"Very well; we will wait. For my part, I think that if his title was rejected, he will find it hard to get it back," said Darrell.

The fact of his going on with his building ought to have been sufficient proof to the other settlers that he had cast his lot with them. But it was not. They feared that at any time he might pay the Don for his land, and cease to be one of them, cease to be a *"squatter."* These doubts, these fears, were the perennial theme of endless discussion with the settlers of Alamar.

With the date of February 14, 1872, the Honorable Legislature of California passed a law *"To protect agriculture, and to prevent the trespassing of animals upon private property in the County of Los Angeles, and the County of San Diego, and parts of Monterey County."*

In the very first section it recited that "every owner *or occupant* of land, *whether it is enclosed or not,"* could take up cattle found in said land, etc., etc. It is not stated to be necessary that the *occupant* should have a good title. All that was required seemed to be that he should *claim to be an occupant* of land, no matter who was the owner.

Before this law came out, Don Mariano had already had a great deal of trouble with the squatters, who kept killing his cattle by the hundred head at times. After this law passed, he had the additional annoyance of having to pay money for the release of cattle taken up by *occupants* who would not fence their ten-acre crops. Thus, the alternative was, that if cattle were not taken up, he was sure to find them shot dead by some invisible hand. He had hoped that the Legislature would pass a law saying that "unless *occupants* of land put fences around their fields, they would not be authorized to take up cattle." But, instead of this, the above-mentioned law was enacted.

This was, of course, ruinous to Don Mariano, as well as to all owners of cattle ranchos where settlers had seen fit to locate homesteads. Now any one man, by planting *one acre* of grain to attract cattle to it, could make useless thousands of acres around it of excellent grazing, because it became necessary to drive cattle away from the vicinity of these unfenced fields.

In view of all this, and seeing that the new law would confirm the right to plant fields without fencing, and take up cattle, horses or any other animals found therein, Don Mariano thought he would call together all the settlers in his rancho, and make some proposition to them that would be fair to everybody and by which he would save his cattle from getting killed or captured (when he must ransom them) all the time.

He told his idea to Mr. Mechlin, who thought it was a good plan, and volunteered to see some of the settlers with whom he was acquainted, thinking that these could see others, and in this manner a meeting be arranged. He started in the morning on his errand, and in the vening, Don Mariano called to learn the result.

"These men are meaner and lower than I had supposed," said Mr. Mechlin, whose very fine nervous organization ill-fitted him for the rough contact of Gasbangs. "Would you believe it, they suspected I wanted to lay a trap in which the innocent lambs would fall, and you—the wolf—catch them. If it had not been that I saw Darrell, I would have been utterly discouraged. And I suspect he would not have been half so polite and considerate but for the influence of his son, who has just arrived."

"I heard he had. You saw him?"

"Yes; and a very gentlemanly, handsome young fellow he is. He made his father promise to go with him to see the settlers in person, and arrange for you to meet them; he will report to me in the evening the result of their embassy."

Clarence kept his word to Mr. Mechlin, and immediately after breakfast he had his buggy and horses (a fine turnout he had brought from San Francisco) at the door. Darrell smiled, and good-naturedly took his seat beside his son, saying it would be best to begin by seeing Gasbang and Mathews. Fortunately they met these men, who were driving to see him, to ask his opinion about agreeing to meet Don Mariano. Darrell promptly told them that he thought no one of the settlers should refuse a request so easy to grant.

"But don't you think there is a trap in it?" Mathews asked.

"None whatever. We are not children," Darrell replied.

"But suppose he makes us promise something?" Mathews asked.

"How can he coerce anyone against his will," said Darrell.

"No one will be obliged to accede unwillingly," said Clarence. "Let us at least be courteous."

"Certainly. Have you any idea what it is that he wants to say?" asked Gasbang.

"He wants to make some proposition to the settlers, by which he hopes that the interests of all concerned will be subserved," said Clarence.

"Visionary!" exclaimed Gasbang, tapping his forehead with his forefinger, "not practical."

"But his intentions are perfectly kind and fair," Clarence said.

"That is to say, Mr. Mechlin thinks they are."

"Why shouldn't they be? He certainly can't coerce anybody. Here we are on what he believes to be his land, and we don't think it is. Well, what of that?"

"He certainly won't propose to fight us single-handed. We are the majority," said Darrell.

"All right. We'll see Hager and Miller, and the other fellows in the valley. But we think Mr. Clarence will do better with Hancock, Pittikin and Hughes. The female element is strong there, but it will weaken in his hands, and in that malleable condition, he can shape it to suit himself, with one look out of his eyes at the whole troop of girls," said Gasbang.

"Goodness! You don't suppose I would go to play the sweet fellow to those ugly old girls, and make a fool of myself," said Clarence, with so genuine a look of thorough disgust that it make John Gasbang indulge in one of his loudest fits of hilarity. "Don't be alarmed, my young friend. There is no harm for you there. I could turn you loose among those girls and you would be as safe as Daniel among 'lions' or in 'fiery furnace.' You would not get a single scratch, or feel any flames at all," said he.

"What a low, vulgar fellow this is, even too low for a squatter," said Clarence, driving off.

"Phew!" ejaculated the elder Darrell, "you speak like *a Don.* Your idea of *a squatter* is not flattering."

"It is flattering thus far, that I think Gasbang is too low for the settler who means no wrong-doing—the average squatter. As for Mathews, I am sure he is a cut-throat by instinct."

"That may be; but I think their idea of your seeing Pittikin and Hughes is good. You can have more effect on them than Gasbang or Mathews."

"Oh, I am willing to go to speak to the old men, but why should I see the girls?"

"You manage that part to suit yourself. And now stop. I'll drop here; you needn't go out of your way. I'll walk home. I want to see this piece of land near by. It has not been located. I might put a claim for Everett and another for Webster."

Clarence sighed and silently drove on. He had passed by the Pittikin and Hughes farms the day he arrived, as his father had taken him to see how nicely the settlers were doing in Southern California, all expecting their prosperity to increase by the building of the railroad. Clarence saw the two houses and began to feel like a mariner of old between Scylla and Charybdis. There might be a troop of ugly old girls in each house. If he could only see some men out in the fields. But the fields looked deserted. Where could the men be—this being no Sunday nor Fourth of July, that they should leave off work? On looking about for some human being to guide him, he saw in the distance, under a clump of dark trees, several wagons, and horses unhitched, standing harnessed near them.

He was about to turn to the left, to take the road between two fields, when he heard voices, shouting loudly. He supposed they were calling someone. The shouts were followed by a man on horseback galloping toward him. Clarence stopped and waited. The rider was no other than Mr. Pittikin, who came in person to invite him to join their picnic, in honor of his daughter's wedding. The opportunity to see *the men* together would be excellent, but the *girls* would be there, too, thought Clarence, not over pleased.

"Please excuse me, I am not dressed to appear in company. I came to see you on business," said he.

"The girls said I must bring you." Clarence felt a qualm.

"And even if I have to fight you I must obey; obey the ladies, you know. There ain't many there. Only our two families—Hughes and mine, and neighbor Hancock's and a few friends. Indeed, we will feel slighted if you don't join us. We will feel you think us too humble a class for you to associate with."

"Nothing of the kind. If I thought so, I would not hesitate to present myself before the ladies in this dress."

"Come along, anyhow. We'll make all the allowance you want. But you see, this is my daughter Fanny's birthday and her wedding day. She was married to Romeo Hancock this morning. So we wanted a room as big as all out doors to celebrate the occasion. We thought the best thing would be to have a picnic under those beautiful trees. Come, please. If you ain't with us, you are against us."

"I'll go home and put on other dress and come back immediately," said Clarence.

Pittikin laughed. "Just what Fanny said. I tell you she is an awfully smart girl. She said, 'He'll tell you he is going home to change his clothes, but don't you let him, because he'll only give us the slip.' So you see, I can't let you go. Besides, they are setting the table—I mean to say, spreading the eatables—so you have no time to go home now."

"But, look here, Mr. Pittikin, what is to become of my mission? I came to see you and Mr. Hughes on business, and not on a picnic."

"Can't the business wait till tomorrow?"

"Not very well, as I promised Mr. Mechlin."

"Oh! I know; Hughes told me," interrupted Pittikin. "The Don wants to make speeches to the settlers to fool us into a—into—some terms of his, so that we'll kick ourselves out of our farms."

"Nothing of the kind. He is not going to make any foolish propositions, but even if he were, you can lose nothing by being polite and listening to him."

"I don't know but what you are right. I like always to be polite; and as for Hughes, he is the politest man going, and no mistake. He never speaks loud, and he always listens to you. I think it will be the best thing, perhaps, to see Hughes, now. Then there is neighbor Hancock, and neighbor Miller and Jackson, and the boys. Come along, we'll collar them in a bunch."

"Then, I can count upon your help?"

"Certainly you can; for when it is a question of politeness, I won't be left behind, and if I give you my word, you can bet on me."

Clarence was received with loud demonstrations of pleasure.

"Here he is," said Pittikin, on arriving at the picnic ground; "I got him; but as he has some business to talk to us about, I promised him we would attend to that too, and mix business with pleasure, as it were. So, you talk to them girls, Mr. Darrell, while we old men see what can be done and how, and we'll let you know."

Clarence was presented by Mr. Pittikin to Mrs. Pittikin, and this lady presented him to the company, saying that he must make himself at home, which Clarence did not see well how he could do.

But the young ladies could not boast of having often the good fortune to entertain a young gentleman as elegant, handsome and rich as Clarence, and they made good use of their golden opportunity. Sweet glances and complimentary expressions of pleasure, because the Darrell family were to be their neighbors, were showered upon him, until he was ready to laugh outright. But he was too kind to have done anything so discourteous, and took it all in good part, thinking it was all meant in kindness.

"Come, let us show to Mr. Darrell our ice fountain; it is, I think, a great natural curiosity," said Mrs. Romeo Hancock, the heroine of the day, being the lady in whose honor the hymeneal festivities took place. "Come, girls and boys," said she, and accompanied by Clarence, and followed by eight or ten others, she guided them to a little cave under a large oak, from which a muffled sound of tiny bells that seemed to tinkle and sigh and whisper, came forth. It seemed to Clarence as if the little fountain was in sympathy with the dispossessed owners but did not dare to raise its timid voice in behalf of the vanquished, who no longer had rights in their patrimony, and must henceforth wander off disinherited, despoiled, forgotten.

"This is a lovely place," said Clarence.

"Yes, and Mathews wanted to kill me for it," said Romeo.

"Why so?" asked Clarence.

"Because he had just sold his place to Mr. Mechlin, intending to locate here. So when he went to town to sign his conveyance, I put some boards in a wagon and came here, and in two hours my father and myself had put up my cabin. Then we put up this fence around one acre, and by nightfall we had placed my boundary stakes. That night I brought my blankets and my rifle, to sleep in my cabin. Mother sent father to keep me company, and we slept soundly, in splendid style. I wasn't afraid of Mathews. Next morning, at daybreak, we heard the rumbling of a wagon, and soon after we spied old Mathews sitting on the top of his boards. He came smack against my fence.

"'What the devil is this?' said he, and began to swear a perfect blue streak. Then he took a hammer from his wagon and began hammering.

"I jumped up, took my rifle and hallooed to him, as if I didn't know him, 'Who is there, hammering my fence?'

"'Your fence?' said he; 'your fence?'

"'Yes, sir, mine. I located here yesterday.'

"'You! you! Get a beard first,' said he, and with another streak of oaths, began hammering again.

"I came up nearer, holding my rifle in good position. I said, 'Look here, Mr. Mathews, leave my fence alone, or you will get into trouble.' I leveled my rifle at him. 'Will you stop? I give you just two minutes.'

"He stopped.

"'You have no right to locate—you are a minor,' said he, livid with rage.

"'You just inform yourself better, by asking a polite question or two of my parents. They will tell you that I am just twenty-one and two days old, and I can prove it by our family Bible and certificate of baptism. I am a Christian, I am, though you don't seem to be, judging by your cursing—and as for my beard, you be patient, and you'll see it, for it is coming as fast as your gray hairs.'

"'Why didn't you say you wanted this place?' he growled.

"'What a question!' I answered. 'You ask it because you don't see my beard, but I feel it pushing ahead with all its might. I didn't tell you, because we ain't exactly bosom friends, and because that is not the style in which we settlers do business. I kept dark, hoping that you would hold on a while longer, trying to get a bigger price for your place from Mr. Mechlin. I watched you, and when you let Saturday pass I knew this sweet little spot was mine—for on Saturday I was twenty-one, and you couldn't sign your conveyance to Mr. Mechlin until Monday. Today is Tuesday, Mr. Mathews, I shall be twenty-one years and three days old at 11 o'clock A.M. this day, if I live five hours longer.'

"'I don't believe a word. You ain't twenty-one. 'Tis a lie!'

"'No, it ain't,' my father said, coming from the cabin.

"'Then he's a jumper. He's jumped my claim.'

"'No, he ain't. Look here, Mathews,' said Father, dragging his rifle along as if it was a dead cat, 'you know well it is yourself who is lying when you say that. You had no right to claim while you held the other.'

"'But I put up my notice that I was going to locate here.'

"'Now, don't be silly,' said Father, leaning on his rifle. 'It is painful to my feelings to hear a grey-headed man talk like a child. You might have put twenty notices—what of that? The law don't allow any circus performances like that, and if it did, you ain't a good enough performer to ride two horses at once.'

"'I think it is a mean performance on your part, too, coming here to steal a march on me.'

"'A mean performance, you say? Do you remember how I had my notices up and my stakes on the ground, six years ago, and when I went to town to bring my lumber, you jumped my claim? My boy has just barely returned the compliment.'

"'I'll be even with you yet,' said he, climbing into his wagon, and beginning to whip his horses, and swear at us worse than ever.

"'The same to you; the same to you,' Father would say, as if answering prayers, and then we both laughed heartily."

"That is not the worst, but that you jumped the claim of his affections," said Tom, whereupon all laughed, and Fanny bashfully hung down her head.

Voices calling them to dinner were now heard, and they returned to the picnic grounds.

No banquet of the Iliad warriors surpassed this, showing that the settlers of Alamar had found the Don's land and the laws of Congress very good.

The elder Mrs. Hancock and Mrs. Pittikin were proud of having given a banquet which no other settler would dare surpass in Alamar.

When the dessert was being served, Clarence said, "We must drink to the bride and groom." All agreed that it should be done.

He arose and made a neat little speech, which was so *"sweetly pretty,"* Mr. P. said, that it brought tears to the eyes of Mrs. Pittikin and Mrs. Hancock the elder.

This put Clarence's popularity beyond doubt.

"Fill your glasses, for I have something to say to Mr. Clarence Darrell, but we must first drink his health," said Mr. Pittikin.

"Here is to our friends, the Darrell family, but more particularly to Mr. Clarence. We respect him, we like him, we are proud of him"—all drank—"and I now take the occasion to say to Mr. Darrell, in the presence of our friends here, that I fulfilled my promise to him, and have spoken to our friends here, the heads of families, and they will speak to those who are not present, and we will meet to hear what the Don has to say."

"But we don't promise to accept any proposition, if it don't suit each one, no matter what anybody votes," said old Hughes.

"That is understood; we want to be polite, that's all," explained Mr. Pittikin.

"And that is all I have requested," Clarence said. "I do not ask anyone to accept any proposition against his will."

"That is fair enough," said old Hancock.

"And little enough, considering we are in possession of land that the Don believes to be his own," said Romeo.

"But it ain't," said old Hager.

"It has been for more than fifty years," Romeo asserted.

"But he lost it by not complying with the law," said Hughes.

"Yes, if he had not neglected his rights, his title would not have been rejected; he went to sleep for eight years, and his right was outlawed," said Miller.

"That was the fault of his lawyers, perhaps," Clarence said.

"Of course it was, but he should have watched his lawyers. The trouble is, that you can't teach 'an old dog new tricks.' Those old Spaniards never will be business men," said Pittikin, sententiously.

It was finally agreed that Clarence would call on Mr. Mechlin that evening to notify him that the settlers would meet the Don on Monday afternoon at 2 o'clock on the porch of Gasbang's house.

A CORRIDO

At its most basic, a corrido *is a song-like ballad that expresses the emotions or political views of a community. Like the Scottish ballads of the thirteenth through eighteenth centuries, most are anonymous.*

The word "corrido" derives from the Spanish verb "correr," which means "to run" or "to flow." As a literary/song form, the corrido first appeared in Mexican-American traditions along the United States–Mexico border during the nineteenth century. Although variations are not unusual, a corrido typically has eight-syllable quatrains of four to six lines. In terms of rhyme, corridos most often pair the first two lines of each quatrain as one set and the second two lines as another.

Traditionally, corridos offer an interpretation of events known to a particular community. They focus on local or regional historical events or people. While some deal with themes of love, border conflict, or the tragedy of losing a friend, others portray heroic figures, such as Gregorio Cortez (a rancher from South Texas who defended his family and his beliefs in the face of overwhelming opposition).

THE BALLAD OF GREGORIO CORTEZ

In the county of Karnes
Look what has happened;
The Major Sheriff died,
Leaving Román badly wounded.

It must have been two in the afternoon
When people arrived;
They said to one another,
"It is not known who killed him."

They went around asking questions,
About half an hour afterward,
They found that the wrongdoer
Had been Gregorio Cortez.

Now they have outlawed Cortez
Throughout the whole state;
Let him be taken, dead or alive;
He has killed several men.

Then said Gregorio Cortez,
With his pistol in his hand,
"I don't regret that I killed him;
I regret my brother's death."

Then said Gregorio Cortez,
And his soul was all aflame,
"I don't regret that I killed him;
A man must defend himself."

The Americans were coming,
They were whiter than a dove,
From the fear that they had
Of Cortez and of his pistol.

Then the Americans said,
Then they said fearfully,
"Come, let us follow the trail;
The wrongdoer is Cortez."

They set the bloodhounds on him,
So they could follow his trail,
But trying to overtake Cortez
Was like following a star.

He struck out for Gonzales
Without showing any fear,
"Follow me, cowardly rangers,
I am Gregorio Cortez."

From Belmont he went to the ranch,
They succeeded in surrounding him,
Quite a few more than three hundred,
But there he jumped their corral.

When he jumped their corral,
According to what we hear,
They got into a gunfight,
And he killed then another sheriff.

Then said Gregorio Cortez,
With his pistol in his hand,
"Don't run, you cowardly rangers,
From just one Mexican."

Gregorio Cortez went out,
He went toward Laredo
They decided not to follow
Because they were afraid of him.

Then said Gregorio Cortez,
"What is the use of your scheming?
You cannot catch me,
Even with those bloodhounds."

Then the Americans said,
"If we catch up with him, what shall we do?
If we fight him man to man,
Very few of us will return."

Over by El Encinal,
According to what we hear,
They made him a corral,
And he killed then another sheriff.

Then said Gregorio Cortez,
Shooting out a lot of bullets,
"I have weathered thunderstorms;
This little mist doesn't bother me."

Now he has met a Mexican;
He says to him haughtily,
"Tell me the news;
I am Gregorio Cortez."

"It is said that because of me
Many people have been killed;
I will surrender now
Because such things are not right."

Cortez says to Jesús,
"At last you are going to see it;
Go tell the rangers
To come and arrest me."

All the rangers were coming,
Coming so fast they even flew,
For they wanted to get
The thousand dollars they were offered.

When they surrounded the house,
Cortez suddenly appeared before them,
"You will take me if I'm willing,
But not any other way."

Then the Major Sheriff said,
As if he was going to cry,
"Cortez, hand over your weapons;
We are not going to kill you."

Then said Gregorio Cortez,
Shouting to them in a loud voice,
"I won't surrender my arms
Until I am in a cell."

Then said Gregorio Cortez,
He said in his godly voice,
"I won't surrender my arms
Until I'm inside a jail."

Now they have taken Cortez,
Now matters are at an end;
His poor family
Are suffering in their hearts.

Now with this I say farewell,
In the shade of a cypress tree;
This is the end of the singing
Of the ballad of Cortez.

PAT MORA

(1942-)

Patricia Estella Mora was born in El Paso, Texas. She earned her bachelor's degree from Texas Western College in 1963. While teaching at the El Paso Independent School, she worked on her master's degree at the University of Texas, El Paso. After completing this degree in 1967, Mora taught English at El Paso Community College for a number of years.

Mora admits that as a teenager she felt ambivalent about her Mexican-American heritage. However, as an adult, she became (and remains) a prominent spokesperson for cultural appreciation, conservation, and education. As a writer, she has achieved considerable acclaim, including awards from the National Association for Chicano Studies and the Southwest Council of Latin American Studies. She has published several poetry collections: Chants *(1984),* Borders *(1986), and* Communion *(1991). In addition to a collection of lectures, essays, poems, and vignettes entitled* Nepantla: Essays from the Land in the Middle *(1993), Mora has also published several books for children:* A Birthday Basket for Tia *(1992),* Pablo's Tree *(1992), and* Tomás and the Library Lady *(1992). In 1997 she published* House of Houses, *a memoir of her family and childhood told through the voices of family members.*

Mora's poem "Immigrants" speaks directly of the anxieties about their children's acceptance in the new society felt by immigrants everywhere.

IMMIGRANTS

wrap their babies in the American flag,
feed them mashed hot dogs and apple pie,
name them Bill and Daisy,
buy them blonde dolls that blink blue
eyes or a football and tiny cleats
before the baby can even walk,
speak to them in thick English,
hallo, babee, hallo,
whisper in Spanish or Polish
when the babies sleep, whisper
in a dark parent bed, that dark
parent fear, "Will they like
our boy, our girl, our fine american
boy, our fine american girl?"

STEPHEN SONDHEIM

(1930-)

Born in New York and educated at Williams College, where he majored in music, Stephen Sondheim began his career in the theater as a lyricist, providing words for musicals by Leonard Bernstein, Jule Styne, and Richard Rodgers. His first successful outing as both composer and lyricist was A Funny Thing Happened on the Way to the Forum *(1962). He has since composed and written lyrics for about a dozen musicals, including* Company *(1970),* A Little Night Music *(1973),* Sweeney Todd *(1979),* Sundays in the Park with George *(1984),* Into the Woods *(1992), and* Passion *(1996). While these mature later works are all distinguished by their unconventional, often sardonic humor about the emotional lives of adults, his work in collaboration with Leonard Bernstein in 1957's* West Side Story *fully supports its romantic reshaping of the Romeo and Juliet story. In the musical's text by playwright Arthur Laurents, the warring Capulets and Montagues are replaced by rival New York youth gangs, the Sharks and the Jets, one composed of Puerto Ricans and the other of Poles and Irish. In one scene, excerpted here, the Sharks' girls discuss the "old country" with conflicting ideas about life back on the island.*

AMERICA

ROSALIA
Puerto Rico . . .
You lovely island . . .
Island of tropical breezes.
Always the pineapples growing,
Always the coffee blossoms blowing . . .

ANITA *(mockingly)*
Puerto Rico . . .
You ugly island . . .
Island of tropic diseases.
Always the hurricanes blowing,
Always the population growing . . .
And the money owing,
And the babies crying,
And the bullets flying.
I like the island Manhattan—
Smoke on your pipe and put that in!

OTHERS *(except Rosalia)*
I like to be in America!
Okay by me in America!
Everything free in America
For a small fee in America!

ROSALIA
I like the city of San Juan.

ANITA
I know a boat you can get on.

ROSALIA
Hundreds of flowers in full bloom.

ANITA
Hundreds of people in each room!

ALL *(except Rosalia)*
Automobile in America,
Chromium steel in America,
Wire-spoke wheel in America,
Very big deal in America!

ROSALIA
I'll drive a Buick through San Juan.

ANITA
If there's a road you can drive on.

ROSALIA
I'll give my cousins a free ride.

ANITA
How you get all of them inside?

ALL *(except Rosalia)*
Immigrant goes to America,
Many hellos in America,
Nobody knows in America
Puerto Rico's in America!

(The girls dance around Rosalia.)

ROSALIA
I'll bring a TV to San Juan.

ANITA
If there's a current to turn on!

ROSALIA
I'll give them new washing machine.

ANITA
What have they got there to keep clean?

ALL *(except Rosalia)*
I like the shores of America!
Comfort is yours in America!
Knobs on the doors in America,
Wall-to-wall floors in America!

(They dance)

ROSALIA
When I will go back to San Juan—

ANITA
When you will shut up and get gone!

ROSALIA
Ev'ryone there will give big cheer!

ANITA
Ev'ryone there will have moved here!

(More dancing)

JÉSUS COLÓN
(1901-1974)

Born in Cayey, Puerto Rico, in 1901, Jésus Colón immigrated to New York City at age 16, in the same year that residents of the island became American citizens. He worked a variety of jobs—stevedore, dishwasher, postal clerk—while attending high school at night; he graduated in 1922, and later attended St. John's University for two years. Always a progressive activist—he had organized a strike against an unjust teacher in his school in San Juan the year before his departure for the mainland—Colón was a member of the Puerto Rican Socialist Party before he left home for New York. He was soon deeply involved in writing for community and socialist newspapers. He wrote columns, at first in Spanish, later in English, for newspapers and magazines, including The Daily Worker *(1928-1958) and its successor,* The Worker *(1958-1971), organs of the socialist worker's movement and of the Communist Party. While writing nearly weekly for almost fifty years, Colón was also active in a variety of other labor and political organizations. He published a collection of his writings,* A Puerto Rican in New York and Other Sketches, *in 1961, and at the time of his death in 1974 was at work on a second collection, published posthumously as* The Way It Was and Other Writings *in 1993.*

Colón's brief, journalistic essays are part of a Latino tradition, the testimonial, or personal essay on public matters, in which the author relates personal experience to communal or national experience. As such Colón's writing on issues of racial and economic justice, international politics, anti-Semitism, color prejudice, corrupt and repressive Latin American governments, and police brutality are addressed to all of the American people and not only to his immediate Puerto Rican audience.

Bitter Sugar:
Why Puerto Ricans Leave Home

I still remember the day my teacher in San Juan gave me that fat history book: *A History of the United States.* It was around 1915. I was in the eighth grade, elementary school. I looked curiously at the maps and pictures, and for the first time looked at the oval face of George Washington and the Christlike figure of Abraham Lincoln.

Thumbing through the book, I chanced upon a phrase in one of the documents reproduced at the end of the book. The phrase was: *"We, the people of the United States . . ."* The phrase somehow evoked a picture of all those people about whom we had been studying in our flat, cream-colored geography book. The people who picked cotton in Alabama, raised wheat in the Dakotas, and grew grapes in California. The people in the big, faraway American cities who manufactured my mother's Singer machine and the shoes we saw on sale. The people in Brooklyn and other shipyards who built the great big ships that plied the waters of the Caribbean. All these people and I, and my father and the poor Puerto Rican sugar workers and tobacco workers, we were, all together, *"the people of the United States."* We all belonged! That is what the words meant to me, a little schoolboy in Spanish-speaking Puerto Rico, colony of the United States.

My eighth-grade teacher was a six-foot Montanan, Mr. Whole, by name. He was very friendly. There was always a fading smile on his lips. One day he was sitting on the wide porch of the Y.M.C.A. All of us in school had been politely obliged to bring in a quarter each as a contribution for the construction of the building. Mr. Whole hailed me from the porch and invited me to play a game of checkers. I sat in front of him, with the checkerboard between us. Somebody in authority came out and told Mr. Whole that I could not play there with him because I did not belong to the white race.

That incident started me thinking. In this "we the people" phrase that I admired so much, were there first and second class people? Were there other distinctions and classifications based not only on "race" but on money or social position?

Life and reading gave me the answer. Yes, there were classifications and divisions. The rich and the poor. The sugar planter and the sugar peon. And I soon discovered that the rich Puerto Rican sugar planter and the rich American investor belonged to the same clubs and played golf and danced and dined together. Both despised and exploited the masses of the Puerto Rican people.

I learned that the American did not come to Puerto Rico because of the altruistic and democratic reasons that General Miles had stated in his famous proclamation when the Yankees invaded Puerto Rico in 1898. I learned that a race to gain control of the resources and the markets of the world was then going on. The

United States was first getting into this race in earnest around 1898. I learned the meaning of the word imperialism. I further learned that ever since the Americans had come into Puerto Rico, our country, which had produced the varied products for our daily meals, was converted into a huge sugar factory with absentee owners caring absolutely nothing about the standards of living of the agricultural workers who comprise two-thirds of the Puerto Rican population. A man's sunrise to sunset labor under the burning tropical sun, cutting sugar cane, yielded one dollar and a half a day.

I realized more clearly than before that all our school books, except our Spanish grammar, were written in English. It would be just as if you New Yorkers or Pennsylvanians discovered one good morning that your children's school books were all written in German or Japanese.

In 1917, there was a big strike of the dock workers. The police were ordered to patrol with long range rifles. Right in front of the school in Puerta de Tierra some of the strikers were marching. It was during the noon recess hour. The mounted police charged them. The dock workers and the Puerta de Tierra women—famous for their militancy—stood firm.

The workers were mauled down by the police. One was killed, many were wounded.

During my first year of high school, I was told by the workers that this legalized murder was nothing new. In the sugar plantations the owners used to burn a stretch of planted sugar cane, impute the arson to the workers and kill them like malaria mosquitoes.

The workers and the course of my life kept teaching me. The workers told me that we were a colony. A sort of storage house for cheap labor and a market for second-class industrial goods. That we Puerto Ricans were a part of a vast colonial system, and that not until colonialism was wiped out and full independence achieved by Puerto Rico would the condition by which we were living be remedied.

Colonialism made me get out of Puerto Rico thirty years ago. Colonialism, with its agricultural slavery, monoculture, absenteeism and rank human exploitation are making the young Puerto Ricans of today come in floods to the United States.

I didn't find any bed of roses in the United States. I found poor pay, long hours, terrible working conditions. I met discrimination even in the slums and in the low-paying factories where the bosses very dexterously pitted Italians against Puerto Ricans, and Puerto Ricans against American Negroes and Jews.

The same American trusts that milked us in Puerto Rico were in control in New York. And the trusts—the fountainhead of imperialism and colonialism, the meaning of which I had learned the hard way—were not only oppressing the Puerto Ricans in New York, but the other various national minorities and workers as well.

Today there are approximately 400,000 Puerto Ricans in greater New York. The largest number live in East Harlem, from 98th to 116th Street, between 5th and Lexington Avenues. Then comes the second largest Puerto Rican community, around Longwood and Prospect Avenues in the Bronx. The third largest concentration is around the Williamsburg section in Brooklyn. There are smaller Puerto Rican communities from Bay Ridge in Brooklyn to Yonkers.

Why have the reactionary newspapers unleashed a concerted campaign against the Puerto Ricans coming to New York? Why do they describe the Puerto Ricans in the worst light they can imagine? Simply because they know that colonial conditions of exploitation and the cry for their economic, social and political independence have made the Puerto Ricans a freedom-loving democratic people. Their American idol is Vito Marcantonio.* Because they are progressives with the right to vote as American citizens, the reactionaries hate them and are trying to intimidate them and frighten them into submission.

The Puerto Ricans are joining the unions and the progressive fraternal, civic and political organizations. They are looking for and achieving unity with the other national groups and progressive forces in America today. Increasing numbers are joining the Cervantes Society of the I.W.O.

The Puerto Ricans now arriving are learning the power of unity. At the call of Representative Vito Marcantonio, a broad organization of all Puerto Ricans has been established after two great conferences of representatives from fraternal, religious, civic and political organizations. This Convention for Puerto Rico, as the organization is called, has as its main purpose the ending of the colonial status of Puerto Rico and achievement of the civil rights of the Puerto Ricans in this country.

MARK TWAIN
(SAMUEL LANGHORNE CLEMENS)
(1835-1910)

Samuel Langhorne Clemens was born in 1835 and grew up in the Mississippi River town of Hannibal, Missouri. His father died when he was eleven, and Clemens went to work at a printing shop. There he became interested in the possibility of making a career out of writing. At the age of sixteen, he published his first piece in a Boston magazine. At twenty, he gave up the printing business to work as a riverboat pilot. After briefly serving with a loosely organized Confederate unit during the Civil War, he decided to try his luck out west as a miner. Failing to strike it rich, he soon returned to writing, becoming a reporter for the Virginia City (Nevada) Territorial Enterprise. It was during this period that Clemens began to use the riverboat leadsman's cry "mark twain" (two fathoms of water) as his pen name. In 1864, he moved to California, where he continued his career as a newspaperman and where he met and married Olivia Langdon, the daughter of a coal mining millionaire.

With the publication of "Jim Smiley and His Jumping Frog" in 1865, America began to take notice of Twain. His letters from a voyage to the Mediterranean and the Holy Land, which were syndicated in both San Francisco and New York newspapers and later collected and published as The Innocents Abroad *(1869), solidified his reputation as a satirist. He published short stories, newspaper columns, and essays, as well as longer fictions. His major works include:* Roughing It *(1872),* The Adventures of Tom Sawyer *(1876),* The Adventures of Huckleberry Finn *(1885),* A Connecticut Yankee in King Arthur's Court *(1889), and* The Tragedy of Puddn'head Wilson *(1894).*

---

*Italian-American Congressman from New York active in the Puerto Rican community

Late in his life, Twain reacted strongly to the resurgence of American imperialism. In "To the Person Sitting in Darkness," using the irony characteristic of his style, Twain exposes how Western nations justify their exploitative endeavors in South Africa, China, and the Philippines.

To the Person Sitting in Darkness

"Christmas will dawn in the United States over a people full of hope and aspiration and good cheer. Such a condition means contentment and happiness. The carping grumbler who may here and there go forth will find few to listen to him. The majority will wonder what is the matter with him and pass on."—*New York Tribune*, on Christmas Eve.

From *The Sun*, of New York:

"The purpose of this article is not to describe the terrible offences against humanity committed in the name of Politics in some of the most notorious East Side districts. *They could not be described, even verbally.* But it is the intention to let the great mass of more or less careless citizens of this beautiful metropolis of the New World get some conception of the havoc and ruin wrought to man, woman and child in the most densely populated and least known section of the city. Name, date and place can be supplied to those of little faith—or to any man who feels himself aggrieved. It is a plain statement of record and observation, written without license and without garnish.

"Imagine, if you can, a section of the city territory completely dominated by one man, without whose permission neither legitimate nor illegitimate business can be conducted; *where illegitimate business is encouraged and legitimate business discouraged;* where the respectable residents have to fasten their doors and windows summer nights and sit in their rooms with asphyxiating air and 100-degree temperature, rather than try to catch the faint whiff of breeze in their natural breathing places, the stoops of their homes; *where naked women dance by night in the streets, and unsexed men prowl like vultures through the darkness on 'business'* not only permitted but encouraged by the police; *where the education of infants begins with the knowledge of prostitution* and the training of little girls is training in the arts of Phyrne; where *American* girls brought up with the refinements of *American* homes are imported from small towns up-State, Massachusetts, Connecticut and New Jersey, and kept as virtually prisoners as if they were locked up behind jail bars until they have lost all semblance of womanhood; *where small boys are taught to solicit for the women of disorderly houses;* where there is an organized society of young men *whose sole business in life is to corrupt young girls and turn them over to bawdy houses;* where men walking with their wives along the street are openly insulted; *where children that have adult diseases are the chief patrons of the hospitals and dispensaries;* where it is the rule, rather than the exception, that *murder, rape, robbery and theft go unpunished*—in short where the Premium of the most awful forms of Vice is the Profit of the politicians."

The following news from China appeared in *The Sun*, of New York, on Christmas Eve. The italics are mine:

"The Rev. Mr. Ament, of the American Board of Foreign Missions, has returned from a trip which he made for the purpose of collecting indemnities for damages done by Boxers. *Everywhere he went he compelled the Chinese to pay.* He says that all his native Christians are now provided for. He had 700 of them under his charge, and 300 were killed. He has *collected* 300 *taels for each* of these murders, and has *compelled full payment for all the property belonging to Christians* that was destroyed. He also assessed *fines* amounting to THIRTEEN TIMES the amount of the indemnity. *This money will be used for the propagation of the Gospel.*

"Mr. Ament declares that the compensation he has collected is *moderate,* when compared with the amount secured by the Catholics, who demand, in addition to money, *head for head.* They collect 500 taels for each murder of a Catholic. In the Wenchiu country, 680 Catholics were killed, and for this the European Catholics here demand 750,000 strings of cash and 680 *heads.*

"In the course of a conversation, Mr. Ament referred to the attitude of the missionaries toward the Chinese. He said:

"'I deny emphatically that the missionaries are *vindictive,* that they *generally* looted, or that they have done anything *since* the siege that *the circumstances did not demand.* I criticise the Americans. *The soft hand of the Americans is not as good as the mailed fist of the Germans.* If you deal with the Chinese with a soft hand they will take advantage of it.'

"The statement that the French Government will return the loot taken by the French soldiers, is the source of the greatest amusement here. The French soldiers were more systematic looters than the Germans, and it is a fact that to-day *Catholic Christians,* carrying French flags and armed with modern guns, *are looting villages* in the Province of Chili."

By happy luck, we get all these glad tidings on Christmas Eve—just in time to enable us to celebrate the day with proper gaiety and enthusiasm. Our spirits soar, and we find we can even make jokes: Taels I win, Heads you lose.

Our Reverend Ament is the right man in the right place. What we want of our missionaries out there is, not that they shall merely represent in their acts and persons the grace and gentleness and charity and loving kindness of our religion, but that they shall also represent the American spirit. The oldest Americans are the Pawnees. Macallum's History says:

"When a white Boxer kills a Pawnee and destroys his property, the other Pawnees do not trouble to seek *him* out, they kill any white person that comes along; also, they make some white village pay deceased's heirs the full cash value of deceased, together with full cash value of the property destroyed; they also make the village pay, in addition, *thirteen times* the value of that property into a fund for the dissemination of the Pawnee religion, which they regard as the best of all religions for the softening and humanizing of the heart of man. It is their idea that it is only fair and right that the innocent should be made to suffer for the guilty, and that it is better that ninety and nine innocent should suffer than that one guilty person should escape."

Our Reverend Ament is justifiably jealous of those enterprising Catholics, who not only get big money for each lost convert, but get "head for head" besides. But he should soothe himself with the reflection that the entirety of their exactions are for their own pockets, whereas he, less selfishly, devotes only 300 taels per head to that service, and gives the whole vast thirteen repetitions of the property-indemnity to the service of propagating the Gospel. His magnanimity has won him the approval of his nation, and will get him a monument. Let him be content with these rewards. We all hold him dear for manfully defending his fellow missionaries from exaggerated charges which were beginning to distress us, but which his testimony has so considerably modified that we can now contemplate them without noticeable pain. For now we know that, even before the siege, the missionaries were not "generally" out looting, and that, "since the siege," they have acted quite handsomely, except when "circumstances" crowded them. I am arranging for the monument. Subscriptions for it can be sent to the American Board; designs for it can be sent to me. Designs must allegorically set forth the Thirteen Reduplications of the Indemnity, and the Object for which they were exacted; as Ornaments, the designs must exhibit 680 Heads, so disposed as to give a pleasing and pretty effect; for the Catholics have done nicely, and are entitled to notice in the monument. Mottoes may be suggested, if any shall be discovered that will satisfactorily cover the ground.

Mr. Ament's financial feat of squeezing a thirteen-fold indemnity out of the pauper peasants to square other people's offenses, thus condemning them and their women and innocent little children to inevitable starvation and lingering death, in order that the blood-money so acquired might be *"used for the propagation of the Gospel,"* does not flutter my serenity; although the act and the words, taken together, concrete a blasphemy so hideous and so colossal that, without doubt, its mate is not findable in the history of this or of any other age. Yet, if a layman had done that thing and justified it with those words, I should have shuddered, I know. Or, if I had done the thing and said the words myself—however, the thought is unthinkable, irreverent as some imperfectly informed people think me. Sometimes an ordained minister sets out to be blasphemous. When this happens, the layman is out of the running; he stands no chance.

We have Mr. Ament's impassioned assurance that the missionaries are not "vindictive." Let us hope and pray that they will never become so, but will remain in the almost morbidly fair and just and gentle temper which is affording so much satisfaction to their brother and champion to-day.

The following is from the *New York Tribune* of Christmas Eve. It comes from that journal's Tokio correspondent. It has a strange and impudent sound, but the Japanese are but partially civilized as yet. When they become wholly civilized they will not talk so:

"The missionary question, of course, occupies a foremost place in the discussion. It is now felt as essential that the Western Powers take cognizance of the sentiment here, that religious invasions of Oriental countries by powerful Western organizations are tantamount to filibustering expeditions, and should not only be discountenanced, but that stern measures should be adopted for their suppression. The feeling here is that the missionary organizations constitute a constant menace to peaceful international relations."

Shall we? That is, shall we go on conferring our Civilization upon the peoples that sit in darkness, or shall we give those poor things a rest? Shall we bang right ahead in our old-time, loud, pious way, and commit the new century to the game; or shall we sober up and sit down and think it over first? Would it not be prudent to get our Civilization-tools together, and see how much stock is left on hand in the way of Glass Beads and Theology, and Maxim Guns and Hymn Books, and Trade-Gin and Torches of Progress and Enlightenment (patent adjustable ones, good to fire villages with, upon occasion), and balance the books, and arrive at the profit and loss, so that we may intelligently decide whether to continue the business or sell out the property and start a new Civilization Scheme on the proceeds?

Extending the Blessings of Civilization to our Brother who Sits in Darkness has been a good trade and has paid well, on the whole; and there is money in it yet, if carefully worked—but not enough, in my judgment, to make any considerable risk advisable. The People that Sit in Darkness are getting to be too scarce—too scarce and too shy. And such darkness as is now left is really of but an indifferent quality, and not dark enough for the game. The most of those People that Sit in Darkness have been furnished with more light than was good for them or profitable for us. We have been injudicious.

The Blessings-of-Civilization Trust, wisely and cautiously administered, is a Daisy. There is more money in it, more territory, more sovereignty, and other kinds of emolument, than there is in any other game that is played. But Christendom has been playing it badly of late years, and must certainly suffer by it, in my opinion. She has been so eager to get every stake that appeared on the green cloth, that the People who Sit in Darkness have noticed it—they have noticed it, and have begun to show alarm. They have become suspicious of the Blessings of Civilization. More— they have begun to examine them. This is not well. The Blessings of Civilization are all right, and a good commercial property; there could not be a better, in a dim light. In the right kind of a light, and at a proper distance, with the goods a little out of focus, they furnish this desirable exhibit to the Gentlemen who Sit in Darkness:

LOVE,	LAW AND ORDER,
JUSTICE,	LIBERTY,
GENTLENESS,	EQUALITY,
CHRISTIANITY,	HONORABLE DEALING,
PROTECTION TO THE WEAK,	MERCY,
TEMPERANCE,	EDUCATION,

—and so on.

There. Is it good? Sir, it is pie. It will bring into camp any idiot that sits in darkness anywhere. But not if we adulterate it. It is proper to be emphatic upon that point. This brand is strictly for Export—apparently. *Apparently.* Privately and confidentially, it is nothing of the kind. Privately and confidentially, it is merely an outside cover, gay and pretty and attractive, displaying the special patterns of our Civilization which we reserve for Home Consumption, while *inside* the bale is the Actual Thing that the Customer Sitting in Darkness buys with his blood and tears and land and liberty. That Actual Thing is, indeed, Civilization, but it is only for Export. Is there a difference between the two brands? In some of the details, yes.

We all know that the Business is being ruined. The reason is not far to seek. It is because our Mr. McKinley, and Mr. Chamberlain, and the Kaiser, and the Czar and the French have been exporting the Actual Thing *with the outside cover left off.* This is bad for the Game. It shows that these new players of it are not sufficiently acquainted with it.

It is a distress to look on and note the mismoves, they are so strange and so awkward. Mr. Chamberlain manufactures a war out of materials so inadequate and so fanciful that they make the boxes grieve and the gallery laugh, and he tries hard to persuade himself that it isn't purely a private raid for cash, but has a sort of dim, vague respectability about it somewhere, if he could only find the spot; and that, by and by, he can scour the flag clean again after he has finished dragging it through the mud, and make it shine and flash in the vault of heaven once more as it had shone and flashed there a thousand years in the world's respect until he laid his unfaithful hand upon it. It is bad play—bad. For it exposes the Actual Thing to Them that Sit in Darkness, and they say: "What! Christian against Christian? And only for money? Is *this* a case of magnanimity, forbearance, love, gentleness, mercy, protection of the weak—this strange and over-showy onslaught of an elephant upon a nest of field-mice, on the pretext that the mice had squeaked an insolence at him—conduct which 'no self-respecting government could allow to pass unavenged?' as Mr. Chamberlain said. Was that a good pretext in a small case, when it had not been a good pretext in a large one?—for only recently Russia had affronted the elephant three times and survived alive and unsmitten. Is this Civilization and Progress? Is it something better than we already possess? These harryings and burnings and desert-makings in the Transvaal—is this an improvement on our darkness? Is it, perhaps, possible that there are two kinds of Civilization—one for home consumption and one for the heathen market?"

Then They that Sit in Darkness are troubled, and shake their heads; and they read this extract from a letter of a British private, recounting his exploits in one of Methuen's victories, some days before the affair of Magersfontein, and they are troubled again:

"We tore up the hill and into the intrenchments, and the Boers saw we had them; so they dropped their guns and went down on their knees and put up their hands clasped, and begged for mercy. And we gave it them—*with the long spoon.*"

The long spoon is the bayonet. See *Lloyd's Weekly,* London, of those days. The same number—and the same column—contained some quite unconscious satire in the form of shocked and bitter upbraidings of the Boers for their brutalities and inhumanities!

Next, to our heavy damage, the Kaiser went to playing the game without first mastering it. He lost a couple of missionaries in a riot in Shantung, and in his account he made an overcharge for them. China had to pay a hundred thousand dollars apiece for them, in money; twelve miles of territory, containing several millions of inhabitants and worth twenty million dollars; and to build a monument, and also a Christian church; whereas the people of China could have been depended upon to remember the missionaries without the help of these expensive memorials. This was all bad play. Bad, because it would not, and could not, and will not now or ever, deceive the Person Sitting in Darkness. He knows that it was an overcharge. He knows that a missionary is like any other man: he is worth merely what you can supply his place for, and no more. He is useful, but so is a doctor, so is a sheriff, so is an editor; but a just Emperor does not charge war-prices for such. A diligent, intelligent, but obscure missionary, and a diligent, intelligent country editor are worth much, and we know it; but they are not worth the earth. We esteem such an editor, and we are sorry to see him go; but, when he goes, we should consider twelve miles of territory, and a church, and a fortune, over-compensation for his loss. I mean, if he was a Chinese editor, and we had to settle for him. It is no proper figure for an editor or a missionary; one can get shop-worn kings for less. It was bad play on the Kaiser's part. It got this property, true; but it *produced the Chinese revolt,* the indignant uprising of China's traduced patriots, the Boxers. The results have been expensive to Germany, and to the other Disseminators of Progress and the Blessings of Civilization.

The Kaiser's claim was paid, yet it was bad play, for it could not fail to have an evil effect upon Persons Sitting in Darkness in China. They would muse upon the event, and be likely to say: "Civilization is gracious and beautiful, for such is its reputation; but can we afford it? There are rich Chinamen, perhaps they could afford it; but this tax is not laid upon them, it is laid upon the peasants of Shantung; it is they that must pay this mighty sum, and their wages are but four cents a day. Is this a better civilization than ours, and holier and higher and nobler? Is not this rapacity? Is not this extortion? Would Germany charge America two hundred thousand dollars for two missionaries, and shake the mailed fist in her face, and send warships, and send soldiers, and say: 'Seize twelve miles of territory, worth twenty millions of dollars, as additional pay for the missionaries, and a costly Christian church to remember them by?' And later would Germany say to her soldiers: 'March through America and slay, *giving no quarter*, make the German face there, as has been our Hun-face here, a terror for a thousand years; march through the Great Republic and slay, slay, slay, carving a road for our offended religion through its heart and bowels?' Would Germany do like this to America, to England, to France, to Russia? Or only to China the helpless—imitating the elephant's assault upon the field-mice? Had we better invest in this Civilization—this Civilization which called Napoleon a buccaneer for carrying off Venice's bronze horses, but which steals our ancient astronomical instruments from our walls, and goes looting like common bandits—that is, all the alien soldiers except America's; and (Americans again excepted) storms frightened villages and cables the result to glad journals at home every day: 'Chinese losses, 450 killed; ours, *one officer and two men wounded.* Shall proceed against neighboring village to-morrow, where a *massacre* is reported.' Can we afford Civilization?"

And, next, Russia must go and play the game injudiciously. She affronts England once or twice—with the Person Sitting in Darkness observing and noting; by moral assistance of France and Germany, she robs Japan of her hand-earned spoil, all swimming in Chinese blood—Port Arthur—with the Person again observing and noting; then she seizes Manchuria, raids its villages, and chokes its great river with the swollen corpses of countless massacred peasants—that astonished Person still observing and noting. And perhaps he is saying to himself: "It is yet *another* Civilized Power, with its banner of the Prince of Peace in one hand and its loot-basket and its butcher-knife in the other. Is there no salvation for us but to adopt Civilization and lift ourselves down to its level?"

And by and by comes America, and our Master of the Game plays it badly—plays it as Mr. Chamberlain was playing it in South Africa. It was a mistake to do that; also, it was one which was quite unlooked for in a Master who was playing it so well in Cuba. In Cuba, he was playing the usual and regular *American* game, and it was winning, for there is no way to beat it. The Master, contemplating Cuba, said: "Here is an oppressed and friendless little nation which is willing to fight to be free; we go partners, and put up the strength of seventy million sympathizers and the resources of the United States: play!" Nothing but Europe combined could call that hand: and Europe cannot combine on anything. There, in Cuba, he was following our great traditions in a way which made us very proud of him, and proud of the deep dissatisfaction which his play was provoking in Continental Europe. Moved by a high inspiration, he threw out those stirring words which proclaimed that forcible annexation would be "criminal aggression;" and in that utterance fired another "shot heard round the world." The memory of that fine saying will be outlived by the remembrance of no act of his but one—that he forgot it within the twelvemonth, and its honorable gospel along with it.

For, presently, came the Philippine temptation. It was strong; it was too strong, and he made that bad mistake: he played the European game, the Chamberlain game. It was a pity; it was a great pity, that error; that one grievous error, that irrevocable error. For it was the very place and time to play the American game again. And at no cost. Rich winnings to be gathered in, too; rich and permanent; indestructible; a fortune transmissible forever to the children of the flag. Not land, not money, not dominion—no, something worth many times more than that dross: our share, the spectacle of a nation of long harassed and persecuted slaves set free through our influence; our posterity's share, the golden memory of that fair deed. The game was in our hands. If it had been played according to the American rules, Dewey would have sailed away from Manila as soon as he had destroyed the Spanish fleet—after putting up a sign on shore guaranteeing foreign property and life against damage by the Filipinos, and warning the Powers that interference with the emancipated patriots would be regarded as an act unfriendly to the United States. The Powers cannot combine, in even a bad cause, and the sign would not have been molested.

Dewey could have gone about his affairs elsewhere, and left the competent Filipino army to starve out the little Spanish garrison and send it home, and the Filipino citizens to set up the form of government they might prefer, and deal with the friars and their doubtful acquisitions according to Filipino ideas of fairness and justice—ideas which have since been tested and found to be of as high an order as any that prevail in Europe or America.

But we played the Chamberlain game, and lost the chance to add another Cuba and another honorable deed to our good record.

The more we examine the mistake, the more clearly we perceive that it is going to be bad for the Business. The Person Sitting in Darkness is almost sure to say: "There is something curious about this—curious and unaccountable. There must be two Americas: one that sets the captive free, and one that takes a once-captive's new freedom away from him, and picks a quarrel with him with nothing to found it on; then kills him to get his land."

The truth is, the Person Sitting in Darkness *is* saying things like that; and for the sake of the Business we must persuade him to look at the Philippine matter in another and healthier way. We must arrange his opinions for him. I believe it can be done; for Mr. Chamberlain has arranged England's opinion of the South African matter, and done it most cleverly and successfully. He presented the facts—some of the facts—and showed those confiding people what the facts meant. He did it statistically, which is a good way. He used the formula: "Twice 2 are 14, and 2 from 9 leaves 35." Figures are effective; figures will convince the elect.

Now, my plan is a still bolder one than Mr. Chamberlain's, though apparently a copy of it. Let us be franker than Mr. Chamberlain; let us audaciously present the whole of the facts, shirking none, then explain them according to Mr. Chamberlain's formula. This daring truthfulness will astonish and dazzle the Person Sitting in Darkness, and he will take the Explanation down before his mental vision has had time to get back into focus. Let us say to him:

"Our case is simple. On the 1st of May, Dewey destroyed the Spanish fleet. This left the Archipelago in the hands of its proper and rightful owners, the Filipino nation.

Their army numbered 30,000 men, and they were competent to whip out or starve out the little Spanish garrison; then the people could set up a government of their own devising. Our traditions required that Dewey should now set up his warning sign, and go away. But the Master of the Game happened to think of another plan—the European plan. He acted upon it. This was, to send out an army—ostensibly to help the native patriots put the finishing touch upon their long and plucky struggle for independence, but really to take their land away from them and keep it. That is, in the interest of Progress and Civilization. The plan developed, stage by stage, and quite satisfactorily. We entered into a military alliance with the trusting Filipinos, and they hemmed in Manila on the land side, and by their valuable help the place, with its garrison of 8,000 or 10,000 Spaniards, was captured—a thing which we could not have accomplished unaided at that time. We got their help by—by ingenuity. We knew they were fighting for their independence, and that they had been at it for two years. We knew they supposed that we also were fighting in their worthy cause—just as we had helped the Cubans fight for Cuban independence—and we allowed them to go on thinking so. *Until Manila was ours and we could get along without them.* Then we showed our hand. Of course, they were surprised—that was natural; surprised and disappointed; disappointed and grieved. To them it looked un-American; uncharacteristic; foreign to our established traditions. And this was natural, too; for we were only playing the American Game in public—in private it was the European. It was neatly done, very neatly, and it bewildered them. They could not understand it; for we had been so friendly—so affectionate, even—with those simple-minded patriots! We, our own selves, had brought back out of exile their leader, their hero, their hope, their Washington—Aguinaldo; brought him in a warship, in high honor, under the sacred shelter and hospitality of the flag; brought him back and restored him to his people, and got their moving and eloquent gratitude for it. Yes, we had been so friendly to them, and had heartened them up in so many ways! We had lent them guns and ammunition; advised with them; exchanged pleasant courtesies with them; placed our sick and wounded in their kindly care; entrusted our Spanish prisoners to their humane and honest hands; fought shoulder to shoulder with them against 'the common enemy' (our own phrase); praised their courage, praised their gallantry, praised their mercifulness, praised their fine and honorable conduct; borrowed their trenches, borrowed strong positions which they had previously captured from the Spaniard; petted them, lied to them—officially proclaiming that our land and naval forces came to give them their freedom and displace the bad Spanish Government—fooled them, used them until we needed them no longer; then derided the sucked orange and threw it away. We kept the positions which we had beguiled them of; by and by, we moved a force forward and overlapped patriot ground—a clever thought, for we needed trouble, and this would produce it. A Filipino soldier, crossing the ground, where no one had a right to forbid him, was shot by our sentry. The badgered patriots resented this with arms, without waiting to know whether Aguinaldo, who was absent, would approve or not. Aguinaldo did not approve; but that availed nothing. What we wanted, in the interest of Progress and Civilization, was the Archipelago, unencumbered by patriots struggling for independence; and War was what we needed. We clinched our opportunity. It is Mr. Chamberlain's case over again—at least in its motive and intention; and we played the game as adroitly as he played it himself."

   At this point in our frank statement of fact to the Person Sitting in Darkness, we should throw in a little trade-taffy about the Blessings of Civilization—for a change, and for the refreshment of his spirit—then go on with our tale:

"We and the patriots having captured Manila, Spain's ownership of the Archipelago and her sovereignty over it were at an end—obliterated—annihilated—not a rag or shred of either remaining behind. It was then that we conceived the divinely humorous idea of *buying* both of these spectres from Spain! [It is quite safe to confess this to the Person Sitting in Darkness, since neither he nor an other sane person will believe it.] In buying those ghosts for twenty millions, we also contracted to take care of the friars and their accumulations. I think we also agreed to propagate leprosy and smallpox, but as to this there is doubt. But it is not important; persons afflicted with the friars do not mind other diseases.

"With our Treaty ratified, Manila subdued, and our Ghosts secured, we had no further use for Aguinaldo and the owners of the Archipelago. We forced a war, and we have been hunting America's guest and ally through the woods and swamps ever since."

At this point in the tale, it will be well to boast a little of our war-work and our heroisms in the field, so as to make our performance look as fine as England's in South Africa; but I believe it will not be best to emphasize this too much. We must be cautious. Of course, we must read the war-telegrams to the Person, in order to keep up our frankness; but we can throw an air of humorousness over them, and that will modify their grim eloquence a little, and their rather indiscreet exhibitions of gory exultation. Before reading to him the following display heads of the dispatches of November 18, 1900, it will be well to practice on them in private first, so as to get the right tang of lightness and gaiety into them:

"ADMINISTRATION WEARY OF PROTRACTED HOSTILITIES!"
"REAL WAR AHEAD FOR FILIPINO REBELS!"*
"WILL SHOW NO MERCY!"
"KITCHENER'S PLAN ADOPTED!"

Kitchener knows how to handle disagreeable people who are fighting for their homes and their liberties, and we must let on that we are merely imitating Kitchener, and have no national interest in the matter, further than to get ourselves admired by the Great Family of Nations, in which august company our Master of the Game has bought a place for us in the back row.

Of course, we must not venture to ignore our General MacArthur's reports—oh, why do they keep on printing those embarrassing things?—we must drop them trippingly from the tongue and take the chances:

"During the last ten months our losses have been 268 killed and 750 wounded; Filipino loss, *three thousand two hundred and twenty-seven killed,* and 694 wounded."

We must stand ready to grab the Person Sitting in Darkness, for he will swoon away at this confession, saying: "Good God, those 'niggers' spare their wounded, and the Americans massacre theirs!"

We must bring him to, and coax him and coddle him, and assure him that the ways of Providence are best, and that it would not become us to find fault with them; and then, to show him that we are only imitators, not originators, we must read the following passage from the letter of an American soldier-lad in the Philip-

---

*"Rebels!" Mumble that funny word—don't let the Person catch it distinctly.

pines to his mother, published in *Public Opinion,* of Decorah, Iowa, describing the finish of a victorious battle:

"WE NEVER LEFT ONE ALIVE. IF ONE WAS WOUNDED, WE WOULD RUN OUR BAYONETS THROUGH HIM."

Having now laid all the historical facts before the Person Sitting in Darkness, we should bring him to again, and explain them to him. We should say to him:

"They look doubtful, but in reality they are not. There have been lies; yes, but they were told in a good cause. We have been treacherous; but that was only in order that real good might come out of apparent evil. True, we have crushed a deceived and confiding people; we have turned against the weak and the friend-less who trusted us; we have stamped out a just and intelligent and well-ordered republic; we have stabbed an ally in the back and slapped the face of a guest; we have bought a Shadow from an enemy that hadn't it to sell; we have robbed a trust-ing friend of his land and his liberty; we have invited our clean young men to shoulder a discredited musket and do bandit's work under a flag which bandits have been accustomed to fear, not to follow; we have debauched America's honor and blackened her face before the world; but each detail was for the best. We know this. The Head of every State and Sovereignty in Christendom and ninety per cent. of every legislative body in Christendom, including our Congress and our fifty State Legislatures, are members not only of the church, but also of the Blessings-of-Civilization Trust. This world-girdling accumulation of trained morals, high principles, and justice, cannot do an unright thing, an unfair thing, an ungenerous thing, an unclean thing. It knows what it is about. Give yourself no uneasiness; it is all right."

Now then, that will convince the Person. You will see. It will restore the Business. Also, it will elect the Master of the Game to the vacant place in the Trinity of our national gods; and there on their high thrones the Three will sit, age after age, in the people's sight, each bearing the Emblem of his service: Washington, the Sword of the Liberator; Lincoln, the Slave's Broken Chains; the Master, the Chains Repaired.

It will give the Business a splendid new start. You will see.

Everything is prosperous, now; everything is just as we should wish it. We have got the Archipelago, and we shall never give it up. Also, we have every rea-son to hope that we shall have an opportunity before very long to slip out of our Congressional contract with Cuba and give her something better in the place of it. It is a rich country, and many of us are already beginning to see that the con-tract was a sentimental mistake. But now—right now—is the best time to do some profitable rehabilitating work—work that will set us up and make us comfortable, and discourage gossip. We cannot conceal from ourselves that, privately, we are a little troubled about our uniform. It is one of our prides; it is acquainted with honor; it is familiar with great deeds and noble; we love it, we revere it; and so this errand it is on makes us uneasy. And our flag—another pride of ours, our chiefest! We have worshipped it so; and when we have seen it in far lands—glimpsing it unexpectedly in that strange sky, waving its welcome and benedic-tion to us—we have caught our breath, and uncovered our heads, and couldn't speak, for a moment, for the thought of what it was to us and the great ideals it stood for. Indeed, we *must* do something about these things; we must not have the flag out there, and the uniform. They are not needed there; we can manage in some other way. England manages, as regards the uniform, and so can we. We have to send soldiers—we can't get out of that—but we can disguise them. It is the way England does in South Africa. Even Mr. Chamberlain himself takes pride in England's honorable uniform, and makes the army down there wear an ugly and odious and appropriate disguise, of yellow stuff such as quarantine flags are made of, and which are hoisted to warn the healthy away from unclean disease and repulsive death. This cloth is called khaki. We could adopt it. It is light, comfortable, grotesque, and deceives the enemy, for he cannot conceive of a soldier being concealed in it.

And as for a flag for the Philippine Province, it is easily managed. We can have a special one—our States do it: we can have just our usual flag, with the white stripes painted black and the stars replaced by the skull and cross-bones.

And we do not need that Civil Commission out there. Having no powers, it has to invent them, and that kind of work cannot be effectively done by just anybody; an expert is required. Mr. Croker can be spared. We do not want the United States represented there, but only the Game.

By help of these suggested amendments, Progress and Civilization in that country can have a boom, and it will take in the Persons who are Sitting in Darkness, and we can resume Business at the old stand.

BIENVENIDO NUQUI SANTOS

(1911-)

Bienvenido Santos, poet, essayist, novelist, short story writer, and educator, was born March 22, 1911, in Manila, Philippines. He became a citizen of the United States in 1970, after he was exiled from the Philippines following the serial publication of his controversial novel, The Praying Man.

Santos received his B.S. from the University of the Philippines in 1932 and an M.A. from the University of Illinois in 1942. He also pursued studies at Harvard (1945-1946) and the University of Iowa (1958-1961). In addition to teaching grade school and high school in the Philippines (1932-1941), he was a professor at Legazpi College, now Aquinas University (1946-1957), the University of Neuva Caceres (1961-1966, 1969-1970), and, since immigrating to the United States, at the University of Iowa (1966-1969, 1970-1973) and Wichita State University (1973-1982).

Santos has won a number of prestigious writing fellowships, as well as honorary degrees from several universities. He has also won numerous awards for his writing, including The Republic Cultural Heritage Award in Literature for a body of work, and the fiction award from New Letters *for his short story "Immigration Blues." While the figure of the exile often occupies a prominent place in his work, as it does in this story, Santos's work expresses hope for both his homeland and for its emigrant sons and daughters in America.*

His publications include: You Lovely People *(short stories, 1955),* The Wounded Stag *(poems, 1956),* Villa Magdalena *(novel, 1965),* The Day the Dancers Came *(essays, 1967),* Scent of Apples: A Collection of Stories *(1979),* The Praying Man *(novel, 1982), and* What the Hell for You Left Your Heart in San Francisco *(1987).*

IMMIGRATION BLUES

Through the window curtain, Alipio saw two women, one seemed twice as large as the other. In their summer dresses, they looked like the country girls he knew back home in the Philippines, who went around peddling rice cakes. The slim one could have passed for his late wife Seniang's sister whom he remembered only in pictures because she never made it to the United States. Before Seniang's death, the couple had arranged for her coming to San Francisco, filing all the required petition papers to facilitate the approval of her visa. The sister was always "almost ready, all the papers have been signed," but she never showed up. His wife had been ailing and when she died, he thought that hearing of her death would hasten her coming, but the wire he had sent her was neither returned nor acknowledged.

The knocking on the door was gentle. A little hard of hearing, Alipio was not sure it was indeed a knocking on the door, but it sounded different from the little noises that sometimes hummed in his ears in the daytime. It was not yet noon, but it must be warm outside in all that sunshine, otherwise those two women would be wearing spring dresses at the least. There were summer days in San Francisco that were cold like winter in the Midwest.

He limped painfully to the door. Until last month, he wore crutches. The entire year before that, he was bed-ridden, but he had to force himself to walk about in the house after coming from the hospital. After Seniang's death, everything had gone to pieces. It was one bust after another, he complained to the few friends who came to visit him.

"Seniang was my good luck. When God decided to take her, I had nothing but bad luck," he said.

Not long after Seniang's death, he was in a car accident. For almost a year he was in the hospital. The doctors were not sure he was going to walk again. He told them it was God's wish. As it was he was thankful he was still alive. It had been a horrible accident.

The case dragged on in court. His lawyer didn't seem too good about car accidents. He was an expert immigration lawyer, but he was a friend. As it turned out, Alipio lost the full privileges and benefits coming to him in another two years if he had not been hospitalized and had continued working until his official retirement.

However, he was well provided. He didn't spend a cent for doctor and medicine and hospital bills. Now there was the prospect of a few thousand dollars compensation. After deducting his lawyer's fees it would still be something to live on. He had social security benefits and a partial retirement pension. Not too bad, really. Besides, now he could walk a little although he still limped and had to move about with extreme care.

When he opened the door, the fat woman said, "Mr. Palma? Alipio Palma?" Her intonation sounded like the beginning of a familiar song.

"Yes," he said. "Come in, come on in." He had not talked to anyone the whole week. His telephone had not rung all that time, not even a wrong number, and there was nobody he wanted to talk to. The little noises in his ears had somehow kept him company. Radio and television sounds lulled him to sleep.

The thin one was completely out of sight as she stood behind the big one who was doing the talking. "I'm sorry, I should have phoned you first, but we were in a hurry."

"The house is a mess," Alipio said truthfully. Had he been imagining things? He remembered seeing two women on the porch. There was another one, who looked like Seniang's sister. The woman said "we," and just then the other one materialized, close behind the big one, who walked in with the assurance of a social worker, about to do him a favor.

"Sit down. Sit down. Anywhere," Alipio said as he led the two women through the dining room, past a huge rectangular table in the center. It was bare except for a vase of plastic flowers as centerpiece. He passed his hand over his face, a mannerism which Seniang hated. Like you have a hang-over, she chided him, and you can't see straight.

A TV set stood close to a wall in the small living room crowded with an assortment of chairs and tables. An aquarium crowded the mantlepiece of a fake fireplace. A lighted bulb inside the tank showed many colored fish swimming about in a haze of fish food. Some of it lay scattered on the edge of the shelf. The carpet underneath was sodden black. Old magazines and tabloids lay just about everywhere.

"Sorry to bother you like this," the fat one said as she plunked herself down on the nearest chair, which sagged to the floor under her weight. The thin one chose the end of the sofa away from the TV set.

"I was just preparing my lunch. I know it's quite early, but I had nothing to do," Alipio said, pushing down with both hands the seat of the cushioned chair near a moveable partition, which separated the living room from the dining room. "It's painful just trying to sit down. I'm not too well yet," he added as he finally made it.

"I hope we're not really bothering you," the fat one said. The other had not said a word. She looked pale and sick. Maybe she was hungry or cold.

"How's it outside?" Alipio asked. "I've not been out all day." Whenever he felt like it, he dragged a chair to the porch and sat there, watching the construction going on across the street and smiling at the people passing by who happened to look his way. Some smiled back and mumbled something like a greeting or a comment on the beauty of the day. He stayed on until he got bored or it became colder than he could stand.

"It's fine. It's fine outside. Just like Baguio," the fat one said.

"You know Baguio? I was born near there."

"We're sisters."

Alipio was thinking, won't the other one speak at all?

"I'm Mrs. Antonieta Zafra, the wife of Carlito. I believe you know him. He says you're friends. In Salinas back in the thirties. He used to be a cook at the Marina."

"Carlito, yes, yes, Carlito Zafra. We bummed together. We come from Ilocos. Where you from?"

"Aklan. My sister and I speak Cebuano."

"Oh, she speak? You, you don't speak Ilocano?"

"Not much. Carlito and I talk in English. Except when he's real mad, like when his cock don't fight or when he lose, then he speaks Ilocano. Cuss words. I've learned them myself. Some, anyway."

"Yes. Carlito. He love cockfighting. How's he?"

"Retired like you. We're now in Fresno. On a farm. He raises chickens and hogs. I do some sewing in town when I can. My sister here is Monica. She's older than me. Never been married."

Monica smiled at the old man, her face in anguish, as if near to tears.

"Carlito. He got some fighting cocks, I bet."

"Not anymore. But he talks a lot about cockfighting. But nobody, not even the pinoys and the Chicanos are interested in it." Mrs. Zafra appeared pleased at the state of things on her home front.

"I remember. Carlito once promoted a cockfight. Everything was ready, but the roosters won't fight. Poor man, he did everything to make them fight like having them peck on each other's necks and so forth. They were so tame, so friendly with each other. Only thing they didn't do is embrace." Alipio laughed, showing a set of perfectly white and even teeth, obviously dentures.

"He hasn't told me about that, I'll remind him."

"Do that. Where's he? Why isn't he with you?"

"We didn't know we'd find you. While visiting some friends this morning, we learned you live here." Mrs. Zafra was beaming on him.

"I've always lived here, but I got few friends now. So you're Mrs. Carlito. I thought he's dead already. I never hear from him. We're old now. We're old already when we got our citizenship papers right after Japanese surrender. So you and him. Good for Carlito."

"I heard about your accident."

"After Seniang died. She was not yet sixty, but she had this heart trouble. I took care of her." Alipio seemed to have forgotten his visitors. He sat there staring at the fish in the aquarium, his ears perked as though waiting for some sound, like the breaking of the surf not far away, or the TV set suddenly turned on.

The sisters looked at each other. Monica was fidgeting, her eyes seemed to say, let's go, let's get out of here.

"Did you hear that?" the old man said.

Monica turned to her sister, her eyes wild with panic. Mrs. Zafra leaned forward, her hand touching the edge of the chair where Alipio sat, and asked gently, "Hear what?"

"The waves. Listen. They're just outside, you know. The breakers have a nice sound like at home in the Philippines. We lived in a coastal town. Like here, I always tell Seniang, across that ocean is the Philippines, we're not far from home."

"But you're alone now. It's not good to be alone," Mrs. Zafra said.

"At night I hear better. I can see the Pacific Ocean from my bedroom. It sends me to sleep. I sleep soundly like I got no debts. I can sleep all day, too, but that's bad. So I walk. I walk much before. I go out there. I let the breakers touch me. It's nice the touch. Seniang always scold me, she says I'll be catching cold, but I don't catch cold, she catch the cold all the time."

"You must miss her," Mrs. Zafra said. Monica was staring at her hands on her lap while the sister talked. Monica's skin was transparent and the veins showed on the back of her hands like trapped eels.

"I take care of Seniang. I work all day and leave her here alone. When I come home, she's smiling. She's wearing my jacket and my slippers. You look funny, I says, why do you wear my things, you're lost inside them. She chuckles, you keep me warm all day, she says, like you're here, I smell you. Oh, that Seniang. You see, we have no baby. If we have a baby . . ."

"I think you and Carlito have the same fate. We have no baby also."

"God dictates," Alipio said, making an effort to stand. In a miraculous surge of power, Monica rushed to him and helped him up. She seemed astonished and embarrassed at what she had done.

"Thank you," said Alipio. "I have crutches, but I don't want no crutches. They tickle me, they hurt me, too." He watched Monica go back to her seat.

"You need help better than crutches," Mrs. Zafra said.

"God helps," Alipio said, walking towards the kitchen as if expecting to find the Almighty there.

Mrs. Zafra followed him. "What are you preparing?" she asked.

"Let's have lunch," he said, "I'm hungry. I hope you are also."

"We'll help you," Mrs. Zafra said, turning back to where Monica sat staring at her hands again and listening perhaps for the sound of the sea. She had not noticed nor heard her sister when she called, "Monica!"

The second time she heard her. Monica stood up and went to the kitchen.

"There's nothing to prepare," Alipio was saying, as he opened the refrigerator. "What you want to eat? Me, I don't eat bread so I got no bread. I eat rice. I was just opening a can of sardines when you come. I like sardines with lotsa tomato sauce, it's great with hot rice."

"Don't you cook the sardines?" Mrs. Zafra asked. "Monica will cook it for you if you want."

"No! If you cook sardines, it taste bad. Better uncooked. Besides it gets cooked on top of the hot rice. Mix with onions, chopped nice. Raw not cooked. You like it?"

"Monica loves raw onions, don't you, Sis?"

"Yes," Monica said in a low voice.

"Your sister, she is well?" Alipio said, glancing towards Monica.

Mrs. Zafra gave her sister an angry look.

"I'm okay," Monica said, a bit louder this time.

"She's not sick," Mrs. Zafra said, "But she's shy. Her own shadow frightens her. I tell you, this sister of mine, she got problems."

"Oh?" Alipio exclaimed. He had been listening quite attentively.

"I eat onions, raw," Monica said. "Sardines, too, I like uncooked."

Her sister smiled. "What do you say, I run out for some groceries," she said, going back to the living room to get her bag.

"Thanks. But no need for you to do that. I got lotsa food, canned food. Only thing I haven't got is bread," Alipio said.

"I eat rice, too," Monica said.

Alipio reached up to open the cabinet. It was stacked full of canned food: corn beef, pork and beans, vienna sausage, tuna, crab meat, shrimp, chow mein, imitation noodles, and, of course, sardines, in green and yellow labels.

"The yellow ones with mustard sauce, not tomato," he explained.

"All I need is a cup of coffee," Mrs. Zafra said, throwing her handbag back on the chair in the living room.

Alipio opened two drawers near the refrigerator. "Look," he said as Mrs. Zafra came running back to the kitchen. "I got more food to last me . . . a long time."

The sisters gaped at the bags of rice, macaroni, spaghetti sticks, sugar, dried shrimps wrapped in cellophane, bottles of soy sauce and fish sauce, vinegar, ketchup, instant coffee, and more cans of sardines.

The sight of all that foodstuff seemed to have enlivened the old man. After all, food meant life, continuing sustenance, source of energy and health. "Now look here," he said, turning briskly now to the refrigerator, which he opened, the sudden light touching his face with a glow that erased years from his eyes. With a jerk he pulled open the large freezer, cramped full of meats. "Mostly lamb chops," he said, adding, "I like lamb chops."

"Carlito, he hates lamb chops," Mrs. Zafra said.

"I like lamb chops," Monica said, still wild eyed, but now a bit of color tinted her cheeks. "Why do you have so much food?" she asked.

Alipio looked at her before answering. He thought she looked younger than Mrs. Zafra. "You see," he said, closing the refrigerator. He was beginning to chill. "I watch the papers for bargain sales. I can still drive the car when I feel right. It's only now my legs bothering me. So. I buy all I can. Save me many trips. Money, too."

Later they sat around the enormous table in the dining room. Monica shared half a plate of boiling rice topped with a sardine with Alipio. He showed her how to place the sardine on top, pressing it a little and pouring spoonfuls of tomato juice over it.

Mrs. Zafra had coffee and settled for a small can of vienna sausage and a little rice. She sipped her coffee meditatively.

"This is good coffee," she said. "I remember how we used to hoard Hills Bros. coffee at . . . at the convent. The sisters were quite selfish about it."

"Antonieta was a nun, a sister of mercy," Monica said.

"What?" Alipio exclaimed, pointing a finger at her for no apparent reason, an involuntary gesture of surprise.

"Yes, I was," Mrs. Zafra admitted. "When I married, I had been out of the order for more than a year, yes, in California, at St. Mary's."

"You didn't . . ." Alipio began.

"Of course not," she interrupted him. "If you mean did I leave the order to marry Carlito. Oh, no. He was already an old man when I met him."

"I see. We used to joke him because he didn't like the girls too much. He prefer the cocks." The memory delighted him so much, he reared his head up as he laughed, covering his mouth hastily, but too late. Some of the tomato soaked grains had already spilled out on his plate and on the table in front of him.

Monica looked pleased as she gathered carefully some of the grains on the table.

"He hasn't changed," Mrs. Zafra said vaguely. "It was me who wanted to marry him."

"You? After being a nun, you wanted to marry . . . Carlito? But why Carlito?" Alipio seemed to have forgotten for the moment that he was still eating. The steam from the rice touched his face till it glistened darkly. He was staring at Mrs. Zafra as he breathed in the aroma without savoring it.

"It's a long story," Mrs. Zafra said. She stabbed a chunky sausage and brought it to her mouth. She looked pensive as she chewed on it.

"When did this happen?"

"Five, six years ago. Six years ago, almost."

"That long?"

"She had to marry him," Monica said blandly.

"What?" Alipio shouted, visibly disturbed. There was the sound of dentures grating in his mouth. He passed a hand over his face. "Carlito done that to you?"

The coffee spilled a little as Mrs. Zafra put the cup down. "Why no," she said. "What are you thinking of?"

Before he could answer, Monica spoke in the same tone of voice, low, unexcited, saying, "He thinks Carlito got you pregnant, that's what."

"Carlito?" She turned to Monica in disbelief. "Why, Alipio knows Carlito," she said. Monica shrugged her shoulders. "Why don't you tell him why?" she suggested.

"As I said, it's a long story, but I shall make it short," Mrs. Zafra began. She took a sip from her cup and continued, "After leaving the order, I couldn't find a job. I was interested in social work, but I didn't know anybody who could help me."

As she paused, Alipio said, "What the heck does Carlito know about social work?"

"Let me continue," Mrs. Zafra said.

She still had a little money, from home, and she was not too worried about being jobless. But there was the question of her status as an alien. Once out of the community, she was no longer entitled to stay in the United States, let alone secure employment. The immigration office began to hound her, as it did other Filipinos in similar predicaments. They were a pitiful lot. Some hid in the apartments of friends like criminals running away from the law. Of course, they were law breakers. Those with transportation money returned home, which they hated to do. At home they would be forced to invent stories, tell lies to explain away why they returned so soon. All their lives they had to learn how to cope with the stigma of failure in a foreign land. They were losers and no longer fit for anything useful. The more sensitive and weak lost their minds and had to be committed to insane asylums. Others became neurotic, antisocial, depressed in mind and spirit. Some turned to crime. Or just folded up, in a manner of speaking. It was a nightmare. Antonieta didn't want to go back to the Philippines under those circumstances. She would have had to be very convincing to prove that she was not thrown out of the order for immoral reasons. Just when she seemed to have reached the breaking point, she recalled incidents in which women in her situation married American citizens and, automatically, became entitled to permanent residency with an option to become U.S. citizens after five years. At first, she thought the idea of such a marriage was hideous, unspeakable. Perhaps other foreign women in similar situations, could do it—and have done it—but not Philippine girls. But what was so special about Philippine girls? Nothing really, but their upbringing was such that to place themselves in a situation where they had to tell a man that all they wanted was a marriage for convenience, was degrading, an unbearable shame. A form of self-destruction. Mortal sin. Better repatriation. A thousand times better.

When an immigration officer finally caught up with her, he proved to be very understanding and quite a gentleman. Yet he was firm. He was young, maybe of Italian descent, and looked like a salesman for a well-known company in the islands that dealt in farm equipment.

"I'm giving you one week," he said. "You have already overstayed by several months. If in one week's time, you haven't left yet, you might have to wait in jail for deportation proceedings."

She cried, oh, how she cried. She wished she had not left the order, no, not really. She had no regrets about leaving up to this point. Life in the convent had turned sour on her. She despised the sisters and the system, which she found tyrannical, inhuman. In her own way, she had a long series of talks with God and God had approved of the step she had taken. She was not going back to the order. Anyhow, even if she did, she would not be taken back. To jail then?

But why not marry an American citizen? In one week's time? How? Accost the first likely man and say, "You look like an American citizen. If you are, indeed, and you have the necessary papers to prove it, will you marry me? I want to remain in this country."

All week she talked to God. It was the same God she had worshipped and feared all her life. Now they were *palsy walsy,* on the best of terms. As she brooded over her misfortune, He brooded with her, sympathized with her, and finally advised her to go look for an elderly Filipino who was an American citizen, and tell him the truth of the matter. Tell him that if he wished, it could be a marriage in name only. For his trouble, she would be willing to pay. How much? If it's a bit too much, could she pay on the installment plan? If he wished . . . otherwise . . . Meanwhile He would look the other way.

How she found Carlito Zafra was another story, a much longer story, more confused and confusing. It was like a miracle, though. Her friend God could not have sent her to a better instrument to satisfy her need. That was not expressed well, but it amounted to that, a need. Carlito was an instrument necessary for her good. And, as it turned out, a not too unwilling instrument.

"We were married the day before the week was over," Mrs. Zafra said. "And I've been in this country ever since. And no regrets."

They lived well and simply, a country life. True, they were childless, but both of them were helping relatives in the Philippines, sending them money and goods marked Made in U.S.A.

"Lately, however, some of the goods we've been sending do not arrive intact. Do you know that some of the good quality material we send never reach our relatives? It's frustrating."

"We got lotsa thieves between here and there," Alipio said, but his mind seemed to be on something else.

"And I was able to send for Monica. From the snapshots she sent us she seemed to be getting thinner and more sickly, teaching in the barrio. And she wanted so much to come here."

"Seniang was like you also, hiding from immigration. I thank God for her," Alipio told Mrs. Zafra in such a low voice he could hardly be heard.

The sisters pretended they didn't know, but they knew practically everything about him. Alipio appeared tired, pensive, and eager to talk so they listened.

"She went to my apartment and said, without any hesitation, marry me and I'll take care of you. She was thin then and I thought what she said was funny, the others had been matching us, you know, but I was not really interested. I believe marriage mean children. And if you cannot produce children, why get married? Besides, I had ugly experiences, bad moments. When I first arrived in the States, here in Frisco, I was young and there were lotsa blondies hanging around on Kearny Street. It was easy. But I wanted a family and they didn't. None of 'em. So what the heck, I said."

Alipio realized that Seniang was not joking. She had to get married to an American citizen otherwise she would be deported. At that time, Alipio was beginning to feel the disadvantage of living alone. There was too much time in his hands. How he hated himself for some of the things he did. He believed that if he was married, he would be more sensible with his time and his money. He would be happier and live long. So when Seniang showed that she was serious, he agreed to marry her. It was not to be in name only. He wanted a woman. He liked her so much he would have proposed himself had he suspected that he had a chance. She was hard working, decent, and in those days, rather slim.

"Like Monica," he said.

"Oh, I'm thin," Monica protested, blushing deeply, "I'm all bones."

"Monica is my only sister. We have no brother," Mrs. Zafra said, adding more items to her sister's vita.

"Look," Monica said, "I finished everything on my plate. I've never tasted sardines this good. Especially the way you eat them. I'm afraid I've eaten up your lunch. This is my first full meal. And I thought I've lost my appetite already."

The words came out in a rush. It seemed she didn't want to stop and she paused only because she didn't know what else to say. She moved about, gaily and at ease, perfectly at home. Alipio watched her with a bemused look in his face as she gathered the dishes and brought them to the kitchen sink. When Alipio heard the water running, he stood up, without much effort this time, and walked to her saying, "Don't bother. I got all the time to do that. You got to leave me something to do. Come, perhaps your sister wants another cup of coffee."

Mrs. Zafra had not moved from her seat. She was watching the two argue about the dishes. When she heard Alipio mention coffee, she said, "No, no more, thanks. I've drunk enough to keep me awake all week."

"Well, I'm going to wash them myself later," Monica was saying as she walked back to the table, Alipio close behind her.

"You're an excellent host, Alipio." Mrs. Zafra spoke in a tone like a reading from a citation on a certificate of merit or something. "And to two complete strangers at that. You're a good man."

"But you're not strangers. Carlito is my friend. We were young together in this country. And that's something, you know. There are lotsa guys like us here. Old-timers, o.t.'s, they call us. Permanent residents, U.S. Citizens. We all gonna be buried here." He appeared to be thinking deeply as he added, "But what's wrong about that?"

The sisters ignored the question. The old man was talking to himself.

"What's wrong is to be dishonest. Earn a living with both hands, not afraid of any kind of work, that's the best good. No other way. Yes, everything for convenience, why not? That's frankly honest. No pretend. Love comes in the afterwards. When it comes. If it comes."

Mrs. Zafra chuckled, saying, "Ah, you're a romantic, Alipio. I must ask Carlito about you. You seem to know so much about him. I bet you were quite a . . ." she paused because what she wanted to say was "rooster," but she might give the impression of over-familiarity.

Alipio interrupted her, saying, "Ask him, he will say yes, I'm a romantic." His voice held a vibrance that was a surprise and a revelation to the visitors. He gestured as he talked, puckering his mouth every now and then, obviously to keep his dentures from slipping out. "What do you think? We were young, why not? We wowed 'em with our gallantry, with our cooking. Boy those dames never seen anything like us. Also, we were fools, most of us, anyway. Fools on fire."

Mrs. Zafra clapped her hands. Monica was smiling.

"Ah, but that fire's gone. Only the fool's left now," Alipio said, weakly. His voice was low and he looked tired as he passed both hands across his face. Then he raised his head. The listening look came back to his face. When he spoke, his voice shook a little.

"Many times I wonder where are the others. Where are you? Speak to me. And I think they're wondering the same, asking the same, so I say, I'm here, your friend Alipio Palma, my leg is broken, the wife she's dead, but I'm okay. Are you okay also? The dead they can hear even if they don't answer. The alive don't answer. But I know. I feel. Some okay, some not. They old now, all of us, who were very young. All over the United States of America. All over the world . . ."

Abruptly, he turned to Mrs. Zafra, saying, "So. You and Carlito. But Carlito, he never had fire."

"How true, how very very true," Mrs. Zafra laughed. "It would burn him. Can't stand it. Not Carlito. But he's a good man, I can tell you that."

"No question. Dabest," Alipio conceded.

Monica remained silent, but her eyes followed every move Alipio made, straying no further than the reach of his arms as he gestured to help make clear the intensity of his feeling.

"I'm sure you still got some of that fire," Mrs. Zafra said.

Monica gasped, but she recovered quickly. Again a rush of words came from her lips as if they had been there all the time waiting for what her sister had said that touched off the torrent of words. Her eyes shone as in a fever as she talked.

"I don't know Carlito very well. I've not been with them very long, but from what you say, from the way you talk, from what I see, the two of you are very different."

"Oh, maybe not," Alipio said, trying to protest, but Monica went on.

"You have strength, Mr. Palma. Strength of character. Strength in your belief in God. I admire that in a man, in a human being. Look at you. Alone. This huge table. Don't you find it too big sometimes?" Monica paused perhaps to allow her meaning to sink into Alipio's consciousness, as she fixed her eyes on him.

"No, not really. I don't eat at this table. I eat in the kitchen," Alipio said.

Mrs. Zafra was going to say something, but she held back. Monica was talking again.

"But it must be hard, that you cannot deny. Living from day to day. Alone. On what? Memories? Cabinets and a refrigerator full of food? I repeat, I admire you, sir. You've found your place. You're home safe. And at peace." She paused again this time to sweep back the strand of hair that had fallen on her brow.

Alipio had a drugged look. He seemed to have lost the drift of her speech. What was she talking about? Groceries? Baseball? He was going to say, you like baseball also? You like tuna? I have all kinds of fish. Get them at bargain price. But, obviously, it was not the proper thing to say.

"Well, I guess, one gets used to anything. Even loneliness," Monica said in a listless, dispirited tone, all the fever in her voice gone.

"God dictates," Alipio said, feeling he had found his way again and he was now on the right track. What a girl. If she had only a little more flesh. And color.

Monica leaned back on her chair, exhausted. Mrs. Zafra was staring at her in disbelief, in grievous disappointment. Her eyes seemed to say, what happened, you were going great, what suddenly hit you that you had to stop, give up, defeated? Monica shook her head in a gesture that quite clearly said, no, I can't do it, I can't anymore, I give up.

Their eyes kept up a show, a deaf-mute dialogue. Mrs. Zafra: Just when everything was going on fine, you quit. We've reached this far and you quit. I could have done it my way, directly, honestly. Not that what you were doing was dishonest, you were great, and now look at that dumb expression in your eyes. Monica: I can't. I can't anymore. But I tried. It's too much.

"How long have you been in the States?" Alipio asked Monica.

"For almost a year now!" Mrs. Zafra screamed and Alipio was visibly shaken, but she didn't care. This was the right moment. She would take it from here whether Monica went along with her or not. She was going to do it her way. "How long exactly, let's see. Moni, when did you get your last extension?"

"Extension?" Alipio repeated the word. It had such a familiar ring like "visa" or "social security," it broke into his consciousness like a touch from Seniang's fingers. It was quite intimate. "You mean . . ."

"That's right. She's here as a temporary visitor. As a matter of fact, she came on a tourist visa. Carlito and I sponsored her coming, filed all the necessary papers, and everything would have been fine, but she couldn't wait. She had to come here as a tourist. Now she's in trouble."

"What trouble?" Alipio asked.

"She has to go back to the Philippines. She can't stay here any longer."

"I have only two days left," Monica said, her head in her hands. "And I don't want to go back."

Alipio glanced at the wall clock. It was past three. They had been talking for hours. It was visas right from the start. Marriages. The long years and the o.t.'s. Now it was visas again. Were his ears playing a game? They might as well as they did sometimes, but his eyes surely were not. He could see this woman very plainly, sobbing on the table. Boy, she was in big trouble. Visas. Immigration. Boy, oh, boy! He knew all about that. His gleaming dentures showed a crooked smile. He turned to Mrs. Zafra.

"Did you come here," he began, but Mrs. Zafra interrupted him.

"Yes, Alipio. Forgive us. As soon as we arrived, I wanted to tell you without much talk, I wanted to say, 'I must tell you why we're here. I've heard about you. Not only from Carlito, but from other Filipinos who know you, how you're living here in San Francisco alone, a widower, and we heard of the accident, your stay in the hospital, when you were released, everything. Here's my sister, a teacher in the Philippines, never married, worried to death because she's being deported unless something turned up like she could marry a U.S. citizen, like I did, like your late wife Seniang, like many others have done, are doing in this exact moment, who can say? Now look at her, she's good, religious, any arrangement you wish, she'd accept it.' But I didn't have a chance to say it. You welcomed us like old friends, relatives. Later every time I began to say something about why we came, she interrupted me. I was afraid she had changed her mind and then she began to talk, then stopped without finishing what she really wanted to say, that is, why we came to see you, and so forth."

"No, no!" Monica cried, raising her head, her eyes red from weeping, her face damp with tears. "You're such a good man. We couldn't do this to you. We're wrong. We started wrong. We should've been more honest, but I was ashamed. I was afraid. Let's go! let's go!"

"Where you going?" Alipio asked.

"Anywhere," Monica answered. "Forgive us. Forgive me, Mister. Alipio, please."

"What's to forgive? Don't go. We have dinner. But first, let's have *merienda.* I take *merienda.* You do also, don't you? And I don't mean snacks like the Americans."

The sisters exchanged glances, their eyes chattering away.

Alipio chuckled. He wanted to say, talk of lightning striking same fellow twice, but thought better of it. A bad thing to say. Seniang was not lightning. At times only. Mostly his fault. And this girl Monica . . . Moni? Nice name also. How can this one be lightning?

Mrs. Zafra picked up her purse and before anyone could stop her, she was opening the door. "Where's the nearest grocery store around here?" she asked, but she didn't wait for an answer.

"Come back, come back here, we got lotsa food," Alipio called after her, but he might just as well have been calling the Pacific Ocean.

Mrs. Zafra took time although a supermarket was only a few blocks away. When she returned, her arms were full of groceries in paper bags. Alipio and Monica met her on the porch.

"Comusta?" she asked, speaking in the dialect for the first time as Monica relieved her of her load. The one word question seemed to mean much more than "How are you?" or "How has it been?"

Alipio replied in English. "God dictates," he said, his dentures sounding faintly as he smacked his lips, but he was not looking at the foodstuff in the paper bags Monica was carrying. His eyes were on her legs, in the direction she was taking. She knew where the kitchen was, of course. He just wanted to be sure she won't lose her way. Like him. On his way to the kitchen, sometimes he found himself in the bedroom. Lotsa things happened to men his age.

Part II

ACTIONS OF MEMORY: MAKING ETHNIC & RACIAL IDENTITIES

The identities to which Americans cling are complex: variable, multiple; at the same time historically determined and radically free. The mostly British inhabitants of North America reconceived themselves as "Americans" between the political revolution of 1776 and the presidency of Andrew Jackson (1829–1837), absorbing French, Dutch, Spanish, and German cultural elements. These European settlers and later immigrants retained or brought with them bits of cultural and national history from England and Ireland, France and Italy, Germany and Russia. As time distanced them from these various pasts, they forgot or abandoned the official history of their pre-American identity, the documents and officially sanctioned narratives of their place in the world, including, in many cases, the context of their emigration/immigration. The immigrants fled not only oppressive states and failed economies; they also left behind aspects of their identity. Their official history lost or denied, what remained was memory, the unofficial narrative of where they came from and later who they had become. They created, out of memory, a narrative of their displacement and acculturation to the new land that was as much fantasy as fact. No official history supported the memory that *we were all kings in the old country* that became a part of Irish-American cultural memory, for example.

For Native Americans, Asian Americans, and African Americans, the function of memory in creating identity had to counteract the negative official stories of who they were: savage and dependent Indians, foolish and incompetent Negroes, devious and inscrutable Orientals. Their struggle for identity was waged with a tighter grip on the past, for the "old country" of memory often provided a more satisfactory sense of self than did their American experience.

1

MEMORY AND
HISTORY

In *Memory and History* the readings, documents, and artifacts explore the gaps between official history and cultural memory, gaps filled by the creative imaginations of the writers. Robert Hayden in his poem "Runagate, Runagate" gives voice to the silent image of the escaped slave while David Henry Hwang's play *The Dance and the Railroad* re-envisions the Chinese immigrant workers who built the transcontinental railroad. Hisaye Yamamoto's story "The Legend of Miss Sasagawara" tells the tale of a sensitive woman in a concentration camp for Japanese-Americans during World War II. Lorna Dee Cervantes's "Poema para los Californios Muertos" remembers the almost forgotten *Californios*—the Spanish and Mexican inhabitants of *Alta California* after the Mexican-American War made them residents of the United States. All of the readings in this section direct our attention to the historical realities of racial and ethnic conflict. Struggle with political and economic forces helps to define the self-concepts of American ethnic and racial communities; remembering those struggles is an important element in maintaining ethnic identity.

ROBERT HAYDEN
(1913-1980)

Robert Hayden was born on August 4, 1913, in Detroit, Michigan. Originally named Asa Bundy Sheffey, his name was changed by his foster parents to Robert Earl Hayden. Hayden was raised in the Detroit area and attended Detroit City College, now Wayne State University. From 1936 to 1940, he researched black history in the Detroit area for the Federal Writers' Project. He later attended the University of Michigan, where he studied with W. H. Auden and received an M.A. in 1944. In both 1938 and 1942 he won the Hopwood Poetry Award. His first volume of poetry, Heart Shape in the Dust, *was published in 1940. After teaching at Michigan for two years, he moved to Nashville in 1946 and joined the faculty at Fisk University. In 1954, he traveled to Mexico on a Ford Foundation fellowship. He returned to Michigan and taught there until his death in February of 1980. During his career, he published another eight collections of poetry and a volume of prose, and he edited three anthologies of African-American literature. Hayden was a member of the American Academy and Institute of Arts and Letters and received many awards for his poetry, including the Prize for Poetry of the First World Festival of Negro Arts, a Michigan Arts Foundation Award, and a Fellowship of the Academy of American Poets. Two of his books were nominated for the National Book Award and from 1976 to 1978 he served as Consultant in Poetry to the Library of Congress.*

In "Runagate, Runagate" Hayden imagines the situation of the renegade or runaway slave through a variety of voices: some official and documentary, some cultural, some purely subjective.

RUNAGATE, RUNAGATE

I

Runs falls rises stumbles on from darkness into darkness
and the darkness thicketed with shapes of terror
and the hunters pursuing and the hounds pursuing
and the night cold and the night long and the river
to cross and the jack-muh-lanterns beckoning beckoning
and blackness ahead and when shall I reach that
    somewhere
morning and keep on going and never turn back
    and keep on going.

    Runagate
          Runagate
              Runagate

Many thousands rise and go
many thousands crossing over

                    O mythic North
            O star-shaped yonder Bible city

Some go weeping and some rejoicing
some in coffins and some in carriages
some in silks and some in shackles

    Rise and go fare you well

No more auction block for me
no more diver's lash for me

    If you see my Pompey, 30 yrs of age,
    new breeches, plain stockings, negro shoes;
    if you see my Anna, likely young mulatto
    branded E on the right cheek, R on the left,
    catch them if you can and notify subscriber.
    Catch them if you can, but it won't be easy.
    They'll dart underground when you try to catch them,
    plunge into quicksand, whirlpools, mazes,
    turn into scorpions when you try to catch them.

And before I'll be a slave
I'll be buried in my grave

    North star and bonanza gold
    I'm bound for the freedom, freedom-bound
    and oh Susyanna don't you cry for me

                    Runagate
                            Runagate

II

Rises from their anguish and their power,

        Harriet Tubman,

        woman of earth, whipscarred,
        a summoning, a shining

        Mean to be free

    And this was the way of it, brethren brethren,
    way we journeyed from Can't to Can.
    Moon so bright and no place to hide,
    the cry up and the patterollers riding,
    hound dogs belling in bladed air.
    And fear starts a-murbling, Never make it,

we'll never make it. *Hush that now,*
and she's turned upon us, leveled pistol
glinting in the moonlight:
Dead folks can't jaybird-talk, she says;
you keep on going now or die, she says.

Wanted Harriet Tubman alias The General
alias Moses Stealer of Slaves

In league with Garrison Alcott Emerson
Garrett Douglass Thoreau John Brown

Armed and known to be Dangerous

Wanted Reward Dead or Alive

Tell me, Ezekiel, oh tell me do you see
mailed Jehovah coming to deliver me?

Hoot-owl calling in the ghosted air,
five times calling to the hants in the air.
Shadow of a face in the scary leaves,
shadow of a voice in the talking leaves:

Come ride-a my train

Oh that train, ghost-story train
through swamp and savanna movering movering,
over trestles of dew, through caves of the wish,
Midnight Special on a saber track movering movering
first stop Mercy and the last Hallelujah.

Come ride-a my train

Mean mean mean to be free.

LORRAINE HANSBERRY
(1930-1965)

Lorraine Vivian Hansberry was born and raised in Chicago. Hansberry
attended the University of Wisconsin, The Art Institute of Chicago, and Roo-
sevelt University. In 1950, she moved to New York City, where she attended
the New School for Social Research, wrote for Paul Robeson's Freedom *mag-*
azine, and worked a variety of jobs. She married Robert Nemiroff in 1953.
Her first play, A Raisin in the Sun, *opened on Broadway in 1959 and won*

the New York Drama Critics Circle Award. At the time, Hansberry was not only the first African American to receive this award but also the youngest writer ever to win it. A Raisin in the Sun *was later made into a film, and in 1961 Hansberry received a Cannes Film Festival special award and a Screen Writer's Guild nomination for her screenplay.* The Sign in Sidney Brustein's Window *opened in 1964 on Broadway and ran until Hansberry's death from cancer on January 12, 1965. After her death, her husband edited and published three of her unproduced plays, including* The Drinking Gourd, *and an autobiographical work,* To Be Young, Gifted, and Black: A Portrait of Lorraine Hansberry in Her Own Words.

The Drinking Gourd, *a full-length play from which we have here the first scene only, was written for television but was never produced. Hansberry's characters are richly imagined versions of slaves, with wit and imagination often denied to them in earlier writing about pre-Emancipation black America.*

FROM THE DRINKING GOURD

AN ORIGINAL DRAMA FOR TELEVISION

"Our new government is founded upon the great
truth that the Negro is not equal to the white man—
that slavery is his natural and normal condition."

—Alexander H. Stephens,
Vice President of the Confederacy

Cast of Characters
(In order of appearance)

THE SOLDIER
SLAVES—MEN, WOMEN, CHILDREN
RISSA
SARAH
JOSHUA
HANNIBAL

FOLLOWING PRELIMINARY PRODUCTION TITLES: Introduce stark, spirited banjo themes.

MAIN PLAY TITLES AND CREDITS

FADE IN: UNDER TITLES

EXTERIOR. TWO SHOT: HANNIBAL, TOMMY—*BRIGHT DAY.*

HANNIBAL *is a young slave of about nineteen or twenty.*

TOMMY, *about ten, is his master's son. It is* HANNIBAL *who is playing the banjo, the neck of which intrudes into close opening shot frame.*

CAMERA MOVES BACK TO WIDER ANGLE to show that Tommy is vigorously keeping time by clapping his hands to the beat of the music. They are seated in a tiny wooded enclosure. Sunlight and leaf shadow play on their faces, the expressions of which are animated and happy.

If workable, they sing, from top.

At completion of titles:

Fade out

from ACT ONE

FADE IN:
EXTERIOR. HIGH-ANGLED PANNING SHOT: AMERICAN EAST COAST—DUSK.

PAN down a great length of coast until a definitive mood is established. Presently the lone figure of a man emerges from the distance. He is tall and narrow-hipped, suggesting a certain idealized American generality. He is not Lincoln, but perhaps Lincolnesque. He wears the side whiskers of the nineteenth century and his hair is long at the neck after the manner of New England or Southern farmers of the period. He is dressed in dark military trousers and boots which are in no way recognizable as to rank or particular army. His shirt is open at the collar and rolled at the sleeves and he carries his dark tunic across his shoulders. He is not battle-scarred or dirty or in any other way suggestive of the disorder of war; but his gait is that of troubled and reflective meditation. When he speaks his voice is markedly free of identifiable regionalism. His imposed generality is to be a symbolic American specificity. He is the narrator. We come down close in his face as he turns to the sea and speaks.

SOLDIER

This is the Atlantic Ocean. *(He gestures easily when he needs to)* Over there, somewhere, is Europe. And over there, down that way, I guess, is Africa. *(Turning and facing inland)* And all of this, for thousands and thousands of miles in all directions, is the New World.

He bends down and empties a pile of dirt from his handkerchief onto the sand.

And this—this is soil. Southern soil. *(Opening his fist)* And this is cotton seed. Europe, Africa, the New World and Cotton. They have all gotten mixed up together to make the trouble.

He begins to walk inland, a wandering gait, full of pauses and gestures.

You see, this seed and this earth—*(Gesturing now to the land around him)* only have meaning—potency—if you add a third force. That third force is labor.

The landscape turns to the Southern countryside. In the distance, shadowed under the incredibly beautiful willows and magnolias, is a large, magnificently columned, white manor house. As he moves close to it, the soft, indescribably sweet sound of the massed voices of the unseen slaves wafts up in one of the most plaintive of the spirituals.

VOICES

"Steal away, steal away,
Steal away to Jesus.

Steal away, steal away home—
I ain't got long to stay here.

My Lord he calls me,
He calls me by the thunder.
The trumpet sounds
    within-a my soul—
I ain't got long to stay here.

Steal away, steal away,
Steal away to Jesus.
Steal away, steal away home—
I ain't got long to stay here."

Beyond the manor house—cotton fields, rows and rows of cotton fields. And, finally, as the narrator walks on, rows of little white-painted cabins, the slave quarters.

The quarters are, at the moment, starkly deserted as though he has come upon this place in a dream only. He wanders in to what appears to be the center of the quarters with an easy familiarity at being there.

This plantation, like the matters he is going to tell us about, has no secrets from him. He knows everything we are going to see; he knows how most of us will react to what we see and how we will decide at the end of the play. Therefore, in manner and words he will try to persuade *us of nothing; he will only tell us facts and stand aside and let us see for ourselves. Thus, he almost leisurely refreshes himself with a drink from a pail hanging on a nail on one of the cabins. He wanders to the community out-door fireplace at center and lounges against it and goes on with his telling.*

SOLDIER

Labor so plentiful that, for a while, it might be cheaper to work a man to
    death and buy another one than to work the first one less harshly.

The gentle slave hymn ends, and with its end comes the arbitrarily imposed abrupt darkness of true night. Somewhere in the distance a driver's voice calls: "Quittin' time! Quittin' time!" in accompaniment to a gong or a bell. Silent indications of life begin to stir around the narrator. We become aware of points of light in some of the cabins and a great fire has begun to roar silently in the fireplace where he leans. Numbers of slaves begin to file, also silently, into the quarters; some of them immediately drop to the ground and just sit or lie perfectly still, on their backs, staring into space. Others slowly form a silent line in front of the fireplace, holding makeshift eating utensils. The narrator moves to make room for them when it is necessary and occasionally glances from them out to us, as if to see if we are truly seeing.

There is, about all of these people, a grim air of fatigue and exhaustion, reflecting the twelve to fourteen hours of almost unrelieved labor they have just completed. The men are dressed in the main in rough trousers of haphazard lengths and coarse shirts. Some have hats. The women wear single-piece shifts, some of them without sleeves or collars. Some wear their hair bound in the traditional bandana of the black slave women of the Americas; others wear or carry the wide straw hats of the cotton fields.

These people are slaves. They did not come here willingly. Their ancestors
were captured, for the most part, on the West Coast of Africa by men who
made such enterprise their business.

We come in for extreme close-ups of the faces of the people as he talks, moving from men to women to children with lingering intimacy.

Few of them could speak to each other. They came from many different peoples and cultures. The slavers were careful about that. Insurrection is very difficult when you cannot even speak to your fellow prisoner.

All of them did not survive the voyage. Some simply died of suffocation; others of disease and still others of suicide. Others were murdered when they mutinied. And when the trade was finally suppressed—sometimes they were just dumped overboard when a British Man-o'-War got after a slave ship. To destroy the evidence.

That trade went on for three centuries. How many were stolen from their homeland? Some scholars say fifteen million. Others fifty million. No one will ever really know.

In any case, today some planters will tell you with pride that the cost of maintaining one of these human beings need not exceed seven dollars and fifty cents—a year. You see, among other things there is no education to pay for—in fact, some of the harshest laws in the slave code are designed to keep the slave from being educated. The penalties are maiming or mutilation—or death. Usually for he who is taught; but very often also for he who might dare to teach—including white men.

There are of course no minimum work hours and no guaranteed minimum wages. No trade unions. And, above all, no wages at all.

As he talks a murmur of low conversation begins among the people and there is a more conspicuous stir of life among them as the narrator now prepares, picking up his tunic and putting it across his shoulder once again, to walk out of the scene.

Please do not forget that this is the nineteenth century. It is a time when we still allow little children—white children—to labor twelve and thirteen hours in the factories and mines of America. We do not yet believe that women are equal citizens who should have the right to vote. It is a time when we still punish the insane for their madness. It is a time, therefore, when some men can believe and proclaim to the world that this system is the—*(Enunciating carefully but without passion)*—highest form of civilization in the world.

He turns away from us and faces the now-living scene in the background.

This system:

The CAMERA immediately comes in to exclude him and down to a close-up of a large skillet suspended over the roaring fire which now crackles with live sound. Pieces of bacon and corn pone sizzle on it. A meager portion of both is lifted up and onto a plate by Rissa, the cook. She is a woman of late years with an expression of indifference that has already passed resignation. The slave receiving his ration from her casts a slightly hopeful glance at the balance but is waved away by the cook. He gives up easily and moves away and retires and eats his food with relish. A second and a third are similarly served.

The fourth person in line is a young girl of about nineteen. She is SARAH. *She holds out her plate for service but bends as she does so, in spite of her own weariness, to play with a small boy of about seven or eight,* JOSHUA, *who has been lingering about the cook, clutching at her skirts and getting as much in her way as he can manage.*

SARAH

Hello, there, Joshua!

JOSHUA

I got a stomick ache.

RISSA

(Busy with her serving) You ain't got nothing but the devil ache.

SARAH

(To the child, with mock and heavily applied sympathy) Awww, poor little thing! Show Sarah* where it hurt you, honey.
He points his finger to a random place on his abdomen; clearly delighted to have even insincere attention.
Here?
She pokes him—ostensibly to determine the place where the pain is, but in reality only to make him laugh, which they both seem to know.
Or here? Oh, I know—right here!
She pokes him very hard with one finger, and he collapses in her arms in a fit of giggling.

RISSA

If y'all don't quit that foolin' 'round behind me while I got all this here to do—you better!
She swings vaguely behind her with the spatula.
Stop it, I say now! Sarah, you worse than he is.

SARAH

(A little surreptitiously—to Joshua) Where's your Uncle Hannibal?
The child shrugs indifferently.

RISSA

(Who overhears everything that is ever spoken on the plantation) Uh-hunh. I knew we'd get 'round to Mr. Hannibal soon enough.

SARAH

(To Rissa) Do you know where he is?

RISSA

How I know where that wild boy of mine is? If he ain't got sense enough to come for his supper, it ain't no care of mine. He's grown now. Move on out the way now. Step up here, Ben!

SARAH

(Moving around to the other side and standing close) He was out the fields again this afternoon, Aunt Rissa.

RISSA

(Softly, suddenly—but without breaking her working rhythm or changing facial expression) Coffin know?

---

*Invariably pronounced "Say-rah."

SARAH

Coffin know everything. Say he goin' to tell Marster Sweet first thing in the mornin'.

RISSA

(Decision) See if you can find that boy of mine, child.
SARAH *pushes the last of her food in her mouth and starts off.*
RISSA *halts her and hands her a small bundle which has been lying in readiness.*
    His supper.

CUT TO:
EXTERIOR. MOONLIT WOODS

Sarah emerges from the woods into a tiny clearing, bundle in hand.

SARAH

(Calling softly) Hannibal—
The camera pans to a little hillock in deep grass where a lean, vital young man lies, arms folded under his head, staring up at the stars with bright commanding eyes. At the sound of SARAH's *voice off-camera we come down in his eyes. He comes alert. She calls again.*
    Hannibal—
He smiles and hides as she approaches.
    Hannibal—
She whirls about fearfully at the snap of a twig, then reassured crosses in front of his hiding place, searching.
    Hannibal—
He touches her ankle—she screams. Laughing, he reaches for her. With a sigh of exasperation she throws him his food.

HANNIBAL

(Romantically, wistfully—playing the poet-fool)
And when she come to me, it were the moonrise . . . *(He holds out his hand)*
And when she touch my hand, it were the true stars fallin'.
He takes her hand and pulls her down in the grass and kisses her. She pulls away with the urgency of her news.

SARAH

Coffin noticed you was gone first thing!

HANNIBAL

Well, that old driver finally gettin' to be almost smart as a jackass.

SARAH

Say he gona tell Marster Sweet in the mornin'! You gona catch you another whippin', boy. . . ! *(In a mood to ignore peril, Hannibal goes on eating his food)*
Hannibal, why you have to run off like that all the time?

HANNIBAL

(Teasing) Don't run off *all* the time.

SARAH

Oh, Hannibal!

HANNIBAL

(Finishing the meager supper and reaching out for her playfully) "Oh, Hanni-bal. Oh, Hannibal!" Come here. *(He takes hold of her and kisses her once sweetly and lightly)* H'you this evenin', Miss Sarah Mae?

SARAH

You don't know how mad old Coffin was today, boy, or you wouldn't be so smart. He's gona get you in trouble with Marster again.

HANNIBAL

Me and you was *born* in trouble with Marster. *(Suddenly looking up at the sky and pointing to distract her)* Hey, lookathere!—

SARAH

(Noting him and also looking up) What—

HANNIBAL

(Drawing her close) Lookit that big, old, fat star shinin' away up yonder there!

SARAH

(Automatically dropping her voice and looking about a bit) Shhh. Hannibal!

HANNIBAL

(With his hand, as though he is personally touching the stars) One, two, three, four—they makes up the dipper. That's the Big Dipper, Sarah. The old Drinkin' Gourd pointin' straight to the North Star!

SARAH

(Knowingly) Everybody knows that's the Big Dipper and you better hush your mouth for sure now, boy. Trees on this plantation got more ears than leaves!

HANNIBAL

(Ignoring the caution) That's the old Drinkin' Gourd herself!
Releasing the girl's arms and settling down, a little wistfully now.

HANNIBAL

Sure is bright tonight. Sure would make good travelin' light tonight . . .

SARAH

(With terror, clapping her hand over his mouth) Stop it!

HANNIBAL

(Moving her hand)—up there jes pointin' away . . . *due North!*

SARAH

(Regarding him sadly) You're sure like your brother, boy. Just like him.
HANNIBAL *ignores her and leans back in the grass in the position of the opening shot
of the scene, with his arms tucked under his head. He sings softly to himself:*

HANNIBAL

"For the old man is a-waitin'
For to carry you to freedom
If you follow the Drinking Gourd.
Follow—follow—follow . . .
If you follow the Drinking Gourd . . ."

SARAH

(Over the song)—look like him . . . talk like him . . . and God knows, you sure
think like him. *(Pause)* In time, I reckon—*(Very sadly)*—you be gone like him.

HANNIBAL

(Sitting bolt upright suddenly and peering into the woods about them) You think
Isaiah got all the way to Canada, Sarah? Mama says it's powerful far. Farther
than Ohio! *(This last with true wonder)* Sure he did! I bet you old Isaiah is up
there and got hisself a job and is livin' fine. I bet you that! Bet he works in a
lumberyard or something and got hisself a wife and maybe even a house and—

SARAH

(Quietly) You mean if he's alive, Hannibal.

HANNIBAL

Oh, he's alive, all right! Catchers ain't never caught my brother. *(He whistles
through his teeth)* That boy lit out of here in a way somebody go who don't
mean to never be caught by nothin'! *(He waits. Then, having assured himself
within)* Wherever he is, he's alive. And he's free.

SARAH

I can't see how his runnin' off like that did you much good. Or your mama.
Almost broke her heart, that's what. And worst of all, leavin' his poor little
baby. Leavin' poor little Joshua who don't have no mother of his own as it is.
Seem like your brother just went out his head when Marster sold Joshua's
mother. I guess everybody on this plantation knew he wasn't gona be here
long then. Even Marster must of known.

HANNIBAL

But Marster couldn't keep him here then! Not all Marster's dogs and drivers
and guns. Nothin'. *(He looks to the woods, remembering)* I met him here that
night to bring him the food and an extry pair of shoes. He was standin' right
over there, right over there, with the moonlight streamin' down on him and
he was breathin' hard—Lord, that boy was breathin' so's you could almost
hear him on the other side of the woods. *(A sudden pause and then a rush
in the telling)* He didn't say nothin' to me, nothin' at all. But his eyes look like
somebody lit a fire in 'em, they was shinin' so in the dark. I jes hand him the

parcel and he put it in his shirt and give me a kind of push on the shoulder
... *(He touches the place, remembering keenly)* ... Here. And then he turned
and lit out through them woods like lightnin'. He was *bound* out this place!
He is entirely quiet behind the completion of the narrative. SARAH *is deeply affected
by the implications of what she has heard and suddenly puts her arms around his
neck and clings very tightly to him. Then she holds him back from her and looks at
him for the truth.*

SARAH

You aim to go, don't you, Hannibal?
He does not answer and it is clear because of it that he intends to run off.
H'you know it's so much better to run off? *(A little desperately, near tears,
thinking of the terrors involved)* Even if you make it—h'you know what's up
there, what it be like to go wanderin' 'round by yourself in this world?

HANNIBAL

I don't know. Jes know what it is to be a slave!

SARAH

Where would you go—?

HANNIBAL

Jes North, that's all I know. *(Kind of shrugging)* Try to find Isaiah maybe. How
I know what I do? *(Throwing up his hands at the difficult question)* There's
people up there what helps runaways.

SARAH

You mean them aba—aba-litchinists? I heard Marster Sweet say once that
they catches runaways and makes soap out of them.

HANNIBAL

(Suddenly older and wiser) That's slave-owner talk, Sarah. Whatever you hear
Marster say 'bout slavery—you always believe the opposite. There ain't
nothin' hurt slave marster so much—*(Savoring the notion)*—as when his
property walk away from him. Guess that's the worst blow of all. Way I look
at it, ever' slave ought to run off 'fore he die.

SARAH

(Looking up suddenly, absorbing the sense of what he has just said) Oh, Hannibal—I couldn't go! *(She starts to shake all over)* I'm too delicate. My breath
wouldn't hold out from here to the river ...

HANNIBAL

(Starting to laugh at her) No, not you—skeerified as you is! *(He looks at her and
pulls her to him)* But don't you worry, little Sarah. I'll come back. *(He smoothes her
hair and comforts her)* I'll come back and buy you. Mama too, if she's still livin'.
*The girl quivers in his arms and he holds her a little more tightly, looking up once
again to his stars.*
I surely do that thing!

W. E. B. Du Bois
(1 8 6 8 - 1 9 6 3)

William Edward Burghardt Du Bois was born in Great Barrington, Massachusetts, into a family that had not experienced slavery for generations. He graduated from Fisk University in 1880, then enrolled in Harvard University and earned a second bachelor's degree and a master's degree in 1890 and 1891. After studying at the University of Berlin, Du Bois returned to Harvard and in 1896 earned the first doctorate awarded to an African American by that institution. His dissertation, The Suppression of the African Slave Trade to the United States of America, 1638–1870, *inaugurated the university's series of historical studies.*

He was lured away from his first job, teaching Greek and Latin at Wilberforce University in Ohio, by the University of Pennsylvania to work on a research project that resulted in his The Philadelphia Negro *(1899), a pioneering study of race, urban history, and sociology. Blocked by racism from joining the Penn faculty, Du Bois became a professor of economics and history at an African-American college, Atlanta University, where he developed conferences and published studies on significant issues in African-American life. In 1905, he organized African Americans to secure voting rights and education; his Niagara Movement led in 1909 to the development of the National Association for the Advancement of Colored People (NAACP), a coalition of blacks and whites in the struggle for civil rights. Du Bois developed and edited* Crisis, *the NAACP's political and literary magazine, from its inception in 1910 until he returned to Atlanta University in 1934. Du Bois's later years saw his continuing engagement with the pan-African struggle for independence from colonial powers. His work resulted in conflict with the U.S. government, which denied him a passport. Disgusted with this treatment and the slow progress in the civil rights arena, Du Bois moved to Africa and died a citizen of Ghana.*

A prolific writer, Du Bois wrote fiction and poetry in addition to such sociological, political, and historical works as The Gift of Black Folk: The Negro in the Making of America *(1924),* Black Reconstruction *(1935), and* Black Folk, Then and Now *(1939). "Of Our Spiritual Strivings" is the first chapter of his book* The Souls of Black Folk *(1903), which augments social and political commentaries with personal essays and fiction.*

O F   O U R   S P I R I T U A L   S T R I V I N G S

O water, voice of my heart, crying in the sand,
    All night long crying with a mournful cry,
As I lie and listen, and cannot understand
        The voice of my heart in my side or the voice of the sea,
    O water, crying for rest, is it I, is it I?
    All night long the water is crying to me.

Unresting water, there shall never be rest
    Till the last moon droop and the last tide fail,

And the fire of the end begin to burn in the west;
     And the heart shall be weary and wonder and cry like
the sea,
    All life long crying without avail,
      As the water all night long is crying to me.
                         —Arthur Symons

Between me and the other world there is ever an unasked question: unasked by some through feelings of delicacy; by others through the difficulty of rightly framing it. All, nevertheless, flutter round it. They approach me in a half-hesitant sort of way, eye me curiously or compassionately, and then, instead of saying directly, How does it feel to be a problem? they say, I know an excellent colored man in my town; or, I fought at Mechanicsville; or, Do not these Southern outrages make your blood boil? At these I smile, or am interested, or reduce the boiling to a simmer, as the occasion may require. To the real question, How does it feel to be a problem? I answer seldom a word.

And yet, being a problem is a strange experience,—peculiar even for one who has never been anything else, save perhaps in babyhood and in Europe. It is in the early days of rollicking boyhood that the revelation first bursts upon one, all in a day, as it were. I remember well when the shadow swept across me. I was a little thing, away up in the hills of New England, where the dark Housatonic winds between Hoosac and Taghkanic to the sea. In a wee wooden schoolhouse, something put it into the boys' and girls' heads to buy gorgeous visiting-cards—ten cents a package—and exchange. The exchange was merry, till one girl, a tall newcomer, refused my card,—refused it peremptorily, with a glance. Then it dawned upon me with a certain suddenness that I was different from the others; or like, mayhap, in heart and life and longing, but shut out from their world by a vast veil. I had thereafter no desire to tear down that veil, to creep through; I held all beyond it in common contempt, and lived above it in a region of blue sky and great wandering shadows. That sky was bluest when I could beat my mates at examination-time, or beat them at a foot-race, or even beat their stringy heads. Alas, with the years all this fine contempt began to fade; for the words I longed for, and all their dazzling opportunities, were theirs, not mine. But they should not keep these prizes, I said; some, all, I would wrest from them. Just how I would do it I could never decide: by reading law, by healing the sick, by telling the wonderful tales that swam in my head,—some way. With other black boys the strife was not so fiercely sunny: their youth shrunk into tasteless sycophancy, or into silent hatred of the pale world about them and mocking distrust of everything white; or wasted itself in a bitter cry, Why did God make me an outcast and a stranger in mine own house? The shades of the prison-house closed round about us all: walls strait and stubborn to the whitest, but relentlessly narrow, tall, and unscalable to sons of night who must plod darkly on in resignation, or beat unavailing palms against the stone, or steadily, half hopelessly, watch the streak of blue above.

After the Egyptian and Indian, the Greek and Roman, the Teuton and Mongolian, the Negro is a sort of seventh son, born with a veil, and gifted with second-sight in this American world,—a world which yields him no true self-consciousness, but only lets him see himself through the revelation of the other world. It is a peculiar sensation, this double-consciousness, this sense of always looking at one's self through the eyes of others, of measuring one's soul by the tape of a world that looks on in amused contempt and pity. One ever feels his twoness,—an American, a Negro; two souls, two thoughts, two unreconciled strivings; two warring ideals in one dark body, whose dogged strength alone keeps it from being torn asunder.

The history of the American Negro is the history of this strife,—this longing to attain self-conscious manhood, to merge his double self into a better and truer self. In this merging he wishes neither of the older selves to be lost. He would not Africanize America, for America has too much to teach the world and Africa. He would not bleach his Negro soul in a flood of white Americanism, for he knows that Negro blood has a message for the world. He simply wishes to make it possible for a man to be both a Negro and an American, without being cursed and spit upon by his fellows, without having the doors of Opportunity closed roughly in his face.

This, then, is the end of his striving: to be a co-worker in the kingdom of culture, to escape both death and isolation, to husband and use his best powers and his latent genius. These powers of body and mind have in the past been strangely wasted, dispersed, or forgotten. The shadow of a mighty Negro past flits through the tale of Ethiopia the Shadowy and of Egypt the Sphinx. Through history, the powers of single black men flash here and there like falling stars, and die sometimes before the world has rightly gauged their brightness. Here in America, in the few days since Emancipation, the black man's turning hither and thither in hesitant and doubtful striving has often made his very strength to lose effectiveness, to seem like absence of power, like weakness. And yet it is not weakness,—it is the contradiction of double aims. The double-aimed struggle of the black artisan—on the one hand to escape white contempt for a nation of mere hewers of wood and drawers of water, and on the other hand to plough and nail and dig for a poverty-stricken horde—could only result in making him a poor craftsman, for he had but half a heart in either cause. By the poverty and ignorance of his people, the Negro minister or doctor was tempted toward quackery and demagogy; and by the criticism of the other world, toward ideals that made him ashamed of his lowly tasks. The would-be black *savant* was confronted by the paradox that the knowledge his people needed was a twice-told tale to his white neighbors, while the knowledge which would teach the white world was Greek to his own flesh and blood. The innate love of harmony and beauty that set the ruder souls of his people a-dancing and a-singing raised but confusion and doubt in the soul of the black artist; for the beauty revealed to him was the soul-beauty of a race which his larger audience despised, and he could not articulate the message of another people. This waste of double aims, this seeking to satisfy two unreconciled ideals, has wrought sad havoc with the courage and faith and deeds of ten thousand thousand people,—has sent them often wooing false gods and invoking false means of salvation, and at times has even seemed about to make them ashamed of themselves.

Away back in the days of bondage they thought to see in one divine event the end of all doubt and disappointment; few men ever worshipped Freedom with half such unquestioning faith as did the American Negro for two centuries. To him, so far as he thought and dreamed, slavery was indeed the sum of all villainies, the cause of all sorrow, the root of all prejudice; Emancipation was the key to a promised land of sweeter beauty than ever stretched before the eyes of wearied Israelites. In song and exhortation swelled one refrain—Liberty; in his tears and curses the God he implored had Freedom in his right hand. At last it came,—suddenly, fearfully, like a dream. With one wild carnival of blood and passion came the message in his own plaintive cadences:—

"Shout, O children!
Shout, you're free!
For God has bought your liberty!"

Years have passed away since then,—ten, twenty, forty; forty years of national life, forty years of renewal and development, and yet the swarthy spectre sits in its accustomed seat at the Nation's feast. In vain do we cry to this our vastest social problem:—

"Take any shape but that, and my firm nerves
Shall never tremble!"

The Nation has not yet found peace from its sins; the freedman has not yet found in freedom his promised land. Whatever of good may have come in these years of change, the shadow of a deep disappointment rests upon the Negro people,—a disappointment all the more bitter because the unattained ideal was unbounded save by the simple ignorance of a lowly people.

The first decade was merely a prolongation of the vain search for freedom, the boon that seemed ever barely to elude their grasp,—like a tantalizing will-o'-the-wisp, maddening and misleading the headless host. The holocaust of war, the terrors of the Ku-Klux Klan, the lies of carpet-baggers, the disorganization of industry, and the contradictory advice of friends and foes, left the bewildered serf with no new watchword beyond the old cry for freedom. As the time flew, however, he began to grasp a new idea. The ideal of liberty demanded for its attainment powerful means, and these the Fifteenth Amendment gave him. The ballot, which before he had looked upon as a visible sign of freedom, he now regarded as the chief means of gaining and perfecting the liberty with which war had partially endowed him. And why not? Had not votes made war and emancipated millions? Had not votes enfranchised the freedmen? Was anything impossible to a power that had done all this? A million black men started with renewed zeal to vote themselves into the kingdom. So the decade flew away, the revolution of 1876 came, and left the half-free serf weary, wondering, but still inspired. Slowly but steadily, in the following years, a new vision began gradually to replace the dream of political power,—a powerful movement, the rise of another ideal to guide the unguided, another pillar of fire by night after a clouded day. It was the ideal of "book-learning"; the curiosity, born of compulsory ignorance, to know and test the power of the cabalistic letters of the white man, the longing to know. Here at last seemed to have been discovered the mountain path to Canaan; longer than the highway of Emancipation and law, steep and rugged, but straight, leading to heights high enough to overlook life.

Up the new path the advance guard toiled, slowly, heavily, doggedly; only those who have watched and guided the faltering feet, the misty minds, the dull understandings, of the dark pupils of these schools know how faithfully, how piteously, this people strove to learn. It was weary work. The cold statistician wrote down the inches of progress here and there, noted also where here and there a foot had slipped or some one had fallen. To the tired climbers, the horizon was ever dark, the mists were often cold, the Canaan was always dim and far away. If, however, the vistas disclosed as yet no goal, no resting-place, little but flattery and criticism, the journey at least gave leisure for reflection and self-examination; it changed the child of Emancipation to the youth with dawning self-consciousness, self-realization, self-respect. In those sombre forests of his striving his own soul rose before him, and he saw himself,—darkly as through a veil; and yet he saw in himself some faint revelation of his power, of his mission. He began to have a dim feeling that, to attain his place in the world, he must be himself, and not another. For the first time he sought to analyze the burden he bore upon his back, that dead-weight of social degradation partially masked behind a half-named Negro problem. He felt his poverty; without a cent, without a home, without land, tools, or savings, he had entered into competition with rich, landed, skilled neighbors. To be a poor man is hard, but to be a poor race in a land of dollars is the very bottom of hardships. He felt the weight of his ignorance,—not simply of letters, but of life, of business, of the humanities; the accumulated sloth and shirking and awkwardness of decades and centuries shackled his hands and feet. Nor was his burden all poverty and ignorance. The red stain of bastardy, which two centuries of systematic legal defilement of Negro women had stamped upon his race, meant not only the loss of ancient African chastity, but also the hereditary weight of a mass of corruption from white adulterers, threatening almost the obliteration of the Negro home.

A people thus handicapped ought not to be asked to race with the world, but rather allowed to give all its time and thought to its own social problems. But alas! while sociologists gleefully count his bastards and his prostitutes, the very soul of the toiling, sweating black man is darkened by the shadow of a vast despair. Men call the shadow prejudice, and learnedly explain it as the natural defence of culture against barbarism, learning against ignorance, purity against crime, the "higher" against the "lower" races. To which the Negro cries Amen! and swears that to so much of this strange prejudice as is founded on just homage to civilization, culture, righteousness, and progress, he humbly bows and meekly does obeisance. But before that nameless prejudice that leaps beyond all this he stands helpless, dismayed, and well-nigh speechless; before that personal disrespect and mockery, the ridicule and systematic humiliation, the distortion of fact and wanton license of fancy, the cynical ignoring of the better and the boisterous welcoming of the worse, the all-pervading desire to inculcate disdain for everything black, from Toussaint to the devil,—before this there rises a sickening despair that would disarm and discourage any nation save that black host to whom "discouragement" is an unwritten word.

But the facing of so vast a prejudice could not but bring the inevitable self-questioning, self-disparagement, and lowering of ideals which ever accompany repression and breed in an atmosphere of contempt and hate. Whisperings and portents came borne upon the four winds: Lo! we are diseased and dying, cried the dark hosts; we cannot write, our voting is vain; what need of education, since we must always cook and serve? And the Nation echoed and enforced this self-criticism, saying: Be content to be servants, and nothing more; what need of higher culture for half-men? Away with the black man's ballot, by force or fraud,—and behold the suicide of a race! Nevertheless, out of the evil came something of good,—the more careful adjustment of education to real life, the clearer perception of the Negroes' social responsibilities, and the sobering realization of the meaning of progress.

So dawned the time of *Sturm und Drang:* storm and stress to-day rocks our little boat on the mad waters of the worldsea; there is within and without the sound of conflict, the burning of body and rending of soul; inspiration strives with doubt, and faith with vain questionings. The bright ideals of the past,—physical freedom, political power, the training of brains and the training of hands,—all these in turn have waxed and waned, until even the last grows dim and overcast. Are they all wrong,—all false?

No, not that, but each alone was over-simple and incomplete,—the dreams of a credulous race-childhood, or the fond imaginings of the other world which does not know and does not want to know our power. To be really true, all these ideals must be melted and welded into one. The training of the schools we need to-day more than ever,—the training of deft hands, quick eyes and ears, and above all the broader, deeper, higher culture of gifted minds and pure hearts. The power of the ballot we need in sheer self-defence,—else what shall save us from a second slavery? Freedom, too, the long-sought, we still seek,—the freedom of life and limb, the freedom to work and think, the freedom to love and aspire. Work, culture, liberty,—all these we need, not singly but together, not successively but together, each growing and aiding each, and all striving toward that vaster ideal that swims before the Negro people, the ideal of human brotherhood, gained through the unifying ideal of Race; the ideal of fostering and developing the traits and talents of the Negro, not in opposition to or contempt for other races, but rather in large conformity to the greater ideals of the American Republic, in order that some day on American soil two world-races may give each to each those characteristics both so sadly lack. We the darker ones come even now not altogether empty-handed: there are to-day no truer exponents of the pure human spirit of the Declaration of Independence than the American Negroes; there is no true American music but the wild sweet melodies of the Negro slave; the American fairy tales and folklore are Indian and African; and, all in all, we black men seem the sole oasis of simple faith and reverence in a dusty desert of dollars and smartness. Will America be poorer if she replace her brutal dyspeptic blundering with light-hearted but determined Negro humility? or her coarse and cruel wit with loving jovial good-humor? or her vulgar music with the soul of the Sorrow Songs?

Merely a concrete test of the underlying principles of the great republic is the Negro Problem, and the spiritual striving of the freedmen's sons is the travail of souls whose burden is almost beyond the measure of their strength, but who bear it in the name of an historic race, in the name of this the land of their fathers' fathers, and in the name of human opportunity.

And now what I have briefly sketched in large outline let me on coming pages tell again in many ways, with loving emphasis and deeper detail, that men may listen to the striving in the souls of black folk.

DAVID HENRY HWANG
(1957-)

David Henry Hwang was born in 1957 in Los Angeles, California, where he lived until recently. He attended Stanford University, where he received his B.A. in 1979. He attended the Yale University School of Drama from 1980 to 1981. In 1980, Hwang's first play, F.O.B., *appeared Off-Broadway and won the Obie Award as the best new play of the season. The Dance and The Railroad,* Hwang's second play, *was produced in New York City in 1981. In 1988 Hwang received wide acclaim for his play* M. Butterfly, *which appeared on Broadway and received a Tony Award, the Outer Critics Cir-*

cle Award for best Broadway play, and a Pulitzer Prize nomination. It has now been produced in over thirty-six countries. Hwang has received fellowships from the National Endowment for the Arts, the John Simon Guggenheim Memorial Foundation, and the New York State Council on the Arts. He has also directed several plays and produced screenplays for film and television. His plays have been widely anthologized, and in 1997 he was awarded another Obie for his play Golden Child.

The Dance and the Railroad, *one of Hwang's first plays, explores the too little known presence of Chinese immigrant workers on the transcontinental railroad project.*

THE DANCE AND THE RAILROAD

Characters
LONE, twenty years old, *ChinaMan railroad worker.*
MA, eighteen years old, *ChinaMan railroad worker.*

Place *A mountaintop near the transcontinental railroad.*

Time *June, 1867.*

Synopsis of Scenes
Scene 1. *Afternoon.*
Scene 2. *Afternoon, a day later.*
Scene 3. *Late afternoon, four days later.*
Scene 4. *Late that night.*
Scene 5. *Just before the following dawn.*

Scene 1

A mountaintop. LONE *is practicing opera steps. He swings his pigtail around like a fan.* MA *enters, cautiously, watches from a hidden spot.* MA *approaches* LONE.

LONE: So, there are insects hiding in the bushes.
MA: Hey, listen, we haven't met, but—
LONE: I don't spend time with insects.

(LONE *whips his hair into* MA's *face;* MA *backs off;* LONE *pursues him, swiping at* MA *with his hair)*

MA: What the—? Cut it out!

(MA *pushes* LONE *away)*

LONE: Don't push me.
MA: What was that for?
LONE: Don't ever push me again.

MA: You mess like that, you're gonna get pushed.

LONE: Don't push me.

MA: You started it. I just wanted to watch.

LONE: You "just wanted to watch." Did you ask my permission?

MA: What?

LONE: Did you?

MA: C'mon.

LONE: You can't expect to get in for free.

MA: Listen. I got some stuff you'll wanna hear.

LONE: You think so?

MA: Yeah. Some advice.

LONE: Advice? How old are you, anyway?

MA: Eighteen.

LONE: A child.

MA: Yeah. Right. A child. But listen—

LONE: A child who tries to advise a grown man—

MA: Listen, you got this kind of attitude.

LONE: —is a child who will never grow up.

MA: You know, the ChinaMen down at camp, they can't stand it.

LONE: Oh?

MA: Yeah. You gotta watch yourself. You know what they say? They call you "Prince of the Mountain." Like you're too good to spend time with them.

LONE: Perceptive of them.

MA: After all, you never sing songs, never tell stories. They say you act like your spit is too clean for them, and they got ways to fix that.

LONE: Is that so?

MA: Like they're gonna bury you in the shit buckets, so you'll have more to clean than your nails.

LONE: But I don't shit.

MA: Or they're gonna cut out your tongue, since you never speak to them.

LONE: There's no one here worth talking to.

MA: Cut it out, Lone. Look, I'm trying to help you, all right? I got a solution.

LONE: So young yet so clever.

MA: That stuff you're doing—it's beautiful. Why don't you do it for the guys at camp? Help us celebrate?

LONE: What will "this stuff" help celebrate?

MA: C'mon. The strike, of course. Guys on a railroad gang, we gotta stick together, you know.

LONE: This is something to celebrate?

MA: Yeah. Yesterday, the weak-kneed ChinaMen, they were running around like chickens without a head: "The white devils are sending their soldiers! Shoot us all!" But now, look—day four, see? Still in one piece. Those soldiers—we've never seen a gun or a bullet.

LONE: So you're all warrior-spirits, huh?

MA: They're scared of us, Lone—that's what it means.

LONE: I appreciate your advice. Tell you what—you go down—

MA: Yeah?

LONE: Down to the camp—

MA: Okay.

LONE: To where the men are—
MA: Yeah?
LONE: Sit there—
MA: Yeah?
LONE: And wait for me.
MA: Okay. *(Pause)* That's it? What do you think I am?
LONE: I think you're an insect interrupting my practice. So fly away. Go home.
MA: Look, I didn't come here to get laughed at.
LONE: No, I suppose you didn't.
MA: So just stay up here. By yourself. You deserve it.
LONE: I do.
MA: And don't expect any more help from me.
LONE: I haven't gotten any yet.
MA: If one day, you wake up and your head is buried in the shit can—
LONE: Yes?
MA: You can't find your body, your tongue is cut out—
LONE: Yes.
MA: Don't worry, 'cuz I'll be there.
LONE: Oh.
MA: To make sure your mother's head is sitting right next to yours.

(MA *exits*)

LONE: His head is too big for this mountain.

(*Returns to practicing*)

Scene 2

Mountaintop. Next day. LONE *is practicing.* MA *enters.*

MA: Hey.
LONE: You? Again?
MA: I forgive you.
LONE: You . . . what?
MA: For making fun of me yesterday. I forgive you.
LONE: You can't—
MA: No. Don't thank me.
LONE: You can't forgive me.
MA: No. Don't mention it.
LONE: You—! I never asked for your forgiveness.
MA: I know. That's just the kinda guy I am.
LONE: This is ridiculous. Why don't you leave? Go down to your friends and play sol-
diers, sing songs, tell stories.
MA: Ah! See? That's just it. I got other ways I wanna spend my time. Will you teach
me the opera?
LONE: What?
MA: I wanna learn it. I dreamt about it all last night.
LONE: No.

MA: The dance, the opera—I can do it.

LONE: You think so?

MA: Yeah. When I get outa here, I wanna go back to China and perform.

LONE: You want to become an actor?

MA: Well, I wanna perform.

LONE: Don't you remember the story about the three sons whose parents send them away to learn a trade? After three years, they return. The first one says, "I have become a coppersmith." The parents say, "Good. Second son, what have you become?" "I've become a silversmith." "Good—and youngest son, what about you?" "I have become an actor." When the parents hear that their son has become only an actor, they are very sad. The mother beats her head against the ground until the ground, out of pity, opens up and swallows her. The father is so angry he can't even speak, and the anger builds up inside him until it blows his body to pieces—little bits of his skin are found hanging from trees days later. You don't know how you endanger your relatives by becoming an actor.

MA: Well, I don't wanna become an "actor." That sounds terrible. I just wanna perform. Look, I'll be rich by the time I get out of here, right?

LONE: Oh?

MA: Sure. By the time I go back to China, I'll ride in gold sedan chairs, with twenty wives fanning me all around.

LONE: Twenty wives? This boy is ambitious.

MA: I'll give out pigs on New Years's and keep a stable of small birds to give to any woman who pleases me. And in my spare time, I'll perform.

LONE: Between your twenty wives and your birds, where will you find a free moment?

MA: I'll play Gwan Gung and tell stories of what life was like on the Gold Mountain.

LONE: Ma, just how long have you been in "America"?

MA: Huh? About four weeks.

LONE: You are a big dreamer.

MA: Well, all us ChinaMen here are—right? Men with little dreams—have little brains to match. They walk with their eyes down, trying to find extra grains of rice on the ground.

LONE: So, you know all about "America"? Tell me, what kind of stories will you tell?

MA: I'll say, "We laid tracks like soldiers. Mountains? We hung from cliffs in baskets and the winds blew us like birds. Snow? We lived underground like moles for days at a time. Deserts? We—"

LONE: Wait. Wait. How do you know these things after only four weeks?

MA: They told me—the other ChinaMen on the gang. We've been telling stories ever since the strike began.

LONE: They made it sound like it's very enjoyable.

MA: They said it is.

LONE: Oh? And you believe them?

MA: They're my friends. Living underground in winter—sounds exciting huh?

LONE: Did they say anything about the cold?

MA: Oh, I already know about that. They told me about the mild winters and the warm snow.

LONE: Warm snow?

MA: When I go home, I'll bring some back to show my brothers.

LONE: Bring some—? On the boat?

MA: They'll be shocked—they never seen American snow before.

LONE: You can't. By the time you get snow to the boat, it'll have melted, evaporated, and returned as rain already.

MA: No.

LONE: No?

MA: Stupid.

LONE: Me?

MA: You been here awhile, haven't you?

LONE: Yes. Two years.

MA: Then how come you're so stupid? This is the Gold Mountain. The snow here doesn't melt. It's not wet.

LONE: That's what they told you?

MA: Yeah. It's true.

LONE: Did anyone show you any of this snow?

MA: No. It's not winter.

LONE: So where does it go?

MA: Huh?

LONE: Where does it go, it if doesn't melt? What happens to it?

MA: The snow? I dunno. I guess it just stays around.

LONE: So where is it? Do you see any?

MA: Here? Well, no, but . . . (*Pause*) This is probably one of those places where it doesn't snow—even in winter.

LONE: Oh.

MA: Anyway, what's the use of me telling you what you already know? Hey, c'mon—teach me some of that stuff. Look—I've been practicing the walk—how's this? (*Demonstrates*)

LONE: You look like a duck in heat.

MA: Hey—it's a start, isn't it?

LONE: Tell you what—you want to play some *die siu?*

MA: *Die siu?* Sure.

LONE: You know, I'm pretty good.

MA: Hey, I play with the guys at camp. You can't be any better than Lee—he's really got it down.

(LONE *pulls out a case with two dice*)

LONE: I used to play till morning.

MA: Hey, us too. We see the sun start to rise, and say, "Hey, if we got to sleep now, we'll never get up for work." So we just keep playing.

LONE: (*Holding out dice*) *Die* or *siu?*

MA: *Siu.*

LONE: You sure?

MA: Yeah!

LONE: All right. (*He rolls*) *Die!*

MA: *Siu!*

(*They see the result*)

MA: Not bad.

(*They continue taking turns rolling through the following section;* MA *always loses*)

LONE: I haven't touched these in two years.

MA: I gotta practice more.

LONE: Have you lost much money?

MA: Huh? So what?

LONE: Oh, you have gold hidden in all your shirt linings, huh?

MA: Here in "America"—losing is no problem. You know—End of the Year Bonus?

LONE: Oh, right.

MA: After I get that, I'll laugh at what I lost.

LONE: Lee told you there was a bonus, right?

MA: How'd you know?

LONE: When I arrived here, Lee told me there was a bonus, too.

MA: Lee teach you how to play?

LONE: Him? He talked to me a lot.

MA: Look, why don't you come down and start playing with the guys again?

LONE: "The guys."

MA: Before we start playing, Lee uses a stick to write "Kill!" in the dirt.

LONE: You seem to live for your nights with "the guys."

MA: What's life without friends, huh?

LONE: Well, why do *you* think I stopped playing?

MA: Hey, maybe you were the one getting killed, huh?

LONE: What?

MA: Hey, just kidding.

LONE: Who's getting killed here?

MA: Just a joke.

LONE: That's not a joke, it's blasphemy.

MA: Look, obviously you stopped playing 'cause you wanted to practice the opera.

LONE: Do you understand that discipline?

MA: But, I mean, you don't have to overdo it either. You don't have to treat 'em like dirt. I mean, who are you trying to impress?

(*Pause.* LONE *throws dice into the bushes*)

LONE: Ooooops. Better go see who won.

MA: Hey! C'mon! Help me look!

LONE: If you find them, they are yours.

MA: You serious?

LONE: Yes.

MA: Here.

(*Finds the dice*)

LONE: Who won?

MA: I didn't check.

LONE: Well, no matter. Keep the dice. Take them and go play with your friends.

MA: Here. (*He offers them to* LONE) A present.

LONE: A present? This isn't a present!

MA: They're mine, aren't they? You gave them to me, right?

LONE: Well, yes, but—

MA: So now I'm giving them to you.

LONE: You can't give me a present. I don't want them.

MA: You wanted them enough to keep them two years.

LONE: I'd forgotten I had them.

MA: See, I know, Lone. You wanna get rid of me. But you can't. I'm paying for lessons.

LONE: With my dice.

MA: Mine now. (*He offers them again*) Here.

(*Pause.* LONE *runs* MA*'s hand across his forehead*)

LONE: Feel this.

MA: Hey!

LONE: Pretty wet, huh?

MA: Big deal.

LONE: Well, it's not from playing *die siu.*

MA: I know how to sweat. I wouldn't be here if I didn't.

LONE: Yes, but are you willing to sweat after you've finished sweating? Are you willing to come up after you've spent the whole day chipping half an inch off a rock, and punish your body some more?

MA: Yeah. Even after work, I still—

LONE: No, you don't. You want to gamble, and tell dirty stories, and dress up like women to do shows.

MA: Hey, I never did that.

LONE: You've only been here a month. (*Pause*) And what about "the guys"? They're not going to treat you so well once you stop playing with them. Are you willing to work all day listening to them whisper, "That one—let's put spiders in his soup"?

MA: They won't do that to me. With you, it's different.

LONE: Is it?

MA: You don't have to act that way.

LONE: What way?

MA: Like you're so much better than them.

LONE: No. You haven't even begun to understand. To practice every day, you must have a fear to force you up here.

MA: A fear? No—it's 'cause what you're doing is beautiful.

LONE: No.

MA: I've seen it.

LONE: It's ugly to practice when the mountain has turned your muscles to ice. When my body hurts too much to come here, I look at the other ChinaMen and think, "They are dead. Their muscles work only because the white man forces them. I live because I can still force my muscles to work for me." Say it. "They are dead."

MA: No. They're my friends.

LONE: Well, then, take your dice down to your friends.

MA: But I want to learn—

LONE: This is your first lesson.

MA: Look, it shouldn't matter—

LONE: It does.

MA: It shouldn't matter what I think.

LONE: Attitude is everything.

MA: But as long as I come up, do the exercises—

LONE: I'm not going to waste time on a quitter.

MA: I'm not!

LONE: Then say it.—"They are dead men."

MA: I can't.

LONE: Then you will never have the dedication.

MA: That doesn't prove anything.

LONE: I will not teach a dead man.

MA: What?

LONE: If you can't see it, then you're dead too.

MA: Don't start pinning—

LONE: Say it!

MA: All right.

LONE: What?

MA: All right. I'm one of them. I'm a dead man too.

(*Pause*)

LONE: I thought as much. So, go. You have your friends.

MA: But I don't have a teacher.

LONE: I don't think you need both.

MA: Are you sure?

LONE: I'm being questioned by a child.

(LONE *returns to practicing. Silence*)

MA: Look, Lone, I'll come up here every night—after work—I'll spend my time practicing, okay? (*Pause*) But I'm not gonna say that they're dead. Look at them. They're on strike; dead men don't go on strike, Lone. The white devils—they try and stick us with a ten-hour day. We want a return to eight hours and also a fourteen-dollar-a-month raise. I learned the demon English—listen: "Eight hour a day good for white man, all same good for ChinaMan." These are the demands of live ChinaMen, Lone. Dead men don't complain.

LONE: All right, this is something new. No one can judge the ChinaMen till after the strike.

MA: They say we'll hold out for months if we have to. The smart men will live on what we've hoarded.

LONE: A ChinaMan's mouth can swallow the earth. (*He takes the dice*) While the strike is on, I'll teach you.

MA: And afterwards?

LONE: Afterwards—we'll decide then whether these are dead or live men.

MA: When can we start?

LONE: We've already begun. Give me your hand.

Scene 3

LONE *and* MA *are doing physical exercises.*

MA: How long will it be before I can play Gwan Gung?

LONE: How long before a dog can play the violin?

MA: Old Ah Hong—have you heard him play the violin?

LONE: Yes. Now, he should take his violin and give it to a dog.

MA: I think he sounds okay.

LONE: I think he caused that avalanche last winter.

MA: He used to play for weddings back home.

LONE: Ah Hong?

MA: That's what he said.

LONE: You probably heard wrong.

MA: No.

LONE: He probably said he played for funerals.

MA: He's been playing for the guys down at camp.

LONE: He should play for the white devils—that will end this stupid strike.

MA: Yang told me for sure—it'll be over by tomorrow.

LONE: Eight days already. And Yang doesn't know anything.

MA: He said they're already down to an eight-hour day and five-dollar raise at the bargaining sessions.

LONE: Yang eats too much opium.

MA: That doesn't mean he's wrong about this.

LONE: You can't trust him. One time—last year—he went around camp looking in everybody's eyes and saying, "Your nails are too long. They're hurting my eyes." This went on for a week. Finally, all the men clipped their nails, made a big pile, which they wrapped in leaves and gave to him. Yang used the nails to season his food—he put it in his soup, sprinkled it on his rice, and never said a word about it again. Now tell me—are you going to trust a man who eats other men's fingernails?

MA: Well, all I know is we won't go back to work until they meet all our demands. Listen, teach me some Gwan Gung steps.

LONE: I should have expected this. A boy who wants to have twenty wives is the type who demands more than he can handle.

MA: Just a few.

LONE: It takes years before an actor can play Gwan Gung.

MA: I can do it. I spend a lot of time watching the opera when it comes around. Every time I see Gwan Gung, I say, "Yeah. That's me. The god of fighters. The god of adventurers. We have the same kind of spirit."

LONE: I tell you, if you work very hard, when you return to China, you can perhaps be the Second Clown.

MA: Second Clown?

LONE: If you work hard.

MA: What's the Second Clown?

LONE: You can play the *p'i p'a,* and dance and jump all over.

MA: I'll buy them.

LONE: Excuse me?

MA: I'm going to be rich, remember? I'll buy a troupe and force them to let me play Gwan Gung.

LONE: I hope you have enough money, then, to pay audiences to sit through your show.

MA: You mean, I'm going to have to practice here every night—and in return, all I can play is the Second Clown?

LONE: If you work hard.

MA: Am I that bad? Maybe I shouldn't even try to do this. Maybe I should just go down.

LONE: It's not you. Everyone must earn the right to play Gwan Gung. I entered opera school when I was ten years old. My parents decided to sell me for ten years to this opera company. I lived with eighty other boys and we slept in bunks four beds high and hid our candy and rice cakes from each other. After eight years, I was studying to play Gwan Gung.

MA: Eight years?

LONE: I was one of the best in my class. One day, I was summoned by my master, who told me I was to go home for two days because my mother had fallen very ill and was dying. When I arrived home, Mother was standing at the door waiting, not sick at all. Her first words to me, the son away for eight years, were, "You've been playing while your village has starved. You must go to the Gold Mountain and work."

MA: And you never returned to school?

LONE: I went from a room with eighty boys to a ship with three hundred men. So, you see, it does not come easily to play Gwan Gung.

MA: Did you want to play Gwan Gung?

LONE: What a foolish question!

MA: Well, you're better off this way.

LONE: What?

MA: Actors—they don't make much money. Here, you make a bundle, then go back and be an actor again. Best of both worlds.

LONE: "Best of both worlds."

MA: Yeah!

(LONE *drops to the ground, begins imitating a duck, waddling and quacking*)

MA: Lone? What are you doing? (LONE *quacks*) You're a duck? (LONE *quacks*) I can see that. (LONE *quacks*) Is this an exercise? Am I supposed to do this? (LONE *quacks*) This is dumb. I never seen Gwan Gung waddle. (LONE *quacks*) Okay. All right. I'll do it. (MA *and* LONE *quack and waddle*) You know, I never realized before how uncomfortable a duck's life is. And you have to listen to yourself quacking all day. Go crazy! (LONE *stands up straight*) Now, what was that all about?

LONE: No, no. Stay down there, duck.

MA: What's the—

LONE: (*Prompting*) Quack, quack, quack.

MA: I don't—

LONE: Act your species!

MA: I'm not a duck!

LONE: Nothing worse than a duck that doesn't know his place.

MA: All right. (*Mechanically*) Quack, quack.

LONE: More.

MA: Quack.

LONE: More!

MA: Quack, quack, quack!

(MA *now continues quacking, as* LONE *gives commands*)

LONE: Louder! It's your mating call! Think of your twenty duck wives! Good! Louder! Project! More! Don't slow down! Put your tail feathers into it! They can't hear you!

(MA *is now quacking up a storm.* LONE *exits, unnoticed by* MA)

MA: Quack! Quack! Quack! Quack. Quack . . . quack.

(*He looks around*) Quack . . . quack . . . Lone? . . . Lone?
(*He waddles around the stage looking*) Lone, where are you?
Where'd you go? (*He stops, scratches his left leg with his right foot*) C'mon—stop playing around. What is this? (LONE *enters as a tiger, unseen by* MA) Look, let's call it a day, okay? I'm getting hungry. (MA *turns around, notices* LONE *right before* LONE *is to bite him*) Aaaaah! Quack, quack, quack!

(*They face off, in character as animals. Duck-*MA *is terrified*)

LONE: Grrrr!
MA: (*As a cry for help*) Quack, quack, quack!

(LONE *pounces on* MA. *They struggle, in character.* MA *is quacking madly, eyes tightly closed.* LONE *stands up straight.* MA *continues to quack*)

LONE: Stand up.
MA: (*Eyes still closed*) Quack, quack, quack!
LONE: (*Louder*) Stand up!
MA: (*Opening his eyes*) Oh.
LONE: What are you?
MA: Huh?
LONE: A ChinaMan or a duck?
MA: Huh? Gimme a second to remember.
LONE: You like being a duck?
MA: My feet fell asleep.
LONE: You change forms so easily.
MA: You said to.
LONE: What else could you turn into?
MA: Well, you scared me—sneaking up like that.
LONE: Perhaps a rock. That would be useful. When the men need to rest, they can sit on you.
MA: I got carried away.
LONE: Let's try . . . a locust. Can you become a locust?
MA: No. Let's cut this, okay?
LONE: Here. It's easy. You just have to know how to hop.
MA: You're not gonna get me—
LONE: Like this.

(*He demonstrates*)

MA: Forget it, Lone.
LONE: I'm a locust.

(*He begins jumping toward* MA)

MA: Hey! Get away!
LONE: I devour whole fields.
MA: Stop it.
LONE: I starve babies before they are born.

MA: Hey, look, stop it!

LONE: I cause famines and destroy villages.

MA: I'm warning you! Get away!

LONE: What are you going to do? You can't kill a locust.

MA: You're not a locust.

LONE: You kill one, and another sits on your hand.

MA: Stop following me.

LONE: Locusts always trouble people. If not, we'd feel useless. Now, if you became a locust, too . . .

MA: I'm not going to become a locust.

LONE: Just stick your teeth out!

MA: I'm not gonna be a bug! It's stupid!

LONE: No man who's just been a duck has the right to call anything stupid.

MA: I thought you were trying to teach me something.

LONE: I am. Go ahead.

MA: All right. There. That look right?

LONE: Your legs should be a little lower. Lower! There.
That's adequate. So how does it feel to be a locust?

(LONE *gets up*)

MA: I dunno. How long do I have to do this?

LONE: Could you do it for three years?

MA: Three years? Don't be—

LONE: You couldn't, could you? Could you be a duck for that long?

MA: Look, I wasn't born to be either of those.

LONE: Exactly. Well, I wasn't born to work on a railroad, either. "Best of both worlds." How can you be such an insect!

(*Pause*)

MA: Lone . . .

LONE: Stay down there! Don't move! I've never told anyone my story—the story of my parents' kidnapping me from school. All the time we were crossing the ocean, the last two years here—I've kept my mouth shut. To you, I finally tell it. And all you can say is, "Best of both worlds." You're a bug to me, a locust. You think you understand the dedication one must have to be in the opera? You think it's the same as working on a railroad.

MA: Lone, all I was saying is that you'll go back too, and—

LONE: You're no longer a student of mine.

MA: What?

LONE: You have no dedication.

MA: Lone, I'm sorry.

LONE: Get up.

MA: I'm honored that you told me that.

LONE: Get up.

MA: No.

LONE: No?

MA: I don't want to. I want to talk.

LONE: Well, I've learned from the past. You're stubborn. You don't go. All right. Stay there. If you want to prove to me that you're dedicated, be a locust till morning. I'll go.

MA: Lone, I'm really honored that you told me.

LONE: I'll return in the morning.

(*Exits*)

MA: Lone? Lone, that's ridiculous. You think I'm gonna stay like this? If you do, you're crazy. Lone? Come back here.

Scene 4

Night. MA, *alone, as a locust.*

MA: Locusts travel in huge swarms, so large that when they cross the sky, they block out the sun, like a storm. Second Uncle—back home—when he was a young man, his whole crop got wiped out by locusts one year. In the famine that followed, Second Uncle lost his eldest son and his second wife—the one he married for love. Even to this day, we look around before saying the word "locust," to make sure Second Uncle is out of hearing range. About eight years ago, my brother and I discovered Second Uncle's cave in back of the stream near our house. We saw him come out of it one day around noon. Later, just before the sun went down, we sneaked in. We only looked once. Inside, there must have been hundreds—maybe five hundred or more—grasshoppers in huge bamboo cages—and around them—stacks of grasshopper legs, grasshopper heads, grasshopper antennae, grasshoppers with one leg, still trying to hop but toppling like trees coughing, grasshoppers wrapped around sharp branches rolling from side to side, grasshoppers legs cut off grasshopper bodies, then tied around grasshoppers and tightened till grasshoppers died. Every conceivable kind of grasshopper in every conceivable stage of life and death, subject to every conceivable grasshopper torture. We ran out quickly, my brother and I—we knew an evil place by the thickness of the air. Now, I think of Second Uncle. How sad that the locusts forced him to take out his agony on innocent grasshoppers. What if Second Uncle could see me now? Would he cut off my legs? He might as well. I can barely feel them. But then again, Second Uncle never tortured actual locusts, just weak grasshoppers.

Scene 5

Night. MA *still as a locust.*

LONE: (*Off, singing*)

Hit your hardest
Pound out your tears
The more you try
The more you'll cry
At how little I've moved
And how large I loom
By the time the sun goes down

MA: You look rested.

LONE: Me?

MA: Well, you sound rested.

LONE: No, not at all.

MA: Maybe I'm just comparing you to me.

LONE: I didn't even close my eyes all last night.

MA: Aw, Lone, you didn't have to stay up for me. You coulda just come up here and—

LONE: For you?

MA: —apologized and everything woulda been—

LONE: I didn't stay up for you.

MA: Huh? You didn't?

LONE: No.

MA: Oh. You sure?

LONE: Positive. I was thinking, that's all.

MA: About me?

LONE: Well . . .

MA: Even a little?

LONE: I was thinking about the ChinaMen—and you. Get up, Ma.

MA: Aw, do I have to? I've gotten to know these grasshoppers real well.

LONE: Get up. I have a lot to tell you.

MA: What'll they think? They take me in, even though I'm a little large, then they find out I'm a human being. I stepped on their kids. No trust. Gimme a hand, will you? (LONE *helps* MA *up, but* MA*'s legs can't support him*) Aw, shit. My legs are coming off.

(*He lies down and tries to straighten them out*)

LONE: I have many surprises. First, you will play Gwan Gung.

MA: My legs will be sent home without me. What'll my family think? Come to port to meet me and all they get is two legs.

LONE: Did you hear me?

MA: Hold on. I can't be in agony and listen to Chinese at the same time.

LONE: Did you hear my first surprise?

MA: No. I'm too busy screaming.

LONE: I said, you'll play Gwan Gung.

MA: Gwan Gung?

LONE: Yes.

MA: Me?

LONE: Yes.

MA: Without legs?

LONE: What?

MA: That might be good.

LONE: Stop that!

MA: I'll become a legend. Like the blind man who defended Amoy.

LONE: Did you hear?

MA: "The legless man who played Gwan Gung."

LONE: Isn't this what you want? To play Gwan Gung?

MA: No, I just wanna sleep.

LONE: No, you don't. Look. Here. I brought you something.

MA: Food?

LONE: Here. Some rice.

MA: Thanks, Lone. And duck?

LONE: Just a little.

MA: Where'd you get the duck?

LONE: Just bones and skin.

MA: We don't have duck. And the white devils have been blockading the food.

LONE: Sing—he had some left over.

MA: Sing? That thief?

LONE: And something to go with it.

MA: What? Lone, where did you find whiskey?

LONE: You know, Sing—he has almost anything.

MA: Yeah. For a price.

LONE: Once, even some thousand-day-old eggs.

MA: He's a thief. That's what they told me.

LONE: Not if you're his friend.

MA: Sing don't have any real friends. Everyone talks about him bein' tied in to the head of the klan in San Francisco. Lone, you didn't have to do this. Here. Have some.

LONE: I had plenty.

MA: Don't gimme that. This cost you plenty, Lone.

LONE: Well, I thought if we were going to celebrate, we should do it as well as we would at home.

MA: Celebrate? What for? Wait.

LONE: Ma, the strike is over.

MA: Shit, I knew it. And we won, right?

LONE: Yes, the ChinaMen have won. They can do more than just talk.

MA: I told you. Didn't I tell you?

LONE: Yes. Yes, you did.

MA: Yang told me it was gonna be done. He said—

LONE: Yes, I remember.

MA: Didn't I tell you? Huh?

LONE: Ma, eat your duck.

MA: Nine days, we civilized the white devils. I knew it. I knew we'd hold out till their ears started twitching. So that's where you got the duck, right? At the celebration?

LONE: No, there wasn't a celebration.

MA: Huh? You sure? ChinaMen—they look for any excuse to party.

LONE: But I thought *we* should celebrate.

MA: Well, that's for sure.

LONE: So you will play Gwan Gung.

MA: God, nine days. Shit, it's finally done. Well, we'll show them how to party. Make noise. Jump off rocks. Make the mountain shake.

LONE: We'll wash your body, to prepare you for the role.

MA: What role?

LONE: Gwan Gung. I've been telling you.

MA: I don't wanna play Gwan Gung.

LONE: You've shown the dedication required to become my student, so—

MA: Lone, you think I stayed up last night 'cause I wanted to play Gwan Gung?

LONE: You said you were like him.

MA: I am. Gwan Gung stayed up all night once to prove his loyalty. Well, now I have too. Lone, I'm honored that you told me your story.

LONE: Yes . . . That is like Gwan Gung.

MA: Good. So let's do an opera about *me.*

LONE: What?

MA: You wanna party or what?

LONE: About you?

MA: You said I was like Gwan Gung, didn't you?

LONE: Yes, but—

MA: Well, look at the operas he's got. I ain't even got one.

LONE: Still, you can't—

MA: You tell me, is that fair?

LONE: You can't do an opera about yourself.

MA: I just won a victory, didn't I? I deserve an opera in my honor.

LONE: But it's not traditional.

MA: Traditional? Lone, you gotta figure any way I could do Gwan Gung wasn't gonna be traditional anyway. I may be as good a guy as him, but he's a better dancer. (*Sings*)

> Old Gwan Gung, just sits about
> Till the dime-store fighters have had it out
> Then he pitches his peach pit
> Combs his beard
> Draws his sword
> And they scatter in fear

LONE: What are you talking about?

MA: I just won a great victory. I get—whatcha call it?—poetic license. C'mon. Hit the gongs. I'll immortalize my story.

LONE: I refuse. This goes against all my training. I try and give you your wish and—

MA: Do it. Gimme my wish. Hit the gongs.

LONE: I never—I can't.

MA: Can't what? Don't think I'm worth an opera? No, I guess not. I forgot—you think I'm just one of those dead men.

(*Silence.* LONE *pulls out a gong.* MA *gets into position.* LONE *hits the gong. They do the following in a mock-Chinese-opera style*)

MA: I am Ma. Yesterday, I was kicked out of my house by my three elder brothers, calling me the lazy dreamer of the family. I am sitting here in front of the temple trying to decide how I will avenge this indignity. Here comes the poorest beggar in this village. (*He cues* LONE) He is called Fleaman because his body is the most popular meeting place for fleas from around the province.

LONE: (*Singing*)

> Fleas in love,
> Find your happiness
> In the gray scraps of my suit

MA: Hello, Flea—

LONE: (*Continuing*)

> Fleas in need,

Shield your families
In the gray hairs of my beard

MA: Hello, Flea—

(LONE *cuts* MA *off, continues an extended improvised aria*)

MA: Hello, Fleaman.
LONE: Hello, Ma. Are you interested in providing a home for these fleas?
MA: No!
LONE: This couple here—seeking to start a new home. Housing today is so hard to find. How about your left arm?
MA: I may have plenty of my own fleas in time. I have been thrown out by my elder brothers.
LONE: Are you seeking revenge? A flea epidemic on your house? (*To a flea*) Get back there. You should be asleep. Your mother will worry.
MA: Nothing would make my brothers angrier than seeing me rich.
LONE: Rich? After the bad crops of the last three years, even the fleas are thinking of moving north.
MA: I heard a white devil talk yesterday.
LONE: Oh—with hair the color of a sick chicken and eyes round as eggs? The fleas and I call him Chicken-Laying-an-Egg.
MA: He said we can make our fortunes on the Gold Mountain, where work is play and the sun scares off snow.
LONE: Don't listen to chicken-brains.
MA: Why not? He said gold grows like weeds.
LONE: I have heard that it is slavery.
MA: Slavery? What do you know, Fleaman? Who told you? The fleas? Yes, I will go to Gold Mountain.

(*Gongs.* MA *strikes a submissive pose to* LONE)

LONE: "The one hundred twenty-five dollars passage money is to be paid to the said head of said Hong, who will make arrangements with the coolies, that their wages shall be deducted until the debt is absorbed."

(MA *bows to* LONE. *Gongs. They pick up fighting sticks and do a water-crossing dance. Dance ends. They stoop next to each other and rock*)

MA: I have been in the bottom of this boat for thirty-six days now. Tang, how many have died?
LONE: Not me. I'll live through this ride.
MA: I didn't ask how you are.
LONE: But why's the Gold Mountain so far?
MA: We left with three hundred and three.
LONE: My family's depending on me.
MA: So tell me, how many have died?
LONE: I'll be the last one alive.
MA: That's not what I wanted to know.

LONE: I'll find some fresh air in this hole.
MA: I asked, how many have died.
LONE: Is that a crack in the side?
MA: Are you listening to me?
LONE: If I had some air—
MA: I asked, don't you see—?
LONE: The crack—over there—
MA: Will you answer me, please?
LONE: I need to get out.
MA: The rest here agree—
LONE: I can't stand the smell.
MA: That a hundred eighty—
LONE: I can't see the air—
MA: Of us will not see—
LONE: And I can't die.
MA: Our Gold Mountain dream.

(LONE/TANG *dies;* MA *throws his body overboard. The boat docks.* MA *exits, walks through the streets. He picks up one of the fighting sticks, while* LONE *becomes the mountain)*

MA: I have been given my pickax. Now I will attack the mountain.

(MA *does a dance of labor.* LONE *sings)*

LONE:

Hit your hardest
Pound out your tears
The more you try
The more you'll cry
At how little I've moved
And how large I loom
By the time the sun goes down

(*Dance stops)*

MA: This mountain is clever. But why shouldn't it be? It's fighting for its life, like we fight for ours.

(*The* MOUNTAIN *picks up a stick.* MA *and the* MOUNTAIN *do a battle dance. Dance ends)*

MA: This mountain not only defends itself—it also attacks. It turns our strength against us.

(LONE *does* MA*'s labor dance, while* MA *plants explosives in midair. Dance ends)*

MA: This mountain has survived for millions of years. Its wisdom is immense.

(LONE *and* MA *begin a second battle dance. This one ends with them working the battle sticks together.* LONE *breaks away, does a warrior strut)*

LONE: I am a white devil! Listen to my stupid language: "Wha che doo doo blah blah." Look at my wide eyes—like I have drunk seventy-two pots of tea. Look at my funny hair—twisting, turning, like a snake telling lies. (*To* MA) Bla bla doo doo tee tee.

MA: We don't understand English.

LONE: (*Angry*) Bla bla doo doo tee tee!

MA: (*With Chinese accent*) Please you-ah speak-ah Chinese?

LONE: Oh. Work—uh—one—two—more—work—two—

MA: Two hours more? Stupid demons. As confused as your hair. We will strike!

(*Gongs.* MA *is on strike*)

MA: (*In broken English*) Eight hours a day good for white man, all same good for ChinaMan.

LONE: The strike is over! We've won!

MA: I knew we would.

LONE: We forced the white devil to act civilized.

MA: Tamed the Barbarians!

LONE: Did you think—

MA: Who woulda thought?

LONE: —it could be done?

MA: Who?

LONE: But who?

MA: Who could tame them?

MA *and* LONE: Only a ChinaMan!

(*They laugh*)

LONE: Well, c'mon.

MA: Let's celebrate!

LONE: We have.

MA: Oh.

LONE: Back to work.

MA: But we've won the strike.

LONE: I know. Congratulations! And now—

MA: —back to work?

LONE: Right.

MA: No.

LONE: But the strike is over.

(LONE *tosses* MA *a stick. They resume their stick battle as before, but* MA *is heard over* LONE*'s singing*)

LONE:	MA:
Hit your hardest	Wait.
Pound out your	I'm tired of this!
tears	How do we end it?
The more you try	Let's stop now, all
The more you'll cry	right?
At how little I've	Look, I said enough!
moved	

And how large I
    loom
By the time the
    sun goes down.

(MA *tosses his stick away, but* LONE *is already aiming a blow toward it, so that* LONE *hits* MA *instead and knocks him down*)

MA: Oh! Shit . . .

LONE: I'm sorry! Are you all right?

MA: Yeah. I guess.

LONE: Why'd you let go? You can't just do that.

MA: I'm bleeding.

LONE: That was stupid—where?

MA: Here.

LONE: No.

MA: Ow!

LONE: There will probably be a bump.

MA: I dunno.

LONE: What?

MA: I dunno why I let go.

LONE: It was stupid.

MA: But how were we going to end the opera?

LONE: Here. (*He applies whiskey to* MA*'s bruise*) I don't know.

MA: Why didn't we just end it with the celebration? Ow! Careful.

LONE: Sorry. But Ma, the celebration's not the end. We're returning to work. Today. At dawn.

MA: What?

LONE: We've already lost nine days of work. But we got eight hours.

MA: Today? That's terrible.

LONE: What do you think we're here for? But they listened to our demands. We're getting a raise.

MA: Right. Fourteen dollars.

LONE: No. Eight.

MA: What?

LONE: We had to compromise. We got an eight-dollar raise.

MA: But we wanted fourteen. Why didn't we get fourteen?

LONE: It was the best deal they could get. Congratulations.

MA: Congratulations? Look, Lone, I'm sick of you making fun of the ChinaMen.

LONE: Ma, I'm not. For the first time. I was wrong. We got eight dollars.

MA: We wanted fourteen.

LONE: But we got eight hours.

MA: We'll go back on strike.

LONE: Why?

MA: We could hold out for months.

LONE: And lose all that work?

MA: But we just gave in.

LONE: You're being ridiculous. We got eight hours. Besides, it's already been decided.

MA: I didn't decide. I wasn't there. You made me stay up here.

LONE: The heads of the gangs decide.

MA: And that's it?

LONE: It's done.

MA: Back to work? That's what they decided? Lone, I don't want to go back to work.

LONE: Who does?

MA: I forgot what it's like.

LONE: You'll pick up the technique again soon enough.

MA: I mean, what it's like to have them telling you what to do all the time. Using up your strength.

LONE: I thought you said even after work, you still feel good.

MA: Some days. But others . . . (*Pause*) I get so frustrated sometimes. At the rock. The rock doesn't give in. It's not human. I wanna claw it with my fingers, but that would just rip them up. I wanna throw myself head first onto it, but it'd just knock my skull open. The rock would knock my skull open, then just sit there, still, like nothing had happened, like a faceless Buddha. (*Pause*) Lone, when do I get out of here?

LONE: Well, the railroad may get finished—

MA: It'll never get finished.

LONE: —or you may get rich.

MA: Rich. Right. This is the Gold Mountain. (*Pause*) Lone, has anyone ever gone home rich from here?

LONE: Yes. Some.

MA: But most?

LONE: Most . . . do go home.

MA: Do you still have the fear?

LONE: The fear?

MA: That you'll become like them—dead men?

LONE: Maybe I was wrong about them.

MA: Well, I do. You wanted me to say it before. I can say it now: "They are dead men." Their greatest accomplishment was to win a strike that's gotten us nothing.

LONE: They're sending money home.

MA: No.

LONE: It's not much, I know, but it's something.

MA: Lone, I'm not even doing that. If I don't get rich here, I might as well die here. Let my brothers laugh in peace.

LONE: Ma, you're too soft to get rich here, naïve—you believed the snow was warm.

MA: I've got to change myself. Toughen up. Take no shit. Count my change. Learn to gamble. Learn to win. Learn to stare. Learn to deny. Learn to look at men with opaque eyes.

LONE: You want to do that?

MA: I will. 'Cause I've got the fear. You've given it to me.

(*Pause*)

LONE: Will I see you here tonight?

MA: Tonight?

LONE: I just thought I'd ask.

MA: I'm sorry, Lone. I haven't got time to be the Second Clown.

LONE: I thought you might not.

MA: Sorry.

LONE: You could have been a . . . fair actor.

MA: You coming down? I gotta get ready for work. This is gonna be a terrible day. My legs are sore and my arms are outa practice.

LONE: You go first. I'm going to practice some before work. There's still time.

MA: Practice? But you said you lost your fear. And you said that's what brings you up here.

LONE: I guess I was wrong about that, too. Today, I am dancing for no reason at all.

MA: Do whatever you want. See you down at camp.

LONE: Could you do me a favor?

MA: A favor?

LONE: Could you take this down so I don't have to take it all?

(LONE *points to a pile of props*)

MA: Well, okay. (*Pause*) But this is the last time.

LONE: Of course, Ma. (MA *exits*) See you soon. The last time. I suppose so.

(LONE *resumes practicing. He twirls his hair around as in the beginning of the play. The sun begins to rise. It continues rising until* LONE *is moving and seen only in shadow*)

Curtain

COUNTEE CULLEN
(1903-1946)

Born Countee LeRoy Butler on May 13, 1903, Countee Cullen later changed his name after the death of his paternal grandmother, his legal guardian. At the age of fifteen, he moved into the home of the Reverend Frederick A. Cullen, a prominent Harlem clergyman, from whom he acquired the name Cullen. In 1925, he graduated from New York University, where he received a number of awards for his poetry. Also that year his first volume, Color, *was published. He obtained an M.A. from Harvard in 1926, and the following year another volume of his poems appeared. In 1928, Cullen received a Guggenheim fellowship and traveled to France. By 1929, he had four volumes of poetry in print, and he had edited a poetry collection,* Caroling Dusk: An Anthology of Verse by Negro Poets. *He continued to travel between New York and France. By the time his fourth volume of poetry,* The Medea, and Some Poems, *appeared in 1935, Cullen had turned his attention to other genres; a novel,* One Way to Heaven, *was published in 1932. The latter part of his career he devoted mainly to playwriting. From 1934 to 1945 he worked as an educator in the New York City public school system.*

"Incident" dramatizes a scene of confrontation between children, in this case a confrontation between racial oppressor and racial victim.

INCIDENT

Once riding in old Baltimore,
    Heart-filled, head-filled with glee,
I saw a Baltimorean
    Keep looking straight at me.

Now I was eight and very small,
    And he was no whit bigger,
And so I smiled, but he poked out
    His tongue, and called me, "Nigger."

I saw the whole of Baltimore
    From May until December;
Of all the things that happened there
    That's all that I remember.

CIVIL RIGHTS PHOTOGRAPHY

The media—television, radio, newspapers, and magazines—played an important part in the civil rights struggle of the 1960s. Journalistic coverage of civil rights demonstrations and protests kept the nation's attention riveted to the issues of racial inequality, vigilantism, and public repression of citizens' legal action. The public came to hate what they saw and to reject the assertion of racism and white privilege that marked these televised and photographed confrontations. Images of police or mobs beating up integrated groups of peaceful protesters did much to turn people's stomachs and change their minds about the racial status quo, with which they had formerly been comfortable.

Photographers like Charles Moore, whose work is represented here, were thus as much agents for change as the objective journalistic observers they set out to be. Opponents of the civil rights movement recognized this when they attempted to prevent photographers from taking pictures of confrontations between nonviolent demonstrators and angry mobs.

CIVIL RIGHTS MOVEMENT

CYRUS CASSELLS

(1957-)

Cyrus Cassells was born in Dover, Delaware. While still a student in high school, he received awards from the National Council of Teachers of English and Scholastic Magazine *for his poetry. He attended Stanford University and received his B.A. in 1979. His first book of poems,* The Mud Actor, *was a winner of the National Poetry Series Competition. Since 1989, he has taught at several colleges and universities, including the College of the Holy Cross, Northeastern University, George Mason University, and Southwest Texas State University. He was awarded a Lavin Younger Poet Award from the Academy of American Poets in 1992. In 1994, Cassell's second volume of poems,* Soul Make a Path Through Shouting, *was published. It received the William Carlos Williams Award from the Poetry Society of America. His work has also been nominated for the Pulitzer Prize, and he has received fellowships from the Rockefeller Foundation and the National Endowment for the Arts. Cassells has traveled extensively and also works as a professional actor. His most recent collection,* Beautiful Signor, *is a series of love poems and was published in 1997.*

The title poem of his second collection, "Soul Make a Path Through Shouting," is a snapshot of an archetypical moment in the civil rights movement, the confrontation of racist power and the innocence of children.

SOUL MAKE A PATH THROUGH SHOUTING

for Elizabeth Eckford
Little Rock, Arkansas, 1957

Thick at the schoolgate are the ones
Rage has twisted
Into minotaurs, harpies
Relentlessly swift;
So you must walk past the pincers,
The swaying horns,
Sister, sister,
Straight through the gusts
Of fear and fury,
Straight through:
Where are you going?

I'm just going to school.

Here we go to meet
The hydra-headed day,
Here we go to meet
The maelstrom —

Can my voice be an angel-on-the-spot,
An amen corner?
Can my voice take you there,
Gallant girl with a notebook,
Up, up from the shadows of gallows trees
To the other shore:
A globe bathed in light,
A chalkboard blooming with equations —

I have never seen the likes of you,
Pioneer in dark glasses:
You won't show the mob your eyes,
But I know your gaze,
Steady-on-the-North-Star, burning —

With their jerry-rigged faith,
Their spear of the American flag,
How could they dare to believe
You're someone sacred?:
Nigger, burr-headed girl,
Where are you going?

I'm just going to school.

NORMAN ROCKWELL

(1894-1978)

Norman Perceval Rockwell was born in New York City, where he studied at the Chase School of Art. In his teens Rockwell also studied briefly at the National Academy of Design and at the Art Students League before 1920. Between 1916 and 1963 Rockwell produced 322 covers for the Saturday Evening Post, *as well as occasional cover art for other popular magazines. His detailed, almost photographic realism drew him acclaim as America's greatest illustrator. Rockwell's pictures captured popular values of patriotism, family devotion, and community. His scenes were often based on people and sites in the small towns he called home: Arlington, Vermont, and Stockbridge, Massachusetts. He also illustrated books, most notably editions of Mark Twain's* Tom Sawyer *and* Huckleberry Finn. My Adventures as an Illustrator *(1959) is his autobiography.*

After his death, The Norman Rockwell Museum was opened in Stockbridge to display his work, which ultimately included not only the illustrations and magazine covers that made him famous but also portraits, murals, and landscapes. "The Problem We All Live With" (1964), from the Museum's collection, is Rockwell's comment on the civil rights movement then in full cry. The illustration focuses the viewer's attention on the innocence of childhood, a continuing theme in Rockwell's work.

SATURDAY EVENING POST COVER

"THE PROBLEM WE ALL LIVE WITH"

EXECUTIVE ORDER 9066

After the Japanese attacked the United States at Pearl Harbor, Hawaii, on December 7, 1941, the shock and dismay caused some citizens to doubt the loyalty of immigrants from Japan and their American-born sons and daughters. The result was a Presidential Executive Order that mandated the removal of Japanese Americans from "sensitive" sites on the west coast. Internment camps were set up in Central California, Arizona, Idaho, and elsewhere. Over 110,000 Japanese-American men, women, and children were held prisoner in these camps without due process, presumed to be guilty—in clear violation of the Constitution—of unstated crimes. Indeed, no evidence of espionage activities by any interned person was ever presented. With rare exceptions, German-American and Italian-American immigrants and citizens were not interned.

THE PRESIDENT

EXECUTIVE ORDER
AUTHORIZING THE SECRETARY OF WAR
TO PRESCRIBE MILITARY AREAS

WHEREAS the successful prosecution of the war requires every possible protection against espionage and against sabotage to national-defense material, national-defense premises, and national-defense utilities as defined in Section 4, Act of April 20, 1918, 40 Stat. 533, as amended by the Act of November 30, 1940, 54 Stat. 1220, and the Act of August 21, 1941, 55 Stat. 655 (U.S.C., Title 50, Sec. 104);

NOW, THEREFORE, by virtue of the authority vested in me as President of the United States, and Commander in Chief of the Army and Navy, I hereby authorize and direct the Secretary of War, and the Military Commanders whom he may from time to time designate, whenever he or any designated Commander deems such action necessary or desirable, to prescribe military areas in such places and of such extent as he or the appropriate Military Commander may determine, from which any or all persons may be excluded, and with respect to which, the right of any person to enter, remain in, or leave shall be subject to whatever restrictions the Secretary of War or the appropriate Military Commander may impose in his discretion. The Secretary of War is hereby authorized to provide for residents of any such area who are excluded therefrom, such transportation, food, shelter, and other accommodations as may be necessary, in the judgment of the Secretary of War or the said Military Commander, and until other arrangements are made, to accomplish the purpose of this order. The designation of military areas in any region or locality shall supersede designations of prohibited and restricted areas by the Attorney General under the Proclamations of December 7 and 8, 1941, and shall supersede the responsibility and authority of the Attorney General under the said Proclamations in respect of such prohibited and restricted areas.

I hereby further authorize and direct the Secretary of War and the said Military Commanders to take such other steps as he or the appropriate Military Commander may deem advisable to enforce compliance with the restrictions applicable to each Military area hereinabove authorized to be designated, including the use of Federal troops and other Federal Agencies, with authority to accept assistance of state and local agencies.

I hereby further authorize and direct all Executive Departments, independent establishments and other Federal Agencies, to assist the Secretary of War or the said Military Commanders in carrying out this Executive Order, including the furnishing of medical aid, hospitalization, food, clothing, transportation, use of land, shelter, and other supplies, equipment, utilities, facilities, and services.

This order shall not be construed as modifying or limiting in any way the authority heretofore granted under Executive Order No. 8972, dated December 12, 1941, nor shall it be construed as limiting or modifying the duty and responsibility of the Federal Bureau of Investigation, with respect to the investigation of alleged acts of sabotage or the duty and responsibility of the Attorney General and the Department of Justice under the Proclamations of December 7 and 8, 1941, prescribing regulations for the conduct and control of alien enemies, except as such duty and responsibility is superseded by the designation of military areas hereunder.

FRANKLIN D. ROOSEVELT
THE WHITE HOUSE,
February 19, 1942.

[No. 9066]

HISAYE YAMAMOTO
(1921-)

Hisaye Yamamoto was born in Redondo Beach, California, in 1921 and spent her early youth in various farming communities in southern California. She graduated from Compton Junior College with a degree in languages. During World War II, she was interned at the Colorado River Relocation Center (Poston), one of the many sites to which 110,000 Japanese Americans on the west coast were forcibly removed. She briefly evaded the indignities of the internment by going east, to Springfield, Massachusetts, but returned to Poston after the death of her younger brother, who was serving in the 442nd Regimental Combat Team in Europe. After the war, Yamamoto moved to Los Angeles and worked for three years at the Los Angeles Tribune. *In 1949, her essay on sexual harassment, "The High-Heeled Shoes," was published in* Partisan Review, *and since then her short stories have appeared in numerous newspapers, literary magazines, and anthologies. In 1986, she won an American Book Award for Lifetime Achievement from the Before Columbus Foundation. A collection of her fiction,* Seventeen Syllables and Other Stories, *was published in 1988.*

"The Legend of Miss Sasagawara" explores the price paid by a sensitive Japanese-American woman under the stress of the internment experience.

It reminds us of the banality and indirectness of much mental pain and the interaction between paralysis and oppression.

THE LEGEND OF MISS SASAGAWARA

Even in that unlikely place of wind, sand, and heat, it was easy to imagine Miss Sasagawara a decorative ingredient of some ballet. Her daily costume, brief and fitting closely to her trifling waist, generously billowing below, and bringing together arrestingly rich colors like mustard yellow and forest green, appeared to have been cut from a coarse-textured homespun; her shining hair was so long it wound twice about her head to form a coronet; her face was delicate and pale, with a fine nose, pouting bright mouth, and glittering eyes; and her measured walk said, "Look, I'm *walking!*" as though walking were not a common but a rather special thing to be doing. I first saw her so one evening after mess, as she was coming out of the women's latrine, going towards her barracks, and after I thought she was out of hearing, I imitated the young men of the Block (No. 33), and gasped, "Wow! How much does *she* weigh?"

"Oh, haven't you heard?" said my friend Elsie Kubo, knowing very well I had not. "That's Miss Sasagawara."

It turned out Elsie knew all about Miss Sasagawara, who with her father was new to Block 33. Where had she accumulated all her items? Probably a morsel here and a morsel there, and, anyway, I forgot to ask her sources, because the picture she painted was so distracting: Miss Sasagawara's father was a Buddhist minister, and the two had gotten permission to come to this Japanese evacuation camp in Arizona from one farther north, after the death there of Mrs. Sasagawara. They had come here to join the Rev. Sasagawara's brother's family, who lived in a neighboring Block, but there had been some trouble between them, and just this week the immigrant pair had gotten leave to move over to Block 33. They were occupying one end of the Block's lone empty barracks, which had not been chopped up yet into the customary four apartments. The other end had been taken over by a young couple, also newcomers to the Block, who had moved in the same day.

"And do you know what, Kiku?" Elsie continued. "Oooh, that gal is really temperamental. I guess it's because she was a ballet dancer before she got stuck in camp, I hear people like that are temperamental. Anyway, the Sasakis, the new couple at the other end of the barracks, think she's crazy. The day they all moved in, the barracks was really dirty, all covered with dust from the dust storms and everything, so Mr. Sasaki was going to wash the whole barracks down with a hose, and he thought he'd be nice and do the Sasagawaras' side first. You know, do them a favor. But do you know what? Mr. Sasaki got the hose attached to the faucet outside and started to go in the door, and he said all the Sasagawaras' suitcases and things were on top of the Army cots and Miss Sasagawara was trying to clean the place out with a pail of water and a broom. He said, 'Here, let me flush the place out with a hose for you; it'll be faster.' And she turned right around and screamed at him, 'What are you trying to do? Spy on me? Get out of here or I'll throw this water on you!' He said he was so surprised he couldn't move for a minute, and before he knew it, Miss Sasagawara just up and threw that water at him, pail and all. Oh, he said he got out of that place fast, but fast. Madwoman, he called her."

But Elsie had already met Miss Sasagawara, too, over at the apartment of the Murakamis, where Miss Sasagawara was borrowing Mrs. Murakami's Singer, and had found her quite amiable. "She said she was thirty-nine years old—imagine, thirty-nine, she looks so young, more like twenty-five; but she said she wasn't sorry she never got married, because she's had her fun. She said she got to go all over the country a couple of times, dancing in the ballet."

And after we emerged from the latrine, Elsie and I, slapping mosquitoes in the warm, gathering dusk, sat on the stoop of her apartment and talked awhile, jealously of the scintillating life Miss Sasagawara had led until now and nostalgically of the few ballets we had seen in the world outside (how faraway Los Angeles seemed!), but we ended up as we always did, agreeing that our mission in life, pushing twenty as we were, was first to finish college somewhere when and if the war ever ended and we were free again, and then to find good jobs and two nice, clean young men, preferably handsome, preferably rich, who would cherish us forever and a day.

My introduction, less spectacular, to the Rev. Sasagawara came later, as I noticed him, a slight and fragile-looking old man, in the Block mess hall (where I worked as a waitress, and Elsie, too) or laundry room or going to and from the latrine. Sometimes he would be farther out, perhaps going to the post-office or canteen or to visit friends in another Block or on some business to the Administration buildings, but wherever he was headed, however doubtless his destination, he always seemed to be wandering lostly. This may have been because he walked so slowly, with such negligible steps, or because he wore perpetually an air of bemusement, never talking directly to a person, as though, being what he was, he could not stop for an instant his meditation on the higher life.

I noticed, too, that Miss Sasagawara never came to the mess hall herself. Her father ate at the tables reserved for the occupants, mostly elderly, of the end barracks known as the bachelors' dormitory. After each meal, he came up to the counter and carried away a plate of food, protected with one of the pinkish apple wrappers we waitresses made as wrinkleless as possible and put out for napkins, and a mug of tea or coffee. Sometimes Miss Sasagawara could be seen rinsing out her empties at the one double-tub in the laundry that was reserved for private dishwashing.

If any one in the Block or in the entire camp of 15,000 or so people had talked at any length with Miss Sasagawara (everyone happening to speak of her called her that, although her first name, Mari, was simple enough and rather pretty) after her first and only visit to use Mrs. Murakami's sewing machine, I never heard of it. Nor did she ever willingly use the shower room, just off the latrine, when anyone else was there. Once, when I was up past midnight writing letters and went for my shower, I came upon her under the full needling force of a steamy spray, but she turned her back to me and did not answer my surprised hello. I hoped my body would be as smooth and spare and well-turned when I was thirty-nine. Another time, Elsie and I passed in front of the Sasagawara apartment, which was really only a cubicle because the once-empty barracks had soon been partitioned off into six units for families of two, and we saw her there on the wooden steps, sitting with her wide, wide skirt spread splendidly about her. She was intent on peeling a grapefruit, which her father had probably brought to her from the mess hall that morning, and Elsie called out, "Hello there!" Miss Sasagawara looked up and stared, without recognition. We were almost out of earshot when I heard her call, "Do I know you?" and

I could have almost sworn that she sounded hopeful, if not downright wistful, but Elsie, already miffed at having expended friendliness so unprofitably, seemed not to have heard, and that was that.

Well, if Miss Sasagawara was not one to speak to, she was certainly one to speak of, and she came up quite often as topic for the endless conversations which helped along the monotonous days. My mother said she had met the late Mrs. Sasagawara once, many years before the war, and to hear her tell it, a sweeter, kindlier woman there never was. "I suppose," said my mother, "that I'll never meet anyone like her again; she was a lady in every sense of the word." Then she reminded me that I had seen the Rev. Sasagawara before. Didn't I remember him as one of the three bhikshus who had read the sutras at Grandfather's funeral?

I could not say that I did. I barely remembered Grandfather, my mother's father. The only thing that came back with clarity was my nausea at the wake and the funeral, the first and only ones I had ever had occasion to attend, because it had been reproduced several times since—each time, in fact, that I had crossed again the actual scent or a suspicion of burning incense. Dimly I recalled the inside of the Buddhist temple in Los Angeles, an immense, murky auditorium whose high and huge platform had held, centered in the background, a great golden shrine touched with black and white. Below this platform, Grandfather, veiled by gauze, had slept in a long, grey box which just fitted him. There had been flowers, oh, such flowers, everywhere. And right in front of Grandfather's box had been the incense stand, upon which squatted two small bowls, one with a cluster of straw-thin sticks sending up white tendrils of smoke, the other containing a heap of coarse, grey powder. Each mourner in turn had gone up to the stand, bowing once, his palms touching in prayer, before he reached it; had bent in prayer over the stand; had taken then a pinch of incense from the bowl of crumbs and, bowing over it reverently, cast it into the other, the active bowl; had bowed, the hands praying again; had retreated a few steps and bowed one last time, the hands still joined, before returning to his seat. (I knew the ceremony well for having been severely coached in it on the evening of the wake.) There had been tears and tears and here and there a sudden sob.

And all this while, three men in black robes had been on the platform, one standing in front of the shining altar, the others sitting on either side, and the entire trio incessantly chanting a strange, mellifluous language in unison. From time to time there had reverberated through the enormous room, above the singsong, above the weeping, above the fragrance, the sharp, startling whang of the gong.

So, one of those men had been Miss Sasagawara's father. . . . This information brought him closer to me, and I listened with interest later when it was told that he kept here in his apartment a small shrine, much more intricately constructed than that kept by the usual Buddhist household, before which, at regular hours of the day, he offered incense and chanted, tinkling (in lieu of the gong) a small bell. What did Miss Sasagawara do at these prayer periods, I wondered; did she participate, did she let it go in one ear and out the other, or did she abruptly go out on the steps, perhaps to eat a grapefruit?

Elsie and I tired one day of working in the mess hall. And this desire for greener fields came almost together with the Administration announcement that henceforth the wages of residents doing truly vital labor, such as in the hospital or on the garbage trucks that went from mess hall to mess hall, would be upped to nineteen dollars a month instead of the common sixteen.

"Oh, I've always wanted to be a nurse!" Elsie confided, as the Block manager sat down to his breakfast after reading out the day's bulletin in English and Japanese.

"What's stopped you?" I asked.

"Mom," Elsie said. "She thinks it's dirty work. And she's afraid I'll catch something. But I'll remind her of the extra three dollars."

"It's never appealed to me much, either," I confessed. "Why don't we go over to garbage? It's the same pay."

Elsie would not even consider it. "Very funny. Well, you don't have to be a nurse's aide, Kiku. The hospital's short all kinds of help. Dental assistants, receptionists. . . . Let's go apply after we finish this here."

So, willy-nilly, while Elsie plunged gleefully into the pleasures of wearing a trim blue-and-white striped seersucker, into the duties of taking temperatures and carrying bed-pans, and into the fringe of medical jargon (she spoke very casually now of catheters, enemas, primiparas, multiparas), I became a relief receptionist at the hospital's front desk, taking my hours as they were assigned. And it was on one of my midnight-to-morning shifts that I spoke to Miss Sasagawara for the first time.

The cooler in the corridor window was still whirring away (for that desert heat in Summer had a way of lingering intact through the night to merge with the warmth of the morning sun), but she entered bundled in an extraordinarily long black coat, her face made petulant, not unprettily, by lines of pain.

"I think I've got appendicitis," she said breathlessly, without preliminary.

"May I have your name and address?" I asked, unscrewing my pen.

Annoyance seemed to outbalance agony for a moment, but she answered soon enough, in a cold rush, "Mari Sasagawara. Thirty-three-seven C."

It was necessary also to learn her symptoms, and I wrote down that she had chills and a dull aching at the back of her head, as well as these excruciating flashes in her lower right abdomen.

"I'll have to go wake up the doctor. Here's a blanket, why don't you lie down over there on the bench until he comes?" I suggested.

She did not answer, so I tossed the Army blanket on the bench, and when I returned from the doctors' dormitory, after having tapped and tapped on the door of young Dr. Moritomo, who was on night duty, she was still standing where I had left her, immobile and holding onto the wooden railing shielding the desk.

"Dr. Moritomo's coming right away," I said. "Why don't you sit down at least?"

Miss Sasagawara said, "Yes," but did not move.

"Did you walk all the way?" I asked incredulously, for Block 33 was a good mile off, across the canal.

She nodded, as if that were not important, also as if to thank me kindly to mind my own business.

Dr. Moritomo (technically, the title was premature; evacuation had caught him with a few months to go on his degree), wearing a maroon bathrobe, shuffled in sleepily and asked her to come into the emergency room for an examination. A short while later, he guided her past my desk into the laboratory, saying he was going to take her blood count.

When they came out, she went over to the electric fountain for a drink of water, and Dr. Moritomo said reflectively, "Her count's all right. Not appendicitis. We should keep her for observation, but the general ward is pretty full, isn't it? Hm, well, I'll give her something to take. Will you tell one of the boys to take her home?"

This I did, but when I came back from arousing George, one of the ambulance boys, Miss Sasagawara was gone, and Dr. Moritomo was coming out of the laboratory where he had gone to push out the lights. "Here's George, but that girl must have walked home," I reported helplessly.

"She's in no condition to do that. George, better catch up with her and take her home," Dr. Moritomo ordered.

Shrugging, George strode down the hall; the doctor shuffled back to bed; and soon there was the shattering sound of one of the old Army ambulances backing out of the hospital drive.

George returned in no time at all to say that Miss Sasagawara had refused to get on the ambulance. "She wouldn't even listen to me. She just kept walking and I drove alongside and told her it was Dr. Moritomo's orders, but she wouldn't even listen to me."

"She wouldn't?"

"I hope Doc didn't expect me to drag her into the ambulance."

"Oh, well," I said. "I guess she'll get home all right. She walked all the way up here."

"Cripes, what a dame!" George complained, shaking his head as he started back to the ambulance room. "I never heard of such a thing. She wouldn't even listen to me."

Miss Sasagawara came back to the hospital about a month later. Elsie was the one who rushed up to the desk where I was on day duty to whisper, "Miss Sasagawara just tried to escape from the hospital!"

"Escape? What do you mean, escape?" I said.

"Well, she came in last night, and they didn't know what was wrong with her, so they kept her for observation. And this morning, just now, she ran out of the ward in just a hospital nightgown and the orderlies chased after her and caught her and brought her back. Oh, she was just fighting them. But once they got her back to bed, she calmed down right away, and Miss Morris asked her what was the big idea, you know, and do you know what she said? She said she didn't want any more of those doctors pawing her. *Pawing* her, imagine!"

After an instant's struggle with self-mockery, my curiosity led me down the entrance corridor after Elsie, into the longer, wider corridor admitting to the general ward. The whole hospital staff appeared to have gathered in the room to get a look at Miss Sasagawara, and the other patients, or those of them that could, were sitting up attentively in their high, white, and narrow beds. Miss Sasagawara had the corner bed to the left as we entered and, covered only by a brief hospital apron, she was sitting on the edge with her legs dangling over the side. With her head slightly bent, she was staring at a certain place on the floor, and I knew that she must be aware of that concentrated gaze, of trembling old Dr. Kawamoto (he had retired several years before the war, but he had been drafted here), of Miss Morris, the head nurse, of Miss Bowman, the nurse in charge of the general ward during the day, of the other patients, of the nurse's aides, of the orderlies, and of everyone else who tripped in and out abashedly on some pretext or other in order to pass by her bed. I knew this by her smile, for as she continued to look at that same piece of the floor, she continued, unexpectedly, to seem wryly amused with the entire proceedings. I peered at her wonderingly through the triangular peep-hole created by someone's hand on hip, while Dr. Kawamoto, Miss Morris, and Miss Bowman tried to persuade her to lie down and relax. She was as smilingly immune to tactful suggestions as she was to tactless gawking.

There was no future to watching such a war of nerves as this, and besides, I was supposed to be at the front desk, so I hurried back in time to greet a frantic young mother and father, the latter carrying their small son who had had a hemorrhage this morning after a tonsillectomy yesterday in the out-patient clinic.

A couple of weeks later, on the late shift, I found George, the ambulance driver, in high spirits. This time he had been the one selected to drive a patient to Phoenix, where special cases were occasionally sent under escort, and he was looking forward to the moment when, for a few hours, the escort would permit him to go shopping around the city and perhaps take in a new movie. He showed me the list of things his friends had asked him to bring back for them, and we laughed together over the request of one plumpish nurse's aide for the biggest, richest chocolate cake he could find.

"You ought to have seen Mabel's eyes while she was describing the kind of cake she wanted," he said. "Man, she looked like she was eating it already!"

Just then one of the other drivers, Bobo Kunitomi, came up and nudged George, and they withdrew a few steps from my desk.

"Oh, I ain't particularly interested in that," I heard George saying.

There was some murmuring from Bobo, of which I caught the words, "Well, hell, you might as well, just as long as you're getting to go out there."

George shrugged, then nodded, and Bobo came over to the desk and asked for a pencil and paper. "This is a good place . . ." he said, handing George what he had written.

Was it my imagination, or did George emerge from his chat with Bobo a little ruddier than usual? "Well, I guess I better go get ready," he said, taking leave. "Oh, anything you want, Kiku? Just say the word."

"Thanks, not this time," I said. "Well, enjoy yourself."

"Don't worry," he said. "I will!"

He had started down the hall when I remembered to ask, "Who are you taking, anyway?"

George turned around. "Miss Sa-sa-ga-wa-ra," he said, accenting every syllable. "Remember that dame? The one who wouldn't let me take her home?"

"Yes," I said. "What's the matter with her?"

George, saying not a word, pointed at his head and made several circles in the air with his first finger.

"Really?" I said.

Still mum, George nodded in emphasis and pity before he turned to go.

How long was she away? It must have been several months, and when, towards late Autumn, she returned at last from the sanitarium in Phoenix, everyone in Block 33 was amazed at the change. She said hello and how are you as often and easily as the next person, although many of those she greeted were surprised and suspicious, remembering the earlier rebuffs. There were some who never did get used to Miss Sasagawara as a friendly being.

One evening when I was going toward the latrine for my shower, my youngest sister, ten-year-old Michi, almost collided with me and said excitedly, "You going for your shower now, Kiku?"

"You want to fight about it?" I said, making fists.

"Don't go now, don't go now! Miss Sasagawara's in there," she whispered wickedly.

"Well," I demanded. "What's wrong with that, honey?"

"She's scary. Us kids were in there and she came in and we finished, so we got out, and she said, 'Don't be afraid of me. I won't hurt you'. Gee, we weren't even afraid of her, but when she said that, gee!"

"Oh, go on home and go to bed," I said.

Miss Sasagawara was indeed in the shower and she welcomed me with a smile. "Aren't you the girl who plays the violin?"

I giggled and explained. Elsie and I, after hearing Menuhin on the radio, had, in a fit of madness, sent to Sears and Roebuck for beginners' violins that cost five dollars each. We had received free instruction booklets, too, but, unable to make heads or tails from them, we contented ourselves with occasionally taking the violins out of their paper bags and sawing every whichway away.

Miss Sasagawara laughed aloud—a lovely sound. "Well, you're just about as good as I am. I sent for a Spanish guitar. I studied it about a year once, but that was so long ago I don't remember the first thing and I'm having to start all over again. We'd make a fine orchestra."

That was the only time we really exchanged words, and some weeks later, I understood she had organized a dancing class from among the younger girls in the Block. My sister Michi, becoming one of her pupils, got very attached to her and spoke of her frequently at home. So I knew that Miss Sasagawara and her father had decorated their apartment to look oh, so pretty, that Miss Sasagawara had a whole big suitcase full of dancing costumes, and that Miss Sasagawara had just lots and lots of books to read.

The fruits of Miss Sasagawara's patient labor were put on show at the Block Christmas party, the second such observance in camp. Again, it was a gay, if odd, celebration. The mess hall was hung with red and green crepe-paper streamers and the greyish mistletoe that grew abundantly on the ancient mesquite surrounding the camp. There were even electric decorations on the token Christmas tree. The oldest occupant of the bachelors' dormitory gave a tremulous monologue in an exaggerated Hiroshima dialect, one of the young boys wore a bow-tie and whispered a popular song while the girls shrieked and pretended to be growing faint, my mother sang an old Japanese song, four of the girls wore similar blue dresses and harmonized on a sweet tune, a little girl in a grass skirt and superfluous brassiere did a hula, and the chief cook came out with an ample saucepan and, assisted by the waitresses, performed the familiar *dojo-sukui*, the comic dance about a man who is merely trying to scoop up a few loaches from an uncooperative lake. Then Miss Sasagawara shooed her eight little girls, including Michi, in front, and while they formed a stiff pattern and waited, self-conscious in the rustly crepe-paper dresses they had made themselves, she set up a portable phonograph on the floor and vigorously turned the crank.

Something was past its prime, either the machine or the record or the needle, for what came out was a feeble rasp but distantly related to the Mozart minuet it was supposed to be. After a bit I recognized the melody; I had learned it as a child to the words,

> When dames wore hoops and powdered hair,
> And very strict was e-ti-quette,
> When men were brave and ladies fair,
> They danced the min-u-et. . . .

And the little girls, who might have curtsied and stepped gracefully about under Miss Sasagawara's eyes alone, were all elbows and knees as they felt the Block's one-hundred-and-fifty or more pairs of eyes on them. Although there was sustained applause after their number, what we were benevolently approving was the great effort, for the achievement had been undeniably small. Then Santa came with a pillow for a stomach, his hands each dragging a bulging burlap bag. Church people outside had kindly sent these gifts, Santa announced, and every recipient must write and thank the person whose name he would find on an enclosed slip. So saying, he called by name each Block child under twelve and ceremoniously presented each eleemosynary package, and a couple of the youngest children screamed in fright at this new experience of a red and white man with a booming voice.

At the last, Santa called, "Miss Mari Sasagawara!" and when she came forward in surprise, he explained to the gathering that she was being rewarded for her help with the Block's younger generation. Everyone clapped and Miss Sasagawara, smiling graciously, opened her package then and there. She held up her gift, a peach-colored bath towel, so that it could be fully seen, and everyone clapped again.

Suddenly, I put this desert scene behind me. The notice I had long awaited, of permission to relocate to Philadelphia to attend college, finally came, and there was a prodigious amount of packing to do, leave papers to sign, and goodbyes to say. And once the wearying, sooty train trip was over, I found myself in an intoxicating new world of daily classes, afternoon teas, and evening concerts, from which I dutifully emerged now and then to answer the letters from home. When the beautiful semester was over, I returned to Arizona, to the glowing heat, to the camp, to the family, for although the war was still on, it had been decided to close down the camps, and I had been asked to go back and spread the good word about higher education among the young people who might be dispersed in this way.

Elsie was still working in the hospital, although she had applied for entrance into the cadet nurse corps and was expecting acceptance any day, and the long conversations we held were mostly about the good old days, the good old days when we had worked in the mess hall together, the good old days when we had worked in the hospital together.

"What ever became of Miss Sasagawara?" I asked one day, seeing the Rev. Sasagawara go abstractly by. "Did she relocate somewhere?"

"I didn't write you about her, did I?" Elsie said meaningfully. "Yes, she's relocated all right. Haven't seen her around, have you?"

"Where did she go?"

Elsie answered offhandedly. "California."

"California?" I exclaimed. "We can't go back to California. What's she doing in California?"

So Elsie told me: Miss Sasagawara had been sent back there to a state institution, oh, not so very long after I had left for school. She had begun slipping back into her aloof ways almost immediately after Christmas, giving up the dancing class and not speaking to people. Then Elsie had heard a couple of very strange, yes, very strange things about her. One thing had been told by young Mrs. Sasaki, that next-door neighbor of the Sasagawaras.

Mrs. Sasaki said she had once come upon Miss Sasagawara sitting, as was her habit, on the porch. Mrs. Sasaki had been shocked to the core to see that the face of this thirty-nine-year-old woman (or was she forty now?) wore a beatific expression as she watched the activity going on in the doorway of her neighbors across the way, the Yoshinagas. This activity had been the joking and loud laughter of Joe and Frank, the young Yoshinaga boys, and three or four of their friends. Mrs. Sasaki would have let the matter go, were it not for the fact that Miss Sasagawara was so absorbed a spectator of this horseplay that her head was bent to one side and she actually had one finger in her mouth as she gazed, in the manner of a shy child confronted with a marvel. "What's the matter with you, watching the boys like that?" Mrs. Sasaki had cried. "You're old enough to be their mother!" Startled, Miss Sasagawara had jumped up and dashed back into her apartment. And when Mrs. Sasaki had gone into hers, adjoining the Sasagawaras', she had been terrified to hear Miss Sasagawara begin to bang on the wooden walls with something heavy like a hammer. The banging, which sounded as though Miss Sasagawara were using all her strength on each blow, had continued wildly for at least five minutes. Then all had been still.

The other thing had been told by Joe Yoshinaga, who lived across the way from Miss Sasagawara. Joe and his brother slept on two Army cots pushed together on one side of the room, while their parents had a similar arrangement on the other side. Joe had standing by his bed an apple crate for a shelf, and he was in the habit of reading his sports and western magazines in bed and throwing them on top of the crate before he went to sleep. But one morning he had noticed his magazines all neatly stacked inside the crate, when he was sure he had carelessly thrown some on top the night before, as usual. This happened several times, and he finally asked his family whether one of them had been putting his magazines away after he fell asleep. They had said no and laughed, telling him he must be getting absent-minded. But the mystery had been solved late one night, when Joe gradually awoke in his cot with the feeling that he was being watched. Warily, he had opened one eye slightly and had been thoroughly awakened and chilled, in the bargain, by what he saw. For what he saw was Miss Sasagawara sitting there on his apple crate, her long hair all undone and flowing about her. She was dressed in a white nightgown and her hands were clasped on her lap. And all she was doing was sitting there watching him, Joe Yoshinaga. He could not help it, he had sat up and screamed. His mother, a light sleeper, came running to see what had happened, just as Miss Sasagawara was running out the door, the door they had always left unlatched, or even wide open in Summer. In the morning, Mrs. Yoshinaga had gone straight to the Rev. Sasagawara and asked him to do something about his daughter. The Rev. Sasagawara, sympathizing with her indignation in his benign but vague manner, had said he would have a talk with Mari.

And, concluded Elsie, Miss Sasagawara had gone away not long after. I was impressed, although Elsie's sources were not what I would ordinarily pay much attention to, Mrs. Sasaki, that plump and giggling young woman who always felt called upon to explain that she was childless by choice, and Joe Yoshinaga, who had a knack of blowing up, in his drawling voice, any incident in which he personally played even a small part (I could imagine the field day he had had with this one). Elsie puzzled aloud over the cause of Miss Sasagawara's derangement, and I, who had so newly had some contact with the recorded explorations into the virgin territory of the human mind, sagely explained that Miss Sasagawara had no doubt looked upon Joe Yoshinaga as the image of either the lost lover or the lost son. But my words made me uneasy by their glibness, and I began to wonder seriously about Miss Sasagawara for the first time.

Then there was this last word from Miss Sasagawara herself, making her strange legend as complete as I, at any rate, would probably ever know it. This came some time after I had gone back to Philadelphia and the family had joined me there, when

I was neck deep in research for my final paper. I happened one day to be looking through the last issue of a small poetry magazine that had suspended publication midway through the war. I felt a thrill of recognition at the name, Mari Sasagawara, signed to a long poem, introduced as ". . . the first published poem of a Japanese-American woman who is, at present, an evacuee from the West Coast making her home in a War Relocation center in Arizona."

It was a *tour de force,* erratically brilliant and, through the first readings, tantalizingly obscure. It appeared to be about a man whose lifelong aim had been to achieve Nirvana, that saintly state of moral purity and universal wisdom. This man had in his way certain handicaps, all stemming from his having acquired, when young and unaware, a family for which he must provide. The day came at last, however, when his wife died and other circumstances made it unnecessary for him to earn a competitive living. These circumstances were considered by those about him as sheer imprisonment, but he had felt free for the first time in his long life. It became possible for him to extinguish within himself all unworthy desire and consequently all evil, to concentrate on that serene, eight-fold path of highest understanding, highest mindedness, highest speech, highest action, highest livelihood, highest recollectedness, highest endeavor, and highest meditation.

This man was certainly noble, the poet wrote, this man was beyond censure. The world was doubtless enriched by his presence. But say that someone else, someone sensitive, someone admiring, someone who had not achieved this sublime condition and who did not wish to, were somehow called to companion such a man. Was it not likely that the saint, blissfully bent on cleansing from his already radiant soul the last imperceptible blemishes (for, being perfect, would he not humbly suspect his own flawlessness?) would be deaf and blind to the human passions rising, subsiding, and again rising, perhaps in anguished silence, within the selfsame room? The poet could not speak for others, of course; she could only speak for herself. But she would describe this man's devotion as a sort of madness, the monstrous sort which, pure of itself and so with immunity, might possibly bring troublous, scented scenes to recur in the other's sleep.

JAMES HOUSTON
(1933–)

AND

JEANNE WAKATSUKI HOUSTON
(1934–)

James Houston, born November 10, 1933, grew up in northern California. He married Jeanne Toyo Wakatsuki in 1957. Jeanne Wakatsuki Houston was also born in California, on September 26, 1934. During World War II, her family was interned at Manzanar Relocation Center. With her husband, she coauthored Farewell to Manzanar, *an account of her family's experiences during their internment and immediately following the war. The couple also coauthored a screenplay of* Farewell to Manzanar, *which was produced in 1976 and awarded a Humanitas Award and a Christopher Award. Jeanne Wakatsuki Houston received a B.A. from the University of San Jose and also studied at the University of Paris. James Houston attended San Jose College and Stanford University, where he was a Wallace Stegner Fellow. He has taught at the University of Hawaii, Manoa; the University of Michigan; and the University of California, Santa Cruz. He has published several novels, as well as works of nonfiction, and has received grants from the National Endowment for the Arts.* In the Ring of Fire: A Pacific Basin Journey *is an account of the couple's travels around the Pacific Basin region.*

FROM FAREWELL TO MANZANAR

In Spanish, Manzanar means "apple orchard." Great stretches of Owens Valley were once green with orchards and alfalfa fields. It has been a desert ever since its water started flowing south into Los Angeles, sometime during the twenties. But a few rows of untended pear and apple trees were still growing there when the camp opened, where a shallow water table had kept them alive. In the spring of 1943 we moved to Block 28, right up next to one of the old pear orchards. That's where we stayed until the end of the war, and those trees stand in my memory for the turning of our life in camp, from the outrageous to the tolerable.

Papa pruned and cared for the nearest trees. Late that summer we picked the fruit green and stored it in a root cellar he had dug under our new barracks. At night the wind through the leaves would sound like the surf had sounded in Ocean Park, and while drifting off to sleep I could almost imagine we were still living by the beach.

Mama had set up this move. Block 28 was also close to the camp hospital. For the most part, people lived there who had to have easy access to it. Mama's connection was her job as dietician. A whole half of one barracks had fallen empty when another family relocated. Mama hustled us in there almost before they'd snapped their suitcases shut.

For all the pain it caused, the loyalty oath finally did speed up the relocation program. One result was a gradual easing of the congestion in the barracks. A shrewd househunter like Mama could set things up fairly comfortably—by Manzanar standards—if she kept her eyes open. But you had to move fast. As soon as the word got around that so-and-so had been cleared to leave, there would be a kind of tribal restlessness, a nervous rise in the level of neighborhood gossip as wives jockeyed for position to see who would get the empty cubicles.

In Block 28 we doubled our living space—four rooms for the twelve of us. Ray and Woody walled them with sheetrock. We had ceilings this time, and linoleum floors of solid maroon. You had three colors to choose from—maroon, black, and forest green—and there was plenty of it around by this time. Some families would vie with one another for the most elegant floor designs, obtaining a roll of each color from the supply shed, cutting it into diamonds, squares, or triangles, shining it with heating oil, then leaving their doors open so that passers-by could admire the handiwork.

Papa brought his still with him when we moved. He set it up behind the door, where he continued to brew his own sake and brandy. He wasn't drinking as much now, though. He spent a lot of time outdoors. Like many of the older Issei men, he didn't take a regular job in camp. He puttered. He had been working hard for thirty years and, bad as it was for him in some ways, camp did allow him time to dabble with hobbies he would never have found time for otherwise.

Once the first year's turmoil cooled down, the authorities started letting us outside the wire for recreation. Papa used to hike along the creeks that channeled down from the base of the Sierras. He brought back chunks of driftwood, and he would pass long hours sitting on the steps carving myrtle limbs into benches, table legs, and lamps, filling our rooms with bits of gnarled, polished furniture.

He hauled stones in off the desert and built a small rock garden outside our doorway, with succulents and a patch of moss. Near it he laid flat steppingstones leading to the stairs.

He also painted watercolors. Until this time I had not known he could paint. He loved to sketch the mountains. If anything made that country habitable it was the mountains themselves, purple when the sun dropped and so sharply etched in the morning light the granite dazzled almost more than the bright snow lacing it. The nearest peaks rose ten thousand feet higher than the valley floor, with Whitney, the highest, just off to the south. They were important for all of us, but especially for the Issei. Whitney reminded Papa of Fujiyama, that is, it gave him the same kind of spiritual sustenance. The tremendous beauty of those peaks was inspirational, as so many natural forms are to the Japanese (the rocks outside our doorway could be those mountains in miniature). They also represented those forces in nature, those powerful and inevitable forces that cannot be resisted, reminding a man that sometimes he must simply endure that which cannot be changed.

Subdued, resigned, Papa's life—all our lives—took on a pattern that would hold for the duration of the war. Public shows of resentment pretty much spent themselves over the loyalty oath crises. *Shikata ga nai* again became the motto, but under altered circumstances. What had to be endured was the climate, the confinement, the steady crumbling away of family life. But the camp itself had been made livable. The government provided for our physical needs. My parents and older brothers and sisters, like most of the internees, accepted their lot and did what they could to make the best of a bad situation. "We're here," Woody would say. "We're here, and there's no use moaning about it forever."

Gardens had sprung up everywhere, in the firebreaks, between the rows of barracks—rock gardens, vegetable gardens, cactus and flower gardens. People who lived in Owens Valley during the war still remember the flowers and lush greenery they could see from the highway as they drove past the main gate. The soil around Manzanar is alluvial and very rich. With water siphoned off from the Los Angeles-bound aqueduct, a large farm was under cultivation just outside the camp, providing the mess halls with lettuce, corn, tomatoes, eggplant, string beans, horseradish, and cucumbers. Near Block 28 some of the men who had been professional gardeners built a small park, with mossy nooks, ponds, waterfalls and curved wooden bridges. Sometimes in the evenings we could walk down the raked gravel paths. You could face away from the barracks, look past a tiny rapids toward the darkening mountains, and for a while not be a prisoner at all. You could hang suspended in some odd, almost lovely land you could not escape from yet almost didn't want to leave.

As the months at Manzanar turned to years, it became a world unto itself, with its own logic and familiar ways. In time, staying there seemed far simpler than moving once again to another, unknown place. It was as if the war were forgotten, our reason for being there forgotten. The present, the little bit of busywork you had right in front of you, became the most urgent thing. In such a narrowed world, in order to survive, you learn to contain your rage and your despair, and you try to re-create, as well as you can, your normality, some sense of things continuing. The fact that America had accused us, or excluded us, or imprisoned us, or whatever it might be called, did not change the kind of world we wanted. Most of us were born in this country; we had no other models. Those parks and gardens lent it an oriental character, but in most ways it was a totally equipped American small town, complete with schools, churches, Boy Scouts, beauty parlors, neighborhood gossip, fire and police departments, glee clubs, softball leagues, Abbott and Costello movies, tennis courts, and traveling shows. (I still remember an Indian who turned up one Saturday billing himself as a Sioux chief, wearing bear claws and head feathers. In the firebreak he sang songs and danced his tribal dances while hundreds of us watched.)

In our family, while Papa puttered, Mama made her daily rounds to the mess halls, helping young mothers with their feeding, planning diets for the various ailments people suffered from. She wore a bright yellow, long-billed sun hat she had made herself and always kept stiffly starched. Afternoons I would see her coming from blocks away, heading home, her tiny figure warped by heat waves and that bonnet a yellow flower wavering in the glare.

In their disagreement over serving the country, Woody and Papa had struck a kind of compromise. Papa talked him out of volunteering; Woody waited for the army to induct him. Meanwhile he clerked in the co-op general store. Kiyo, nearly thirteen by this time, looked forward to the heavy winds. They moved the sand around and uncovered obsidian arrowheads he could sell to old men in camp for fifty cents apiece. Ray, a few years older, played in the six-man touch football league, sometimes against Caucasian teams who would come in from Lone Pine or Independence. My sister Lillian was in high school and singing with a hillbilly band called The Sierra Stars—jeans, cowboy hats, two guitars, and a tub bass. And my oldest brother, Bill, led a dance band called The Jive Bombers—brass and rhythm, with cardboard fold-out music stands lettered J. B. Dances were held every weekend in one of the recreation halls. Bill played trumpet and took vocals on Glenn Miller arrangements of such tunes as *In the Mood, String of Pearls,* and *Don't Fence Me In.* He didn't sing *Don't Fence Me In* out of protest, as if trying quietly to mock the authorities. It just happened to be a hit song one year, and they all wanted to be an up-to-date American swing band. They would blast it out into recreation barracks full of bobby-soxed, jitterbugging couples:

> *Oh, give me land, lots of land*
> *Under starry skies above,*
> *Don't fence me in.*
> *Let me ride through the wide*
> *Open country that I love . . .*

Pictures of the band, in their bow ties and jackets, appeared in the high school yearbook for 1943-1944, along with pictures of just about everything else in camp that year. It was called *Our World.* In its pages you see school kids with armloads of books, wearing cardigan sweaters and walking past rows of tarpapered shacks. You see chubby girl yell leaders, pompons flying as they leap with glee. You read about the school play, called *Growing Pains* ". . . the story of a typical American home, in this case that of the McIntyres. They see their boy and girl tossed into the normal awkward growing up stage, but can offer little assistance or direction in their turbulent course . . ." with Shoji Katayama as George McIntyre, Takudo Ando as Terry McIntyre, and Mrs. McIntyre played by Kazuko Nagai.

All the class pictures are in there, from the seventh grade through twelfth, with individual head shots of seniors, their names followed by the names of the high schools they would have graduated from on the outside: Theodore Roosevelt, Thomas Jefferson, Herbert Hoover, Sacred Heart. You see pretty girls on bicycles, chicken yards full of fat pullets, patients back-tilted in dental chairs, lines of laundry, and finally, two large blowups, the first of a high tower with a searchlight, against a Sierra backdrop, the next a two-page endsheet showing a wide path that curves among rows of elm trees. White stones border the path. Two dogs are following an old woman in gardening clothes as she strolls along. She is in the middle distance, small beneath the trees, beneath the snowy peaks. It is winter. All the elms are bare. The scene is both stark and comforting. This path leads toward one edge of camp, but the wire is out of sight, or out of focus. The tiny woman seems very much at ease. She and her tiny dogs seem almost swallowed by the landscape, or floating in it.

GARRETT HONGO
(1951-   )

Garrett Hongo was born in Volcano, Hawaii. His most recent work, Volcano: A Memoir of Hawaii, *is a personal account of Hongo's discovery of his family history in this small community on Hawaii. He attended Pomona College and did graduate work at the University of Michigan and at the University of California, Irvine. In 1975, Hongo received the Hopwood Prize from the University of Michigan, and in 1981 the Poetry Center of the 92nd Street Y awarded him a Discovery/The* Nation *award. Hongo's first volume of poetry,* Yellow Light, *was published in 1982. He has taught at several universities, including the University of California, Los Angeles; the University of Southern California; and the University of Missouri, Columbia, where he was poetry editor of* The Missouri Review. *His second volume of poetry,* The River of Heaven, *was awarded the Lamont Poetry Prize of the Academy of American Poets and was a finalist for the 1989 Pulitzer Prize. He has received fellowships from the National Endowment for the Arts and the John Simon Guggenheim Memorial Foundation. Garrett Hongo has also edited* Under Western Eyes: Personal Essays from Asian America; Songs My Mother Taught Me: Stories, Memoir, and Plays by Wakako Yamauchi; *and* The Open Boat: Poems from Asian America. *He is Professor of English and Creative Writing at the University of Oregon and lives in Eugene, Oregon.*

"Something Whispered in the Shakuhachi*" gives a voice to the silent memories and spiritual devastation of a Japanese-American man displaced by the Internment.*

Something Whispered

in the *Shakuhachi*

No one knew the secret of my flutes,
and I laugh now
because some said
I was enlightened.
But the truth is
I'm only a gardener
who before the War
was a dirt farmer and learned
how to grow the bamboo
in ditches next to the fields,
how to leave things alone
and let the silt build up
until it was deep enough to stink
bad as night soil, bad
as the long, witch-grey
hair of a ghost.

No secret in that.

My land was no good, rocky,
and so dry I had to sneak
water from the whites,
hacksaw the locks off the chutes at night,
and blame Mexicans, Filipinos,
or else some wicked spirit
of a migrant, murdered in his sleep
by sheriffs and wanting revenge.
Even though they never believed me,
it didn't matter—no witnesses,
and my land was never thick with rice,
only the bamboo
growing lush as old melodies
and whispering like brush strokes
against the fine scroll of wind.

I found some string in the shed
or else took a few stalks
and stripped off their skins,
wove the fibers, the floss,
into cords I could bind
around the feet, ankles, and throats
of only the best bamboos.
I used an ice pick for an awl,

a fish knife to carve finger holes,
and a scythe to shape the mouthpiece.

I had my flutes.

*

When the War came,
I told myself I lost nothing.
My land, which was barren,
was not actually mine but leased
(we could not own property)
and the shacks didn't matter.

What did were the power lines nearby
and that sabotage was suspected.

What mattered to me
were the flutes I burned
in a small fire
by the bath house.

*

All through Relocation,
in the desert where they put us,
at night when the stars talked
and the sky came down
and drummed against the mesas,
I could hear my flutes
wail like fists of wind
whistling through the barracks.
I came out of Camp,
a blanket slung over my shoulder,
found land next to this swamp,
planted strawberries and beanplants,
planted the dwarf pines and tended them,
got rich enough to quit
and leave things alone,
let the ditches clog with silt again
and the bamboo grow thick as history.

*

So, when it's bad now,
when I can't remember what's lost
and all I have for the world to take
means nothing,
I go out back of the greenhouse
at the far end of my land
where the grasses go wild
and the arroyos come up

with cat's-claw and giant dahlias,
where the children of my neighbors
consult with the wise heads
of sunflowers, huge against the sky,
where the rivers of weather
and the charred ghosts of old melodies
converge to flood my land
and sustain the one thicket
of memory that calls for me
to come and sit
among the tall canes
and shape full-throated songs
out of wind, out of bamboo,
out of a voice
that only whispers.

Lorna Dee Cervantes
(1954-)

Lorna Dee Cervantes is a fifth-generation Californian born in San Francisco. She received a B.A. from San Jose State University and did graduate work at the University of California, Santa Cruz. In 1979, she was awarded a grant from the National Endowment for the Arts. Her first volume of poetry, Emplumada, *was published in 1981 and awarded the American Book Award in 1982. Her second collection of poems,* From the Cables of Genocide: Poems on Love and Hunger, *was published in 1992 and awarded the Patterson Poetry Prize. She has also received fellowships from the Colorado Arts Council and the Lila Wallace-Reader's Digest Fund. She has taught at the University of Houston and currently teaches creative writing at the University of Colorado in Boulder.*

Cervantes's "Poema para los Californios Muertos" [Poem for the Dead Californios], is an elegiac lamentation for the injustices done to the Hispanic Californians who were disposessed by the annexation of Mexico's Northern territories following the Mexican-American War of 1845-1846.

Poema para los Californios Muertos

Once a refuge for Mexican Californios . . .
—plaque outside a restaurant
in Los Altos, California, 1974.

These older towns die
into stretches of freeway,
The high scaffolding cuts a clean cesarean

across belly valleys and fertile dust.
What a bastard child, this city
lost in the soft
llorando de las madres.
Californios moan like husbands of the raped,
husbands de la tierra,
tierra la madre.

I run my fingers
across this brass plaque.
Its cold stirs in me a memory
of silver buckles and spent bullets,
of embroidered shawls and dark rebozos.
Yo recuerdo los antepasados muertos.
Los recuerdo en la sangre,
la sangre fértil.

What refuge did you find here,
ancient Californios?
Now at this restaurant nothing remains
but this old oak and an ill-placed plaque.
Is it true that you still live here
in the shadows of these white, high-class houses?
Soy la hija pobrecita
pero puedo maldecir estas fantasmas blancas.
Las fantasmas tuyas deben aquí quedarse,
solas las tuyas.

In this place I see nothing but strangers.
On the shelves there are bitter antiques,
yanqui remnants
y estos no de los Californios.
A blue jay shrieks
above the pungent odor of crushed
eucalyptus and the pure scent
of rage.

LUIS VALDEZ
(1940-)

Luis Valdez was born on June 26, 1940, in Delano, California. While in college, Valdez first began writing plays. After he graduated from San Jose State University in 1964, he performed in a mime troupe before joining the United Farm Workers as a union organizer. Valdez used theater to explore the concerns of migrant farm workers represented by the union, and the theater company he founded, *El Teatro Campesino*, grew out of this work with the United Farm Workers. *El Teatro Campesino* has produced a number of his plays and has toured extensively in the United States and abroad. In 1978, his play Zoot Suit, *which he also directed, received an award from the Los Ange-les Drama Critics Circle, and its film adaptation was nominated for a Golden Globe for best musical film in 1981. Valdez has written and directed other film projects, including the film* La Bamba. *His work has received numerous prizes, including an Obie Award and an Emmy Award. He has lectured at both the University of California, Santa Cruz, and the University of California, Berke-ley, and has been a member of the California Arts Council and the National Endowment for the Arts Congressional Committee for the State of the Arts.*

Valdez's one-act play, Los Vendidos, *raises the issue of representation. It asks the audience to consider the narrow range of stereotypical images of Mexican-American men that circulated in the public discourse of the 1970s.*

LOS VENDIDOS

Characters

HONEST SANCHO
SECRETARY
FARM WORKER
JOHNNY
REVOLUCIONARIO
MEXICAN-AMERICAN

Scene: HONEST SANCHO's *Used Mexican Lot and Mexican Curio Shop. Three models are on display in* HONEST SANCHO's *shop: to the right, there is a* REVOLUCIONARIO, *complete with sombrero, carrilleras, and carabina 30–30. At center, on the floor, there is the* FARM WORKER, *under a broad straw sombrero. At stage left is the* PACHUCO, *filero in hand.*

(HONEST SANCHO *is moving among his models, dusting them off and preparing for another day of business.*)

SANCHO: Bueno, bueno, mis monos, vamos a ver a quien vendemos ahora, ¿no? (*To audience.*) ¡Quihubo! I'm Honest Sancho and this is my shop. Antes fui con-tratista pero ahora longré tener mi negocito. All I need now is a customer. (*A bell rings offstage.*) Ay, a customer!

SECRETARY: (*Entering*) Good morning, I'm Miss Jiménez from—

SANCHO: ¡Ah, una chicana! Welcome, welcome Señorita Jiménez.

SECRETARY: (*Anglo pronunciation*) JIM-enez.

SANCHO: ¿Qué?

SECRETARY: My name is Miss JIM-enez. Don't you speak English? What's wrong with you?

SANCHO: Oh, nothing, Señorita JIM-enez. I'm here to help you.

SECRETARY: That's better. As I was starting to say, I'm a secretary from Governor Rea-gan's office, and we're looking for a Mexican type for the administration.

SANCHO: Well, you come to the right place, lady. This is Honest Sancho's Used Mexi-can lot, and we got all types here. Any particular type you want?

SECRETARY: Yes, we were looking for somebody suave—

SANCHO: Suave.

SECRETARY: Debonair.

SANCHO: De buen aire.

SECRETARY: Dark.

SANCHO: Prieto.

SECRETARY: But of course not too dark.

SANCHO: No muy prieto.

SECRETARY: Perhaps, beige.

SANCHO: Beige, just the tone. Así como cafecito con leche, ¿no?

SECRETARY: One more thing. He must be hard-working.

SANCHO: That could only be one model. Step right over here to the center of the shop, lady. (*They cross to the* FARM WORKER.) This is our standard farm worker model. As you can see, in the words of our beloved Senator George Murphy, he is "built close to the ground." Also take special notice of his four-ply Goodyear huaraches, made from the rain tire. This wide-brimmed sombrero is an extra added feature—keeps off the sun, rain, and dust.

SECRETARY: Yes, it does look durable.

SANCHO: And our farm worker model is friendly. Muy amable. Watch. (*Snaps his fingers.*)

FARM WORKER: (*Lifts up head*) Buenos días, señorita. (*His head drops.*)

SECRETARY: My, he's friendly.

SANCHO: Didn't I tell you? Loves his patrones! But his most attractive feature is that he's hard-working. Let me show you. (*Snaps fingers.* FARM WORKER *stands.*)

FARM WORKER: ¡El jale! (*He begins to work.*)

SANCHO: As you can see, he is cutting grapes.

SECRETARY: Oh, I wouldn't know.

SANCHO: He also picks cotton. (*Snap.* FARM WORKER *begins to pick cotton.*)

SECRETARY: Versatile isn't he?

SANCHO: He also picks melons. (*Snap.* FARM WORKER *picks melons.*) That's his slow speed for late in the season. Here's his fast speed. (*Snap.* FARM WORKER *picks faster.*)

SECRETARY: ¡Chihuahua! . . . I mean, goodness, he sure is a hard worker.

SANCHO: (*Pulls the* FARM WORKER *to his feet*) And that isn't the half of it. Do you see these little holes on his arms that appear to be pores? During those hot sluggish days in the field, when the vines or the branches get so entangled, it's almost impossible to move; these holes emit a certain grease that allow our model to slip and slide right through the crop with no trouble at all.

SECRETARY: Wonderful. But is he economical?

SANCHO: Economical? Señorita, you are looking at the Volkswagen of Mexicans. Pennies a day is all it takes. One plate of beans and tortillas will keep him going all day. That, and chile. Plenty of chile. Chile jalapenos, chile verde, chile colorado. But, of course, if you do give him chile (*Snap.* FARM WORKER *turns left face. Snap.* FARM WORKER *bends over.*) then you have to change his oil filter once a week.

SECRETARY: What about storage?

SANCHO: No problem. You know these new farm labor camps our Honorable Governor Reagan has built out by Parlier or Raisin City? They were designed with our model in mind. Five, six, seven, even ten in one of those shacks will give you no trouble at all. You can also put him in old barns, old cars, river banks. You can even leave him out in the field overnight with no worry!

SECRETARY: Remarkable.

SANCHO: And here's an added feature: Every year at the end of the season, this model goes back to Mexico and doesn't return, automatically, until next Spring.

SECRETARY: How about that. But tell me: does he speak English?

SANCHO: Another outstanding feature is that last year this model was programmed to go out on STRIKE! (*Snap.*)

FARM WORKER: ¡HUELGA! ¡HUELGA! Hermanos, sálganse de esos files. (*Snap. He stops.*)

SECRETARY: No! Oh no, we can't strike in the State Capitol.

SANCHO: Well, he also scabs. (*Snap.*)

FARM WORKER: Me vendo barato, ¿y qué? (*Snap.*)

SECRETARY: That's much better, but you didn't answer my question. Does he speak English?

SANCHO: Bueno . . . no pero he has other—

SECRETARY: No.

SANCHO: Other features.

SECRETARY: NO! He just won't do!

SANCHO: Okay, okay pues. We have other models.

SECRETARY: I hope so. What we need is something a little more sophisticated.

SANCHO: Sophisti—¿qué?

SECRETARY: An urban model.

SANCHO: Ah, from the city! Step right back. Over here in this corner of the shop is exactly what you're looking for. Introducing our new 1969 JOHNNY PACHUCO model! This is our fast-back model. Streamlined. Built for speed, low-riding, city life. Take a look at some of these features. Mag shoes, dual exhausts, green chartreuse paint-job, dark-tint windshield, a little poof on top. Let me just turn him on. (*Snap.* JOHNNY *walks to stage center with a pachuco bounce.*)

SECRETARY: What was that?

SANCHO: That, señorita, was the Chicano shuffle.

SECRETARY: Okay, what does he do?

SANCHO: Anything and everything necessary for city life. For instance, survival: He knife fights. (*Snap.* JOHNNY *pulls out switch blade and swings at* SECRETARY.)

(SECRETARY *screams.*)

SANCHO: He dances. (*Snap.*)

JOHNNY: (*Singing*) "Angel Baby, my Angel Baby . . ." (*Snap.*)

SANCHO: And here's a feature no city model can be without. He gets arrested, but not without resisting, of course. (*Snap.*)

JOHNNY: ¡En la madre, la placa! I didn't do it! I didn't do it! (JOHNNY *turns and stands up against an imaginary wall, legs spread out, arms behind his back.*)

SECRETARY: Oh no, we can't have arrests! We must maintain law and order.

SANCHO: But he's bilingual!

SECRETARY: Bilingual?

SANCHO: Simón que yes. He speaks English! Johnny, give us some English. (*Snap.*)

JOHNNY: (*Comes downstage.*) Fuck-you!

SECRETARY: (*Gasps*) Oh! I've never been so insulted in my whole life!

SANCHO: Well, he learned it in your school.

SECRETARY: I don't care where he learned it.

SANCHO: But he's economical!

SECRETARY: Economical?

SANCHO: Nickels and dimes. You can keep Johnny running on hamburgers, Taco Bell tacos, Lucky Lager beer, Thunderbird wine, yesca—

SECRETARY: Yesca?

SANCHO: Mota.

SECRETARY: Mota?

SANCHO: Leños . . . Marijuana. (*Snap;* JOHNNY *inhales on an imaginary joint.*)

SECRETARY: That's against the law!

JOHNNY: (*Big smile, holding his breath*) Yeah.

SANCHO: He also sniffs glue. (*Snap.* JOHNNY *inhales glue, big smile.*)

JOHNNY: Tha's too much, ése.

SECRETARY: No, Mr. Sancho, I don't think this—

SANCHO: Wait a minute, he has other qualities I know you'll love. For example, an inferiority complex. (*Snap.*)

JOHNNY: (*To* SANCHO) You think you're better than me, huh ése? (*Swings switch blade.*)

SANCHO: He can also be beaten and he bruises, cut him and he bleeds; kick him and he— (*He beats, bruises and kicks* PACHUCO.) would you like to try it?

SECRETARY: Oh, I couldn't.

SANCHO: Be my guest. He's a great scapegoat.

SECRETARY: No, really.

SANCHO: Please.

SECRETARY: Well, all right. Just once. (*She kicks* PACHUCO.) Oh, he's so soft.

SANCHO: Wasn't that good? Try again.

SECRETARY: (*Kicks* PACHUCO) Oh, he's so wonderful! (*She kicks him again.*)

SANCHO: Okay, that's enough, lady. You ruin the merchandise. Yes, our Johnny Pachuco model can give you many hours of pleasure. Why, the L.A.P.D. just bought twenty of these to train their rookie cops on. And talk about maintenance. Señorita, you are looking at an entirely self-supporting machine. You're never going to find our Johnny Pachuco model on the relief rolls. No, sir, this model knows how to liberate.

SECRETARY: Liberate?

SANCHO: He steals. (*Snap.* JOHNNY *rushes the* SECRETARY *and steals her purse.*)

JOHNNY: ¡Dame esa bolsa, vieja! (*He grabs the purse and runs. Snap by* SANCHO. *He stops.*)

(SECRETARY *runs after* JOHNNY *and grabs purse away from him, kicking him as she goes.*)

SECRETARY: No, no, no! We can't have any *more* thieves in the State Administration. Put him back.

SANCHO: Okay, we still got other models. Come on, Johnny, we'll sell you to some old lady. (SANCHO *takes* JOHNNY *back to his place.*)

SECRETARY: Mr. Sancho, I don't think you quite understand what we need. What we need is something that will attract the women voters. Something more traditional, more romantic.

SANCHO: Ah, a lover. (*He smiles meaningfully.*) Step right over here, señorita. Introducing our standard Revolucionario and/or Early California Bandit type. As you can see he is well-built, sturdy, durable. This is the International Harvester of Mexicans.

SECRETARY: What does he do?

SANCHO: You name it, he does it. He rides horses, stays in the mountains, crosses deserts, plains, rivers, leads revolutions, follows revolutions, kills, can be killed, serves as a martyr, hero, movie star—did I say movie star? Did you ever see *Viva Zapata? Viva Villa? Villa Rides? Pancho Villa Returns? Pancho Villa Goes Back? Pancho Villa Meets Abbot and Costello*—

SECRETARY: I've never seen any of those.

SANCHO: Well, he was in all of them. Listen to this. (*Snap.*)

REVOLUCIONARIO: (*Scream.*) ¡VIVA VILLAAAAA!

SECRETARY: That's awfully loud.

SANCHO: He has a volume control. (*He adjusts volume. Snap.*)

REVOLUCIONARIO: (*Mousey voice*) ¡Viva Villa!

SECRETARY: That's better.

SANCHO: And even if you didn't see him in the movies, perhaps you saw him on TV. He makes commercials. (*Snap.*)

REVOLUCIONARIO: Is there a Frito Bandito in your house?

SECRETARY: Oh yes, I've seen that one!

SANCHO: Another feature about this one is that he is economical. He runs on raw horsemeat and tequila!

SECRETARY: Isn't that rather savage?

SANCHO: Al contrario, it makes him a lover. (*Snap.*)

REVOLUCIONARIO: (*To* SECRETARY) ¡Ay, mamasota, cochota, ven pa'ca! (*He grabs* SECRETARY *and folds her back—Latin-lover style.*)

SANCHO: (*Snap.* REVOLUCIONARIO *goes back upright.*) Now wasn't that nice?

SECRETARY: Well, it was rather nice.

SANCHO: And finally, there is one outstanding feature about this model I KNOW the ladies are going to love: He's a GENUINE antique! He was made in Mexico in 1910!

SECRETARY: Made in Mexico?

SANCHO: That's right. Once in Tijuana, twice in Guadalajara, three times in Cuernavaca.

SECRETARY: Mr. Sancho, I thought he was an American product.

SANCHO: No, but—

SECRETARY: No, I'm sorry. We can't buy anything but American-made products. He just won't do.

SANCHO: But he's an antique!

SECRETARY: I don't care. You still don't understand what we need. It's true we need Mexican models such as these, but it's more important that he be *American*.

SANCHO: American?

SECRETARY: That's right, and judging from what you've shown me, I don't think you have what we want. Well, my lunch hour's almost over; I better—

SANCHO: Wait a minute! Mexican but American?

SECRETARY: That's correct.

SANCHO: Mexican but . . . (*A sudden flash.*) AMERICAN! Yeah, I think we've got exactly what you want. He just came in today! Give me a minute. (*He exits. Talks from backstage.*) Here he is in the shop. Let me just get some papers off. There. Introducing our new 1970 Mexican-American! Ta-ra-ra-ra-ra-ra-RA-RAAA!

(SANCHO *brings out the* MEXICAN-AMERICAN *model, a clean-shaven middle-class type in business suit, with glasses.*)

SECRETARY: (*Impressed*) Where have you been hiding this one?

SANCHO: He just came in this morning. Ain't he a beauty? Feast your eyes on him! Sturdy US STEEL frame, streamlined, modern. As a matter of fact, he is built exactly like our Anglo models except that he comes in a variety of darker shades: naugahyde, leather, or leatherette.

SECRETARY: Naugahyde.

SANCHO: Well, we'll just write that down. Yes, señorita, this model represents the apex of American engineering! He is bilingual, college educated, ambitious! Say the world "acculturate" and he accelerates. He is intelligent, well-mannered, clean—did I say clean? (*Snap.* MEXICAN-AMERICAN *raises his arm.*) Smell.

SECRETARY: (*Smells*) Old Sobaco, my favorite.

SANCHO: (*Snap.* MEXICAN-AMERICAN *turns toward* SANCHO.) Eric! (*To* SECRETARY.) We call him Eric Garcia. (*To* ERIC.) I want you to meet Miss JIM-enez, Eric.

MEXICAN-AMERICAN: Miss JIM-enez, I am delighted to make your acquaintance. (*He kisses her hand.*)

SECRETARY: Oh, my, how charming!

SANCHO: Did you feel the suction? He has seven especially engineered suction cups right behind his lips. He's a charmer all right!

SECRETARY: How about boards? Does he function on boards?

SANCHO: You name them, he is on them. Parole boards, draft boards, school boards, taco quality control boards, surf boards, two-by-fours.

SECRETARY: Does he function in politics?

SANCHO: Señorita, you are looking at a political MACHINE. Have you ever heard of the OEO, EOC, COD, WAR ON POVERTY? That's our model! Not only that, he makes political speeches.

SECRETARY: May I hear one?

SANCHO: With pleasure. (*Snap.*) Eric, give us a speech.

MEXICAN-AMERICAN: Mr. Congressman, Mr. Chairman, members of the board, honored guests, ladies and gentlemen. (SANCHO *and* SECRETARY *applaud.*) Please, please, I come before you as a Mexican-American to tell you about the problems of the Mexican. The problems of the Mexican stem from one thing and one thing alone: He's stupid. He's uneducated. He needs to stay in school. He needs to be ambitious, forward-looking, harder-working. He needs to think American, American, American, AMERICAN, AMERICAN, AMERICAN. GOD BLESS AMERICA! GOD BLESS AMERICA!! (*He goes out of control.*)

(SANCHO *snaps frantically and the* MEXICAN-AMERICAN *finally slumps forward, bending at the waist.*)

SECRETARY: Oh my, he's patriotic too!

SANCHO: Sí, señorita, he loves his country. Let me just make a little adjustment here. (*Stands* MEXICAN-AMERICAN *up.*)

SECRETARY: What about upkeep? Is he economical?

SANCHO: Well, no, I won't lie to you. The Mexican-American costs a little bit more, but you get what you pay for. He's worth every extra cent. You can keep him running on dry martinis, Langendorf bread.

SECRETARY: Apple pie?

SANCHO: Only Mom's. Of course, he's also programmed to eat Mexican food on ceremonial functions, but I must warn you: an overdose of beans will plug up his exhaust.

SECRETARY: Fine! There's just one more question: HOW MUCH DO YOU WANT FOR HIM?

SANCHO: Well, I tell you what I'm gonna do. Today and today only, because you've been so sweet, I'm gonna let you steal this model from me! I'm gonna let you drive him off the lot for the simple price of—let's see taxes and license included—$15,000.

SECRETARY: Fifteen thousand DOLLARS? For a MEXICAN!

SANCHO: Mexican? What are you talking, lady? This is a Mexican-AMERICAN! We had to melt down two pachucos, a farm worker and three gabachos to make this model! You want quality, but you gotta pay for it! This is no cheap run-about. He's got class!

SECRETARY: Okay, I'll take him.

SANCHO: You will?

SECRETARY: Here's your money.

SANCHO: You mind if I count it?

SECRETARY: Go right ahead.

SANCHO: Well, you'll get your pink slip in the mail. Oh, do you want me to wrap him up for you? We have a box in the back.

SECRETARY: No, thank you. The Governor is having a luncheon this afternoon, and we need a brown face in the crowd. How do I drive him?

SANCHO: Just snap your fingers. He'll do anything you want.

(SECRETARY *snaps.* MEXICAN-AMERICAN *steps forward.*)

MEXICAN-AMERICAN: RAZA QUERIDA, ¡VAMOS LEVANTANDO ARMAS PARA LIBER-ARNOS DE ESTOS DESGRACIADOS GABACHOS QUE NOS EXPLOTAN! VAMOS.

SECRETARY: What did he say?

SANCHO: Something about lifting arms, killing white people, etc.

SECRETARY: But he's not supposed to say that!

SANCHO: Look, lady, don't blame me for bugs from the factory. He's your Mexican-American; you bought him, now drive him off the lot!

SECRETARY: But he's broken!

SANCHO: Try snapping another finger.

(SECRETARY *snaps.* MEXICAN-AMERICAN *comes to life again.*)

MEXICAN-AMERICAN: ¡ESTA GRAN HUMANIDAD HA DICHO BASTA! Y SE HA PUESTO EN MARCHA! ¡BASTA! ¡BASTA! ¡VIVA LA RAZA! ¡VIVA LA CAUSA! ¡VIVA LA HUELGA! ¡VIVAN LOS BROWN BERETS! ¡VIVAN LOS ESTUDIANTES! ¡CHICANO POWER!

(*The* MEXICAN-AMERICAN *turns toward the* SECRETARY, *who gasps and backs up. He keeps turning toward the* PACHUCO, FARM WORKER, *and* REVOLUCIONARIO, *snapping his fingers and turning each of them on, one by one.*)

PACHUCO: (*Snap. To* SECRETARY) I'm going to get you, baby! ¡Viva La Raza!

FARM WORKER: (*Snap. To* SECRETARY) ¡Viva la huelga! ¡Viva la Huelga! ¡VIVA LA HUELGA!

REVOLUCIONARIO: (*Snap. To* SECRETARY) ¡Viva la revolución! ¡VIVA LA REVOLUCIÓN!

REVOLUCIONARIO: (*Snap. To* SECRETARY) ¡Viva la revolución! ¡VIVA LA REVOLUCIÓN!

(*The three models join together and advance toward the* SECRETARY *who backs up and runs out of the shop screaming.* SANCHO *is at the other end of the shop holding his money in his hand. All freeze. After a few seconds of silence, the* PACHUCO *moves and stretches, shaking his arms and loosening up. The* FARM WORKER *and* REVOLUCIONARIO *do the same.* SANCHO *stays where he is, frozen to his spot.*)

JOHNNY: Man, that was a long one, ése. (*Others agree with him.*)

FARM WORKER: How did we do?

JOHNNY: Pretty good, look all that lana, man! (*He goes over to* SANCHO *and removes the money from his hand.* SANCHO *stays where he is.*)

REVOLUCIONARIO: En la madre, look at all the money.

JOHNNY: We keep this up, we're going to be rich.

FARM WORKER: They think we're machines.

REVOLUCIONARIO: Burros.

JOHNNY: Puppets.

MEXICAN-AMERICAN: The only thing I don't like is—how come I always got to play the goddamn Mexican-American?

JOHNNY: That's what you get for finishing high school.

FARM WORKER: How about our wages, ése?

JOHNNY: Here it comes right now. $3,000 for you, $3,000 for you, $3,000 for you, and $3,000 for me. The rest we put back into the business.

MEXICAN-AMERICAN: Too much, man. Heh, where you vatos going tonight?

FARM WORKER: I'm going over to Concha's. There's a party.

JOHNNY: Wait a minute, vatos. What about our salesman? I think he needs an oil job.

REVOLUCIONARIO: Leave him to me.

(*The* PACHUCO, FARM WORKER, *and* MEXICAN-AMERICAN *exit, talking loudly about their plans for the night. The* REVOLUCIONARIO *goes over to* SANCHO, *removes his derby hat and cigar, lifts him up and throws him over his shoulder.* SANCHO *hangs loose, lifeless.*)

REVOLUCIONARIO: (*To audience*) He's the best model we got! ¡Ajua! (*Exit.*)

2

RESENTMENTS AND
NOSTALGIAS

In *Resentments and Nostalgias* the selections explore the ways Americans have imagined their identities in the context of history, including the struggle within individuals to balance the memory of their communal ethnic or racial past against the opportunity to forget—to assimilate, to disconnect, sometimes to betray or deny. These selections present individuals who struggle with stereotyped images of their ethnic and racial selves, some explicitly—like Alice Childress's domestic servant, Mildred, and Diane Burns in "Sure You Can Ask Me a Personal Question"—and some subtly and psychologically, like the narrators in John A. Williams's "Son in the Afternoon" and John Fante's "The Odyssey of a Wop," who both encounter the complex burden of an internalized negative self-image. In the poems of Lawson Fusao Inada and Gina Valdes on the ironies of a bilingual heritage, yet another area of conflict between official history and communal memory is engaged. All of the writers gathered here similarly explore the many painful ironies involved in belonging to a national community that does not always accept all of its citizens as equals.

AUNT JEMIMA ADVERTISEMENT

Aunt Jemima is a brand-name image based on the Mammy stereotypes of black women as domestic workers on the slave plantations. These Mammy stereotypes sentimentalized the role of slave women as wet-nurses, cooks, and housekeepers for wealthy white families during slavery and after Emancipation. The advertising image allowed white consumers to continue the distorted vision of African-American women as primarily caretakers of other people's households.

Promotional artifacts with the Aunt Jemima image were used during the 1940s and 1950s by Aunt Jemima clubs for working-class white women. At the meetings of these clubs new recipes were developed and disseminated.

ALICE CHILDRESS
(1920-1994)

Born in Charleston, South Carolina, Alice Childress had a varied career as an actor, playwright, director, and novelist. She worked as both an actor and director for the American Negro Theatre in New York City, which in 1949 produced her first play, Florence. *During her career she wrote several plays, and in 1956 she was awarded an Obie for best original Off-Broadway play for* Trouble in Mind. *She also appeared as an actress on Broadway and television. Later in her life, she wrote a number of novels for young*

adults and screenplays of her works. In 1973 her novel A Hero Ain't Nothin'
but a Sandwich *was named one of the Outstanding Books of the Year by the*
New York Times Book Review, *was awarded Best Young Adult Book of 1975*
by the American Library Association, and was nominated for the National
Book Award. In 1956 a collection of monologues (originally written for Paul
Robeson's paper Freedom *and for the* Baltimore Afro-American), *Like One*
of the Family: Conversations from a Domestic's Life, was published. She
lectured at several universities and colleges and received a Lifetime
Achievement Award from the Association for Theatre in Higher Education,
a Radcliffe Graduate Society Medal, and two Paul Robeson Awards.

These two examples of her newspaper feature "Here's Mildred," taken
from the collection Like One of the Family, *represent a kind of public resis-*
tance to the image of the black woman as only a domestic servant. Chil-
dress's Mildred leads a vibrant life outside her employer's kitchen. And she
is in no way docile or passive at work either.

FROM LIKE ONE OF THE FAMILY

Like One of the Family

Hi Marge! I have had me one hectic day. . . . Well, I had to take out my crystal ball
and give Mrs. C . . . a thorough reading. She's the woman that I took over from
Naomi after Naomi got married. . . . Well, she's a pretty nice woman as they go and
I have never had too much trouble with her, but from time to time she really gripes
me with her ways.

When she has company, for example, she'll holler out to me from the living room
to the kitchen: "Mildred dear! Be sure and eat *both* of those lamb chops for your
lunch!" Now you know she wasn't doing a thing but tryin' to prove to the company
how "good" and "kind" she was to the servant, because she had told me *already* to
eat those chops.

Today she had a girl friend of hers over to lunch and I was real busy afterwards
clearing the things away and she called me over and introduced me to the woman.
. . . Oh no, Marge! I didn't object to that at all. I greeted the lady and then went back
to my work. . . . And then it started! I could hear her talkin' just as loud . . . and she
says to her friend, "We *just* love her! She's *like* one of the family and she *just adores*
our little Carol! We don't know *what* we'd do without her! We don't think of her as
a servant!" And on and on she went . . . and every time I came in to move a plate off
the table both of them would grin at me like chessy cats.

After I couldn't stand it any more, I went in and took the platter off the table and
gave 'em both a look that would have frizzled a egg. . . . Well, you might have heard
a pin drop and then they started talkin' about something else.

When the guest leaves, I go in the living room and says, "Mrs. C . . . , I want to
have a talk with you."

"By all means," she says.

I drew up a chair and read her thusly: "Mrs. C . . . , you are a pretty nice person
to work for, but I wish you would please stop talkin' about me like I was a *cocker*
spaniel or a *poll parrot* or a *kitten.* . . . Now you just sit there and hear me out.

"In the first place, you do not *love* me; you may be fond of me, but that is all. . . . In the second place, I am *not* just like one of the family at all! The family eats in the dining room and I eat in the kitchen. Your mama borrows your lace tablecloth for her company and your son entertains his friends in your parlor, your daughter takes her afternoon nap on the living room couch and the puppy sleeps on your satin spread . . . and whenever your husband gets tired of something you are talkin' about he says, 'Oh, for Pete's sake, forget it. . . .' So you can see I am not *just* like one of the family.

"Now for another thing, I do not *just* adore your little Carol. I think she is a likable child, but she is also fresh and sassy. I know you call it 'uninhibited' and that is the way you want your child to be, but *luckily* my mother taught me some inhibitions or else I would smack little Carol once in a while when she's talkin' to you like you're a dog, but as it is I just laugh it off the way you do because she is *your* child and I am *not* like one of the family.

"Now when you say, 'We don't know *what* we'd do without her' this is a polite lie . . . because I know that if I dropped dead or had a stroke, you would get somebody to replace me.

"You think it is a compliment when you say, 'We don't think of her as a servant. . . .' but after I have worked myself into a sweat cleaning the bathroom and the kitchen . . . making the beds . . . cooking the lunch . . . washing the dishes and ironing Carol's pinafores . . . I do not feel like no weekend house guest. I feel like a servant, and in the face of that I have been meaning to ask you for a slight raise which will make me feel much better toward everyone here and make me know my work is appreciated.

"Now I hope you will stop talkin' about me in my presence and that we will get along like a good employer and employee should."

Marge! She was almost speechless but she *apologized* and said she'd talk to her husband about the raise. . . . I knew things were progressing because this evening Carol came in the kitchen and she did not say, "I want some bread and jam!" but she did say, "*Please,* Mildred, will you fix me a slice of bread and jam."

I'm going upstairs, Marge. Just look . . . you done messed up that buttonhole!

If You Want to Get Along with Me

Marge, ain't it strange how the two of us get along so well? . . . Now you see there! Why do you have to get so sensitive? . . . No, I was not reflecting on your personality or making any kind of digs! . . . Well, if you'll give me a chance I'll try to explain what I mean. . . . I've known you for years and although you've got your ways . . . Yes, yes, I know I've got mine . . . but the important thing is that we go right on being friends . . . for example, remember the time you borrowed my best white gloves and lost them? . . . I know that I spilled punch on your blue satin blouse! . . . Now, wait a minute, girl! Are we goin' to have a big argument over how friendly we are!

I said all of that to say this. Today I worked for Mrs. M . . . and she is an awful nice lady when she wants to be, but she can get on my nerves something terrible. . . . No, I do not mean that you get on my nerves too, and if you keep pickin' up every little thing I say, I'm gonna get up and go on home. . . . Well, gettin' back to Mrs. M . . . , she can make me downright uncomfortable! . . . Yes, you know what I mean, she turns my workday into a real socializin' session, and her idea of socializin' is to ask me a million questions. . . . "What do you do after work, Mildred?" and "Do you have a lot of friends?" and "Are you married?" and "Do you have a boyfriend?" and "Do you save your money?" and "Do you like to read?" and "Do *you people* like this or that?" . . . By *you people* she means colored people . . . and I can tell you she can wear my nerve-cells pretty near the breaking point. . . . I know you know!

Well, at first I tried to get used to it because she is so nice in other ways . . . I mean like not followin' me around and dippin' into every thing I'm doing . . . yes, I appreciate that. . . . She lets me do my work, and then if anything isn't quite pleasin' to her she will tell me afterwards but it usually turns out that she's satisfied. Also I like the fact that she is not afraid of a little work herself, and many a day we've worked side by side on jobs that was too much for me to handle all alone. Also she makes the children call me *Miss* Johnson. . . . Sure, whenever anybody has so many good ways, you hate to be pointin' out the bad ones. . . . But question, question, question . . . and it wasn't only the questions. . . . Honey, she could come out with the most gratin' remarks! . . . Honestly, she made such a point of tellin' me about how much she liked and admired Negroes, and how sorry she felt for their plight, and what a *fine, honest, smart,* and *attractive* woman was workin' for her mother and so forth and so on and so forth until it was all I could do to keep from screamin', "All right, back up there and take it easy!"

Well, the upshot of it all was that I began to pick her up a little here and there in order to put her on the right track. For example, I'd say to her, "What's so strange about that woman being *honest* and *attractive?*" Well, Marge, she'd look so stricken and hurt and confused that I'd find myself feelin' sorry for her. . . . No, I didn't stop altogether but I'd let things go along a bit and then I'd have to pick her up on something again, and over a period of five or six weeks I had to jack her up several times. . . . Girl! all of a sudden she turned coldly polite and quiet and I can tell you that it was awful uncomfortable and strained in the house.

I guess I could have stood the strain but it began to tear me up when she'd say things like "May I suggest" and "Do you mind if I say" and "If it's all right with you." . . . When I had my fill of that I came right out and asked her, "Mrs. M . . . , what is the matter, you look so grieved and talk so strange 'til I don't know what to think?" She looked at me accusingly and said, "I'm afraid to say anything to you, Mildred. It seems that every time I open my mouth something wrong comes out and you have to correct me. It makes me very nervous because the last thing I want to do is hurt your feelings. I mean well, but I guess that isn't enough. I try to do the right thing and since it keeps coming out wrong I figured I'd just keep quiet. I . . . I . . . want to get along but I don't know how."

Marge, in that minute I understood her better and it came to my mind that she was doing her best to make me comfortable and havin' a doggone hard go of it. After all, everything she's ever been taught adds up to her being better than me in every way and on her own she had to find out that this was wrong. . . . That's right, she was tryin' to treat me very special because she still felt a bit superior but wanted me to know that she admired me just the same.

"Mrs. M . . . ," I said, "you just treat me like you would anybody else that might be workin' for you in any kind of job. Don't be afraid to talk to me because if you say the wrong thing I promise to correct you, and if you want to get along you won't mind me doing so. After all, if I got into all your personal business and wanted to know everything about your life and your husband and your friends, pretty soon you would be forced to correct me even though it might make me uncomfortable." "Oh, Mildred," she says, "I didn't realize . . ." "Of course you didn't," I cut in, "but can't you see that it's unfair to push a one-sided friendship on me?" "Mildred," she says, "I wanted to be friendly." "Now of course you did," I answered, "but, for example, when you told me the other day that you're going to drop by my house and see me sometime I don't appreciate that because I never invited you, and you never had me to your house except to do a day's work." She looked down at her hands as I went on. "I don't think it's fair that you can invite yourself to my house and I can't tell you that I'll be over here for tea on Sunday afternoon."

Marge, she shook her head sadly. "You mean that there is nothing that we have in common, nothing that we can talk about?" "I didn't say that at all," I said, "but let's just relax and feel our way along and not try to prove anything, and before you know it everything will go along easy-like."

She smiled then, "You mean you don't want to be treated *special?*" "Well, I do and I don't," I answered; "because I knew a woman once who was awful rude to me and said that was the way she was with everybody, no matter what color, and she didn't want to treat me *special*. I told her that if that was her general way then I'd appreciate her treatin' me special and I'd bet that other folks would like the change too." Marge, Mrs. M . . . fell out laughin' and says "Mildred, people are the limit!" . . . And I guess she's right too. . . . No indeed, I don't take that time and bother with most folks because when I run into a mean, hateful one who comes chatterin' around me about "What do you do after work?" I just give her a short smile and say, "Oh, first one thing then another." And by the time she's figured that out, I'm in another room busy doin' something else! . . . That's right, but, as I said, Mrs. M . . . is a nice person, so I told her.

JOHN A. WILLIAMS
(1925-)

John Alfred Williams was born in Jackson, Mississippi, and served in the United States Navy during World War II. In 1950, he received a B.A. from Syracuse University and pursued graduate study there during 1950-1951. Williams later worked as a welfare case worker, a publicity director, and a European correspondent for two magazines. He is the author of over a dozen books, including the novels Night Song *(1961),* The Man Who Cried I Am *(1967),* Captain Blackman *(1972), and more recently,* The Berhama Account *(1985) and* Clifford's Blues *(1996). Williams has taught at several schools, including Sarah Lawrence College, Boston University, and Rutgers University, where he was Professor of English from 1979 to 1990 and Paul Robeson Professor from 1990 to 1993. He has received an award from the National Institute of Arts and Letters and has twice received the American Book Award from the Before Columbus Foundation.*

Williams's best-known short story, "Son in the Afternoon," is about the expression of resentment by an African-American man toward his mother's other "son"—the white child she cares for as a domestic servant.

SON IN THE AFTERNOON

It was hot. I tend to be a bitch when it's hot. I goosed the little Ford over Sepulveda Boulevard toward Santa Monica until I got stuck in the traffic that pours from L.A. into the surrounding towns. I'd had a very lousy day at the studio.

I was—still am—a writer and this studio had hired me to check scripts and films with Negroes in them to make sure the Negro moviegoer wouldn't be offended. The signs were already clear one day the whole of American industry would be racing pell-mell to get a Negro, showcase a spade. I was kind of a pioneer. I'm a *Negro* writer, you see. The day had been tough because of a couple of verbs—slink and walk. One of those Hollywood hippies had done a script calling for a Negro waiter to slink away from the table where a dinner party was glaring at him. I said the waiter should walk, not slink, because later on he becomes a hero. The Hollywood hippie, who understood it all because he had some colored friends, said that it was essential to the plot that the waiter slink. I said you don't slink one minute and become a hero the next; there has to be some consistency. The Negro actor I was standing up for said nothing either way. He had played Uncle Tom roles so long that he had become Uncle Tom. But the director agreed with me.

Anyway . . . hear me out now. I was on my way to Santa Monica to pick up my mother, Nora. It was a long haul for such a hot day. I had planned a quiet evening: a nice shower, fresh clothes, and then I would have dinner at the Watkins and talk with some of the musicians on the scene for a quick taste before they cut to their gigs. After, I was going to the Pigalle down on Figueroa and catch Earl Grant at the organ, and still later, if nothing exciting happened, I'd pick up Scottie and make it to the Lighthouse on the Beach or to the Strollers and listen to some of the white boys play. I liked the long drive, especially while listening to Sleepy Stein's show on the radio. Later, much later of course, it would be home, back to Watts.

So you see, this picking up Nora was a little inconvenient. My mother was a maid for the Couchmans. Ronald Couchman was an architect, a good one I understood from Nora who has a fine sense for this sort of thing; you don't work in some hundred-odd houses during your life without getting some idea of the way a house should be laid out. Couchman's wife, Kay, was a playgirl who drove a white Jaguar from one party to another. My mother didn't like her too much; she didn't seem to care much for her son, Ronald, junior. There's something wrong with a parent who can't really love her own child, Nora thought. The Couchmans lived in a real fine residential section, of course. A number of actors lived nearby, character actors, not really big stars.

Somehow it is very funny. I mean that the maids and butlers knew everything about these people, and these people knew nothing at all about the help. Through Nora and her friends I knew who was laying whose wife; who had money and who *really* had money; I knew about the wild parties hours before the police, and who smoked marijuana, when, and where they got it.

To get to Couchman's driveway I had to go three blocks up one side of a palm-planted center strip and back down the other. The driveway bent gently, then swept back out of sight of the main road. The house, sheltered by slim palms, looked like a transplanted New England Colonial. I parked and walked to the kitchen door, skirting the growling Great Dane who was tied to a tree. That was the route to the kitchen door.

I don't like kitchen doors. Entering people's houses by them, I mean. I'd done this thing most of my life when I called at places where Nora worked to pick up the patched or worn sheets or the half-eaten roasts, the battered, tarnished silver—the fringe benefits of a housemaid. As a teen-ager I'd told Nora I was through with that crap; I was not going through anyone's kitchen door. She only laughed and said I'd learn. One day soon after, I called for her and without knocking walked right through the front door of this house and right on through the living room. I was almost out of the room when I saw feet behind the couch. I leaned over and there was Mr. Jorgensen and his wife making out like crazy. I guess they thought Nora had gone and it must have hit them sort of suddenly and they went at it like the hell-bomb was due to drop any minute. I've been that way too, mostly in the spring. Of course, when Mr. Jorgensen looked over his shoulder and saw me, you know what happened. I was thrown out and Nora right behind me. It was the middle of winter, the old man was sick and the coal bill three months overdue. Nora was right about those kitchen doors: I learned.

My mother saw me before I could ring the bell. She opened the door. "Hello," she said. She was breathing hard, like she'd been running or something. "Come in and sit down. I don't know *where* that Kay is. Little Ronald is sick and she's probably out gettin' drunk again." She left me then and trotted back through the house, I guess to be with Ronnie. I hated the combination of her white nylon uniform, her dark brown face and the wide streaks of gray in her hair. Nora had married this guy from Texas a few years after the old man had died. He was all right. He made out okay. Nora didn't have to work, but she just couldn't be still; she always had to be doing something. I suggested she quit work, but I had as much luck as her husband. I used to tease her about liking to be around those white folks. It would have been good for her to take an extended trip around the country visiting my brothers and sisters. Once she got to Philadelphia, she could go right out to the cemetery and sit awhile with the old man.

I walked through the Couchman home. I liked the library. I thought if I knew Couchman I'd like him. The room made me feel like that. I left it and went into the big living room. You could tell that Couchman had let his wife do that. Everything in it was fast, dart-like, with no sense of ease. But on the walls were several of Couchman's conceptions of buildings and homes. I guess he was a disciple of Wright. My mother walked rapidly through the room without looking at me and said, "Just be patient, Wendell. She should be here real soon."

"Yeah," I said, "with a snootful." I had turned back to the drawings when Ronnie scampered into the room, his face twisted with rage.

"Nora!" he tried to roar, perhaps the way he'd seen the parents of some of his friends roar at their maids. I'm quite sure Kay didn't shout at Nora, and I don't think Couchman would. But then no one shouts at Nora. "Nora, you come right back here this minute!" the little bastard shouted and stamped and pointed to a spot on the floor where Nora was supposed to come to roost. I have a nasty temper. Sometimes it lies dormant for ages and at other times, like when the weather is hot and nothing seems to be going right, it's bubbling and ready to explode. "Don't talk to *my* mother like that, you little—!" I said sharply, breaking off just before I cursed. I wanted him to be large enough for me to strike. "How'd you like for me to talk to *your* mother like that?"

The nine-year-old looked up at me in surprise and confusion. He hadn't expected me to say anything. I was just another piece of furniture. Tears rose in his eyes and spilled out onto his pale cheeks. He put his hands behind him, twisted them. He moved backwards, away from me. He looked at my mother with a "Nora, come help me" look. And sure enough, there was Nora, speeding back across the room, gathering the kid in her arms, tucking his robe together. I was too angry to feel hatred for myself.

Ronnie was the Couchman's only kid. Nora loved him. I suppose that was the trouble. Couchman was gone ten, twelve hours a day. Kay didn't stay around the house any longer than she had to. So Ronnie had only my mother. I think kids should have someone to love, and Nora wasn't a bad sort. But somehow when the six of us, her own children, were growing up we never had her. She was gone, out scuffling to get those crumbs to put into our mouths and shoes for our feet and praying for something to happen so that all the space in between would be taken care of. Nora's affection for us took the form of rushing out into the morning's five o'clock blackness to wake some silly bitch and get her coffee; took form in her trudging five miles home every night instead of taking the streetcar to save money to buy tablets for us, to use at school, we said. But the truth was that all of us liked to draw and we went through a writing tablet in a couple of hours every day. Can you imagine? There's not a goddamn artist among us. We never had the physical affection, the pat on the head, the quick, smiling kiss, the "gimmee a hug" routine. All of this Ronnie was getting.

Now he buried his little blond head in Nora's breast and sobbed. "There, there now," Nora said. "Don't you cry, Ronnie. Ol' Wendell is just jealous, and he hasn't much sense either. He didn't mean nuthin'."

I left the room. Nora had hit it of course, hit it and passed on. I looked back. It didn't look so incongruous, the white and black together, I mean. Ronnie was still sobbing. His head bobbed gently on Nora's shoulder. The only time I ever got that close to her was when she trapped me with a bearhug so she could whale the daylights out of me after I put a snowball through Mrs. Grant's window. I walked outside and lit a cigarette. When Ronnie was in the hospital the month before, Nora got me to run her way over to Hollywood every night to see him. I didn't like that worth a damn. All right, I'll admit it: it did upset me. All that affection I didn't get nor my brothers and sisters going to that little white boy who, without a doubt, when away from her called her the names he'd learned from adults. Can you imagine a nine-year-old calling Nora a "girl," "our girl"? I spat at the Great Dane. He snarled and then I bounced a rock off his fanny. "Lay down, you bastard," I muttered. It was a good thing he was tied up.

I heard the low cough of the Jaguar slapping against the road. The car was throttled down, and with a muted roar it swung into the driveway. The woman aimed it for me. I was evil enough not to move. I was tired of playing with these people. At the last moment, grinning, she swung the wheel over and braked. She bounded out of the car like a tennis player vaulting over a net.

"Hi," she said, tugging at her shorts.

"Hello."

"You're Nora's boy?"

"I'm Nora's son." Hell, I was as old as she was; besides, I can't stand "boy."

"Nora tells us you're working in Hollywood. Like it?"

"It's all right."

"You must be pretty talented."

We stood looking at each other while the dog whined for her attention. Kay had a nice body and it was well tanned. She was high, boy, was she high. Looking at her, I could feel myself going into my sexy bastard routine; sometimes I can swing it great. Maybe it all had to do with the business inside. Kay took off her sunglasses and took a good look at me. "Do you have a cigarette?"

I gave her one and lit it. "Nice tan," I said. Most white people I know think it's a great big deal if a Negro compliments them on their tans. It's a large laugh. You have all this volleyball about color and come summer you can't hold the white folks back from the beaches, anyplace where they can get some sun. And of course the blacker they get, the more pleased they are. Crazy. If there is ever a Negro revolt, it will come during the summer and Negroes will descend upon the beaches around the nation and paralyze the country. You can't conceal cattle prods and bombs and pistols and police dogs when you're showing your birthday suit to the sun.

"You like it?" she asked. She was pleased. She placed her arm next to mine. "Almost the same color," she said.

"Ronnie isn't feeling well," I said.

"Oh, the poor kid. I'm so glad we have Nora. She's such a charm. I'll run right in and look at him. Do have a drink in the bar. Fix me one too, will you?" Kay skipped inside and I went to the bar and poured out two strong drinks. I made hers stronger than mine. She was back soon. "Nora was trying to put him to sleep and she made me stay out." She giggled. She quickly tossed off her drink. "Another, please?" While I was fixing her drink she was saying how amazing it was for Nora to have such a talented son. What she was really saying was that it was amazing for a servant to have a son who was not also a servant. "Anything can happen in a democracy," I said. "Servants' sons drink with madames and so on."

"Oh, Nora isn't a servant," Kay said. "She's part of the family."

Yeah, I thought. Where and how many times had I heard *that* before?

In the ensuing silence, she started to admire her tan again. "You think it's pretty good, do you? You don't know how hard I worked to get it." I moved closer to her and held her arm. I placed my other arm around her. She pretended not to see or feel it, but she wasn't trying to get away either. In fact she was pressing closer and the register in my brain that tells me at the precise moment when I'm in, went off. Kay was very high. I put both arms around her and she put both hers around me. When I kissed her, she responded completely.

"Mom!"

"Ronnie, come back to bed," I heard Nora shout from the other room. We could hear Ronnie running over the rug in the outer room. Kay tried to get away from me, push me to one side, because we could tell that Ronnie knew where to look for his Mom: he was running right for the bar, where we were. "Oh, please," she said, "don't let him see us." I wouldn't let her push me away. "Stop!" she hissed. "He'll *see* us!" We stopped struggling just for an instant, and we listened to the echoes of the word *see.* She gritted her teeth and renewed her efforts to get away.

Me? I had the scene laid right out. The kid breaks into the room, see, and sees his mother in this real wriggly clinch with this colored guy who's just shouted at him, see, and no matter how his mother explains it away, the kid has the image—the colored guy and his mother—for the rest of his life, see?

That's the way it happened. The kid's mother hissed under her breath, *"You're crazy!"* and she looked at me as though she were seeing me or something about me for the very first time. I'd released her as soon as Ronnie, romping into the bar, saw us and came to a full, open-mouthed halt. Kay went to him. He looked first at me, then at his mother. Kay turned to me, but she couldn't speak.

Outside the living room my mother called, "Wendell, where are you? We can go now."

I started to move past Kay and Ronnie. I felt many things, but I made myself think mostly, *There you little bastard, there.*

My mother thrust her face inside the door and said, "Good-bye, Mrs. Couchman. See you tomorrow. 'Bye, Ronnie."

"Yes," Kay said, sort of stunned. "Tomorrow." She was reaching for Ronnie's hand as we left, but the kid was slapping her hand away. I hurried quickly after Nora, hating the long drive back to Watts.

CIGAR STORE INDIAN STATUE

Throughout the latter part of the nineteenth century and deep into the twentieth, statues of Native Americans were symbols of tobacco shops, as familiar to most Americans as the striped poles that had come to indicate barber shops. Most of these statues, carved by folk-sculptors, depicted conventional, often fanciful, versions of Native Americans. As the Indian Wars raged between the end of the Civil War in 1865 and the 1890s, the stylization of the statues came increasingly to represent Plains Indians rather than the Algonquian communities from whom the use of tobacco had actually been learned. Thus the cigar store Indian is an ambiguous monument, at once a reminder of indebtedness and a silent representative of the vanquished.

Diane Burns

(1957-)

Diane Burns is of Chemehuevi and Anishinabe heritage. She attended the Institute of American Indian Art in Santa Fe, New Mexico, and Barnard College in New York City. She is a painter and illustrator as well as a poet. Her collection, Riding the One-Eyed Ford, *was published in 1981. The book was nominated for the Poetry Society of America's William Carlos Williams Award.*

First published in an anthology in 1983, "Sure You Can Ask Me a Personal Question" encapsulates the resentment of Native people who are constantly being objectified by outsiders.

Sure You Can Ask Me a Personal Question

How do you do?
   No, I am not Chinese.
No, not Spanish.
   No, I am American Indi-uh, Native American.
No, not from India.
   No, not Apache.
No, not Navajo.
   No, not Sioux.
No, we are not extinct.
   Yes, Indian.
Oh?
   So that's where you got those high cheekbones.
Your great grandmother, huh?
   An Indian Princess, huh?
Hair down to there?
   Let me guess. Cherokee?
Oh, so you've had an Indian friend?
   That close?
Oh, so you've had an Indian lover?
   That tight?
Oh, so you've had an Indian servant?
   That much?
Yeah, it was awful what you guys did to us.
   It's real decent of you to apologize.
No, I don't know where you can get peyote.
   No, I don't know where you can get Navajo rugs real cheap.
No, I didn't make this. I bought it at Bloomingdale's.
   Thank you. I like your hair too.

I don't know if anyone knows whether or not Cher is really Indian.
No, I didn't make it rain tonight.
Yeah. Uh-huh. Spirituality.
Uh-huh. Yeah. Spirituality. Uh-huh. Mother
Earth. Yeah. Uh'huh. Uh'huh. Spirituality.
No, I didn't major in archery.
Yeah, a lot of us drink too much.
Some of us can't drink enough.
This ain't no stoic look.
This is my face.

PAULA GUNN ALLEN
(1939-)

Paula Gunn Allen is a poet, novelist, and critic who is part Native American and part Lebanese American. She was born and raised in New Mexico, where her father was Lieutenant Governor from 1967 to 1970. She obtained a B.A. in 1966 and an M.F.A. in 1968 from the University of Oregon. She published her first volume of poetry, The Blind Lion, *in 1974. The following year she received a Ph.D. from the University of New Mexico. She has been awarded fellowships from the National Endowment for the Arts, the University of California, and the Ford Foundation. In addition to several volumes of poetry, she has also published works on Native-American women's issues and literature. In 1990 she received the American Book Award from the Before Columbus Foundation for* Spider Woman's Granddaughters: Traditional Tales and Contemporary Writing. *She teaches at the University of California, Los Angeles.*

"Where I Come From Is Like This" is excerpted from Allen's The Sacred Hoop: Recovering the Feminine in American Indian Traditions *(1985), a book of political and cultural criticism that argues for the recognition of Native women's political and cultural presence in pre-assimilation Native life.*

WHERE I COME FROM IS LIKE THIS

I

Modern American Indian women, like their non-Indian sisters, are deeply engaged in the struggle to redefine themselves. In their struggle they must reconcile traditional tribal definitions of women with industrial and postindustrial non-Indian definitions. Yet while these definitions seem to be more or less mutually exclusive, Indian women must somehow harmonize and integrate both in their own lives.

An American Indian woman is primarily defined by her tribal identity. In her eyes, her destiny is necessarily that of her people, and her sense of herself as a woman is first and foremost prescribed by her tribe. The definitions of woman's roles are as diverse as tribal cultures in the Americas. In some she is devalued, in others she wields considerable power. In some she is a familial/clan adjunct, in some she is as close to autonomous as her economic circumstances and psychological traits permit. But in no tribal definitions is she perceived in the same way as are women in Western industrial and postindustrial cultures.

In the West, few images of women form part of the cultural mythos, and these are largely sexually charged. Among Christians, the Madonna is the female prototype, and she is portrayed as essentially passive: her contribution is simply that of birthing. Little else is attributed to her and she certainly possesses few of the characteristics that are attributed to mythic figures among Indian tribes. This image is countered (rather than balanced) by the witch-goddess/whore characteristics designed to reinforce cultural beliefs about women, as well as Western adversarial and dualistic perceptions of reality.

The tribes see women variously, but they do not question the power of femininity. Sometimes they see women as fearful, sometimes peaceful, sometimes omnipotent and omniscient, but they never portray women as mindless, helpless, simple, or oppressed. And while the women in a given tribe, clan, or band may be all these things, the individual woman is provided with a variety of images of women from the interconnected supernatural, natural, and social worlds she lives in.

As a half-breed American Indian woman, I cast about in my mind for negative images of Indian women, and I find none that are directed to Indian women alone. The negative images I do have are of Indians in general and in fact are more often of males than of females. All these images come to me from non-Indian sources, and they are always balanced by a positive image. My ideas of womanhood, passed on largely by my mother and grandmothers, Laguna Pueblo women, are about practicality, strength, reasonableness, intelligence, wit, and competence. I also remember vividly the women who came to my father's store, the women who held me and sang to me, the women at Feast Day, at Grab Days, the women in the kitchen of my Cubero home, the women I grew up with; none of them appeared weak or helpless, none of them presented herself tentatively. I remember a certain reserve on those lovely brown faces; I remember the direct gaze of eyes framed by bright-colored shawls draped over their heads and cascading down their backs. I remember the clean cotton dresses and carefully pressed hand-embroidered aprons they always wore; I remember laughter and good food, especially the sweet bread and the oven bread they gave us. Nowhere in my mind is there a foolish woman, a dumb woman, a vain woman, or a plastic woman, though the Indian women I have known have shown a wide range of personal style and demeanor.

My memory includes the Navajo woman who was badly beaten by her Sioux husband; but I also remember that my grandmother abandoned her Sioux husband long ago. I recall the stories about the Laguna woman beaten regularly by her husband in the presence of her children so that the children would not believe in the strength and power of femininity. And I remember the women who drank, who got into fights with other women and with the men, and who often won those battles. I have memories of tired women, partying women, stubborn women, sullen women, amicable women, selfish women, shy women, and aggressive women. Most of all I remember the women who laugh and scold and sit uncomplaining in the long sun on feast days and who cook wonderful food on wood stoves, in beehive mud ovens, and over open fires outdoors.

Among the images of women that come to me from various tribes as well as my own are White Buffalo Woman, who came to the Lakota long ago and brought them the religion of the Sacred Pipe which they still practice; Tinotzin the goddess who came to Juan Diego to remind him that she still walked the hills of her people and sent him with her message, her demand, and her proof to the Catholic bishop in the city nearby. And from Laguna I take the images of Yellow Woman, Coyote Woman, Grandmother Spider (Spider Old Woman), who brought the light, who gave us weaving and medicine, who gave us life. Among the Keres she is known as Thought Woman who created us all and who keeps us in creation even now. I remember Iyatiku, Earth Woman, Corn Woman, who guides and counsels the people to peace and who welcomes us home when we cast off this coil of flesh as huskers cast off the leaves that wrap the corn. I remember Iyatiku's sister, Sun Woman, who held metals and cattle, pigs and sheep, highways and engines and so many things in her bundle, who went away to the east saying that one day she would return.

II

Since the coming of the Anglo-Europeans beginning in the fifteenth century, the fragile web of identity that long held tribal people secure has gradually been weakened and torn. But the oral tradition has prevented the complete destruction of the web, the ultimate disruption of tribal ways. The oral tradition is vital; it heals itself and the tribal web by adapting to the flow of the present while never relinquishing its connection to the past. Its adaptability has always been required, as many generations have experienced. Certainly the modern American Indian woman bears slight resemblance to her forebears—at least on superficial examination—but she is still a tribal woman in her deepest being. Her tribal sense of relationship to all that is continues to flourish. And though she is at times beset by her knowledge of the enormous gap between the life she lives and the life she was raised to live, and while she adapts her mind and being to the circumstances of her present life, she does so in tribal ways, mending the tears in the web of being from which she takes her existence as she goes.

My mother told me stories all the time, though I often did not recognize them as that. My mother told me stories about cooking and childbearing; she told me stories about menstruation and pregnancy; she told me stories about gods and heroes, about fairies and elves, about goddesses and spirits; she told me stories about the land and the sky, about cats and dogs, about snakes and spiders; she told me stories about climbing trees and exploring the mesas; she told me stories about going to dances and getting married; she told me stories about dressing and undressing, about sleeping and waking; she told me stories about herself, about her mother, about her grandmother. She told me stories about grieving and laughing, about thinking and doing; she told me stories about school and about people; about darning and mending; she told me stories about turquoise and about gold; she told me European stories and Laguna stories; she told me Catholic stories and Presbyterian stories; she told me city stories and country stories; she told me political stories and religious stories. She told me stories about living and stories about dying. And in all of those stories she told me who I was, who I was supposed to be, whom I came from, and who would follow me. In this way she taught me the meaning of the words she said, that all life is a circle and everything has a place within it. That's what she said and what she showed me in the things she did and the way she lives.

Of course, through my formal, white, Christian education, I discovered that other people had stories of their own—about women, about Indians, about fact, about reality—and I was amazed by a number of startling suppositions that others made about tribal customs and beliefs. According to the un-Indian, non-Indian view, for instance, Indians barred menstruating women from ceremonies and indeed segregated them from the rest of the people, consigning them to some space specially designed for them. This showed that Indians considered menstruating women unclean and not fit to enjoy the company of decent (nonmenstruating) people, that is, men. I was surprised and confused to hear this because my mother had taught me that white people had strange attitudes toward menstruation: they thought something was bad about it, that it meant you were sick, cursed, sinful, and weak and that you had to be very careful during that time. She taught me that menstruation was a normal occurrence, that I could go swimming or hiking or whatever else I wanted to do during my period. She actively scorned women who took to their beds, who were incapacitated by cramps, who "got the blues."

As I struggled to reconcile these very contradictory interpretations of American Indians' traditional beliefs concerning menstruation, I realized that the menstrual taboos were about power, not about sin or filth. My conclusion was later borne out by some tribes' own explanations, which, as you may well imagine, came as quite a relief to me.

The truth of the matter as many Indians see it is that women who are at the peak of their fecundity are believed to possess power that throws male power totally out of kilter. They emit such force that, in their presence, any male-owned or -dominated ritual or sacred object cannot do its usual task. For instance, the Lakota say that a menstruating woman anywhere near a yuwipi man, who is a special sort of psychic, spirit-empowered healer, for a day or so before he is to do his ceremony will effectively disempower him. Conversely, among many if not most tribes, important ceremonies cannot be held without the presence of women. Sometimes the ritual woman who empowers the ceremony must be unmarried and virginal so that the power she channels is unalloyed, unweakened by sexual arousal and penetration by a male. Other ceremonies require tumescent women, others the presence of mature women who have borne children, and still others depend for empowerment on post-menopausal women. Women may be segregated from the company of the whole band or village on certain occasions, but on certain occasions men are also segregated. In short, each ritual depends on a certain balance of power, and the positions of women within the phases of womanhood are used by tribal people to empower certain rites. This does not derive from a male-dominant view; it is not a ritual observance imposed on women by men. It derives from a tribal view of reality that distinguishes tribal people from feudal and industrial people.

Among the tribes, the occult power of women, inextricably bound to our hormonal life, is thought to be very great; many hold that we possess innately the blood-given power to kill—with a glance, with a step, or with a judicious mixing of menstrual blood into somebody's soup. Medicine women among the Pomo of California cannot practice until they are sufficiently mature; when they are immature, their power is diffuse and is likely to interfere with their practice until time and experience have it under control. So women of the tribes are not especially inclined to see themselves as poor helpless victims of male domination. Even in those tribes where something akin to male domination was present, women are perceived as powerful, socially, physically, and metaphysically. In times past, as in times present, women carried enormous burdens with aplomb. We were far indeed from the "weaker sex," the designation that white aristocratic sisters unhappily earned for us all.

I remember my mother moving furniture all over the house when she wanted it change. She didn't wait for my father to come home and help—she just went ahead and moved the piano, a huge upright from the old days, the couch, the refrigerator. Nobody had told her she was too weak to do such things. In imitation of her, I would delight in loading trucks at my father's store with cases of pop or fifty-pound sacks of flour. Even when I was quite small I could do it, and it gave me a belief in my own physical strength that advancing middle age can't quite erase. My mother used to tell me about the Acoma Pueblo women she had seen as a child carrying huge ollas (water pots) on their heads as they wound their way up the tortuous stairwell carved into the face of the "Sky City" mesa, a feat I tried to imitate with books and tin buckets. ("Sky City" is the term used by the chamber of commerce for the mother village of Acoma, which is situated atop a high sandstone table mountain.) I was never very successful, but even the attempt reminded me that I was supposed to be strong and balanced to be a proper girl.

Of course, my mother's Laguna people are Keres Indian, reputed to be the last extreme mother-right people on earth. So it is no wonder that I got notably nonwhite notions about the natural strength and prowess of women. Indeed, it is only when I am trying to get non-Indian approval, recognition, or acknowledgment that my "weak sister" emotional and intellectual ploys get the better of my tribal woman's good sense. At such times I forget that I just moved the piano or just wrote a competent paper or just completed a financial transaction satisfactorily or have supported myself and my children for most of my adult life.

Nor is my contradictory behavior atypical. Most Indian women I know are in the same bicultural bind: we vacillate between being dependent and strong, self-reliant and powerless, strongly motivated and hopelessly insecure. We resolve the dilemma in various ways: some of us party all the time; some of us drink to excess; some of us travel and move around a lot; some of us land good jobs and then quit them; some of us engage in violent exchanges; some of us blow our brains out. We act in these destructive ways because we suffer from the societal conflicts caused by having to identify with two hopelessly opposed cultural definitions of women. Through this destructive dissonance we are unhappy prey to the self-disparagement common to, indeed demanded of, Indians living in the United States today. Our situation is caused by the exigencies of a history of invasion, conquest, and colonization whose searing marks are probably ineradicable. A popular bumper sticker on many Indian cars proclaims: "If You're Indian You're In," to which I always find myself adding under my breath, "Trouble."

No Indian can grow to any age without being informed that her people were "savages" who interferred with the march of progress pursued by respectable, loving, civilized white people. We are the villains of the scenario when we are mentioned at all. We are absent from much of white history except when we are calmly, rationally, succinctly, and systematically dehumanized. On the few occasions we are noticed in any way other than as howling, bloodthirsty beings, we are acclaimed for our noble quaintness. In this definition, we are exotic curios. Our ancient arts and customs are used to draw tourist money to state coffers, into the pocketbooks and bank accounts of scholars, and into support of the American-in-Disneyland promoters' dream.

As a Roman Catholic child I was treated to bloody tales of how the savage Indians martyred the hapless priests and missionaries who went among them in an attempt to lead them to the one true path. By the time I was through high school I had the idea that Indians were people who had benefited mightily from the advanced knowledge and superior morality of the Anglo-Europeans. At least I had, perforce, that idea to lay beside the other one that derived from my daily experience of Indian life, an idea less dehumanizing and more accurate because it came from my mother and the other Indian people who raised me. That idea was that Indians are a people who don't tell lies, who care for their children and their old people. You never seen an Indian orphan, they said. You always know when you're old that someone will take care of you—one of your children will. Then they'd list the old folks who were being taken care of by this child or that. No child is ever considered illegitimate among the Indians, they said. If a girl gets pregnant, the baby is still part of the family, and the mother is too. That's what they said, and they showed me real people who lived according to those principles.

Of course the ravages of colonization have taken their toll; there are orphans in Indian country now, and abandoned, brutalized old folks; there are even illegitimate children, though the very concept still strikes me as absurd. There are battered children and neglected children, and there are battered wives and women who have been raped by Indian men. Proximity to the "civilizing" effects of white Christians has not improved the moral quality of life in Indian country, though each group, Indian and white, explains the situation differently. Nor is there much yet in the oral tradition that can enable us to adapt to these inhuman changes. But a force is growing in that direction, and it is helping Indian women reclaim their lives. Their power, their sense of direction and of self will soon be visible. It is the force of the women who speak and work and write, and it is formidable.

Through all the centuries of war and death and cultural and psychic destruction have endured the women who raise the children and tend the fires, who pass along the tales and the traditions, who weep and bury the dead, who are the dead, and who never forget. There are always the women, who make pots and weave baskets, who fashion clothes and cheer their children on at powwow, who make fry bread and piki bread, and corn soup and chili stew, who dance and sing and remember and hold within their hearts the dream of their ancient peoples—that one day the woman who thinks will speak to us again, and everywhere there will be peace. Meanwhile we tell the stories of fun and scandal and laugh over all manner of things that happen every day. We watch and we wait.

My great-grandmother told my mother: Never forget you are Indian. And my mother told me the same thing. This, then, is how I have gone about remembering, so that my children will remember too.

LESLIE MARMON SILKO
(1948-)

Leslie Marmon Silko was born in Albuquerque, New Mexico, and grew up on the Laguna Pueblo Reservation. She attended the University of New Mexico. In 1974 she published her first book, Laguna Woman: Poems, *and was awarded a grant from the National Endowment for the Arts. Her first novel,* Ceremony, *was published in 1977 and brought her wide critical acclaim. That same year she received a Pushcart Prize for poetry. Her collection of*

poems and stories, Storyteller, *was published in 1981, and* Almanac of the
Dead, *her controversial second novel, was published in 1991. Her most
recent work is* Yellow Woman and a Beauty of the Spirit: Essays on Native
American Life Today *(1996), and a third novel,* Gardens in the Dunes
*(1999). She has taught at the University of Arizona and is the recipient of a
John D. and Catherine T. MacArthur Foundation grant.*

Silko's short story "The Man to Send Rain Clouds" from her collection
Storyteller *recounts the conflict between the oppressed and colonized
Laguna Pueblo people and the forces of colonization, including Christian
religion and the Catholic church.*

THE MAN TO SEND RAIN CLOUDS

One

They found him under a big cottonwood tree. His Levi jacket and pants were faded
light-blue so that he had been easy to find. The big cottonwood tree stood apart
from a small grove of winterbare cottonwoods which grew in the wide, sandy
arroyo. He had been dead for a day or more, and the sheep had wandered and scattered up and down the arroyo. Leon and his brother-in-law, Ken, gathered the sheep
and left them in the pen at the sheep camp before they returned to the cottonwood
tree. Leon waited under the tree while Ken drove the truck through the deep sand
to the edge of the arroyo. He squinted up at the sun and unzipped his jacket—it
sure was hot for this time of year. But high and northwest the blue mountains were
still deep in snow. Ken came sliding down the low, crumbling bank about fifty yards
down, and he was bringing the red blanket.

Before they wrapped the old man, Leon took a piece of string out of his pocket
and tied a small gray feather in the old man's long white hair. Ken gave him the
paint. Across the brown wrinkled forehead he drew a streak of white and along the
high cheekbones he drew a strip of blue paint. He paused and watched Ken throw
pinches of corn meal and pollen into the wind that fluttered the small gray feather.
Then Leon painted with yellow under the old man's broad nose, and finally, when
he had painted green across the chin, he smiled.

"Send us rain clouds, Grandfather." They laid the bundle in the back of the
pickup and covered it with a heavy tarp before they started back to the pueblo.

They turned off the highway onto the sandy pueblo road. Not long after they
passed the store and post office they saw Father Paul's car coming toward them.
When he recognized their faces he slowed his car and waved for them to stop. The
young priest rolled down the car window.

"Did you find old Teofilo?" he asked loudly.

Leon stopped the truck. "Good morning, Father. We were just out to the sheep
camp. Everything is O.K. now."

"Thank God for that. Teofilo is a very old man. You really shouldn't allow him to
stay at the sheep camp alone."

"No, he won't do that any more now."

"Well, I'm glad you understand. I hope I'll be seeing you at Mass this week—we
missed you last Sunday. See if you can get old Teofilo to come with you." The priest
smiled and waved at them as they drove away.

Two

Louise and Teresa were waiting. The table was set for lunch, and the coffee was boiling on the black iron stove. Leon looked at Louise and then at Teresa.

"We found him under a cottonwood tree in the big arroyo near sheep camp. I guess he sat down to rest in the shade and never got up again." Leon walked toward the old man's bed. The red plaid shawl had been shaken and spread carefully over the bed, and a new brown flannel shirt and pair of stiff new Levis were arranged neatly beside the pillow. Louise held the screen door open while Leon and Ken carried in the red blanket. He looked small and shriveled, and after they dressed him in the new shirt and pants he seemed more shrunken.

It was noontime now because the church bells rang the Angelus. They ate the beans with hot bread, and nobody said anything until after Teresa poured the coffee.

Ken stood up and put on his jacket. "I'll see about the gravediggers. Only the top layer of soil is frozen. I think it can be ready before dark."

Leon nodded his head and finished his coffee. After Ken had been gone for a while, the neighbors and clanspeople came quietly to embrace Teofilo's family and to leave food on the table because the gravediggers would come to eat when they were finished.

Three

The sky in the west was full of pale-yellow light. Louise stood outside with her hands in the pockets of Leon's green army jacket that was too big for her. The funeral was over, and the old men had taken their candles and medicine bags and were gone. She waited until the body was laid into the pickup before she said anything to Leon. She touched his arm, and he noticed that her hands were still dusty from the corn meal that she had sprinkled around the old man. When she spoke, Leon could not hear her.

"What did you say? I didn't hear you."

"I said that I had been thinking about something."

"About what?"

"About the priest sprinkling holy water for Grandpa. So he won't be thirsty."

Leon stared at the new moccasins that Teofilo had made for the ceremonial dances in the summer. They were nearly hidden by the red blanket. It was getting colder, and the wind pushed gray dust down the narrow pueblo road. The sun was approaching the long mesa where it disappeared during the winter. Louise stood there shivering and watching his face. Then he zipped up his jacket and opened the truck door. "I'll see if he's there."

Four

Ken stopped the pickup at the church, and Leon got out; and then Ken drove down the hill to the graveyard where people were waiting. Leon knocked at the old carved door with its symbols of the Lamb. While he waited he looked up at the twin bells from the king of Spain with the last sunlight pouring around them in their tower.

The priest opened the door and smiled when he saw who it was. "Come in! What brings you here this evening?"

The priest walked toward the kitchen, and Leon stood with his cap in his hand, playing with the earflaps and examining the living room—the brown sofa, the green armchair, and the brass lamp that hung down from the ceiling by links of chain. The priest dragged a chair out of the kitchen and offered it to Leon.

"No thank you, Father. I only came to ask you if you would bring your holy water to the graveyard."

The priest turned away from Leon and looked out the window at the patio full of shadows and the dining-room windows of the nuns' cloister across the patio. The curtains were heavy, and the light from within faintly penetrated; it was impossible to see the nuns inside eating supper. "Why didn't you tell me he was dead? I could have brought the Last Rites anyway."

Leon smiled. "It wasn't necessary, Father."

The priest stared down at his scuffed brown loafers and the worn hem of his cassock. "For a Christian burial it was necessary."

His voice was distant, and Leon thought that his blue eyes looked tired.

"It's O.K. Father, we just want him to have plenty of water."

The priest sank down into the green chair and picked up a glossy missionary magazine. He turned the colored pages full of lepers and pagans without looking at them.

"You know I can't do that, Leon. There should have been the Last Rites and a funeral Mass at the very least."

Leon put on his green cap and pulled the flaps down over his ears. "It's getting late, Father. I've got to go."

When Leon opened the door Father Paul stood up and said, "Wait." He left the room and came back wearing a long brown overcoat. He followed Leon out the door and across the dim churchyard to the adobe steps in front of the church. They both stooped to fit through the low adobe entrance. And when they started down the hill to the graveyard only half of the sun was visible above the mesa.

The priest approached the grave slowly, wondering how they had managed to dig into the frozen ground; and then he remembered that this was New Mexico, and saw the pile of cold loose sand beside the hole. The people stood close to each other with little clouds of steam puffing from their faces. The priest looked at them and saw a pile of jackets, gloves, and scarves in the yellow, dry tumbleweeds that grew in the graveyard. He looked at the red blanket, not sure that Teofilo was so small, wondering if it wasn't some perverse Indian trick—something they did in March to ensure a good harvest—wondering if maybe old Teofilo was actually at sheep camp corraling the sheep for the night. But there he was, facing into a cold dry wind and squinting at the last sunlight, ready to bury a red wool blanket while the faces of his parishioners were in shadow with the last warmth of the sun on their backs.

His fingers were stiff, and it took him a long time to twist the lid off the holy water. Drops of water fell on the red blanket and soaked into dark icy spots. He sprinkled the grave and the water disappeared almost before it touched the dim, cold sand; it reminded him of something—he tried to remember what it was, because he thought if he could remember he might understand this. He sprinkled more water; he shook the container until it was empty, and the water fell through the light from sundown like August rain that fell while the sun was still shining, almost evaporating before it touched the wilted squash flowers.

The wind pulled at the priest's brown Franciscan robe and swirled away the corn meal and pollen that had been sprinkled on the blanket. They lowered the bundle into the ground, and they didn't bother to untie the stiff pieces of new rope that were tied around the ends of the blanket. The sun was gone, and over on the highway the eastbound lane was full of headlights. The priest walked away slowly. Leon watched him climb the hill, and when he had disappeared within the tall, thick walls, Leon turned to look up at the high blue mountains in the deep snow that reflected a faint red light from the west. He felt good because it was finished, and he was happy about the sprinkling of the holy water; now the old man could send them big thunderclouds for sure.

JOHN FANTE
(1909-1983)

Born in Colorado, John Fante moved to Los Angeles, California, in the 1930s to pursue a writing career. He attended the University of Colorado and later Long Beach City College. He published his first short story in 1932 and his subsequent stories appeared in numerous publications, including The Atlantic Monthly, Esquire, *and* Harper's Bazaar. *In 1938 he published his first novel,* Wait Until Spring, Bandini. *During his early career, he held a variety of jobs, but beginning in 1940 he worked steadily as a screenwriter for the next thirty years. He produced novels such as* Ask the Dust *(1939), a collection of short stories,* Dago Red *(1940), and numerous screenplays. In 1957, his screenplay of his novel* Full of Life *was nominated for an Academy Award.*

Fante's story "The Odyssey of a Wop" reminds us that one of the consequences of minority status in a white supremacist and anti-immigrant environment is self-hatred.

THE ODYSSEY OF A WOP

I pick up little bits of information about my grandfather. My grandmother tells me of him. She tells me that when he lived he was a good fellow whose goodness evoked not admiration but pity. He was known as a good little Wop. Of an evening he liked to sit at a table in a saloon sipping a tumbler of anisette, all by himself. He sat there like a little girl nipping an ice-cream cone. The old boy loved that green stuff, that anisette. It was his passion, and when folks saw him sitting alone it tickled them, for he was a good little Wop.

One night, my grandmother tells me, my grandfather was sitting in the saloon, he and his anisette. A drunken teamster stumbled through the swinging doors, braced himself at the bar, and bellowed:

"All right, everybody! Come an' get 'em! They're on me!"

And there sat my grandfather, not moving, his old tongue coquetting with the anisette. Everyone but he stood at the bar and drank the teamster's liquor. The teamster swung round. He saw my grandfather. He was insulted.

"You too, Wop!" said he. "Come up and drink!"

Silence. My grandfather arose. He staggered across the floor, passed the teamster, and then what did he do but go through the swinging doors and down the snowy street! He heard laughter coming after him from the saloon and his chest burned. He went home to my father.

"*Mamma mia!*" he blubbered. "Tummy Murray, he calla me Wopa."

"*Sangue della Madonna!*"

Bareheaded, my father rushed down the street to the saloon. Tommy Murray was not there. He was in another saloon half a block away, and there my father found him. He drew the teamster aside and spoke under his breath. A fight! Immediately blood and hair began to fly. Chairs were drawn back. The customers applauded. The two men fought for an hour. They rolled over the floor, kicking, cursing, biting. They were in a knot in the middle of the floor, their bodies wrapped around each other. My father's head, chest, and arms buried the teamster's face. The teamster screamed. My father growled. His neck was rigid and trembling. The teamster screamed again, and lay still. My father got to his feet and wiped blood from his open mouth with the back of his hand. On the floor the teamster lay with a loose ear hanging from his head. . . . This is the story my grandmother tells me.

I think about the two men, my father and the teamster, and I picture them struggling on the floor. Boy! *Can* my father fight!

I get an idea. My two brothers are playing in another room. I leave my grandmother and go to them. They are sprawled on the rug, bent over crayons and drawing-paper. They look up and see my face flaming with my idea.

"What's wrong?" one asks.

"I dare you to do something!"

"Do what?"

"I dare you to call me a Wop!"

My youngest brother, barely six, jumps to his feet, and dancing up and down, screams: "Wop! Wop! Wop! Wop!"

I look at him. Pooh! He's too small. It's that other brother, that bigger brother, I want. He's got ears too, he has.

"I bet *you're* afraid to call me Wop."

But he senses the devil in the woodpile.

"Nah," says he. "I don't wanna."

"Wop! Wop! Wop! Wop!" screams my little brother.

"Shut your mouth, you!"

"I won't neither. You're a Wop! Wop! Woppedy Wop!"

My older brother's box of crayons lies on the floor in front of his nose. I put my heel upon the box and grind it into the carpet. He yells, seizing my leg. I back away, and he begins to cry.

"Aw, that was sure dirty," he says.

"I dare you to call me a Wop!"

"Wop!"

I charge, seeking his ear. But my grandmother comes into the room flourishing a razor strop.

II

From the beginning, I hear my mother use the words Wop and Dago with such vigor as to denote violent distaste. She spits them out. They leap from her lips. To her, they contain the essence of poverty, squalor, filth. If I don't wash my teeth, or hang up my cap, my mother says: "Don't be like that. Don't be a Wop." Thus, as I begin to acquire her values, Wop and Dago to me become synonymous with things evil. But she's consistent.

My father isn't. He's loose with his tongue. His moods create his judgments. I at once notice that to him Wop and Dago are without any distinct meaning, though if one not an Italian slaps them onto him, he's instantly insulted. Christopher Columbus was the greatest Wop who ever lived, says my father. So is Caruso. So is this fellow and that. But his very good friend Peter Ladonna is not only a drunken pig, but a Wop on top of it; and of course all his brothers-in-law are good-for-nothing Wops.

He pretends to hate the Irish. He really doesn't, but he likes to think so, and he warns us children against them. Our grocer's name is O'Neil. Frequently and inadvertently he makes errors when my mother is at his store. She tells my father about short weights in meats, and now and then of a stale egg.

Straightway my father grows tense, his lower lip curling. "This is the last time that Irish bum robs me!" And he goes out, goes to the grocery-store, his heels booming.

Soon he returns. He's smiling. His fists bulge with cigars. "From now on," says he, "everything's gonna be all right."

I don't like the grocer. My mother sends me to his store every day, and instantly he chokes up my breathing with the greeting: "Hello, you little Dago! What'll you have?" So I detest him, and never enter his store if other customers are to be seen, for to be called a Dago before others is a ghastly, almost a physical humiliation. My stomach expands and contracts, and I feel naked.

I steal recklessly when the grocer's back is turned. I enjoy stealing from him—candy bars, cookies, fruit. When he goes into his refrigerator I lean on his meat scales, hoping to snap a spring; I press my toe into egg baskets. Sometimes I pilfer too much. Then, what a pleasure it is to stand on the curb, my appetite gorged, and heave *his* candy bars, *his* cookies, *his* apples into the high yellow weeds across the street! . . . "Damn you, O'Neil, you can't call me a Dago and get away with it!"

His daughter is of my age. She's cross-eyed. Twice a week she passes our house on her way to her music lesson. Above the street, and high in the branches of an elm tree, I watch her coming down the sidewalk, swinging her violin case. When she is under me, I jeer in sing-song:

> *Martha's crooooooss-eyed!*
> *Martha's crooooooss-eyed!*
> *Martha's crooooooss-eyed!*

III

As I grow older, I find out that Italians use Wop and Dago much more than Americans. My grandmother, whose vocabulary of English is confined to the commonest of nouns, always employs them in discussing contemporary Italians. The words never come forth quietly, unobtrusively. No; they bolt forth. There is a blatant intonation, and then the sense of someone being scathed, stunned.

I enter the parochial school with an awful fear that I will be called a Wop. As soon as I find out why people have such things as surnames, I match my own against such typically Italian cognomens as Bianchi, Borello, Pacelli—the names of other students. I am pleasantly relieved by the comparison. After all, I think, people will say I am French. Doesn't my name sound French? Sure! So thereafter, when people ask me my nationality, I tell them I am French. A few boys begin calling me Frenchy. I like that. It feels fine.

Thus I begin to loathe my heritage. I avoid Italian boys and girls who try to be friendly. I thank God for my light skin and hair, and I choose my companions by the Anglo-Saxon ring of their names. If a boy's name is Whitney, Brown, or Smythe, then he's my pal; but I'm always a little breathless when I am with him; he may find me out. At the lunch hour I huddle over my lunch pail, for my mother doesn't wrap my sandwiches in wax paper, and she makes them too large, and the lettuce leaves protrude. Worse, the bread is homemade; not bakery bread, not "American" bread. I make a great fuss because I can't have mayonnaise and other "American" things.

The parish priest is a good friend of my father's. He comes strolling through the school grounds, watching the children at play. He calls to me and asks about my father, and then he tells me I should be proud to be studying about my great countrymen, Columbus, Vespucci, John Cabot. He speaks in a loud, humorous voice. Students gather around us, listening, and I bite my lips and wish to Jesus he'd shut up and move on.

Occasionally now I hear about a fellow named Dante. But when I find out that he was an Italian I hate him as if he were alive and walking through the classrooms, pointing a finger at me. One day I find his picture in a dictionary. I look at it and tell myself that never have I seen an uglier bastard.

We students are at the blackboard one day, and a soft-eyed Italian girl whom I hate but who insists that I am her beau stands beside me. She twitches and shuffles about uneasily, half on tiptoe, smiling queerly at me. I sneer and turn my back, moving as far away from her as I can. The nun sees the wide space separating us and tells me to move nearer the girl. I do so, and the girl draws away, nearer the student on her other side.

Then I look down at my feet, and there I stand in a wet, spreading spot. I look quickly at the girl, and she hangs her head and looks at me in a way that begs me to take the blame for her. We attract the attention of others, and the classroom becomes alive with titters. Here comes the nun. I think I am in for it again but she embraces me and murmurs that I should have raised two fingers and of course I would have been allowed to leave the room. But, says she, there's no need for that now; the thing for me to do is go out and get the mop. I do so, and amid the hysteria I nurse my conviction that only a Wop girl, right out of a Wop home, would ever do such a thing as this.

Oh, you Wop! Oh, you Dago! You bother me even when I sleep. I dream of defending myself against tormentors. One day I learn from my mother that my father went to the Argentine in his youth, and lived in Buenos Aires for two years. My mother tells me of his experiences there, and all day I think about them, even to the time I go to sleep. That night I come awake with a jerk. In the darkness I grope my way to my mother's room. My father sleeps at her side, and I awaken her gently, so that he won't be aroused.

I whisper: "Are you sure Papa wasn't *born* in Argentina?"

"No. Your father was born in Italy."

I go back to bed, disconsolate and disgusted.

IV

During a ball game on the school grounds, a boy who plays on the opposing team begins to ridicule my playing. It is the ninth inning, and I ignore his taunts. We are losing the game, but if I can knock out a hit our chances of winning are pretty strong. I am determined to come through, and I face the pitcher confidently. The tormentor sees me at the plate.

"Ho! Ho!" he shouts. "Look who's up! The Wop's up. Let's get rid of the Wop!"

This is the first time anyone at school has ever flung the word at me, and I am so angry that I strike out foolishly. We fight after the game, this boy and I, and I make him take it back.

Now school days become fighting days. Nearly every afternoon at 3:15 a crowd gathers to watch me make some guy take it back. This is fun; I am getting somewhere now, so come on, you guys, I dare you to call me a Wop! When at length there are no more boys who challenge me, insults come to me by hearsay, and I seek out the culprits. I strut down the corridors. The smaller boys admire me. "Here he comes!" they say, and they gaze and gaze. My two younger brothers attend the same school, and the smallest, a little squirt seven years old, brings his friends to me and asks me to roll up my sleeve and show them my muscles. Here you are, boys. Look me over.

My brother brings home furious accounts of my battles. My father listens avidly, and I stand by, to clear up any doubtful details. Sadly happy days! My father gives me pointers: how to hold my fist, how to guard my head. My mother, too shocked to hear more, presses her temples and squeezes her eyes and leaves the room.

I am nervous when I bring friends to my house; the place looks so Italian. Here hangs a picture of Victor Emmanuel, and over there is one of the cathedral of Milan, and next to it one of St. Peter's, and on the buffet stands a wine pitcher of medieval design; it's forever brimming, forever red and brilliant with wine. These things are heirlooms belonging to my father, and no matter who may come to our house, he likes to stand under them and brag.

So I begin to shout to him. I tell him to cut out being a Wop and be an American once in a while. Immediately he gets his razor strop and whales hell out of me, clouting me from room to room and finally out the back door. I go into the woodshed and pull down my pants and stretch my neck to examine the blue slices across my rump. A Wop, that's what my father is! Nowhere is there an American father who beats his son this way. Well, he's not going to get away with it; some day I'll get even with him.

I begin to think that my grandmother is hopelessly a Wop. She's a small, stocky peasant who walks with her wrists crisscrossed over her belly, a simple old lady fond of boys. She comes into the room and tries to talk to my friends. She speaks English with a bad accent, her vowels rolling out like hoops. When, in her simple way, she confronts a friend of mind and says, her old eyes smiling: "You lika go the Seester scola?" my heart roars. *Mannaggia!* I'm disgraced; now they all know that I'm an Italian.

My grandmother has taught me to speak the native tongue. By seven, I know it pretty well, and I always address her in it. But when friends are with me, when I am twelve and thirteen, I pretend ignorance of what she says, and smirk stiffly; my friends daren't know that I can speak any language but English. Sometimes this infuriates her. She bristles, the loose skin at her throat knits hard, and she blasphemes with a mighty blasphemy.

V

When I finish in the parochial school my people decide to send me to a Jesuit academy in another city. My father comes with me on the first day. Chiseled into the stone coping that skirts the roof of the main building of the academy is the Latin inscription: *Religioni et Bonis Artibus.* My father and I stand at a distance, and he reads it aloud and tells me what it means.

I look up at him in amazement. Is this man my father? Why, look at him! Listen to him! He reads with an Italian inflection! He's wearing an Italian mustache. I have never realized it until this moment, but he looks exactly like a Wop. His suit hangs carelessly in wrinkles upon him. Why the deuce doesn't he buy a new one? And look at his tie! It's crooked. And his shoes: they need a shine. And, for the Lord's sake, will you look at his pants! They're not even buttoned in front. And oh, damn, damn, damn, you can see those dirty old suspenders that he won't throw away. Say, Mister, are you really my father? You there, why, you're such a little guy, such a runt, such an old-looking fellow! You look exactly like one of those immigrants carrying a blanket. You can't be *my* father! Why, I thought . . . I've always thought . . .

I'm crying now, the first time I've ever cried for any reason excepting a licking, and I'm glad he's not crying too. I'm glad he's as tough as he is, and we say good-bye quickly, and I go down the path quickly, and I do not turn to look back, for I know he's standing there and looking at me.

I enter the administration building and stand in line with strange boys who also wait to register for the autumn term. Some Italian boys stand among them. I am away from home, and I sense the Italians. We look at one another and our eyes meet in an irresistible amalgamation, a suffusive consanguinity; I look away.

A burly Jesuit rises from his chair behind the desk and introduces himself to me. Such a voice for a man! There are a dozen thunderstorms in his chest. He asks my name, and writes it down on a little card.

"Nationality?" he roars.

"American."

"Your father's name?"

I whisper it: "Guido."

"How's that? Spell it out. Talk louder."

I cough. I touch my lips with the back of my hand and spell out the name.

"Ha!" shouts the registrar. "And still they come! Another Wop! Well, young man, you'll be at home here! Yes, sir! Lots of Wops here! We've even got Kikes! And, you know, this place reeks with shanty Irish!"

Dio! How I hate that priest!

He continues: "Where was your father born?"

"Buenos Aires, Argentina."

"Your mother?"

At last I can shout with the gusto of truth.

"Denver!" Aye, just like a conductor.

Casually, by way of conversation, he asks: "You speak Italian?"

"Nah! Not a word."

"Too bad," he says.

"You're nuts," I think.

VI

That semester I wait on table to defray my tuition fee. Trouble ahead; the chef and his assistants in the kitchen are all Italians. They know at once that I am of the breed. I ignore the chef's friendly overtures, loathing him from the first. He understands why, and we become enemies. Every word he uses has a knife in it. His remarks cut me to pieces. After two months I can stand it no longer in the kitchen, and so I write a long letter to my mother; I am losing weight, I write; if you don't let me quit this job, I'll get sick and flunk my tests. She telegraphs me some money and tells me to quit at once; oh, I feel so sorry for you, my boy; I didn't dream it would be so hard on you.

I decide to work just one more evening, to wait on table for just one more meal. That evening, after the meal, when the kitchen is deserted save for the cook and his assistants, I remove my apron and take my stand across the kitchen from him, staring at him. This is my moment. Two months I have waited for this moment. There is a knife stuck into the chopping block. I pick it up, still staring. I want to hurt the cook, square things up.

He sees me, and he says: "Get out of here, Wop!"

An assistant shouts: "Look out, he's got a knife!"

"You won't throw it, Wop," the cook says. I am not thinking of throwing it, but since he says I won't, I do. It goes over his head and strikes the wall and drops with a clatter to the floor. He picks it up and chases me out of the kitchen. I run, thanking God I didn't hit him.

That year the football team is made up of Irish and Italian boys. The linemen are Irish, and we in the backfield are four Italians. We have a good team and win a lot of games, and my teammates are excellent players who are unselfish and work together as one man. But I hate my three fellow-players in the backfield; because of our nationality we seem ridiculous. The team makes a captain of me, and I call signals and see to it my fellow-Italians in the backfield do as little scoring as possible. I hog the play.

The school journal and the town's sport pages begin to refer to us as the Wop Wonders. I think it an insult. Late one afternoon, at the close of an important game, a number of students leave the main grandstand and group themselves at one end of the field, to improvise some yells. They give three big ones for the Wop Wonders. It sickens me. I can feel my stomach move; and after that game I turn in my suit and quit the team.

I am a bad Latinist. Disliking the language, I do not study, and therefore I flunk my examinations regularly. Now a student comes to me and tells me that it is possible to drop Latin from my curriculum if I follow his suggestion, which is that I fail deliberately in the next few examinations, fail hopelessly. If I do this, the student says, the Jesuits will bow to my stupidity and allow me to abandon the language.

This is an agreeable suggestion. I follow it out. But it backtracks, for the Jesuits are wise fellows. They see what I'm doing, and they laugh and tell me that I am not clever enough to fool them, and that I must keep on studying Latin, even if it takes me twenty years to pass. Worse, they double my assignments and I spend my recreation time with Latin syntax. Before examinations in my junior year the Jesuit who instructs me calls me to his room and says:

"It is a mystery to me that a thoroughbred Italian like yourself should have any trouble with Latin. The language is in your blood and, believe me, you're a darned poor Wop."

Abbastanza! I go upstairs and lock my door and sit down with my book in front of me, my Latin book, and I study like a wild man, tearing crazily into the stuff until, lo, what is this? What am I studying here? Sure enough, it's a lot like the Italian my grandmother taught me so long ago—this Latin, it isn't so hard, after all. I pass the examination, I pass it with such an incredibly fine grade that my instructor thinks there is knavery somewhere.

Two weeks before graduation I get sick and go to the infirmary and am quarantined there. I lie in bed and feed my grudges. I bite my thumbs and ponder old grievances. I am running a high fever, and I can't sleep. I think about the principal. He was my close friend during my first two years at the school, but in my third year, last year, he was transferred to another school. I lie in bed thinking of the day we met again in this, the last year. We met again on his return that September, in the principal's room. He said hello to the boys, this fellow and that, and then he turned to me, and said:

"And you, the Wop! So you're still with us."

Coming from the mouth of the priest, the word had a lumpish sound that shook me all over. I felt the eyes of everyone, and I heard a giggle. So that's how it is! I lie in bed thinking of the priest and now of the fellow who giggled.

All of a sudden I jump out of bed, tear the fly-leaf from a book, find a pencil, and write a note to the priest. I write: "Dear Father: I haven't forgotten your insult. You called me a Wop last September. If you don't apologize right away there's going to be trouble." I call the brother in charge of the infirmary and tell him to deliver the note to the priest.

After a while I hear the priest's footsteps rising on the stairs. He comes to the door of my room, opens it, looks at me for a long time, not speaking, but only looking querulously. I wait for him to come in and apologize, for this is a grand moment for me. But he closes the door quietly and walks away. I am astonished. A double insult!

I am well again on the night of graduation. On the platform the principal makes a speech and then begins to distribute the diplomas. We're supposed to say: "Thank you," when he gives them to us. So thank you, and thank you, and thank you, everyone says in his turn. But when he gives me mine, I look squarely at him, just stand there and look, and I don't say anything, and from that day we never speak to each other again.

The following September I enroll at the university.

"Where was your father born?" asks the registrar.

"Buenos Aires, Argentina."

Sure, that's it. The same theme, with variations.

VII

Time passes, and so do school days. I am sitting on a wall along the plaza in Los Angeles, watching a Mexican *fiesta* across the street. A man comes along and lifts himself to the wall beside me, and asks if I have a cigarette. I have, and, lighting the cigarette, he makes conversation with me, and we talk of casual things until the *fiesta* is over. Then we get down from the wall and, still talking, go walking through the Los Angeles Tenderloin. This man needs a shave and his clothes do not fit him;

it's plain that he's a bum. He tells one lie upon another, and not one is well told. But I am lonesome in this town, and a willing listener.

We step into a restaurant for coffee. Now he becomes intimate. He has bummed his way from Chicago to Los Angeles, and has come in search of his sister; he has her address, but she is not at it, and for two weeks he has been looking for her in vain. He talks on and on about this sister, seeming to gyrate like a buzzard over her, hinting to me that I should ask some questions about her. He wants me to touch off the fuse that will release his feelings.

So I ask: "Is she married?"

And then he rips into her, hammer and tongs. Even if he does find her, he will not live with her. What kind of a sister is she to let him walk these streets without a dime in his pocket, and she married to a man who has plenty of money and can give him a job? He thinks she has deliberately given him a false address so that he will not find her, and when he gets his hands on her he's going to wring her neck. In the end, after he has completely demolished her; he does exactly what I think he is going to do.

He asks: "Have *you* got a sister?"

I tell him yes, and he waits for my opinion of her; but he doesn't get it.

We meet again a week later.

He has found his sister. Now he begins to praise her. She has induced her husband to give him a job, and tomorrow he goes to work as a waiter in his brother-in-law's restaurant. He tells me the address, but I do not think more of it beyond the fact that it must be somewhere in the Italian quarter.

And so it is, and by a strange coincidence I know his brother-in-law, Rocco Saccone, an old friend of my people and a *paesano* of my father's. I am in Rocco's place one night a fortnight later. Rocco and I are speaking in Italian when the man I have met on the plaza steps out of the kitchen, an apron over his legs. Rocco calls him and he comes over, and Rocco introduces him as his brother-in-law from Chicago. We shake hands.

"We've met before," I say, but the plaza man doesn't seem to want this known, for he lets go of my hand quickly and goes behind the counter, pretending to be busy with something back there. Oh, he's bluffing; you can see that.

In a loud voice, Rocco says to me: "That man is a skunk. He's ashamed of his own flesh and blood." He turns to the plaza man. "Ain't you?"

"Oh, yeah?" the plaza man sneers.

"How do you mean—he's ashamed? How do you mean?

"Ashamed of being an Italian," Rocco says.

"Oh, yeah?" from the plaza man.

"That's all he knows," Rocco says. "Oh, yeah? That's all he knows. Oh, yeah? Oh, yeah? Oh, yeah? That's all he knows."

"Oh, yeah?" the plaza man says again.

"Yah," Rocco says, his face blue. *"Animale codardo!"*

The plaza man looks at me with peaked eyebrows, and he doesn't know it, he standing there with his black, liquid eyes, he doesn't know that he's as good as a god in his waiter's apron; for he is indeed a god, a miracle worker; no, he doesn't know; no one knows; just the same, he is that—he, of all people. Standing there and looking at him, I feel like my grandfather and my father and the Jesuit cook and Rocco; I seem to have come home, and I am surprised that this return, which I have somehow always expected, should come so quietly, without trumpets and thunder.

"If I were you, I'd get rid of him," I say to Rocco.

"Oh, yeah?" the plaza man says again.

I'd like to paste him. But that won't do any good. There's no sense in hammering your own corpse.

LLOYD VAN BRUNT
(1936-)

Lloyd Van Brunt, who uses the pen name H. L. Van Brunt, was born in Tulsa, Oklahoma, and attended Allan Hancock Junior College. Early in his career, he worked as a reporter and editor. His first collection of poetry, Uncertainties, *was published in 1968, and he has since published several more volumes and contributed poems to numerous literary magazines and anthologies. He has received awards from the Pennsylvania Council for the Arts and the Maryland State Arts Council and has lectured at several colleges and universities. He is the poetry editor of the* Oconee Review *and founding poetry editor of the* Pushcart Prize. *His most recent work is a memoir of growing up in Oklahoma orphanages. He lives in New York City.*

"Whites Without Money" first appeared in the "About Men" feature of the New York Times. *In a time of affluence, Van Brunt's brief essay speaks to the oppression and self-hatred among "poor whites" who often disappear from the cultural radar screens during such periods.*

WHITES WITHOUT MONEY

Poor whites in this country—whether they're called woodchucks in certain parts of New England, lunch pails in the industrial Midwest or rednecks and crackers in the southern reaches of Appalachia—are often made fun of and referred to as "welfare cheats," since many of them survive on public assistance of one kind or another.

Unlike blacks and other racial minorities, poor and mostly rural whites have few defenders, no articulated cause (although a very small proportion may belong to certain ideological groups). And they have been made to feel deeply ashamed of themselves—as I was. This shame, this feeling of worthlessness, is one of the vilest and most self-destructive emotions to be endured. To be poor in a country that places a premium on wealth is in itself shameful. To be white and poor is unforgivable.

Discussing this issue with a black novelist friend of mine recently, I was surprised at his reaction to my assertion that prejudice against poor whites was still prejudice. I had mentioned Tonya Harding's case, how most of the press had "trashed" her for her "lowlife" life style. My friend had little sympathy for Harding: "Come on. You've never walked into a restaurant and had people raise their eyebrows and frown at you—and neither has she. That's prejudice, or at least the tip of the iceberg of it. We're talking apples and oranges here. What poor whites suffer from mostly is envy of power. They don't have any."

What my friend was too polite to tell me, what would have made conversation awkward between us, was that poor whites are also this country's most bigoted citizens. That's why I call them the Polish-joke class, the one group everybody feels free to belittle, knowing that no politically correct boundaries will be violated. It's mostly poor whites who join the Klan or become skinheads who tattoo themselves with swastikas. They're angry, and ashamed of their origins. That rage projects itself against minorities. In turn the poor members of minority groups despise and look down on poor whites, especially the men. The unspoken assumption here is that if they had been born white there wouldn't have been anything they couldn't have done.

That attitude was first brought home to me when I worked in several Pennsylvania prisons in the late 70's, teaching creative-writing workshops. Most of my students were either African-American or Hispanic. The most hated members of the groups were the white prisoners. The other men's contempt for these white failures was endless.

I wore a suit and tie and handmade shoes and had long ago lost my Okie accent; I grew up mostly in Oklahoma orphanages. When asked where I was from, I lied and told the men I was a native of Manhattan—New York City; so that placed me in a special category of white men. At least I was successful—or so they had been led to believe.

But the "honkies" in the joints were just honkies—alkies and bums and punks—losers who weren't even good thieves or robbers, many convicted for low-status crimes like child molestation or cashing stolen welfare checks. The real men, the bank robbers and armored-car hijackers, were almost all members of minorities. "We're talkin' white trash here, my man," I was told. "That's for real." His friends agreed. "White trash." That said it all.

I wished then I could have told them the truth about my background, that I had been born "white trash" in Oklahoma. How that fact had been spelled out to me again and again by matrons at the orphanages and, on one occasion, by a schoolteacher who called me a "welfare cheat" in front of a whole class of staring kids. I was so embarrassed, so mortified, that I ran off and was nearly sent to a state reformatory.

I was sure the men would think me a phony if I told them I could have ended up in the joint—one of the despised white failures. If it hadn't been for the right people at the right time encouraging me, I might never have got through a childhood that featured a father who abandoned my mother and me, a mother who died when I was 8 and years and years in orphanages and foster homes where I was abused. As I escorted the men back to their cell blocks, I thought of trying to explain these things—but it wouldn't have worked.

They admired my London-tailored suits, my Turnbull & Asser shirts and ties and silk handkerchiefs that were oh-so-carefully folded and arranged. They admired success, wanted to be next to it, associated with it. "Feel these threads," a prisoner once said to me. He put his hand on my shoulder as if to rub an ache out. "Fine, fine." They could never have suspected that for two decades I had kept about $10,000 in debt with credit cards, trying to make myself look like an English gentleman.

These men, I realized, had a considerable investment in me. To them I was a big shot, not a little-known writer who taught creative writing for a living—and one who had had considerable misgivings about teaching in prisons. They had leafed through my four books of poetry and wanted me to be a celebrity, one whose signature on the certificates they would receive on completing the workshop would mean something, could be bragged about, could be shown to the parole board. A honky in disguise? Forget it!

Yet no matter how expensive my apparel, I could never have the self-assurance that goes with such clothes. That quality was not for sale. One had to be brought up in a certain way—as many of the students I worked with in a Maryland prep school had. One had to have the easy assumptions of one's class. Teaching in that private school, I was astounded by my students' sense of privilege. They acted as though they owned the space they walked around in. Not all of them were happy or satisfied or had great parents, but most of them had this aura of self-assurance. They seemed sure that no matter what happened they would be protected—as a matter of course.

My novelist friend was right. I had envied these children of the upper middle class—not for the wealth they might inherit (a couple of them already drove $50,000 sports cars, which made all the teachers cat-tongued) but for their indefinable feeling of well-being. I knew that no matter how far I ran from my origins, I could never possess their sense of owning the earth—not even a piece of it. For after 10 years of psychotherapy, I still have to remind myself not to walk around in my fine clothes with head down, eyes averted, as if trying to hide some shameful secret, some deep and unreachable sense of worthlessness. That is the legacy of America's poor whites, their only inheritance.

NICHOLASA MOHR
(1938–)

Nicholasa Mohr was born and raised in New York City. Mohr is both a visual artist and a writer. She attended the Art Students League, the Brooklyn Museum of Art School, and the Pratt Institute Center for Printmaking. She has held appointments at several institutions, including Rutgers University, Queens College of the City University of New York, the Smithsonian Institution, and the Center for American Culture Studies at Columbia University. She has written novels, including her first, the autobiographical Nilda *(1973), and* Going Home *(1986), and two collections of short stories,* In Nueva York *(1977) and* Rituals of Survival: Woman's Portfolio *(1985). In 1975 her stories collected in* El Bronx Remembered—A Novella and Stories *was a finalist for the National Book Award. Her novel* Felita *was awarded the American Book Award in 1981.*

"The English Lesson" from Mohr's In Nueva York *exposes the complex human interaction in a class ostensibly devoted to "learning English," a scene and topic for which some feel nostalgia while others seethe with resentment.*

THE ENGLISH LESSON

"Remember our assignment for today everybody! I'm so confident that you will all do exceptionally well!" Mrs. Susan Hamma smiled enthusiastically at her students. "Everyone is to get up and make a brief statement as to why he or she is taking this course in Basic English. You must state your name, where you originally came from, how long you have been here, and . . . uh . . . a little something about yourself, if you wish. Keep it brief, not too long; remember, there are twenty-eight of us. We have a full class, and everyone must have a chance." Mrs. Hamma waved a forefinger at her students. "This is, after all, a democracy, and we have a democratic class; fairness for all!"

Lali grinned and looked at William, who sat directly next to her. He winked and rolled his eyes toward Mrs. Hamma. This was the third class they had attended together. It had not been easy to persuade Rudi that Lali should learn better English.

"Why is it necessary, eh?" Rudi had protested. "She works here in the store with me. She don't have to talk to nobody. Besides, everybody that comes in speaks Spanish—practically everybody, anyway."

But once William had put the idea to Lali and explained how much easier things would be for her, she kept insisting until Rudi finally agreed. "Go on, you're both driving me nuts. But it can't interfere with business or work—I'm warning you!"

Adult Education offered Basic English, Tuesday evenings from 6:30 to 8:00, at a local public school. Night customers did not usually come into Rudi's Luncheonette until after eight. William and Lali promised that they would leave everything prepared and make up for any inconvenience by working harder and longer than usual, if necessary.

The class admitted twenty-eight students, and because there were only twenty-seven registered, Lali was allowed to take the course even after missing the first two classes. William had assured Mrs. Hamma that he would help Lali catch up; she was glad to have another student to make up the full registration.

Most of the students were Spanish speaking. The majority were American citizens—Puerto Ricans who had migrated to New York and spoke very little English. The rest were immigrants admitted to the United States as legal aliens. There were several Chinese, two Dominicans, one Sicilian, and one Pole.

Every Tuesday Mrs. Hamma traveled to the Lower East Side from Bayside, Queens, where she lived and was employed as a history teacher in the local junior high school. She was convinced that this small group of people desperately needed her services. Mrs. Hamma reiterated her feelings frequently to just about anyone who would listen. "Why, if these people can make it to class after working all day at those miserable, dreary, uninteresting, and often revolting jobs, well, the least I can do is be there to serve them, making every lesson count toward improving their conditions! My grandparents came here from Germany as poor immigrants, working their way up. I'm not one to forget a thing like that!"

By the time class started most of the students were quite tired. And after the lesson was over, many had to go on to part-time jobs, some even without time for supper. As a result there was always sluggishness and yawning among the students. This never discouraged Mrs. Hamma, whose drive and enthusiasm not only amused the class but often kept everyone awake.

"Now this is the moment we have all been preparing for." Mrs. Hamma stood up, nodded, and blinked knowingly at her students. "Five lessons, I think, are enough to prepare us for our oral statements. You may read from prepared notes, as I said before, but please try not to read every word. We want to hear you speak; conversation is what we're after. When someone asks you about yourself, you cannot take a piece of paper and start reading the answers, now can you? That would be foolish. So . . ."

Standing in front of her desk, she put her hands on her hips and spread her feet, giving the impression that she was going to demonstrate calisthenics.

"Shall we begin?"

Mrs. Hamma was a very tall, angular woman with large extremities. She was the tallest person in the room. Her eyes roamed from student to student until they met William's.

"Mr. Colón, will you please begin?"

Nervously William looked around him, hesitating.

"Come on now, we must get the ball rolling. All right now . . . did you hear what I said? Listen, 'getting the ball rolling' means getting started. Getting things going, such as—" Mrs. Hamma swiftly lifted her right hand over her head, making a fist, then swung her arm around like a pitcher and, with an underhand curve, forcefully threw an imaginary ball out at her students. Trying to maintain her balance, Mrs. Hamma hopped from one leg to the other. Startled, the students looked at one another. In spite of their efforts to restrain themselves, several people in back began to giggle. Lali and William looked away, avoiding each other's eyes and trying not to laugh out loud. With assured countenance, Mrs. Hamma continued.

"An idiom!" she exclaimed, pleased. "You have just seen me demonstrate the meaning of an idiom. Now I want everyone to jot down this information in his notebook." Going to the blackboard, Mrs. Hamma explained, "It's something which literally says one thing, but actually means another. Idiom . . . idiomatic." Quickly and obediently, everyone began to copy what she wrote. "Has everyone got it? O.K., let's GET THE BALL ROLLING, Mr. Colón!"

Uneasily William stood up; he was almost the same height standing as sitting. When speaking to others, especially in a new situation, he always preferred to sit alongside those listening; it gave him a sense of equality with other people. He looked around and cleared his throat; at least everyone else was sitting. Taking a deep breath, William felt better.

"My name is William Horacio Colón," he read from a prepared statement. "I have been here in New York City for five months. I coming from Puerto Rico. My town is located in the mountains in the central part of the island. The name of my town is Aibonito, which means in Spanish 'oh how pretty.' It is name like this because when the Spaniards first seen that place they was very impressed with the beauty of the section and—"

"Make it brief, Mr. Colón," Mrs. Hamma interrupted, "there are others, you know."

William looked at her, unable to continue.

"Go on, go on, Mr. Colón, please!"

"I am working here now living with my mother and family in Lower East Side of New York City," William spoke rapidly. "I study Basic English por que . . . because my ambition is to learn to speak and read English very good. To get a better job. Y— y también, to help my mother y familia." He shrugged. "Y do better, that's all."

"That's all? Why, that's wonderful! Wonderful! Didn't he do well class?" Mrs. Hamma bowed slightly toward William and applauded him. The students watched her and slowly each one began to imitate her. Please, Mrs. Hamma looked around her; all together they gave William a healthy round of applause.

Next, Mrs. Hamma turned to a Chinese man seated at the other side of the room. "Mr. Fong, you may go next."

Mr. Fong stood up; he was a man in his late thirties, of medium height and slight build. Cautiously he looked at Mrs. Hamma, and waited.

"Go on, Mr. Fong. Get the ball rolling, remember?"

"All right. Get a ball rolling . . . is idiot!" Mr. Fong smiled.

"No, Mr. Fong, idio*mmmmmm*!" Mrs. Hamma hummed her *m*'s, shaking her head. "Not an— It's idiomatic!"

"What I said!" Mr. Fong responded with self-assurance, looking directly at Mrs. Hamma. "Get a ball rolling, idiomit."

"Never mind." She cleared her throat. "Just go on."

"I said O.K.?" Mr. Fong waited for an answer.

"Go on, please."

Mr. Fong sighed, "My name is Joseph Fong. I been here in this country United States New York City for most one year." He too read from a prepared statement. "I come from Hong Kong but original born in city of Canton, China. I working delivery food business and live with my brother and his family in Chinatown. I taking the course in Basic English to speak good and improve my position better in this country. Also to be eligible to become American citizen."

Mrs. Hamma selected each student who was to speak from a different part of the room, rather than in the more conventional orderly fashion of row by row, or front to back, or even alphabetical order. This way, she reasoned, no one will know who's next; it will be more spontaneous. Mrs. Hamma enjoyed catching the uncertain looks on the faces of her students. A feeling of control over the situation gave her a pleasing thrill, and she made the most of these moments by looking at several people more than once before making her final choice.

There were more men than women, and Mrs. Hamma called two or three men for each woman. It was her way of maintaining a balance. To her distress, most read from prepared notes, despite her efforts to discourage this. She would interrupt them when she felt they went on too long, then praise them when they finished. Each statement was followed by applause from everyone.

All had similar statements. They had migrated here in search of a better future, were living with relatives, and worked as unskilled laborers. With the exception of Lali, who was childless, every woman gave the ages and sex of her children; most men referred only to their "family." And, among the legal aliens, there was only one who did not want to become an American citizen, Diego Torres, a young man from the Dominican Republic, and he gave his reasons.

". . . and to improve my economic situation." Diego Torres hesitated, looking around the room. "But is one thing I no want, and is to become American citizen"— he pointed to an older man with a dark complexion, seated a few seats away—"like my fellow countryman over there!" The man shook his head disapprovingly at Diego Torres, trying to hide his annoyance. "I no give up my country, Santo Domingo, for nothing," he went on, "nothing in the whole world. O.K., man? I come here, pero I cannot help. I got no work at home. There, is political. The United States control most the industry which is sugar and tourismo. Y—you have to know somebody. I tell you, is political to get a job, man! You don't know nobody and you no work, eh? So I come here from necessity, pero this no my country—"

"Mr. Torres," Mrs. Hamma interrupted, "we must be brief, please, there are—"

"I no finish lady!" he snapped. "You wait a minute when I finish!"

There was complete silence as Diego Torres glared at Susan Hamma. No one had ever spoken to her like that, and her confusion was greater than her embarrassment. Without speaking, she lowered her eyes and nodded.

"O.K., I prefer live feeling happy in my country, man. Even I don't got too much. I live simple but in my own country I be contento. Pero this is no possible in the situation of Santo Domingo now. Someday we gonna run our own country and be jobs for everybody. My reasons to be here is to make money, man, and go back home buy my house and property. I no be American citizen, no way. I'm Dominican and proud! That's it. That's all I got to say." Abruptly, Diego Torres sat down.

"All right." Mrs. Hamma had composed herself. "Very good; you can come here and state your views. That is what America is all about! We may not agree with you, but we defend your right to an opinion. And as long as you are in this classroom, Mr. Torres, you are in America. Now, everyone, let us give Mr. Torres the same courtesy as everyone else in this class." Mrs. Hamma applauded with a polite light clap, then turned to find the next speaker.

"Bullshit," whispered Diego Torres.

Practically everyone had spoken. Lali and the two European immigrants were the only ones left. Mrs. Hamma called upon Lali.

"My name is Rogelia Dolores Padillo. I come from Canovanas in Puerto Rico. Is a small village in the mountains near El Yunque Rain Forest. My family is still living there. I marry and live here with my husband working in his business of restaurant. Call Rudi's Luncheonette. I been here New York City Lower East Side since I marry, which is now about one year. I study Basic English to improve my vocabulario and learn more about here. This way I help my husband in his business and I do more also for myself, including to be able to read better in English. Thank you."

Aldo Fabrizi, the Sicilian, spoke next. He was a very short man, barely five feet tall. Usually he was self-conscious about his height, but William's presence relieved him of these feelings. Looking at William, he thought being short was no big thing; he was, after all, normal. He told the class that he was originally from Palermo, the capital of Sicily, and had gone to Milano, in the north of Italy, looking for work. After three years in Milano, he immigrated here six months ago and now lived with his sister. He had a good steady job, he said, working in a copper wire factory with his brother-in-law in Brooklyn. Aldo Fabrizi wanted to become an American citizen and spoke passionately about it, without reading from his notes.

"I be proud to be American citizen. I no come here find work live good and no have responsibility or no be grateful." He turned and looked threateningly at Diego Torres. "Hey? I tell you all one thing, I got my nephew right now fighting in Vietnam for this country!" Diego Torres stretched his hands over his head, yawning, folded his hands, and lowered his eyelids. "I wish I could be citizen to fight for this country. My whole family is citizens—we all Americans and we love America!" His voice was quite loud. "That's how I feel."

"Very good," Mrs. Hamma called, distracting Aldo Fabrizi. "That was well stated. I'm sure you will not only become a citizen, but you will also be a credit to this country."

The last person to be called on was the Pole. He was always neatly dressed in a business suit, with a shirt and tie, and carried a briefcase. His manner was reserved but friendly.

"Good evening fellow students and Madame Teacher." He nodded politely to Mrs. Hamma. "My name is Stephan Paczkowski. I am originally from Poland about four months ago. My background is I was born in capital city of Poland, Warsaw. Being educated in capital and also graduating from the University with degree of professor of music with specialty in the history of music."

Stephan Paczkowski read from his notes carefully, articulating every word. "I was given appointment of professor of history of music at University of Krakow. I work there for ten years until about year and half ago. At this time the political situation in Poland was so that all Jewish people were requested by the government to leave Poland. My wife who also is being a professor of economics at University of Krakow is of Jewish parents. My wife was told she could not remain in position at University or remain over there. We made arrangements for my wife and daughter who is seven years of age and myself to come here with my wife's cousin who is to be helping us.

"Since four months I am working in large hospital as position of porter in maintenance department. The thing of it is, I wish to take Basic English to improve my knowledge of English language, and be able to return to my position of professor of history of music. Finally, I wish to become a citizen of United States. That is my reasons. I thank you all."

After Stephan Paczkowski sat down, there was a long awkward silence and everyone turned to look at Mrs. Hamma. Even after the confrontation with Diego Torres, she had applauded without hesitation. Now she seemed unable to move.

"Well," she said, almost breathless, "that's admirable! I'm sure, sir, that you will do very well . . . a person of your . . . like yourself, I mean . . . a professor, after all, it's really just admirable." Everyone was listening intently to what she said. "That was well done, class. Now, we have to get to next week's assignment." Mrs. Hamma realized that no one had applauded Stephan Paczkowski. With a slightly pained expression, she began to applaud. "Mustn't forget Mr. Paczkowski; everybody here must be treated equally. This is America!" The class joined her in a round of applause.

As Mrs. Hamma began to write the next week's assignment on the board, some students looked anxiously at their watches and others asked about the time. Then they all quickly copied the information into their notebooks. It was almost eight o'clock. Those who had to get to second jobs did not want to be late; some even hoped to have time for a bite to eat first. Others were just tired and wanted to get home.

Lali looked at William, sighing impatiently. They both hoped Mrs. Hamma would finish quickly. There would be hell to pay with Rudi if the night customers were already at the luncheonette.

"There, that's next week's work, which is very important, by the way. We will be looking at the history of New York City and the different ethnic groups that lived here as far back as the Dutch. I can't tell you how proud I am of the way you all spoke. All of you—I have no favorites, you know."

Mrs. Hamma was interrupted by the long, loud buzzing sound bringing the lesson to an end. Quickly everyone began to exit.

"Good night, see you all next Tuesday!" Mrs. Hamma called out. "By the way, if any of you here wants extra help, I have a few minutes this evening." Several people bolted past her, excusing themselves. In less than thirty seconds, Mrs. Hamma was standing in an empty classroom.

William and Lali hurried along, struggling against the cold, sharp March wind that whipped across Houston Street, stinging their faces and making their eyes tear.

In a few minutes they would be at Rudi's. So far, they had not been late once.

"You read very well—better than anybody in class. I told you there was nothing to worry about. You caught up in no time."

"Go on. I was so nervous, honestly! But, I'm glad she left me for one of the last. If I had to go first, like you, I don't think I could open my mouth. You were so calm. You started the thing off very well."

"You go on now, I was nervous myself!" He laughed, pleased.

"Mira, Chiquitín," Lali giggled, "I didn't know your name was Horacio. William Horacio. Ave María, so imposing!"

"That's right, because you see, my mother was expecting a valiant warrior! Instead, well"—he threw up his hands—"no one warned me either. And what a name for a Chiquitín like me."

Lali smiled, saying nothing. At first she had been very aware of William's dwarfishness. Now it no longer mattered. It was only when she saw others reacting to him for the first time that she was once more momentarily struck with William's physical difference.

"We should really try to speak in English, Lali. It would be good practice for us."

"Dios mío . . . I feel so foolish, and my accent is terrible!"

"But look, we all have to start some place. Besides, what about the Americanos? When they speak Spanish, they sound pretty awful, but we accept it. You know I'm right. And that's how people get ahead, by not being afraid to try."

They walked in silence for a few moments. Since William had begun to work at Rudi's, Lali's life had become less lonely. Lali was shy by nature; making friends was difficult for her. She had grown up in the sheltered environment of a large family living in a tiny mountain village. She was considered quite plain. Until Rudi had asked her parents for permission to court her, she had only gone out with two local boys. She had accepted his marriage proposal expecting great changes in her life. But the age difference between her and Rudi, being in a strange country without friends or relatives, and the long hours of work at the luncheonette confined Lali to a way of life she could not have imagined. Every evening she found herself waiting for William to come in to work, looking forward to his presence.

Lali glanced over at him as they started across the wide busy street. His grip on her elbow was firm but gentle as he led her to the sidewalk.

"There you are, Miss Lali, please to watch your step!" he spoke in English.

His thick golden-blond hair was slightly mussed and fell softly, partially covering his forehead. His wide smile, white teeth and large shoulders made him appear quite handsome. Lali found herself staring at William. At that moment she wished he could be just like everybody else.

"Lali?" William asked, confused by her silent stare. "Is something wrong?"

"No." Quickly Lali turned her face. She felt herself blushing. "I . . . I was just thinking how to answer in English, that's all."

"But that's it . . . don't think! What I mean is, don't go worrying about what to say. Just talk natural. Get used to simple phrases and the rest will come, you'll see."

"All right," Lali said, glad the strange feeling of involvement had passed, and William had taken no notice of it. "It's an interesting class, don't you think so? I mean—like that man, the professor. Bendito! Imagine, they had to leave because they were Jewish. What a terrible thing!"

"I don't believe he's Jewish; it's his wife who is Jewish. She was a professor too. But I guess they don't wanna be separated . . . and they have a child."

"Tsk, tsk, los pobres! But, can you imagine, then? A professor from a university doing the job of a porter? My goodness!" Lali sighed. "I never heard of such a thing!"

"But you gotta remember, it's like Mrs. Hamma said, this is America, right? So . . . everybody got a chance to clean toilets! Equality, didn't she say that?"

They both laughed loudly, stepping up their pace until their reached Rudi's Luncheonette.

The small luncheonette was almost empty. One customer sat at the counter.

"Just in time," Rudi called out. "Let's get going. People gonna be coming in hungry any minute. I was beginning to worry about you two!"

William ran in the back to change into his workshirt.

Lali slipped into her uniform and soon was busy at the grill.

"Well, did you learn anything tonight?" Rudi asked her.

"Yes."

"What?"

"I don't know," she answered, without interrupting her work. "We just talked a little bit in English."

"A little bit in English—about what?"

Lali busied herself, ignoring him. Rudi waited, then tried once more.

"You remember what you talked about?" He watched her as she moved, working quickly, not looking in his direction.

"No." Her response was barely audible.

Lately Rudi had begun to reflect on his decision to marry such a young woman. Especially a country girl like Lali, who was shy and timid. He had never had children with his first wife and wondered if he lacked the patience needed for the young. They had little in common and certainly seldom spoke about anything but the business. Certainly he could not fault her for being lazy; she was always working without being asked. People would accuse him in jest of overworking his young wife. He assured them there was no need, because she had the endurance of a country mule. After almost one year of marriage, he felt he hardly knew Lali or what he might do to please her.

William began to stack clean glasses behind the counter.

"Chiquitín! How about you and Lali having something to eat? We gotta few minutes yet. There's some fresh rice pudding."

"Later . . . I'll have mine a little later, thanks."

"Ask her if she wants some." Rudi whispered, gesturing toward Lali.

William moved close to Lali and spoke softly to her.

"She said no." William continued his work.

"Listen, Chiquitín, I already spoke to Raquel Martinez who lives next door. You know, she's got all them kids? In case you people are late, she can cover for you and Lali. She said it was O.K."

"Thanks, Rudi, I appreciate it. But we'll get back on time."

"She's good, you know. She helps me out during the day whenever I need extra help. Off the books, I give her a few bucks. But, mira, I cannot pay you and Raquel both. So if she comes in, you don't get paid. You know that then, O.K.?"

"Of course. Thanks, Rudi."

"Sure, well, it's a good thing after all. You and Lali improving yourselves. Not that she really needs it, you know. I provide for her. As I said, she's my wife, so she don't gotta worry. If she wants something, I'll buy it for her. I made it clear she didn't have to bother with none of that, but"—Rudi shrugged—"if that's what she wants, I'm not one to interfere."

The door opened. Several men walked in.

"Here they come, kids!"

Orders were taken and quickly filled. Customers came and went steadily until about eleven o'clock, when Rudi announced that it was closing time.

The weeks passed, then the months, and this evening, William and Lali sat with the other students listening to Mrs. Hamma as she taught the last lesson of the Basic English course.

"It's been fifteen long hard weeks for all of you. And I want you to know how proud I am of each and every one here."

William glanced at Lali; he knew she was upset. He felt it too, wishing that this was not the end of the course. It was the only time he and Lali had free to themselves. Tuesday had become their evening.

Lali had been especially irritable that week, dreading this last session. For her, Tuesday meant leaving the world of Rudi, the luncheonette, that street, everything that she felt imprisoned her. She was accomplishing something all by herself, and without the help of the man she was dependent upon.

Mrs. Hamma finally felt that she had spent enough time assuring her students of her sincere appreciation.

"I hope some of you will stay and have a cup of coffee or tea, and cookies. There's plenty over there." She pointed to a side table where a large electric coffeepot filled with hot water was steaming. The table was set for instant coffee and tea, complete with several boxes of assorted cookies. "I do this every semester for my classes. I think it's nice to have a little informal chat with one another; perhaps discuss our plans for the future and so on. But it must be in English! Especially those of you who are Spanish speaking. Just because you outnumber the rest of us, don't you think you can get away with it!" Mrs. Hamma lifted her forefinger threateningly but smiled. "Now, it's still early, so there's plenty of time left. Please turn in your books."

Some of the people said good-bye quickly and left, but the majority waited, helping themselves to coffee or tea and cookies. Small clusters formed as people began to chat with one another.

Diego Torres and Aldo Fabrizi were engaged in a friendly but heated debate on the merits of citizenship.

"Hey, you come here a minute, please," Aldo Fabrizi called out to William, who was standing with a few people by the table, helping himself to coffee. William walked over to the two men.

"What's the matter?"

"What do you think of your paisano. He don't wanna be citizen. I say—my opinion—he don't appreciate what he got in this country. This is great country! You the same like him, what do you think?"

"Mira, please tell him we no the same," Diego Torres said with exasperation. "You a citizen, pero not me. Este tipo no comprende, man!"

"Listen, yo comprendo . . . yo capito! I know what you say. He be born in Puerto Rico. But you see, we got the same thing. I be born in Sicily—that is another part of the country, separate. But I still Italiano, capito?"

"Dios mío!" Diego Torres smacked his forehead with an open palm. "Mira"—he turned to William—"explain to him, por favor."

William swallowed a mouthful of cookies. "He's right. Puerto Rico is part of the United States. And Sicily is part of Italy. But not the Dominican Republic where he been born. There it is not the United States. I was born a citizen, do you see?"

"Sure!" Aldo Fabrizi nodded. "Capito. Hey, but you still no can vote, right?"

"Sure I can vote; I got all the rights. I am a citizen, just like anybody else," William assured him.

"You some lucky guy then. You got it made! You don't gotta worry like the rest of—"

"Bullshit," Diego Torres interrupted. "Why he got it made, man? He force to leave his country. Pendejo, you no capito nothing, man . . ."

As the two men continued to argue, William waited for the right moment to slip away and join Lali.

She was with some of the women, who were discussing how sincere and devoted Mrs. Hamma was.

"She's hardworking . . ."

"And she's good people . . ." an older woman agreed.

Mr. Fong joined them, and they spoke about the weather and how nice and warm the days were.

Slowly people began to leave, shaking hands with their fellow students and Mrs. Hamma, wishing each other luck.

Mrs. Hamma had been hoping to speak to Stephan Paczkowski privately this evening, but he was always with a group. Now he offered his hand.

"I thank you very much for your good teaching. It was a fine semester."

"Oh, do you think so? Oh, I'm so glad to hear you say that. You don't know how much it means. Especially coming from a person of your caliber. I am confident, yes, indeed, that you will soon be back to your profession, which, after all, is your true calling. If there is anything I can do, please . . ."

"Thank you, miss. This time I am registering in Hunter College, which is in Manhattan on Sixty-fifth Street in Lexington Avenue, with a course of English Literature for beginners." After a slight bow, he left.

"Good-bye." Mrs. Hamma sighed after him.

Lali, William, and several of the women picked up the paper cups and napkins and tossed them into the trash basket.

"Thank you so much, that's just fine. Luis the porter will do the rest. He takes care of these things. He's a lovely person and very helpful. Thank you."

William shook hands with Mrs. Hamma, then waited for Lali to say good-bye. They were the last ones to leave.

"Both of you have been such good students. What are your plans? I hope you will continue with your English."

"Next term we're taking another course," Lali said, looking at William.

"Yes," William responded, "it's more advance. Over at the Washington Irving High School around Fourteenth Street."

"Wonderful." Mrs. Hamma hesitated. "May I ask you a question before you leave? It's only that I'm a little curious about something."

"Sure, of course." They both nodded.

"Are you two related? I mean, you are always together and yet have different last names, so I was just . . . wondering."

"Oh, we are just friends," Lali answered, blushing.

"I work over in the luncheonette at night, part-time."

"Of course." Mrs. Hamma looked at Lali. "Mrs. Padillo, your husband's place of business. My, that's wonderful, just wonderful! You are all just so ambitious. Very good . . ."

They exchanged farewells.

Outside, the warm June night was sprinkled with the sweetness of the new buds sprouting on the scrawny trees and hedges planted along the sidewalks and in the housing project grounds. A brisk breeze swept over the East River on to Houston Street, providing a freshness in the air.

This time they were early, and Lali and William strolled at a relaxed pace.

"Well," Lali shrugged, "that's that. It's over!"

"Only for a couple of months. In September we'll be taking a more advanced course at the high school."

"I'll probably forget everything I learned by then."

"Come on, Lali, the summer will be over before you know it. Just you wait and see. Besides, we can practice so we don't forget what Mrs. Hamma taught us."

"Sure, what do you like to speak about?" Lali said in English.

William smiled, and clasping his hands, said, "I would like to say to you how wonderful you are, and how you gonna have the most fabulous future . . . after all, you so ambitious!"

When she realized he sounded just like Mrs. Hamma, Lali began to laugh.

"Are you"—Lali tried to keep from giggling, tried to pretend to speak in earnest—"sure there is some hope for me?"

"Oh, heavens, yes! You have shown such ability this"—William was beginning to lose control, laughing loudly—"semester!"

"But I want"—Lali was holding her sides with laughter—"some guarantee of this. I got to know."

"Please, Miss Lali." William was laughing so hard tears were coming to his eyes. "After . . . after all, you now a member in good standing . . . of the promised future!"

William and Lali broke into uncontrollable laughter, swaying and limping, oblivious to the scene they created for the people who stared and pointed at them as they continued on their way to Rudi's.

LAWSON FUSAO INADA
(1938-)

Lawson Inada was born and raised in Fresno, California. A third-generation Japanese American, Inada was interned during World War II with his family in California, Arkansas, and Colorado. He attended the University of California, Berkeley, and Fresno State, where he obtained a B.A. He received an M.F.A. from the University of Oregon in 1966. In 1971 his first book, Before the War: Poems as They Happen, *was published, and the following year he received his first of two creative writing fellowships from the National Endowment for the Arts. In 1994 he was awarded the American Book Award for his second collection of poems,* Legends from Camp. *Inada is a coeditor of* Aiiieeee! (1974), *a pioneer anthology of Asian-American writing. Since 1966 he has taught at Southern Oregon State University. His most recent collection of poems is* Drawing the Line (1997), *from which "Kicking the Habit" has been taken.*

Originally published under the title "Anglophilia," "Kicking the Habit" explores the complex, sometimes painful, sometimes comical relationships among poet, ethnic identity, and language.

KICKING THE HABIT

Late last night, I decided to
stop using English.
I had been using it all day—

    talking all day,
    listening all day,
    thinking all day,
    reading all day,
    remembering all day,
    feeling all day,

    and even driving all day,
    in English—

when finally I decided to
stop.

So I pulled off the main highway
onto a dark country road
and kept on going and going
until I emerged in another nation and . . .
stopped.

There, the insects
inspected my passport, the frogs
investigated my baggage, and the trees
pointed out lights in the sky,
saying,
    "Shhhhlllyyymmm"—

and I, of course, replied.
After all, I was a foreigner,
and had to comply . . .

Now don't get me wrong:
There's nothing "wrong"
with English,

and I'm not complaining
about the language
which is my native tongue.
I make my living with the lingo;
I was even in England once.
So you might say I'm actually
addicted to it;
yes, I'm an Angloholic,
and I can't get along without the stuff:
It controls my life.

Until last night, that is.
Yes, I had had it
with the habit.

I was exhausted,
burned out,
by the habit.
And I decided to
kick the habit,
cold turkey,
right then and there
on the spot!

And, in so doing, I kicked
open the door of a cage
and stepped out from confinement
into the greater world.

Tentatively, I uttered,

    "Chemawa?   Chinook?"

and the pines said

    "Clackamas, Siskiyou."

And before long, everything else
chimed in with their two cents' worth
and we had a fluid and fluent
conversation going,

    communicating, expressing,
    echoing whatever we needed to
    know, know, know . . .

What was it like?
Well, just listen:

Ah, the exquisite seasonings
of syllables, the consummate consonants, the vigorous
vowels of varied vocabularies

      clicking, ticking, humming,
      growling, throbbing, strumming—

coming from all parts of orifices, surfaces,
in creative combinations, orchestrations,
resonating in rhythm with the atmosphere!

I could have remained there
forever—as I did, and will.
And when I resumed my way,
my stay could no longer be

      "ordinary"—

as they say,
as *we* say, in English.

For on the road to life,
in the code of life,

there's much more to red than

      "stop,"

there's much more to green than

      "go,"

and there's much, much more to yellow than

      "caution,"

for as the yellow
sun clearly enunciated to me this morning:

      "Fusao. Inada."

GINA VALDÉS
(1943-)

Gina Valdés writes both fiction and poetry and was born in Los Angeles, California, but raised in both Mexico and the United States. Along with a novel, There Are No Madmen Here *(1981), she has published two bilingual collections of poetry,* Comiendo Lumbe/Eating Fire *(1986) and* Puentes y Fronteras/Bridges and Frontiers *(1996). She has taught in the San Diego public schools, as well as at several colleges and universities, including the University of California, Los Angeles. Her poetry and fiction have appeared in anthologies in the United States, Europe, and Mexico.*

"English con Salsa" was published in 1993, during the controversy over massive immigration, legal and illegal, from Latin American nations and the reactionary pressure for English-only legislation.

ENGLISH CON SALSA

Welcome to ESL 100, English Surely Latinized,
inglés con chile y cilantro, English as American
as Benito Juárez. Welcome, muchachos from Xochicalco,
learn the language of dólares and dolores, of kings
and queens, of Donald Duck and Batman. Holy Toluca!
In four months you'll be speaking like George Washington,
in four weeks you can ask, More coffee? In two months
you can say, May I take your order? In one year you
can ask for a raise, cool as the Tuxpan River.

Welcome, muchachas from Teocaltiche, in this class
we speak English refrito, English con sal y limón,
English thick as mango juice, English poured from
a clay jug, English tuned like a requinto from Uruapán,
English lighted by Oaxacan dawns, English spiked
with mezcal from Juchitán, English with a red cactus
flower blooming in its heart.

Welcome, welcome, amigos del sur, bring your Zapotec
tongues, your Nahuatl tones, your patience of pyramids,
your red suns and golden moons, your guardian angels,
your duendes, your patron saints, Santa Tristeza,
Santa Alegría, Santo Todolopuede. We will sprinkle
holy water on pronouns, make the sign of the cross
on past participles, jump like fish from Lake Pátzcuaro
on gerunds, pour tequila from Jalisco on future perfects,
say shoes and shit, grab a cool verb and a pollo loco
and dance on the walls like chapulines.

When a teacher from La Jolla or a cowboy from Santee
asks you, Do you speak English? You'll answer, Sí,
yes, simón, of course. I love English!

And you'll hum
a Mixtec chant that touches la tierra and the heavens.

ENGLISH-ONLY CAMPAIGN

*Beginning about 1980, campaigns to make English the legally constituted
official language were mounted in several states but were especially strong
in California and Florida, states where the English-speaking majority was
challenged by large numbers of Spanish-speaking immigrants from Mexico
and/or Cuba and Central America. These campaigns produced over a
dozen constitutional amendments to effect a change from the de facto dominance of English to a mandated dominance. Some would have forbid the
federal government from producing material in any other language, while
others would have left it up to the individual states to implement and
enforce "English only." Congressional committees took testimony on the
issue in 1984 and 1988, but no bill was ever reported out of either House
or Senate, and the issue faded away as the realization grew that English
was not only securely dominant in the United States but was also fast
becoming the world's language.*

ENGLISH AS THE OFFICIAL LANGUAGE: THREE PROPOSED AMENDMENTS TO THE CONSTITUTION OF THE UNITED STATES

S.J. RES. 72 (1981)

Sponsored by Senator S. I. Hayakawa (R-Calif.)

Section 1. The English language shall be the official language of the United States.

Section 2. Neither the United States nor any State shall make or enforce any law which requires the use of any language other than English.

Section 3. This article shall apply to laws, ordinances, regulations, orders, programs, and policies.

Section 4. No order or decree shall be issued by any court of the United States or of any State requiring that any proceedings, or matters to which this article applies, be in any language other than English.

Section 5. This article shall not prohibit educational instruction in a language other than English as required as a transitional method of making students who use a language other than English proficient in English.

Section 6. The Congress and the States shall have power to enforce this article by appropriate legislation.

S.J. RES. 167 (1983)

Sponsored by Senators Walter Huddleston (D-Ky.) and Steve Symms (R-Idaho)

Section 1. The English language shall be the official language of the United States.

Section 2. The Congress shall have the power to enforce this article by appropriate legislation.

H.J. RES. 81 (1989)

Sponsored by Representative Norman Shumway (R-Calif.)

Section 1. The English language shall be the official language of the United States.

Section 2. Neither the United States nor any State shall require, by law, ordinance, regulation, order, decree, program, or policy, the use in the United States of any language other than English.

Section 3. This article shall not prohibit any law, ordinance, regulation, order, decree, program, or policy—

(1) to provide educational instruction in a language other than English for the purpose of making students who use a language other than English proficient in English,

(2) to teach a foreign language to students who are already proficient in English,

(3) to protect public health and safety, or

(4) to allow translators for litigants, defendants, or witnesses in court cases.

Section 4. The Congress and the States may enforce this article by appropriate legislation.

3

TRANSITION AND TRANSCENDENCE: CONNECTING PAST AND FUTURE

Coming to terms with the actions of memory is the theme of the third section, *Transition and Transcendence: Connecting Past and Future.* The stories, essays, and poems gathered here record the effort to connect various versions of the self—ethnic and personal, gendered and racialized, rich and poor, young and old— through memory.

Thus, Paule Marshall memorializes an ancestor she has come to understand better as an adult. Adrienne Rich, in her essay "Split at the Root: An Essay on Jewish Identity," remembers coming to terms with her understanding of Jewishness as a late development of social and religious consciousness, a special kind of maturation, while Joy Harjo's poem "Remember" portrays memory as the way to a salutary self-image for Native Americans. These and the other readings in this section provide images of "the way out"—ideas and actions that enable us to encompass and perhaps to control the conflict between ethnic and national identities.

RALPH FASANELLA
(1914–1997)

Born in the Bronx, Ralph Fasanella attended the New York City public schools but was essentially self-taught as an artist. He grew up in the Greenwich Village neighborhood of Manhattan, where Italian Americans mingled with bohemian writers and artists from all over the country. In early life Fasanella worked as an iceman, then became a union organizer in about 1940. The first exhibition of his paintings came in 1944, when he was thirty years old. Recognition of his urban folk style developed during the 1970s. His leftist political view is reflected in his themes and subjects: factories and workers, storefronts and sidewalks, baseball, subway travel, and political and labor struggles. In 1996, his painting "Subway Riders" was installed in the New York City subway station at Fifth Avenue and 53rd Street.

"SUBWAY RIDERS"

MONICA KRAWCZYK
(1887–1954)

Monica Krawczyk was born in Winona, Minnesota, the first child of Polish immigrants. She worked as both a teacher and social worker and was an active promoter of Polish culture, helping to organize the Minneapolis Polonia Club. In such national magazines as Woman's Day *and* Good Housekeeping *she published dozens of stories detailing the lives of rural Polish Americans. Many of these stories were collected in her only book,* If the Branch Blossoms and Other Stories, *which was published in 1950.*

"For Dimes and Quarters" examines one of the ways that immigrants like Krawczyk's immigrant mother bought into the American dream of material advancement and self-fulfillment through education.

FOR DIMES AND QUARTERS

Antosia, living in her little four-room house, often dreamed about the whole world. Her big blue eyes sparkled with every new idea, every new thing that came to her. In the old country her mother had often reminded her, "Antosia, be not too bold, for curiosity is the first step to hell. Look what happened to Eve and her apple." When Antosia was leaving her mother's side to venture with her man and their two children into the wilds of America, her mother warned her with a threat in her voice, "Antosia, you are such a crazy one to see . . . to know everything. Just stay home and take care of your man and your children."

She did. But on Sunday she went to church, and after mass she lingered to speak with Zosia Krukowska, who no longer wore old-country shawls. Instead, she paraded a hat with huge red roses. Antosia shook her head. She could not go "down-town" buying new things. No money to spare. She just had to stay at home.

Once a year in early September she felt great joy in making a visit to Columbia School to enroll one of her children in kindergarten. She would comb her thick brown hair and roll it on the back of her head. She would take out her feshly ironed white shawl, and standing before a small wall mirror, she would carefully place it over her head and tie it under her chin. She smiled with the excitement of the visit to school. "Miss Cook," she had said on her last visit, "Today I bring my Jozka. Ah, such a nice big building. I like if I myself come to school. Always I want to learn." Miss Cook laughed. "Why not? We have night school for mothers and fathers, like you." Antosia shrugged her shoulders. "Ah, yes, my man no like if I go. Children small, lots of work." And the curious one that she was, she still hoped and dreamed that some day she would learn to know more of the big new world.

One sunny day in November, Miss Cook called after school, leading Jozka by the hand. Antosia was pleased, for her floor had been neatly scrubbed, there were clean stiffly-ironed curtains to the windows, and there was a row of six loaves of warm good-smelling bread on the table.

"Good afternoon, Mrs. Milewski," Miss Cook greeted.

Antosia pulled out a chair, brushed it quickly, and smiling, said, "Miss Cook, I am glad . . . you come to my house."

"Indeed, I am happy too," Miss Cook responded. "What a nice home, clean, comfortable." And after a few remarks about Jozka's progress in kindergarten, she said, "I came to ask if you could find someone to help my mother clean her house."

Antosia was surprised. "I? Find someone?" In the next moment she asked, right out, "Miss Cook, how you like if I come?"

"That would be wonderful, Mrs. Milewski," said Miss Cook. "Mother would be delighted with you . . ." Miss Cook gave her the address and the name of the street car.

Antosia closed the door carefully, and reflected dizzily on this new thing.

She liked Miss Cook's mother, a kind and patient old lady, wearing a black, snug-fitting dress, with a dainty white collar at her neck. And Miss Cook's house was a castle, like in the old country. She saw the sun streaming through tall, wide windows to floors that shone like glass. Chairs with graceful legs were upholstered in heavy flowered brocade. And when Antosia walked over the thick, soft rugs in deep wine colors, she laughed. Like a queen she felt.

But most of all Antosia enjoyed cleaning the library. It was a room full of books, on every shelf from the floor to the ceiling. To Antosia a book was a most precious thing, like her own prayer book. Otherwise, how could she ever say the many beautiful thoughts to God. Books were stories. She lingered in the room with a feeling of admiration, of awe. She handled each book tenderly as she wiped away every speck of harmful dust.

Going home that day she thought of how fortunate she was, for besides living in Miss Cook's home for the seven hours that day, she received good pay for her work. She must not put the money in her purse where it would get mixed with the everyday cash for bread and salt. It must go for something special, something that she could not afford to buy with her man's shoe-mending money.

One day an idea came into her mind. She could save the money for a gift, something new, like a reward for her husband, who each day went into his little shoe shop, and for hours upon hours bent over his work, tearing off old soles and heels from shoes, and sewing and hammering on new ones. Besides, for three evenings a week he went to night school to learn to speak English. Yes, he deserved the reward.

Ah, how she, too, would have liked to have gone to night school, the curious one that ever she was! But her man always objected. "A woman's place is in the home." Still Antosia was not content.

One evening, she said to her husband, "Bring your book home and show it to me. Maybe I could learn, too."

Milewski, a tall, pale, worried man, looked at her with displeasure. "With everything you want to get mixed up," he said. "Better you just watch the kettles on the stove."

By chance one day, Antosia came across her man's book when she was taking coats out of the tall wardrobe for an airing. A bright red book it was, and not very large. During the day after this, in her spare moments, she would sit with Jozef's book in her hand, looking at the words made up of letters that were like the Polish ones in her prayer book, but strangely put together. Smiling, she tried to give them sound.

It was during one such lesson that a loud knock came upon the quiet of the kitchen. Antosia opened the door to a man with a huge book under his arm. He was smooth-shaven and tall, with a good face. He stood with his hat raised.

"Good afternoon, Mrs. Milewski," he greeted cheerfully. "May I come in?" he asked. "I have something to show you."

Antosia liked his manner, her smile gave him a friendly welcome.

Immediately he saw the little red book in her hand. " I see you like to read, Mrs. Milewski," he praised. "I, too, have a book, a big one, with a lot of pictures. May I show it to you? Just sit where you are." Had this agent come with a rug or a brush, Antosia would have said quickly, "No, no, Mister, I do not buy. No money." But a book, one even larger than any in Miss Cook's house—that was another matter.

He picked up Mileweski's reader. "Some one goes to night school?"

"Yes, my man," Antosia told him, and added hurriedly, "I learn too, in day time."

"You are wise," he said. "Now this book that I have will help your husband learn his lessons, and you, too. Your children also. I see the little coats and sweaters on the hooks."

"Yes, we got four children. I like if it help my man, and my boys, Franek and Kazek. Girls, they study good."

"Excellent for all of them," he went on. "Every subject, about everything you can think of. And you know what else?" Like the magician bringing out his best trick, he said with emphasis, "A story of every country . . . in the whole world!"

Antosia listened wide-eyed. She asked quickly, "Is there story about Poland, too?"

"Oh, yes." He turned the pages and ran his finger down the index. "Here it is—Poland. Pages and pages about it."

To Antosia it seemed like a miracle. "In that one book?" she asked. "Show me pages, please."

"Not in this volume," he explained. "There are thirty-six such books." Antosia felt hot, her heart pounded. Thirty-six books . . . He must have the wrong house.

"You don't have to buy them, Mrs. Milewski." He was sitting beside her now, like her man sometimes did, and speaking slowly. "You see, this is a new company. We can deliver all thirty-six books to your house, on trial, to see if you like them. You can keep them as long as you like, while you are trying them out."

"You mean . . . for nothing I try them?" Antosia asked, and was sorry in the next moment that she had asked, for who in this world would give her something for nothing?

"Almost for nothing," he said. "And think of having the story of the world right in your house."

Antosia nodded. She remembered the delight, the wonder she had felt in Miss Cook's library. Then her face dropped

The salesman must have guessed her thoughts. "You need to pay only two dollars down, and then one dollar or so a month."

Antosia thought hard. Always she sought advice from her man in money matters, like buying a new stove on payment, or an extra bed for her growing children. But Jozef's mind was already heavy with payments on the house, and sick and worried with the three-times-a-week night school. She must not trouble him. Unless, like a flash it came to her mind, it could be out of the extra special savings she had hid away for a gift for her man. The books, to be sure, would be a reward for Jozef! For the children! For herself—for the whole house!

At once she said, "I pay the two dollars." She went to the reed chest quickly, and with trembling fingers took out the money. What better use could she make of her earnings. . . .

The books came. The truck had backed up to the front door of the house, and two men carried them in heavy boxes, grunting under their weight.

From his shoe shop next door, Milewski ran in. "Some mistake, not?" he asked Antosia.

The men brushed past him to the front room where Antosia directed, and the first book fell to the floor with a heavy thud.

Milewski stood in one spot, pale, his eyes burning with anger. After the men were let out, he demanded, "What the devil is in there?"

Antosia smiled nervously and touched the first box. "Books."

Like a thunderclap the words struck Milewski. "Are you crazy? Books are not bread. They cost money. . . ."

At first Antosia wanted to walk away. This gift had not come at a good moment. She would have liked them to come when she was alone. Once they had been arranged in their place on the table against the wall, they would have looked alive, like those in Miss Cook's house. Now the books were nailed in a box and her man was making war upon them. She stood still, her hands pinching her apron. She was completely crushed.

"There must be a hundred of them," Milewski stormed. "And who will read them? The children have books at school. I already pay taxes for them. What craziness got into your head? Remember," he shouted, "I do not pay a cent!" He walked out slamming the door.

Her man's words rumbled through her head until it ached. Truly, she was out of her mind. Books cost money, and there were other needs—the clothes wringer needed fixing, Franek had to have new shoes, there was the new dress she wanted to buy for Manka for the school program. But thirty-six books in her house! Suddenly her mouth tightened in determination. The books would be paid from her savings.

Antosia waited anxiously for the children coming from school. Franek was the first to see the boxes. "What's in there? Can I open them? Can I have the boxes?"

"There are many books," Antosia said, as though it were a promise of great joy.

Franek scowled. "Books!" What for?" With hammer in hand, he attacked the job of prying the boxes open.

"Careful," Antosia warned, "so you do not hurt them."

Franek laughed. "You can't hurt books."

Manka ran in, the oldest of her children, and eagerly pulled out the first book. "*Mamo,* are these ours? How wonderful! Just look at them. All kinds of topics for my studies. *Mamo,* it's like a library right in our house!"

Little Jozka appeared, with a jumping rope in her hand, and quickly leaned over Manka to see the book. "Oh, Mamo, a whole bunch of pictures to draw. This will be my book."

Kazek was stepping into his overalls, always in a hurry to be out of the house.

"Look at one book, Kazek," Antosia urged. He, too, needed the learning—so wild and rough he was, so full of life.

"Mom, the boys are waiting," Kazek's even teeth sparkled as he talked. "I'm pitcher today," he boasted, patting her hand lovingly. "Honest, I got to go." Like a flash he was out.

"*Mamo,* where did you get them?" Manka asked.

Antosia smiled a little, her husband's slamming of the door still a shadow on her mind. "The books are a present . . . for the whole family," she said. Silently she prayed, "They will all come to them in time."

From this day each morning after the family left, Antosia was down on her knees in the front room, looking over the books, studying the pictures, giving sound to the words. Sometimes she stayed with them so long that the bread dough was running out of the pan, or her lunch was late, or beds had gone unmade. She scolded herself, "Curiosity, woman, will bring you trouble. And the books are here to stay. . . ." It seemed she never could have enough of them.

In the evenings, both Manka and Jozka were quick to reach for a book, and Antosia was pleased and proud that the books were in use.

When Kazek brought his six-weeks report card one day, Antosia frowned. "Kazek, I know the marks would be higher if you studied out of these big books."

"Mom, I learn in school," he said.

"Not enough," Antosia told him. "Try these books."

"Wait till it's winter and too cold out. I'm getting a paper route, too, so I won't have much time. Honest, Mom, the kids are waiting. Say, where's my ball and bat? I left it right here."

Such a one that Kazek was. But Antosia would remind him, let come the first cold day.

Late that same evening, before Milewski had returned from night school, and the others were asleep, Franek was sitting in his father's chair, waiting to talk to his mother. It struck Antosia this moment how much he looked like his father, in his growing up. His blue eyes were wide and soft, his brown hair combed back from his forehead. Something was on his mind.

"Mom, why did you buy all those books?" he asked.

"I thought you would like them, Franek," Antosia said. "From these books you can learn the ways of men. A few years yet and you will be among them, working for your bread."

"I don't like books. For that money I would have liked something else," Franek said.

Antosia's heart ached for this big boy. "What, Franek, would you like for the money?" she asked warmly, putting down her mending.

"Well, Jimmie has some chickens to sell, I would like to raise chickens and I could earn some money selling eggs."

Antosia was not surprised. Franek had his own ideas. She remembered his rabbits and pigeons. He would have no books stuffed into his head.

Franek went on, "Jimmie's family is moving to Wisconsin, so he's got to sell them quick. Two dollars for the six chickens. And you know what else," his eyes were shining with excitement. "his mother says I can have their chicken coop, too. For nothing. Only I have to take it apart. Then I can build my own coop. You know how I learned when I helped Pa build his shoe shop."

Antosia laughed with tears in her eyes. All this planning in Franek's head. He knew what he wanted. And he had a way with growing things! "Franek, tomorrow I will give you the money for the chickens."

"But the books. . . ."

"Miss Cook will have to find me one more cleaning place. Now to bed."

Milewski, for whom the books were meant especially, had not mentioned them since the day they had arrived. In addition to his little red reader, he now carried two other books, one about law, and the other about the constitution of this country.

One evening Antosia, mending Kasek's stockings, watched her man as he sat at the table studying out of his book.

"Tell me, Jozef, what is it you study now?"

He did not answer. Antosia continued her sewing and the room became very still.

Suddenly the book fell out of Jozef's tired hands and his eyes were shut in sleep. His head slowly dropped to his arms on the table. An hour later Antosia helped him to bed, and wondered how he could ever get to the thirty-six books. . . .

The next day Antosia was surprised when a letter came addressed to Mrs. A. Milewski, looking suspiciously like a bill. As soon as Manka came from school, Antosia said, "Read it, Manka, please."

"It says here," Manka read slowly, "for thirty-six books . . . encyclopedia set . . . one hundred fifty-eight dollars."

Antosia put her hand to her face as if someone had struck her. She sat down with a heavy sigh. She recalled the clean-shaven, polite man with all his promises. A bill for one-hundred fifty-eight dollars . . . a punishment for her!

After supper, when she was alone with her man she showed him the bill. Now he must know about it.

"All the time I knew it," Jozef said. "You get nothing . . . for nothing."

He said much more, his eyes flashing angrily at her. "One hundred fifty-eight dollars! You are crazy. From where can we get so much money?"

Antosia took the words to herself calmly and penitently. "You are right," she told him.

The next morning it rained. Today she could not look at the books. They were cold, reminding her only of her great worry. She stacked the breakfst dishes, put on her coat and hurried to school to see Miss Cook.

"I come today for help." Antosia told her story quickly. "I can't pay so much money!" she asserted. "What should I do?"

Miss Cook looked at the bill. "Those are splendid books," she said. "Your family should have them."

"I like to keep them," Antosia said, "but only my man works, fixing shoes. We have expenses, for children, for house, insurance. Sometimes extra, like chickens for Franek or for doctor. Not enough money," she shrugged her shoulders helplessly.

"The children could help when they start working," Miss Cook suggested.

"No, no! My man cannot sleep nights with worry."

"It's true, it is hard," Miss Cook sympathized. "You really don't have to keep the books. Just write and tell them."

"Miss Cook, please, you be so kind and write me letter. Say, thank you very much for trial. . . ."

That evening, as soon as the lamp was lit, Antosia cleared the table and sat to it. This night she must look at the books for the last time.

Jozef had gone to bed, and Franek had not yet come in—he was locking up his chickens. Kazek was sewing on his baseball and both Manka and Jozka were absorbed in the books.

Antosia said to Manka, "Have you finished your studying?"

"No, but I have time until next week. What is it, *Mamo*?"

"Bring out the book that has the story about Poland."

Manka soon opened to the pages and showed Antosia the pictures.

"God give those people health," Antosia said, "for making such nice books. Now see, a *chatka* with a stork on the roof of it. This, old, old wooden church could be the one from my village. See this *teatr* building in Warsaw, the *Wawel* in Krakow. And the flag of Poland. . . ." Her throat choked with tears.

"Let me read you the story, *Mamo*," Manka offered.

She read in a clear young voice, slowly, without hesitation, about the land that Antosia had come from, about all her people, their ideals, traditions, their customs.

A tender loneliness came over Antosia. She was back in Poland, a little girl in her full, wide skirts, picking buttercups in the meadow with the sweet, stirring song of the *slowik* overhead; she was at the carnival dance, with Jozef swinging her in a lively *krakoviak* and whispering sweet words into her ear; she thought of the day when the two of them spoke brief words of parting to their parents, and went forth, far away, to a free land. . . .

Antosia listened intently. How good it was that Manka could read Jozef's and her story now, here, in the language of the free land, of the country that was theirs.

"Copy the address of the company, so you may some day buy these books." Her voice shook as she said, "Soon the truck comes to take them away."

"*Mamo*, no, no!" Manka cried. "We need them. All my lessons. . . ."

Jozka was alarmed. "We won't let them take the books," she said, standing up to the door as if to block the way this moment.

Now Kazek, too, was aroused. "Mom, why do you let them go?" he asked.

Franek walked in. "What's all the noise?"

"Sh . . ." Antosia tried to quiet them. "So you do not awaken Father. The bill came yesterday, for one hundred fifty-eight dollars! The books have to go!"

"How about on payments," Kazek suggested. "I've got a paper route now. I can pay fifty cents or a dollar."

Franek spoke up. "I already talked to the manual training teacher about making a nice bookcase for 'em."

"There, see *Mamo*?" Manka was enthusiastic. "I can help, too, watching the kids for the Canfields. We'll all pitch up our dimes and quarters."

Antosia was delighted as with the taste of milk and honey. Her children knew what was good; her children, all of them, wanted to help save the books.

Two days went by, and no truck arrived. Three days, four, and then on the fifth, there was the knock, cheerful, not heavy-knuckled like that of a truck man.

It really frightened Antosia, for all these days she had been moving about her house with a heavy heart.

She opened the door, and there he was, smooth-shaven, smiling, his hat raised. "How do you do, Mrs. Milewski," he said. "May I come in?"

Antosia stepped back, her face tense with anger. What could he want now, the deceiver! Should she slam the door in his face?

He was rustling a paper. "It's about this letter. . . ."

"I told Miss Cook to write it," Antosia said coldly.

"Yes, I know. You have had the books a while now and that's why I came. I want to know what you think of them?"

"I?" she looked at him, unbelieving. With some hesitation, she said, "I like them very much." Seeing his smile broaden, she added, "And my children, too, like them."

"Then you keep them," he said, emphatically. Before she had a chance to protest, he went on, "Look, how much can you pay a month?"

"You mean. . . ."

"Yes, I mean you should keep the books. Can you pay," he was doing some figuring in a little black notebook, "say three or four or five dollars a month? You get it paid up sooner, that's all. Or, just the two dollars we agreed. We know you're honest."

The gates of heaven were open again and Antosia's heart nearly burst with joy. She wanted to take his hand in hers. "Mister," she said, "you are a good man. How would it be . . . I pay you every month?" On her fingers she counted her children's dimes and quarters; then, after a moment's hesitation, she said, "I pay you every month just how much I can!"

"Very fine, very fine," he told her.

Antosia hardly heard his words. To her, it was a real wonder—the books would remain in her house.

ADRIENNE RICH

(1929-)

Adrienne Rich, one of America's most prominent poets, was born in Baltimore, Maryland, and educated at Radcliffe College, where she graduated with honors. Her first book, A Change of the World, *was published in 1951 and received the Yale Series of Younger Poets Award. Since then she has published over fifteen volumes of poetry and six collections of prose. She has taught at Swarthmore College, Columbia University, Cornell University, and most recently Stanford University. She has received numerous awards for her work, including the National Institute of Arts and Letters award for poetry and the National Book Award, which she received for her book* Diving into the Wreck: Poems, 1971-1972. *Adrienne Rich has also been the recipient of grants from the National Endowment for the Arts and the Ingram Merrill Foundation and two fellowships from the Guggenheim Foundation. In 1994, she was awarded a MacArthur Fellowship. Her most recent work is* Midnight Salvage: Poems 1995-1998.*

"Split at the Root: An Essay on Jewish Identity" explores Rich's somewhat delayed realization of the importance of her religious and cultural heritage in defining who she has become, and how that realization will influence her future as a woman and a citizen.

FROM SPLIT AT THE ROOT: AN ESSAY ON JEWISH IDENTITY

For about fifteen minutes I have been sitting chin in hand in front of the typewriter, staring out at the snow. Trying to be honest with myself, trying to figure out why writing this seems to be so dangerous an act, filled with fear and shame, and why it seems so necessary. It comes to me that in order to write this I have to be willing to do two things: I have to claim my father, for I have my Jewishness from him and not from my gentile mother; and I have to break his silence, his taboos; in order to claim him I have in a sense to expose him.

And there is, of course, the third thing: I have to face the sources and the flickering presence of my own ambivalence as a Jew; the daily, mundane anti-Semitisms of my entire life.

These are stories I have never tried to tell before. Why now? Why, I asked myself sometime last year, does this question of Jewish identity float so impalpably, so ungraspably around me, a cloud I can't quite see the outlines of, which feels to me to be without definition?

And yet I've been on the track of this longer than I think.

. . .

In a long poem written in 1960, when I was thirty-one years old, I described myself as "Split at the root, neither Gentile nor Jew, / Yankee nor Rebel."* I was still trying to have it both ways: to be neither/nor, trying to live (with my Jewish husband and three children more Jewish in ancestry than I) in the predominantly gentile Yankee academic world of Cambridge, Massachusetts.

But this begins, for me, in Baltimore, where I was born in my father's workplace, a hospital in the Black ghetto, whose lobby contained an immense white marble statue of Christ.

. . .

My father was then a young teacher and researcher in the department of pathology at the Johns Hopkins Medical School, one of the very few Jews to attend or teach at that institution. He was from Birmingham, Alabama; his father, Samuel, was Ashkenazic, an immigrant from Austria-Hungary, and his mother, Hattie Rice, a Sephardic Jew from Vicksburg, Mississippi. My grandfather had had a shoe store in Birmingham, which did well enough to allow him to retire comfortably and to leave my grandmother income on his death. The only souvenirs of my grandfather, Samuel Rich, were his ivory flute, which lay on our living-room mantel and was not to be played with; his thin gold pocket watch, which my father wore; and his Hebrew prayer book, which I discovered among my father's books in the course of reading my way through his library. In this prayer book there was a newspaper clipping about my grandparents' wedding, which took place in a synagogue.

My father, Arnold, was sent in adolescence to a military school in the North Carolina mountains, a place for training white southern Christian gentlemen. I suspect that there were few, if any, other Jewish boys at Colonel Bingham's, or at "Mr. Jefferson's university" in Charlottesville, where he studied as an undergraduate. With whatever conscious forethought, Samuel and Hattie sent their son into the dominant southern WASP culture to become an "exception," to enter the professional class. Never, in describing these experiences, did he speak of having suffered—from loneliness, cultural alienation, or outsiderhood. Never did I hear him use the word *anti-Semitism.*

. . .

It was only in college, when I read a poem by Karl Shapiro beginning "To hate the Negro and avoid the Jew / is the curriculum," that it flashed on me that there was an untold side to my father's story of his student years. He looked recognizably Jewish, was short and slender in build with dark wiry hair and deep-set eyes, high forehead and curved nose.

My mother is a gentile. In Jewish law I cannot count myself a Jew. If it is true that "we think back through our mothers if we are women" (Virginia Woolf)—and I myself have affirmed this—then even according to lesbian theory, I cannot (or need not?) count myself a Jew.

The white southern Protestant woman, the gentile, has always been there for me to peel back into. That's a whole piece of history in itself, for my gentile grand-

---

*Adrienne Rich, "Readings of History," in *Snapshots of a Daughter-in-Law* (New York: W. W. Norton, 1967), pp. 35–40.

mother and my mother were also frustrated artists and intellectuals, a lost writer and a lost composer between them. Readers and annotators of books, note takers, my mother a good pianist still, in her eighties. But there was also the obsession with ancestry, with "background," the southern talk of family, not as people you would necessarily know and depend on, but as heritage, the guarantee of "good breeding." There was the inveterate romantic heterosexual fantasy, the mother telling the daughter how to attract men (my mother often used the word "fascinate"); the assumption that relations between the sexes could only be romantic, that it was in the woman's interest to cultivate "mystery," conceal her actual feelings. Survival tactics of a kind, I think today, knowing what I know about the white woman's sexual role in the southern racist scenario. Heterosexuality as protection, but also drawing white women deeper into collusion with white men.

It would be easy to push away and deny the gentile in me—that white southern woman, that social christian. At different times in my life I have wanted to push away one or the other burden of inheritance, to say merely *I am a woman; I am a lesbian*. If I call myself a Jewish lesbian, do I thereby try to shed some of my southern gentile white woman's culpability? If I call myself only through my mother, is it because I pass more easily through a world where being a lesbian often seems like outsiderhood enough?

. . .

According to Nazi logic, my two Jewish grandparents would have made me a *Mischling, first-degree*—nonexempt from the Final Solution.

. . .

The social world in which I grew up was christian virtually without needing to say so—christian imagery, music, language, symbols, assumptions everywhere. It was also a genteel, white, middle-class world in which "common" was a term of deep opprobrium. "Common" white people might speak of "niggers"; *we* were taught never to use that word—*we* said "Negroes" (even as we accepted segregation, the eating taboo, the assumption that Black people were simply of a separate species). Our language was more polite, distinguishing us from the "rednecks" or the lynch-mob mentality. But so charged with negative meaning was even the word "Negro" that as children we were taught never to use it in front of Black people. We were taught that any mention of skin color in the presence of colored people was treacherous, forbidden ground. In a parallel way, the word "Jew" was not used by polite gentiles. I sometimes heard my best friend's father, a Presbyterian minister, allude to "the Hebrew people" or "people of the Jewish faith." The world of acceptable folk was white, gentile (christian, really), and had "ideals" (which colored people, white "common" people, were not supposed to have). "Ideals" and "manners" included not hurting someone's feelings by calling her or him a Negro or a Jew—naming the hated identity. This is the mental framework of the 1930s and 1940s in which I was raised.

(Writing this, I feel dimly like the betrayer; of my father, who did not speak the word; of my mother, who must have trained me in the messages; of my caste and class; of my whiteness itself.)

Two memories: I am in a play reading at school of *The Merchant of Venice*. Whatever Jewish law says, I am quite sure I was *seen* as Jewish (with a reassuringly gentile mother) in that double vision that bigotry allows. I am the only Jewish girl in the class, and I am playing Portia. As always, I read my part aloud for my father the night before, and he tells me to convey, with my voice, more scorn and contempt with the word "Jew": "Therefore, Jew . . ." I have to say the word out, and say it loudly. I was encouraged to pretend to be a non-Jewish child acting a non-Jewish character who has to speak the word "Jew" emphatically. Such a child would not have had trouble with the part. But *I* must have had trouble with the part, if only because the word itself was really taboo. I can see that there was a kind of terrible, bitter bravado about my father's way of handling this. And who would not dissociate from Shylock in order to identify with Portia? As a Jewish child who was also a female, I loved Portia—and, like every other Shakespearean heroine, she proved a treacherous role model.

A year or so later I am in another play, *The School for Scandal,* in which a noto-rious spendthrift is described as having "many excellent friends . . . among the Jews." In neither case was anything explained, either to me or to the class at large, about this scorn for Jews and the disgust surrounding Jews and money. Money, when Jews wanted it, had it, or lent it to others, seemed to take on a peculiar nasti-ness; Jews and money had some peculiar and unspeakable relation.

At this same school—in which we had Episcopalian hymns and prayers, and read aloud through the Bible morning after morning—I gained the impression that Jews were in the Bible and mentioned in English literature, that they had been persecuted centuries ago by the wicked Inquisition, but that they seemed not to exist in every-day life. These were the 1940s, and we were told a great deal about the Battle of Britain, the noble French Resistance fighters, the brave, starving Dutch—but I did not learn of the resistance of the Warsaw ghetto until I left home.

I was sent to the Episcopal church, baptized and confirmed, and attended it for about five years, though without belief. That religion seemed to have little to do with belief or commitment; it was liturgy that mattered, not spiritual passion. Neither of my parents ever entered that church, and my father would not enter *any* church for any reason—wedding or funeral. Nor did I enter a synagogue until I left Baltimore. When I came home from church, for a while, my father insisted on reading aloud to me from Thomas Paine's *The Age of Reason*—a diatribe against institutional reli-gion. Thus, he explained, I would have a balanced view of these things, a choice. He—they—did not give me the choice to be a Jew. My mother explained to me when I was filling out forms for college that if any question was asked about "religion," I should put down "Episcopalian" rather than "none"—to seem to have no religion was, she implied, dangerous.

But it was white social christianity, rather than any particular christian sect, that the world was founded on. The very word *Christian* was used as a synonym for virtuous, just, peace-loving, generous, etc., etc.* The norm was christian: "reli-gion: none" was indeed not acceptable. Anti-Semitism was so intrinsic as not to have a name. I don't recall exactly being taught that the Jews killed Jesus—"Christ killer" seems too strong a term for the bland Episcopal vocaculary—but certainly we got the impression that the Jews had been caught out in a terrible mistake, fail-ing to recognize the true Messiah, and were thereby less advanced in moral and spiritual sensibility. The Jews had actually allowed *moneylenders in the Temple* (again, the unexplained obsession with Jews and money): They were of the past, archaic, primitive, as older (and darker) cultures are supposed to be primitive; christianity was lightness, fairness, peace on earth, and combined the feminine

---

*In a similar way the phrase "That's white of you" implied that you were behaving with the superior decency and morality expected of white but not of Black people.

appeal of "The meek shall inherit the earth" with the masculine stride of "Onward, Christian Soldiers."

. . .

Sometime in 1946, while still in high school, I read in the newspaper that a theater in Baltimore was showing films of the Allied liberation of the Nazi concentration camps. Alone, I went downtown after school one afternoon and watched the stark, blurry, but unmistakable newsreels. When I try to go back and touch the pulse of that girl of sixteen, growing up in many ways so precocious and so ignorant, I am overwhelmed by a memory of despair, a sense of inevitability more enveloping than any I had ever known. Anne Frank's diary and many other personal narratives of the Holocaust were still unknown or unwritten. But it came to me that every one of those piles of corpses, mountains of shoes and clothing had contained, simply, individuals, who had believed, as I now believed of myself, that they were intended to live out a life of some kind of meaning, that the world possessed some kind of sense and order; yet *this* had happened to them. And I, who believed my life was intended to be so interesting and meaningful, was connected to those dead by something— not just mortality but a taboo name, a hated identity. Or was I—did I really have to be? Writing this now, I feel belated rage that I was so impoverished by the family and social worlds I lived in, that I had to try to figure out by myself what this did indeed mean for me. That I had never been taught about resistance, only about passing. That I had no language for anti-Semitism itself.

When I went home and told my parents where I had been, they were not pleased. I felt accused of being morbidly curious, not healthy, sniffing around death for the thrill of it. And since, at sixteen, I was often not sure of the sources of my feelings or of my motives for doing what I did, I probably accused myself as well. One thing was clear: there was nobody in my world with whom I could discuss those films. Probably at the same time, I was reading accounts of the camps in magazines and newspapers; what I remember were the films and having questions that I could not even phrase, such as *Are those men and women "them" or "us"?*

To be able to ask even the child's astonished question *Why do they hate us so?* means knowing how to say "we." The guilt of not knowing, the guilt of perhaps having betrayed my parents or even those victims, those survivors, through mere curiosity—these also froze in me for years the impulse to find out more about the Holocaust.

. . .

1947: I left Baltimore to go to college in Cambridge, Massachusetts, left (I thought) the backward, enervating South for the intellectual, vital North. New England also had for me some vibration of higher moral rectitude, of moral passion even, with its seventeenth-century Puritan self-scrutiny, its nineteenth-century literary "flowering," its abolitionist righteousness, Colonel Shaw and his Black Civil War regiment depicted in granite on Boston Common. At the same time, I found myself, at Radcliffe, among Jewish women. I used to sit for hours over coffee with what I thought of as the "real" Jewish students, who told me about middle-class Jewish culture in America. I described my background—for the first time to strangers—and they took me on, some with amusement at my illiteracy, some arguing that I could never marry into a strict Jewish family, some convinced I didn't "look Jewish," others that I did. I learned the names of holidays and foods, which surnames are Jewish and which are "changed names"; about girls who had had their noses "fixed," their hair straightened. For these young Jewish women, students in the late 1940s, it was acceptable, perhaps even necessary, to strive to look as gentile as possible; but they stuck proudly to being Jewish, expected to marry a Jew, have children, keep the holidays, carry on the culture.

I felt I was testing a forbidden current, that there was danger in these revelations. I bought a reproduction of a Chagall portrait of a rabbi in striped prayer shawl and hung it on the wall of my room. I was admittedly young and trying to educate myself, but I was also doing something that *is* dangerous: I was flirting with identity.

. . .

One day that year I was in a small shop where I had bought a dress with a too-long skirt. The shop employed a seamstress who did alterations, and she came in to pin up the skirt on me. I am sure that she was a recent immigrant, a survivor. I remember a short, dark woman wearing heavy glasses, with an accent so foreign I could not understand her words. Something about her presence was very powerful and disturbing to me. After marking and pinning up the skirt, she sat back on her knees, looked up at me, and asked in a hurried whisper: "You Jewish?" Eighteen years of training in assimilation sprang into the reflex by which I shook my head, rejecting her, and muttered, "No."

What was I actually saying "no" to? She was poor, older, struggling with a foreign tongue, anxious; she had escaped the death that had been intended for her, but I had no imagination of her possible courage and foresight, her resistance—I did not see in her a heroine who had perhaps saved many lives, including her own. I saw the frightened immigrant, the seamstress hemming the skirts of college girls, the wandering Jew. But I was an American college girl having her skirt hemmed. And I was frightened myself, I think, because she had recognized me ("It takes one to know one," my friend Edie at Radcliffe had said) even if I refused to recognize myself or her, even if her recognition was sharpened by loneliness or the need to feel safe with me.

But why should she have felt safe with me? I myself was living with a false sense of safety.

There are betrayals in my life that I have known at the very moment were betrayals: this was one of them. There are other betrayals committed so repeatedly, so mundanely, that they leave no memory trace behind, only a growing residue of misery, of dull, accreted self-hatred. Often these take the form not of words but of silence. Silence before the joke at which everyone is laughing; the anti-woman joke, the racist joke, the anti-Semitic joke. Silence and then amnesia. Blocking it out when the oppressor's language starts coming from the lips of one we admire, whose courage and eloquence have touched us: *She didn't really mean that; he didn't really say that.* But the accretions build up out of sight, like scale inside a kettle.

. . .

1948: I come home from my freshman year at college, flaming with new insights, new information. I am the daughter who has gone out into the world, to the pinnacle of intellectual prestige, Harvard, fulfilling my father's hopes for me, but also exposed to dangerous influences. I have already been reproved for attending a rally for Henry Wallace and the Progressive party. I challenge my father: "Why haven't you told me that I am Jewish? Why do you never talk about being a Jew?" He answers measuredly, "You know that I have never denied that I am a Jew. But it's not important to me. I am a scientist, a deist. I have no use for organized religion. I choose to live in a world of many kinds of people. There are Jews I admire and others who I despise. I am a person, not simply a Jew." The words are as I remember them, not perhaps exactly as spoken. But that was the message. And it contained enough truth—as all denial drugs itself on partial truth—so that it remained for the time being unanswerable, leaving me high and dry, split at the root, gasping for clarity, for air.

At that time Arnold Rich was living in suspension, waiting to be appointed to the professorship of pathology at Johns Hopkins. The appointment was delayed for years, no Jew ever having held a professional chair in that medical school. And he wanted it badly. It must have been a very bitter time for him, since he had believed so greatly in the redeeming power of excellence, of being the most brilliant, inspired man for the job. With enough excellence, you could presumably make it stop mattering that you were Jewish; you could become the *only* Jew in the gentile world, a Jew so "civilized," so far from "common," so attractively combining southern gentility with European cultural values that no one would ever confuse you with the raw, "pushy" Jew of New York, the "loud, hysterical" refugees from eastern Europe, the "overdressed" Jews of the urban South.

We—my sister, mother, and I—were constantly urged to speak quietly in public, to dress without ostentation, to repress all vividness or spontaneity, to assimilate with a world which might see us as too flamboyant. I suppose that my mother, pure gentile though she was, could be seen as acting "common" or "Jewish" if she laughed too loudly or spoke aggressively. My father's mother, who lived with us half the year, was a model of circumspect behavior, dressed in dark blue or lavender, retiring in company, ladylike to an extreme, wearing no jewelry except a good gold chain, a narrow brooch, or a string of pearls. A few times, within the family, I saw her anger flare, felt the passion whe was repressing. But when Arnold took us out to a restaurant or on a trip, the Rich women were always tuned down to some WASP level my father believed, surely, would protect us all—maybe also make us unrecognizable to the "real Jews" who wanted to seize us, drag us back to the *shtetl,* the ghetto, in its many manifestations.

For, yes, that *was* a message—that some Jews would be after you, once they "knew," to rejoin them, to re-enter a world that was messy, noisy, unpredictable, maybe poor—"even though," as my mother once wrote me, criticizing my largely Jewish choice of friends in college, "some of them will be the most brilliant, fascinating people you'll ever meet." I wonder if that isn't one message of assimilation—of America—that the unlucky or the unachieving want to pull you backward, that to identify with them is to court downward mobility, lose the precious chance of passing, of token existence. There was always within this sense of Jewish identity a strong class discrimination. Jews might be "fascinating" as individuals but came with huge unruly families who "poured chicken soup over everyone's head" (in the phrase of a white southern male poet). Anti-Semitism could thus be justified by the bad behavior of certain Jews; and if you did not effectively deny family and community, there would always be a remote cousin claiming kinship with you who was the "wrong kind" of Jew.

I have always believed his attitude toward other Jews depended on who they were. . . . It was my impression that Jews of this background looked down on Eastern European Jews, including Polish Jews and Russian Jews, who generally were not as well educated. This from a letter written to me recently by a gentile who had worked in my father's department, whom I had asked about anti-Semitism there and in particular regarding my father. This informant also wrote me that it was hard to perceive anti-

Semitism in Baltimore because the racism made so much more intense an impression: *I would almost have to think that blacks went to a different heaven than the whites, because the bodies were kept in a separate morgue, and some white persons did not even want blood transfusions from black donors.* My father's mind was predictably racist and misogynist; yet as a medical student he noted in his journal that southern male chivalry stopped at the point of any white man in a streetcar giving his seat to an old, weary Black woman standing in the aisle. Was this a Jewish insight—an outsider's insight, even though the outsider was striving to be on the inside?

Because what isn't named is often more permeating than what is, I believe that my father's Jewishness profoundly shaped my own identity and our family existence. They were shaped both by external anti-Semitism and my father's self-hatred, and by his Jewish pride. What Arnold did, I think, was call his Jewish pride something else: achievement, aspiration, genius, idealism. Whatever was unacceptable got left back under the rubric of Jewishness or the "wrong kind" of Jews—uneducated, aggressive, loud. The message I got was that we were really superior: nobody else's father had collected so many books, had traveled so far, knew so many languages. Baltimore was a musical city, but for the most part, in the families of my school friends, culture was for women. My father was an amateur musician, read poetry, adored encyclopedic knowledge. He prowled and pounced over my school papers, insisting I use "grownup" sources; he criticized my poems for faulty technique and gave me books on rhyme and meter and form. His investment in my intellect and talent was egotistical, tyrannical, opinionated, and terribly wearing. He taught me, nevertheless, to believe in hard work, to mistrust easy inspiration, to write and rewrite; to feel that I *was* a person of the book, even though a woman; to take ideas seriously. He made me feel, at a very young age, the power of language and that I could share in it.

The Riches were proud, but we also had to be very careful. Our behavior had to be more impeccable than other people's. Strangers were not to be trusted, nor even friends; family issues must never go beyond the family; the world was full of potential slanderers, betrayers, *people who could not understand.* Even within the family, I realize that I never in my whole life knew what my father was really feeling. Yet he spoke—monologued—with driving intensity. You could grow up in such a house mesmerized by the local electricity, the crucial meanings assumed by the merest things. This used to seem to me a sign that we were all living on some high emotional plane. It was a difficult force field for a favored daughter to disengage from.

Easy to call that intensity Jewish; and I have no doubt that passion is one of the qualities required for survival over generations of persecution. But what happens when passion is rent from its original base, when the white gentile world is softly saying "Be more like us and you can be almost one of us"? What happens when survival seems to mean closing off one emotional artery after another? His forebears in Europe had been forbidden to travel or expelled from one country after another, had special taxes levied on them if they left the city walls, had been forced to wear special clothes and badges, restricted to the poorest neighborhoods. He had wanted to be a "free spirit," to travel widely, among "all kinds of people." Yet in his prime of life he lived in an increasingly withdrawn world, in his house up on a hill in a neighborhood where Jews were not supposed to be able to buy property, depending almost exclusively on interactions with his wife and daughters to provide emotional connectedness. In his home, he created a private defense system so elaborate that even as he was dying, my mother felt unable to talk freely with his colleagues or others who might have helped her. Of course, she acquiesced in this.

The loneliness of the "only," the token, often doesn't feel like loneliness but like a kind of dead echo chamber. Certain things that ought to don't resonate. Somewhere Beverly Smith writes of women of color "inspiring the behavior" in each other. When there's nobody to "inspire the behavior," act out of the culture, there is an atrophy, a dwindling, which is partly invisible.

. . .

Sometimes I feel I have seen too long from too many disconnected angles: white, Jewish, anti-Semite, racist, anti-racist, once-married, lesbian, middle-class, feminist, ex-matriate southerner, *split at the root*—that I will never bring them whole. I would have liked, in this essay, to bring together the meanings of anti-Semitism and racism as I have experienced them and as I believe they intersect in the world beyond my life. But I'm not able to do this yet. I feel the tension as I think, make notes: *If you really look at the one reality, the other will waver and disperse.* Trying in one week to read Angela Davis and Lucy Davidowicz;* trying to hold throughout to a feminist, a lesbian, perspective—what does this mean? Nothing has trained me for this. And sometimes I feel inadequate to make any statement as a Jew; I feel the history of denial within me like an injury, a scar. For assimilation has affected *my* perceptions; those early lapses in meaning, those blanks, are with me still. My ignorance can be dangerous to me and to others.

Yet we can't wait for the undamaged to make our connections for us; we can't wait to speak until we are perfectly clear and righteous. There is no purity and, in our lifetimes, no end to this process.

This essay, then, has no conclusions: it is another beginning for me. Not just a way of saying, in 1982 Right Wing America, *I too, will wear the yellow star.* It's a moving into accountability, enlarging the range of accountability. I know that in the rest of my life, the next half century or so, every aspect of my identity will have to be engaged. The middle-class white girl taught to trade obedience for privilege. The Jewish lesbian raised to be a heterosexual gentile. The woman who first heard oppression named and analyzed in the Black Civil Rights struggle. The woman with three sons, the feminist who hates male violence. The woman limping with a cane, the woman who has stopped bleeding are also accountable. The poet who knows that beautiful language can lie, that the oppressor's language sometimes sounds beautiful. The woman trying, as part of her resistance, to clean up her act.

PAULE MARSHALL
(1929-)

Paule Marshall was born in Brooklyn, New York, to parents who had immigrated from Barbados in the West Indies. She attended Brooklyn College and Hunter College. For three years she was a writer for Our World *magazine,*

---

*Angela Y. Davis, *Woman, Race and Class* (New York: Random House, 1981); Lucy S. Davidowicz, *The War against the Jews 1933–1945* (1975; New York: Bantam, 1979).

and in 1959 she published her first novel, Brown Girl, Brownstones. *The following year she was awarded a fellowship from the Guggenheim Foundation. She has published four novels and two collections of short fiction. Among her awards are a Ford Foundation grant, the Rosenthal Award from the National Institute of Arts and Letters, a National Endowment for the Arts grant, and a MacArthur fellowship. Her novel* Praisesong for the Widow *was awarded the Before Columbus Foundation American Book Award in 1984. She has taught at numerous colleges and universities and is currently the Gould Sheppard Professor of Literature and Culture at New York University. Her novel* Daughters *won the 1991 Booklist Award for Best Adult Fiction. Her most recent work is* The Fisher King (2000).*

Marshall's autobiographical story "To Da-duh, In Memoriam" is a consideration of the people from the past whom we come to realize embodied values we depend upon for guidance and spiritual comfort. Mourning Daduh allows Marshall to connect her past and her present.

TO DA-DUH, IN MEMORIAM

I did not see her at first I remember. For not only was it dark inside the crowded disembarkation shed in spite of the daylight flooding in from outside, but standing there waiting for her with my mother and sister I was still somewhat blinded from the sheen of tropical sunlight on the water of the bay which we had just crossed in the landing boat, leaving behind us the ship that had brought us from New York lying in the offing. Besides, being only nine years of age at the time and knowing nothing of islands I was busy attending to the alien sights and sounds of Barbados, the unfamiliar smells.

I did not see her, but I was alerted to her approach by my mother's hand which suddenly tightened around mine, and looking up I traced her gaze through the gloom in the shed until I finally made out the small, purposeful, painfully erect figure of the old woman headed our way.

Her face was drowned in the shadow of an ugly rolled-brim brown felt hat, but the details of her slight body and of the struggle taking place within it were clear enough—an intense, unrelenting struggle between her back which was beginning to bend ever so slightly under the weight of her eighty-odd years and the rest of her which sought to deny those years and hold that back straight, keep it in line. Moving swiftly toward us (so swiftly it seemed she did not intend stopping when she reached us but would sweep past us out the doorway which opened onto the sea and like Christ walk upon the water!), she was caught between the sunlight at her end of the building and the darkness inside—and for a moment she appeared to contain them both: the light in the long severe old-fashioned white dress she wore which brought the sense of a past that was still alive into our bustling present and in the snatch of white at her eye; the darkness in her black high-top shoes and in her face which was visible now that she was closer.

It was as stark and fleshless as a death mask, that face. The maggots might have already done their work, leaving only the framework of bone beneath the ruined skin and deep wells at the temple and jaw. But her eyes were alive, unnervingly so for one so old, with a sharp light that flicked out of the dim clouded depths like a lizard's tongue to snap up all in her view. Those eyes betrayed a child's curiosity about the world, and I wondered vaguely seeing them, and seeing the way the bodice of her ancient dress had collapsed in on her flat chest (what had happened to her breasts?) whether she might not be some kind of child at the same time that she was a woman, with fourteen children, my mother included, to prove it. Perhaps she was both, both child and woman, darkness and light, past and present, life and death— all the opposites contained and reconciled in her.

"My Da-duh," my mother said formally and stepped forward. The name sounded like thunder fading softly in the distance.

"Child," Da-duh said, and her tone, her quick scrutiny of my mother, the brief embrace in which they appeared to shy from each other rather than touch, wiped out the fifteen years my mother had been away and restored the old relationship. My mother, who was such a formidable figure in my eyes, had suddenly with a word been reduced to my status.

"Yes, God is good," Da-duh said with a nod that was like a tic. "He has spared me to see my child again."

We were led forward then, apologetically because not only did Da-duh prefer boys but she also liked her grandchildren to be "white," that is, fair-skinned; and we had, I was to discover, a number of cousins, the outside children of white estate managers and the like, who qualified. We, though, were as black as she.

My sister being the oldest was presented first. "This one takes after the father," my mother said and waited to be reproved.

Frowning, Da-duh tilted my sister's face toward the light. But her frown soon gave way to a grudging smile, for my sister with her large mild eyes and little broad winged nose, with our father's high-cheeked Barbadian cast to her face, was pretty.

"She's goin' be lucky," Da-duh said and patted her once on the cheek. "Any girl child that takes after the father does be lucky."

She turned then to me. But oddly enough she did not touch me. Instead leaning close, she peered hard at me, and then quickly drew back. I thought I saw her hand start up as though to shield her eyes. It was almost as if she saw not only me, a thin truculent child who it was said took after no one but myself, but something in me which for some reason she found disturbing, even threatening. We looked silently at each other for a long time there in the noisy shed, our gaze locked. She was the first to look away.

"But Adry," she said to my mother and her laugh was cracked, thin, apprehensive. "Where did you get this one here with this fierce look?"

"We don't know where she came out of, my Da-duh," my mother said, laughing also. Even I smiled to myself. After all I had won the encounter. Da-duh had recognized my small strength—and this was all I ever asked of the adults in my life then.

"Come, soul," Da-duh said and took my hand. "You must be one of those New York terrors you hear so much about."

She led us, me at her side and my sister and mother behind, out of the shed into the sunlight that was like a bright driving summer rain and over to a group of people clustered beside a decrepit lorry. They were our relatives, most of them from St. Andrews although Da-duh herself lived in St. Thomas, the women wearing bright print dresses, the colors vivid against their darkness, the men rusty black suits that encased them like straightjackets. Da-duh, holding fast to my hand, became my anchor as they circled round us like a nervous sea, exclaiming, touching us with their calloused hands, embracing us shyly. They laughed in awed bursts: "But look Adry got big-big children!"/"And see the nice things they wearing, wrist watch and all!"/"I tell you, Adry has done all right for sheself in New York. . . ."

Da-duh, ashamed at their wonder, embarrassed for them, admonished them the while. "But oh Christ," she said, "why you all got to get on like you never saw people from 'Away' before? You would think New York is the only place in the world to hear wunna. That's why I don't like to go anyplace with you St. Andrews people, you know. You all ain't been colonized."

We were in the back of the lorry finally, packed in among the barrels of ham, flour, cornmeal and rice and the trunks of clothes that my mother had brought as gifts. We made our way slowly through Bridgetown's clogged streets, part of a funereal procession of cars and open-sided buses, bicycles and donkey carts. The dim little limestone shops and offices along the way marched with us, at the same mournful pace, toward the same grave ceremony—as did the people, the women balancing huge baskets on top their heads as if they were no more than hats they wore to shade them from the sun. Looking over the edge of the lorry I watched as their feet slurred the dust. I listened, and their voices, raw and loud and dissonant in the heat, seemed to be grappling with each other high overhead.

Da-duh sat on a trunk in our midst, a monarch amid her court. She still held my hand, but it was different now. I had suddenly become her anchor, for I felt her fear of the lorry with its asthmatic motor (a fear and distrust, I later learned, she held of all machines) beating like a pulse in her rough palm.

As soon as we left Bridgetown behind though, she relaxed, and while the others around us talked she gazed at the canes standing tall on either side of the winding marl road. "C'dear," she said softly to herself after a time. "The canes this side are pretty enough."

They were too much for me. I thought of them as giant weeds that had overrun the island, leaving scarcely any room for the small tottering houses of sunbleached pine we passed or the people, dark streaks as our lorry hurtled by. I suddenly feared that we were journeying, unaware that we were, toward some dangerous place where the canes, grown as high and thick as a forest, would close in on us and run us through with their stiletto blades. I longed then for the familiar: for the street in Brooklyn where I lived, for my father who had refused to accompany us ("Blowing out good money on foolishness," he had said of the trip), for a game of tag with my friends under the chestnut tree outside our aging brownstone house.

"Yes, but wait till you see St. Thomas canes," Da-duh was saying to me. "They's canes father, bo," she gave a proud arrogant nod. "Tomorrow, God willing, I goin' take you out in the ground and show them to you."

True to her word Da-duh took me with her the following day out into the ground. It was a fairly large plot adjoining her weathered board and shingle house and consisting of a small orchard, a good-sized cane-piece and behind the canes, where the land sloped abruptly down, a gully. She had purchased it with Panama money sent her by her eldest son, my uncle Joseph, who had died working on the canal. We entered the ground along a trail no wider than her body and as devious and complex as her reasons for showing me her land. Da-duh strode briskly ahead, her slight form filled out this morning by the layers of sacking petticoats she wore under her working dress to protect her against the damp. A fresh white cloth, elaborately arranged around her head, added to her height, and lent her a vain, almost roguish air.

Her pace slowed once we reached the orchard, and glancing back at me occasionally over her shoulder, she pointed out the various trees.

"This here is a breadfruit," she said. "That one yonder is a papaw. Here's a guava. This is a mango. I know you don't have anything like these in New York. Here's a sugar apple." (The fruit looked more like artichokes than apples to me.) "This one bears limes. . . ." She went on for some time, intoning the names of the trees as though they were those of her gods. Finally, turning to me, she said, "I know you don't have anything this nice where you come from." Then, as I hesitated, "I said I know you don't have anything this nice where you come from. . . ."

"No," I said and my world did seem lacking.

Da-duh nodded and passed on. The orchard ended and we were on the narrow cart road that led through the canepiece, the canes clashing like swords above my cowering head. Again she turned and her thin muscular arms spread wide, her dim gaze embracing the small field of canes, she said—and her voice almost broke under the weight of her pride, "Tell me, have you got anything like these in that place where you were born?"

"No."

"I din't think so. I bet you don't even know that these canes here and the sugar you eat is one and the same thing. That they does throw the canes into some damn machine at the factory and squeeze out all the little life in them to make sugar for you all so in New York to eat. I bet you don't know that."

"I've got two cavities and I'm not allowed to eat a lot of sugar."

But Da-duh didn't hear me. She had turned with an inexplicably angry motion and was making her way rapidly out of the canes and down the slope at the edge of the field which led to the gully below. Following her apprehensively down the incline amid a stand of banana plants whose leaves flapped like elephants ears in the wind, I found myself in the middle of a small tropical wood—a place dense and damp and gloomy and tremulous with the fitful play of light and shadow as the leaves high above moved against the sun that was almost hidden from view. It was a violent place, the tangled foliage fighting each other for a chance at the sunlight, the branches of the trees locked in what seemed an immemorial struggle, one both necessary and inevitable. But despite the violence, it was pleasant, almost peaceful in the gully, and beneath the thick undergrowth the earth smelled like spring.

This time Da-duh didn't even bother to ask her usual question, but simply turned and waited for me to speak.

"No," I said, my head bowed. "We don't have anything like this in New York."

"Ah," she cried, her triumph complete. "I din' think so. Why, I've heard that's a place where you can walk till you near drop and never see a tree."

"We've got a chestnut tree in front of our house," I said.

"Does it bear?" She waited. "I ask you, does it bear?"

"Not anymore," I muttered. "It used to, but not anymore."

She gave the nod that was like a nervous twitch. "You see," she said, "Nothing can bear there." Then, secure behind her scorn, she added, "But tell me, what's this snow like that you hear so much about?"

Looking up, I studied her closely, sensing my chance, and then I told her, describing at length and with as much drama as I could summon not only what snow in the city was like, but what it would be like here, in her perennial summer kingdom.

". . . And you see all these trees you got here," I said. "Well, they'd be bare. No leaves, no fruit, nothing. They'd be covered in snow. You see your canes. They'd be buried under tons of snow. The snow would be higher than your head, higher than your house, and you wouldn't be able to come down into this here gully because it would be snowed under. . . ."

She searched my face for the lie, still scornful but intrigued. "What a thing, huh?" she said finally, whispering it softly to herself.

"And when it snows you couldn't dress like you are now," I said. "Oh no, you'd freeze to death. You'd have to wear a hat and gloves and galoshes and ear muffs so your ears wouldn't freeze and drop off, and a heavy coat. I've got a Shirley Temple coat with fur on the collar. I can dance. You wanna see?"

Before she could answer I began, with a dance called the Truck which was popular back then in the 1930's. My right forefinger waving, I trucked around the nearby trees and around Da-duh's awed and rigid form. After the Truck I did the Suzy-Q, my lean hips swishing, my sneakers sidling zigzag over the ground. "I can sing," I said and did so, starting with "I'm Gonna Sit Right Down and Write Myself a Letter," then without pausing, "Tea For Two," and ending with "I Found a Million Dollar Baby in a Five and Ten Cent Store."

For long moments afterwards Da-duh stared at me as if I were a creature from Mars, an emissary from some world she did not know but which intrigued her and whose power she both felt and feared. Yet something about my performance must have pleased her, because bending down she slowly lifted her long skirt and then, one by one, the layers of petticoats until she came to a drawstring purse dangling at the end of a long strip of cloth tied round her waist. Opening the purse she handed me a penny. "Here," she said half-smiling against her will. "Take this to buy yourself a sweet at the shop up the road. There's nothing to be done with you, soul."

From then on, whenever I wasn't taken to visit relatives, I accompanied Da-duh out into the ground, and alone with her amid the canes or down in the gully I told her about New York. It always began with some slighting remark on her part: "I know they don't have anything this nice where you come from," or "Tell me, I hear those foolish people in New York does do such and such. . . ." But as I answered, recreating my towering world of steel and concrete and machines for her, building the city out of words, I would feel her give way. I came to know the signs of her surrender: the total stillness that would come over her little hard dry form, the probing gaze that like a surgeon's knife sought to cut through my skull to get at the images there, to see if I were lying; above all, her fear, a fear nameless and profound, the same one I had felt beating in the palm of her hand that day in the lorry.

Over the weeks I told her about refrigerators, radios, gas stoves, elevators, trolley cars, wringer washing machines, movies, airplanes, the cyclone at Coney Island, subways, toasters, electric lights: "At night, see, all you have to do is flip this little switch on the wall and all the lights in the house go on. Just like that. Like magic. It's like turning on the sun at night."

"But tell me," she said to me once with a faint mocking smile, "do the white people have all these things too or it's only the people looking like us?"

I laughed. "What d'ya mean," I said. "The white people have even better." Then: "I beat up a white girl in my class last term."

"Beating up white people!" Her tone was incredulous.

"How you mean!" I said, using an expression of hers. "She called me a name."

For some reason Da-duh could not quite get over this and repeated in the same, shocked voice, "Beating up white people now! Oh, the lord, the world's changing up so I can scarce recognize it anymore."

One morning toward the end of our stay, Da-duh led me into a part of the gully that we had never visited before, an area darker and more thickly overgrown than the rest, almost impenetrable. There in a small clearing amid the dense bush, she stopped before an incredibly tall royal palm which rose cleanly out of the ground, and drawing the eye up with it, soared high above the trees around it into the sky. It appeared to be touching the blue dome of sky, to be flaunting its dark crown of fronds right in the blinding white face of the late morning sun.

Da-duh watched me a long time before she spoke, and then she said, very quietly, "All right, now, tell me if you've got anything this tall in that place you're from."

I almost wished, seeing her face, that I could have said no. "Yes," I said. "We've got buildings hundreds of times this tall in New York. There's one called the Empire State Building that's the tallest in the world. My class visited it last year and I went all the way to the top. It's got over a hundred floors. I can't describe how tall it is. Wait a minute. What's the name of that hill I went to visit the other day, where they have the police station?"

"You mean Bissex?"

"Yes, Bissex. Well, the Empire State Building is way taller than that."

"You're lying now!" she shouted, trembling with rage. Her hand lifted to strike me.

"No, I'm not," I said. "It really is, if you don't believe me I'll send you a picture postcard of it soon as I get back home so you can see for yourself. But it's way taller than Bissex."

All the fight went out of her at that. The hand poised to strike me fell limp to her side, and as she stared at me, seeing not me but the building that was taller than the highest hill she knew, the small stubborn light in her eyes (it was the same amber as the flame in the kerosene lamp she lit at dusk) began to fail. Finally, with a vague gesture that even in the midst of her defeat still tried to dismiss me and my world, she turned and started back through the gully, walking slowly, her steps groping and uncertain, as if she were suddenly no longer sure of the way, while I followed triumphant yet strangely saddened behind.

The next morning I found her dressed for our morning walk but stretched out on the Berbice chair in the tiny drawing room where she sometimes napped during the afternoon heat, her face turned to the window beside her. She appeared thinner and suddenly indescribably old.

"My Da-duh," I said.

"Yes, nuh," she said. Her voice was listless and the face she slowly turned my way was, now that I think back on it, like a Benin mask, the features drawn and almost distorted by an ancient abstract sorrow.

"Don't you feel well?" I asked.

"Girl, I don't know."

"My Da-duh, I goin' boil you some bush tea?," my aunt, Da-duh's youngest child, who lived with her, called from the shed roof kitchen.

"Who tell you I need bush tea?" she cried, her voice assuming for a moment its old authority. "You can't even rest nowadays without some malicious person looking for you to be dead. Come girl," she motioned me to a place beside her on the old-fashioned lounge chair, "give us a tune."

I sang for her until breakfast at eleven, all my brash irreverent Tin Pan Alley songs, and then just before noon we went out into the ground. But it was a short, dispirited walk. Da-duh didn't even notice that the mangoes were beginning to ripen and would have to be picked before the village boys got to them. And when she paused occasionally and looked out across the canes or up at her trees it wasn't as if she were seeing them but something else. Some huge, monolithic shape had imposed itself, it seemed, between her and the land, obstructing her vision. Return-ing to the house she slept the entire afternoon on the Berbice chair.

She remained like this until we left, languishing away the mornings on the chair at the window gazing out at the land as if it were already doomed; then, at noon, taking the brief stroll with me through the ground during which she seldom spoke and afterwards returning home to sleep till almost dusk sometimes.

On the day of our departure she put on the austere, ankle length white dress, the black shoes and brown felt hat (her town clothes she called them), but she did not go with us to town. She saw us off on the road outside her house and in the midst of my mother's tearful protracted farewell, she leaned down and whispered in my ear, "Girl, you're not to forget now to send me the picture of that building, you hear."

By the time I mailed her the large colored picture postcard of the Empire State Building she was dead. She died during the famous '37 strike which began shortly after we left. On the day of her death England sent planes flying low over the island in a show of force—so low, according to my aunt's letter, that the downdraft from them shook the ripened mangoes from the trees in Da-duh's orchard. Frightened, everyone in the village fled into the canes. Except Da-duh. She remained in the house at the window so my aunt said, watching as the planes came swooping and scream-ing like monstrous birds down over the village, over her house, rattling her trees and flattening the young canes in her field. It must have seemed to her lying there that they did not intend pulling out of their dive, but like the hardback beetles which hurled themselves with suicidal force against the walls of the house at night, those menacing silver shapes would hurl themselves in an ecstasy of self-immola-tion onto the land, destroying it utterly.

When the planes finally left and the villagers returned they found her dead on the Berbice chair at the window.

She died and I lived, but always, to this day even, within the shadow of her death. For a brief period after I was grown I went to live alone, like one doing penance, in a loft above a noisy factory in downtown New York and there painted seas of sugar-cane and huge swirling Van Gogh suns and palm trees striding like brightly-plumed Tutsi warriors across a tropical landscape, while the thunderous tread of the machines downstairs jarred the floor beneath my easel, mocking my efforts.

LOUISE ERDRICH
(1954-)

Louise Erdrich is a novelist, short story writer, poet, essayist, and critic and one of the country's most successful Native-American authors. She was born in Little Falls, Minnesota, and grew up in Wahpeton, North Dakota, where her parents were teachers for the Bureau of Indian Affairs. She attended Dartmouth College and then The Johns Hopkins University, where she received an M.A. in creative writing in 1979. After receiving her degree, she returned to Dartmouth to teach writing. In 1984 she published her first novel, Love Medicine; *it received wide critical acclaim and was a national best seller. Erdrich was awarded the National Book Critics Circle Award, the*

American Book Award, and the Sue Kaufman Prize for the Best First Novel from the American Academy and Institute of Arts and Letters. Since then she has published a half dozen novels, as well as works of poetry, memoir, and children's fiction. She has received fellowships from the Guggenheim Foundation and the National Endowment for the Arts.

"The Bingo Van" was first published in The New Yorker *and later incorporated into Erdrich's novel* The Bingo Palace. *It features Lipsha Morrissey, a young Chippewa man who first appeared in* Love Medicine. *Here Lipsha learns a lesson about the complications inherent in getting what you desire, especially when it is entangled with issues like gambling.*

THE BINGO VAN

When I walked into bingo that night in early spring, I didn't have a girlfriend, a home or an apartment, a piece of land or a car, and I wasn't tattooed yet, either. Now look at me. I'm walking the reservation road in borrowed pants, toward a place that isn't mine, downhearted because I'm left by a woman. All I have of my temporary riches is this black pony running across the back of my hand—a tattoo I had Lewey's Tattoo Den put there on account of a waking dream. I'm still not paid up. I still owe for the little horse. But if Lewey wants to repossess it, then he'll have to catch me first.

Here's how it is on coming to the bingo hall. It's a long, low quonset barn. Inside, there used to be a pall of smoke, but now the smoke-eater fans in the ceiling take care of that. So upon first entering you can pick out your friends. On that night in early spring, I saw Eber, Clay, and Robert Morrissey sitting about halfway up toward the curtained stage with their grandmother Lulu. By another marriage, she was my grandma, too. She had five tickets spread in front of her. The boys each had only one. When the numbers rolled, she picked up a dabber in each hand. It was the Earlybird game, a one-hundred-dollar prize, and nobody had got too wound up yet or serious.

"Lipsha, go get us a Coke," said Lulu when someone else bingoed. "Yourself, too."

I went to the concession with Eber, who had finished high school with me. Clay and Robert were younger. We got our soft drinks and came back, set them down, pulled up to the table, and laid out a new set of tickets before us. Like I say, my grandmother, she played five at once, which is how you get the big money. In the long run, much more than breaking even, she was one of those rare Chippewas who actually profited by bingo. But, then again, it was her only way of gambling. No pull-tabs, no blackjack, no slot machines for her. She never went into the back room. She banked all the cash she won. I thought I should learn from Lulu Lamartine, whose other grandsons had stiff new boots while mine were worn down into the soft shape of moccasins. I watched her.

Concentration. Before the numbers even started, she set her mouth, snapped her purse shut. She shook her dabbers so that the foam-rubber tips were thoroughly inked. She looked at the time on her watch. The Coke, she took a drink of that, but no more than a sip. She was a narrow-eyed woman with a round jaw, curled hair. Her eyeglasses, blue plastic, hung from her neck by a gleaming chain. She raised the ovals to her eyes as the caller took the stand. She held her dabbers poised while he plucked the ball from the chute. He read it out: B-7. Then she was absorbed, scanning, dabbing, into the game. She didn't mutter. She had no lucky piece to touch in front of her. And afterward, even if she lost a blackout game by one square, she never sighed or complained.

All business, that was Lulu. And all business paid.

I think I would have been all business too, like her, if it hadn't been for what lay behind the stage curtain to be revealed. I didn't know it, but that was what would change the order of my life. Because of the van, I'd have to get stupid first, then wise. You see, I had been floundering since high school, trying to catch my bearings in the world. It all lay ahead of me, spread out in the sun like a giveaway at a naming ceremony. Only thing was, I could not choose a prize. Something always stopped my hand before it reached.

"Lipsha Morrissey, you got to go for a vocation." That's what I told myself, in a state of nervous worry. I was getting by on almost no money, relying on my job as night watchman in a bar. That earned me a place to sleep, twenty dollars per week, and as much beef jerky, Beer Nuts, and spicy sausage sticks as I could eat.

I was now composed of these three false substances. No food in a bar has a shelf life of less than forty months. If you are what you eat, I would live forever, I thought.

And then they pulled aside the curtain, and I saw that I wouldn't live as long as I had coming unless I owned that van. It had every option you could believe—blue plush on the steering wheel, diamond side windows, and complete carpeted interior. The seats were easy chairs, with little headphones, and it was wired all through the walls. You could walk up close during intermission and touch the sides. The paint was cream, except for the design picked out in blue, which was a Sioux drum border. In the back there was a small refrigerator and a carpeted platform for sleeping. It was a home, a portable den with front-wheel drive. I could see myself in it right off. I could see I *was* it.

On TV, they say you are what you drive. Let's put it this way: I wanted to be that van.

Now, I know that what I felt was a symptom of the national decline. You'll scoff at me, scorn me, say, What right does that waste Lipsha Morrissey, who makes his living guarding beer, have to comment outside of his own tribal boundary? But I was able to investigate the larger picture, thanks to Grandma Lulu, from whom I learned to be one-minded in my pursuit of a material object.

I went night after night to the bingo. Every hour I spent there, I grew more certain I was close. There was only one game per night at which the van was offered, a blackout game, where you had to fill every slot. The more tickets you bought, the more your chances increased. I tried to play five tickets, like Grandma Lulu did, but they cost five bucks each. To get my van, I had to shake hands with greed. I got unprincipled.

You see, my one talent in this life is a healing power I get passed down through the Pillager branch of my background. It's in my hands. I snap my fingers together so hard they almost spark. Then I blank out my mind, and I put on the touch. I had a reputation up to then for curing sore joints and veins. I could relieve ailments caused in an old person by a half century of grinding stoop-over work. I had a power in myself that flowed out, resistless. I had a richness in my dreams and waking thoughts. But I never realized I would have to give up my healing source once I started charging for my service.

You know how it is about charging. People suddenly think you are worth something. Used to be, I'd go anyplace I was called, take any price or take nothing. Once

I let it get around that I charged a twenty for my basic work, however, the phone at the bar rang off the hook.

"Where's that medicine boy?" they asked. "Where's Lipsha?"

I took their money. And it's not like beneath the pressure of a twenty I didn't try, for I did try, even harder than before. I skipped my palms together, snapped my fingers, positioned them where the touch inhabiting them should flow. But when it came to blanking out my mind I consistently failed. For each time, in the center of the cloud that came down into my brain, the van was now parked, in perfect focus.

I suppose I longed for it like for a woman, except I wasn't that bad yet, and, anyway, then I did meet a woman, which set me back in my quest.

Instead of going for the van with everything, saving up to buy as many cards as I could play when they got to the special game, for a few nights I went short term, for variety, with U-Pickem cards, the kind where you have to choose the numbers for yourself.

First off, I wrote in the shoe and pants sizes of those Morrissey boys. No luck. So much for them. Next I took my birth date and a double of it—still no go. I wrote down the numbers of my grandma's address and her anniversary dates. Nothing. Then one night I realized if my U-Pickem was going to win it would be more like *revealed*, rather than forced kind of thing. So I shut my eyes, right there in the middle of the long bingo table, and I let my mind blank out, white and fizzing like the screen of a television, until something formed. The van, as always. But on its tail this time a license plate was officially fixed and numbered. I used that number, wrote it down in the boxes, and then I bingoed.

I got two hundred dollars from that imaginary license. The money was in my pocket when I left. The next morning, I had fifty cents. But it's not like you think with Serena, and I'll explain that. She didn't want something from me; she didn't care if I had money, and she didn't ask for it. She was seventeen and had a two-year-old boy. That tells you about her life. Her last name was American Horse, an old Sioux name she was proud of even though it was strange to Chippewa country. At her older sister's house Serena's little boy blended in with the younger children, and Serena herself was just one of the teen-agers. She was still in high school, a year behind the year she should have been in, and she had ambitions. Her idea was to go into business and sell her clothing designs, of which she had six books.

I don't know how I got a girl so decided in her future to go with me, even that night. Except I told myself, "Lipsha, you're a nice-looking guy. You're a winner." And for the moment I was. I went right up to her at the Coin-op and said, "Care to dance?," which was a joke—there wasn't anyplace to dance. Yet she liked me. We had a sandwich and then she wanted to take a drive, so we tagged along with some others in the back of their car. They went straight south, toward Hoopdance, off the reservation, where action was taking place.

"Lipsha," she whispered on the way, "I always liked you from a distance."

"Serena," I said, "I liked you from a distance, too."

So then we moved close together on the car seat. My hand was on my knee, and I thought of a couple of different ways I could gesture, casually pretend to let it fall on hers, how maybe if I talked fast she wouldn't notice, in the heat of the moment, her hand in my hand, us holding hands, our lips drawn to one another. But then I decided to boldly take courage, to take her hand as, at the same time, I looked into her eyes. I did this. In the front, the others talked among themselves. Yet we just sat there. After a while she said, "You want to kiss me?"

But I answered, not planning how the words would come out, "Our first kiss has to be a magic moment only we can share."

Her eyes went wide as a deer's, and her big smile bloomed. Her skin was dark, her long hair a burnt-brown color. She wore no jewelry, no rings, just the clothing she had sewed from her designs—a suit jacket and pair of pants that were the tan of eggshells, with symbols picked out in blue thread on the borders, the cuffs, and the hem. I took her in, admiring, for some time on that drive before I realized that the reason Serena's cute outfit nagged me so was on account of she was dressed up to match my bingo van. I could hardly tell her this surprising coincidence, but it did convince me that the time was perfect, the time was right.

They let us off at a certain place just over the reservation line, and we got out, hardly breaking our gaze from each other. You want to know what this place was? I'll tell you. O.K. So it was a motel—a long, low double row of rooms, painted white on the outside, with brown wooden doors. There was a beautiful sign set up, featuring a lake with some fish jumping out of it. We stood beside the painted water.

"I haven't done this since Jason," she said. That was the name of her two-year-old son. "I have to call up my sister first."

There was a phone near the office, inside a plastic shell. She went over there.

"He's sleeping," she said when she returned.

I went into the office, stood before the metal counter. There was a number floating in my mind.

"Is Room 22 available?" I asked.

I suppose, looking at me, I look too much like an Indian. The owner, a big sandy-haired woman in a shiny black blouse, noticed that. You get so you see it cross their face the way wind blows a disturbance on water. There was a period of contemplation, a struggle in this woman's thinking. Behind her the television whispered. Her mouth opened, but I spoke first.

"This here is Andrew Jackson," I said, tenderizing the bill. "Known for setting up our Southern relatives for the Trail of Tears. And to keep him company we got two Mr. Hamiltons."

The woman turned shrewd, and took the bills.

"No parties." She held out a key attached to a square of orange plastic.

"Just sex." I could not help but reassure her. But that was talk, big talk from a person with hardly any experience and nothing that resembled a birth-control device. I wasn't one of those so-called studs who couldn't open up their wallets without dropping a foil-wrapped square. No, Lipsha Morrissey was deep at heart a romantic, a wild-minded kind of guy, I told myself, a fool with no letup. I went out to Serena, and took her hand in mine. I was shaking inside but my voice was steady and my hands were cool.

"Let's go in." I showed the key. "Let's not think about tomorrow."

"That's how I got Jason," said Serena.

So we stood there.

"I'll go in," she said at last. "Down two blocks, there's an all-night gas station. They sell 'em."

I went. O.K. Life in this day and age might be less romantic in some ways. It seemed so in the hard twenty-four-hour fluorescent light, as I tried to choose what I needed from the rack by the counter. It was quite a display; there were dazzling choices—textures, shapes. I saw I was being watched, and I suddenly grabbed what was near my hand—two boxes, economy size.

"Heavy date?"

I suppose the guy on the late shift was bored, could not resist. His T-shirt said "Big Sky Country." He was grinning in an ugly way. So I answered.

"Not really. Fixing up a bunch of my white buddies from Montana. Trying to keep down the sheep population."

His grin stayed fixed. Maybe he had heard a lot of jokes about Montana blondes, or maybe he was from somewhere else. I looked at the boxes in my hand, put one back.

"Let me help you out," the guy said. "What you need is a bag of these."

He took down a plastic sack of little oblong party balloons, Day-Glo pinks and oranges and blues.

"Too bright," I said. "My girlfriend's a designer. She hates clashing colors." I was breathing hard suddenly and so was he. Our eyes met and narrowed.

"What does she design?" he said. "Bedsheets?"

"What does yours design?" I said. "Wool sweaters?"

I put money between us. "For your information, my girlfriend's not only beautiful but she and I are the same species."

"Which is?"

"Take the money," I said. "Hand over my change and I'll be out of here. Don't make me do something I'd regret."

"I'd be real threatened." The guy turned from me, ringing up my sale. "I'd be shaking, except I know you Indian guys are chickenshit."

I took my package, took my change.

"Baaaaa," I said, and beat it out of there. It's strange how a bashful kind of person like me gets talkative in some of our less pleasant border-town situations.

I took a roundabout way back to Room 22 and tapped on the door. There was a little window right beside it. Serena peeked through, and let me in.

"Well," I said then, in that awkward interval, "guess we're set."

She took the bag from my hand and didn't say a word, just put it on the little table beside the bed. There were two chairs. Each of us took one. Then we sat down and turned on the television. The romance wasn't in us now for some reason, but there was something invisible that made me hopeful about the room.

It was just a small place, a modest kind of place, clean. You could smell the faint chemical of bug spray the moment you stepped inside. You could look at the television hung on the wall, or examine the picture of golden trees and a waterfall. You could take a shower for a long time in the cement shower stall, standing on your personal shower mat for safety. There was a little tin desk. You could sit down there and write a letter on a sheet of plain paper from the drawer. The lampshade was made of reeds, pressed and laced tight together. The spread on the double mattress was reddish, a rusty cotton material. There was an air-conditioner, with a fan we turned on.

"I don't know why we're here," I said at last. "I'm sorry."

Serena took a small brush from her purse.

"Comb my hair?"

I took the brush and sat on the bed, just behind her. I began at the ends, very careful, but there were hardly any tangles to begin with. Her hair was a quiet brown without variation. My hand followed the brush, smoothing after each stroke, until the fall of her hair was a hypnotizing silk. I could lift my hand away from her head and the hair would follow, electric to my touch, in soft strands that hung suspended until I returned to the brushing. She never moved, except to switch off the light and then the television. She sat down again in the total dark and said, "Please, keep on," so I did. The air got thick. Her hair got lighter, full of blue static, charged so that I was held in place by the attraction. A golden spark jumped on the carpet. Serena turned toward me. Her hair floated down around her at that moment like a tent of energy.

Well, the money part is not related to that. I gave it all to Serena, that's true. Her intention was to buy material and put together the creations that she drew in her notebooks. It was fashion with a Chippewa flair, as she explained it, and sure to win prizes at the state home-ec. contest. She promised to pay me interest when she opened her own shop. The next day, after we had parted, after I had checked out the bar I was supposed to night-watch, I went off to the woods to sit and think. Not about the money, which was Serena's—and good luck to her—but about her and me.

She was two years younger than me, yet she had direction and a child, while I was aimless, lost in hyperspace, using up my talent, which was already fading from my hands. I wondered what our future could hold. One thing was sure: I never knew a man to support his family by playing bingo, and the medicine calls for Lipsha were getting fewer by the week, and fewer, as my touch failed to heal people, fled from me, and lay concealed.

I sat on ground where, years ago, my greats and my great-greats, the Pillagers, had walked. The trees around me were the dense birch and oak of old woods. The lake drifted in, gray waves, white foam in a bobbing lace. Thin gulls lined themselves up on a sandbar. The sky went dark. I closed my eyes, and that is when the little black pony galloped into my mind. It sped across the choppy waves like a skipping stone, its mane a banner, its tail a flag, and vanished on the other side of the shore.

It was luck. Serena's animal. American Horse.

"This is the last night I'm going to try for the van," I told myself. I always kept three twenties stuffed inside the edging of my blanket in back of the bar. Once that stash was gone I'd make a real decision. I'd open the yellow pages at random, and where my finger pointed I would take that kind of job.

Of course, I never counted on winning the van.

I was playing for it on the shaded side of a blackout ticket, which is always hard to get. As usual, I sat with Lulu and her boys. Her vigilance helped me. She let me use her extra dabber and she sat and smoked a filter cigarette, observing the quiet frenzy that was taking place around her. Even though that van had sat on the stage for five months, even though nobody had yet won it and everyone said it was a scam, when it came to playing for it most people bought a couple of tickets. That night, I went all out and purchased eight.

A girl read out the numbers from the hopper. Her voice was clear and light on the microphone. I didn't even notice what was happening—Lulu pointed out one place I had missed on the winning ticket. Then I had just two squares left to make a bingo and I suddenly sweated, I broke out into a chill, I went cold and hot at once. After all my pursuit, after all my plans, I was N-6 and G-60. I had narrowed myself, shrunk into the spaces on the ticket. Each time the girl read a number and it wasn't that 6 or 60 I sickened, recovered, forgot to breathe.

She must have read twenty numbers out before N-6. Then, right after that, G-60 rolled off her lips.

I screamed. I am ashamed to say how loud I yelled. That girl came over, got the manager, and then he checked out my numbers slow and careful while everyone hushed.

He didn't say a word. He checked them over twice. Then he pursed his lips together and wished he didn't have to say it.

"It's a bingo," he finally told the crowd.

Noise buzzed to the ceiling—talk of how close some others had come, green talk—and every eye was turned and cast on me, which was uncomfortable. I never was the center of looks before, not Lipsha, who everybody took for granted around here. Not all those looks were for the good, either. Some were plain envious and ready to believe the first bad thing a sour tongue could pin on me. It made sense in a way. Of all those who'd stalked that bingo van over the long months, I was now the only one who had not lost money on the hope.

O.K., so what kind of man does it make Lipsha Morrissey that the keys did not tarnish his hands one slight degree, and that he beat it out that very night in the van, completing only the basic paperwork? I didn't go after Serena, and I can't tell you why. Yet I was hardly ever happier. In that van, I rode high, but that's the thing. Looking down on others, even if it's only from the seat of a van that a person never really earned, does something to the human mentality. It's hard to say. I changed. After just one evening riding the reservation roads, passing with a swish of my tires, I started smiling at the homemade hot rods, at the clunkers below me, at the old-lady cars nosing carefully up and down the gravel hills.

I started saying to myself that I should visit Serena, and a few nights later I finally did go over there. I pulled into her sister's driveway with a flourish I could not help, as the van slipped into a pothole and I roared the engine. For a moment, I sat in the dark, letting my headlamps blaze alongside the door until Serena's brother-in-law leaned out.

"Cut the lights!" he yelled. "We got a sick child."

I rolled down my window, and asked for Serena.

"It's her boy. She's in here with him." He waited. I did, too, in the dark. A dim light was on behind him and I saw some shadows, a small girl in those pajamas with the feet tacked on, someone pacing back and forth.

"You want to come in?" he called.

But here's the gist of it: I just said to tell Serena hi for me, and then I backed out of there, down the drive, and left her to fend for herself. I could have stayed there. I could have drawn my touch back from wherever it had gone to. I could have offered my van to take Jason to the I.H.S. I could have sat there in silence as a dog guards its mate, its own blood. I could have done something different from what I did, which was to hit the road for Hoopdance and look for a better time.

I cruised until I saw where the party house was located that night. I drove the van over the low curb, into the yard, and I parked there. I watched until I recognized a couple of cars and saw the outlines of Indians and mixed, so I knew that walking in would not involve me in what the newspapers term an episode. The door was white, stained and raked by a dog, with a tiny fan-shaped window. I went through and stood inside. There was movement, a kind of low-key swirl of bright hair and dark hair tossing alongside each other. There were about as many Indians as there weren't. This party was what we call around here a Hairy Buffalo, and most people were grouped around a big brown plastic garbage can that served as the punch bowl for the all-purpose stuff, which was anything that anyone brought, dumped in along with pink Hawaiian Punch. I grew up around a lot of the people, and others I knew by sight. Among those last, there was a young familiar-looking guy.

It bothered me. I recognized him, but I didn't know him. I hadn't been to school with him, or played him in any sport, because I did not play sports. I couldn't think where I'd seen him until later, when the heat went up and he took off his bomber jacket. Then "Big Sky Country" showed, plain letters on a bright-blue background.

I edged around the corner of the room, into the hall, and stood there to argue with myself. Would he recognize me, or was I just another face, a customer? He probably wasn't really from Montana, so he might not even have been insulted by our little conversation, or remember it anymore. I reasoned that he had probably picked up the shirt vacationing, though who would want to go across that border, over to where the world got meaner? I told myself that I should calm my nerves, go back into the room, have fun. What kept me from doing that was the sudden thought of Serena, of our night together and what I had bought and used.

Once I remembered, I was lost to the present moment. One part of me caught up with the other. I realized that I had left Serena to face her crisis, alone, while I took off in my brand new van.

I have a hard time getting drunk. It's just the way I am. I start thinking and forget to fill the cup, or recall something I have got to do, and just end up walking from a party. I have put down a full can of beer before and walked out to weed my grandma's rhubarb patch, or work on a cousin's car. Now I was putting myself in Serena's place, feeling her feelings.

What would he want to do that to me for?

I heard her voice say this out loud, just behind me, where there was nothing but wall. I edged along until I came to a door, and then I went through, into a tiny bedroom full of coats, and so far nobody either making out or unconscious upon the floor. I sat on a pile of parkas and jean jackets in this little room, an alcove in the rising buzz of the party outside. I saw a phone, and I dialled Serena's number. Her sister answered.

"Thanks a lot," she said when I said it was me. "You woke up Jason."

"What's wrong with him?" I asked.

There was a silence, then Serena's voice got on the line. "I'm going to hang up."

"Don't."

"He's crying. His ears hurt so bad he can't stand it."

"I'm coming over there."

"Forget it. Forget you."

She said the money I had loaned her would be in the mail. She reminded me it was a long time since the last time I had called. And then the phone went dead. I held the droning receiver in my hand, and tried to clear my mind. The only thing I saw in it, clear as usual, was the van. I decided this was a sign for me to get in behind the wheel. I should drive straight to Serena's house, put on the touch, help her son out. So I set my drink on the windowsill. Then I slipped out the door and I walked down the porch steps, only to find them waiting.

I guess he had recognized me after all, and I guess he was from Montana. He had friends, too. They stood around the van, and their heads were level with the roof, for they were tall.

"Let's go for a ride," said the one from the all-night gas pump.

He knocked on the window of my van with his knuckles. When I told him no thanks, he started karate-kicking the door. He wore black cowboy boots, pointy-toed, with hard-edged new heels. They left ugly dents everytime he landed a blow.

"Thanks anyhow," I repeated. "But the party's not over." I tried to get back into the house, but, like in a bad dream, the door was stuck, or locked. I hollered, pounded, kicked at the very marks that desperate dog had left, but the music rose and nobody heard. So I ended up in the van. They acted very gracious. They urged me to drive. They were so polite that I tried to tell myself they weren't all that bad. And sure enough, after we had drove for a while, these Montana guys said they had chipped in together to buy me a present.

"What is it?" I asked. "Don't keep me in suspense."

"Keep driving," said the pump jockey.

"I don't really go for surprises," I said. "What's your name, anyhow?"

"Marty."

"I got a cousin named Marty," I said.

"Forget it."

The guys in the back exchanged a grumbling kind of laughter, a knowing set of groans. Marty grinned, turned toward me from the passenger seat.

"If you really want to know what we're going to give you, I'll tell. It's a map. A map of Montana."

Their laughter got wild and went for too long.

"I always liked the state," I said in a serious voice.

"No shit," said Marty. "Then I hope you like sitting on it." He signalled where I should turn, and all of a sudden I realized that Lewey's lay ahead. Lewey ran his Tat-too Den from the basement of his house, kept his equipment set up and ready for the weekend.

"Whoa," I said. I stopped the van. "You can't tattoo a person against his will. It's illegal."

"Get your lawyer on it tomorrow." Marty leaned in close for me to see his eyes. I put the van back in gear but just chugged along, desperately thinking. Lewey was a strange kind of guy, an old Dutch sailor who got beached here, about as far as you can get from salt water. I decided that I'd ask Marty, in a polite kind of way, to beat me up instead. If that failed, I would tell him that there were many states I would not mind so much—smaller, rounder ones.

"Are any of you guys from any other state?" I asked, anxious to trade.

"Kansas."

"South Dakota."

It wasn't that I really had a thing against those places, understand; it's just that the straight-edged shape is not a Chippewa preference. You look around you, and everything you see is round, everything in nature. There are no perfect boundaries, no borders. Only human-made things tend toward cubes and squares—the van, for instance. That was an example. Suddenly I realized that I was driving a wheeled version of the state of North Dakota.

"Just beat me up, you guys. Let's get this over with. I'll stop."

But they laughed, and then we were at Lewey's.

The sign on his basement door said "COME IN." I was shoved from behind and strapped together by five pairs of heavy, football-toughened hands. I was the first to see Lewey, I think, the first to notice that he was not just a piece of all the trash and accumulated junk that washed through the concrete-floored cellar but a person, sitting still as any statue, in a corner, on a chair that creaked and sang when he rose and walked over.

He even looked like a statue—not the type you see in history books, I don't mean those, but the kind you see for sale as you drive along the highway. He was a Paul Bunyan, carved with a chain saw. He was rough-looking, finished in big strokes.

"Please," I said, "I don't want . . ."

Marty squeezed me around the throat and tousled up my hair, like friendly.

"He's just got cold feet. Now remember, Lewey, map of Montana. You know where. And put in a lot of detail."

I tried to scream.

"Like I was thinking," Marty went on, "of those maps we did in grade school showing products from each region. Cows' heads, oil wells, those little sheaves of wheat, and so on."

"Tie him up," said Lewey. His voice was thick, with a commanding formal accent. "Then leave."

They did. They took my pants and the keys to the van. I heard the engine roar and die away, and I rolled from side to side in my strict bindings. I felt Lewey's hand on my shoulder.

"Be still." His voice had changed, now that the others were gone, to a low sound that went with his appearance and did not seem at all unkind. I looked up at him. A broke-down God is who he looked like from my worm's-eye view. His beard was pure white, long and patchy, and his big eyes frozen blue. His head was half bald, shining underneath the brilliant fluorescent tubes in the ceiling. You never know where you're going to find your twin in the world, your double. I don't mean in terms of looks—I'm talking about mind-set. You never know where you're going to find the same thoughts in another brain, but when it happens you know it right off, just like the two of you were connected by a small electrical wire that suddenly glows red-hot and sparks. That's what happened when I met Lewey Koep.

"I don't have a pattern for Montana," he told me. He untied my ropes with a few quick jerks, sneering at the clumsiness of the knots. Then he sat in his desk chair again, and watched me get my bearings.

"I don't want anything tattooed on me, Mr. Koep," I said. "It's a kind of revenge plot."

He sat in silence, in a waiting quiet, hands folded and face composed. By now I knew I was safe, but I had nowhere to go, and so I sat down on a pile of magazines. He asked, "What revenge?" and I told him the story, the whole thing right from the beginning, when I walked into the bingo hall. I left out the personal details about Serena and me, but he got the picture. I told him about the van.

"That's an unusual piece of good fortune."

"Have you ever had any? Good fortune?"

"All the time. Those guys paid plenty, for instance, though I suppose they'll want it back. You pick out a design. You can owe me."

He opened a book he had on the table, a notebook with plastic pages that clipped in and out, and handed it over to me. I didn't want a tattoo, but I didn't want to disappoint this man, either. I leafed through the dragons and the hearts, thinking how to refuse, and then suddenly I saw the horse. It was the same picture that had come into my head as I sat in the woods. Now here it was. The pony skimmed, legs outstretched, reaching for the edge of the page. I got a thought in my head, clear and vital, that this little horse would convince Serena I was serious about her.

"This one."

Lewey nodded, and heated his tools.

That's why I got it put on, that little horse, and suffered pain. Now my hand won't let me rest. It throbs and aches as if it was coming alive again after a hard frost had made it numb. I know I'm going somewhere, taking this hand to Serena. Even walking down the road in a pair of big-waisted green pants belonging to Lewey Koep, toward the So Long Bar, where I keep everything I own in life, I'm going forward. My hand is a ball of pins, but when I look down I see the little black horse running hard, fast, and serious.

I'm ready for what will come next. That's why I don't fall on the ground, and I don't yell, when I come across the van in a field. At first, I think it is the dream van, the way I always see it in my vision. Then I look, and it's the real vehicle. Totalled.

My bingo van is smashed on the sides, kicked and scratched, and the insides are scattered. Stereo wires, glass, and ripped pieces of carpet are spread here and there among the new sprouts of wheat. I force open a door that is bent inward. I wedge myself behind the wheel, which is tipped over at a crazy angle, and I look out. The windshield is shattered in a sunlight burst, through which the world is cut to bits.

I've been up all night, and the day stretches long before me, so I decide to sleep where I am. Part of the seat is still wonderfully upholstered, thick and plush, and it reclines now—permanently, but so what? I relax into the small comfort, my body as warm as an animal, my thoughts drifting. I know I'll wake to nothing, but at this moment I feel rich. Sinking away, I feel like everything worth having is within my grasp. All I have to do is put my hand into the emptiness.

JOY HARJO
(1951-)

Born into the Creek community in Tulsa, Oklahoma, Joy Harjo attended the University of New Mexico. She then studied at the University of Iowa, where she received an M.F.A. in 1978. Her first collection of poetry was published in 1975 and three years later she received her first fellowship from the National Endowment for the Arts. Her fourth collection, In Mad Love and War, *was awarded the William Carlos Williams Award from the Poetry Society of America and the American Book Award from the Before Columbus Foundation. Joy Harjo has taught at Arizona State University, the Institute of American Indian Arts, the University of Colorado, and the University of New Mexico. In addition to her writing, she plays saxophone and performs with the band Poetic Justice. In 1998, she received a Lila Wallace–Reader's Digest Fund Writer's Award to work with a nonprofit group that brings literary resources to Native-American communities.*

Harjo's poem "Remember" from her 1983 collection She Had Some Horses *displays her chacteristic lyric and rhythmic qualities, as well as her sense of the human connection to nature. She calls us to remember not what has happened to us, but the spiritual context in which everything happens.*

REMEMBER

Remember the sky that you were born under,
know each of the star's stories.
Remember the moon, know who she is.
Remember the sun's birth at dawn, that is the
strongest point of time. Remember sundown
and the giving away to night.
Remember your birth, how your mother struggled
to give you form and breath. You are evidence of
her life, and her mother's, and hers.
Remember your father. He is your life, also.
Remember the earth whose skin you are:
red earth, black earth, yellow earth, white earth
brown earth, we are earth.
Remember the plants, trees, animal life who all have their
tribes, their families, their histories, too. Talk to them,
listen to them. They are alive poems.
Remember the wind. Remember her voice. She knows the
origin of this universe.
Remember you are all people and all people are you.
Remember you are this universe and this
universe is you.
Remember all is in motion, is growing, is you.
Remember language comes from this.
Remember the dance language is, that life is.
Remember.

HANAY GEIOGAMAH
(1945-)

Hanay Geiogamah, a playwright and a leading figure in Native-American theater, was born in Lawton, Oklahoma. He studied journalism at the University of Oklahoma, and then theater and drama at Indiana University, where he received a B.A. in 1980. He has worked as artistic director for the Native American Theater Ensemble, Native Americans in the Arts, and the American Indian Dance Theater. He has also taught at Colorado College, the University of Washington, and the University of California, Los Angeles.

Foghorn, like most of Geiogamah's short plays, makes use of theatrical techniques that imitate the fluidity of film. Within this style, the play is both a critical exploration of historical stereotypes of Native Americans and a critique of the images developed to counter them.

FOGHORN

The People of the Play

NARRATOR, a spokesman for the Indians
NUN
ALTAR BOY
SCHOOLTEACHER, circa 1900, in stars and stripes skirt
THE PRINCESS POCAHONTAS
POCAHONTAS'S HANDMAIDENS, three or four
LONE RANGER
TONTO
FIRST LADY OF THE UNITED STATES
U.S. GOVERNMENT SPY
VOICE OF THE SPY'S CONTACT (can be acted)
BULL
GIRL (reading treaties)

Wild West Show

SHOW CARD GIRL
HEAD WARRIOR
TWO INDIAN BRAVES (performing "hand-to-hand" combat)
TWO CHIEFS AND ASSORTED BRAVES (for Indian war council)
INDIAN INTERPRETER
LOVELY WHITE MAIDEN (wearing bright blonde wig)
LECHEROUS INDIAN MAN (who chases her)

Music

ELECTRONIC COMPOSITION FOR JOURNEY (4 or 5 minutes)
ZUNI SUNRISE CHANT
PLAINS INDIAN WAR DANCE SONG
VERY LOFTY CHURCH-ORGAN MUSIC (Nun Scene)
GOOD MORNING TO YOU (Schoolteacher Scene)
THE STAR SPANGLED BANNER (Schoolteacher Scene)
THE INDIAN LOVE CALL (Pocahontas Scene)
WILLIAM TELL OVERTURE ("Lone Ranger" Theme)
AMERICA THE BEAUTIFUL (First Lady Scene)
PASS THAT PEACE PIPE (AND BURY THAT HATCHET) (Special Arrangement)
WILD WEST SHOW ACCOMPANIMENT (special composition on show organ or piano; mock drumming rhythms for Indian Council of War, Authentic Indian War Dance, and Savage Brutal Scalp Dance. Old-fashioned piano for chasing of Lovely White Maiden.)
THE AIM SONG ("Indian people will be free When we win at Wounded Knee")

Author's Note

Almost all the characters in this play are stereotypes pushed to the point of absurdity. The satire proceeds by playful mockery rather than bitter denunciation. A production should aim at a light, almost frivolous effect (the basic seriousness of the play will emerge all the more effectively if the heavy hand is avoided). The actors should never appear to be preaching, nor should they strive too much for laughs; they should simply let them occur.

It is vital that there be a minimum of delay between scenes. The drilling sounds and the visuals of earth being drilled form a bridge between scenes, but they should be kept brief.

The stage can be decorated to reflect a mixture of the prison yard on Alcatraz Island during the 1969–71 occupation; the terrain around Wounded Knee, South Dakota, during the 1973 incident; a composite Indian reservation; and various national monuments across the United States, such as Mount Rushmore and the Jefferson Memorial. The visuals are intended to counterpoint the action and to give a feeling that the audience is actually present yet not directly participating in the action of the play.

It is desirable that the actors know how to sing, for live performance of the songs makes for a much stronger production. Some of the songs, such as "Pass That Peace Pipe and Bury That Hatchet," can be recorded on tape and the performance synchronized with them. The Wild West Show composition should almost certainly be taped. All traditional drumming should be performed live if possible.

It is not important if the audience can see offstage into the wings or if other elements of the production are exposed. The actors should pay no attention to this informality and take any accidents that may occur in their stride.

There should be a lot of color, but not so riotous that it distracts the attention of the audience. Props should be of slapstick proportions in the Nun, Peace Pipe, and Wild West Show scenes.

1

The opening section of the play, until the appearance of the religious personnel, is performed against a background of progressive electronic sound, one that evokes a journey through time and space, perhaps composed on a synthesizer or possibly with string instruments and percussion. The performing group follows a stylized choreography that is patterned to follow the electronic score. The "parts" are distributed among members of the performing group who form an ensemble for the production. They carry bundles of belongings, pull travois, and so forth. The costumes and movement should suggest a forced journey, such as the Trail of Tears, spanning the centuries from 1492 to the present and stretching geographically from the West Indies to Alcatraz Island. The delivery of the first six statements must be timed as a narration for the journey, and must convey an evolving attitude toward Indians. If enough performers are available, the company members can portray the Spanish sailor, senator, and others in spotlighted areas about the stage. Or the lines can be recorded on tape with the electronic score.

The stage is dark. Suddenly a large, painted Indian face appears, apparitionlike, moving slowly as it is projected about the stage, its eyes gazing toward the audience. The electronic music begins.

SPANISH SAILOR
  (*very excited*) ¡Señor Capitan Columbus! ¡Mire! ¡Mire! ¡Mire! ¡Alla! ¡Mire! ¡Dios mio!
  ¡Estos hombres, cho-co-la-tes! ¡Los indios! ¡Los indios! ¡Ellos son los indios!

*The face fades as lights come up dimly, revealing the performing group frozen in
position onstage. They begin moving slowly as the electronic journey music resumes.*

MALE SETTLER
  You're only an Injun. Don't talk back! (*now louder*)
  You're only an Injun! Don't talk back!

*Sounds of mixed gunfire: rifles, old muskets, and so forth, followed by a pause. Then
more gunfire.*

TWO WHITE MEN
  (*voices colliding*) Vermin! Varmits! Vermin! Varmits! Vermin! Varmits!

Electronic journey music, group movement.

FEMALE SETTLER
  Filthy savages. Murderers! Scalpers!

Electronic journey music, group movement.

ANGRY MALE VIGILANTE
  I say let's force 'em off the land! Move 'em with force, guns! Now!

*Electronic journey music, group movement, mixed gunshots, high volume. Electronic
journey music and group movement continue. More gunshots. Electronic journey
music and group movement now becoming fragmented.*

UNITED STATES SENATOR
  The Indian problem is a matter for the courts and the Congress to deal with.
  We've been victorious over them on the battlefield, now they must settle on the
  reservations we have generously set aside for them. They have stood in the way
  of our great American Manifest Destiny long enough.

Electronic journey music concludes as performers exit.

2

*The performing group returns to the stage one by one as a panoramic view of Alca-
traz Island is projected onto the cyclorama or back wall of the playing area. Photographs of the occupation are seen in a dissolving sequence as the group sings the
Zuni Sunrise Chant.*

GROUP
  Following a leader, with respectful expressions
  BAH HEY BA HO
  BAH HEY BA HO

EYE YA NE NAH WAY
EE I YA HO. I YA HO WAY.
SHEY-NE NAH-WAY.

BAH HO. BA HEY.
BA HO. BA HEY.

NARRATOR

Thanksgiving Day, 1969. Alcatraz Island, San Francisco Bay. We are discovered, again. It was the first time that we had taken back land that already was ours. Indian people everywhere felt good about our having the island, about our determination.

The visuals continue, their projection punctured by the silhouettes of the performing group members, who stand attentively about the playing area.

We planned to develop the island, to build a cultural and spiritual center for all tribes, all people. Nineteen months. It was a good beginning.

Alcatraz fades. A gigantic map of the United States, blank except for delineations of the Indian reservations, comes into focus. The performing group now pantomimes boarding a boat, sailing across the bay. A low flute is heard. The players form a phalanx across the front of the stage as they disembark, and the narrator moves to downstage center.

NARRATOR

We, the Native Americans, reclaim this land, known as America, in the name of all American Indians, by right of discovery. We wish to be fair and honorable with the Caucasian inhabitants of this land, who as a majority wrongfully claim it as theirs, and hereby pledge that we shall give to the majority inhabitants of this country a portion of the land for their own, to be held in trust by the American Indian people—for as long as the sun shall rise and the rivers go down to the sea! We will further guide the majority inhabitants in the proper way of living. We will offer them our religion, our education, our way of life—in order to help them achieve our level of civilization and thus raise them and all their white brothers from their savage and unhappy state.

3

The performing group loudly sings and drums a Plains Indian War Dance song in celebration. When the singing ends, an organ blasts out church music, bringing on a Catholic nun and Indian altar boy, who carries a cross covered with paper money. Members of the performing group, wrapped in blankets and with poker-faced expressions, take places right and left of the nun and altar boy who are standing stage center, smiling.

NUN

(*As church music fades, she speaks first calmly, then gradually up to a frenzy.*)

My blessed savages.
Children of the unknown, of the wilderness.

You are most fortunate that we have found you.

You have been smiled favorably upon by the holy father in Rome.

He has seen fit to send us out to this New World to impart the divine wisdom of God to you. (*She pauses, fondles her book, then raises it in front of the Indians.*)

This book contains all of His holy teachings.

I am going to give His teachings to you.

For no soul must be without knowledge of the Almighty.

No soul must be allowed to wander in the darkness, as yours have for so long, and never know the Kingdom of God.

You do not have religion!

You do not have an all-forgiving father like ours.

You are heathens.

Pagans.

Poor, miserable, ignorant, uncivilized, NAKED!

(*She calms herself.*)

We are going to take you out of this darkness and show you His way. And you will be happy and grateful, forever, that we have found you.

Our faith, our beautiful faith, that has been the salvation of so many millions of souls, will now be yours.

For without faith in God, the one, true Christian God, you will never have the hope of becoming civilized, of knowing a way of life other than this pitiful existence of yours.

And!

If we did not find you, your souls would burn! Burn forever, for eternity! In HELL!

She and the altar boy, who has been raising and lowering the cross behind her as she is speaking, now stand triumphantly before the group. The Indians attack them as the church music blasts through the theater. Then a sharp drilling noise is heard, the lights flash, and action visuals of giant chunks of earth flying through space are projected on the playing area.

4

A clownish schoolteacher dances onstage, ringing a bell, carrying a bundle of small American flags, singing "Good Morning to You." She has been preceded by a group of very young Indian students who run onstage playfully, taking seats on two wooden benches. They respond to the teacher with awe, surprise, mild defiance, and fear. The teacher is snobbish, nervous, rude, feisty, and blusterous.

TEACHER

(*very overdone, but with control*) Good morning, boys and girls, er, squaws and bucks. Good morning.

(*She puts the bell down, fusses with her hair and dress. The students pay no attention. She becomes angry.*)

G—ood morning, savages! (*She busily arranges them in "order."*) I see that this is going to be more difficult than they told me it would be. You are all totally ignorant. You might as well be deaf and dumb! Do any of you understand any English? Not a single one of you?

(*to the audience*) I wonder if the people in Washington really know what they're doing by trying to teach these savages how to speak English, how to live like civilized human beings. These stupid children should be left on their reservations and forgotten about. What a bunch of worthless things.

(*She sees one of the girls gesture to one of the others, and pummels the girls, who pulls back wide-eyed with surprise.*) What are you doing there? What was that? Was that an Indian sign-language gesture I saw you making there? Was it? Was it sign language? Well, there won't be any more of that in this classroom, none of that! I'll rap your knuckles hard if you do that again. Do you hear me? Do you understand me? It'll be the dark room for you. (*pause*) That's one step out of savagery for you.

(*Suddenly pinching her nose in broad gesture*) Ooooooooh, oooooh! What an odor! (*She lifts the blanket of a girl pupil.*) Oooooohweeeeee, young lady, ooooohweeeee! You don't smell like a white woman! You smell like a . . . like . . . a . . . Oh, my goodness, you are going to have to learn how to take a nice, civilized ladylike bath and keep your body clean. Do you hear me? That will be another step out of your darkness!

(*looking in one of the boys' hair*) Oh, heavens alive! Oh, good heavens! Nits! Nits! Oh, and they're alive, they're real! Oh, oh! Lice! How disgusting, how utterly disgusting! (*She scratches herself wildly.*) Well, this can be easily solved. Everyone of you, everyone of you will have your hair cut off tonight. Tonight! Girls and boys. We will not have a bunch of lousy Indians in this classroom! No, oh, no!

(*after a short pause*) Sign language! Stinking bodies! Blankets! Deaf and dumb! How did these people ever get themselves in this condition?

The students are giggling again, she reestablishes order, continues.

You Indians are going to become educated, educated! That's spelled E-D-U-C-A-T-E-D, ed-u-ca-ted! Here in this school you are going to learn the English language. You are going to learn how to be Christians, how to worship God and live a clean, wholesome, decent life. You are going to learn how to be civilized people, civilized Indians, Indians who can earn an honest living, Indians that the American people can be proud of, not shamed by, so that we can hold our heads up high and say, "They are just like us, they are civilized. They aren't wild and on the warpath anymore. They are living the American way."

(*She sings a line of "Star Spangled Banner," then sees the girl make the gesture again, lunges at her, yanks up the child, shouts directly into her face.*) This is not the reservation, child! This is not that awful place you came from where you all run around half naked, filthy, living in sin! This is a white man's schoolhouse. I told you not to do that again. I told you what I'd do. (*She shakes the child violently.*) You are going to be a lesson for the others. You, child, are going to be punished. (*She pulls out a bottle of castor oil and pours it down the struggling child's mouth.*) It's the dark room for you. (*She pushes the child into a dark closet space.*) You will stay in here all day. No food! No water! And no toilet! (*turns to others*) She is a lesson for all of you to follow. I caught her doing a sign-language gesture. No more of that in this classroom, do you hear me? You are going to forget all of your Indian ways, all of them. You can start erasing them from your minds right now, right here, right this instant. No more of your disgusting sign language. No more of your savage tongue. No more greasy, lousy hair. No more blankets. You are going to learn the English language. That is what you were brought here for. (*turning to the audience*) The English language. The most beautiful language in all the world. The language that has brought hope and civilization to people everywhere. The one true language, OUR language!

(*Quickly turning her back to the students*) Now, listen to me carefully, very carefully. I am going to teach you your first word of English. Listen carefully, for it is the word, the one word, you must know first to become civilized. You must say this word to all of the white people you see, all of them, men and ladies. They'll be proud of you when they hear you say it, yes, proud, and when they hear you say it, they'll know that you are being relieved of your savage, uncivilized ways. They'll smile back at you and say the same thing. All right? Okay? Listen closely. The word is hell-o. Hell-o. H-E-L-L-O. Hello. Listen to the way I say it. Hello. Hell-o. It's the first word of the American way. The American way begins with hello. Say it, children, say it. Hell-O. Hell-O.

One of the pupils timidly tries the word and giggles as the others show amusement. The teacher hears her, yanks her to the front of the class with much flourish.

She said it! She said it! She said the word. She's on the road to the American way now! She said hello!

The teacher hands the girl a small American flag, then takes it back to demonstrate how to wave it while repeating hello. The girl clowns crudely with the flag in her hand as the teacher turns to coax the class one by one to say hello. The students ape the teacher with strong gestures as she continues to instruct the remaining students. The teacher soars on her success. The pupils form into a tight group, fists clenched, close in on her, and attack. The lights fade on the drilling sound, earth visuals.

5

The Princess Pocahontas runs onstage carrying flowers and singing "The Indian Love Call." Her handmaidens follow, giggling. As Pocahontas flutters about, the handmaidens seat themselves in a semicircle for gossip.

HANDMAIDENS
   (*very eager*) How was it, Princess Pocahontas? How was it? Tell us.
POCAHONTAS
   (*a languid smile on her face*) I couldn't take my eyes off him when I first saw him. He was so . . . so . . . ooh!

The handmaidens twitter excitedly, Pocahontas flutters back and forth.

HANDMAIDENS

So, so what, Pocahontas? Tell us, please.

POCAHONTAS

(*gesturing with her hands*) He was so . . . big. Ooooooh, uuuh.

HANDMAIDENS

(*puzzled*) Big? How do you mean, Pocahontas, big?

POCAHONTAS

(*enjoying the handmaidens' curiosity*) He had such big legs. Such big, uh, arms, such big, uh, uh, chest. Such big, big head. Such big, big hands. Such big, big feet. Such big eyes. Such big mouth. Such big ears. Ooooooh, aaahaaa.

HANDMAIDENS

And? And?

POCAHONTAS

And his hat was big. And his cape was big. And his boots and his sword and his. . . . And all of the other white men with him were big. Oooooooh, uuuh.

The handmaidens squeal loudly as they pant for more details.

POCAHONTAS

(*eyes becoming dreamy*) Be quiet and I will tell you about the big captain. The big, big captain.

The handmaidens calm down, move in closer to hear.

POCAHONTAS

First, first he took me to his dwelling and he seemed, uh, kind of, of nervous about me being with him. He told one of the other captains that nobody was to . . . to come into the hut. This made me a little bit afraid at first, but he took hold of my hand and smiled at me. He kept smiling at me, and then he asked me, he asked me if I was a . . . a . . . vir-gin. When he said enough so that I knew what he was talking about, I . . . I said to him, "Yes, yes, I am a vir-gin." When I said this, he seemed to get kind of nervous, excited. He looked at me deeply with his big blue eyes and told me that he was . . . in . . . in *luff* with me and he wanted me to . . . to . . . know his body and that he wanted to know, know my body too. Then he pulled me gently down on the bed and began to put his lips on mine. He did this several times, and each time his breathing became more, more nervous, like he was getting very warm. Then he began to kiss my neck and my cheeks. (*The handmaidens urge her on.*) And then he touched my breasts. And then he stood up, suddenly, and began to take off his clothes. He took off his boots, his shirt, his pants, all that he was wearing. He stood over me, his big, big, big body naked like one of the little children. There was so much hair on his body, it made me a little afraid. (*She giggles to herself.*)

HANDMAIDENS

(*interrupting*) Did you . . . did you take off . . . ?

POCAHONTAS

Yes, I did, slowly, I didn't know what . . . I was doing, but I felt happy and warm and . . .

One of the older handmaidens casts an unbelieving glance to one of her companions on the last remark.

HANDMAIDENS
Yes, yes! Tell us all of it!

POCAHONTAS
And the big captain was standing above me, looking down at me, breathing like a boy after a footrace, and I saw that his . . .

The handmaidens huddle closely with Pocahontas for the intimate details. One of them pops up, exclaiming "Pink?" Then Pocahontas rises above them, lifts her arms in a manner to suggest an erect phallus. The handmaidens gasp. Then a kazoo whistle indicates that the erection falls quickly, and the handmaidens explode with laughter.

POCAHONTAS
(*fighting for their attention*) He said to me, I love you, dear Pocahontas. I promise you it won't happen the next time, I promise, I promise, I promise.

The lights fade on the handmaidens squealing with laughter. Drilling sound, earth visuals.

6

Tonto and the Lone Ranger enter with horse-riding pantomime as a piano thumps out familiar Lone Ranger theme. Piano stops and starts, giving Tonto an opportunity to make mocking gestures toward the Lone Ranger. Entrance music ends; they dismount. Lone Ranger takes a seat, exhales, motions to Tonto to shine his boots.

LONE RANGER
(*worried*) You know, Tonto, I've been thinking.

TONTO
(*impassively*) Kemo Sabay.

LONE RANGER
I've been thinking, Tonto. The way you always bail me out of the crisis right at the last minute with your clever thinking sure doesn't look too good for me. You know what I mean? It looks maybe like I'm not too smart having to rely on an illiterate Injun like you to do all the clever thinking, and even outsmarting the white man.

TONTO
(*briskly shining the boots*) Kemo Sabay.

LONE RANGER
Tonto, can you think of any way that I can come to your rescue and save you from the hands of death? Just once, Tonto? I'm really feeling insecure about this, old partner. You always come up with something good.

TONTO
Kemo Sabay.

LONE RANGER
People might start losing faith in me if they keep seeing you doing all the smart stuff. It's bad for business, Tonto.

TONTO
(*shifting to Lone Ranger's other boot*) Kemo Sabay.

LONE RANGER

(*inspired*) I got it! I got it! (*piano interlude suggesting wickedness, villainy*) Tonto, you get shot, real badly, right smack in the chest by a no-good Injun varmit who says you stole his squaw. You're about to die, and I find you. I get you to a friendly rancher's house, one where they'll let me bring my Injun friend inside, and do an operation on you to remove the bullet. How's that, Tonto?

TONTO

Kemo Sabay.

LONE RANGER

(*excited*) You're just about to bleed to death, and I know all this doctor's learning about surgery. Your life is fast slipping away. I'm trying hard to save you, me in my mask and my doctor's outfit and my scalpel and other tools, and suddenly you rise up to tell me which aorta in your heart to bypass, and the shock from this kills you instantly, and you fall back, dead. And, and, and I say: "I did what I could for my Injun friend, I tried to save him. I almost did, but he killed himself before I could finish the operation." How's that? Huh, Tonto, how's that? That'll show I'm not so reliant on you, right? It'd be the end of the Lone Ranger and Tonto, his faithful Injun companion. Then, there'd be just the Lone Ranger. How's that, Tonto? Sound like it'll work to you?

The Lone Ranger stands staring out toward the audience, caught up by the story. Tonto rises from the floor, taps him lightly on the shoulder, he turns, and Tonto cuts his throat with a knife. Drilling sound on tape, earth visuals, lights out fast.

7

The performing group becomes an audience for a dedication ceremony. "America the Beautiful" is heard, then scattered applause, all on tape.

DEEP MALE VOICE

(*velvety and awestruck, on tape*) Ladies and gentlemen, I give you, the First Lay—dee of the United States.

Thunderous applause.

FIRST LADY

(*A bit daffy and with fluttery happiness "to be here."*) Thank you. Thank yooou. I want to say right away that I have never seen such lovely, stoic faces as those of our Indian friends here with us today. Just look at those beautiful facial lines, those high cheekbones, those wonderfully well-rounded lips, those big dark eyes. And their costumes. Aren't they simply tooo beautiful? Let's-give-them-a-big-hand-ladies-and-gentlemen, let's give-them-a-big-hand. (*The Indians applaud, rib each other.*) Their radiance has made this day truly one to remember.

(*She clears her throat, quickly checks her makeup.*) I know, I just know they are going to be wonderful assets to the new national recreational park which I am here with you today to dedicate. In the next few years, there will be hundreds-of-pretty-pictures-of-these-colorful, uh, Indian natives, taken-here-in-this-neeyew park of ours, adding the excitement of a great outdoors vacation in the great American West to family photo albums in homes all across our land. Isn't-that-wonderful?

Applause cut short on tape, she fidgets nervously, smiles widely, hurries on with her speech.

The idea for this new park came directly from my husband, the pres-i-dent, and his assistant, the secretary of the interior. The three of us were having tea and ladyfingers in my sitting room in the family quarters of the White House, discussing ways to beautify America, and the secretary said to the pres-i-dent, "Mr. Pres-i-dent, I have a great idea. As you know sir, some of nature's most spectacular scenery is located right on many of the Indian reservations out West. Why don't we declare one of these reservations as a national park?

(*pause*) It'll be a first. (*There is a stir in the Indian group.*) The Indians get very little use of them anyway. The pres-i-dent said he thought it was a great idea, and time an entire Indian reservation be made a national park.

INDIAN

(*with prop camera in hand, interrupting*) Hey, First Lady, would you smile for me?

FIRST LADY

Why, why I'd be mighty happy to.

She strikes a lavish pose as the Indian clicks his shutter. A puff of smoke, sparks fly, the First Lady lets out a very ladylike scream. The Indians break up. Drilling sound, lights out, earth visuals.

8

The lights reveal an isolated telephone booth at corner stage left. Flashes of light pepper the distant background. A racing siren wails faintly. A suggestion of the Washington Monument can also be seen in the shadowy background. A man comes on, wrapped in an Indian blanket, and anxiously enters the telephone booth.

SPY

(*dialing furtively*) My God! Those damned Indians are crazier than the Afghans, the Congolese, the . . .

His call number goes through, the sound of the telephone clicking musically comes on tape.

VOICE

Hell . . . o. White . . . uh, excuse me, I mean, thank you for calling, and how is the weather today?

SPY

I'm not worried about the weather, pal. Who is this? Dwight? Gordon? Bob? Who? Which one of you guys am I talking with?

VOICE

You . . . you know better than to refer directly to . . . uh, uh, the names of the innocent, oh, excuse me, I mean, certain individuals. Haven't we warned you enough times about doing that?

SPY

Be serious. Who would dare listen in on a direct call to the White House? How could anybody be smart enough to tape, I mean tap, this call box? (*confusion*) Wait a minute. I'm not calling to argue about that, my friend, you know I'm here on assignment. The Indians are going to blow the hell out of the Bureau of Indian Affairs building any time now. They have every kind of revolutionary armament and defensive device you can think of in that place. The entire joint is wired. I managed to infiltrate by wrapping a blanket around myself and putting on a braided wig. I look pretty convincing.

VOICE

What tribe were you passing for? Oh, never mind!

SPY

(*pleased*) As a matter of fact, I thought I looked like a Sioux (*pronounces it "Si-ox"*) or an Apache.

VOICE

And what is your reading of the situation? The boss has no time to devote to this matter just now. You know the election is just two days away. It cannot be blown. Do you understand that?

SPY

Yes, yes, yes! You know I understand. I'm just trying to be helpful, that's all. Helpful as long as you pay me, goddammit!

VOICE

Please, don't use profanity on this line!

SPY

Oh, excuse me, I forgot I was talking to the White . . . oh!

VOICE

Don't say it!

SPY

Okay! Okay! Now listen, the only way we can save the building and prevent a bloody massacre of all those Indians and head off an explosive situation which could turn into an extremely embarrassing mess for the administration in the eyes of the world is to . . .

VOICE

Yes, we're waiting.

SPY

Is to bribe 'em, buy 'em off! (*He looks around to see if he is being watched.*)

VOICE

How do you mean that? With beads, blankets, and whiskey?

SPY

No, hell no, dammit!

VOICE

Stop cursing, please!

SPY

No, no, we pay them cash, cold, hard cash. You know what that is, don't you? I know you do.

VOICE

> How much?

SPY

> I managed to do some figuring while I was inside the building. If my figures are correct, Indians are about two-thirds of one percent of the total population of the country, right? So, give them something like, uh, $66,500. Say to the press it's for travel expenses, to get the Indians back to their reservations. The public'll be impressed that even the poor old Indians are getting a little of the dole from Washington. Deliver the money to them in a briefcase. Or two if it all won't fit into one. Get it in and get out quick.

VOICE

> (*indignant*) Hush money?

SPY

> No, perfectly legal. Travel expenses. They're all government consultants. You can put it down as that.

VOICE

> And yourself, how much for you?

SPY

> My fee for this national security operation will be $250,000, in cold, cold, hard, hard cash, of course.

VOICE

> (*disbelief*) Two hundred and fifty . . .

SPY

> (*cutting him off*) You heard me, $250,000, in cold, hard cash!

VOICE

> If we had to we could raise that, no problem. But we, we could use troops and tear gas to get those redskins out; why pay them? This is an unnecessary extravagance, highway robbery, plain old extortion.

SPY

> Who says so?

VOICE

> Well, you're getting more than the Indians will get, if this outrageously expensive transaction is approved.

SPY

> This is dangerous work. I could have been scalped or killed if I had been caught in my disguise. And besides, the election will be in two days. You don't want a big bloody mess over here to foul things up, do you?

VOICE

> Hang up now. I'll have to check this out with the Committee to Re . . . oh, pardon me, please. I need to consult my superiors. We'll be right back to you.

SPY

> Don't take all night. This is an explosive situation over here. The specters of death and disaster are everywhere in the air. Have you ever been in the middle of a wild mob of hot-blooded warriors, buddy?

VOICE

> Thank you so much for the weather report, Mr. Smith, uh, Jones.

Spy hangs up, looks again to see if he is watched. Phone rings intermittently.

SPY

This is Neptune. The fish are running.

VOICE

What kind of fish?

SPY

Red snappers.

VOICE

The word is go. We'll make the arrangements on this end to get the money to the Indians. It will look very proper. The public knows how money-happy all Indians are, so miserable and poor, and our most isolated minority. They'll do anything to get their hands on some. Giving them money is a wonderful way to show them and the voters how much this administration cares. How do we get yours to you?

SPY

The usual way.

VOICE

Thank you for this weather report.

SPY

Sure, any time.

He hangs up, steps outside the booth, is showered with money. Drilling sound, earth visuals. Lights out.

9

The performing group lines up in a choreographed pattern as the piano begins "Pass That Peace Pipe."* Between each of the stanzas of the song, delivered as a wild production number, an actor wearing a bull's head is spotlighted with a pretty girl in pigtails, who reads from a giant roll of toilet tissue. The bull also holds a roll, and unwinds enough tissue to wipe his behind each time a treaty is called out.

CHORUS

IF YOUR TEMPER'S GETTIN' THE TOP HAND

ALL YOU GOTTA DO IS JUST STOP AND

PASS THAT PEACE PIPE AND BURY THAT HATCHET

LIKE THE CHOCTAWS, CHICKASAWS, CHATTAHOOCHIES,

CHIPPEWAS DO!

GIRL

(leading the bull to front of stage)

THE TREATY OF ATOKA!

(action)

THE TREATY OF NEW ECHOTA!

(action)

THE TREATY OF DANCING RABBIT CREEK.

(action)

THE TREATY OF 1851.

(*action*)

CHORUS

IF YOU'RE FEELIN' MAD AS A WET HEN

MAD AS YOU CAN POSSIBLY GET, THEN

PASS THAT PEACE PIPE AND BURY THAT TOMAHAWK

LIKE THOSE CHICHIMECS, CHEROKEES, CHEPULTEPECS,

TOO!

GIRL

THE TREATY OF MEDICINE LODGE CREEK!

(*action*)

THE TREATY OF PORT ELLIOTT!

(*action*)

THE TREATY OF THE LITTLE ARKANSAS!

(*action*)

THE TREATY OF FORT WISE!

(*action*)

CHORUS

DON'T BE CRANKY, TRY TO USE A LITTLE RESTRAINT

FOLD THAT HANKY, AND WIPE OFF ALL OF THAT WAR PAINT!

AND IF YOU FIND YOURSELF IN A FURY, BE YOUR

    OWN JUDGE AND YOUR OWN JURY!

PASS THAT PEACE PIPE AND BURY THAT HATCHET

LIKE THE CHOCTAWS, CHICKASAWS, CHATTAHOOCHIES,

CHIPPEWAS, DO!

GIRL

THE TREATY OF FORT LARAMIE!

(*action*)

THE TREATY OF MEDICINE LODGE!

(*action*)

THE TREATY OF FORT KLAMATH!

(*action*)

AND THE TREATY OF POINT NO POINT!

(*action*)

CHORUS

WRITE THAT APOLOGY, AND DISPATCH IT,

WHEN YOU'VE QUARRELED, IT'S BETTER TO PATCH IT.

PASS THAT PEACE PIPE AND BURY THAT HATCHET

LIKE THE CHOCTAWS, CHICKASAWS, CHATTAHOOCHIES, CHIPPEWAS,

AND THOSE CHICHIMECS, CHEROKEES, CHEPULTEPECS,

AND THOSE CHICUTIMEES, CHEPECHETS AND CHICAPEES,

CHO-CHOS, CHANGOS, CHATTANOOGAS, CHEECAROWS, DO!

Drilling sound, earth visuals, lights

10

The choreography and music for this Wild West Show sequence provides the performing group members wide latitude for clowning. A girl in flimsy costume runs onstage with a show card to announce each scene. (The show cards will read: WILD APACHES; INDIAN COUNCIL OF WAR; LOVELY WHITE MAIDEN; SCALP DANCE; *and* TRIUMPH OF THE WHITES.) *The Indians wear fake war bonnets, ride stick horses and yelp war whoops.*

ANNOUNCER'S VOICE
(*on tape*) COMING SOON! COMING SOON! TO THE OLYMPIC THEATER! DIRECTLY FROM THEIR HOMES IN THE WILD, WILD WEST!! THE WI—LD APACHES OF ARIZONA!

(*music up, Indians ride onstage.*) Stalwart Braves and Squaws, Without Doubt the Finest Specimens of the Aborigines Ever Seen in this City in a Live Show of this Kind! THIS ENTERTAINMENT WILL CONSIST OF A SERIES OF STIRRING TABLEAUX, INTENSELY AND ACCU-RATELY ILLUSTRATIVE OF INDIAN MODES AND CUSTOMS, NEVER BEFORE SO FAITHFULLY SET FORTH!!

(*music up*)
See Unbelievable, Breathtaking Scenes
Of Thrilling Hand-To-Hand Combat.
A True-To-Life Indian Council of War!
Featuring Speeches in the Actual Indian Tongues,
By the Noted Chiefs and Braves.
The Breaking of the Arrow!

(*music up*)
An original, authentic WAAARRR DANCE!

Music and drumming create transition: all performers exit for entrance of Lovely White Maiden.

See the Lovely White Maiden!
The surprise!
  The chase!
    The taking of the scalp!
A Savage, Brutal SCALP DANCE!
THE TRIUMPH OF THE WHITES!

Loud drumbeat for shotgun blast ends scalp dance and knocks the Indians dead on stage floor.

These, as well as many other fascinating true-to-life scenes of this vanishing specimen of primitive mankind.

Piano now fading. Show-card girl tiptoes among the Indian bodies with her final card.

Special matinees of this fantastic spectacle will be given on Saturdays and Sun-days, as well as all national and civic holidays.

Show-card girl flits off. With the bodies on the floor, the drilling sound and earth slides are now more intense than before. In an instant they change to rifle fire and vistas of the ter-rain around Wounded Knee, South Dakota. The visuals stop on a single picture of a mar-shal peering through a rifle scope that is aimed toward the performers and the audience.

11

The performing group members now rise from the floor and form a semicircle around the drummer, who is bare-chested. He drums and sings The AIM Song, building to a spirited pitch. A single rifle shot rings out and the drummer falls forward, his body taut, glistening in the lights. The helicopters, armored cars, and more gunfire are heard. The picture of the marshal switches to a sequence of action shots of the siege of Wounded Knee in 1973.

MARSHAL'S VOICE

(*mixed with sounds of siege on tape*) May I please have your attention! I am the United States District Marshal from Rapid City, and I am at the head of a force of 500 federal officers and deputies. We have the entire area surrounded. You cannot escape.

The performers lift the drummer's body, raise it above their heads, and begin a slow procession offstage.

It is my duty to inform you that you are all under arrest on the charge of unlawfully trespassing on private property. Warrants for your arrest have been issued in federal district court. I must caution all of you not to make any sudden moves. We are armed and are prepared to take any necessary defensive action. All of you who do not surrender without resistance are hereby warned that additional charges will be filed against you for resisting arrest.

Your hands must be held high above your heads until the handcuffs are placed on you.

Again, I warn you, do not make any sudden moves.

Your cooperation will help to speed this procedure.

Move forward, stay at absolute arms length.

The siege visuals end as the performing group files back on the darkened stage in a funeral procession, led by a drummer who sounds a single heavy beat. The men carry the body of the dead drummer covered by a star blanket. A series of visuals showing the hands of the performing group members being handcuffed are projected as they file off. Then, one by one, they return to the stage, handcuffed, with their arms raised above their heads. The narrator steps to the front of the group.

NARRATOR

We move on. To a courtroom in Rapid City, South Dakota. To a courtroom in Sioux Falls, Iowa.

PERFORMER

(*Moving out from the group, he thrusts his hands toward audience.*) I am Pawnee.

NARRATOR

We move on.

PERFORMER

(*repeating the action*) I am Creek.

NARRATOR

Back to our homes, our people.

PERFORMER
> I am Winnebago.

NARRATOR
> We move on.

PERFORMER
> I am Sioux.

NARRATOR
> To the land.

PERFORMER
> I am Apache.

NARRATOR
> To the sky.

PERFORMER
> I am Ojibwa.

The lights dim as the apparition of the Indian face again appears on the stage backside and moves slowly around the playing area.

VOICE OF SPANISH SAILOR
> (*on tape*) ¡Capitan! ¡Capitan! ¡Dios mio! ¡Muchas gracias! ¡Madre mia! ¡Los indios! ¡Los indios! ¡India! ¡Ellos son los indios!

NARRATOR
> (*very compassionately*) I am . . . NOT GUILTY!

Lights fade slowly. Performing group exits.

END

MARTÍN ESPADA
(1957-)

Martín Espada was born in Brooklyn, New York, and educated at the University of Wisconsin at Madison, where he studied history. His first collection of poems, The Immigrant Iceboy's Bolero, *was published in 1982. In 1985, he received a J.D. from the Northeastern University School of Law, and he worked as a tenant lawyer and supervisor of Su Clinica Legal in Boston. Among the awards he has received for his six volumes of poetry are the Paterson Poetry Prize and the American Book Award, as well as fellowships from the National Endowment for the Arts and the PEN/Revson Foundation. He also edited two collections of poetry and authored a collection of essays,* Zapata's Disciple: Essays. *He teaches at the University of Massachusetts at Amherst.*

Espada's work unites passionate social and political commitment to a lyric and richly metaphoric poetic language. "Imagine the Angels of Bread," the title poem of Espada's 1999 collection, imagines the feeling of triumph over ethnic and economic oppression that lies—perhaps—ahead.

IMAGINE THE ANGELS OF BREAD

This is the year that squatters evict landlords,
gazing like admirals from the rail
of the roofdeck
or levitating hands in praise
of steam in the shower;
this is the year
that shawled refugees deport judges
who stare at the floor
and their swollen feet
as files are stamped
with their destination;
this is the year that police revolvers,
stove-hot, blister the fingers
of raging cops,
and nightsticks splinter
in their palms;
this is the year
that darkskinned men
lynched a century ago
return to sip coffee quietly
with the apologizing descendants
of their executioners.

This is the year that those
who swim the border's undertow
and shiver in boxcars
are greeted with trumpets and drums
at the first railroad crossing
on the other side;
this is the year that the hands
pulling tomatoes from the vine
uproot the deed to the earth that sprouts the vine,
the hands canning tomatoes
are named in the will
that owns the bedlam of the cannery;
this is the year that the eyes
stinging from the poison that purifies toilets
awaken at last to the sight
of a rooster-loud hillside,
pilgrimage of immigrant birth;
this is the year that cockroaches
become extinct, that no doctor
finds a roach embedded
in the ear of an infant;
this is the year that the food stamps

of adolescent mothers
are auctioned like gold doubloons,
and no coin is given to buy machetes
for the next bouquet of severed heads
in coffee plantation country.

If the abolition of slave-manacles
began as a vision of hands without manacles,
then this is the year;
if the shutdown of extermination camps
began as imagination of a land
without barbed wire or the crematorium,
then this is the year;
if every rebellion begins with the idea
that conquerors on horseback
are not many-legged gods, that they too drown
if plunged in the river,
then this is the year.

So may every humiliated mouth,
teeth like desecrated headstones,
fill with the angels of bread.

RUDOLFO ANAYA
(1937-)

Rudolfo Anaya was born in Pastura, New Mexico. He attended the University of New Mexico, where he received both a B.A. and M.A. in English. In 1972, he received another M.A. from the University of New Mexico in guidance and counseling, and he worked briefly as director of counseling at the University of Albuquerque. In 1972 he published his first novel, Bless Me, Ultima. *Since then he has published another seven novels, plays, and a collection of short stories, as well as works of nonfiction and children's literature. He has also edited anthologies of Chicano literature and a collection of essays,* Aztlan: Essays on the Chicano Homeland. *In 1980 he received a fellowship from the National Endowment for the Arts as well as the American Book Award for his novel,* Tortuga. *From 1974 until his retirement in 1993 he taught literature and writing at the University of New Mexico.*

"In Search of Epifano" follows the journey of an old woman who seeks to understand her life by finding an ancestor in the "Old Country," in this case, Mexico.

IN SEARCH OF EPIFANO

She drove into the desert of Sonora in search of Epifano. For years, when summer came and she finished her classes, she had loaded her old Jeep with supplies and gone south into Mexico.

Now she was almost eighty and, she thought, ready for death but not afraid of death. It was the pain of the bone-jarring journey which was her reality, not thoughts of death. But that did not diminish the urgency she felt as she drove south, across the desert. She was following the north rim of El Cañon de Cobre towards the land of the Tarahumaras. In the Indian villages there was always a welcome and fresh water.

The battered Jeep kicked up a cloud of chalky dust which rose into the empty and searing sky of summer. Around her, nothing moved in the heat. Dry mirages rose and shimmered, without content, without form. Her bright, clear eyes remained fixed on the rocky, rutted road in front. Around her there was only the vast and empty space of the desert. The dry heat.

The Jeep wrenched sideways, the low gear groaning and complaining. It had broken down once, and had cost her many days' delay in Mexicali. The mechanic at the garage told her not to worry. In one day the parts would be in Calexico and she would be on her way.

But she knew the way of the Mexican, so she rented a room in a hotel nearby. Yes, she knew the Mexican. Part of her blood was Mexican, wasn't it? Her great-grandfather, Epifano, had come north to Chihuahua to ranch and mine. She knew the stories whispered about the man, how he had built a great ranch in the desert. His picture was preserved in the family album, at his side his wife, a dark-haired woman. Around them, their sons.

The dry desert air burned her nostrils. A scent of the green ocotillo reached her, reminded her of other times, other years. She knew how to live in the sun, how to travel and how to survive, and she knew how to be alone under the stars. Night was her time in the desert. She liked to lie in her bedroll and look up at the swirling dance of the stars. In the cool of evening, her pulse would quicken. The sure path of the stars was her map, drawing her south.

Sweat streaked her wrinkled skin. Sweat and dust, the scent commingling. She felt alive. "At least I'm not dry and dead," she said aloud. Sweat and pleasure, it came together.

The Jeep worried her now. A sound somewhere in the gearbox was not right. "It has trouble," the mechanic had said, wiping his oily hands on a dirty rag. What he meant was that he did not trust his work. It was best to return home, he suggested with a shrug. He had seen her musing over the old and tattered map, and he was concerned about the old woman going south. Alone. It was not good.

"We all have trouble," she mumbled. We live too long and the bones get brittle and the blood dries up. Why can't I taste the desert in my mouth? Have I grown so old? Epifano? How does it feel to become a spirit of the desert?

Her back and arms ached from driving; she was covered with the dust of the desert. Deep inside, in her liver or in her spleen, in one of those organs that the ancients called the seat of life, there was an ache, a dull, persistent pain. In her heart there was a tightness. Would she die and never reach the land of Epifano?

She slept while she waited for the Jeep to be repaired. Slept and dreamed under the shade of the laurel in the patio of the small hotel. Around her, Mexican sounds and colors permeated her dream. What did she dream? That it was too late in her life to go once again into the desert? That she was an old woman and her life was lived, and the only evidence she would leave of her existence would be her sketches and paintings? Even now, as weariness filled her, the dreams came, and she slipped in and out of past and present. In her dreams she heard the voice of the old man, Epifano.

She saw his eyes, blue and bright like hers, piercing but soft. The eyes of a kind man. He had died. Of course, he had died. He belonged to the past. But she had not forgotten him. In the family album, which she carried with her, his gaze was the one that looked out at her and drew her into the desert. She was the artist of the family. She had taken up painting. She heard voices. The voice of her great-grandfather. The rest of her family had forgotten the past, forgotten Mexico and the old man, Epifano.

The groaning of the Jeep shattered the silence of the desert. She tasted dust in her mouth, she yearned for a drink of water. She smiled. A thirst to be satisfied. Always there was one more desire to be satisfied. Her paintings were like that, a desire from within to be satisfied, a call to do one more sketch of the desert in the molten light before night came. And always the voice of Epifano drawing her to the trek into the past.

The immense solitude of the desert swallowed her. She was only a moving shadow in the burning day. Overhead, vultures circled in the sky, the heat grew intense. She was alone on a dirt road she barely remembered, taking her bearings only by instinct, roughly following the north rim of the Cañon de Cobre, drawn by the thin line of the horizon, where the dull peaks of las montañas met the dull blue of the sky. Whirlwinds danced in her eyes, memories flooded at her soul.

She had married young. She thought she was in love; he was a man of ambition. It took her years to learn that he had little desire or passion. He could not, or would not, fulfill her. What was the fulfillment she sought? It had to do with something that lay even beneath the moments of love or children carried in the womb. Of that she was sure.

She turned to painting, she took classes, she traveled alone. She came to understand that she and the man were not meant for each other.

She remembered a strange thing had happened in the chapel where the family gathered to attend her marriage. An Indian had entered and stood at the back of the room. She had turned and looked at him. Then he was gone, and later she was not sure if the appearance was real or imagined.

But she did not forget. She had looked into his eyes. He had the features of a Tarahumara. Was he Epifano's messenger? Had he brought a warning? For a moment she hesitated, then she had turned and said yes to the preacher's question. Yes to the man who could never understand the depth of her passion. She did what was expected of her there in the land of ocean and sun. She bore him a daughter and a son. But in all those years, the man never understood the desire in her, he never explored her depth of passion. She turned to her dreams, and there she heard the voice of Epifano, a resonant voice imparting seductive images of the past.

Years later she left her husband, left everything, left the dream of southern California where there was no love in the arms of the man, no sweet juices in the nights of love pretended. She left the circle of pretend. She needed a meaning, she needed desperately to understand the voices which spoke in her soul. She drove south, alone, in search of Epifano. The desert dried her by day, but replenished her at night. She learned that the mystery of the stars at night was like the mystery in her soul.

She sketched, she painted, and each year in springtime she drove farther south. On her map she marked her goal, the place where once stood Epifano's hacienda.

In the desert the voices were clear. She followed the road into Tarahumara country, she dreamed of the old man, Epifano. She was his blood, the only one who remembered him.

At the end of the day she stood at the side of a pool of water, a small, desert spring surrounded by desert trees. The smell of the air was cool, wet. At her feet, tracks of deer, a desert cat. Ocelot. She stooped to drink, like a cautious animal.

"Thank the gods for this water which quenches our thirst," she said, splashing the precious water on her face, knowing there is no life in the desert without the water which flows from deep within the earth. Around her, the first stars of dusk began to appear.

She had come at last to the ranch of Epifano. There, below the spring where she stood, on the flat ground, was the hacienda. Now could be seen only the outlines of the foundation and the shape of the old corrals. From here his family had spread, northwest, up into Mexicali and finally into southern California. Seeds. Desert seeds seeking precious water. The water of desire. And only she had returned.

She sat and gazed at the desert, the peaceful, quiet mauve of the setting sun. She felt a deep sadness within. An old woman, sitting alone in the wide desert, her dream done.

A noise caused her to turn. Perhaps an animal come to drink at the spring, the same spring where Epifano had once wet his lips. She waited, and in the shadows of the palo verde and the desert willows she saw the Indian appear. She smiled.

She was dressed in white, the color of desire not consummated. Shadows moved around her. She had come home, home to the arms of Epifano. The Indian was a tall, splendid man. Silent. He wore paint, as they did in the old days when they ran the game of the pelota up and down las montañas of the Cañon de Cobre.

"Epifano," she said, "I came in search of Epifano." He understood the name. Epifano. He held his hand to his chest. His eyes were bright and blue, not Tarahumara eyes, but the eyes of Epifano. He had known she would come. Around her, other shadows moved, the women. Indian women of the desert. They moved silently around her, a circle of women, an old ceremony about to begin.

The sadness left her. She struggled to rise, and in the dying light of the sun a blinding flash filled her being. Like desire, or like an arrow from the bow of the Indian, the light filled her and she quivered.

The moan of love is like the moan of life. She was dressed in white.

III

Reconstitut(ion)ing the Nation: Problems and Solutions

The idea of the United States as a nation has never actually been a stable reality. We have grown comfortable with some kinds of instability—such as the gradual addition of new states throughout the nineteenth century—and forgotten what wrenching cultural displacements were involved in the annexation of Florida in 1819, the implementation of the Louisiana Purchase after 1804, the acquisition of Texas, California, and the rest of the Southwest after the Mexican War of 1846. We forget how the admissions of other territories as states were charged with the volatility of the slavery/antislavery conflict that finally resulted in civil war. Less distant, and therefore more volatile, perhaps, are the dislocations of the idea of the nation engendered by immigration over the last hundred years. Immigration challenged the nation's sense of itself as an "Anglo-Saxon civilization" and created cultural anxieties expressed in discriminatory policies, xenophobic literature, and anti-immigrant legislation.

The immigrants persisted, however, and finally prevailed. The citizens who can trace their roots to post-Revolutionary immigration far outnumber those whose ancestors predated the Revolution. Far from coalescing into a homogenized whole, the American people become more diverse as time goes on, while immigrants from nations in Asia, Africa, and South America enrich the mixture and extend the process. New people from foreign lands not only changed the population as they became the American people, they also, over time and in connection with other forces, have inevitably changed the American society's sense of itself.

1

DESIRES AND
IDENTITIES

Various institutions and organizations help to move the process of American re-definition and reconstruction along. The advertising, information, and entertainment industries, for example, shape the nation's sense of self in many important ways, reporting—selectively—on "events" and "personalities" that are presumed to interest everyone, creating more desire by promoting commodities so that we will want to purchase them, defining who and what is and is not of interest to "average Americans." *Desires and Identities* focuses attention on the struggle within American popular culture as people attempt to resist or control the desires represented in magazine advertising, film, television, and other media. Diana Chang in "Saying Yes" speaks of the ironies of a Chinese-American identity ill-understood by outsiders. Michael Ventura in his essay "Report from El Dorado" assesses the impact of television on our sense of self, while Lee Smith's short story "Dear Phil Donahue" explores an example of destructive over-involvement with celebrity. Ross Chambers offers a personal reflection on the privileges of whiteness from the point of view of a late-twentieth-century immigrant. Both Bharati Mukherjee in her story "A Father" and Sherman Alexie in his story "A Drug Called Tradition" explore ways that contemporary life shapes the processes of assimilation and acculturation differently for members of different ethnic and racialized groups. These and the other works included in this section demonstrate a variety of ways that we as Americans have responded to the struggle between traditions of identity and cultural forces that attempt to subvert them.

MINSTRELSY MUSIC COVER

During most of the nineteenth century and well into the twentieth, the minstrel show was the most popular form of public entertainment in the United States. In these shows, white actors and singers blackened their faces with burnt cork and imitated the speech, music, and dancing of slaves and other blacks. They mocked African-American oratory and dancing, while producing reams of music on plantation themes. As immigration developed, Irish, Jewish, and Italian stereotypes were added to the repertoire. Late in the century, when black entertainers took over the minstrel show as an acceptable outlet for their desire to perform, they found themselves trapped in the long-established stereotypes and only very slowly began to change them. A major influence for change was "the ragtime craze" (1895–1915), the overwhelming popularity in the white middle classes of the syncopated African-American piano music that preceded jazz. When this music was published, however, many of the minstrel stereotypes were repeated. Thus while the music was more authentically African American than the minstrel songs and was enormously popular, the culture continued to place a mask of mockery and disapproval over the face of its creators.

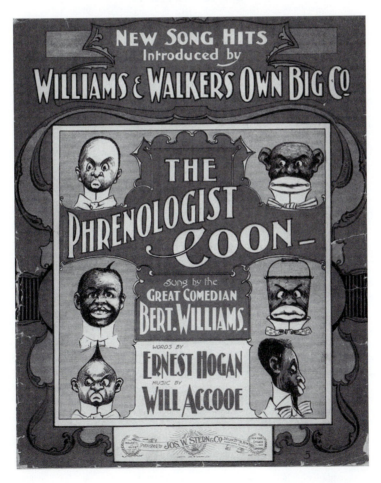

PAUL LAURENCE DUNBAR
(1872-1906)

*Paul Laurence Dunbar began showing literary promise in his Dayton, Ohio,
hometown high school where he became the class president and class poet
even though he was the only African American in his class. While still in
high school, he published poems in the* Dayton Herald *and worked as editor of the short-lived* Dayton Tattler, *a newspaper for African Americans.
Although Dunbar enjoyed popularity with the publication of collections of
his dialect verse, beginning with* Oak and Ivy *in 1893, his canon largely consists of short stories, novels, plays, poems, and essays in standard English.
As a poet, he is best remembered for "We Wear the Mask" (1896), "When
Malindy Sings" (1903), and the following poem, "Sympathy" (1899). Dunbar
died of tuberculosis in 1906; his collected poems—over 400 of them—were
published in 1913.*

SYMPATHY

I know what the caged bird feels, alas!
    When the sun is bright on the upland slopes;
When the wind stirs soft through the springing grass,
And the river flows like a stream of glass;
    When the first bird sings and the first bud opens,
And the faint perfume from its chalice steals—
I know what the caged bird feels!

I know why the caged bird beats his wing
    Till its blood is red on the cruel bars;
For he must fly back to his perch and cling
When he fain would be on the bough a-swing;
    And a pain still throbs in the old, old scars
And they pulse again with a keener sting—
I know why he beats his wing!

I know why the caged bird sings, ah me,
    When his wing is bruised and his bosom sore,—
When he beats his bars and he would be free;
It is not a carol of joy or glee,
    But a prayer that he sends from his heart's deep core,
But a plea, that upward to Heaven he flings—
I know why the caged bird sings!

ITABARI NJERI

(1953-)

Born Jill Stacey Moreland in New York City, Itabari Njeri has had a varied career as a journalist, reporter, author, singer, actress, and radio producer. Njeri is of African, East Indian, English, Native American, and French ancestry and describes herself as "a typical descendant of the African diaspora." A graduate of the High School of Music and Art in New York City, where she studied singing, Njeri earned a B.S. at Boston University's School of Public Communications and a M.S. from the Columbia University School of Journalism. She has won awards and recognition in all the arenas of her career. Njeri was named "Best New Pop Vocalist" by MGM Records and was awarded a National Endowment for the Humanities Fellowship. She has worked as a reporter and arts critic for the Miami Herald *and the* Los Angeles Times. *She received the American Book Award for her memoir,* Every Good-bye Ain't Gone: Family Portraits and Personal Escapades *(1990). Other publications include* Sushi & Grits: The Challenge of Diversity *(1993), and* The Last Plantation: Color, Conflict, and Identity; Reflections of a New World Black *(1997).*

"What's in a Name?" first appeared in the Miami Herald *and was incorporated into* Every Good-bye Ain't Gone. *Here Njeri explores the desire of African Americans like herself for a self-invented identity, one not defined by the stereotypes of outsiders.*

WHAT'S IN A NAME?

The decade was about to end when I started my first newspaper job. The seventies might have been the disco generation for some, but it was a continuation of the Black Power, post–civil rights era for me. Of course in some parts of America it was still the pre–civil rights era. And that was the part of America I wanted to explore. As a good reporter I needed a sense of the whole country, not just the provincial Northeast Corridor in which I was raised.

I headed for Greenville ("Pearl of the Piedmont"), South Carolina.

"Wheeere," some people snarled, their nostrils twitching, their mouths twisted so their top lips went slightly to the right, the bottom ones way down and to the left, "did you get *that* name from?"

Itabiddy, Etabeedy. Etabeeree. Eat a berry. Mata Hari. Theda Bara. And one secretary in the office of the Greenville Urban League told her employer: "It's Ms. Idi Amin."

Then, and now, there are a whole bunch of people who greet me with: "Hi, Ita." They think "Bari" is my last name. Even when they don't, they still want to call me "Ita." When I tell them my first name is Itabari, they say, "Well, what do people call you for short?"

"They don't call me anything for short," I say. "The name is Itabari."

Sophisticated white people, upon hearing my name, approach me as would a cultural anthropologist finding a piece of exotica right in his own living room. This happens a lot, still, at cocktail parties.

"Oh, what an unusual and beautiful name. Where are you from?"

"Brooklyn," I say. I can see the disappointment in their eyes. Just another home-grown Negro.

Then there are other white people who, having heard my decidedly northeastern accent, will simply say, "What a lovely name," and smile knowingly, indicating that they saw Roots and understand.

Then there are others, black and white, who for different reasons take me through this number:

"What's your *real* name?"

"Itabari Njeri is my real, legal name," I explain.

"Okay, what's your original name?" they ask, often with eyes rolling, exasperation in their voices.

After Malcolm X, Muhammad Ali, Kareem Abdul-Jabbar, Ntozake Shange, and Kunta Kinte, who, I ask, should be exasperated by this question-and-answer game?

Nevertheless, I explain, "Because of slavery, black people in the Western world don't usually know their original names. What you really want to know is what my slave name was."

Now this is where things get tense. Four hundred years of bitter history, culture, and politics between blacks and whites in America is evoked by this one term, "slave name."

Some white people wince when they hear the phrase, pained and embarrassed by this reminder of their ancestors' inhumanity. Further, they quickly scrutinize me and conclude that mine was a post–Emancipation Proclamation birth. "You were never a slave."

I used to be reluctant to tell people my slave name unless I surmised that they wouldn't impose their cultural values on me and refuse to use my African name. I don't care anymore. When I changed my name, I changed my life, and I've been Itabari for more years now than I was Jill. Nonetheless, people will say: "Well, that's your *real* name, you were born in America and that's what I am going to call you." My mother tried a variation of this on me when I legalized my traditional African name. I respectfully made it clear to her that I would not tolerate it. Her behavior, and subsequently her attitude, changed.

But many black folks remain just as skeptical of my name as my mother was.

"You're one of those black people who changed their name, huh," they are likely to begin. "Well, I still got the old slave master's Irish name," said one man named O'Hare at a party. This man's defensive tone was a reaction to what I called the "blacker than thou" syndrome perpetrated by many black nationalists in the sixties and seventies. Those who reclaimed their African names made blacks who didn't do the same thing feel like Uncle Toms.

These so-called Uncle Toms couldn't figure out why they should use an African name when they didn't know a thing about Africa. Besides, many of them were proud of their names, no matter how they had come by them. And it should be noted that after the Emancipation Proclamation in 1863, four million black people changed their names, adopting surnames such as Freeman, Freedman, and Liberty. They eagerly gave up names that slave masters had imposed upon them as a way of identifying their human chattel.

Besides names that indicated their newly won freedom, blacks chose common English names such as Jones, Scott, and Johnson. English was their language. America was their home, and they wanted names that would allow them to assimilate as easily as possible.

Of course, many of our European surnames belong to us by birthright. We are the legal as well as "illegitimate" heirs to the names Jefferson, Franklin, Washington, et al., and in my own family, Lord.

Still, I consider most of these names to be by-products of slavery, if not actual slave names. Had we not been enslaved, we would not have been cut off from our culture, lost our indigenous languages, and been compelled to use European names.

The loss of our African culture is a tragic fact of history, and the conflict it poses is a profound one that has divided blacks many times since Emancipation: do we accept the loss and assimilate totally or do we try to reclaim our culture and synthesize it with our present reality?

A new generation of black people in America is reexamining the issues raised by the cultural nationalists and Pan-Africanists of the sixties and seventies: what are the cultural images that appropriately convey the "new" black aesthetic in literature and art?

The young Afro-American novelist Trey Ellis has asserted that the "New Black Aesthetic shamelessly borrows and reassembles across both race and class lines." It is not afraid to embrace the full implications of our hundreds of years in the New World. We are a new people who need not be tied to externally imposed or self-inflicted cultural parochialism. Had I understood that as a teenager, I might still be singing today.

Even the fundamental issue of identity and nomenclature, raised by Baraka and others twenty years ago, is back on the agenda: are we to call ourselves blacks or African-Americans?

In reality, it's an old debate. "Only with the founding of the American Colonization Society in 1816 did blacks recoil from using the term African in referring to themselves and their institutions," the noted historian and author Sterling Stuckey pointed out in an interview with me. They feared that using the term "African" would fuel white efforts to send them back to Africa. But they felt no white person had the right to send them back when they had slaved to build America.

Many black institutions retained their African identification, most notably the African Methodist Episcopal Church. Changes in black self-identification in America have come in cycles, usually reflecting the larger dynamics of domestic and international politics.

The period after World War II, said Stuckey, "culminating in the Cold War years of Roy Wilkins's leadership of the NAACP," was a time of "frenzied integrationism." And there was "no respectable black leader on the scene evincing any sort of interest in Africa—neither the NAACP or the Urban League."

This, he said, "was an example of historical discontinuity, the likes of which we, as a people, had not seen before." Prior to that, for more than a century and a half, black leaders were Pan-Africanists, including Frederick Douglass. "He recognized," said Stuckey, "that Africa was important and that somehow one had to redeem the motherland in order to be genuinely respected in the New World."

The Reverend Jesse Jackson has, of course, placed on the national agenda the importance of blacks in America restoring their cultural, historical, and political links with Africa.

But what does it really mean to be called an African-American?

"Black" can be viewed as a more encompassing term, referring to all people of African descent. "Afro-American" and "African-American" refer to a specific ethnic group. I use the terms interchangeably, depending on the context and the point I want to emphasize.

But I wonder: as the twenty-first century breathes down our necks—prodding us to wake up to the expanding mélange of ethnic groups immigrating in record numbers to the United States, inevitably intermarrying, and to realize the eventual reshaping of the nation's political imperatives in a newly multicultural society—will the term "African-American" be as much of a racial and cultural obfuscation as the term "black"? In other words, will we be the only people, in a society moving toward cultural pluralism, viewed to have no history and no culture? Will we just be a color with a new name: African-American?

Or will the term be—as I think it should—an ethnic label describing people with a shared culture who descended from Africans, were transformed in (as well as transformed) America, and are genetically intertwined with myriad other groups in the United States?

Such a definition reflects the historical reality and distances us from the fallacious, unscientific concept of separate races when there is only one: *Homo sapiens.*

But to comprehend what should be an obvious definition requires knowledge and a willingness to accept history.

When James Baldwin wrote *Nobody Knows My Name*, the title was a metaphor—at the deepest level of the collective African-American psyche—for the blighting of black history and culture before the nadir of slavery and since.

The eradication or distortion of our place in world history and culture is most obvious in the popular media. Liz Taylor—and, for an earlier generation, Claudette Colbert—still represent what Cleopatra—a woman of color in a multiethnic society, dominated at various times by blacks—looks like.

And in American homes, thanks to reruns and cable, a new generation of black kids grow up believing that a simpleton shouting "Dy-no-mite!" is a genuine reflection of Afro-American culture, rather than a white Hollywood writer's stereotype.

More recently, *Coming to America*, starring Eddie Murphy as an African prince seeking a bride in the United States, depicted traditional African dancers in what amounted to a Las Vegas stage show, totally distorting the nature and beauty of real African dance. But with every burlesque-style pelvic thrust on the screen, I saw blacks in the audience burst into applause. They think that's African culture, too.

And what do Africans know of us, since blacks don't control the organs of communication that disseminate information about us?

"No!" screamed the mother of a Kenyan man when he announced his engagement to an African-American woman who was a friend of mine. The mother said marry a European, marry a white American. But please, not one of those low-down, ignorant, drug-dealing, murderous black people she had seen in American movies. Ultimately, the mother prevailed.

In Tanzania, the travel agent looked at me indignantly. "Njeri, that's Kikuyu. What are you doing with an African name?" he demanded.

I'd been in Dar es Salaam about a month and had learned that Africans assess in a glance the ethnic origins of the people they meet.

Without a greeting, strangers on the street in Tanzania's capital would comment, "Oh, you're an Afro-American or West Indian."

"Both."

"I knew it," they'd respond, sometimes politely, sometimes not.

Or, people I got to know while in Africa would mention, "I know another half-caste like you." Then they would call in the "mixed-race" person and say, "Please meet Itabari Njeri." The darker-complected African, presumably of unmixed ancestry, would then smile and stare at us like we were animals in the zoo.

Of course, this "half-caste" (which I suppose is a term preferable to "mulatto," which I hate, and which every person who understands its derogatory meaning— "mule"—should never use) was usually the product of a mixed marriage, not generations of ethnic intermingling. And it was clear from most "half-castes" I met that they did not like being compared to so mongrelized and stigmatized a group as Afro-Americans.

I had minored in African studies in college, worked for years with Africans in the United States, and had no romantic illusions as to how I would be received in the motherland. I wasn't going back to find my roots. The only thing that shocked me in Tanzania was being called, with great disdain, a "white woman" by an African waiter. Even if the rest of the world didn't follow the practice, I then assumed everyone understood that any known or perceptible degree of African ancestry made one "black" in America by law and social custom.

But I was pleasantly surprised by the telephone call I received two minutes after I walked into my Dar es Salaam hotel room. It was the hotel operator. "Sister, welcome to Tanzania. . . . Please tell everyone in Harlem hello for us." The year was 1978, and people in Tanzania were wearing half-foot-high platform shoes and dancing to James Brown wherever I went.

Shortly before I left, I stood on a hill surrounded by a field of endless flowers in Arusha, near the border of Tanzania and Kenya. A toothless woman with a wide smile, a staff in her hand, and two young girls at her side, came toward me on a winding path. I spoke to her in fractured Swahili and she to me in broken English.

"I know you," she said smiling. "Wa-Negro." "Wa" is a prefix in Bantu languages meaning people. "You are from the lost tribe," she told me. "Welcome," she said, touching me, then walked down a hill that lay in the shadow of Mount Kilimanjaro.

I never told her my name, but when I told other Africans, they'd say: *Emmmm Itabari. Too long. How about I just call you Ita."

JULIA FIELDS
(1938-)

Born in Perry County, Alabama, Julia Fields is known for her poetry and short stories that probe the political, social, and moral status of African Americans. She earned a bachelor's degree at Knoxville College and received a master's from The Bread Loaf School of English. Fields began her writing career as a playwright in 1966 with the production of All Day Tomorrow? *at the Knoxville College Drama Workshop. She received a National Endowment for the Arts grant in 1967. Her publications include* I Heard a Young Man Saying *(1967),* A Summoning, A Shining *(1976),* Slow Coins: New Poems (& Some Old Ones) *(1981), and* The Green Lion of Zion Street *(1988). Fields has taught at colleges and universities including Mills College, Hampton University, and Howard University.*

Like many of her poems, "High on the Hog" plays with the African-American vernacular voice. Here Fields is imitating the rhythmic play and word invention of the oral tradition to articulate desires the poet shares with other members of her racialized community.

HIGH ON THE HOG

Take my share of Soul Food—
I do not wish
To taste of pig
    Of either gut
        or Grunt
        from bowel
            Or jowl
I want caviar
Shrimp soufflé
Sherry
      Champagne
          And not because
    These are the
    Whites' domain
    But just because
    I'm entitled —

For I've been
          V.d.'d enough
          T.b.'d enough
    and
    Hoe-cake fed Knock-Knee'd enough
    Spindly led-bloodhound tree'd enough
To eat
High on the Hog
    I've been
        Hired last
        Fired first enough
    I've sugar-watered my
        Thirst enough —

Been lynched enough
        Slaved enough
        Cried enough
        Died enough
Been deprived —
        Have survived enough
          To eat
    High on the Hog

Keep the black-eyed peas
          And the grits
          The high blood-pressure chops
          And gravy sops

I want apertifs supreme
          Baked Alaska —
       Something suave, cool
       For I've been considered faithful fool
       From 40 acres and a mule . . .

I've been
       Slighted enough
       Sever-righted enough
       And up tighted enough
    And I want
       High on the Hog

For dragging the cotton sack
       On bended knees
       In burning sun
       In homage to the
             Great-King cotton
       For priming the money-green tobacco
             And earning pocket-change

       For washing in iron pots
       For warming by coal and soot
       For eating the leavings from
           Others' tables

I've lived my wretched life
       Between domestic rats
          And foreign wars

Carted to my final rest
       In second-hand cars

But I've been leeched enough
       Dixie-peached enough
       Color bleached enough

       And I want
       High on the Hog!

Oh, I've heard the Mau Mau
       Screaming

Romanticising Pain
      I hear them think
      They go against the Grain

But I've lived in shacks
               Long enough
      Had strong black beaten
               Backs long enough

And I've been
      Urban-planned
               Been moynihanned
               Enough
      And I want
      High on the Hog

STUDS TERKEL

(1912–   )

Born Louis Terkel in New York City, Studs Terkel has had a varied career as a biographer, memoirist, journalist, critic, and dramatist. Terkel earned a bachelor's degree and a law degree from the University of Chicago and later worked as a broadcaster for various Chicago radio and television stations. Through his experience as an interviewer, Terkel developed a rapport with people of diverse backgrounds and occupations. He used his experience as a music critic in his first book, Giants of Jazz *(1957). Similarly, his broadcasting experience led to the publication of several best-selling oral histories based on interviews with average Americans. Terkel received the Pulitzer Prize in nonfiction in 1985 for* "The Good War": An Oral History of World War II *(1984). Terkel was also awarded the George Foster Peabody Broadcasting Award in 1980. Other publications include* The Great Divide: Second Thoughts on the American Dream *(1988) and* RACE: How Blacks and Whites Think and Feel about the American Obsession *(1992), in which the following interview with Frank Chin appeared.*

Frank Chin was born in 1940 in Sacramento, California. He was educated at the University of California, Berkeley. Chin's literary career took off with the production of his play The Chickencoop Chinaman *in New York in 1980. Another play,* The Year of the Dragon, *was also produced there. His later work is as a critic and theorist of Asian-American writing, as one of the editors of* Aiiieee! An Anthology of Asian American Writing *(1974), and as the author of fiction: a collection of short stories,* The Chinaman Pacific and Frisco Railroad *(1988), and two novels,* Donald Duk *(1991) and* Gunga Din Highway *(1994). A collection of nonfiction appeared as* Bulletproof Buddhists and Other Essays *in 1998.*

An Interview with Frank Chin

A *Chinese-American playwright and novelist.*

"When I was a little kid, during World War II, I was raised by white folks: a retired vaudeville acrobat and a retired silent-screen bit player. We lived in a tarpaper shanty, outside Sacramento.

"A war veteran, with one eye missing and a few drinks, said to them, 'What are you doin' with that Jap kid?' I said, 'I'm no Jap kid. I'm an American of Chinese descent.' I didn't know what it was, but he didn't either. The rest of my life, I've been trying to find out exactly what it is." [Laughs.]

He later moved in with his grandmother and aunts in Oakland. "All we spoke in the family was Cantonese."

I hung out with blacks. I learned if I could make them laugh, I wouldn't get beat up and I could walk away and maintain my dignity. They actually came to respect me because I could talk my way out of fights in a way that would make them feel good. They would walk me to school.

Some people looked at this as a rejection of things Chinese. On the other hand, the blacks would say, and the whites, too, why was I talking about all this Chinese stuff? "We think of you as a member of the family." That always bothered me.

The Tower of Babel story always bothered me, too.

Oakland is the Tower of Babel. All these languages. And nobody even speaks English like everybody else. I've come to believe that monotheism encourages racism, whoever practices it. There is only one God and everyone else is an infidel, a pagan, or a goy. The Chinese look on all behavior as tactics and strategy. It's like war. You have to know the terrain. You don't destroy the terrain, you deal with it. We get along, not because we share a belief in God or Original Sin or a social contract, but because we make little deals and alliances with each other.

I like whites and blacks. I take them as individuals. I admire white culture: Shakespeare, the great ideas of Western Civilization. I also like black culture. In the sixties, it became a force in Asian-America. It always had a large presence in Oakland. I grew up with rhythm-and-blues, jazz, our original American art forms.

The fifties was still our age of innocence: the Eisenhower era. Everything was looking up: Perry Como. Since I grew up a loner, without any idea of parents, I thought Mommy and Daddy were just nicknames, like Shorty and Skinny. The idea that parents had a proprietary right over children was alien to me. A lot of the ideas of Chinese inferiority came late to me, from the outside. The one thing that saved me from being raised in the stereotype was my isolation during World War II, being raised by these white folks.

The sixties and the civil-rights movement came along, and the blacks were asserting themselves and getting our attention with phrases like "Power to the People." These wonderful black-leather jackets and the shades and the black berets were new even to the blacks themselves. It was like a parade, everyone in uniform.

As for the yellows, the civil-rights movement made us aware that we had no presence, no image in American culture as men, as people. We were preceived as being bright but with less physical prowess than the blacks and whites. We were more favored than the blacks, but we lacked their manhood. So a bunch of us began to appropriate "blackness." We'd wear the clothes, we'd affect the walk and we began talking black. We'd call our selves "Bro" and began talking Southern: "Hey, man."

We started talking about the sisters in the street and the brothers in the joint. I'd been in the joint and I didn't see any yellows there. I didn't see so many of our sisters walking the streets. That wasn't our thing. If it had been, we might have had a better sex life. [Laughs.]

[He imitates the Black Panther rap.] "Brothers and sisters, we've gotta organize, get together, and fight the pig. Brothers and sisters, Power to the People. Right on!" I said, "What is this? This isn't Chinese. It's a yellow minstrel show."

At this time, the government was throwing a lot of money at the gangs. The War on Poverty was on. Chinatown gangs, whose main business was being criminals, suddenly had social significance. They were perfectly happy to collect chump change.

I was teaching a class in Asian-American studies. My students were Chinese-Americans and Japanese-Americans. They were from the suburbs, outside China-town. My purpose was to break down stereotypes. So I decided to do an agit-prop thing, having them play the stereotypes.

We were rehearsing, doing a rock-and-roll version of

> Ching-chong Chinaman,
> sitting on a rail,
> along come a choo-choo train,
> cut off his tail.

Guitars, everything. The Lum gang walks in, walks up to the singer [Simulates a deep, menacing voice.]: "Stop singing that song. We don't like it." Lum comes up to me, he's holding his fist down, staring a hole through my chest. A student, a quiet little girl, who'd become a militant, is behind me saying, "Don't take no shit from nobody." I'm saying, "Shhh, shhh!" Porky, who's standing behind Lum, is yelling, "Kill 'im! Kill 'im!"

Lum is growling, "Stop singing that song. It makes fun of Chinese people." I say, in my gentlest voice, "Have you ever heard of satire? We know it's a racist song. That's why we're singing it. We're making fun of the people who make fun of Chinese. Do you understand?" I could see I wasn't cutting it. Porky is hollering, "Kill 'im! Kill 'im!" Finally, in frustration, because I wasn't responding to a fight, they walk out.

The gang council decides that we're too controversial. They call me to a meeting. The leader of the Chinatown Red Guard taps me on the shoulder and says, "I want to talk to you." I turn around and just like in the movies, his fist is coming toward me. He knocks me down, my glasses go flying, he punches me in the stomach. Just like in the movies, he hits me in the back of the neck. While I'm on my hands and knees, he stomps on me and starts kicking me. I'm saying [in a whining voice], "This is the wrong movie, guys."

He says, "Identify with China!" I say, "Wait a minute. We're in America. This is where we are, where we live and where we're going to die. There's not going to be any revolution. That's crazy." He can't hit me anymore. He's already done that and it's not working. I've interrupted his speech. This had never happened to him before. He curls his lip and says, "You cultural nationalist!" I go, "What? What's a cultural nationalist? Don't you know how to swear? Call me motherfucker, call me asshole, call me anything you want, but what's a cultural nationalist?" He doesn't know what to say to that, so they leave.

George Woo, a big guy, who's now teaching Asian-American Studies at San Francisco State, was pretty tight with the gangs then. He runs after the Red Guard and tells them if they ever beat me up again, he'll take it personally, that I'm his friend. All of a sudden, the leader of the gang council comes up to me and says, "I want to shake your hand. No one ever talked back to Alex that way before." We're all buddy-buddy now, because George said he'll take it personally.

The word flashes through Chinatown. Twenty-five minutes later, another gang of kids shows up. Must be fifteen, sixteen years old. One of them has a Tommy gun. "*Where are they?* We heard someone beat up a friend of George's." [*Laughs.*] I said "No, no, that's not my style. Let's do it with words."

The civil-rights movement of the sixties affected the Chinese-American community in a number of ways. In ways that aren't very flattering to us. When I went to interview some Asian-American actors who played Charlie Chan's Number One, Two, Three, and Four sons, they were blaming the blacks for the yellows not getting more parts. "Here we've been good people, keeping our noses clean—" Suddenly they realized what I was up to and they saw *me* as a threat. I was making Chinese-Americans controversial by speaking out against racism.

It's an old story. The good Chinese were the Christian Chinese. The good Chinese were the ones who shucked all Chinese ways. They revere Pearl Buck and the missionaries that worked Chinatown. That's what bothered me, our history in Chinatown, San Francisco.

In Chinatown's twelve blocks, there are forty-two Christian churches. On the walls of Chinatown, there's a plaque honoring Ross Hunter, who produced *The Flower Drum Song*; a plaque honoring the song "Grant Avenue"; a plaque marking the birthplace of the first white child in San Francisco; a monument to the first white school. *Nothing* for the Chinese. There is one exception: a monument to Sun Yat Sen. He was a Christian.

Most in the community saw the civil-rights movement as a threat. They objected to school integration because they didn't want their children to be influenced by blacks. The fact is the mimicking of blacks that I experienced were of a few. White journalists have emphasized that aspect. As though the Chinese don't think of themselves as Chinese-Americans. As though we're an enclave, like Americans working for Aramco in Saudi Arabia.

Chinatown may be a stronghold of Chinese culture, but we're Chinese-Americans. We saw the movement as a threat because we might be identified as a minority. We were thinking of ourselves as being assimilated. We had worked so hard at being acculturated that we didn't know anything about China anymore.

During the Depression, my uncle was raised in a Chinese Baptist Home for Boys. To raise money, they put on a show. It was the first Chinese-American blackface minstrel show in the history of the world. I came across the autobiography of the founder. I showed my uncle a picture in the book; the boys in blackface. He burst into tears. He was one of the Chung-mai minstrels. He got sad and I got angry. It was humiliating.

At the same time, we thought we were above the blacks. My family owned some property in the black district of Oakland. I once went with my mother to collect the rent. I said, "These places are terrible." She says, "Yeah, but they drive Cadillacs. It's what you call nigger-rich." That struck me so hard. I had never heard my folks put down blacks, denigrate people that way. Yet we were slumlords, taking advantage, exploiting them. It was a moment of moral confusion. I was eight at the time.

We feel because we're more civilized, quote unquote, because we're more middle-class, that we deserve more acceptance than the blacks. We don't riot, we don't make waves, we didn't protest, we're more American. We don't see that we've described ourselves as a race of Helen Kellers, mute, blind and deaf. We're the perfect minority.

We embrace Charlie Chan as an image of racist love. Most of us still think the good Chinaman is the Christian, Charlie Chan. There's a Chinese-American sociologist who said, "The Chinese, much to their credit, have never been overly bitter about racial prejudice. They have gone into jobs that reduced visibility and are moving out of population vortices of New York and San Francisco's Chinatown to outlying areas. Such a movement should be encouraged, because dispersion discourages visibility." The stereotype is embraced as a strategy for white acceptance.

The prejudice against blacks still continues, but we're smart enough to know it isn't quite civilized. We're also smart enough to use it to get our share. It happened to me. It was in the sixties. The railroads were taken to court for failing to integrate. They fell under ICC rules. So they put up a call: they were hiring brakemen. I was encouraged to apply. I was a clerk for a railroad company. It was the lowest of the low. I was fairly assured I'd be hired, implying I'd be more acceptable than a black. By default, I became the first Chinese-American brakeman on the Southern Pacific. I was the lesser of the two evils.

We believed what whites believed about blacks. We adopted all the white prejudice. The blacks adopted the same prejudices about us. David Hilliard of the Black Panthers got up in Portsmouth Square—luckily most Chinese there didn't understand English—and said, "You Chinese are the Uncle Toms of the colored peoples." It was apt. At the same time, the solution was not for us to become black.

The new immigrants, the Indochinese are a revelation. They still speak all the dialects of Indochina: Lao, Viet, or Cambodian. They pick up English as a matter of necessity, as a language of commerce. It's strategic. It's a white-man's world and you have to get along. Yet, all these languages are being spoken. They're using English as a dialect of Chinese and not following the rules. In Chinese-America, it is the new immigrants threatening our relationship with the whites, not the blacks. They are the unredeemed Chinese Chinese. It's an interesting, exciting time.

TOSHIO MORI
(1910-1980)

Born in Oakland, California, Toshio Mori was one of the first native-born Japanese-Americans to publish fiction. During World War II, Mori was relocated to the Topaz center in Utah, where he served as camp historian. Mori began publishing in 1949 with the short story collection, Yokohama, California, *which had been scheduled for publication before the war. His other works include* Woman from Hiroshima *(1979) and another short story collection,* The Chauvinist and Other Stories *(1979).*

Mori's story "Japanese Hamlet" looks at the desire of a Japanese-American to become a great Shakespearean actor. Without articulating the cultural and historical barriers to Tom's achievement of this goal, the story suggests, among other things, the sacrifices a man will make for the dream of art.

JAPANESE HAMLET

He used to come to the house and ask me to hear him recite. Each time he handed me a volume of *The Complete Works of William Shakespeare.* He never forgot to do that. He wanted me to sit in front of him, open the book and follow him as he recited his lines. I did willingly. There was little for me to do in the evenings so when Tom Fukunaga came over I was ready to help out almost any time. And as his love for Shakespeare's plays grew with the years he did not want anything else in the world but to be a Shakespearean actor.

Tom Fukunaga was a schoolboy in a Piedmont home. He had been one since his freshman days in high school. When he was thirty-one he was still a schoolboy. Nobody knew his age but he and the relatives. Every time his relatives came to the city they put up a roar and said he was a good-for-nothing loafer and ought to be ashamed of himself for being a schoolboy at this age.

"I am not loafing," he told his relatives. "I am studying very hard."

One of his uncles came often to the city to see him. He tried a number of times to persuade Tom to quit stage hopes and schoolboy attitude. "Your parents have already disowned you. Come to your senses," he said. "You should go out and earn a man's salary. You are alone now. Pretty soon even your relatives will drop you."

"That's all right," Tom Fukunaga said. He kept shaking his head until his uncle went away.

When Tom Fukunaga came over to the house he used to tell me about his parents and relatives in the country. He told me in particular about the uncle who kept coming back to warn and persuade him. Tom said he really was sorry for Uncle Bill to take the trouble to see him.

"Why don't you work for someone in the daytime and study at night?" I said to Tom.

"I cannot be bothered with such a change at this time," he said. "Besides, I get five dollars a week plus room and board. That is enough for me. If I should go out and work for someone I would have to pay for room and board besides carfare so I would not be richer. And even if I should save a little more it would not help me become a better Shakespearean actor."

When we came down to the business of recitation there was no recess. Tom Fukunaga wanted none of it. He would place a cup of water before him and never touch it. "Tonight we'll begin with Hamlet," he said many times during the years. *Hamlet* was his favorite play. When he talked about Shakespeare to anyone he began by mentioning Hamlet. He played parts in other plays but always he came back to Hamlet. This was his special role, the role which would establish him in Shakespearean history.

There were moments when I was afraid that Tom's energy and time were wasted and I helped along to waste it. We were miles away from the stage world. Tom Fukunaga had not seen a backstage. He was just as far from the stagedoor in his thirties as he was in his high school days. Sometimes as I sat holding Shakespeare's book and listening to Tom I must have looked worried and discouraged.

"Come on, come on!" he said. "Have you got the blues?"

One day I told him the truth: I was afraid we were not getting anywhere, that perhaps we were attempting the impossible. "If you could contact the stage people it might help," I said. "Otherwise we are wasting our lives."

"I don't think so," Tom said. "I am improving every day. That is what counts. Our time will come later."

That night we took up Macbeth. He went through his parts smoothly. This made him feel good. "Some day I'll be the ranking Shakespearean actor," he said.

Sometimes I told him I liked best to hear him recite the sonnets. I thought he was better with the sonnets than in the parts of Macbeth or Hamlet.

"I'd much rather hear you recite his sonnets, Tom," I said.

"Perhaps you like his sonnets best of all," he said. "Hamlet is my forte. I know I am at my best playing Hamlet."

For a year Tom Fukunaga did not miss a week coming to the house. Each time he brought a copy of Shakespeare's complete works and asked me to hear him say the lines. For better or worse he was not a bit downhearted. He still had no contact with the stage people. He did not talk about his uncle who kept coming back urging him to quit. I found out later that his uncle did not come to see him any more.

In the meantime Tom stayed at the Piedmont home as a schoolboy. He accepted his five dollars a week just as he had done years ago when he was a freshman at Piedmont High. This fact did not bother Tom at all when I mentioned it to him. "What are you worrying for?" he said. "I know I am taking chances. I went into this with my eyes open, so don't worry."

But I could not get over worrying about Tom Fukunaga's chances. Every time he came over I felt bad for he was wasting his life and for the fact that I was mixed in it. Several times I told him to go somewhere and find a job. He laughed. He kept coming to the house and asked me to sit and hear him recite Hamlet.

The longer I came to know Tom the more I wished to see him well off in business or with a job. I got so I could not stand his coming to the house and asking me to sit while he recited. I began to dread his presence in the house as if his figure reminded me of my part in the mock play that his life was, and the prominence that my house and attention played.

One night I became desperate. "That book is destroying you, Tom. Why don't you give this up for awhile?"

He looked at me curiously without a word. He recited several pages and left early that evening.

Tom did not come to the house again. I guess it got so that Tom could not stand me any more than his uncle and parents. When he quit coming I felt bad. I knew he would never abandon his ambition. I was equally sure that Tom would never rank with the great Shakespearean actors, but I could not forget his simple persistence.

One day, years later, I saw him on the Piedmont car at Fourteenth and Broadway. He was sitting with his head buried in a book and I was sure it was a copy of Shakespeare's. For a moment he looked up and stared at me as if I were a stranger. Then his face broke into a smile and he raised his hand. I waved back eagerly.

"How are you, Tom?" I shouted.

He waved his hand politely again but did not get off, and the car started up Broadway.

DIANA CHANG

(1934-)

Born in New York City to a Chinese father and a Eurasian mother, Diana Chang has had a varied career as a poet, novelist, teacher, editor, and painter. Her writing spans several genres including poetry, short stories, and novels. Chang earned a bachelor's degree in English from Barnard College of Columbia University and was awarded a John Hay Whitney Foundation Fellowship. She has published six novels including her first, The Frontiers of Love, *in 1956 and the most recent,* Earth Water Light *(1991). Chang's short story, "Falling Tree," was adapted as a radio play and broadcast over National Public Radio in more than thirty-five cities across the United States. Chang was professor of creative writing at Barnard College until 1989. Also a painter, Chang's acrylics, pastels, and watercolors have been exhibited at various galleries in New York.*

Chang's poem "Saying Yes" addresses the duality inherent in an identity racialized and exoticized by her countrymen.

SAYING YES

"Are you Chinese?"
"Yes."

"American?"
"Yes."

"*Really* Chinese?"
"No . . . not quite."

"*Really* American?"
"Well, actually, you see . . ."

But I would rather say
yes

Not neither-nor,
not maybe,
but both, and not only

The homes I've had,
the ways I am

I'd rather say it
twice,
yes.

CHERYL SAVAGEAU

(1950-)

Born in Worcester, Massachusetts, Cheryl Savageau is noted for her poetry that centers on family, poverty, and mixed ancestry and is rooted in her Native American (Abenaki) and French-Canadian ancestry. Her first collection, Home Country, *was published in 1992. Other publications include* Dirt Road Home *(1995) and* Muskrat Will Be Swimming *(1996). In addition to her poetry, she has worked as a storyteller and writer-in-residence in Massachusetts schools. Savageau has also taught at Holy Cross College, Clark University, and the University of New Mexico. Savageau is presently teaching at the University of Massachusetts at Amherst where she is also pursuing a doctorate in English.*

"Grandmother" from Savageau's 1995 collection expresses the speaker's desire to connect the red and white parts of her heritage, disjointed by time and racism.

GRANDMOTHER

Grandmother, you don't know me
but they say I walk as you did,
in touch with the earth.

Grandmother, when you met him
did you unbraid your hair?
Nobody will tell me, Grandmother,
what happened to your hair.

You bore him fine white babies, Grandmother,
their cheekbones high, eyes black,
noses never quite European.

Did you love him, Grandmother,
this white man, this cutter
of trees?

He was a strong man, they say,
walked over half the continent,
lived to be two weeks short of a hundred.
He's legend in these parts.

Grandmother, why
are there no stories
about you?
Grandmother, nobody will tell me
what happened to your hair.

When I was a child, Grandmother,
the earth was my body
and I played in the rain
happy as a frog.
And Grandmother, the hurricane
was my raindance
and the trees
sheltered me
and the sun, the sun
made my body
as red as yours, Grandmother,
as brown as yours.

Grandmother, they knew about you.
And Grandmother, they told me my eyes
are blue.
And Grandmother, they wouldn't tell me
your name.
Grandmother, Grandmother,
I was singing to you,
and they cut off
my hair.

DESI ARNAZ AND LUCILLE BALL

Lucille Ball and her Cuban-born husband Desi Arnaz were the first super-stars of broadcast television. Their show, "I Love Lucy," ran for ten years (1951–1961) and can still be seen in reruns on cable channels both here and abroad. The show was important beyond its timeless comedic appeal: Ball and Arnaz invented the now standard three-camera setup for television drama and comedy. They also developed their own studio for the production of other television programs.

Lucille Ball came to television from a successful career as a Hollywood actress who had worked with the Marx Brothers among others. The character she played on the show, a middle-class housewife who hungers to share in her husband's show-business life, provided a comic image of the American woman straining against domestic constraints and thwarted in her ambitions. When her adventure in show business or the work world is over, Lucy always settles for the life she has as beloved wife and home-maker, thus reinforcing the sense of the audience that the domestic sphere is her "place."

Desiderio Arnaz was, like Ricky Ricardo, his character on the show, a bandleader who played the night club circuit, where Latin American and Caribbean music had been prominent for over a decade. He proved himself to be a fine comedic straight man as well as an excellent businessman. The show played out the ancient ethnic joke about his Spanish-accented English but only rarely touched upon other aspects of Cuban-American culture. Stereotypes of Latino machismo and exuberance were played for laughs, but Desi's character represented the middle-class American man of the 1950s, caught in a never-ending struggle to contain a wife he dearly loves who will not behave as she ought.

MICHAEL VENTURA

(1945-)

Michael Ventura is a poet, editor, and journalist who was born in the Bronx, New York. Ventura began his career as the arts editor of the Austin Sun *in 1974. In 1978 he cofounded the* Los Angeles Weekly *and served as its senior editor until 1993. Ventura began publishing as a poet with* The Mollyhawk

Poems *(1977). Other publications include* Shadow Dancing in the USA *(1985),* Night Time, Losing Time *(1989),* Letters at Three A. M.: Reports on Endarkenment *(1993), and* The Zoo Where You're Fed to God *(1994).*

"Report from El Dorado" from Shadow Dancing in the USA *addresses the central location of entertainment media in American life and our relationship with the media as both our creation and our creator.*

REPORT FROM EL DORADO

To go from a job you don't like to watching a screen on which others live more intensely than you . . . is American life, by and large.

This is our political ground. This is our artistic ground. This is what we've done with our immense resources. We have to stop calling it "entertainment" or "news" or "sports" and start calling it what it is: our most immediate environment.

This is a very, very different America from the America that built the industrial capacity to win the Second World War and to surge forward on the multiple momentums of that victory for thirty years. That was an America that worked at mostly menial tasks during the day (now we work at mostly clerical tasks) and had to look at each other at night.

I'm not suggesting a nostalgia for that time. It was repressive and bigoted to an extent that is largely forgotten today, to cite only two of its uglier aspects. But in that environment America meant *America*: the people and the land. The land was far bigger than what we'd done with the land.

This is no longer true. Now the environment of America is media. Not the land itself, but the image of the land. The focus is not on the people so much as it is on the interplay between people and screens. What we've done with the land is far more important now than the land—we're not even dealing with the land anymore, we're dealing with our manipulation and pollution of it.

And what we've done with the very concept of "image" is taking on far more importance for many of us than the actual sights and sounds of our lives.

For instance: Ronald Reagan stands on a cliff in Normandy to commemorate the day U.S. Army Rangers scaled those cliffs in the World War II invasion. Today's Rangers reenact the event while some of the original Rangers, in their sixties now, look on. Except that it is the wrong cliff. The cliff that was actually scaled is a bit further down the beach, but it's not as photogenic as this cliff, so this cliff has been chosen for everybody to emote over. Some of the old Rangers tell reporters that the historical cliff is over yonder, but the old Rangers are swept up (as well they might be) in the ceremonies, and nobody objects enough. This dislocation, this choice, this stance that the real cliff is not important, today's photograph is more important, is a media event. It insults the real event, and overpowers it. Multiplied thousands of times over thousands of outlets of every form and size, ensconced in textbooks as well as screenplays, in sales presentations as well as legislative packages, in religious revivals as well as performance-art pieces, this is the process that has displaced what used to be called "culture."

. . .

"I'm not even sure it's a culture anymore. It's like this careening hunger splattering out in all directions."

Jeff Nightbyrd was trying to define "culture" in the wee hours at the Four Queens in Las Vegas. It was a conversation that had been going on since we'd become friends working on the *Austin Sun* in 1974, trying to get our bearings now that the sixties were *really over*. He'd spent that tripletime decade as an SDS organizer and editor of *Rat*, and I'd hit Austin after a few years of road-roving, commune-hopping, and intensive (often depressive) self-exploration—getting by, as the song said, with a little help from my friends, as a lot of us did then. This particular weekend Nightbyrd had come to Vegas from Austin for a computer convention, and I had taken off from my duties at the *L.A. Weekly* for some lessons in craps (at which Jeff is quite good) and to further our rap. The slot machines clattered around us in unison, almost comfortingly, the way the sound of a large shaky air-conditioner can be comforting in a cheap hotel room when you're trying to remember to forget. We were, after all, trying to fathom an old love: America.

There are worse places to indulge in this obsession than Las Vegas. It is the most American, the most audacious, of cities. Consuming unthinkable amounts of energy in the midst of an unlivable desert (Death Valley is not far away), its decor is based on various cheap-to-luxurious versions of a 1930's Busby Berkeley musical. Indeed, no studio backlot could ever be more of a set, teeming with extras, people who come from all over America, and all over the world, to see the topless, tasteless shows, the Johnny Carson guests on parade doing their utterly predictable routines, the dealers and crap-table croupiers who combine total boredom with ruthless efficiency and milk us dry—yet at least these tourists are risking something they genuinely value: money. It's a quiz show turned into a way of life, where you can get a good Italian dinner at dawn. Even the half-lit hour of the wolf doesn't faze Las Vegas. How could it, when the town has survived the flash of atom bombs tested just over the horizon?

The history books will tell you that, ironically enough, the town was founded by Mormons in 1855. Even their purity of vision couldn't bear the intensity of this desert, and they abandoned the place after just two years. But they had left a human imprint, and a decade later the U.S. Army built a fort here. The settlement hung on, and the railroad came through in 1905. During the Second World War the Mafia started to build the city as we know it now. Religious zealots, the Army, and the Mafia—quite a triad of founding fathers.

Yet one could go back even further, some 400 years, when the first Europeans discovered the deserts of the American West—Spaniards who, as they slowly began to believe that there might be no end to these expansive wilds, became more and more certain that somewhere, somewhere to the north, lay El Dorado—a city of gold. Immeasurable wealth would be theirs, they believed, and eternal youth. What would they have thought if they had suddenly come upon modern Las Vegas, lying as it does in the midst of this bleached nowhere, glowing at night with a brilliance that would have frightened them? We have built our desert city to their measure—for they were gaudy and greedy, devout and vicious, jovial and frenzied, like this town. They had just wasted the entire Aztec civilization because their fantasies were so strong they couldn't see the ancient cultural marvels before their eyes. The Aztecs, awed and terrified, believed they were being murdered by gods; and in the midst of such strangeness, the Spaniards took on godlike powers even in their own eyes. As many Europeans would in America, they took liberties here they would never have taken within sight of their home cathedrals. Their hungers dominated them, and in their own eyes the New World seemed as inexhaustible as their appetites. So when Nightbyrd described our present culture as "a careening hunger splattering out in all directions," he was also, if unintentionally, speaking about our past. Fittingly, we were sitting in the midst of a city that had been fantasized by those seekers of El Dorado 400 years ago. In that sense, America had Las Vegas a century before it had Plymouth Rock. And our sensibility has been caught between the fantasies of the conquistadors and the obsessions of the Puritans ever since.

Yes, a fitting place to try to think about American culture.

"There are memories of culture," Nightbyrd was saying, "but the things that have given people strength have dissolved. And because they're dissolved, people are into distractions. And distractions aren't culture."

Are there even memories? The media have taken over our memories. That day Nightbyrd had been driving through the small towns that dot this desert, towns for which Vegas is only a dull glow to the southwest. In a bar in one of those towns, "like that little bar in *The Right Stuff*," he'd seen pictures of cowboys on the wall. "Except that they weren't cowboys. They were movie stars. Guys who grew up in Glendale [John Wayne] and Santa Monica [Robert Redford]." Surely this desert had its own heroes once, in the old gold-mining towns where a few people still hang on, towns like Goldfield and Tonopah. Remembering those actual heroes would be "culture." Needing pictures of movie stars for want of the real thing is only a nostalgia for culture.

Nostalgia is not memory. Memory is specific. One has a relationship to a memory, and it may be a different relationship, because a memory always makes a demand upon the present. But nostalgia is vague, a sentimental wash that obscures memory and acts as a narcotic to dull the importance of the present.

Media as we know it now thrives on nostalgia and is hostile to memory. In a television bio-pic, Helen Keller is impersonated by Mare Winningham. But the face of Helen Keller was marked by her enormous powers of concentration, while the face of Mare Winningham is merely cameo-pretty. A memory has been stolen. It takes a beauty in you to see the beauty in Helen Keller's face, while to cast the face of a Mare Winningham in the role is to suggest, powerfully, that one can come back from the depths unscathed. No small delusion is being sold here. Yet this is a minor instance in a worldwide, twenty-four-hour-a-day onslaught.

An onslaught that gathers momentum every twenty-four hours. Remember that what drew us to Las Vegas was a computer fair. One of these new computers does interesting things with photographs. You can put a photograph into the computer digitally. This means the photograph is in there without a negative or print, each element of the image stored separately. In the computer, you can change any element of the photograph you wish, replacing it or combining it with elements from other photographs. In other words, you can take composites of different photographs and put them into a new photograph of your own composition. Combine this with computer drawing, and you can touch up shadows that don't match. When it comes out of the computer the finished product bears no evidence of tampering with any negative. The possibilities for history books and news stories are infinite. Whole new histories can now be written. Events which never happened can be fully documented.

The neo-Nazis who are trying to convince people that the Holocaust never happened will be able to show the readers of their newsletter an Auschwitz of well-fed, happy people being watched over by kindly S.S. men while tending gardens. And they will be able to make the accusation that photographs of the *real* Auschwitz were created in a computer by manipulative Jews. The Soviet Union can rewrite Czechoslovakia and Afghanistan, the United States can rewrite Vietnam, and atomic weapons proponents can prove that the average resident of Hiroshima was unharmed by the blast. On a less sinister, but equally disruptive, level, the writers of business prospectuses and real-estate brochures can have a field day.

Needless to say, when any photograph can be processed this way then all photographs become suspect. It not only becomes easier to lie, it becomes far harder to tell the truth.

But why should this seem shocking when under the names of "entertainment" and "advertising" we've been filming history, and every facet of daily life, in just this way for nearly a century now? It shouldn't surprise us that the ethics of our entertainment have taken over, and that we are viewing reality itself as a form of entertainment. And, as entertainment, reality can be rewritten, transformed, played with, in any fashion.

These considerations place us squarely at the center of our world—and we have no choice, it's the only world there is anymore. *Electronic media has done for everyday reality what Einstein did for physics:* everything is shifting. Even the shifts are shifting. And a fact is not so crucial anymore, not so crucial as the process that turns a fact into an image. For we live now with images as much as facts, and the images seem to impart more life than facts *precisely because they are so capable of transmutation, of transcendence, able to transcend their sources and their uses.* And all the while the images goad us on, so that we become partly images ourselves, imitating the properties of images as we surround ourselves with images.

This is most blatant in our idea of "a vacation"—an idea only about 100 years old. To "vacation" is to enter an image. Las Vegas is only the most shrill embodiment of this phenomenon. People come here not so much to gamble (individual losses are comparatively light), nor for the glittery entertainment, but to step into an image, a daydream, a filmlike world where "everything" is promised. No matter that the Vegas definition of "everything" is severely limited, what thrills tourists is the sense of being surrounded in "real life" by the same images that they see on TV. But the same is true of the Grand Canyon, or Yellowstone National Park, or Yosemite, or Death Valley, or virtually any of our "natural" attractions. What with all their roads, telephones, bars, cable-TV motels, the visitors are carefully protected from having to *experience* the place. They view its image, they camp out in its image, ski down or climb up its image, take deep breaths of its image, let its image give them a tan. Or, when they tour the cities, they ride the quaint trolley cars of the city's image, they visit the Latin Quarter of its image, they walk across the Brooklyn Bridge of its image—our recreation is a *re*-creation of America into one big Disneyland.

And this is only one way we have stripped the very face of America of any content, any reality, concentrating only on its power as image. We also elect images, groom ourselves as images, make an image of our home, our car, and now, with aerobics, of our very bodies. For in the aerobics craze the flesh becomes a garment, susceptible to fashion. So it becomes less *our* flesh, though the exercise may make it more serviceable. It becomes "my" body, like "my" car, "my" house. What, within us, is saying "my"? What is transforming body into image? We shy away from asking. In this sense it can be said that after the age of about twenty-five we no longer *have* bodies anymore—we have possessions that are either more or less young, which we are constantly trying to transform and through which we try to breathe.

It's not that all this transformation of realities into un- or non- or supra-realities is "bad," but that it's unconscious, compulsive, reductive. We rarely make things more than they were; we simplify them into less. Though surely the process *could*— at least theoretically—go both ways. Or so India's meditators and Zen's monks say. But that would be to *increase* meaning, and we seem bent on the elimination of meaning. We're Reagon's Rangers, climbing a cliff that *is* a real cliff, except it's not the cliff we say it is, so that the meaning of both cliffs—not to mention of our act of climbing—is reduced.

As I look out onto a glowing city that is more than 400 years old but was built only during the last forty years, as I watch it shine in blinking neon in a desert that has seen the flash of atom bombs, it becomes more and more plain to me that America is at war with meaning. America is form opposed to content. Not just form *instead* of content. Form opposed. Often violently. There are few things resented so much among us as the suggestion that what we do *means*. It *means* something to watch so much TV. It *means* something to be obsessed with sports. It *means* something to vacation by indulging in images. It means something, and therefore it has consequences. Other cultures have argued over their meanings. We tend to deny that there is any such thing, insisting instead that what you see is what you get and that's *it*. All we're doing is having a *good time*. All we're doing is making a buck. All we're doing is enjoying the spectacle, we insist. So that when we export American culture what we are really exporting is an attitude toward content. Media is the American war on content with all the stops out, with meaning in utter rout, frightened nuances dropping their weapons as they run.

. . .

"Media is the history that forgives," my friend Dave Johnson told me on a drive through that same desert a few months later. We love to take a weekend every now and again and just *drive*. Maybe it started with reading *On the Road* when we were kids, or watching a great old TV show called *Route 66* about two guys who drove from town to town working at odd jobs and having adventures with intense women who, when asked who they were, might say (as one did), "Suppose I said I was the Queen of Spain?" Or maybe it was all those rock 'n' roll songs about "the road"—the road, where we can blast our tape-decks as loud as we want, and watch the world go by without having to touch it, a trip through the greatest hologram there is, feeling like neither boys nor men but both and something more, embodiments of some ageless, restless principle of movement rooted deep in our prehistory. All of which is to say that we're just as stuck with the compulsion to enter the image as anybody, and that we love the luxuries of fossil fuel just as much as any other red-blooded, thickheaded Americans.

Those drives are our favorite time to talk, and, again, America is our oldest flame. We never tire of speaking of her, nor of our other old girlfriends. For miles and miles of desert I thought of what Dave had said.

"Media is the history that forgives." A lovely way to put it, and quite un-Western. We Westerners tend to think in sets of opposites: good/bad, right/wrong, me/you, past/present. These sets are often either antagonistic (East/West, commie/capitalist, Christian/heathen) or they set up a duality that instantly calls out to be bridged (man/woman). But Dave's comment sidesteps the dualities and suggests something more complex: a lyrical impulse is alive somewhere in all this media obfuscation. It is the impulse to redeem the past—in his word, to *forgive* history—by presenting it as we would have most liked it to be.

It is one thing to accuse the media of lying. They are, and they know it, and they know we know, and we know they know that we know, and nothing changes. It is another to recognize the rampant lying shallowness of our media as a massive united longing for . . . innocence? For a sheltered childlike state in which we need not know about our world or our past. We are so desperate for this that we are willing to accept ignorance as a substitute for innocence. For there can be no doubt anymore that this society *knowingly* accepts its ignorance as innocence—we have seen so much in the last twenty years that now we know what we *don't* see. Whenever a TV show or a movie or a news broadcast leaves out crucial realities for the sake of sentimentality, we pretty much understand the nature of what's been left out and why.

But American media *forgives* the emptiness and injustice of our daily life by presenting our daily life as innocent. Society, in turn, forgives American media for lying because if we accept the lie as truth then we needn't *do* anything, we needn't change.

I like Dave's line of thought because it suggests a motive—literally, a motive force—for these rivers of glop that stream from the screens and loudspeakers of our era. Because, contrary to popular belief, profit is *not* the motive. That seems a rash statement to make in the vicinity of Las Vegas, but the profit motive merely begs the question: *why* is it profitable? Profit, in media, is simply a way of measuring attention. Why does what we call "media" attract so much attention?

The answer is that it is otherwise too crippling for individuals to bear the strain of accepting the unbalanced, unrewarding, uninspiring existence that is advertised as "normal daily life" for most people who have to earn a living every day.

Do those words seem too strong? Consider: to go to a job you don't value in itself but for its paycheck, while your kids go to a school that is less and less able to educate them; a large percentage of your pay is taken by the government for defenses that don't defend, welfare that doesn't aid, and the upkeep of a government that is impermeable to the influence of a single individual; while you are caught in a value system that judges you by what you own, in a society where it is taken for granted now that children can't communicate with their parents, that old people have to be shut away in homes, and that no neighborhood is *really* safe; while the highest medical costs in the world don't prevent us from having one of the worst health records in the West (for instance, New York has a far higher infant mortality rate than Hong Kong), and the air, water, and supermarket food are filled with God-knows-what; and to have, at the end of a busy yet uneventful life, little to show for enduring all this but a comfortable home if you've "done well" enough; yet to *know* all along that you're living in the freest, most powerful country in the world, though you haven't had time to exercise much freedom and don't personally have any power—this is to be living a life of slow attrition and maddening contradictions.

Add to this a social style that values cheerfulness more than any other attribute, and then it is not so strange or shocking that the average American family watches six to eight hours of network television a day. It is a cheap and sanctioned way to partake of this world without having actually to live in it.

Certainly they don't watch so much TV because they're bored—there's far too much tension in their lives to call them bored, and, in fact, many of the products advertised on their favorite programs feature drugs to calm them down. Nor is it because they're stupid—a people managing the most technically intricate daily life in history can hardly be written off as stupid; nor because they can't entertain themselves—they are not so different from the hundreds of generations of their forebears who entertained themselves very well as a matter of course. No, they are glued to the TV because one of the most fundamental messages of television is: "It's all right."

Every sitcom and drama says: "It's all right." Those people on the tube go through the same—if highly stylized—frustrations, and are exposed to the same dangers as we are, yet they reappear magically every week (every day on the soap operas) ready for more, always hopeful, always cheery, never questioning the fundamental premise that this is the way a great culture behaves and that all the harassments are the temporary inconveniences of a beneficent society. It's going to get even *better*, but even now *it's all right.* The commercials, the Hollywood movies, the universal demand in every television drama or comedy that no character's hope can ever be exhausted, combine in a deafening chorus of: *It's all right.*

As a screenwriter I have been in many a film production meeting, and not once have I heard any producer or studio executive say, "We have to lie to the public." What I have heard, over and over, is, "They have to leave the theater feeling good." This, of course, easily (though not always) translates into lying—into simplifying emotions and events so that "it's all right." You may measure how deeply our people know "it" is *not* all right, not at all, by how much money they are willing to pay to be ceaselessly told that it is. The more they feel it's not, the more they need to be told it is—hence Mr. Reagan's popularity.

Works that don't say "It's all right" don't get much media attention or make much money.

The culture itself is in the infantile position of needing to be assured, every day, all day, that this way of life is good for you. Even the most disturbing news is dispensed in the most reassuring package. As world news has gotten more and more disturbing, the trend in broadcast journalism has been to get more and more flim-flam, to take it less seriously, to keep up the front of "It's really quite all right." This creates an enormous tension between the medium and its messages, because everybody knows that what's on the news is *not* all right. That is why such big money is paid to a newscaster with a calm, authoritative air who, by his presence alone, seems to resolve the contradictions of his medium. Walter Cronkite was the most popular newscaster in broadcast history because his very presence implied: "As long as I'm on the air, you can be sure that, no matter what I'm telling you, *it's still all right.*"

Which is to say that the media has found it profitable to do the mothering of the mass psyche. But it's a weak mother. It cannot nurture. All it can do is say it's all right, tuck us in, and hope for the best.

Today most serious, creative people exhaust themselves in a sideline commentary on this state of affairs, a commentary that usually gets sucked up into the media and spewed back out in a format that says "It's all right. What this guy's saying is quite all right, what this woman's singing is all right, all right." This is what "gaining recognition" virtually always means now in America: your work gets turned inside out so that its meaning becomes "It's all right."

Of course, most of what exists *to make media of*, to make images of, is more and more disorder. Media keeps saying, "It's all right" while being fixated upon the violent, the chaotic, and the terrifying. So the production of media becomes more and more schizoid, with two messages simultaneously being broadcast: "It's all right. We're dying. It's all right. We're all dying." The other crucial message—"We're dying"—runs right alongside *It's all right.*

Murder is the crux of much media "drama." But it's murder presented harmlessly, with trivial causes cited. Rare is the attempt, in all our thousands of murder dramas, to delve below the surface. We take for granted now, almost as an immutable principle of dramatic unity, that significant numbers of us want to kill significant numbers of the rest of us. And what are all the murders in our media but a way of saying "We are being killed, we are killing, we are dying"? Only a people dying and in the midst of death would need to see so much of it in such sanitized form *in order to make death harmless.* This is the way we choose to share our death.

Delete the word "entertainment" and say instead, North Americans devote an enormous amount of time to the ritual of sharing death. If this were recognized as a ritual, and if the deaths were shared with a respect for the realities and the mysteries of death, this might be a very useful thing to do. But there is no respect for death in our death-dependent media, there is only the compulsion to display death. As for the consumers, they consume these deaths like sugar pills. Their ritual goes on far beneath any level on which they'd be prepared to admit the word "ritual." So we engage in a ritual we pretend isn't happening, hovering around deaths that we say aren't real.

It is no coincidence that this practice has thrived while the Pentagon uses the money of these death watchers to create weapons for death on a scale that is beyond the powers of human imagination—the very same human imagination that is stunting itself by watching ersatz deaths, as though intentionally crippling its capacity to envision the encroaching dangers. It is possible that the Pentagon's process could not go on without the dulling effects of this "entertainment."

When we're not watching our screens, we're listening to music. And, of course, North Americans listen to love songs at every possible opportunity, through every possible orifice of media. People under the strain of such dislocating unrealities need to hear "I love you, I love you," as often as they can. "I love you" or "I used to love you" or "I ought to love you" or "I need to love you" or "I want to love you." It is the fashion of pop-music critics to discount the words for the style, forgetting that most of the world's cultures have had songs about *everything*, songs about work, about the sky, about death, about the gods, about getting up in the morning, about animals, about children, about eating, about dreams—about everything, along with love. These were songs that everybody knew and sang. For a short time in the late sixties we moved toward such songs again, but that was a brief digression; since the First World War the music that most North Americans listen to has been a music of love lyrics that rarely go beyond adolescent yearnings. Either the song is steeped in the yearnings themselves, or it is saturated with a longing for the days when one could, shamelessly, feel like an adolescent. The beat has changed radically from decade to decade, but with brief exceptions that beat has carried the same pathetic load. (The beat, thankfully, has given us other gifts.)

It can't be over-emphasized that these are entertainments of a people whose basic imperative is the need not to think about their environment. The depth of their need may be measured by the hysterical popularity of this entertainment; it is also the measure of how little good it does them.

. . .

Media is not experience. In its most common form, media substitutes a fantasy of experience or (in the case of news) an abbreviation of experience for the living fact. But in our culture the absorption of media has become a substitute for experience. We absorb media, we don't live it—there is a vast psychological difference, and it is a difference that is rarely brought up.

For example, in the 1940's, when one's environment was still one's *environment,* an experience to be lived instead of a media-saturation to be absorbed, teenagers like Elvis Presley and Jerry Lee Lewis didn't learn their music primarily from the radio. Beginning when they were small boys they sneaked over to the black juke joints of Louisiana and Mississippi and Tennessee, where they weren't supposed to go, and they listened and learned. When Lewis and Presley began recording, even though they were barely twenty they had tremendous authority because they had experience—a raw experience of crossing foreign boundaries, of streets and sounds and peoples, of the night-to-night learning of ways that could not be taught at home.

This is very different from young musicians now who learn from a product, not a living ground. Their music doesn't get to them till it's been sifted through elaborate corporate networks of production and distribution. It doesn't smack of the raw world that exists before "product" can even be thought of.

The young know this, of course. They sense the difference intensely, and often react to it violently. So white kids from suburban media culture invented slam dancing (jumping up and down and slamming into each other) while black kids from the South Bronx, who have to deal with realities far more urgent than media, were elaborating the astounding graces of break dancing.

Slam dancing was a dead end. Break dancing, coming from a living ground, goes out through media but becomes ultimately transformed into another living ground—the kids in the elementary school down the street in Santa Monica break dance. Which is to say, a grace has been added to their lives. A possibility of grace. With the vitality that comes from having originated from a living ground. The media here is taking its proper role as a channel, not as a world in itself. It's possible that these kids are being affected more in their bodies and their daily lives by the South Bronx subculture than by high-gloss films like *Gremlins* or *Indiana Jones and the Temple of Doom.* Even through all this static, life can speak to life.

Of course, break dancing inevitably gets hyped, and hence devalued, by the entertainment industry, the way Elvis Presley ended up singing "Viva Las Vegas" as that town's most glamorous headliner. He went from being the numinous son of a living ground to being the charismatic product of a media empire—the paradigm of media's power to transform the transformers. The town veritably glows in the dark with the strength of media's mystique.

We do not yet know what life *is* in a media environment. We have not yet evolved a contemporary culture that can supply the definition—or rather, supply the constellation of concepts in which that definition would live and grow. These seem such simple statements, but they are at the crux of the American dilemma now. An important aspect of this dilemma is that we've barely begun a body of thought and art which is focused on what is really *alive* in the ground of a media-saturated daily life. For culture always proceeds from two poles: one is the people of the land and the street; the other is the thinker. You see this most starkly in revolutions: the ground swell on the one hand, the thinker (the Jefferson, for instance) on the other. Or religiously, the ground swell of belief that is articulated by a Michelangelo or a Dante. The two poles can exist without each other but they cannot be effective without each other.

Unless a body of thought connects with a living ground, there is no possibility that this era will discover itself within its cacophony and create, one day, a post-A.D. culture. It is ours to attempt the thought and seek the ground—for all of us exist between those poles. We are not only dying. We are living. And we are struggling to share our lives, which is all, finally, that "culture" means.

LEE SMITH

(1944-)

Born in Grundy, Virginia, Lee Smith is noted for fictions that transcend but never break with her rural Appalachian heritage. She earned a bachelor's degree at Hollins College and turned her senior creative writing project into her first novel, The Last Day the Dogbushes Bloomed *(1968), winning the first of many writing prizes. Her fifth novel,* Oral History *(1983), marked Smith's emergence as a major voice in contemporary American literature. Later publications include* Family Linen *(1985),* Fair and Tender Ladies *(1988),* Me and My Baby View the Eclipse *(1990), and* The Devil's Dream *(1992).*

"Dear Phil Donahue," from Smith's short story collection Cakewalk *(1981), details the kind of trouble we can get into when we are over-involved with the images and figures of popular culture.*

DEAR PHIL DONAHUE

I used to be so cute and so gay, I can't tell you. The quote under my picture in the high school yearbook was all about "trodding" and "springtime" and "gay." Sometimes I still trod gaily such as yesterday even, I picked up both babies and danced all over the house to "Boogie Shoes" on Jerry's *Saturday Night Fever* album. While I was doing this Jerry came in to get some more of his stuff, including that album, as it turned out. He turned down the volume and went to the refrigerator and got some yogurt (Jerry never used to eat yogurt) and stood there eating and watching me with this weird expression. It was a party before he came in.

But now I've blown it, Phil. I mean when you opened this letter and saw that first line you probably thought it was from some brilliant bisexual celebrity who wanted to be on your show. Well now you know. This letter is from me: Martha Rasnick, age twenty-eight, currently separated from my husband because I kept a man in our garage for three days. Three days is not a lifetime. I realize I'm writing this letter in a tone of what I would call (from my dim past as an English major before I dropped out) quirky desperation.

You probably wonder why I'm writing to you at all, Phil. Why I picked you out from among the hundreds of celebrities who grace my screen. It's because you talked to me, Phil, all those mornings.

Not only that but you've taught me all kinds of things on your show. I know about child psychology, common sexual myths, investing, acupuncture, birth control, problems of aging, politics, stress, and *anorexia nervosa.* I even know Rosalynn Carter. One thing I love about you, Phil, is that you've kept my brain from drying up. I mean that literally: you kept my head from caving in. Another thing I love about you is the way you look everybody in the eye. It's perfectly clear that if some radical Californian sat down on your show and announced that he had just planted a bomb in the studio you would be so terrific, so cool, you would look him straight in the eye and say, "Now tell us, Mr. Blah, how you first became interested in explosive devices."

As a matter of fact my house is an explosive device. It never goes off, though. It never goes off because I, tricky little dervish that I am, whirl through it every day wielding vacuum cleaner and dust rags, sticking in pacifiers and baby supppositories, watering plants and changing diapers, turning the dials to their proper positions for the specific time of day OFF ON PRESOAK BROIL, emptying and consuming, maintaining this equilibrium. But let me tell you that it's barely, just barely, maintained. Chaos is right around the corner in my house and explosions lurk everywhere.

This is what I do, Phil. The thing I'm trying to determine is whether or not it is separate from what I am. And whether either of those things has anything to do with this man I kept in the garage. If I were on your show, Phil, you could ask me pertinent questions and I could give you informative answers and we could get it all worked out before the station break. As it is, you're not here with your questions and I don't know where to start since there's no real beginning to this story at all. People who have been to China are always showing you slides. I've got some slides of my own, Phil, and they're pretty colorful. I'll provide the commentary—and here are some interesting tapes.

Look at our house. Glass and stone, somebody said it "approaches the organic." Approach our organic house. Look at our huge shag-carpeted living room (you rake a shag rug), with its lower "conversation center" around the fireplace. In the conversation center, I've never been able to say a word. Look at our glass coffee table, our mushroom chairs, the little geometric tables that fit together to make a big table, the antique grandfather clock, the carved frog, the split-leaf philodendron tree, the Oriental ashtrays, the fake Calder mobile. In the white kitchen, look at the gleaming espresso coffee maker, which I don't know how to use. You'll notice several things on this tour. One is that the stuff we have is good. The other is that we really don't have very much. You'll notice a lot of long, bare non-organic spaces. This stuff is all new and none of it is paid for.

We never had anything until two years ago when Jerry finally finished graduate school and got this good job. I quit college myself and worked as a secretary while he was an undergraduate, then while he was in the Army, and then while he was in graduate school. Believe me, I was ready to quit when the time came. Now suddenly we have all this stuff because Jerry said we had to have a house where we could "entertain." I don't work anymore and we have two babies because Jerry said he wanted a "family." But I always wanted babies, so that's all right. I wanted a house, too.

It's just that when you get *things*, and they're your things, then they take over. You have to take care of them. You have to dust them and polish them and fix their cords. I was born to do that, however, right here in Nashville. My mother was a home ec teacher for thirty years until she died. And I always knew what I wanted to do: take care of my home and my family. It should be a joy to take care of our things. In fact I enjoyed it. At least I thought I was a snappy little dervish full of joy.

JERRY: Well, we did it.

ME: Did what?

JERRY: Bought the block. The whole damn block. There was this one guy holding out but he finally came across. He finally saw the light.

ME: The what?

JERRY: The *light*, Martha. Christ, are you deaf?

ME: Does anybody live there now? I mean, what happens to the people who live there now?

JERRY: They *move*, baby.

ME: But, Jerry.

JERRY: *What?* Look, come over here, Martha. Give your old man a kiss.

ME: A what?

JERRY: A *kiss.* You're deaf, Martha.

ME: Yes. (I give him that kiss.)

This is an aerial slide, showing our whole neighborhood. Our address is 28 Country Club Circle. Jerry loves our address. A funny thing about the neighborhood, though. The circle is OK. But this circle is surrounded by lowlife. By houses that change hands, houses that different people sleep in, houses with flamingos and hubcaps in the front yards, houses where men sit outside on the steps barechested in summer drinking beer and in the windows behind them you can see women through the slats of the venetian blinds, ironing in their slips, pale strange women with cigarettes hanging out of their mouths.

The country club golf course is laid out so that sometimes the fairways pass close to these houses and the people who live there come out in their dirt yards to stare at the bright golfers. What are they thinking? Some of the golfers have complained.

One of these houses, pretty close to our own house if you cut through the yards and driveways, is run by a widow who lets her rooms only to psychiatric outpatients of the Veterans Administration Hospital. They're allowed to live here and hold jobs in the community while they reorient themselves to the outside world. Let's go in closer for a better look at the crazy veterans. See the fat man with the three-piece suit, sitting Indian fashion in the grass? He must be hot in that suit. See the little dude in the red baseball cap? The doctors must urge them to dress in loud colors. Look at their shirts. The doctors must urge them to walk, too, as a part of their therapy. On Saturday afternoons they walk to town, going to see a movie. I know they're going to see a movie because somebody told me that's what they do. But they walk as though they're not quite sure where they're going or why they're out walking at all. Sometimes they go single file. It upsets me to see them walking and if I have to go someplace on Saturday afternoons I take another street.

Now we have a conversation between me and my mother-in-law, one Tuesday morning when she has unexpectedly dropped by. (I almost wrote *dead* instead of *by.*) Mrs. Rasnick has stopped in on her way home from the beauty shop where they have curled her, sprayed her, massaged her, pedicured her, and filed her nails to silver points. She's wearing some kind of classy pantsuit and silver loafers with Lucite heels. I'm wearing blue jeans (too tight). I'm folding diapers. *Sesame Street* is on. Will is riding his fire engine. Linda is in the playpen chewing up a Metropolitan Museum of Art calendar. Mrs. Rasnick's name is Charlsie and she's always asking me to call her that.

MRS. RASNICK: And anyway I went by Michael Corzine's, just to look, you know, I thought I might pick up a christening present for Louise's new grandson, and they had this marvelous little man down in the basement giving lessons on how to make leather bottles. Incredibly attractive bottles, sort of Spanishy, only the secret is that *they're not leather at all!*

WILL: (screaming) Doose!

ME: Juice, please.

WILL: Doose, pee. (I give him some apple juice.)

MRS. RASNICK: They're just old bottles covered with newspaper! Isn't that the cleverest thing? You take old bottles and put a layer of newspaper around them and then a layer of varnish and then a stain and then another layer of newspaper and so on and it's absolutely amazing, they look just like leather! They would fool anybody. I can't wait to try it. I bought all the stuff, doesn't it sound like fun?

ME: Great!

WILL: (loud) Fruck!

MRS. RASNICK: *What did he say?*

ME: Ha, ha, *truck,* Mrs. Rasnick. He can't say T's yet.

MRS. RASNICK: Oh, isn't that cute? Fruck, I'll have to tell Louise.

Linda gets her toes caught in the playpen mesh and starts yelling. I untangle them but she's still yelling so I pick her up and get a Playtex bottle out of the refrigerator to start running hot water over it.

MRS. RASNICK: You know dear. (Hesitates.)

ME: What's that, Mrs. Rasnick?

MRS. RASNICK: Well, pardon me if I'm speaking out of turn, but you really look a little wan this morning. I have plenty of varnish, why don't I leave a can with you? You know you really ought to do something with your *hands.* (Mrs. Rasnick looks at her hands, holding them out so that I can see them too, making graceful arcs in the air.)

Conversation between me and my old friend Mare, about two months ago. Mare's real name is Mary but lately she styles herself "Mare." She sits in her yellow Porsche in our driveway, sounding the musical horn. I go out carrying Linda, and look in at Mare who is surrounded by wig boxes and Mark Cross luggage and Kleenex.

MARE: I'm leaving. (Mare is big on drama.)

ME: Oh, are you going on a trip?

MARE: Yes, I'm going to Chicago, but not really—well I *am* going to Chicago but it's only to stay with my sister for a little while. To forget.

OF COURSE I SAY: Forget what?

MARE: Oh, Willis. Willis moved out. He just said he couldn't take it anymore and he wouldn't even say what. He moved out while I was at Kroger's and when I came back I found a note. (She shows me the note. Willis is the man she's been living with.) I'd just bought a leg of lamb and everything. I just had to come by and tell you. I knew you'd want to know. And Martha (leans out, grabs my arm; I almost drop Linda), I might as well tell you, whenever I'm really depressed I come to see you. You and Jerry, well, you're just special people, you know? I mean you're so happy and everything, it gives me faith. Willis was wrong for me anyway, you know that. We never would have had a thing like you and Jerry have, not in a million years. (Mare nibbles her long streaked hair. Linda is getting very heavy and I switch arms.) Well, see you in a week or so. I have to regroup my forces, that's all. Or is it recoup? (Giggles weirdly.) Tell me you're happy, Martha. You and Jerry. Somebody's got to be happy.

ME: I'm happy, Mare. We're very lucky. See you when you get back from Chicago.

A brave wave from Mare. A sad, reckless (she's loving it) smile and she backs out, turns, spinning loose gravel, while I stand in the driveway holding Linda. It's a warm clear day. Oddly enough I do feel happy and lucky and I mean every word I just said, yet I feel strangly fake, too. This air is so clear it's hurting my face.

Jerry at a party, in conversation with a girl in purple velvet pants, overheard by me sliding up behind to get a cigarette.

SHE: What do you do, then?

JERRY: Well, it's hard to describe. I think of myself as an artist, an urban creator, you might say. I'm in the conceptual end of the business, pure thought. On one hand, it's a very intricate process of matching people with places, habitats, filling their little needs. Anticipating their creature comforts. On the other hand, it's like sculpture, dealing with space and form.

SHE: Oh, that must be very exciting.

Jerry sells real estate.

A quick slide of Jerry: you think you've seen him before. He looks like the men who stand beside the cars in car ads: you know the look. Blond, lean, and meaningful as hell. Jerry's looks are deceptive, though. They change. When I started going with Jerry, it was in high school and he had a crewcut and pink shirts. He was a senior, the president of the student government. He went off to college and during the first two years he pledged a fraternity and drank a lot of beer. The last two years he let his hair grow long and protested everything he could think of. Now he has a straight job and straight clothes to fit it but once he gets home—on weekends or when we go out—he looks like he's auditioning for a motorcycle movie. He has all this turquoise jewelry, too. We live in Nashville and there are a lot of music people around and Jerry likes that, he likes to try to hang around with them. Nobody big, though: for instance we know somebody who knows Kris Kristofferson. We go to parties where everyone smokes dope and we also go to straight parties, ornate cocktail suppers with shrimp trees, given by Jerry's business friends. I've always enjoyed being with all our friends but now that this has happened, Phil, nobody much has come around. I thought they were my good friends but I guess they were Jerry's friends and instead of being Martha I was Jerry's wife. I don't know. I mean I'm trying to figure all this out now that it's too late.

But look at the man on the slide: Jerry. My high school honey. I always knew we'd get married and we did, and it was just exactly like I had dreamed it would be, and I've been happy ever since. This is Jerry, ready to go out now: ruffled shirt, leather vest, jeans, boots, a belt with a turquoise buckle. I don't know, I can't seem to get a fix on Jerry even when I show you this slide. Jerry used to say "movie." Then he said "flick." Now he says "film." I mean I've known him so long but there is something I don't know.

Later in October. Late afternoon. Will is running around the yard. Linda is on a blanket on the grass. I'm digging holes in the yard around the cedars, with a spoon. I put a bulb into each hole and then I cover it back up. Will keeps trying to dig up the bulbs but I keep him away by saying "I bet you can't run all the way around the house" and so on. I feel good, the way you feel when you plant something.

Then a man I've seen before walks around the circle and stops in front of our house, on the sidewalk, staring at us. I've never actually noticed him before, but now that he's here I know I've seen him before, walking. I don't know why I say "man." He's just a boy. About nineteen or twenty years old, tall and thin. He has long hair and he wears jeans and an orange windbreaker and I know immediately, from the windbreaker, that he is one of the psychiatric boarders. But the awful thing, Phil, is that he stops walking and stares at me as if I'm somebody he has known very well in the past but has not expected to see again. His hair is feathery and almost white. His eyes are surprisingly dark. They glitter. He stares at me. I move toward Linda on the blanket, thinking *where is Will?* But I can't look away from this boy. His eyes are black and crazy. As I edge toward Linda I feel it, in spite of everything I can do, I feel that answering recognition come into my own face.

"Hiya!" shrieks Will, suddenly at my side, and I grab his hand and jerk Linda up from the blanket and, pulling Will, get inside the house as fast as I can. From the window I see that he's still standing there on the sidewalk for a long time, half an hour, after I have closed and locked the door. I surprise myself. Now I'm concerned that one of the neighbors will notice him there and call the police. When Jerry comes home, I don't tell him about it at all.

The secret madness starts here. But that's the wrong name, Phil. It isn't madness; it's simply something different. Something different starts here. This is when I start being different from what I do. OK: I feed Jerry, I feed the babies. I sleep with Jerry, we go out, the babies are fine, Will starts to catch on to the potty. We have a party. I get a frizzy permanent. Mare comes back from Chicago and starts dating a veterinarian/songwriter.

During all this time it gets worse and worse. I wake up cold and panicked, it's like dying when I wake up. Finally at nine thirty you come on the TV, Phil, and believe me I'm ready for you. I watch as hard as I can. I hoard opinions and facts; what consumers really think, what blacks really think, how Viet Nam veterans really feel. If I listen hard enough, maybe I can collect enough interesting opinions and strong feelings to get me through the day. Getting through the day becomes a major project. I buy a big calendar with spaces for every hour. I know that it's absolutely necessary for me to be as busy as possible at all times. If I slip or relax for even one minute, something horrible will happen. I don't know what. Sometimes I think about it in terms of my head falling apart, caving in or splintering grotesquely outward in all directions. That would frighten the babies. Other times I think about it as something worse: if I relax, if I sit still, something will slip in and take possession. I don't know what. Some sort of insect, creepy.

The things that actually happened during this period are pretty much of a blur, even though it was only two or three weeks ago. Nothing happened, actually. Out of a period of about two weeks there, all you get is a few short tapes.

WILL: Read, read.

ME: OK. Just a minute.

WILL: Read, read, *want.*

ME: OK. Let me get your book.

WILL: Book.

ME: That's right. Now, what's this?

WILL: Airplane in the sky!

ME: Smart boy! Now what's this?

WILL: Airplane in the sky!

ME: No, it's an elephant. El-e-phant. Can you say elephant?

WILL: Efem.

ME: Good. Will, what would you say if Mommy told you she's going crazy?

WILL: Airplane in the sky!

I call my old friend Janice, after staring at the telephone for fifteen minutes. Janice and Mare are my two best friends. Once, years ago, the three of us shared an apartment for the summer. Since then, Mare has gone in one direction and Janice has gone the opposite way and I guess I've just stayed put. Janice is a member of the Junior League. She has three kids and goes to church. I decide to tell her everything.

ME: Janice, this is Martha. Are you busy? I mean, can you talk for a little while?

JANICE: Well, actually, I was just on my way out the door.

ME: Oh, well, I just wondered. This will only take a minute.

JANICE: Yes?

ME: I mean, well it's a little hard to put into words.

JANICE: What is it, Martha? Is something wrong?

ME: No, no, nothing like that. Listen, you go ahead, and we'll talk about it another time. Maybe you can come over for coffee soon.

JANICE: Tell me.

ME: No, it's not anything, really.

JANICE: (relieved) Great. I'll be looking forward to it. (Click. Click. Two very loud clicks. I sit looking at the phone. First I want it to ring and then I don't want it to ring, but in any case, it doesn't.)

The boy walks around our circle every day now, Phil. He slows down when he passes our house. He wears blue jeans and his windbreaker and tennis shoes. On Tuesday, November 3, he walks up the driveway and into that side of the garage we never use, the side where the junk and the suitcases and tools are stored. He stays in there for about five minutes and then comes out. The next day he goes into the garage again, carrying a cardboard box. On November 5 he goes into the garage again, carrying an airlines bag. This time he doesn't come out.

While the babies are taking their naps, I hold a long excited debate with myself. What should I do? Should I call the police? Should I call Jerry? It would be fun to tell him something exciting for a change. I haven't had anything exciting to tell him for years. Or should I march right out to the garage and say OK, what are you doing here? Get out.

In the end I do none of these things. I wash my hair and set it (usually I don't set it) and then I cook beef stroganoff for dinner, early. After I feed the babies—Jerry won't be home for an hour—I fix up this little guest tray for the boy in the garage. I'm humming to myself, tra la, a strange operatic humming that I've never done before. I put a plate of beef stroganoff and noodles, two Pepperidge Farm rolls, a nice tossed salad, and some peanut butter cookies and an apple on the tray. I'm not pleased with the peanut butter cookies but I hadn't planned on dessert. I put Will in front of the TV to watch *Misterogers*, go out to the garage, knock on the door of the closed side, and set the tray down right in front of it. I leave immediately. I take the cat inside with me so she won't bother the tray.

Now I'm in suspense. I flit around the kitchen windows, even though I know there's no possible way to see that door from the house. But I keep looking. In fifteen minutes I go back out to check, and the tray has disappeared. As if by magic. No tray, closed door. I'm delighted. I go back into the house, make two martinis, put the pitcher in the refrigerator and continue humming, refining my style.

When Jerry comes in he says, "Hey, great, Martha, what's the occasion?"

"All for you," I tell him. "Have a drink."

The next morning I wake up free of fear. After Jerry leaves, I fix a breakfast tray. It occurs to me that there's no bathroom in there, but I can't be bothered with such details. I fix poached eggs and bacon, and fifteen minutes later the tray is gone. Now both trays are inside the room.

I had thought that he might put the one from supper outside the door, so that I can wash the dishes. Now I imagine dishes stacked up to the low ceiling of the storage room—all my dishes, all my silverware. I'll have to feed my family on paper plates. I start giggling and Will catches it and giggles too. Sooner or later I'll go in there and talk to that boy. I savor it, putting it off. He's mine to talk to and I can go in there and talk to him whenever I want. Whenever I'm ready. I hold long conversations in my head. I tell him everything.

I finally decide to go in later that day, while the babies are asleep. My hand shakes as I brush my hair. Ever since that boy has been in the garage, the fear is gone. As swiftly and as mysteriously as it came. Now I feel weird and lightheaded, constantly on the verge of laughter. I take a long time with my hair. When I'm ready the doorbell rings, scaring me to death. It's Janice in a boxy brown suit.

"I thought I'd run over for a minute while Mattie's still at my house to watch Lisa. You're looking good."

I say thanks, holding back the laughter.

Janice lights a Salem and frowns. "What was the matter the other day?" she asks, looking carefully at my left ear. "You want to talk about it?" She hates conversations like this.

"Oh, nothing," I say. "I mean, just nothing at all. I think my pills are depressing me, some days I really drag around. I've decided to call Dr. Lassiter and see if I can get the sequential kind, isn't that what you call them?"

"Oh *listen!*" Janice says. "You really should. I mean, they can be so dangerous. I had this friend who—" Janice is off and running. She loves a good pill reaction better than anything in the world except an unusual pregnancy. Janice tells me five true case stories involving terrible pill reactions. All through the conversation, I keep thinking Janice would *die* if I told her I have a boy in the garage. She would *die*. At the end of Janice's pill act, Linda wakes up. Janice leaves, I am annoyed yet also relieved, in a funny way, that I haven't spoken to him yet. I have to get my head completely right. I have to save him as long as I can.

I fix roast pork for supper and that night Jerry and I watch Anthony Quinn on Dick Cavett. Anthony Quinn is good. I feel very relaxed, as if I've melted and I'm sloshing around inside my skin. I realize how long it's been since I've relaxed.

Morning. The third day. I call Charlsie, actually calling her Charlsie. She always offers to babysit and I know she never means it; this time she's caught.

ME: Hi, Charlsie. Put your money where your mouth is. (I feel giddy now and out of control. I've just taken him his breakfast; it's going on too long.)

CHARLSIE: What? Is this *Martha*? (This is the first time I've ever called her Charlsie. No wonder she's surprised.)

ME: Yes, it is. Listen, I forgot that I have a doctor's appointment this afternoon and I don't have a sitter and I wondered if you could possibly babysit for about an hour? I can't tell you how much I would appreciate it if you could. (Afterthought:) *Charlsie.*

MRS. RASNICK: Well, let me see, I suppose so. Actually I'm knee-deep in these bottles . . . (This vision of Mrs. Rasnick literally knee-deep in bottles nearly cracks me up. But I recover. I give no ground.)

ME: Both the babies will be asleep.

MRS. RASNICK: Well, all right, dear. I suppose I could bring my bottles with me—

ME: Oh, yes. By all means. Bring your bottles. See you about one.

I don't know why I made such an elaborate plan, Phil. I could have walked out to the garage while the babies were asleep. I didn't need a sitter. God knows, I didn't need Mrs. Rasnick. Probably by then I wanted to be found out; I don't know.

I mop the kitchen. Then I get all dressed up, like I'm going to the doctor. Mrs. Rasnick appears, armed with her bottles and goo. She carries everything in a burlap bag covered with seashells. Making seashell bags was her thing two years ago. I sail out of the house, go to the garage, start the car noisily, back out the driveway and park immediately on our side street, cleverly out of view of Mrs. Rasnick. I am so taken with my own cleverness. I sneak through our boxwood and into our garage.

I knock on the door. "It's me," I say.

No response.

"Can I come in?"

No answer.

I knock again: nothing. Now I'm really frightened. What if he's dead in my garage? Somehow that strikes me as funny and then I open the door. I'm still laughing as I open the door.

It doesn't hit me until then, Phil. What I've done. The storage room smells awful; I told you there was no bathroom in there. There are rotten food smells and sweat smells also. It's so bad that I retch at the door. Oddly enough I'm still so conditioned by what I do that I almost go back to get the Lysol spray. But I step inside. It's dark and at first I can't see anything. I remember now that the light in here burned out a month ago and I've been meaning to replace it ever since. There's no window, which means that the boy has been here in the dark for almost exactly three days.

I can't see him. I can't see anything. I wait until my eyes adjust to the darkness and then gradually I see him, curled up in the corner by the lawnmower. I had been staring at him all along. I walk over there, picking my way through the mess. He's curled up, asleep. I realize he doesn't know whether it's night or day. I bend down. He breathes slowly and regularly, as deeply as a child. He has crumpled his orange windbreaker into a sort of pillow and has put it under his head. That windbreaker is the final thing, Phil.

I kneel down and shake his shoulder, gently. I can feel the bones. He murmurs and I keep shaking him and suddenly he bolts up, wild-eyed, like an animal. He tries to stand, loses his footing, and crashes back on some plates and knocks over a tool box. The noise is deafening because it has been so quiet. He hasn't heard any noise at all for three days, remember. He cringes. I cringe. He's breathing hard now, with a sharp sobbing intake of breath.

"Don't be afraid," I say. "I won't hurt you. Don't be afraid." I move a little closer, sort of crawling. I reach out for his hand but touch instead something slimy and wet that he's holding. He makes an unintelligible sound, pulls his hand back and puts it to his mouth. Finally I realize what he has: the piece of chamois that was in the tool box, that Jerry uses to polish the car. He is chewing it. Apparently he has been chewing it for some time.

"Oh, Christ," I say out loud. I feel dead and I can see that I have finally gotten there, dead center. His eyes dart back and forth, back and forth. Looking into them I see how far I've come along the way to where he is. I feel awful so I hold him in my arms and begin rocking slightly back and forth. He goes limp and I hold him, saying things that are meant to comfort him, all lies, like "That's all right," and I hold him for a long time. Looking around I see all the mess and the filth, and the door blows open more and the bright fall sunlight is coming in a straight path from the door and falling short of us by a few feet. I hold him until the sunlight is blocked by Mrs. Rasnick, black avenging angel silhouetted in her too-young pantsuit against the door frame. This is the last slide: Mrs. Rasnick's silhouette.

MRS. RASNICK: I thought I heard—

MRS. RASNICK: (rising pitch) Martha, are you all right?

MRS. RASNICK: My God.

Mrs. Rasnick starts to scream.

That just about wraps it up, Phil, except for one painful interview with Jerry. You don't want to hear the whole thing, it's repetitive. I'll start about the middle.

JERRY: Martha, Christ, Martha, why did you have to get my mother to babysit for Christ's sake? That's what I can't understand. My mother. She's been in bed ever since, you know that? She's never been so upset in her life. The least, the very least you could have done would be to have said he raped you or something.

ME: But he didn't rape me.

JERRY: I know that, Martha. We both know that. But couldn't you have said that, just to soften the blow a little? I mean, she's got chest pains.

ME: Well, look, Jerry, I'm sorry that your mother has got chest pains but that's hardly the point of this whole discussion. Don't you want to hear my side of it?

JERRY: You haven't got a side of it. Martha, I told you, I'm arranging for you to see a doctor. That's all I can do. We'll discuss this whole thing some other time. (I forgot to tell you, Phil, Jerry is packing. He's folding his cowboy shirt.)

ME: Well, if you think I'm so crazy, how come you're willing to leave the babies with me? (Not that I would ever let him take them, of course; I'm merely testing.)

JERRY: I can't take care of them, I have to work. My mother can't take care of them, she's sick. That's one thing I'll say for you, Martha, at least you didn't lock the babies up out there too.

ME: I keep telling you, I didn't lock *anyone* up out there. That boy went into the storage room himself and all I did was take him some food. That's all—I mean, that's hardly a capital crime, is it? The door was open the whole time. Three lousy little days. I didn't even go in there until the third day when I went in to talk to him and your mother came in and that's all that happened. That's *all*, Jerry.

JERRY: Sure it is.

ME: Jerry, I don't like what you're insinuating. All I did was take him some food and then try to talk to him.

JERRY: That's a real nice, normal thing to do, Martha.

ME: I don't see why you're leaving.

JERRY: Look, I said I don't want to talk about it anymore, Martha. I'm upset, I don't know what I might say to you right now. All along, you've been right there, I could depend on you. This is really a shock.

ME: Do you mean you think I've been a good wife or something? Wow, Jer, that's real nice. That's real touching. (Long silence.) Jerry, I've been a *bore!* a horrible, lousy bore!

JERRY: I just don't understand how you could do it. You endangered the children, my mother, me, my job, everything. You don't know anything about that guy. He could be an ax murderer for all you know.

ME: He's not.

JERRY: You *don't know*, Martha. You don't know anything about him. You still don't. And whatever he is, you've retarded his progress about a million percent. They're probably going to file charges, you know that? *File charges.* That's what the doctor who came with the ambulance said. The Veterans Administration versus Mrs. Martha Rasnick, how's that? Really great, huh? You've outdone yourself.

ME: I don't care about all that stuff.

JERRY: Well just what exactly do you care about? You obviously don't give a damn about me or the children or anything else I can think of. It's more than a little embarrassing, Martha, what you've done.

ME: Jerry, Jerry, please listen to me.

JERRY: You haven't got anything to say that I want to hear right now, Martha.

So that's the way it is, Phil. that's why I'm writing to you. I didn't have anything to say for a long time, and now that I'm ready to talk, no one is here to listen. That's my fault. I've done these things: closed my mind, failed to grow or change, failed to understand Jerry, used my job and then my babies as shields, and—worst of all, last of all—used that boy. Some of it is not my fault, however. A lot of it is not my fault. Anyway it's all done: water under the bridge. I'm sorry, really sorry, about the boy— if I hurt him, that is. If I made him worse. I'm not so sure I did, though. Anyway I am so sorry about the boy. But I'm not sorry about anything else. If Jerry was inconvenienced, if the neighbors were embarrassed by the scene, if Mrs. Rasnick has chest pains, those are their problems. I would do it again. No, I wouldn't, actually. I wouldn't need to do it now. See what I've learned, Phil, from by "experience." See what fine conclusions I've reached. The only thing is that it doesn't do me much good right now, does it, if you're still the only one I have to talk to?

S T U D S   T E R K E L

(1912-)

Born Louis Terkel in New York City, Studs Terkel has had a varied career as a biographer, memoirist, journalist, critic, and dramatist. Terkel earned a bachelor's degree and a law degree from the University of Chicago and later worked as a broadcaster for various Chicago radio and television stations. Through his experience as an interviewer, Terkel developed a rapport with people of diverse backgrounds and occupations. He used his experience as a music critic in his first book, Giants of Jazz *(1957). Similarly, his broadcasting experience led to the publication of several best-selling oral histories based on interviews with average Americans. Terkel received the Pulitzer Prize in nonfiction in 1985 for* "The Good War": An Oral History of World War II *(1984). Terkel was also awarded the George Foster Peabody Broadcasting Award in 1980. Other publications include* The Great Divide: Second Thoughts on the American Dream *(1988) and* RACE: How Blacks and Whites Think and Feel about the American Obsession *(1992), in which the following interview with Peggy Terry appeared.*

In many ways a typically anonymous Terkel subject, Peggy Terry represents both the desire to make amends for personal error that characterizes many white Americans' attitudes toward racial questions and the development of a political consciousness that more is required.

An Interview with Peggy Terry

She lives in Chicago with her daughter and grandson. "My dad worked in the oil fields of Oklahoma, where I was born. He was a coal miner in Kentucky. None of these jobs was too steady, so we went back and forth."

I knew black people were around, but I didn't know where they lived, in Oklahoma City. In Paducah, we lived on the edge. We could sit on the porch and hear the singing from the black church. That's where I really learned to love gospel singing. I never made friends with any of them because I was brought up in prejudice. How can you be raised in garbage and not stink from it? You pick it up. It's like the air you breathe. There wasn't anyone saying any different. Until I heard Reverend King, I never heard any black person say, "I'm as good as you are." Out in the open.

I picked it up from everyone in the family. My father never changed. In one of our trips from Kentucky to Oklahoma in 1929, we went there in a Model T Ford. Daddy slid the car off into a ditch. We were just laying sidewise. This old black man came by on a wagon and offered to pull Daddy out. Daddy says, "Nigger, you better get your black ass on down the road. I don't need any help from you!" Here was my mother, pregnant—she had the baby two weeks after we got there—and three other little children in the car. I was eight. I remember it was so cold. Here's this bigoted man, cutting off his nose to spite his face. That's what a lot of white people do.

Oh, sure, my father was sympathetic to the Klan. So was my grandfather. When they started lynching black people, my grandfather quit. One of my earliest memories is in Littleville, the poor section of Paducah. Blacks and poor whites lived out there together. My grandfather had a buggy with a fringe around the top. We all met at Fletcher's grocery and went to the Ku Kluck Klan meeting. I remember all those hoods. I was about three. My mother says I couldn't have remembered it, but I do. I lost my shoe at that meeting.

Funny thing, my father was a strong union man and always fought the bosses. He always spoke out and stuck up for the workingman. Walked off many jobs, without a penny in his pocket. But he had this blind spot when it came to color.

1970
She recalls her feelings of white superiority, her discoveries.

I didn't like black people. In fact, I hated 'em. If they just shipped 'em all out, I don't think it woulda bothered me. If I really knew what changed me . . . I've thought about it and thought about it.

You don't go anywhere because you always see yourself as something you're not. As long as you can say, "I'm better than they are," then there's somebody below you can kick. But once you get over that, you see that you're not any better off than they are. In fact, you're worse off because you're livin' a lie. And it was right there, in front of us. In the cotton field, choppin' cotton, and right over in the next field, there's these black people—Alabama, Texas, Kentucky. Never once did it occur to me that we had anything in common.

After I was up here for a while and I saw how poor white people were treated, poor white Southerners, they were treated just as badly as black people are. I think maybe that crystallized the whole thing.

I didn't feel any identification with the Mexicans either. My husband and me were migrant workers. We were just kids. I was fifteen and he was sixteen. We were on the road for three years in the thirties. I got pregnant along the way.

We went down in the valley of Texas, which is very beautiful. We picked oranges and grapefruits, lemons and limes in the Rio Grande Valley. We got a nickel a bushel for citrus fruits.

I remember this one little Mexican boy in particular. I felt all right toward him. The Mexican men and the women I worked with, they were just spics and they should be sent back to Mexico. I remember I was very irritated because there were very few gringos in this little Texas town where we lived. Hardly anybody spoke English. When you tried to talk to the Mexicans, they couldn't understand English. It never occurred to us that we should learn to speak Spanish. It's really hard to talk about a time like that, 'cause it seems like a different person. When I remember those times, it's like looking into a world where another person is doing those things.

1990

I was living in Montgomery, Alabama, during the bus boycott and that absolutely changed my life. It forced white people to take a new look at the situation. Not all of them changed the way I did. It didn't leave you in the same comfortable spot you were in. You had to be either for it or against it. I saw grown white men pick black women up and throw them into buses trying to force them to ride. I saw Reverend King beat up at the jail. He would be released on bond and they would pick him up again on some trifling thing. They just kept repeatedly doing these things.

I remember one time he came out of jail in all white clothes. About five or six white men jumped him. Suddenly something says to me, "Two on one is nigger fun." That's what they always said when they saw two white kids beatin' up on a black kid. When I saw 'em beatin' up on Reverend King, something clicked.

When I heard he was gonna get out of jail, me and some other white women wanted to see this smart-aleck nigger. I'm so thankful I went down there that day because I might have gone all my life just the way I was. When I saw all those people beating up on him and he didn't fight back, and didn't cuss like I would have done, and he didn't say anything, I was just turned upside down.

I'm sure it didn't happen in just that instant. I'm sure there must have been something within me before that. You know, poor white women don't see too much of the violence. The men, they *do* the violence. We women knew it went on but we never *saw* it. This was my first seeing it, actually.

While the boycott was still goin' on, I came to Chicago. Down South, they always said that black people run the cities up north. They'd say, "You don't want to go up there, niggers run the workplace." I really expected to see that. I was ready to cope with it as best I could. But I didn't see any black people, except early in the morning. They were going north on the buses and streetcars and el trains to work in kitchens and homes. In the evening, they'd all go south. That was the only time I saw any of them.

The nearest I came to making a black friend in the South was this lady who lived behind us in Littleville. This was during the Depression. My dad was working on the WPA, but we still didn't make enough money to eat properly. This black woman used to call us kids over and feed us. Maybe that's one of the things that lodged in my heart and in my mind, this woman was so good to us. In Chicago, I met this black woman, she from Texas, me from Oklahoma. We'd say we're black and white hillbillies. I learned so much from her. My second husband knew her and invited her for supper. I didn't want it, but I didn't make a fuss. It had never happened to me, eating at the same table with a black. It was a cold winter. She had on galoshes and my husband helped take them off. I'm sitting there just wide-eyed. A white person helping a black person off with her coat and boots. I was so mixed up.

With all my feelings and what happened in Montgomery, I was ready to take a step forward and try to undilute all the damage. When I believe in something, I act on it. I went down and joined CORE.* I was in jail before the night came. They were having sit-ins at the Board of Education. Protesting the Willis Wagons. Instead of letting black children go to integrated schools, they had all these mobile trailers parked around the black schools on the South and West Side. I was in jail, oh, at least half a dozen times and loved every minute of it. I felt I was doing something. I don't belong to any church but I'm a deeply religious person. I believe that you act on your beliefs.

I enjoy picketing, too. I don't remember who we were picketing, but this really well-dressed white woman said, "Why are you out there doing this?" I had about six kids with me, mine and my girlfriend's. I said, "Well, where else could I go and be treated with this respect that I've been treated with by Reverend King, the Nobel Prize Peace winner? No white Nobel Prize winner would pay poor white trash like me the slightest attention. Reverend King does."†

We reached a period in the movement when black people felt they weren't given the respect they should have. White liberals ran everything. They made the final decisions. Blacks said, "We want to do it under our own power." There was a rift, but not in my mind. I felt black people were doing what they should be doing.

I heard about these white Southerners in Uptown. I didn't want anything to do with them, because, oh God, I just got out of that jackpot. But this black guy told me about JOIN—Jobs or Income Now. Either give us a job or give us money. I went to a couple of meetings and I realized that's where I should be. White people, go organize your own. There were two black women in the group. Big Dovie Coleman and Little Dovie Thurman. The rest were southern whites.

My great discovery was that poor people, no matter what color they are, have a hard time. They should stop fighting among themselves and get together. We were having a meeting one night. Both Dovies were there. It did deteriorate into nigger this and nigger that. I finally said, "I heard all I want to hear. You don't want to talk about welfare rights and decent housing. All you want to do is sit around and talk about niggers. I'm going home."

I'm walking down the sidewalk and I hear three or four women behind me, these hillbilly women. I think, oh God, they're gonna beat the heck out of me. They came up to me and one of 'em—she was no bigger'n a bar of soap—was crying. She said, "Peggy, we never thought of things like that. You come back and we'll talk about something else."

---

*Congress of Racial Equality.
†As she recounted this incident at an Operation PUSH rally which I attended, the overwhelmingly black audience rose to its feet, cheering, stamping, and singing.

Peggy Terry has suffered a series of illnesses during the past several years and has been, to some degree, housebound.

I'm not into much of anything these days, but I do watch all the black talk shows. From what I hear on these programs, it's better for some but worse for the majority. That goes for poor whites, too. The good thing is that it's out in the open. We're talking about it. Before the boycott in Montgomery, nobody talked about it. All this garbage existed but we ignored it. The black is now highly visible, thank goodness.

Sure there's an antiwhite feeling among blacks. Not in everyone, but in a lot. To me, that's understandable. It's unspeakable what black people have gone through since they were first brought to this country.

What about the young blue-collar white guy, who's out of a job, which he attributes to affirmative action? He says, "I had nothing to do with the past. Why should I be the fall guy?"

Oh, but he did. Just by existing. Whites had always been given better treatment. Even coal miners like my father, who had a terrible time, were treated better than blacks.* The white in many cases is better qualified because he had all these years a better chance at an education, a better chance at a job.

I don't think it's up to any white person to say what black people want or how they go about getting it. I'm not talking about open warfare in the streets. But the kindest, gentlest man that could have led us into great changes was shot and killed. Reverend King. How come's there's no white Martin Luther King?

If there was enough work for everybody, there wouldn't be so much animosity. We wouldn't have this fear of a black person getting a job, who may not be qualified. I think most black people before they get a job have to be doubly qualified. It's changed a lot, but not that much. The media makes a big deal of it whenever a black goofs up on a job, whereas "A white would have handled it. There's affirmative action for you." But what percentage of the workforce is really affected by it? We have a long, long way to go.

We look at crooked black politicians and say, "See? Once they get in, see what happens?" Black men are American men just like white men are American men. They go into a corrupt system. Why expect them to be different? They're not.

What makes white people afraid of blacks in power is that they know deep in their heart black people have not been treated right. They're afraid with the shoe on the other foot, it will all come home. No matter how much they may deny it, my God, they've got to know.

To a certain extent, we're all racists. Maybe not to the point of burning crosses, but we have attitudes that we don't even recognize in ourselves. I know I'll never be free of it. I fight it all the time. It's things you've grown up with all your life. I will never reach the point where I can sit with black people and be unaware of their

---

*Lord, I'm so lowdown, baby.
I declare I'm lookin' up at down.
The men in the mine, baby,
They all lookin' down at me.
A Big Bill Broonzy blues, 1930s

being black. I'm always afraid I'm going to say something wrong, even with those I love and trust.

There were all those years when I said and believed horrible things. I'm afraid that sometimes that will come out. Remember, I was forty years old before I went into the civil-rights movement. Being a Southerner makes it worse because Southerners say what they think. A lot of times they say it *before* they think.

I was raised to hate Jews, too. They killed Christ and all that. It went along with being antiblack. I heard black people say that Jewish people should be thankful every day that black people are here, because if they weren't, the Jews would be catching it. When each wave of immigrants came here, there was always someone just above them. The way I see it, Jewish people are just above black people. There has to be a top crust and a bottom crust in our society. Somebody has to be on the bottom.

I think you become an adult when you reach a point where you don't need anybody underneath you. When you can look at yourself and say I'm okay the way I am. I don't need anybody underneath me. One of the things that keeps my class of people from having any vision is race hatred. You're so busy hating somebody else, you're not gonna realize how beautiful you are and how much you destroy all that's good in the world.

ROSS CHAMBERS
(1940?–)

Born in Australia, Ross Chambers is the Marvin Felheim Distinguished Professor of French and comparative literature at the University of Michigan. Chambers's works include contemporary cultural studies as well as studies of nineteenth century French literature. He is the author of many books including Loiterature *(1999),* Room for Maneuver: Reading Oppositional Narratives *(1991), and* Story and Situation *(1984).*

Chambers's essay "The Unexamined" turns the light on the desired/undesired nature of white privilege.

THE UNEXAMINED

Who Was That Marked Man?

A long time ago, perhaps 1963, I took a flight from Sydney to Rome. It's a long flight, so there's time to chat with your neighbor. On this occasion, mine was a fellow Australian, a bit younger than I and smartly dressed. Although his accent was proletarian, I judged him to be a successful businessman (in Australia there's no real incompatibility). I was even a bit intimidated, as his cool urbanity contrasted more than favorably, I thought, with the veneer of citified ways I had recently picked up after spending my early years in "the bush." (There must have been sexual attraction, too; why else would I remember all this so vividly?) We chatted pleasantly, breaking the ice—since he was from Melbourne and I from Sydney, then as now rival cities—with well-tried pleasantries (Melbourne's unaccountable passion for Aussie Rules football, the difficulty of finding decent beer in Sydney). Oh, I forgot to tell you that we both were white, male, and English speaking—but you knew that, didn't you? Some things can be taken for granted.

As the flight approached Rome, my companion reached into a bag and pulled out his disembarkation card; could I help him with it? My first thought was that he needed assistance with a document in Italian—but then I suddenly realized the problem was of another order. He could read and write, but only very laboriously, and it quickly came out that after emigrating to Australia in early adolescence, he was now returning for the first time in more than ten years to visit his family in Sicily and demonstrate his wealth and social success. I couldn't have been more surprised. But now I looked again: yes, how had I failed to notice the black hair, the olive complexion, the dark eyes? Suddenly my companion had slipped from the unexamined, all-purpose category of (male) "Australian" into another, *marked* group, one that could not so easily be taken for granted and instead invited examination. In the awkward government-sponsored euphemism of the day, he was now a "New Australian."

At that moment, I began to learn about the contingent, context-bound character of social classification, but I confess that my first feeling, along with surprise, was one of reassurance. The man's "whiteness" was not (quite) at issue, but it was more compromised by his Mediterranean origins than mine could ever be by my countrified crudeness, since I belonged to the "naturally" superior category of the native born. The quality of my whiteness was enhanced, in other words, to the same degree that his was damaged. He was a marked man in a way that I was not, even though we both were soon to emerge into the streets of Rome where he would pass unnoticed and I would stick out like the proverbial sore thumb.[1]

Markedness and unmarkedness, then, are relative categories; who is marked and who not is ultimately a matter of context. In linguistics, from which social semiotics borrowed the concept of markedness, there is no sense that the unmarked/marked pair lines up with concepts like normalcy and deviation or unexaminedness and unexaminability. Those linguistic features designated as marked or unmarked form part of a single paradigm, so that a zero-degree feature (e.g., the unpronounced ending of the French verb *j'aime*) is in differential relation not with the general category of marked features but with each member of the paradigm, whether marked or unmarked. Thus, *j'aime* contrasts with *tu aimes* or *il/elle aime,* in which the ending also is unpronounced, in a way no different from its contrast with, say, *j'aimais* or *j'aimerai* with their marked endings.

In the social sphere, however, things work otherwise. The differential structures that mediate social relations are themselves mediated by the phenomena we call power and desire. One of the effects of such phenomena is to distribute to unmarkedness the privileges of normalcy and unexaminedness and to reserve for markedness the characteristics of derivedness, deviation, secondariness, and examinability, which function as indices of disempowerment (although, oddly, not always of undesirability).

There are plenty of unmarked categories (maleness, heterosexuality, and middle classness being obvious ones), but whiteness is perhaps the primary unmarked and so unexamined—let's say "blank"—category. Like other unmarked categories, it has a touchstone quality of the normal, against which the members of marked categories are measured and, of course, found deviant, that is, wanting. It is thus (unlike linguistic unmarkedness) situated outside the paradigm that it defines. Whiteness is not itself compared with anything, but other things are compared unfavorably with it, and their own comparability with one another derives from their distance from the touchstone. In other words, unmarked or "blank" categories are *aparadigmatic.* Only the marked categories form part of the paradigm and may therefore be compared with one another.

As a result, the marked categories' relation to the unmarked ones that define their paradigmaticity is that of a *plural* (having the characteristic of comparability) to a *singular* (having the characteristic of incomparability). For example, in championship tennis, as Freadman and Macdonald point out, men's singles (there being no "mixed singles") is the touchstone game. Men's singles is in a different category, since it alone determines who the "top" players are from the various other singles and mixed games that (together with men's singles, however) constitute the field of "tennis." In the field of "race," whiteness occupies the position of men's singles with respect to the many categories of nonwhite, determining who the "top" people are.

Something similar could be argued for all the big binaries, whose unmarked-versus-marked structure is more frequently bound up with a singular-versus-plural (or indivisible-versus-divided) distinction than is generally recognized. Like the difference between white and nonwhite, that between masculine and nonmasculine or metropolitan and nonmetropolitan (notice that I don't say white and black or masculine and feminine or metropolitan and colonial) is the difference between an incomparable singular and a plural—the plural of "colors" and "ethnicities," of straight women/lesbians/gay men, of the different kinds of colonies, "client states," and provinces—whose members are subject to comparison among themselves. Thus, gay men are "like women"; Asians are "better immigrants" than Latinos; Thailand is "third world," even though it was never strictly a colony.

Notice also that this result is produced by a certain "contamination" among the binaries themselves. To enable the pluralization of the nonmasculine other, it is necessary for the gender binary (masculine/feminine) to be contaminated by sexuality (heterosexual/homosexual), so that it becomes what is familiar to us as the sex–gender system. Similarly, the configuration of the postcolonial world results from a contamination of the metropolitan/colonial binary with a European/non-European or West/rest binary that is itself modeled on the city/country or capital/provinces distinction.

In the same way, in a country such as the United States, the racial binary (white/colored) is contaminated by the concept of ethnicity (with whiteness constituting the "blank"—nonracial or nonethnic—category). It thus becomes a race-ethnicity system in which Jews and "white ethnics" mingle with Latinos, Asian Americans, and blacks to form a variegated class of "others." By means of a similar system, a young Australian of Anglo-Celtic ancestry (the blank category) was able, in 1963, to put a young Australian of Mediterranean extraction into a category that might have been labeled "off-white," where he began to rub shoulders with *who knows whom?* (that was my mother's catchall phrase for the innumerable set of marked groups from which our white, lower-middle-class family knew itself to be significantly different). The class contamination according to which—at that time and in that culture—it was better to be a white, urban, working-class businessman than a white, countrified, middle-class teacher, a contamination that might in other circumstances have made me the marked category and compromised my social status, faded into insignificance by comparison with the power of the race-ethnicity system to determine prestige, privilege, and power.

I am arguing that the difference between white and nonwhite depends in crucial ways on there also being differences among the multiple categories that constitute the paradigm of the nonwhite, since it is only by differentiation from a pluralized paradigm that the singularity of whiteness as nonparadigmatic, its undivided touchstone character, can be produced. Thus, the fact that nonwhiteness can be black or coffee colored or yellow or olive, African, Asian, or Latino, mestizo, or "pure" is, according to this argument, the essential feature by which whiteness enjoys its privileged, aparadigmatic status. In short, to pluralize the other is to produce one's own singularity.

The case of the countrified white Australian and the new Australian from Sicily on that Quantas flight demonstrates that the tactic of pluralization (like all scapegoating tactics)[2] can backfire. A singularity that is the product of the pluralization of its other can be vulnerable, in turn, to a pluralization, a divisibility of its own. There are "degrees" or "shades" of whiteness, which is a quality that can be inflected by the same operators (of color, ethnicity, class, and the like) needed to pluralize the other.

Mine is an argument from example, but it is confirmed by deconstructive philosophy, which teaches that there is no difference without mixture. The equation "whiteness is to nonwhiteness as the aparadigmatic is to the paradigmatic" implies a sense in which the supposedly aparadigmatic category actually forms part of the paradigm, and whiteness—thus brought within the purview of difference—is therefore "tinged" with nonwhiteness. Only if whiteness were opposed to an equally homogeneous category of nonwhiteness and only if there were no other systems of social classification could an absolute distinction between the categories be maintained and the purity of each sustained.

Questions arise, however, as they did on that Quantas flight. Is a Jewish lesbian as white as a sraight male WASP? How does southern white "trash" measure up against a light-skinned, blue-eyed, college-educated, second- or third-generation, non-Spanish-speaking Cuban American? In South Africa under apartheid, visiting Japanese businessmen enjoyed the status and perks of honorary whites. Light-skinned, middle-class, educated African Americans in the United States can seem well on the way to becoming white by comparison with cousins or even siblings who may be darker skinned or have remained working class, rural, or poor. In the end, identity becomes a bit like a poker hand, in which the value of the ace (whiteness) can be enhanced, if one holds a couple of face cards or another ace (masculinity, heterosexuality, middle classness) or, alternatively, depreciated by association with cards of lower value (ethnicity, color, lack of education, working classness).

My question now is why these facts are so widely ignored, misrepresented, and misrecognized. How does whiteness retain its mythic status of aparadigmaticity? It is not enough, it seems, for whiteness to pluralize its other. It must also protect itself from scrutiny, for fear that it will lead to the kind of awkward questions asked on my Signey-to Rome flight. In addition to singularity, whiteness needs another quality to ensure tht its highly vulnerable claim to the indivisibility of an aparadigmatic norm will not be examined. That is, it needs to be not only indivisible but also invisible.

Examinability and In(di)visibility

Indivisibility ensures that whiteness is considered to be, contrary to the evidence, a uniform quality that one either possesses or does not, whereas the pluralization of the other produces nonwhiteness as a multiplicity of different ways of being (of being nonwhite). The invisibility of whiteness, however—its ability to elude examination—depends on a further dichotomizaion of the white/nonwhite relation, one that inverts in an apparently contradictory way the relation of white singularity to the pluralized other. Whereas the other is *pluralized* in order to produce whiteness as indivisible and singular, the groups that compose this pluralized other are *homogenized* in this new relation, through what is called *stereotyping*, that is, the belief that "all Xs are the same" (where X refers to the members of marked, examinable groups and perhaps, at a certain horizon, to the whole set of members of all such groups).

In contrast to those whose identity is defined by their classificatory status as members of a given group, whites are perceived as individual historical agents whose unclassifiable difference from one another is their most prominent trait. Whiteness itself is thus atomized into invisibility through the individualization of white subjects. Whereas nonwhites are perceived first and foremost as a function of their group belongingness, that is, as black or Latino or Asian (and then as individuals), whites are perceived first as individual people (and only secondarily, if at all, as whites). Their essential identity is thus their individual self-identity, to which whiteness as such is a secondary, and so a negligible, factor.[3]

The pluralization of the *other* and the homogenization of *others* are not contradictory, however, because each depends on the classification of non-whites into groups. The nonwhite is pluralized by being divided into groups, each of which is homogenizable through stereotyping, either as an autonomous group or in association with other groups with which it may be thought to have an affinity (thus, at some official level in the United States, "Asians and Pacific Islanders" are thought to be "all the same"). In contrast, the category of the individual is the key to white hegemony, that is, to the unexaminedness of the degrees and divisions in whiteness (its own forms of nonwhiteness). The reason is that whiteness's indivisibility (as a function of the pluralization of the other) can be maintained only through the production of an invisibility that depends on atomizing whiteness (as a function of the homogenization of others), distributing it among individual historical agents whose common whiteness thus is unperceived and escapes examination.

Since the category of the individual shares with the singularity of whiteness the quality of undividedness (that is what "individual" means etymologically) and is simultaneously the factor of white invisibility, we can encapsulate the secret of whiteness's unmarked, unexamined quality in a single word, *in(di)visibility*. We also can state that in(di)visibility has as its opposite the examinability resulting from the pluralization of the other (its divisibility), in conjunction with the homogenization of the others resulting from pluralization. What does it mean, then, to be examinable—what form of visibility, as well of divisibility, does this imply—and what does it mean to be unexamined?

First, the category of examinability has not one but two alternatives: one can either be unexaminable (out of reach of examination), or examinable but nevertheless be unexamined (which is the case, I claim, of whiteness). Christopher Miller points out that in European "Africanist" discourse, Africa was perceived as a place of "blank darkness."[4] It was so other that other was not the word; there was nothing to be perceived there and no knowledge to be had of it. According to this definition, "blank darkness" exemplifies the category of the unexaminable, and in(di)visibility can therefore be said to produce, at the other end of the spectrum, something like "blank whiteness." It is as much outside the paradigm of divisible otherness as blank darkness is, but normalized into familiarity rather than exoticized and taken for granted rather than posing a challenge by virtue of its extreme otherness. Blank whiteness is therefore in the category of the unexamined. It is as if the system encompassed two mythic (or incomparable) categories, blank whiteness and absolute blackness, each of which is held to lie outside the sphere of examinability. One is unexamined "norm," and the other is unknowable "other" (or extreme of otherness), and between them lies the pluralized area of the multiple categories that come under scrutiny, constituting the knowable others of whiteness as the domain of the examinable. These in-between categories are disqualified for their otherness from the status of the unexamined, but they are not consigned, beyond the limits of the knowable, to the category of unexaminability.

As a result of a long history of European colonization, "darkest Africa" has moved from its status of absolute and unexamined alterity to the category of the examinable other. One may think that blackness, as the category diametrically opposed to whiteness, has retained from this history a certain characteristic of extremity that gives it a particular status among whiteness' pluralized others. In the United States, for example, it is clear that the system of racial categories is bookended by whiteness and blackness, as if the in(di)visibility of whiteness were matched by the blank inscrutability of blackness.[5]

This category of absolute blackness is necessary, it seems, only so that there can be, for symmetry, a category of unexamined whiteness, since blacks do not enjoy the same privilege of aparadigmaticity as whites do and are included in the general mix of the pluralized other even as they are viewed as the polar opposite of whiteness. In other words, the special status of blackness derives from an ambiguity: it forms part of a (white/black) dichotomy while simultaneously functioning as only one category—the "extreme" one—among those that constitute whiteness's pluralized other.[6] The special status of whiteness derives from its being opposed to blackness as an absolute term, and so it lies (unlike blackness) outside the pluralized group that constitutes its others.

As a product of in(di)visibility, blank whiteness escapes examination by being unexamined, but all other nonwhite categories, including blackness, belong to the field of examinable others. Examinability, as I am using the term here, refers to the unfavorable attention to certain groups that is recognized, in its overtly hostile forms, by terms like *misogyny, homophobia,* and *racism* but that has many other more covert, polite, hypocritical, and even sanctimonious forms. It is not in principle the same as the practice of examination that Foucault identified as the key practice of disciplinary knowledge, which is thought of as an objective scrutiny characterized by the supposed neutrality of the examiner and based on the false assumption of the separability of the examining subject and the object of examination.[7] Historically, the disciplinary examination of marked categories (nonwhite, women, homosexuals, criminals, the insane) has been difficult to distinguish from the prejudiced attention paid to socially marked others, so illusory is the alleged neutrality of examination as a practice.

Examination, furthermore, is not solely an operation performed by members of unexamined groups on members of examinable groups, as the phenomena of "internalized" misogny, homophobia, and racism demonstate. What all these cases of examination (disciplinaary, prejudiced, internalized) have in common, however, is the examining subject's desire not to be confused with those who, because of their examinability, are its objects, even when the subject and the object of examination are housed in the same person. It is as if the practice of examination itself resulted in the desired separation of the (unexamined) examiner from the (examinable) examined, by producing as its object an area of examinability that can imply a space exempt from examination that is occupied by the examiner. Examining thus turns out to have the structure of scapegoating: one classifies oneself as a member of the category of the unexamined through the very act of examining others.

If this analysis is correct, examination expresses a desire for the separation of examiner and examined that is itself an acknowledgment that the two are in fact connected. Examinability, in other words, is a device of disconnection: it presupposes the denegation of contexts—that is, of a history—in which the relatedness of the subjects and objects of examination becomes apparent. The act of examining (think of this next time you have a medical, or academic, or judicial examination) is a device for denying the contexts that join people. As it happens, the idea that such disconnectedness, as the denial of historical context, is what defines both the familiarity of the "everyday" and the strangeness of the "exotic" is something that I have argued elsewhere.[8]

A radical disconnection of subject and object causes the object-world to fade into insignificance and become unworthy of examination, so that only the doings and concerns of the subject (to the extent that they are separable from the mere "decor" that surrounds them) are perceived as interesting and important. This is the structure of the "everyday," which is unexamined as an object (like the invisibility of whiteness) because it is presumed to be already known, as opposed to the concerns, tasks, and negotiations in which the subjects of history engage.

The "exotic," on the other hand, results from a disconnection that brings the object-world into prominence and visibility, with a concomitant backgrounding of the viewing subjectivity. Its examinability is proportionate to the degree to which the subject and object are connected (otherwise it would simply be "blank darkness," the unknowable). These disconnections of subject and object are what permit historical contexts to be forgotten, ignored, or at least backgrounded (in sort, denied), because the stories that actually connect the subject and the object come to be identified exclusively with either the overlooked object (in the case of the everyday) or the underrated subject (in the case of the exotic).

My claim is now, therefore, that at the two extremes, unexamined whiteness can be mapped onto the familiar invisibility of the everyday, and unexaminable blackness (as blank darkness) can be projected onto the strange unknowability of the exotic. Each is a product of disconnectedness and of the denial of those historical contexts by virtue of which we all are brought together. If so, in light of this mapping, it becomes possible to describe the intervening area of whiteness's pluralized and examinable other(s) as one that has mixed characteristics. It is neither wholly familiar nor completely exotic because it is at one and the same time both familiar and exotic. We can then understand the trick of othering—from the point of view of ensuring the unexamined in(di)visibility of whiteness—as the production of forms of disconnectedness that correspond, on the one hand, to the homogenized other's status as familiar and already known and, on the other, to the pluralized other's status as exotic. More particularly, the pluralization of the other is a practice of exoticization, and the homogenization of others is a practice of familiarization, with the outcome of the two being examinability.

By relation to the exoticization of the plural other as a multitude of diverse and colorful forms and practices, the normalcy of singular, undivided whiteness is produced as part of the familiarity of the everyday, unworthy of examination. At the same time, because of the homogenization of marked categories, these categories are themselves produced as familiar and always already known (since "all Xs are the same"). They become part of the ordinary surroundings and trappings, the decor of everyday life. In contrast, the individuality of white subjects—their essential difference from one another as the markers of history—is highlighted, their common whiteness receding into the invisibility of the unexamined. The exotic quality of the pluralized other produces white indivisibility as something relatively unworthy of note, and the actual invisibility of whiteness is a function of the foregrounding of white subjects as active and diverse agents, in contrast to their homogenized and so already familiar others.

The pluralization of the other and the homogenization of othered groups are thus part of the same ploy—the ploy of in(di)visibility. The ploy in turn is possible because of the definitional fact that the other is constitutively split between familiarity and strangeness (as in the Freudian understanding of the unconscious as *un/heimlich*). Finally, this split furnishes the means by which corresponding fissures in the category of whiteness are able to escape examination. Whiteness—like other "blank" categories—is the denial of its own dividedness through the production of its other(s) as examinable, because they are split. Examinability, producing the separation of the unexamined and the examined, is the scapegoating device through which the distinction between the in(di)visible (those individuals whose whiteness is simultaneously invisible and undivided) and the (di)visible (those groups whose visibility is a function of their split identity as others and produces them as examinable) is enforced.

The (di)visibility of the examinable other has more obviously "political" advantages as well. Groups that are produced, through pluralization, as different from one another while simultaneously sharing a relatively small proportion of the available power, wealth, and social prestige can readily become mutually suspicious, envious, and hostile. These qualities are enhanced as the hegemony of whiteness breeds specific subforms of racism (such as "black anti-Semitism"), and the differential system that governs the identity of homogenized others can be used to justify an unequal distribution of the relatively few social advantages that are available. The pluralization of the other translates, in other words, into political disunity and competitive victimhood and forces disadvantages groups, whose common interests are obscured by their pluralized differences, into the complexities and frustrations of alliance politics.

Meanwhile, white people, whose solidarity is ensured by the singularity and indivisibility of whiteness, have little trouble identifying their common interests and pursuing the policies that those interests dictate. (This does not preclude the possibility of internal divisions between groups of white people—say, white feminists against white male chauvinists—but it predicts the difficulty of their being perceived as divisions among white people as opposed to divisions among [kinds of] "people.")

Such difficulties, bred as they are by the pluralization of the other, are exacerbated by the effects of homogenization and stereotyping. To internalize the doctrine that "all Xs are the same" is to produce forms of chauvinism (e.g., racial "pride") that can obscure people's common interests across the lines of social categorization, producing in many cases conflicts of "loyalty" (should my lesbianism, my feminism, or my racial allegiance take political priority?) and the kind of "loyalty oath" that activists sometimes extract. Political chauvinisms are readily identified (from the point of view of a white politics that passes for "mainstream" because its whiteness is unexamined) as "special interests" and their insistent claims can be all the more easily ignored because of the principle that "all Xs are the same," so whatever a given X may have to say can always be assumed, like women's "nagging," either to have been heard before or else to be entirely predictable, given one's foreknowledge of Xs.

It is against this picture of disunity and militancy that white politics comes to look democratic, reaonable, and (not "white" at all but) mainstream. The in(di)visibility of whiteness ensures that white people doing what is in effect their own brand of special-interest politics look like so many individual agents getting on with the business of expressing, exploring, negotiating, and even settling their legitimate differences—differences that define them not as white people (a classificatory identity) but as "people." Identity politics is alien to white people as white people (I'm obviously not talking about white women as women or white gay men as gay men) because whiteness is not a classificatory identity but just the unexamined norm against which such identities are defined, compared, and examined. Their whiteness (our whiteness) being too in(di)visible to define them (us), they (we) have only the self-identities of individual agents. Whereas others may have group identities, white people as a group are just the unexamined. But there is more political strength in that than in all the identity politics in the world.

Buzzing at the Glass Door

What must be done? I have been describing, in a too schematic and abstract way, the operation of a hegemony, and I would not have been able to describe it if it weren't already beginning to come under attack, to falter, and to fail. (As I write, Nelson Mandela is being sworn in as president of South Africa). But the hegemony is far from dead, and the question is how to hasten its demise. In which direction should we push? Should the breakdown of the power differential separating the unexamined from the examinable take the form of bringing the pluralized/homogenized other(s), with their group identities, into the capacious mansion of whiteness, where individuality reigns and racial identity becomes invisible? Or should it take the form of bringing whiteness out of its aparadigmaticity and having it join those whose differences form a paradigm, in which it would become one group—a classificatory, not a normative, identity—among many other, comparable groups? Can both these operations be pursued at the same time? Are they incompatible, or are they in a relation of solidarity with each other? Whatever the theoretical issues, the actual structure and distribution of power, which make the attributes of whiteness widely desirable, suggest that the priority is likely to go toward bringing nonwhite others into the sphere previously defined by whiteness, in which individuality defines subjects as historical agents, regardless of racial or ethnic identity. If so, the story of Patricia Williams's attempt to enter the Benetton's store in SoHo has a certain emblematic significance.[9]

Patricia Williams is a black woman law professor. To judge by the photo on the cover of her book, she also is quite light skinned. As an African American woman, she still has a couple of face cards in her poker hand. One day she saw a sweater in the window of a Benetton's store and, thinking of buying it as a Christmas present for her mother, buzzed—"Buzzers are big in New York City"—for admittance.

> A narrow-eyed, white teenager, wearing running shoes and feasting on bubble gum glared out, evaluating me for signs that would pit me against the limits of his social understanding. After about five seconds, he mouthed: "We're closed," and blew pink rubber at me. It was two Saturdays before Christmas, at one o'clock in the afternoon; there were several white people in the store who appeared to be shopping for things for *their* mothers. (44-45)

The buzzer, of course, signified that admission to the store was conditioned on a test of examinability, a test that Patricia Williams failed. Through a homogenization ("all Xs are the same") that made her excludable on the strength of a classificatory identity, she was denied the unexamined status that would have made her welcome in the store as an individual member of the buying public. Her examinability meant that she and her desire to buy a sweater could be ignored, referred back to the everyday decor of a New York City street where they "belonged," while the white people in the store went on with the important business of shopping. "No words, no gestures, no prejudices of my own would make a bit of difference to [the clerk]; his refusal to let me into the store was an outward manifestation of his never having let someone like me into the realm of his reality." And so she was left pressing "[her] round brown face to the window and [her] finger to the buzzer" (44-45), an exemplary victim of the glass divide—a window for some, a door for others, a partition for all—that separates, as a form of apartheid without segregation, the unexamined from the examinable in American society.

As Williams observes, the exclusion of blacks from the marketplace has its historical roots in slavery, when they (like sweaters) were the objects of transactions between historical white subjects to whom they were simply chattel:

> Blacks went from being owned to having everything around them owned by others. In a civilization that values private property above all else, this means a devaluation of the person, a removal of blacks not just from the market but from the pseudo-spiritual circle of psychic and civic communion. As illustrated in microcosm by my exclusion from Benetton's, this limbo of disownedness keeps blacks beyond the pale of those who are entitled to receive the survival gifts of commerce, the life, liberty and happiness whose fruits our culture locates in the marketplace. (71)

Notice that Williams refers quite naturally here to "our culture"—of which she is part—even as she laments the exclusion of blacks from its fruits. They have a function in the culture, which is to be excludable, on the grounds of examinability, from those historical activities the culture holds to be central; they thus help define those activities as historical and central.

Our analysis could be extended (minus the heritage of slavery, a large omission) to the various other groups whose markedness—similarly, but in different ways and to different degrees—justifies their reclusion behind the glass door that divides the national culture of the United States into those who partake and those who, at best, are permitted to buzz for admission. In her role as X, Patricia Williams, testing the salesclerk's "social understanding," stood for the homogenized category of blacks in general. But also and by extension—in the way that Asian American and Pacific

Islanders can be "all the same"—she stood for all the examinable/excludable social categories that Benetton's did not wish to admit "into the realm of [its] reality."

This role played by the buzzer in Williams's story interests me. It is provided as a means to get attention so that the owner of the face and the finger behind the glass can, on occasion, be excluded from attention, ignored. Ironically enough, it means that white people, as the unexamined, are subject to a prior examinability that establishes their "unexamined" status. But for others, the buzzer stands for examinability as a form of noticeability that serves to mark certain people as not worthy of notice—a truly curious form of attention. It is a bit like the hypocritical slide of the eyes performed in the street (I know, I've done it) by those who identify, say, a homeless or handicapped person only to look immediately away, as if the person had not been seen at all. Had I been in that Benetton's on that December Saturday afternoon, intent on selecting a sweater or engaged in making a purchase, would I have allowed the buzzer to distract me? Would I have noticed the "round brown face" pressed to the glass or perceived the "saleschild's" mouthed (unspoken, silent) words: "We're closed"? Maybe I would have—but it is possible, more than possible, that I would just have vaguely looked up and gone straight back to the sweaters.

In this case, the buzzer is not so much about averting the gaze as about not hearing messages, about selectively not hearing messages. A glass door permits visibility (Williams can see the white shoppers inside; the saleschild can subject her to scrutiny) while by promoting inaudibility, it makes communication—in particular, two-way communication—problematic. The clerk's rather straightforward message can be "mouthed" (it doesn't need to be spoken in order to be understood), whereas any of the necessarily more complex arguments Williams might try to make in reply will be—literally as well as figuratively—unheard, given the glass and the hum of commerce inside the store and the street din outside.

In her account of the incident, Williams quite logically talks about the difficulty she had in publishing her story in a law review that insisted on neutralizing it into aspecificity and pointlessness; and then of how, when she told the story in a public lecture, it was misheard and misreported in the press, its meaning distorted into a critique of affirmative action. A system of apartheid without segregation is one in which people share cultural "space" but communication between them is seriously muffled.

Examinability in this context—the buzzer system—means, as I mentioned, producing certain groups of people as noticeable in the sense that they, their desires and projects, and their messages can be ignored. To return to my previous analysis of otherness as split, their noticeability is a function of their relative strangeness, and their ignorability results from the relative familiarity of their otherness, its everyday, already known quality. Examinability in this sense is the metaphorical glass in the door that separates the members of a racially divided society, as sharers in a common history whose relevance is denied by the practice of examination, so that communication is basically limited to the one-way message: "We're closed." But the system cannot work without a buzzer; a shared (but denied) history implies the necessity of a means for sorting the candidates for admission into those—the unexamined—who will be admitted and the examinable, who will be excluded (so that the "unexamined" is itself a category subject to examination).

Conversely to the way that examinability presupposes a shared history that it is the function of examination to deny, the buzzer therefore figures all the inescapable reminders of shared historical context—those that enable, for example, a Patricia Williams, excluded from Benetton's, to refer nevertheless to "our culture." And people who are not allowed in and whose argument may be inaudible can still keep on buzzing, buzzing, and buzzing again.

That is, they can exploit cultural commonality in order to assert their status as individuals, the status implied by shared history, as opposed to the classificatory identity and the excludability that examinability foists on them. Patricia Williams's book, with its insistence on her singularity as a person and its analysis of shared U.S. history, but taken also as a rhetorical performance (its foregrounding of her personality, its performance of "craziness"), is a fine example of what it takes to be heard when one is on the wrong side of the glass, pressing one's face to the window and one's finger to the buzzer, in a society in which "the rules may be colorblind but people are not" (126). The trick is to convert the background buzz of speech that, like nagging, attracts attention only to be ignored, to a claim for admission that cannot be denied.

But this puts the whole burden on the excluded to demonstrate their admissibility, as individuals, into the world of the unexamined. Would it be too much to expect that the unexamined themselves might dismantle the glass doors and disconnect the buzzers? Thus, they (we) might substitute for the attention characteristic of examinability—quick-to-notice classificatory identities so that their bearers can be relegated behind the glass—a form of attention that would watch for signs of individuality, signs that would be indistinguishable from the evidence of a given person's historical relevance and so the legitimacy of her or his participation in whatever the business at hand might be. For all of her criticism of the law, Williams puts her faith in affirmative action: "It is thus that affirmative action is an affirmation, the affirmative act of hiring—and hearing—blacks as a recognition of individuality that re-places blacks as a social statistic, that is profoundly connected to the fate of blacks and whites either as sub-groups or as one group" (50).

But given a world of apartheid without segregation, in which the rules may be color blind but the people are not, the success of affirmative action itself depends on the fulfillment of a cultural precondition, one that the law itself cannot legislate. The recognition of individuality that Williams seeks presupposes the abandonment of both the categories of examinability and the practices of examination.

In their place, we need to substitute the concept of readability and modes of reading, understanding "reading" to name a relational practice that does not deny but actually recognizes the mutual dependence of subject and object, the relevance, therefore, of context, and finally the particularity of social interactions, mediated as they may be by the codes and conventions without which sociality itself would be impossible.

A reader does not "examine" a text, presumed to be disconnected from the reading subject, but enters into an interaction in which the other (the text) is understood as relevant to (connected with) the self. And finally, reading does not imply a distinction between the readable and the unread in the way that examination presupposes the separability of the examinable and the unexamined. Rather, the act of reading, as I have discussed elsewhere,[10] presupposes the possibility of the readers being read in turn. Such an understanding would be the condition, I suggest (with an apology for bringing this idea so suddenly and so briefly out of my hat; I plan to return to it on another occasion), for social relations of genuine mutuality, as opposed to the glass doors and the buzzers, the system of marked and unmarked, examinable and unexamined categories, that still plagues even the best-intentioned relations today.

But how to achieve this? I hear you ask. Well, we're just going to have to work at it, that's all.[11]

Notes

1. I begin with a story that illustrates my own racism, among other reasons because in my experience it's rare for the critics of racism to confess the racist structure of their own subjectivity. Yet it's impossible to live in a racist society, that is, to be subject to a racist culture, without being a racist cultural subject. It is ourselves we are trying to change, and it does no good, therefore, to begin by pretending that we are outselves exempt from the problems we describe.

That said, the date of the story is important: few contemporary Australians, I surmise, are likely to recognize themselves in it. Particularly offensive is the conflation of whiteness with Australianness, as if the country had not been inhabited for forty thousand years before the white people came. But an elderly aunt of mine, born at the turn of the century (about the same time as modern Australia) and recently deceased, steadfastly refused to take a taxi unless it was driven by an "Australian," by which she meant a person, preferably male, of Anglo-Celtic extraction.

2. Scapegoating consists of singling out for blame and exclusion an individual or group that is charged with the evils of a community. It follows that scapegoaters are, by definition, guilty of that with which the scapegoat is charged, as it is the general function of the act of scapegoating to produce a kind of magical exemption of the scapegoater—a pseudoinnocence that can always be called into question.

3. For a similar argument (with less stress on individualization as such) see Richard Dyer, "White," *Screen* 29 (Autumn 1988): 46. "White people—not there as a category and everywhere everything as a fact—are difficult if not impossible to analyze *qua* white" because they are always represented as something else instead (middle-class English people, the lesbians who live around the corner, or a "boy from the bush"). My thanks to Ian Leong for directing my attention to this article.

4. Christopher Miller, *Blank Darkness: Africanist Discourse in French* (Chicago: University of Chicago Press, 1985).

5. The word *inscrutability*, which I use here as a synonym for unexaminability, has a parallel colonial and racist history of its own, as witness the cliché of "oriental inscrutability."

6. The same analysis applies to the dichotomization of masculine–feminine or metropolitan–colonial in conjunction with the pluralization of the (nonmasculine or the nonmetropolitan) other.

7. Michel Foucault, *Discipline and Punish: The Birth of the Prison* (New York: Vintage Books, 1979).

8. Ross Chambers, "Pointless Stories and Storyless Points: Roland Barthes Between 'Soirées de Paris' and 'Incidents,'" *L'Ésprit créateur* 34 (Summer 1994): 12–30.

9. Patricia Williams, *The Alchemy of Race and Rights: Diary of a Law Professor* (Cambridge, MA: Harvard University Press, 1991), pp. 44–51.

10. Ross Chambers, "Reading and Being Read: Irony and Critical Practices in Cultural Studies," *the minnesota review* 43/44 (Fall 1996): 113–30.

11. An enabling step would consist of substituting an understanding of the (negotiable) genre of specific social interactions for that of the (nonnegotiable because pre-given) identity of the participants in interactions. Genre is the mediator of reading, whereas identity is the object of examinability. It would take a long essay to explore this idea. See Anne Freadman and Amanda Macdonald, *What Is This Thing . . . "Called Genre"?* (Mount Nebo, Qsld: Boombana Publications, 1992).

MAY SWENSON
(1919-1989)

May Swenson was a prolific poet noted for her use of experimental forms and visual design in her poetry. Born in Logan, Utah, Swenson earned a B.A. at Utah State University. She won numerous awards including the Robert Frost Poetry fellowship of the Bread Loaf Writers' Conference, a Guggenheim Fellowship, a Ford Foundation Grant, a Rockefeller Writing Fellowship, a National Endowment for the Arts Grant, a MacArthur Award, a National Book Award nomination for New and Selected Things Taking Place *(1987), and the National Book Critics Circle Award Nomination in poetry for* In Other Words *(1988). Other publications include* Another Animal *(1954) and* May Out West *(1996).*

Swenson's "Black Tuesday" is among the best of the poems written to express the national grief over the assassination of Martin Luther King, Jr. Swenson's white and feminist perspectives are in play here, as is her experimentation with the appearance of the poem on the page.

BLACK TUESDAY

```
                    M
                    A
                    Y

                    S
                    W
                    E      *ICONOGRAPHS
                    N              O
                    S              E
                    O              M
          I C O N O G R A P H S
```

BLACKTUESDAYBLACKTUESDAYBLACKTUESDAY

Blesséd is the man of color
for his blood is rich with
the nuclear sap of the sun.
Blesséd is his spirit which
a savage history has
refined to intercept
whitest lightnings of
vision. Blesséd the neck
of the black man made
muscular by the weight of
the yoke made proud
bursting the lynch rope.
Blesséd his body meek on
the slave block thunderous
on the porch of revolt.
Blesséd his head hewn with

animal beauty for he has
grappled as the lion bled
as the lamb and extracted
the excellence of each for
his character. Blesséd the
black and the white of his
eye.

For Martin Luther King
April 4, 1968

SHERMAN ALEXIE

(1966-)

Born in Spokane, Washington, Sherman Alexie is a Spokane/Coeur d'Alene Indian who grew up and still lives on the Spokane Indian Reservation in Wellpinit, Washington. Alexie is noted for his poetry and short stories on contemporary Native American reservation life. He earned his B.A. at Washington State University and published his first collection of short fiction, The Lone Ranger and Tonto Fistfight in Heaven, *in 1993.*

Alexie was awarded the American Book Award of the Before Columbus Foundation in 1996 for his novel Reservation Blues *(1995); a second novel,* Indian Killer, *was published in 1996, and a second collection of stories,* The Toughest Indian in the World, *in 2000. Alexie is also a poet whose collections include* The Business of Fancydancing *(1992),* I Would Steal Horses *(1992), and* First Indian on the Moon *(1993). Alexie has also been awarded poetry fellowships by the Washington State Arts Commission in 1991 and the National Endowment for the Arts in 1992. His film "Smoke Signals" (1998) was adapted from one of his short stories.*

"A Drug Called Tradition" exemplifies Alexie's ironic vision, in which Native people often seem to make startling and unusual accommodations between the desire to be "modern" and the desire to retain traditional or "tribal" ties.

A DRUG CALLED TRADITION

"Goddamn it, Thomas," Junior yelled. "How come your fridge is always fucking empty?"

Thomas walked over to the refrigerator, saw it was empty, and then sat down inside. "There," Thomas said. "It ain't empty no more."

Everybody in the kitchen laughed their asses off. It was the second-largest party in reservation history and Thomas Builds-the-Fire was the host. He was the host because he was the one buying all the beer. And he was buying all the beer because he had just got a ton of money from Washington Water Power. And he just got a ton of money from Washington Water Power because they had to pay for the lease to have ten power poles running across some land that Thomas had inherited.

When Indians make lots of money from corporations that way, we can all hear our ancestors laughing in the trees. But we never can tell whether they're laughing at the Indians or the whites. I think they're laughing at pretty much everybody.

"Hey, Victor," Junior said. "I hear you got some magic mushrooms."

"No way," I said. "Just Green Giant mushrooms. I'm making salad later."

But I did have this brand new drug and had planned on inviting Junior along. Maybe a couple Indian princesses, too. But only if they were full-blood. Well, maybe if they were at least half-Spokane.

"Listen," I whispered to Junior to keep it secret. "I've got some good stuff, a new drug, but just enough for me and you and maybe a couple others. Keep it under your warbonnet."

"Cool," Junior said. "I've got my new car outside. Let's go."

We ditched the party, decided to save the new drug for ourselves, and jumped into Junior's Camaro. The engine was completely shot but the exterior was good. You see, the car looked mean. Mostly we just parked it in front of the Trading Post and tried to look like horsepowered warriors. Driving it was a whole other matter, though. It belched and farted its way down the road like an old man. That definitely wasn't cool.

"Where do you want to go?" Junior asked.

"Benjamin Lake," I said, and we took off in a cloud of oil and exhaust. We drove down the road a little toward Benjamin Lake when we saw Thomas Builds-the-Fire standing by the side of the road. Junior stopped the car and I leaned out the window.

"Hey, Thomas," I asked. "Shouldn't you be at your own party?"

"You guys know it ain't my party anyway," Thomas said. "I just paid for it."

We laughed. I looked at Junior and he nodded his head.

"Hey," I said. "Jump in with us. We're going out to Benjamin Lake to do this new drug I got. It'll be very fucking Indian. Spiritual shit, you know?"

Thomas climbed in back and was just about ready to tell another one of his god-damn stories when I stopped him.

"Now, listen," I said. "You can only come with us if you don't tell any of your stories until after you've taken the drug."

Thomas thought that over awhile. He nodded his head in the affirmative and we drove on. He looked so happy to be spending the time with us that I gave him the new drug.

"Eat up, Thomas," I said. "The party's on me now."

Thomas downed it and smiled.

"Tell us what you see, Mr. Builds-the-Fire," Junior said.

Thomas looked around the car. Hell, he looked around our world and then poked his head through some hole in the wall into another world. A better world.

"Victor," Thomas said. "I can see you. God, you're beautiful. You've got braids and you're stealing a horse. Wait, no. It's not a horse. It's a cow."

Junior almost wrecked because he laughed so hard.

"Why the fuck would I be stealing a cow?" I asked.

"I'm just giving you shit," Thomas said. "No, really, you're stealing a horse and you're riding by moonlight. Van Gogh should've painted this one, Victor. Van Gogh should've painted you."

It was a cold, cold night. I had crawled through the brush for hours, moved by inches so the Others would not hear me. I wanted one of their ponies. I needed one of their ponies. I needed to be a hero and earn my name.

I crawl close enough to their camp to hear voices, to hear an old man sucking the last bit of meat off a bone. I can see the pony I want. He is black, twenty hands high. I can feel him shiver because he knows I have come for him in the middle of this cold night.

Crawling more quickly now, I make my way to the corral, right between the legs of a young boy asleep on his feet. He was supposed to keep watch for men like me. I barely touch his bare leg and he swipes at it, thinking it is a mosquito. If I stood and kissed the young boy full on the mouth, he would only think he was dreaming of the girl who smiled at him earlier in the day.

When I finally come close to the beautiful black pony, I stand up straight and touch his nose, his mane.

I have come for you, I tell the horse, and he moves against me, knows it is true. I mount him and ride silently through the camp, right in front of a blind man who smells us pass by and thinks we are just a pleasant memory. When he finds out the next day who we really were, he will remain haunted and crowded the rest of his life.

I am riding that pony across the open plain, in moonlight that makes everything a shadow.

What's your name? I ask the horse, and he rears back on his hind legs. He pulls air deep into his lungs and rises above the ground.

Flight, he tells me, *my name is Flight.*

"That's what I see," Thomas said. "I see you on that horse."

Junior looked at Thomas in the rearview mirror, looked at me, looked at the road in front of him.

"Victor," Junior said. "Give me some of that stuff."

"But you're driving," I said.

"That'll make it even better," he said, and I had to agree with him.

"Tell us what you see," Thomas said and leaned forward.

"Nothing yet," Junior said.

"Am I still on that horse?" I asked Thomas.

"Oh, yeah."

We came up on the turnoff to Benjamin Lake, and Junior made it into a screaming corner. Just another Indian boy engaged in some rough play.

"Oh, shit," Junior said. "I can see Thomas dancing."

"I don't dance," Thomas said.

"You're dancing and you ain't wearing nothing. You're dancing naked around a fire."

"No, I'm not."

"Shit, you're not. I can see you, you're tall and dark and fucking huge, cousin."

. . .

They're all gone, my tribe is gone. Those blankets they gave us, infected with small-pox, have killed us. I'm the last, the very last, and I'm sick, too. So very sick. Hot. My fever burning so hot.

I have to take off my clothes, feel the cold air, splash the water across my bare skin. And dance. I'll dance a Ghost Dance. I'll bring them back. Can you hear the drums? I can hear them, and it's my grandfather and my grandmother singing. Can you hear them?

I dance one step and my sister rises from the ash. I dance another and a buffalo crashes down from the sky onto a log cabin in Nebraska. With every step, an Indian rises. With every other step, a buffalo falls.

I'm growing, too. My blisters heal, my muscles stretch, expand. My tribe dances behind me. At first they are no bigger than children. Then they begin to grow, larger than me, larger than the trees around us. The buffalo come to join us and their hooves shake the earth, knock all the white people from their beds, send their plates crashing to the floor.

We dance in circles growing larger and larger until we are standing on the shore, watching all the ships returning to Europe. All the white hands are waving good-bye and we continue to dance, dance until the ships fall off the horizon, dance until we are so tall and strong that the sun is nearly jealous. *We dance that way.*

"Junior," I yelled. "Slow down, slow down."

Junior had the car spinning in circles, doing donuts across empty fields, coming too close to fences and lonely trees.

"Thomas," Junior yelled. "You're dancing, dancing hard."

I leaned over and slammed on the brakes. Junior jumped out of the car and ran across the field. I turned the car off and followed him. We'd gotten about a mile down the road toward Benjamin Lake when Thomas came driving by.

"Stop the car," I yelled, and Thomas did just that.

"Where were you going?" I asked him.

"I was chasing you and your horse, cousin."

"Jesus, this shit is powerful," I said and swallowed some. Instantly I saw and heard Junior singing. He stood on a stage in a ribbon shirt and blue jeans. Singing. With a guitar.

Indians make the best cowboys. I can tell you that. I've been singing at the Plantation since I was ten years old and have always drawn big crowds. All the white folks come to hear my songs, my little pieces of Indian wisdom, although they have to sit in the back of the theater because all the Indians get the best tickets for my shows. It's not racism. The Indians just camp out all night to buy tickets. Even the President of the United States, Mr. Edgar Crazy Horse himself, came to hear me once. I played a song I wrote for his great-grandfather, the famous Lakota warrior who helped us win the war against the whites:

> *Crazy Horse, what have you done?*
> *Crazy Horse, what have you done?*
> *It took four hundred years*
> *and four hundred thousand guns*
> *but the Indians finally won.*
> *Ya-hey, the Indians finally won.*

> *Crazy Horse, are you still singing?*
> *Crazy Horse, are you still singing?*
> *I honor your old songs*
> *and all they keep on bringing*
> *because the Indians keep winning.*
> *Ya-hey, the Indians keep winning.*

Believe me, I'm the best guitar player who ever lived. I can make my guitar sound like a drum. More than that, I can make any drum sound like a guitar. I can take a single hair from the braids of an Indian woman and make it sound like a promise come true. *Like a thousand promises come true.*

"Junior," I asked. "Where'd you learn to sing?"

"I don't know how to sing," he said.

We made our way down the road to Benjamin Lake and stood by the water. Thomas sat on the dock with his feet in the water and laughed softly. Junior sat on the hood of his car, and I danced around them both.

After a little bit, I tired out and sat on the hood of the car with Junior. The drug was beginning to wear off. All I could see in my vision of Junior was his guitar. Junior pulled out a can of warm Diet Pepsi and we passed it back and forth and watched Thomas talking to himself.

"He's telling himself stories," Junior said.

"Well," I said. "Ain't nobody else going to listen."

"Why's he like that?" Junior asked. "Why's he always talking about strange shit? Hell, he don't even need drugs."

"Some people say he got dropped on his head when he was little. Some of the old people think he's magic."

"What do you think?"

"I think he got dropped on his head and I think he's magic."

We laughed, and Thomas looked up from the water, from his stories, and smiled at us.

"Hey," he said. "You two want to hear a story?"

Junior and I looked at each other, looked back at Thomas, and decided that it would be all right. Thomas closed his eyes and told his story.

It is now. Three Indian boys are drinking Diet Pepsi and talking out by Benjamin Lake. They are wearing only loincloths and braids. Although it is the twentieth century and planes are passing overhead, the Indian boys have decided to be real Indians tonight.

They all want to have their vision, to receive their true names, their adult names. That is the problem with Indians these days. They have the same names all their lives. Indians wear their names like a pair of bad shoes.

So they decided to build a fire and breathe in that sweet smoke. They have not eaten for days so they know their visions should arrive soon. Maybe they'll see it in the flames or in the wood. Maybe the smoke will talk in Spokane or English. Maybe the cinders and ash will rise up.

The boys sit by the fire and breathe, their visions arrive. They are all carried away to the past, to the moment before any of them took their first drink of alcohol.

The boy Thomas throws the beer he is offered into the garbage. The boy Junior throws his whiskey through a window. The boy Victor spills his vodka down the drain.

Then the boys sing. They sing and dance and drum. They steal horses. I can see them. *They steal horses.*

"You don't really believe that shit?" I asked Thomas.

"Don't need to believe anything. It just is."

Thomas stood up and walked away. He wouldn't even try to tell us any stories again for a few years. We had never been very good to him, even as boys, but he had always been kind to us. When he stopped even looking at me, I was hurt. How do you explain that?

Before he left for good, though, he turned back to Junior and me and yelled at us. I couldn't really understand what he was saying, but Junior swore he told us not to slow dance with our skeletons.

"What the hell does that mean?" I asked.

"I don't know," Junior said.

There are things you should learn. Your past is a skeleton walking one step behind you, and your future is a skeleton walking one step in front of you. Maybe you don't wear a watch, but your skeletons do, and they always know what time it is. Now, these skeletons are made of memories, dreams, and voices. And they can trap you in the in-between, between touching and becoming. But they're not necessarily evil, unless you let them be.

What you have to do is keep moving, keep walking, in step with your skeletons. They ain't ever going to leave you, so you don't have to worry about that. Your past ain't going to fall behind, and your future won't get too far ahead. Sometimes, though, your skeletons will talk to you, tell you to sit down and take a rest, breathe a little. Maybe they'll make you promises, tell you all the things you want to hear.

Sometimes your skeletons will dress up as beautiful Indian women and ask you to slow dance. Sometimes your skeletons will dress up as your best friend and offer you a drink, one more for the road. Sometimes your skeletons will look exactly like your parents and offer you gifts.

But, no matter what they do, keep walking, keep moving. And don't wear a watch. Hell, Indians never need to wear a watch because your skeletons will always remind you about the time. See, it is always now. That's what Indian time is. The past, the future, all of it is wrapped up in the now. That's how it is. *We are trapped in the now.*

Junior and I sat out by Benjamin Lake until dawn. We heard voices now and again, saw lights in the trees. After I saw my grandmother walking across the water toward me, I threw away the rest of my new drug and hid in the backseat of Junior's car.

Later that day we were parked in front of the Trading Post, gossiping and laughing, talking stories when Big Mom walked up to the car. Big Mom was the spiritual leader of the Spokane Tribe. She had so much good medicine I think she may have been the one who created the earth.

"I know what you saw," Big Mom said.

"We didn't see nothing," I said, but we all knew that I was lying.

Big Mom smiled at me, shook her head a little, and handed me a little drum. It looked like it was about a hundred years old, maybe older. It was so small it could fit in the palm of my hand.

"You keep that," she said. "Just in case."

"Just in case of what?" I asked.

"That's my pager. Just give it a tap and I'll be right over," she said and laughed as she walked away.

Now, I'll tell you that I haven't used the thing. In fact, Big Mom died a couple years back and I'm not sure she'd come even if the thing did work. But I keep it really close to me, like Big Mom said, just in case. I guess you could call it the only religion I have, one drum that can fit in my hand, but I think if I played it a little, it might fill up the whole world.

BHARATI MUKHERJEE

(1 9 4 0 -   )

Bharati Mukherjee is noted for her writings that reflect her personal experiences in immigrating to the United States and Canada. Mukherjee earned her B.A. at the University of Calcutta, where she was born. She received an M.A. from the University of Baroda and both an M.F.A. and a Ph.D from the University of Iowa. She was awarded the National Book Critics Circle Award for her collection, The Middleman and Other Stories *(1988). As a novelist, Mukherjee's publications include* The Tiger's Daughter *(1972),* Jasmine *(1989),* The Holder of the World *(1993), and* Leave It to Me *(1997). She has been a teacher for over thirty years at universities including the University of Wisconsin, Emory University, City University of New York, and the University of California, Berkeley, where she currently teaches.*

Mukherjee's short story "A Father" gives a very contemporary twist to the perennial tale of the struggle within immigrant households between the desire for conformity to traditions of the older generation and the desire to "Americanize" of the younger.

A FATHER

One Wednesday morning in mid-May Mr. Bhowmick woke up as he usually did at 5:43 A.M., checked his Rolex against the alarm clock's digital readout, punched down the alarm (set for 5:45), then nudged his wife awake. She worked as a claims investigator for an insurance company that had an office in a nearby shopping mall. She didn't really have to leave the house until 8:30, but she liked to get up early and cook him a big breakfast. Mr. Bhowmick had to drive a long way to work. He was a naturally dutiful, cautious man, and he set the alarm clock early enough to accommodate a margin for accidents.

While his wife, in a pink nylon negligee she had paid for with her own Master-Card card, made him a new version of French toast from a clipping ("Eggs-cellent Recipes!") Scotchtaped to the inside of a kitchen cupboard, Mr. Bhowmick brushed his teeth. He brushed, he gurgled with the loud, hawking noises that he and his brother had been taught as children to make in order to flush clean not merely teeth but also tongue and palate.

After that he showered, then, back in the bedroom again, he recited prayers in Sanskrit to Kali, the patron goddess of his family, the goddess of wrath and vengeance. In the pokey flat of his childhood in Ranchi, Bihar, his mother had given over a whole bedroom to her collection of gods and goddesses. Mr. Bhowmick couldn't be that extravagant in Detroit. His daughter, twenty-six and an electrical engineer, slept in the other of the two bedrooms in his apartment. But he had done his best. He had taken Woodworking I and II at a nearby recreation center and built a grotto for the goddess. Kali-Mata was eight inches tall, made of metal and painted a glistening black so that the metal glowed like the oiled, black skin of a peasant woman. And though Kali-Mata was totally nude except for a tiny gilt crown and a garland strung together from sinners' chopped off heads, she looked warm, cozy, *pleased,* in her makeshift wooden shrine in Detroit. Mr. Bhowmick had gathered quite a crowd of admiring, fellow woodworkers in those final weeks of decoration.

"Hurry it up with the prayers," his wife shouted from the kitchen. She was an agnostic, a believer in ambition, not grace. She frequently complained that his prayers had gotten so long that soon he wouldn't have time to go to work, play duplicate bridge with the Ghosals, or play the tabla in the Bengali Association's one Sunday per month musical soirees. Lately she'd begun to drain him in a wholly new way. He wasn't praying, she nagged; he was shutting her out of his life. There'd be no place in the house until she hid Kali-Mata in a suitcase.

She nagged, and he threatened to beat her with his shoe as his father had threatened his mother: it was the thrust and volley of marriage. There was no question of actually taking off a shoe and applying it to his wife's body. She was bigger than he was. And, secretly, he admired her for having the nerve, the agnosticism, which as a college boy in backward Bihar he too had claimed.

"I have time," he shot at her. He was still wrapped in a damp terry towel.

"You have time for everything but domestic life."

It was the fault of the shopping mall that his wife had started to buy pop psychology paperbacks. These paperbacks preached that for couples who could sit down and talk about their "relationship," life would be sweet again. His engineer daughter was on his wife's side. She accused him of holding things in.

"Face it, Dad," she said. "You have an affect deficit."

But surely everyone had feelings they didn't want to talk about or talk over. He definitely did not want to blurt out anything about the sick-in-the-guts sensations that came over him most mornings and that he couldn't bubble down with Alka-Seltzer or smother with Gas-X. The women in his family were smarter than him. They were cheerful, outgoing, more American somehow.

How could he tell these bright, mocking women that, in the 5:43 A.M. darkness, he sensed invisible presences: gods and snakes frolicked in the master bedroom, little white sparks of cosmic static crackled up the legs of his pajamas. Something was out there in the dark, something that could invent accidents and coincidences to remind mortals that even in Detroit they were no more than mortal. His wife would label this paranoia and dismiss it. Paranoia, premonition: whatever it was, it had begun to undermine his composure.

Take this morning, Mr. Bhowmick had woken up from a pleasant dream about a man taking a Club Med vacation, and the postdream satisfaction had lasted through the shower, but when he'd come back to the shrine in the bedroom, he'd noticed all at once how scarlet and saucy was the tongue that Kali-Mata stuck out at the world. Surely he had not lavished such alarming detail, such admonitory colors on that flap of flesh.

Watch out, ambulatory sinners. Be careful out there, the goddess warned him, and not with the affection of Sergeant Esterhaus, either.

"French toast must be eaten hot-hot," his wife nagged. "Otherwise they'll taste like rubber."

Mr. Bhowmick laid the trousers of a two-trouser suit he had bought on sale that winter against his favorite tweed jacket. The navy stripes in the trousers and the small, navy tweed flecks in the jacket looked quite good together. So what if the Chief Engineer had already started wearing summer cottons?

"I am coming, I am coming," he shouted back. 'You want me to eat hot-hot, you start the frying only when I am sitting down. You didn't learn anything from Mother in Ranchi?"

'Mother cooked French toast from fancy recipes? I mean French Sandwich Toast with complicated filling?"

He came into the room to give her his testiest look. "You don't know the meaning of complicated cookery. And mother had to get the coal fire of the *chula* going first."

His daughter was already at the table. "Why don't you break down and buy her a microwave oven? That's what I mean about sitting down and talking things out." She had finished her orange juice. She took a plastic measure of Slim-Fast out of its can and poured the powder into a glass of skim milk. "It's ridiculous."

Babli was not the child he would have chosen as his only heir. She was brighter certainly than the sons and daughters of the other Bengalis he knew in Detroit, and she had been the only female student in most of her classes at Georgia Tech, but as she sat there in her beige linen business suit, her thick chin dropping into a polka-dotted cravat, he regretted again that she was not the child of his dreams. Babli would be able to help him out moneywise if something happened to him, something so bad that even his pension plans and his insurance policies and his money market schemes wouldn't be enough. But Babli could never comfort him. She wasn't womanly or tender the way that unmarried girls had been in the wistful days of his adolescence. She could sing Hindi film songs, mimicking exactly the high, artiificial voice of Lata Mungeshkar, and she had taken two years of dance lessons at Sona Devi's Dance Academy in Southfield, but these accomplishments didn't add up to real femininity. Not the kind that had given him palpitations in Ranchi.

Mr. Bhowmick did his best with his wife's French toast. In spite of its filling of marshmallows, apricot jam and maple syrup, it tasted rubbery. He drank two cups of Darjeeling tea, said,"Well, I'm off," and took off.

All might have gone well if Mr. Bhowmick hadn't fussed longer than usual about putting his briefcase and his trenchcoat in the backseat. He got in behind the wheel of his Oldsmobile, fixed his seatbelt and was just about to turn the key in the ignition when his neighbor, Al Stazniak, who was starting up his Buick Skylark, sneezed. A sneeze at the start of a journey brings bad luck. Al Stazniak's sneeze was fierce, made up of five short bursts, too loud to be ignored.

Be careful out there! Mr. Bhowmick could see the goddess's scarlet little tongue tip wagging at him.

He was a modern man, an intelligent man. Otherwise he couldn't have had the options in life that he did have. He couldn't have given up a good job with perks in Bombay and found a better job with General Motors in Detroit. But Mr. Bhowmick was also a prudent enough man to know that some abiding truth lies bunkered within each wanton Hindu superstition. A sneeze was more than a sneeze. The heedless are carried off in ambulances. He had choices to make. He could ignore the sneeze, and so challenge the world unseen by men. Perhaps Al Stazniak had hayfever. For a sneeze to be a potent omen, surely it had to be unprovoked and terrifying, a thunderclap cleaving the summer skies. Or he could admit the smallness of mortals, undo the fate of the universe by starting over, and go back inside the apartment, sit for a second on the sofa, then re-start his trip.

Al Stazniak rolled down his window. "Everything okay?"

Mr. Bhowmick nodded shyly. They weren't really friends in the way neighbors can sometimes be. They talked as they parked or pulled out of their adjacent parking stalls. For all Mr. Bhowmick knew, Al Stazniak had no legs. He had never seen the man out of his Skylark.

He let the Buick back out first. Everything was okay, yes, please. All the same he undid his seatbelt. Compromise, adaptability, call it what you will. A dozen times a day he made these small trade-offs between new-world reasonableness and old-world beliefs.

While he was sitting in his parked caar, his wife's ride came by. For fifty dollars a month, she was picked up and dropped off by a hard up, newly divorced woman who worked at a florist's shop in the same mall. His wife came out the front door in brown K-Mart pants and a burgundy windbreaker. She waved to him, then slipped into the passenger seat of the florist's rusty Japanese car.

He was a metallurgist. He knew about rust and ways of preventing it, secret ways, thus far unknown to the Japanese.

Babli's fiery red Mitsubishi was still in the lot. She wouldn't leave for work for another eight minutes. He didn't want her to know he'd been undone by a sneeze. Babli wasn't tolerant of superstitions. She played New Wave music in her tapedeck. If asked about Hinduism, all she'd ever said to her American friends was that "it's neat." Mr. Bhowmick had heard her on the phone years before. The cosmos balanced on the head of a snake was like a beach ball balanced on the snout of a circus seal. "This Hindu myth stuff," he'd heard her say, "is like a series of super graphics."

He'd forgiven her. He could probably forgive her anything. It was her way of surviving high school in a city that was both native to her, and alien.

There was no question of going back where he'd come from. He hated Ranchi. Ranchi was no place for dreamers. All through his teenage years, Mr. Bhowmick had dreamed of success abroad. What form that success would take he had left vague. Success had meant to him escape from the constant plotting and bitterness that wore out India's middle class.

Babli should have come out of the apartment and driven off to work by now. Mr. Bhowmick decided to take a risk, to dash inside and pretend he'd left his briefcase on the coffee table.

When he entered the living room, he noticed Babli's spring coat and large vinyl pocketbook on the sofa. She was probably sorting through the junk jewelry on her dresser to give her business suit a lift. She read hints about dressing in women's magazines and applied them to her person with seriousness. If his luck held, he could sit on the sofa, say a quick prayer and get back to the car without her catching on.

It surprised him that she didn't shout out from her bedroom, "Who's there?" What if he had been a rapist?

Then he heard Babli in the bathroom. He heard unladylike squawking noises. She was throwing up. A squawk, a spitting, then the horrible gurgle of a waterfall.

A revelation came to Mr. Bhowmick. A woman vomiting in the privacy of the bathroom could mean many things. She was coming down with the flu. She was nervous about a meeting. But Mr. Bhowmick knew at once that his daughter, his untender, unloving daughter whom he couldn't love and hadn't tried to love, was not, in the larger world of Detroit, unloved. Sinners are everywhere, even in the bosom of an upright, unambitious family like the Bhowmicks. It was the goddess sticking out her tongue at him.

The father sat heavily on the sofa, shrinking from contact with her coat and pocketbook. His brisk, bright engineer daughter was pregnant. Someone had taken time to make love to her. Someone had thought her tender, feminine. Someone even now was perhaps mooning over her. The idea excited him. It was so grotesque and wondrous. At twenty-six Babli had found the man of her dreams; whereas at twenty-six Mr. Bhowmick had given up on truth, beauty, and poetry and exchanged them for two years at Carnegie Tech.

Mr. Bhowmick's tweed-jacketed body sagged against the sofa cushions. Babli would abort, of course. He knew his Babli. It was the only possible option if she didn't want to bring shame to the Bhowmick family. All the same, he could see a chubby baby boy on the rug, crawling to his granddaddy. Shame like that was easier to hide in Ranchi. There was always a barren womb sanctified by marriage that could claim sudden fructifying by the goddess Parvati. Babli would do what she wanted. She was headstrong and independent and he was afraid of her.

Babli staggered out of the bathroom. Damp stains ruined her linen suit. It was the first time he had seen his daughter look ridiculous, quite unprofessional. She didn't come into the living room to investigate the noises he'd made. He glimpsed her shoeless stockinged feet flip-flop on collapsed arches down the hall to her bedroom.

"Are you all right?" Mr. Bhowmick asked, standing in the hall. "Do you need Sinutab?"

She wheeled around. "What're you doing here?"

He was the one who should be angry. "I'm feeling poorly too," he said. "I'm taking the day off."

"I feel fine," Babli said.

Within fifteen minutes Babli had changed her clothes and left. Mr. Bhowmick had the apartment to himself all day. All day for praising or cursing the life that had brought him along with its other surprises an illegitimate grandchild.

It was his wife that he blamed. Coming to America to live had been his wife's idea. After the wedding, the young Bhowmicks had spent two years in Pittsburgh on his student visa, then gone back home to Ranchi for nine years. Nine crushing years. Then the job in Bombay had come through. All during those nine years his wife had screamed and wept. She was a woman of wild, progressive ideas—she'd called them her "American" ideas—and she'd been martyred by her neighbors for them. American *memsahib. Markin mem, Markin mem.* In bazaars the beggar boys had trailed her and hooted. She'd done provocative things. She'd hired a *chamar* woman who by caste rules was forbidden to cook for higher caste families, especially for widowed mothers of decent men. This had caused a blowup in the neighborhood. She'd made other, lesser errors. While other wives shopped and cooked every day, his wife had cooked the whole week's menu on weekends.

"What's the point of having a refrigerator, then?" She'd been scornful of the Ranchi women.

His mother, an old-fashioned widow, had accused her of trying to kill her by poisoning. "You are in such a hurry? You want to get rid of me quick-quick so you can go back to the States?"

Family life had been turbulent.

He had kept aloof, inwardly siding with his mother. He did not love his wife now, and he had not loved her then. In any case, he had not defended her. He felt some affection, and he felt guilty for having shunned her during those unhappy years. But he had thought of it then as revenge. He had wanted to marry a beautiful woman.

Not being a young man of means, only a young man with prospects, he had had no right to yearn for pure beauty. He cursed his fate and after a while, settled for a barrister's daughter, a plain girl with a wide, flat plank of a body and myopic eyes. The barrister had sweetened the deal by throwing in an all-expenses-paid two years' study at Carnegie Tech to which Mr. Bhowmick had been admitted. Those two years had changed his wife from pliant girl to ambitious woman. She wanted America, nothing less.

It was his wife who had forced him to apply for permanent resident status in the U.S. even though he had a good job in Ranchi as a government engineer. The putting together of documents for the immigrant visa had been a long and humbling process. He had had to explain to a chilly clerk in the Embassy that, like most Indians of his generation, he had no birth certificate. He had to swear out affidavits, suffer through police checks, bribe orderlies whose job it was to move his dossier from desk to desk. The decision, the clerk had advised him, would take months, maybe years. He hadn't dared hope that merit might be rewarded. Merit could collapse under bad luck. It was for grace that he prayed.

While the immigration papers were being processed, he had found the job in Bombay. So he'd moved his mother in with his younger brother's family, and left his hometown for good. Life in Bombay had been lighthearted, almost fulfilling. His wife had thrown herself into charity work with the same energy that had offended the Ranchi women. He was happy to be in a big city at last. Bombay was the Rio de Janeiro of the East; he'd read that in a travel brochure. He drove out to Nariman Point at least once a week to admire the necklace of municipal lights, toss coconut shells into the dark ocean, drink beer at the Oberoi-Sheraton where overseas Indian girls in designer jeans beckoned him in sly ways. His nights were full. He played duplicate bridge, went to the movies, took his wife to Bingo nights at his club. In Detroit he was a lonelier man.

Then the green card had come through. For him, for his wife, and for the daughter who had been born to them in Bombay. He sold what he could sell, and put in his brother's informal trust what he couldn't to save on taxes. Then he had left for America, and one more start.

All through the week, Mr. Bhowmick watched his daughter. He kept furtive notes on how many times she rushed to the bathroom and made hawking, wrenching noises, how many times she stayed late at the office, calling her mother to say she'd be taking in a movie and pizza afterwards with friends.

He had to tell her that he knew. And he probably didn't have much time. She shouldn't be on Slim-Fast in her condition. He had to talk things over with her. But what would he say to her? What position could he take? He had to choose between public shame for the family, and murder.

For three more weeks he watched her and kept his silence. Babli wore shifts to the office instead of business suits, and he liked her better in those garments. Perhaps she was dressing for her young man, not from necessity. Her skin was pale and blotchy by turn. At breakfast her fingers looked stiff, and she had trouble with silverware.

Two Saturdays running, he lost badly at duplicate bridge. His wife scolded him. He had made silly mistakes. When was Babli meeting this man? Where? He must be American; Mr. Bhowmick prayed only that he was white. He pictured his grandson crawling to him, and the grandson was always fat and brown and buttery-skinned, like the infant Krishna. An American son-in-law was a terrifying notion. Why was she not mentioning men, at least, preparing the way for the major announcement? He listened sharply for men's names, rehearsed little lines like, "Hello, Bob, I'm Babli's old man," with a cracked little laugh. Bob, Jack, Jimmy, Tom. But no names surfaced. When she went out for pizza and a movie it was with the familiar set of Indian girls and their strange, unpopular, American friends, all without men. Mr. Bhowmick tried to be reasonable. Maybe she had already gotten married and was keeping it secret. "Well, Bob, you and Babli sure had Mrs. Bhowmick and me going there, heh-heh," he mumbled one night with the Sahas and Ghosals, over cards. "Pardon?" asked Pronob Saha. Mr. Bhowmick dropped two tricks, and his wife glared. "Such stupid blunders," she fumed on the drive back. A new truth was dawning; there would be no marriage for Babli. Her young man probably was not so young and not so available. He must be already married. She must have yielded to passion or been raped in the office. His wife seemed to have noticed nothing. Was he a murderer, or a conspirator? He kept his secret from his wife; his daughter kept her decision to herself.

Nights, Mr. Bhowmick pretended to sleep, but as soon as his wife began her snoring—not real snores so much as loud, gaspy gulpings for breath—he turned on his side and prayed to Kali-Mata.

In July, when Babli's belly had begun to push up against the waistless dresses she'd bought herself, Mr. Bhowmick came out of the shower one weekday morning and found the two women screaming at each other. His wife had a rolling pin in one hand. His daughter held up a *National Geographic* as a shield for her head. The crazy look that had been in his wife's eyes when she'd shooed away beggar kids was in her eyes again.

"Stop it!" His own boldness overwhelmed him. "Shut up! Babli's pregnant, so what? It's your fault, you made us come to the States."

Girls like Babli were caught between rules, that's the point he wished to make. They were too smart, too impulsive for a backward place like Ranchi, but not tough nor smart enough for sex-crazy places like Detroit.

"My fault?" his wife cried. " I told her to do hanky-panky with boys? I told her to shame us like this?"

She got in one blow with the rolling pin. The second glanced off Babli's shoulder and fell on his arm which he had stuck out for his grandson's sake.

"I'm calling the police," Babli shouted. She was out of the rolling pin's range. "This is brutality. You can't do this to me."

"Shut up! Shut your mouth, foolish woman." He wrenched the weapon from his wife's fist. He made a show of taking off his shoe to beat his wife on the face.

"What do you know? You don't know anything." She let herself down slowly on a dining chair. Her hair, curled overnight, stood in wild whorls around her head. "Nothing."

"And you do!" He laughed. He remembered her tormentors, and laughed again. He had begun to enjoy himself. Now *he* was the one with the crazy, progressive ideas.

"Your daughter is pregnant, yes," she said, "any fool knows that. But ask her the name of the father. Go, ask."

He stared at his daughter who gazed straight ahead, eyes burning with hate, jaw clenched with fury.

"Babli?"

"Who needs a man?" she hissed. "The father of my baby is a bottle and a syringe. Men louse up your lives. I just want a baby. Oh, don't worry—he's a certified fit donor. No diseases, college graduate, above average, and he made the easiest twenty-five dollars of his life—

"Like animals," his wife said. For the first time he heard horror in her voice. His daughter grinned at him. He saw her tongue, thick and red, squirming behind her row of perfect teeth.

"Yes, yes, yes," she screamed, "like livestock. Just like animals. You should be happy—that's what marriage is all about, isn't it? Matching bloodlines, matching horoscopes, matching castes, matching, matching, matching . . ." and it was difficult to know if she was laughing or singing, or mocking and like a madwoman.

Mr. Bhowmick lifted the rolling pin high above his head and brought it down hard on the dome of Babli's stomach. In the end, it was his wife who called the police.

LEROY QUINTANA
(1944-)

Leroy Quintana has had a varied career as a poet, editor, educator, and counselor. Born in Albuquerque, New Mexico, Quintana earned a B.A. at the University of New Mexico and received two graduate degree, a master's in English from New Mexico State and a master's in counseling from Western New Mexico University. He won the first of two American Book Awards for his first collection of poetry, Hijo del Pueblo: New Mexico Poems *(1976). In 1993 his second collection,* Sangre *(1981), won the award again. Other collections include* The History of Home *(1993) and* My Hair Turning Grey Among Strangers *(1996). He is presently a professor of English at San Diego Mesa College.*

Quintana's poem "Legacy II" expresses the desire for continuity with the cultural past that dominates many ethnic Americans' view of their situation.

LEGACY II

Grandfather never went to school
spoke only a few words of English,
a quiet man; when he talked
talked about simple things
planting corn or about the weather
sometimes about herding sheep as a child.
One day pointed to the four directions
taught me their names

El Norte
Poniente   Oriente
El Sur

He spoke their names as if they were
one of only a handful of things
a man needed to know

Now I look back
only two generations removed
realize I am nothing but a poor fool
who went to college

trying to find my way back
to the center of the world
where Grandfather stood
that day

2

MIXED RELATIONS

With greater interaction between previously segregated groups has come increased opportunity for friendship and emotional relationships. Contemporary Americans are revising long-held prohibitions about who they may love, mate, and marry. *Mixed Relations* examines some of the ways race and ethnicity interact with sexuality. The prohibition of sexual relations between members of different racialized groups is part of our American heritage, reinforced by hundreds of state laws. William Faulkner's story "Dry September" measures the price a Southern white family pays for supporting interracial sexual taboos to the point of lynching an alleged black violator. Daniela Gioseffi in her poem "The Exotic Enemy" explores the dangerous attraction of the forbidden other. Willie Perdomo and Langston Hughes examine in their poems the impact of racially mixed heritages on individuals. All of the readings in this section explore the complications and contradictions that racism and oppression make for our most personal relations.

ANTIMISCEGENATION LAWS

Laws regulating the potential sexual and marital interaction between slaves and masters developed early on in the colonial period. In some colonies similar laws regulated sexual and marital relations between whites and Natives as well, but these were harder to enforce, as white partners in such relations usually joined the Native community and were out of the reach of the disapproving Europeans. The slaves, of course, were constantly under supervision. They rarely had the opportunity to exercise free choice in sexual and marital matters. To the contrary, slaveowners turned increasingly to the sexual management of their slaves, as a way of increasing the supply. Slave children were a profitable commodity, especially as the volume of the slave trade dwindled and then was interdicted by the British navy during the 1830s. The anxiety about sexual relations across racial lines that is expressed in these laws never extended to the protection of slave women from the sexual advances of slaveowners and overseers. After ther Emancipation the white majority's cultural anxiety shifted to the maintenance of social distance between whites and blacks; despite cultural agreement on the inferiority of blacks, laws seemed to be neeeded to restrain whites from sexual and marital relations with them.

The following outline of the history of laws concerning interracial sex and marriage, compiled by Werner Sollors for his book Neither Black nor White, Yet Both *(1997), while in no way complete, maps the breadth and the extent over time of the effort made by the white majority to prevent sexual and marital relations between members of different races.*

PROHIBITIONS OF INTERRACIAL MARRIAGE AND COHABITATION

1638   Ordinance of the Director and Council of New Netherland prohibits adulterous intercourse between whites and heathens, blacks or other persons, upon threat of exemplary punishment of the white party.

1661   Maryland act condemns free-born English women who intermarry with Negro slaves: "whatsoever free-born woman shall intermarry with any slave, shall serve the master of such slave during the life of her husband; all the issues of such free-born women, so married, shall be slaves as their fathers were."

1685   Article 9 of *Code noir* of Louis XIV threatens those men who live in concubinage with a (Negro) slave woman with the high fine of 2000 livres (pounds of sugar). Penalty could be avoided if the man so charged was unmarried and married the slave woman, which also legitimated any earlier offspring.

1686   *Code noir* permits intermarriage between white men and slave women, but penalizes cohabitation.

1705   Massachusetts "Act for the Better Preventing of a Spurious and Mixt Issue" bans interracial fornication and marriage by statute. Section 1 prohibits fornication of "any negro or molatto man" "with an English woman, or a woman of any other Christian nation with this province," punishable by whipping of both partners, the selling of the man out of the province within six months (after continuous imprisonment), and pressing the woman into servitude if she is unable to maintain a child.

1725   Pennsylvania forbids interracial marriage and cohabitation.

1771   Viceroy of Portuguese Brazil orders degradation of an Amerindian chief, who, "disregarding the signal honours which he had received from the Crown, had sunk so low as to marry a Negress, staining his blood with this alliance."

1778   5 April: "Order of the Council of State forbidding all marriages between whites and blacks in France, on penalty of being expelled at once to the colonies."

1786   Virginia bill, drafted by Thomas Jefferson, revises colonial marriage law, omitting reference to ecclesiastical authority but reenacting the following:

          "A marriage between a person of free condition and a slave, or between a white person of free condition and a slave, or between a white person and a negro, or between a white person and a mulatto, shall be null."

1786   22 June: Massachusetts reenacts the colonial law, "That no person by this Act authorized to marry, shall join in marriage any white person with any Negro, Indian or Mulatto, on penalty of the sum of *fifty pounds* . . . ; and that all such marriages shall be absolutely null and void."

1800–1900 During the nineteenth century, as many as thirty-eight [U.S.] states prohibited interracial marriages.

1819   *Midway v. Needham*, 16 Mass. 157, upheld the validity of a marriage between a Mulatto man and a white woman, both domiciled in Massachusetts, "although celebrated in Rhode Island in order to avoid the Massachusetts law."

1825   Louisiana Civil Code continues the prohibition of marriage between slaves, free persons of color, and whites.

1841   Rhode Island repeals its law banning intermarriage.

1843   Massachusetts repeals law.

1861   Ohio law forbids intermarriage between a person of pure white blood and one having a visible admixture of African blood.

1869   *Scott v. Georgia*, 39 Ga. rep. 321, 324 (1869): "The amalgamation of the races is not only unnatural, but is always productive of deplorable results. Our daily observation shows us, that the off-spring of these unnatural connections are generally sickly and effeminate, and that they are inferior in physical development and strength, to the full-blood of either race. It is sometimes urged that such marriages should be encouraged, for the purpose of elevating the inferior race. The reply is, that such connections never elevate the inferior race to the position of the superior, but they bring down the superior to that of the inferior. They are productive of evil, and evil only, without any corresponding good."

1877   Alabama supreme court, in *Green v. State*, 58 Ala. 190, 195, asserts state's right to enforce intermarriage bans: "Manifestly, it is for the peace and happiness of the black race, as well as of the white, that such laws should exist. And surely there can not be any tyranny or injustice in requiring both alike, to form this union with those of their own race only, whom God hath joined together by indelible peculiarities, which declare that He has made the two races distinct."

1877   In the Virginia case of *McPherson v. Commonwealth*, 69 Va. 292, Judge Moncure decided that Rowena McPherson was permitted to marry a white man because "less than one-fourth of her blood is negro blood. If it be but one drop less, she is not a negro."

1881   Alabama supreme court, in *Pace v. State*, 69 Ala. 231, 232, upholds a statute more severely punishing adultery when it is interracial and stresses the hazardous effects of racial mixing: "Its result may be the amalgamation of the two races, producing a mongrel population and a degraded civilization, the prevention of which is dictated by a sound public policy affecting the highest interests of society and government."

1881   Florida act provides twelve months' imprisonment and a maximum fine of $500 for a Negro and a white person of opposite sex who occupy the same room habitually. Penalty for violation of intermarriage prohibition is prison up to ten years and a maximum fine of $500; for clergymen, priests, or public officials who solemnize such a union, it is prison up to one year and a fine up to $1000.

1882   U.S. Supreme Court rules the Alabama Code's harsher punishment of interracial fornication constitutional in *Pace v. Alabama*, 106 U.S. 583— on the grounds that both black and white get punished more severely for interracial than for intraracial fornication.

1883   Maine and Michigan laws repealed.

1883	Missouri: *State v. Jackson*, Mo. 175, 179: "It is stated as a well authenticated fact that if the issue of a black man and a white woman, and a white man and a black woman, intermarry, they cannot possibly have any progeny, and such a fact sufficiently justifies those laws which forbid the intermarriage of blacks and whites, laying out of view other sufficient grounds for such enactments."
1883	Constitution of North Carolina, art. 14, sec. 8: "All marriages between a white person and a Negro, or between a white person and a person of Negro descent to the third generation inclusive, are hereby forever prohibited."
1886	New Mexico repeals its law.
1887	Ohio legislature repeals all laws establishing or permitting distinctions of color, including intermarriage bans.
1889	Georgia II Code, sec. 2422: "The marriage relation between white persons and persons of African descent is forever prohibited, and such marriage shall be null and void."
1890	Constitution of Mississippi, art. 14, sec. 263: "The marriage of a white person with a negro or mulatto, or person who shall have one-eighth or more of negro blood, shall be unlawful and void."
1892	State Constitution of Florida, art. 16, sec. 24: "All marriages between a white person and a negro, or between a white person and a person of negro descent to the fourth generation, inclusive, are hereby forever prohibited."
1895	The Constitution of South Carolina, art. 3, sec. 33: "The marriage of a white person with a negro or mulatto, or person who shall have one-eighth or more of negro blood, shall be unlawful and void."
1896	Constitution of Tennessee, art. 11, sec. 14: "The intermarriage of white persons with negroes, mulattoes, or persons of mixed blood, descended from a negro to the third generation, inclusive, or their living together as man and wife in this State is prohibited. The legislature shall enforce this section by appropriate legislation."
1898	Utah Revised Statutes, sec. 1184: "Marriage is prohibited and declared void: between a negro and a white person" and "between a Mongolian and a white person."
1901	Alabama State Constitution (amended), sec. 102: "The legislature shall never pass any law to authorize or legalize any marriage between any white person and a negro, or a descendant of a negro."

1901   Arizona Revised Statutes, sec. 3092: "All marriages of persons of Caucasian blood, or their descendants, with Negroes, Mongolians or Indians, and their descendants, shall be null and void."

1902   Oregon: Bellinger and Cotton Code, sec. 5217: "What marriages are void. 3. When either of the parties is a white person and the other negro, or Mongolian or a person of one-fourth or more of negro or Mongolian Blood." Sec. 1999: "Hereafter it shall not be lawful within this state for any white person, male or female, to intermarry with any negro, Chinese, or any person having one fourth or more negro, Chinese or Kanaka blood, or any person having more than one-half Indian blood, . . . and all such marriages, or attempted marriages, shall be absolutely null and void."

1906   *Kerr's Code of California*, vol. 2, part 3, paragraph 60: "All marriages of white persons with negroes, mongolians, or mulattoes are illegal and void."

1906   Texas Criminal Statutes, art. 346: "If any white person and negro shall knowingly intermarry with each other within this state, or, having so intermarried, in or out of the state, shall continue to live together as man and wife within this state, they shall be punished by confinement in the penitentiary for a term not less than two or more than five years."

1908   Indiana statutes make void marriage between a white person and one of one-eighth or more of Negro blood.

1908   Louisiana Act 87 makes "concubinage between a person of the Caucasian race and a person of the negro race a felony, fixing the punishment therefore and defining what shall constitute the concubinage"; penalty imprisonment of one month to one year with or without hard labor.

In the same year the Louisiana Supreme Court in *State v. Treadaway* (126 La. 1908) acquits Treadaway of miscegenation charge "because his companion was an octoroon, and an octoroon was not 'a person of the negro blood or black race.'" This, the court argues, is because "[t]here are no negroes who are not persons of color; but there are persons of color who are not negroes."

1909   Montana statutes passed declaring marriages between whites and persons of whole or part Negro blood or Chinese or Japanese null and void.

1910   Oklahoma Revised Laws, sec. 3894: "The marriage of any person of African descent, as defined by the constitution of this State to any person not of African descent to any person of African descent, shall be unlawful and is hereby prohibited within this State." The state constitution, art. 23, sec. 11, defines races as follows: "Wherever in this Constitution and laws of the State the word or words 'colored' or 'colored race,' 'negro' or 'negro race' are used the same shall be construed to mean or apply to all persons of African descent. The term 'white race' shall include all other persons."

1912   Nevada Revised Laws, sec. 6517: "If any white person shall live and cohabit with any black person, mulatto, Indian, or any person of the Malay or brown race or of the Mongolian or yellow race, in a state of fornication, such person so offending shall, on conviction thereof, be fined in any sum not exceeding five hundred dollars, and not less than one hundred dollars, or be imprisoned in the county jail not less than six months or more than one year, or both."

1913   South Dakota Compiled Laws, ch. 166, sec. 1: "The intermarriage or illicit cohabitation of any persons belonging to the African, Corean, Malayan or Mongolian race, with any person of the opposite sex, belonging to the Caucasian or white race, is hereby prohibited, and any person who shall hereafter enter into any such marriage, or who shall indulge in any such illicit cohabitation shall be deemed guilty of a felony and upon conviction thereof shall be punished by a fine of not exceeding ten years or both such fine and imprisonment."

1915   28 U.S. states have statutes prohibiting interracial marriages or cohabitation; ten among them have constitutional prohibitions.

1920   Statutes of Louisiana act 220 prohibits marriage between persons of Indian race and of colored or black race; act 230 forbids cohabitation between Negroes and Indians.

1920   Wyoming Compiled Statutes prohibit marriage of a white and a Negro, Mulatto, Mongolian, or Malay.

1921   Georgia act makes felonious and void the intermarriage of whites and persons with an ascertainable trace of African, West Indian, Asiatic Indian, or Mongolian blood. Provisions for detecting such blood could not be enforced for lack of appropriations.

1923   Public Acts of Michigan, no. 7, declares intermarriages legal.

1923   Oklahoma Supreme Court, in *Blake v. Sessions*, declares void the marriage between a man of ¾ Indian and ¼ Negro blood and a woman with ¾ Indian and ¼ white blood (reason: 1910 Oklahoma Laws, sec. 1677, prohibits marriages between persons of African descent and persons of non-African descent).

1924   27 February: Virginia Senate passes 23 to 4 the "Act to Preserve Racial Integrity," requiring racial ancestry certificate for all citizens born before 14 June 1912 and sharpening previous intermarriage bans: "It shall be unlawful for any white person in this state to marry any save a white person, or a person with no other admixture of blood other than white and American Indian. For the purpose of this act, the term 'white person' shall apply only to the person who has no trace whatsoever of any blood other than Caucasian; but persons who have one-sixteenth or less of the blood of the American Indian and have no other non-caucasic blood shall be deemed to be white" (previously persons of less than one-quarter Negro blood did not count as Negroes).

1927   Georgia passes law requiring citizens to provide information on racial antecedents.

1930   Virginia requires persons to provide racial genealogy.

1945   End of World War II; racial legislation in Italy and Germany annulled.

1948   California supreme court case of *Perez v. Sharp*, 32 Cal. 2d 711, 198 P. 2d 17, declares state miscegenation laws unconstitutional.

1950   Intermarriage prohibited in 30 of 48 U.S. states (same figure for 1944; by the 1967 Supreme Court ruling, 13 states had repealed their laws).

1951   Oregon repeals interdiction.

1953   Montana terminates prohibition.

1955   North Dakota laws voided.

1955   In *Naim v. Naim*, 197 Va. 80, 87 S.E. 2d 749, Virginia supreme court sustains miscegenation statute; state's legislative purpose was "to preserve the racial integrity of its citizens" and to prevent "the corruption of blood," "the obliteration of racial pride," and the creation of "a mongrel breed of citizens."

1957   South Dakota and Colorado repeal laws.

1959   Louisiana supreme court upholds the state's miscegenation law, arguing that the state could protect the children from such marriages from "a feeling of inferiority as to their status in the community that may affect their hearts and minds in a way unlikely ever to be undone."

1962   Arizona law repealed.

1963   Nebraska and Utah revoke intermarriage prohibitions.

1964   In *McLaughlin et al. v. Florida*, U.S. Supreme Court strikes down Florida criminal statute 798.05, which prohibits an "unmarried interracial couple from habitually living in and occupying the same room in the nighttime" with a penalty of jail up to one year and a fine up to $500; ruling explicitly overturns *Pace v. Alabama* (1882).

1967   12 June: *Loving v. Virginia.* U.S. Supreme Court rules (9 to 0) that anti-miscegenation laws are unconstitutional within the equal protection clause of the Fourteenth Amendment. Chief Justice Warren: "There can be no question that Virginia's miscegenation statutes rest solely upon distinctions drawn according to race. . . . Marriage is one of 'the basic civil rights of man,' fundamental to our very existence and survival. . . . To deny this fundamental freedom on so unsupportable a basis as the racial classifications embodied in these statutes, classifications so directly subversive of the principle of equality at the heart of the Fourteenth Amendment, is surely to deprive all the State's citizens of liberty without due process of law. The Fourteenth Amendment requires that freedom of choice to marry not be restricted by invidious racial discriminations. Under our Constitution, the freedom to marry or not marry, a person of another race resides with the individual and cannot be infringed by the State."

1978   31 March: Tennessee proclaims repeal of the 1896 constitution's art. 11, sec. 14, prohibiting racial intermarriage after narrow approval of electorate with 199,742 against 191,745 votes.

1987   4 December: Mississippi Secretary of State proclaims that section 263 of 1890 constitution, prohibiting interracial marriage, is deleted based upon House Concurrent Resolution #13 (Laws 1987, ch. 672) and ratification by the electorate on November 3.

WILLIAM FAULKNER
(1897-1962)

Mississippi born and bred, William Faulkner is considered one of the greatest twentieth-century novelists. He spent most of his literary career in the South, which both inspired and informed his fiction. Faulkner's canon spans many genres: poetry, novels, short stories, screenplays, dramas, and essays. He was elected to the American Academy of Arts and Letters in 1948 and was awarded the Nobel Prize of Literature in 1949. He received a National Book Award for Collected Stories in 1951 and a National Book Award and a Pulitzer Prize in 1955 for A Fable *(1954). His most influential publications include* The Sound and the Fury *(1929),* Light in August *(1932), and* Absalom, Absalom! *(1936). Faulkner ended his literary career as a writer in residence at the University of Virginia.*

Many of Faulkner's stories, reflecting the social dimensions of Southern life, touch upon the relations among white Southerners, African Americans, and Native Americans. These relations, in the view of stories like "Dry September," are charged with sexual as well as racial tensions.

DRY SEPTEMBER

I

Through the bloody September twilight, aftermath of sixty-two rainless days, it had gone like a fire in dry grass—the rumor, the story, whatever it was. Something about Miss Minnie Cooper and a Negro. Attacked, insulted, frightened: none of them, gathered in the barber shop on that Saturday evening where the ceiling fan stirred, without freshening it, the vitiated air, sending back upon them, in recurrent surges of stale pomade and lotion, their own stale breath and odors, knew exactly what had happened.

"Except it wasn't Will Mayes," a barber said. He was a man of middle age; a thin, sand-colored man with a mild face, who was shaving a client. "I know Will Mayes. He's a good nigger. And I know Miss Minnie Cooper, too."

"What do you know about her?" a second barber said.

"Who is she?" the client said. "A young girl?"

"No," the barber said. "She's about forty, I reckon. She aint married. That's why I dont believe—"

"Believe, hell!" a hulking youth in a sweat-stained silk shirt said. "Wont you take a white woman's word before a nigger's?"

"I dont believe Will Mayes did it," the barber said. "I know Will Mayes."

"Maybe you know who did it, then. Maybe you already got him out of town, you damn niggerlover."

"I dont believe anybody did anything. I dont believe anything happened. I leave it to you fellows if them ladies that get old without getting married dont have notions that a man cant—"

"Then you are a hell of a white man," the client said. He moved under the cloth. The youth had sprung to his feet.

"You dont?" he said. "Do you accuse a white woman of lying?"

The barber held the razor poised above the half-risen client. He did not look around.

"It's this durn weather," another said. "It's enough to make a man do anything. Even to her."

Nobody laughed. The barber said in his mild, stubborn tone: "I aint accusing nobody of nothing. I just know and you fellows know how a woman that never—"

"You damn niggerlover!" the youth said.

"Shut up, Butch," another said. "We'll get the facts in plenty of time to act."

"Who is? Who's getting them?" the youth said. "Facts, hell! I—"

"You're a fine white man," the client said. "Aint you?" In his frothy beard he looked like a desert rat in the moving pictures. "You tell them, Jack," he said to the youth. "If there aint any white men in this town, you can count on me, even if I aint only a drummer and a stranger."

"That's right, boys," the barber said. "Find out the truth first. I know Will Mayes."

"Well, by God!" the youth shouted. "To think that a white man in this town—"

"Shut up, Butch," the second speaker said. "We got plenty of time."

The client sat up. He looked at the speaker. "Do you claim that anything excuses a nigger attacking a white woman? Do you mean to tell me you are a white man and you'll stand for it? You better go back North where you came from. The South dont want your kind here."

"North what?" the second said. "I was born and raised in this town."

"Well, by God!" the youth said. He looked about with a strained, baffled gaze, as if he was trying to remember what it was he wanted to say or to do. He drew his sleeve across his sweating face. "Damn if I'm going to let a white woman—"

"You tell them, Jack," the drummer said. "By God, if they—"

The screen door crashed open. A man stood in the floor, his feet apart and his heavy-set body poised easily. His white shirt was open at the throat; he wore a felt hat. His hot, bold glance swept the group. His name was McLendon. He had commanded troops at the front in France and had been decorated for valor.

"Well," he said, "are you going to sit there and let a black son rape a white woman on the streets of Jefferson?"

Butch sprang up again. The silk of his shirt clung flat to his heavy shoulders. At each armpit was a dark halfmoon. "That's what I been telling them! That's what I—"

"Did it really happen?" a third said. "This aint the first man scare she ever had, like Hawkshaw says. Wasn't there something about a man on the kitchen roof, watching her undress, about a year ago?"

"What?" the client said. "What's that?" The barber had been slowly forcing him back into the chair; he arrested himself reclining, his head lifted, the barber still pressing him down.

McLendon whirled on the third speaker. "Happen? What the hell difference does it make? Are you going to let the black sons get away with it until one really does it?"

"That's what I'm telling them!" Butch shouted. He cursed, long and steady, pointless.

"Here, here," a fourth said. "Not so loud. Dont talk so loud."

"Sure," McLendon said; "no talking necessary at all. I've done my talking. Who's with me?" He poised on the balls of his feet, roving his gaze.

The barber held the drummer's face down, the razor poised. "Find out the facts first, boys. I know Willy Mayes. It wasn't him. Let's get the sheriff and do this thing right."

McLendon whirled upon him his furious, rigid face. The barber did not look away. They looked like men of different races. The other barbers had ceased also above their prone clients. "You mean to tell me," McLendon said, "that you'd take a nigger's word before a white woman's? Why, you damn niggerloving—"

The third speaker rose and grasped McLendon's arm; he too had been a soldier. "Now, now. Let's figure this thing out. Who knows anything about what really happened?"

"Figure out hell!" McLendon jerked his arm free. "All that're with me get up from there. The ones that aint—" He roved his gaze, dragging his sleeve across his face.

Three men rose. The drummer in the chair sat up. "Here," he said, jerking at the cloth about his neck; "get this rag off me. I'm with him. I dont live here, but by God, if our mothers and wives and sisters—" He smeared the cloth over his face and flung it to the floor. McLendon stood in the floor and cursed the others. Another rose and moved toward him. The remainder sat uncomfortable, not looking at one another, then one by one they rose and joined him.

The barber picked the cloth from the floor. He began to fold it neatly. "Boys, dont do that. Will Mayes never done it. I know."

"Come on," McLendon said. He whirled. From his hip pocket protruded the butt of a heavy automatic pistol. They went out. The screen door crashed behind them reverberant in the dead air.

The barber wiped the razor carefully and swiftly, and put it away, and ran to the rear, and took his hat from the wall. "I'll be back as soon as I can," he said to the other barbers. "I cant let—" He went out, running. The two other barbers followed him to the door and caught it on the rebound, leaning out and looking up the street after him. The air was flat and dead. It had a metallic taste at the base of the tongue.

"What can he do?" the first said. The second one was saying "Jees Christ, Jees Christ" under his breath. "I'd just as lief be Will Mayes as Hawk, if he gets McLendon riled."

"Jees Christ, Jees Christ," the second whispered.

"You reckon he really done it to her?" the first said.

II

She was thirty-eight or thirty-nine. She lived in a small frame house with her invalid mother and a thin, sallow, unflagging aunt, where each morning between ten and eleven she would appear on the porch in a lace-trimmed boudoir cap, to sit swinging in the porch swing until noon. After dinner she lay down for a while, until the afternoon began to cool. Then, in one of the three or four new voile dresses which she had each summer, she would go downtown to spend the afternoon in the stores with the other ladies, where they would handle the goods and haggle over the prices in cold, immediate voices, without any intention of buying.

She was of comfortable people—not the best in Jefferson, but good people enough—and she was still on the slender side of ordinary looking, with a bright, faintly haggard manner and dress. When she was young she had had a slender, nervous body and a sort of hard vivacity which had enabled her for a time to ride upon the crest of the town's social life as exemplified by the high school party and church social period of her contemporaries while still children enough to be unclassconscious.

She was the last to realize that she was losing ground; that those among whom she had been a little brighter and louder flame than any other were beginning to learn the pleasure of snobbery—male—and retaliation—female. That was when her face began to wear that bright, haggard look. She still carried it to parties on shadowy porticoes and summer lawns, like a mask or a flag, with that bafflement of furious repudiation of truth in her eyes. One evening at a party she heard a boy and two girls, all schoolmates, talking. She never accepted another invitation.

She watched the girls with whom she had grown up as they married and got homes and children, but no man ever called on her steadily until the children of the other girls had been calling her "aunty" for several years, the while their mothers told them in bright voices about how popular Aunt Minnie had been as a girl. Then the town began to see her driving on Sunday afternoons with the cashier in the bank. He was a widower of about forty—a high-colored man, smelling always faintly of the barber shop or of whiskey. He owned the first automobile in town, a red runabout; Minnie had the first motoring bonnet and veil the town ever saw. Then the town began to say: "Poor Minnie." "But she is old enough to take care of herself," others said. That was when she began to ask her old schoolmates that their children call her "cousin" instead of "aunty."

It was twelve years now since she had been relegated into adultery by public opinion, and eight years since the cashier had gone to a Memphis bank, returning for one day each Christmas, which he spent at an annual bachelors' party at a hunting club on the river. From behind their curtains the neighbors would see the party pass, and during the over-the-way Christmas day visiting they would tell her about him, about how well he looked, and how they heard that he was prospering in the city, watching with bright, secret eyes her haggard, bright face. Usually by that hour there would be the scent of whiskey on her breath. It was supplied her by a youth, a clerk at the soda fountain: "Sure; I buy it for the old gal. I reckon she's entitled to a little fun."

Her mother kept to her room altogether now; the gaunt aunt ran the house. Against that background Minnie's bright dresses, her idle and empty days, had a quality of furious unreality. She went out in the evenings only with women now, neighbors, to the moving pictures. Each afternoon she dressed in one of the new dresses and went downtown alone, where her young "cousins" were already strolling in the late afternoons with their delicate, silken heads and thin, awkward arms and conscious hips, clinging to one another or shrieking and giggling with paired boys in the soda fountain when she passed and went on along the serried store fronts, in the doors of which the sitting and lounging men did not even follow her with their eyes any more.

III

The barber went swiftly up the street where the sparse lights, insect-swirled, glared in rigid and violent suspension in the lifeless air. The day had died in a pall of dust; above the darkened square, shrouded by the spent dust, the sky was as clear as the inside of a brass bell. Below the east was a rumor of the twice-waxed moon.

When he overtook them McLendon and three others were getting into a car parked in an alley. McLendon stooped his thick head, peering out beneath the top. "Changed your mind, did you?" he said. "Damn good thing; by God, tomorrow when this town hears about how you talked tonight—"

"Now, now," the other ex-soldier said. "Hawkshaw's all right. Come on, Hawk; jump in."

"Will Mayes never done it, boys," the barber said. "If anybody done it. Why, you all know well as I do there aint any town where they got better niggers than us. And you know how a lady will kind of think things about men when there aint any reason to, and Miss Minnie anyway—"

"Sure, sure," the soldier said. "We're just going to talk to him a little; that's all."

"Talk, hell!" Butch said. "When we're through with the—"

"Shut up, for God's sake!" the soldier said. "Do you want everybody in town—"

"Tell them, by God!" McLendon said. "Tell every one of the sons that'll let a white woman—"

"Let's go; let's go: here's the other car." The second car slid squealing out of a cloud of dust at the alley mouth. McLendon started his car and took the lead. Dust lay like fog in the street. The street lights hung nimbused as in water. They drove on out of town.

A rutted lane turned at right angles. Dust hung above it too, and above all the land. The dark bulk of the ice plant, where the Negro Mayes was night watchman, rose against the sky. "Better stop here, hadn't we?" the soldier said. McLendon did not reply. He hurled the car up and slammed to a stop, the headlights glaring on the blank wall.

"Listen here, boys," the barber said; "if he's here, dont that prove he never done it? Dont it? If it was him, he would run. Dont you see he would?" The second car came up and stopped. McLendon got down; Butch sprang down beside him. "Listen, boys," the barber said.

"Cut the lights off!" McLendon said. The breathless dark rushed down. There was no sound in it save their lungs as they sought air in the parched dust in which for two months they had lived; then the diminishing crunch of McLendon's and Butch's feet, and a moment later McLendon's voice:

"Will! . . . Will!"

Below the east the wan hemorrhage of the moon increased. It heaved above the ridge, silvering the air, the dust, so that they seemed to breathe, live, in a bowl of molten lead. There was no sound of nightbird nor insect, no sound save their breathing and a faint ticking of contracting metal about the cars. Where their bodies touched one another they seemed to sweat dryly, for no more moisture came. "Christ!" a voice said; "let's get out of here."

But they didn't move until vague noises began to grow out of the darkness ahead; then they got out and waited tensely in the breathless dark. There was another sound: a blow, a hissing expulsion of breath and McLendon cursing in undertone. They stood a moment longer, then they ran forward. They ran in a stumbling clump, as though they were fleeing something. "Kill him, kill the son," a voice whispered. McLendon flung them back.

"Not here," he said. "Get him into the car." "Kill him, kill the black son!" the voice murmured. They dragged the Negro to the car. The barber had waited beside the car. He could feel himself sweating and he knew he was going to be sick at the stomach.

"What is it, captains?" the Negro said. "I aint done nothing. 'Fore God, Mr John." Someone produced handcuffs. They worked busily about the Negro as though he were a post, quiet, intent, getting in one another's way. He submitted to the handcuffs, looking swiftly and constantly from dim face to dim face. "Who's here, captains?" he said, leaning to peer into the faces until they could feel his breath and smell his sweaty reek. He spoke a name or two. "What you all say I done, Mr John?"

McLendon jerked the car door open. "Get in!" he said.

The Negro did not move. "What you all going to do with me, Mr John? I aint done nothing. White folks, captains, I aint done nothing: I swear 'fore God." He called another name.

"Get in!" McLendon said. He struck the Negro. The others expelled their breath in a dry hissing and struck him with random blows and he whirled and cursed them, and swept his manacled hands across their faces and slashed the barber upon the mouth, and the barber struck him also. "Get him in there," McLendon said. They pushed at him. He ceased struggling and got in and sat quietly as the others took their places. He sat between the barber and the soldier, drawing his limbs in so as not to touch them, his eyes going swiftly and constantly from face to face. Butch clung to the running board. The car moved on. The barber nursed his mouth with his handkerchief.

"What's the matter, Hawk?" the soldier said.

"Nothing," the barber said. They regained the highroad and turned away from town. The second car dropped back out of the dust. They went on, gaining speed; the final fringe of houses dropped behind.

"Goddamn, he stinks!" the soldier said.

"We'll fix that," the drummer in front beside McLendon said. On the running board Butch cursed into the hot rush of air. The barber leaned suddenly forward and touched McLendon's arm.

"Let me out, John," he said.

"Jump out, niggerlover," McLendon said without turning his head. He drove swiftly. Behind them the sourceless lights of the second car glared in the dust. Presently McLendon turned into a narrow road. It was rutted with disuse. It led back to an abandoned brick kiln—a series of reddish mounds and weed- and vine-choked vats without bottom. It had been used for pasture once, until one day the owner missed one of his mules. Although he prodded carefully in the vats with a long pole, he could not even find the bottom of them.

"John," the barber said.

"Jump out, then," McLendon said, hurling the car along the ruts. Beside the barber the Negro spoke:

"Mr Henry."

The barber sat forward. The narrow tunnel of the road rushed up and past. Their motion was like an extinct furnace blast: cooler, but utterly dead. The car bounded from rut to rut.

"Mr Henry," the Negro said.

The barber began to tug furiously at the door. "Look out, there!" the soldier said, but the barber had already kicked the door open and swung onto the running board. The soldier leaned across the Negro and grasped at him, but he had already jumped. The car went on without checking speed.

The impetus hurled him crashing through dust-sheathed weeds, into the ditch. Dust puffed about him, and in a thin, vicious crackling of sapless stems he lay choking and retching until the second car passed and died away. Then he rose and limped on until he reached the highroad and turned toward town, brushing at his clothes with his hands. The moon was higher, riding high and clear of the dust at last, and after a while the town began to glare beneath the dust. He went on, limping. Presently he heard cars and the glow of them grew in the dust behind him and he left the road and crouched again in the weeds until they passed. McLendon's car came last now. There were four people in it and Butch was not on the running board.

They went on; the dust swallowed them; the glare and the sound died away. The dust of them hung for a while, but soon the eternal dust absorbed it again. The barber climbed back onto the road and limped on toward town.

IV

As she dressed for supper on that Saturday evening, her own flesh felt like fever. Her hands trembled among the hooks and eyes, and her eyes had a feverish look, and her hair swirled crisp and crackling under the comb. While she was still dressing the friends called for her and sat while she donned her sheerest underthings and stockings and a new voile dress. "Do you feel strong enough to go out?" they said, their eyes bright too, with a dark glitter. "When you have had time to get over the shock, you must tell us what happened. What he said and did; everything."

In the leafed darkness, as they walked toward the square, she began to breathe deeply, something like a swimmer preparing to dive, until she ceased trembling, the four of them walking slowly because of the terrible heat and out of solicitude for her. But as they neared the square she began to tremble again, walking with her head up, her hands clenched at her sides, their voices about her murmurous, also with that feverish, glittering quality of their eyes.

They entered the square, she in the center of the group, fragile in her fresh dress. She was trembling worse. She walked slower and slower, as children eat ice cream, her head up and her eyes bright in the haggard banner of her face, passing the hotel and the coatless drummers in chairs along the curb looking around at her: "That's the one: see? The one in pink in the middle." "Is that her? What did they do with the nigger? Did they—?" "Sure. He's all right." "All right, is he?" "Sure. He went on a little trip." Then the drug store, where even the young men lounging in the doorway tipped their hats and followed with their eyes the motion of her hips and legs when she passed.

They went on, passing the lifted hats of the gentlemen, the suddenly ceased voices, deferent, protective. "Do you see?" the friends said. Their voices sounded like long, hovering sighs of hissing exultation. "There's not a Negro on the square. Not one."

They reached the picture show. It was like a miniature fairyland with its lighted lobby and colored lithographs of life caught in its terrible and beautiful mutations. Her lips began to tingle. In the dark, when the picture began, it would be all right; she could hold back the laughing so it would not waste away so fast and so soon. So she hurried on before the turning faces, the undertones of low astonishment, and they took their accustomed places where she could see the aisle against the silver glare and the young men and girls coming in two and two against it.

The lights flicked away; the screen glowed silver, and soon life began to unfold, beautiful and passionate and sad, while still the young men and girls entered, scented and sibilant in the half dark, their paired backs in silhouette delicate and sleek, their slim, quick bodies awkward, divinely young, while beyond them the silver dream accumulated, inevitably on and on. She began to laugh. In trying to suppress it, it made more noise than ever; heads began to turn. Still laughing, her friends raised her and led her out, and she stood at the curb, laughing on a high, sustained note, until the taxi came up and they helped her in.

They removed the pink voile and the sheer underthings and the stockings, and put her to bed, and cracked ice for her temples, and sent for the doctor. He was hard to locate, so they ministered to her with hushed ejaculations, renewing the ice and fanning her. While the ice was fresh and cold she stopped laughing and lay still for a time, moaning only a little. But soon the laughing welled again and her voice rose screaming.

"Shhhhhhhhhhhh! Shhhhhhhhhhhhhhh!" they said, freshening the icepack, smoothing her hair, examining it for gray; "poor girl!" Then to one another: "Do you suppose anything really happened?" their eyes darkly aglitter, secret and passionate. "Shhhhhhhhhh! Poor girl! Poor Minnie!"

V

It was midnight when McLendon drove up to his neat new house. It was trim and fresh as a birdcage and almost as small, with its clean, green-and-white paint. He locked the car and mounted the porch and entered. His wife rose from a chair beside the reading lamp. McLendon stopped in the floor and stared at her until she looked down.

"Look at that clock," he said, lifting his arm, pointing. She stood before him, her face lowered, a magazine in her hands. Her face was pale, strained, and weary-looking. "Haven't I told you about sitting up like this, waiting to see when I come in?"

"John," she said. She laid the magazine down. Poised on the balls of his feet, he glared at her with his hot eyes, his sweating face.

"Didn't I tell you?" He went toward her. She looked up then. He caught her shoulder. She stood passive, looking at him.

"Don't, John. I couldn't sleep . . . The heat; something. Please, John. You're hurting me."

"Didn't I tell you?" He released her and half struck, half flung her across the chair, and she lay there and watched him quietly as he left the room.

He went on through the house, ripping off his shirt, and on the dark, screened porch at the rear he stood and mopped his head and shoulders with the shirt and flung it away. He took the pistol from his hip and laid it on the table beside the bed, and sat on the bed and removed his shoes, and rose and slipped his trousers off. He was sweating again already, and he stooped and hunted furiously for the shirt. At last he found it and wiped his body again, and, with his body pressed against the dusty screen, he stood panting. There was no movement, no sound, not even an insect. The dark world seemed to lie stricken beneath the cold moon and the lidless stars.

DANIELA GIOSEFFI
(1941-)

Born in Orange, New Jersey, Daniela Gioseffi has written in many forms: poetry, plays, stories, and novels. Gioseffi earned her bachelor's degree from Montclair State College and received her M.F.A. at Catholic University of America. She began her professional career as an actress, playing in stock resident and touring companies from 1964 through 1969. Gioseffi has had several multimedia works produced in New York on Broadway and off. These include "Care of the Body" (1970), "The Birth Dance of Earth" (1972), "The Golden Daffodil Dwarf and Other Works" (1973), and "Fathers and Sons" (1973). Her publications include the novel, The Great American Belly Dance *(1977);* Eggs in the Lake *(1979), poems; and* Earth Dancing: Mother Nature's Oldest Rite *(1980), nonfiction.*

Gioseffi's poem "The Exotic Enemy" articulates the existential issues behind the often destructive attraction of Otherness, which she sees operating between humans and nature, between men and women, and between persons of different races or colors.

THE EXOTIC ENEMY

Deep in us this fascination with the exotic other—
no sentiment about it—this passion
with the blood of the other
stains our hands and tongues—

to poke at the fruit until its juices run on the ground,
to tear the rose from its stem, scatter petals to the wind,
to pluck the butterfly's wings for the microscope's lens,
to plunge a fist
into a teetering tower of bricks,
watch the debris sail, explode fireworks
until all crumbles to dust and is undone, open
to the curious eye.

Does this or that creature die as I die,
cry as I cry, writhe as I if my guts were ripped
from the walls of my flesh,
my ripe heart eaten alive.

The probing questions of sacred exploration,
as if science can
progress without
empathy.

Does a penis feel as a clitoris feels?
Do slanted eyes see as I see? Is a white or black skin
or sin the same as a red one;
is it like me? Does it burn, does it peel, does it boil
in oil or reel in pain?

The obsession to possess the other so completely that his blood
fills the mouth and you eat of her flesh from its bone,
and then know if she, if he, feels as you feel,
if your world
is
real.

WILLIE PERDOMO
(1960?–)

*Willie Perdomo is a poet of Puerto Rican heritage who lives in East Harlem,
New York City. He is a winner of the Nuyorican Poets Cafe Grand Slam, a
performance contest among poets. He was featured in PBS's Alive from Off-
Center series' program "Words in Your Face." His book,* Where a Nickel
Costs a Dime, *was published in 1996.*

*Perdomo's poem "Nigger-Reecan Blues" confronts the complexity of
identity behind the simple appellation "Puerto Rican," for the island has a
history involving Native Americans, Spanish and other European colonizers
and immigrants, and African slaves.*

NIGGER-REECAN BLUES

(for Piri Thomas)

Hey, Willie. What are you, man? Boricua? Moreno? Que?

I am.

No, silly. You know what I mean: What are you?

I am you. You are me. We the same. Can't you feel our veins
drinking the same blood?

    –But who said you was a Porta Reecan?
    –Tu no ere Puerto Riqueno, brother.
    –Maybe Indian like Ghandi Indian.
    –I thought you was a Black man.
    –Is one of your parents white?
    –You sure you ain't a mix of something like
    –Portuguese and Chinese?
    –Naaaahhhh . . . You ain't no Porta Reecan.
    –I keep telling you: The boy is a Black man with an accent.

If you look closely you will see that your spirits are standing
right next to our songs. Yo soy Boricua! Yo soy Africano! I
ain't lyin'. Pero mi pelo es kinky y kurly y mi skin no es negro
pero it can pass . . .

    –Hey, yo. I don't care *what* you say—you Black.

I ain't Black! Everytime I go downtown la madam blankeeta de
madeeson avenue sees that I'm standing right next to her and
she holds her purse just a bit tighter. I can't even catch a
taxi late at night and the newspapers say that if I'm not in
front of a gun, chances are that I'll be behind one. I wonder why . . .

    –Cuz you Black, nigger.

I ain't Black, man. I had a conversation with my professor. Went
like this:

    –Where are you from, Willie?
    –I'm from Harlem.
    –Ohh! Are you Black?
    –No, but—
    –Do you play much basketball?

–Te lo estoy diciendo, brother. Ese hombre es un moreno!
Miralo!

Mira yo no soy moreno! I just come out of Jerry's Den and the
coconut
spray off my new shape-up sails around the corner, up to the Harlem
River and off to New Jersey. I'm lookin' slim and I'm lookin' trim
and when my homeboy Davi saw me, he said: "Coño, Papo. Te
parece como
un moreno, brother. Word up, bro. You look like a stone black
kid."

   –I told you-you was Black.

Damn! I ain't even Black and here I am sufferin' from the young
Black man's plight/the old white man's burden/and I ain't even
Black, man/A Black man/I am not/Boricua I am/ain't never really
was/Black/like me . . .

   –Leave that boy alone. He got the Nigger-Reecan Blues

I'm a Spic!
I'm a Nigger!
Spic! Spic! No different than a Nigger!
Neglected, rejected, oppressed and depressed
From banana boats to tenements
Street gangs to regiments . . .
Spic! Spic! I ain't nooooo different than a Nigger.

LANGSTON HUGHES
(1902–1967)

Born in Joplin, Missouri, Langston Hughes was first recognized in the 1920s
as an important literary figure of the Harlem Renaissance (1920-1940)
before going on to a varied and illustrious career as a poet, novelist, short
story writer, playwright, song lyricist, author of juvenile books, editor,
translator, journalist, and lecturer. Although he graduated from Lincoln
University in 1929, Hughes had attended Columbia University before publishing his first book of poems, The Weary Blues, in 1926. Hughes was perhaps the first African American to make a living entirely from his writing.
His poetry is both popular and accessible—making use of such African
American lyric forms as the spiritual, the gospel, and the blues—and critical—presenting, as "Cross" does, the social and political challenges faced by

his people. *Among his major works are* The Ways of White Folks, *stories (1934)*, Jim Crow's Last Stand, *poems (1943), and* Montage of a Dream Deferred, *poems (1951). His most popular work in his lifetime was the series of sketches published in African American newspapers that features Jesse B. Semple, a Harlem "everyman."* Simple on my Mind *(1950) was the first of five collections of these sketches. Nonfiction publications include two autobiographies,* The Big Sea *(1940) and* I Wonder as I Wander *(1956), and* The Sweet Flypaper of Life *with photographs by Roy De Carava (1955).*

CROSS

My old man's a white old man
And my old mother's black.
If ever I cursed my white old man
I take my curses back.

If ever I cursed my black old mother
And wished she were in hell,
I'm sorry for that evil wish
And now I wish her well.

My old man died in a fine big house.
My ma died in a shack.
I wonder where I'm gonna die,
Being neither white nor black?

DAVID MURA
(1952-)

David Mura, of Japanese ancestry, was born in Great Lakes, Illinois. He earned his B.A. from Grinnell College and received an M.F.A. at Vermont College. Mura has won a host of awards and accolades, including the Fanny Fay Wood Memorial Prize of the American Academy of Poets (1977), a National Endowment for the Arts Literature Fellowship (1985), the Loft McKnight Award of Distinction for Poetry (1992), the U.S./Japan Creative Artist Fellowship, and a Lila Wallace-Reader's Digest Writers Award. Mura has published in varied genres including A Male Grief: Notes on Pornography and Addiction, *nonfiction (1987);* After We Lost Our Way, *poems (1989);* Turning Japanese: Memoirs of a Sansei, *autobiography (1991);* The Colors of Desire, *poems (1995); and* Where the Body Meets Memory: An Odyssey of Race, Sexuality, and Identity, *essays (1996). A special interest, reflected in the following essay, "Secrets and Anger," is in the personal, psy-*

chological situation of the American of mixed racial background and/or assimilated ethnicity. In addition to teaching at St. Olaf College and the University of Oregon as a visiting professor, Mura has also held administrative and teaching positions in secondary education including the Writers-and-Artists-in-the-Schools program.

SECRETS AND ANGER

On the day our daughter was born, as my wife, Susie, and I waited for the doctor to do a cesarean section, we talked about names. Standing at the window, I looked out and said, "Samantha, the day you were born was a gray and blustery day." We decided on Samantha Lyn, after my sisters, Susan Lynn and Lynda. I felt to give the baby a Japanese name might mark her as too different, especially since we live in St. Paul, where Asian Americans are a small minority. I had insisted that her last name be hyphenated, Sencer-Mura. My wife had argued that such a name was unwieldy. "What happens when Samantha Sencer-Mura marries Bob Rodriguez-Stein?" she asked. "That's her generation's problem," I said, laughing.

I sometimes wish now we'd given her a Japanese middle name, as Susie had wanted. Perhaps it's because I sense that the world Samantha's inheriting won't be dominated by the melting-pot model, that multiculturalism is not a project but a reality, that in the next century there will no longer be a white majority in this country. Or perhaps I simply feel guilty about having given in to the dominant culture once again.

I am working on a poem about my daughter, about trying to take in her presence, her life, about trying to link her with my sense of the past—my father and mother, the internment camps, my grandparents. I picture myself serving her sukiyaki, a dish I shunned as a child, and her shouting for more rice, brandishing her *hashi* (a word for chopsticks, which I never used as a child and only began to use after my trip to Japan). As I describe Samantha running through the garden, scattering petals, squashing tomatoes, I suddenly think of how someone someday will call her a "gook," that I know this with more certainty than I know she'll find happiness in love.

I speak to my wife about moving out to the West Coast or to Hawaii, where there would be more Asian Americans. In Hawaii, more than a third of the children are *happa* (mixed race); Samantha would be the norm, not the minority. I need to spend more time living in an Asian-American community: I can't tell its stories if I'm not a part of it. As I talk about moving one evening, Susie starts to feel uneasy. "I'm afraid you'll cross this bridge and take Sam with you, and leave me here," she says.

"But I've lived all my life on your side of the bridge. At most social gatherings, I'm the only person of color in the room. What's wrong with living awhile on my side of the bridge? What keeps you from crossing?"

Susie, a pediatric oncologist, works with families of all colors. Still, having a hybrid daughter is changing her experience. Often when she's in the grocery with Sam, someone will come up to her and say: "Oh, she's such a beautiful little girl. Where did you get her?" This has happened so often Susie swears she's going to teach Sam to say: "Fuck you. My genes came all the way over on the *Mayflower*, thank you."

These incidents mark ways Susie has experienced something negative over race that I have not. No one asks me where Sam came from: they assume I'm her father. For Susie, the encounters are a challenge to her position as Samantha's biological mother, the negation of an arduous pregnancy and the physical work of birth and motherhood. For me, they stir an old wound. The people who mistake Sam for an adopted child can't picture a white woman married to an Asian man.

Six ways of viewing identity: Identity is a social and historical construction. Identity is formed by political and economic and cultural exigencies. Identity is a fiction. Identity is a choice. Identity may appear unitary but is always fragmentary. Identity is deciding to acknowledge or not acknowledge political and economic and cultural exigencies.

When I address the question of raising my daughter, I address the question of her identity, which means I address the question of my identity, her mother's, our parents', and so on. But this multiplication of the self takes place along many lines. Who knows where it stops? At my grandparents? At the woman in the grocery store? At you, the imagined reader of this piece?

In the matrix of race and color in our society, there is the binary opposition of black and white. And then there are the various Others, determined by race or culture or gender or sexual preference—Native Americans, Hispanic Americans, Asian Americans, Japanese Americans, women, men, heterosexuals, homosexuals. None of these definitions stands alone; together they form an intricate, mazelike weave that's impossible to disentangle.

I wrote my memoir, *Turning Japanese*, to explore the cultural amnesia of Japanese Americans, particularly those of the third generation, like myself, who speak little or no Japanese. When I give readings, people often ask if I'm going to raise Samantha with a greater awareness of Japanese culture than I received as a child. The obvious answer is yes. I also acknowledge that the prospects of teaching her about Japanese culture feel to me rather daunting, and I now have more sympathy for my nisei parents, whom I used to criticize for forgetting the past.

And yet, near the end of my stay in Japan, I decided that I was not Japanese, that I was never going to be Japanese, and that I was not even going to be an expert on Japanese culture. My identity was as a Japanese American. That meant claiming the particularities of Japanese-American history; it meant coming to terms with how the dominant culture had formed me; it meant realizing my identity would always be partially occluded. Finally, it meant that the issues of race were central to me, that I would see myself as a person of color.

Can I teach these things to my daughter? My Japanese-American identity comes from my own experience. But I am still trying to understand that experience and still struggling to find language to talk about the issues of race. My failures are caused by more than a lack of knowledge; there's the powerful wish not to know. How, for instance, can I talk to my daughter about sexuality and race? My own life is so filled with shame and regret, so filled with experiences I would rather not discuss, that it seems much easier to opt for silence. It's simpler to pretend multiculturalism means teaching her *kanji* and how to conjugate Japanese verbs.

I know that every day Samantha will be exposed to images telling her that Asian bodies are marginalized, that the women are exotic or sensual or submissive, that the men are houseboys or Chinatown punks, kung fu warriors or Japanese businessmen—robotlike and powerful or robotlike and comic. I know that she will face constant pressure to forget that she is part Japanese American, to assume a basically white middle-class identity. When she reaches adolescence, there will be strong messages for her to dissociate herself from other people of color, perhaps from the children of recent Asian immigrants. She may find herself wanting to assume a privilege and status that come from not calling attention to her identity or from playing into the stereotype that makes Asian women seem so desirable to certain white men. And I know I will have no power over these forces.

Should I tell her of how, when I look at her mother, I know my desire for her cannot be separated from the way the culture has inculcated me with standards of white beauty? Should I tell her of my own desire for a "hallucinatory whiteness," of how in my twenties such a desire fueled a rampant promiscuity and addiction to pornography, to the "beautiful" bodies of white women? It's all too much to expect Samantha to take in. It should not even be written down. It should be kept hidden, unspoken. These forces should not exist.

Samantha's presence has made me more willing to speak out on issues of race, to challenge the status quo. I suppose I want her to inherit a different world than the one I grew up in.

One day last year, I was talking with two white friends about the landmark controversy over the Broadway production of *Miss Saigon.* Like many Asian Americans, I agreed with the protest by Actor's Equity against the producer's casting. I felt disturbed that again a white actor, the British Jonathan Pryce, was playing a Eurasian and that no Asian-American actor had been given a chance to audition for that role. Beyond that, I was upset by the Madame Butterfly plot of *Miss Saigon,* where an Asian woman pines for her white male lover.

Both my friends—Paula, a painter, and Mark, a writer—consider themselves liberals; Mark was active in the antiwar movement during the sixties. He was part of my wedding and, at the time, perhaps my closest male friend. But neither agreed with me about *Miss Saigon.* They argued that art represented freedom of the imagination, that it meant trying to get inside other people's skin. Isn't color-blind casting what we're striving for? they said.

"Why is it everyone gets so upset when a white actor may be denied a role?" I asked. "What about every time an Asian-American actor tries out for a part that says 'lawyer' or 'doctor' and is turned down?"

But reverse discrimination isn't the answer, they replied.

I don't recall exactly what happened after this. I think the argument trailed off into some safer topic, as such arguments often do. But afterward, I felt angrier and angrier and, at the same time, more despairing. I realized that for me the fact that Warner Oland, a Swede, played Charlie Chan was humiliating. It did not show me that art was a democracy of the imagination. But for Paula and Mark, my sense of shame was secondary to their belief in "freedom" in the arts.

When I talked to my wife about my anger and despair, she felt uncomfortable. These were her friends, too. She said I'd argued before with them about the role of politics in art. Mark had always looked ruefully at his political involvement in the sixties, when he felt he had gone overboard with his zealous self-righteousness. "He's threatened by your increasing political involvement," Susie said. She felt I should take our disagreement as just another incident in a long friendly dialogue.

But when I talked with a black friend, Garth, who's a writer, he replied: "Yeah, I was surprised too at the reaction of some of my white artist friends to *Miss Saigon.* It really told me where they were. It marked a dividing line."

For a while, I avoided talking about my feelings when Paula and Mark came by. Susie urged me to talk to them, to work it out. "You're trying to get me to have sympathy with how difficult this is for them or for you, how this creates tensions between you and them," I said. "But I have to have this conversation about *Miss Saigon* with every white friend I have. Each of you only has to have it with me." My wife said that I was taking my anger out on her—which, in part, I was.

Finally, in a series of telephone calls, I told Paula and Mark I not only felt that their views about *Miss Saigon* were wrong but that they were racially based. In the emotionally charged conversations, I don't think I used the word "racist," but I know my friends objected to my lumping them together with other whites. Paula said I was stereotyping them, that she wasn't like other whites. She told me of her friendships with a few blacks when she lived back East, of the history of her mother's involvement in supporting civil rights. "It's not like I don't know what discrimination is," she said. "Women get discriminated against, so do artists." Her tone moved back and forth between self-righteousness and resentment to distress and tears about losing our friendship.

Mark talked of his shame about being a WASP. "Do you know that I don't have a single male friend who is a WASP?" he said. I decided not to point out that, within the context of color, the difference between a WASP male and, say, an Irish Catholic, isn't much of a difference. And I also didn't remark that he had no friends of color, other than myself. I suppose I felt such remarks would hurt him too much. I also didn't feel it was safe to say them.

A few months later, I had calmer talks with Mark, but they always ended with this distance between us. I needed some acknowledgment from him that, when we began talking about race, I knew more about it than he did, that our arguing about race was not the same as our arguing about free verse versus formal verse. That my experience gave me insights he didn't have.

"Of course, that's true," he said. "I know you've had different experiences." But for him, we had to meet on an equal basis, where his views on race were considered at the start as just as valid as mine. Otherwise, he felt he was compromising himself, giving away his soul. He likened it to the way he gave away his self in his alcoholic family, where he denied his own feelings. He would be making himself a "victim" again.

At one point, I suggested we do some sessions with a therapist who was counseling him and whom I had also gone to. "No," said Mark. "I can't do that now. I need him on my side."

I can still see us sitting there on my front steps, on a warm early-spring day. I looked at this man with whom I'd shared my writing and my most intimate secrets, with whom I'd shared the process of undergoing therapy and recovery, and I realized we were now no longer intimates. I felt that I had embarked on a journey to discover myself as a person of color, to discover the rage and pain that had formed my Japanese-American identity, and that he would deny me this journey. He saw me as someone who would make him a victim, whose feelings on race were charged with arrogance and self-righteousness. And yet, on some level, I know he saw that my journey was good for me. I felt I was asking him to come on that journey with me.

Inevitably I wonder if my daughter will understand my perspective as a person of color. Will she identify with white friends, and be fearful and suspicious of my anger and frustration? Or will she be working from some viewpoint I can't quite conceive, some line that marks her as a person of color and white and neither, all at the same time, as some new being whose experiences I will have to listen to and learn from? How can I prepare her for that new identity?

Will it be fair or accurate or helpful for me to tell her, "Unless the world is radically different, on some level, you will still have to choose: Are you a person of color or not?"

It took me many months to figure out what had gone down with Paula and Mark. Part of me wanted to let things go, but part of me knew that someday I'd have to talk to Samantha about race. If I avoided what was difficult in my own life, what would I be able to say to her? My black friend Alexs and I talked about how whites deperately want to do "the victim limbo," as he called it. Offered by many as a token of solidarity—"I'm just the same as you"—it's really a way of depoliticizing the racial question; it ignores the differences in power in this country that result from race.

When white people engage in conversation about racism, the first thing they often do, as Paula did with me, is the victim limbo: "I'm a woman, I know what prejudice is, I've experienced it." "I'm Jewish/working class/Italian in a WASP neighborhood, I know what prejudice is." The purpose of this is to show the person of color that he or she doesn't really experience anything the white person hasn't experienced, that the white person is a victim too. But Alexs and I both knew that the positions of a person of color and a white person in American society are not the same. "Whites don't want to give up their privilege and psychic comforts," said Alexs. "That's really why they're so angry. They have to choose whether they're going to give up power or fight for it."

Thinking this through, though, does not assuage the pain and bitterness I feel about losing white friendships over race, or the distance I have seen open up between me and my white friends. Nor does it help me explain to my daughter why we no longer see Paula or Mark. The compensation has been the numerous friendships that I've begun to have with people of color. My daughter will grow up in a household where the people who visit will be from a wider spectrum than were those Japanese Americans and whites who visited my parents' house in the suburbs of Chicago.

Not that teaching her about her Asian-American self has become any easier. My wife has been more conscious than I've been about telling Sam that she's Japanese. After playing with blond Shannon, the girl from next door, Sam said: "She's not Japanese, Mom. We're Japanese." "No," said Susie. "Daddy's Japanese, and you're part Japanese, but I'm not Japanese." Sam refused to believe this: "No, you're Japanese." After a few minutes, Susie finally sorted out the confusion. Sam thought being Japanese meant you had black hair.

For many liberal whites, what seems most important in any discussion of race is the need for hope, the need to find some link with people of color. They do not see how much that need serves as a tool of denial, how their claims of solidarity not only ignore real differences but also blot out the reality of people of color. How can we move forward, they ask, with all this rage you seem to feel? How can you stereotype me or group me in this category of whiteness?

I tell them they are still unwilling to examine what being white has meant to their existence. They think their rage at being classified as a white person is the same rage that people of color feel when they are being stereotyped. It is not. When whites feel anger about race, almost always they are feeling a threat to their comfort or power.

In the end, whites must exchange a hope based on naiveté and ignorance for one based on knowledge. For this naive hope denies connections, complexities. It is the drug of amnesia. It says there is no thread from one moment to the next, no cause and effect. It denies consequence and responsibility.

For my wife, this journey has been a difficult one. The arguments we have over race mirror our other arguments; at the same time, they exist in another realm, where I am a person of color and Susie is white. "I realize that in a way I've been passing too," she said a few months ago. "There's this comfort I've got to give up, this ease." At her clinic, she challenges the mainly white children's books in the waiting room, or a colleague's unconscious assumptions about Hmong families. More and more, she finds herself at gatherings where she as a white person is in the minority.

Breaking through denial, seeing how much needs to be changed, does not have to blunt the capacity for hope. For both of us, our daughter is proof of that capacity. And if I know that someday someone will call Samantha a gook, I know today she's a happy child. The love her mother and I share, the love we bear for her, cannot spare her from pain over race, and yet it can make her stronger. Sam will go further than we will, she will know more. She will be like nothing I can imagine, as I am like nothing my parents imagined.

Today my daughter told me she will grow up and work with her mother at the hospital. I'll be a grandpa and stay home and write poems and be with her children. Neither race nor ethnicity enters into her vision of the future. And yet they are already there, with our hopes, gathering shape.

WENDY ROSE
(1948-)

Born in Oakland, California, Wendy Rose, a Native American of Hopi ancestry, is noted for poetry that explores the experiences of mixed-blood Natives who are estranged from both Native and white societies. Rose earned a B.A. and an M.A. from the University of California, Berkeley, where she began writing poetry. Her collections include Hopi Roadrunner Dancing *(1973),* What Happened When the Hopi Hit New York *(1981),* Halfbreed Chronicles *(1985), and* Now Poof She is Gone *(1994). Rose is also an illustrator, with numerous books to her credit. She has taught at the University of California, Berkeley, California State University, Fresno, and Fresno City College.*

Rose's poem "If I Am Too Brown or Too White for You," from Halfbreed Chronicles, *moves the question of caste and color prejudices that operate both within minority communities and within American culture generally so that we see it from a new angle.*

If I Am Too Brown
or Too White for You

remember I am a garnet woman
whirling into precision
as a crystal arithmetic
or a cluster and so

why the dream
in my mouth,
the flutter of blackbirds
at my wrists?

In the morning
there you are
at the edge of the river
on one knee

and you are selecting me
from among polished stones
more definitely red or white
between which tiny serpents swim

and you see that my body
is blood frozen
into giving birth
over and over in a single motion

and you touch the matrix
shattered in winter
and begin to piece together
the shape of me

wanting the fit in your palm
to be perfect
and the image less
clouded, less mixed

but you always see
just in time
working me around
in the evening sun

there is a small light
in the smoke, a tiny sun
in the blood, so deep
it is there and not there,

so pure
it is singing.

3

TOWARD THE

MULTICULTURE

In this last section, *Toward the Multiculture*, the selections develop the reinvention of American identity, a process that is always under way but has accelerated in the post–World War II period. Greater self-consciousness about race and immigration as defining forces in shaping the nation and new openness about interracial and inter-ethnic relations interact with developments such as the emigration of educated elites from war-torn or poverty-stricken countries to move Americans toward more complex notions of American identity. We can see the roots of such a revision in José Martí's essay "Our America" which reminded readers early in the twentieth cen-tury that "American" was an identity shared with millions of people in the hemi-sphere outside of the United States. Ishmael Reed explores in his essay "America: The Multinational Society" a vision of the U.S. as a purposefully multiethnic civi-lization, quite a different view than the model of assimilation summed up in the widespread "melting pot" metaphor. Jessica Hagedorn in her essay "Homesick" offers a take on a complex, binational identity made possible by such realities as high-speed international travel and the exportation of American culture around the globe. John Leguizamo in his sketch "The Crossover King" and Trey Ellis in his short story "Guess Who's Coming to Seder" explore the personal impact of new social relations, public and private. Arjun Appadurai in his essay "The Heart of Whiteness" examines the possible meaning for Americans of the ongoing dissolution of the assumed bond between nations and states. Other works in this section suggest how matters as disparate as style, language, and geography influence our developing redefinition of America.

ADRIAN WONG SHUE
(1952-)

Adrian Wong Shue was born in Jamaica, West Indies, and is of Afro-Caribbean and Chinese heritage. He began studying art at the age of fourteen with an immigrant artist from China, Alfred Chin. He later continued his studies at Kingston College in Jamaica and in California. Wong Shue traveled throughout the Caribbean and to Brazil and China as he developed his art. He received his B.A. degree from Antioch University in 1987. He has exhibited his work widely in his adopted country, Asia, Europe, and the Caribbean.

Deeply influenced by the Hunan school of Chinese artists, Wong Shue's work in many media—pastels, oils, ink, charcoals, woodcuts, lithographs, watercolors—is both richly colorful and culturally evocative.

"TROPICAL DAYDREAM"

J O S É   M A R T Í
(1853~1895)

In January 1880 José Martí arrived in New York City as a recognized writer, patriot, and orator exiled from Spanish-ruled Cuba. In New York, he worked as a translator, teacher, and correspondent for newspapers in Venezuela, Argentina, and Mexico. Martí also wrote articles on his life in the United States for the New York Sun. *However, his main objective in the U.S. was to unite the rival factions of the Cuban independence movement under the Cuban Revolutionary Party. To support this goal, he traveled from New York to Central America, Mexico, and the Caribbean and eventually died on the battlefield in eastern Cuba in 1895. Martí's ultimate concern is for "one America based on its Native American uniqueness, without racial hatred," a desire expressed in his essay, "Our America." Martí's works include* The America of José Martí: Selected Writings *(1954), translated by Juan de Onis;* Inside the Monster: Writings on the United States and American Imperialism *(1975), edited by Philip S. Foner; and* Our America: Writings on Latin America and the Struggle for Cuban Independence *(1978), also edited by Philip S. Foner.*

O U R   A M E R I C A

The villager fondly believes that the world is contained in his village, and he thinks the universal order good if he can be mayor, humiliate the rival who stole his sweetheart, or add to the savings in his sock—unaware of the giants with seven-league boots who can crush him under foot, or the strife in the heavens between comets, which streak through space, devouring worlds. What remains of the parochial in America must awake. These are not times for sleeping in a nightcap, but rather with weapons for a pillow, like the warriors of Juan de Castellanos: weapons of the mind, which conquer all others. Barricades of ideas are worth more than barricades of stone.

There is no prow that can cleave a cloud-bank of ideas. An energetic idea, unfurled in good season before the world, turns back a squadron of ironsides with the power of the mystic banner of the judgement day. Nations that do not know one another should make haste to do so, as brothers-in-arms. Those who shake their fists at each other, like jealous brothers who covet the same land, or the cottager who envies the squire his manor, should clasp hands until they are one. Those who allege the sanction of a criminal tradition to lop off the lands of their brother, with a sword dipped in his own blood, had best return the lands to the brother punished far beyond his due, if they do not want to be called thieves. The honorable do not seek money in satisfaction of debts of honor, at so much a slap. We can no longer be a people like foliage, living in the air, heavy with blossoms, bursting and fluttering at the whim of light's caress, or buffeted and tossed by the tempest: the trees must form ranks so the giant with seven-league boots shall not pass! It is the hour of muster and the united march. We must advance shoulder-to-shoulder, one solid mass like the silver lodes in the depths of the Andes.

Only the seven-month birthling will lack the courage. Those who do not have faith in their country are seven-month men. They cannot reach the first limb with their puny arms, arms with painted nails and bracelets, arms of Madrid or Paris; and they say the lofty tree cannot be climbed. The ships must be loaded with these destructive insects, who gnaw the marrow of the country that nourishes them. If they are Parisians or Madrilenians, let them stroll along the Prado under the lamplights, or take sherbet at Tortoni's. These carpenter's sons who are ashamed of their father for his trade! These American sons who are ashamed of the mother that loves them because she wears an Indian apron, and disown their sick mother, the scoundrels, abandoning her on her sick bed! Well, who is the man worthy of the name? The one who stays with his mother to nurse her in her sickness, or the one who puts her to work out of the sight of the world and lives off her labors in the decadent lands, affecting fancy cravats, cursing the womb that carried him, displaying the sign of traitor on the back of his paper cassock? These children of our America, which will be saved by its Indians, and goes from less to more, these deserters who take up arms in the armies of North America, which drowns its Indians in blood, and goes from more to less! These delicate beings, who are men but do not want to do the work of men! The Washington who forged this land, did he go to live with the English, to live with them during the years in which he saw them coming against his own country? These *incroyables* of their honor, who trail it through alien lands, like their counterparts in the French Revolution, with their dancing, their affectations, their drawling speech!

For in what lands can a man take greater pride than in our long-suffering republics of America, raised up from among the mute Indian masses by the bleeding arms of a hundred apostles to the sounds of battle between the book and the thurible. Never in history have such advanced and unified nations been forged in less time from such disordered elements. The fool in his pride believes that the earth was created to serve him as a pedestal because words flow easily from his pen, or his speech is colorful, and he charges his native land with being worthless and beyond salvation because its virgin jungles do not provide him with means to travel continuously abroad, driving Persian ponies and lavishing champagne, like a tycoon. The incapacity does not lie with the nascent country, which seeks suitable forms and greatness that will serve, but with those who attempt to rule nations of a unique character, and singular, violent composition, with laws that derive from four centuries of operative liberty in the United States, and nineteen centuries of French monarchy. A decree by Hamilton does not halt the charge of the *llanero*'s pony. A phrase of Sièyes does nothing to quicken the stagnant blood of the Indian race. One must see things as they are, to govern well; the good governor in America is not one who knows how government is conducted in France or Germany, but who knows the elements of which his country is composed and how they can be marshaled so that by methods and institutions native to the country the desirable state may be attained wherein every man realizes himself, and all share in the abundance that Nature bestowed for the common benefit on the nation they enrich with their labor and defend with their lives. The government must be the child of the country. The spirit of the government must be the same as that of the country. The form of government must conform to the natural constitution of the country. Good government is nothing more than the true balance between the natural elements of the nation.

For that reason, the foreign book has been conquered in America by the natural man. The natural men have vanquished the artificial, lettered men. The native-born half-breed has vanquished the exotic Creole. The struggle is not between barbarity and civilization, but between false erudition and nature. The natural man is good. He respects and rewards superior intelligence, as long as his submission is not turned against him, or he is not offended by being disregarded, a thing the natural man does not forgive, prepared as he is to regain by force the respect of whoever has wounded his pride or threatened his interests. Tyrants in America have risen to power serving these scorned natural elements, and have fallen the moment they betrayed them. Republics have paid in tyrannies for their inability to recognize the true elements of their countries, to derive from them the proper form of government, and govern accordingly. To be a governor of a new country means to be a creator.

In nations of cultured and uncultured elements, the uncultured will govern, because it is their habit to strike and resolve all doubts by force, whenever the cultured prove incapable in office. The uncultured mass is lazy, and timid in matters of the mind. It asks only to be well-governed. But if the government hurts it, it rebels and governs itself. How can the universities be expected to produce governors, if there is not one university in America that teaches the rudimentary in the art of government, which is the analysis of the elements peculiar to America? Young men go out into the world wearing Yankee or French spectacles, and hope to govern by guesswork a nation they do not know. In the political race, all entries should be scratched who do not demonstrate a knowledge of the political rudiments. The prize in literary contests should go not to the best ode, but to the best study of the political factors in one's country. Newspapers, universities, and schools should foment the study of their country's dynamic factors. They have only to be stated, straightforward and in plain language. For whoever disregards any portion of the truth, whether by ignorance or design, is doomed to fall; the truth he lacked grows in the negligence and brings down whatever was erected without it. It is easier to determine the elements and attack the problem, than to attack the problem without knowing the elements. The natural man arrives, indignant and strong, and topples the authority based on books because he was not governed according to the obvious realities of the country. Knowledge holds the key. To know one's country, and govern it with that knowledge, is the only alternative to tyranny. The European university must give way to the American university. The history of America, from the Incas to the present, must be taught until it is known by heart, even if the Archons of the Greeks go by the board. Our Greece must take priority over the Greece that is not ours: we need it more. Nationalist statesmen must replace cosmopolitan statesmen. Let the world be grafted on our republics; but the trunk must be our own. And let the vanquished pedant hold his tongue: for there are no lands in which a man can take greater pride than our long-suffering American republics.

With the rosary as our guide, our head white and our body mottled, being Indian and Creole, we intrepidly entered the community of nations. We set out to conquer liberty under the standard of the Virgin. A priest, a handful of lieutenants, and a woman raised the Mexican Republic on the shoulders of the Indians. A few heroic students instructed in French liberty by a Spanish cleric, raised Central America against Spain under a Spanish general. In the oriflammed habits of monarchy, Venezuelans and Argentinians struck out, from north to south, to deliver nations. When the two heroes collided and the continent almost rocked, one, and not the lesser, turned back. But when the wars ended, heroism, by being less glorious, became rarer; it is easier for men to die with honor than to think with order. It was discovered that it is simpler to govern when sentiments are exalted and united, than in the wake of battle when divisive, arrogant, exotic, and ambitious ideas emerge. The forces routed in the epic conflict sought, with the feline cunning of their species, and utilizing the weight of realities, to undermine the new structure, which embraced at once the rude and singular provinces of our half-breed America, and the cities of silken hose and Parisian frock coats beneath the unfamiliar flag of reason and liberty, borrowed from nations skilled in the arts of government. The hierarchical constitution of the colonies resisted the democratic organization of the republics. The capitals of stock and collar kept the countryside of horse-hide boots cooling its heels in the vestibule. The cultured leaders did not realize that the revolution had triumphed because their words had unshackled the soul of the nation, and that they had to govern with that soul, and not against it or without it. America began to suffer, and still suffers, from the effort of trying to find an adjustment between the discordant and hostile elements it inherited from a despotic and perverse colonizer, and the imported ideas and forms which have retarded the logical government because of their lack of local reality. The continent, disjointed by three centuries of a rule that denied men the right to use their reason, embarked on a form of government based on reason, without thought or reflection on the unlettered hordes which had helped in its redemption; it was to be the reason of all in matters of general concern, not the reason of the university over the reason of the province. The problem of the Independence was not the change in forms, but the change in spirit.

It was necessary to make common cause with the downtrodden, to secure the new system against the interests and habits of rule of the oppressors. The tiger, frightened off by the powder flash, returns at night to the haunts of his prey. When he dies, it is with flames shooting from his eyes and claws unsheathed. But his step cannot be heard, for he comes on velvet paws. When the prey awakes, the tiger is upon him. The colony lives on in the republic; and our America is saving itself from its grave errors—the arrogance of the capital cities, the blind triumph of the scorned country people, the influx of foreign ideas and formulas, the wicked and unpolitic disdain in which the aboriginal race is held—through the superior virtue, backed by the necessary conviction, of the republic that struggles against the colony. The tiger lurks behind each tree, waiting at every turn. He will die with his claws unsheathed and flames shooting from his eyes.

But "these countries will be saved," as the Argentine Rivadavia announced, whose sin was to be gentlemanly in crude times; a silk scabbard does not become the *machete*, nor can the lance be discarded in a country won by the lance, for it becomes angry, and presents itself at the door of Iturbide's congress demanding that "the blond one be made emperor." These countries will be saved because a genius for moderation, found in Nature's imperturbable harmony, seems to prevail in the continent of light, where there emerges a new realistic man schooled for these realistic times in the critical philosophy, which in Europe has succeeded the literature of sect and opinion in which the previous generation was steeped.

We were a strange sight with the chest of an athlete, the hands of a coxcomb, and the brain of a child. We were a masquerade in English trousers, Parisian vest, North American jacket, and Spanish hat. The Indian circled about us in silent wonder, and went to the mountains to baptize his children. The runaway Negro poured out the music of his heart on the night air, alone and unknown among the rivers and wild beasts. The men of the land, the creators, rose up in blind indignation against the scornful city, against their own child. We were all epaulets and tunics in countries that came into the world with hemp sandals on their feet and head-bands for hats. The stroke of genius would have been to couple the headband and tunic with the charity of heart and daring of the founding father; to rescue the Indian; to make a place for the able Negro; to fit liberty to the body of those who rose up and triumphed in its name. We were left with the judge, the general, the scholar and the prebendary. As if caught in the tentacles of an octopus, the angelic young men lunged toward Heaven, only to fall back, crowned with clouds, in sterile glory. The natural people, driven by instinct, swept away the golden staffs of office in blind triumph. The European or Yankee book could not provide the answer to the Hispanic-American enigma. Hate was tried, and the countries wasted away, year by year. Exhausted by the senseless struggle between the book and the lance, of reason against dogma, of the city against the country, of the impossible rule by rival city cliques over the natural nation alternately tempestuous and inert, we begin almost without realizing it to try love. The nations stand up and salute each other. "What are we like?" they ask; and they begin to tell one another what they are like. When a problem arises in Cojimar, they do not send to Danzig for the answer. The frock coat is still French, but thought begins to be American. The youth of America roll up their sleeves and plunge their hands into the dough; it rises with the leavening of their sweat. They understand that there is too much imitation, and that creation holds the key to salvation. "Create" is the password of this generation. The wine is from plantain, and if it proves sour, it is our wine! It is understood that the forms of government must accommodate themselves to the natural elements of the country, that absolute ideas must take relative forms if they are to escape emasculation by the failure of the form, that liberty, if it is to be viable, must be sincere and complete, that the republic which does not open its arms to all, and move ahead with all, must die. The tiger within enters through the fissure, and the tiger from without. The general restrains his cavalry to a pace that suits his infantry, for if the infantry be left behind, the cavalry is surrounded by the enemy. Politics is strategy. Nations should live in continual self-criticism, because criticism is healthy; but always with one heart and one mind. Go down to the unfortunate and take them in your arms! Dissolve what is clotted in America with the fire of the heart! Make the natural blood of the nations course and throb through their veins! Erect, with the happy, sparkling eyes of workingmen, the new Americans salute one another from country to country. The natural statesman appears, schooled in the direct study of Nature. He reads to apply what he reads, not to copy. Economists study the problems at their origin. Orators begin to be lofty. Dramatists bring native characters to the stage. Academics consider practical subjects. Poetry shears off its romantic locks and hangs its red vest on the glorious tree. Prose, lively and discriminating, is charged with ideas. Governors study Indian in republics of Indians.

America is escaping all its dangers. The octopus still sleeps on some republics; but others, in contrast, drain the ocean from their lands with a furious, sublime haste, as if to make up for lost centuries. Some, forgetting that Juárez rode in a mule-drawn coach, hitch their coach to the wind and entrust the reins to a soap-bubble; poisonous luxury, the enemy of liberty, corrupts the frivolous and opens the door to the outlander. In others, where independence is threatened, an epic spirit produces a heightened manliness. Still others spawn a rabble-in-arms in rapacious wars against their neighbors which may yet turn and devour them. But there is yet another danger which does not come from within, but from the difference in origins, methods and interests between the two halves of the continent. The hour is fast approaching when our America will be confronted by an enterprising and energetic nation seeking close relations, but with indifference and scorn for us and our ways. And since strong countries, self-made by the rifle and the law, love, and love only, strong countries; since the hour of recklessness and ambition, of which North America may be freed if that which is purest in her blood predominates, or on which she may be launched by her vengeful and sordid masses, her tradition of expansion or the ambition of some powerful leaders, is not so near at hand, even to the most timorous eye, that there is not time to show the self-possessed and unwavering pride that would confront and dissuade her; since her good name as a republic in the eyes of the world puts on the America of the North a brake which cannot be removed even by the puerile grievances, the pompous arrogance, or parricidal discords of our American nations, the pressing need for our America, is to show herself as she is, one in soul and purpose, swift conqueror of a suffocating tradition, stained only by the blood drawn from hands that struggle to clear away ruins, and the scars left us by our masters. The scorn of our formidable neighbor, who does not know us, is the greatest danger for our America; and it is imperative that our neighbor know us, and know us soon, so she shall not scorn us, for the day of the visit is at hand. Through ignorance, she might go so far as to lay hands on us. From respect, once she came to know us, she would remove her hands. One must have faith in the best in men and distrust the worst. If not, the worst prevails. Nations should have a pillory for whoever fans useless hates; and another for whoever does not tell them the truth in time.

There can be no racial hate, because there are no races. The rachitic thinkers and theorists juggle and warm over the library-shelf races, which the open-minded traveler and well-disposed observer seek in vain in Nature's justice, where the universal identity of man leaps forth from triumphant love and the turbulent lust for life. The soul emanates, equal and eternal, from bodies distinct in shape and color. Whoever foments and propagates antagonism and hate between races, sins against Humanity. But as nations take shape among other different nations, they acquire distinctive and vital characteristics of thought and habit, of expansion and conquest, of vanity and greed, which from the latent state of national preoccupation could be converted in a period of internal unrest, or precipitation of the accumulated character of the nation, into a serious threat to the neighboring countries, isolated and weak, which the strong country declares perishable and inferior. The thought is father to the deed. But it must not be supposed, from a parochial animus, that there is a fatal and ingrained evil in the blond nation of the continent, because it does not speak our tongue, nor see the world as we do, nor resemble us in its political faults, which are of a different order, nor favorably regard the excitable, dark-skinned people, nor look charitably, from its still uncertain eminence, on those less favored by History, who climb the road of republicanism by heroic stages. The self-evident facts of the problem should not be obscured for it can be resolved, to the benefit of peaceful centuries yet to come, by timely study and the tacit, immediate union of the continental soul. The hymn of oneness sounds already; the actual generation carries a purposeful America along the road enriched by their sublime fathers; from the Rio Grande to the straits of Magellan, the Great Semi, seated on the flank of the condor, sows the seed of the new America through the romantic nations of the continent and the sorrowful islands of the sea!

JESSICA HAGEDORN
(1949-)

An international artist born in the Philippines, Jessica Hagedorn is known for her controversial subjects, including male prostitution, drugs, and political corruption on both sides of the Pacific. Hagedorn is a versatile artist, working as a poet, novelist, performance artist, singer, and radio commentator. She received a National Book Award nomination for her first novel, Dogeaters *(1989). Hagedorn published a second novel,* The Gangster of Love, *in 1996. As a poet, she has published* Dangerous Music *(1975),* Pet Food and Tropical Apparitions *(1981), and* Danger and Beauty *(1993). As a playwright, Hagedorn cowrote* Where the Mississippi Meets the Amazon *with Thulani Nkabinda and Ntozake Shange, produced in New York City in 1977. She also wrote the screenplay* Fresh Kill *(1994). As a performance artist, Hagedorn created* Airport Music *in the late 1970s. She is the editor of* Charlie Chan Is Dead: An Anthology of Contemporary Asian-American Writing *(1989). She lives in New York and Manila.*

"Homesick" from her collection of poems Danger and Beauty *expresses Hagedorn's complex emotions abut her complex international identity.*

HOMESICK

Blame it on the mambo and the cha-cha, voodoo amulets worn on the same chain with tiny crucifixes and scapulars blessed by the Pope. Chains of love, medals engraved with the all-seeing Eye, ascending Blessed Virgins floating towards heaven surrounded by erotic cherubs and archangels, the magnificent torso of a tormented, half-naked Saint Sebastian pierced by arrows dripping blood. A crown of barbed-wire thorns adorns the holy subversive's head, while we drown in the legacy of brutal tropical generals stuffed in khaki uniforms, their eyes shielded by impenetrable black sunglasses, Douglas MacArthur-style.

And Douglas MacArthur and Tom Cruise are painted on billboards lining Manila's highways, modelling Ray-Ban shades and Jockey underwear. You choose between the cinema version starring Gregory Peck smoking a corncob pipe, or the real thing. "I shall return," promised the North American general, still revered by many as the savior of the Filipino people, who eagerly awaited his return. As the old saying goes, this is how we got screwed, screwed real good. According to Nick Joaquin, "The Phillippines spent three hundred years trapped in a convent, and fifty-eight years in Hollywood . . . ." Or was it four hundred years? No matter—there we were, seduced and abandoned in a confusion of identities, then granted our independence. Hollywood pretended to leave us alone. An African American saying goes: "Nobody's *given* freedom." Being granted our independence meant we were owned all along by someone other than ourselves.

I step off the crowded plane on to the tarmac of the newly named Ninoy Aquino airport. It is an interesting appropriation of the assassinated senator's name, don't you think? So I think, homesick for this birthplace, my country of supreme ironies and fatalistic humor, mountains of foul garbage and breathtaking women, men with the fierce faces of wolves and steamy streets teeming with abandoned children.

The widow of the assassinated senator is Corazon Aquino, now President of the Republic of the Philippines in a deft stroke of irony that left the world stunned by a sudden turn of events in February, 1986. She is a beloved figurehead, a twentieth-century icon who has inherited a bundle of cultural contradictions and an economic nightmare in a lush paradise of corrupt, warring factions. In a Manila department store, one of the first souvenirs I buy my daughter is a rather homely Cory Aquino doll made out of brown cloth; the doll wears crooked wire eyeglasses, a straw shoulderbag, plastic high-heeled shoes, and Cory's signature yellow dress, with "I Love Cory" embroidered on the front. My daughter seems delighted with her doll and the notion of a woman president.

Soldiers in disguise, patrol the countryside . . . Jungle not far away. So goes a song I once wrote, pungent as the remembered taste of mangoes overripe as my imagination, the memory of Manila the central character of the novel I am writing, the novel which brings me back to this torrid zone, my landscape haunted by ghosts and movie-lovers.

Nietzsche once said, "A joke is an epitaph for an emotion." Our laughter is pained, self-mocking. Blake it on *Rambo, Platoon,* and *Gidget Goes Hawaiian.* Cory Aquino has inherited a holy war, a class war, an amazing nation of people who've endured incredible poverty and spiritual loss with inherent humor and grace. Member of the ruling class, our pious President has also inherited an army of divided, greedy men. Yet no one will probably bother assassinating her, as icons are always useful.

My novel sits in its black folder, an obsession with me for over ten years. Home is now New York, but home in my heart will also always be Manila, and the rage of a marvelous culture stilled, confused, and diverted. Manila is my river of dreams choked with refuse, the refuse of refusal and denial, a denial more profound than the forbidding Catholic Church in all its ominous presence.

Blame it on the mambo and the cha-cha, a Cardinal named Sin and an adviser named Joker. Blame it on *Imeldification,* a former beauty queen with a puffy face bailed out of a jam by Doris Duke. Blame it on children named Lourdes, Maria, Jesus, Carlos, Peachy, Baby, and Elvis. Blame it on the rich, who hang on in spite of everything. Blame it on the same people who are still in power, before Marcos, after Marcos. You name it, we'll blame it. The NPR, the vigilantes, rebel colonels nicknamed "Gringo" and a restless army plotting coups. Blame it on signs in nightclubs that warn: NO GUNS OR DRUGS.

Cards have been reshuffled, roles exchanged. The major players are the same, even those who suffered long years in prison under one regime, even those who died by the bullet. Aquino, Lopez, Cojuangco, Zobel, Laurel, Enrile, etc. Blood against blood, controlling the destinies of so many disparate tribes in these seven thousand islands.

I remember my grandmother, Lola Tecla, going for drives with me as a child down the boulevard along Manila Bay. The boulevard led to Luneta Park, where Rizal was executed by the Spanish colonizers; it was then known as "Dewey Boulevard," after an American admiral. From history books forced on me as a child at a convent school run by strict nuns, I learned a lopsided history of myself, one full of lies and blank spaces, a history of omission—a colonial version of history which scorned the "savage" ways of precolonial Filipinos. In those days, even our language was kept at a distance; Tagalog was studied in a course called "National Language" (sic), but it was English that was spoken, English that was preferred. Tagalog was a language used to address servants. I scorned myself, and it was only later, after I had left the Philippines to settle in the country of my oppressor, that I learned to confront my demons and reinvent my own history.

I am writing a novel set in the contemporary Philippines. It is a novel of fiction, a journey back I am always taking. I leave one place for the other, welcomed and embraced by the family I have left—fathers and brothers and cousins and uncles and aunts. Childhood sweethearts, now with their own children. I am unable to stay. I make excuses, adhere to tight schedules. I return, only to depart, weeks or months later, depending on finances and the weather, obligations to my daughter, my art, my addiction to life in the belly of one particular beast. I am the other, the exile within, afflicted with permanent nostalgia for the mud. I return only to depart: Manila, New York, San Francisco, Manila, Honolulu, Detroit, Manila, Guam, Hong Kong, Zamboanga, Manila, New York, San Francisco, Tokyo, Manila again, Manila again, Manila again.

ROBERT N. HOPKINS

The author of the following essay on late-twentieth-century immigration anxiety left no trace of his identity. However, the essay and its attitudes have a distinguished lineage in American culture. The debate over immigration that raged during the period 1890–1920, when large numbers of Italian, Polish, and Russian immigrants were arriving in American cities, produced a great deal of writing that predicted similar disastrous outcomes. Essays very much like this one appeared in popular magazines throughout the period. At the end of the twentieth century, the fear that inspired the renewed debate was fear of immigration from the South and the East, from Asia and Latin America.

CAN THE UNITED STATES ASSIMILATE THE WAVE OF NEW IMMIGRANTS?

The problem of assimilating immigrant peoples into the United States culture and society has had a varied history, depending largely on who the immigrant peoples were and what the dominant culture of America was at that time.

When the majority population of the United States was still British by origin, the ideal of "Anglo-conformity" was the standard. This demanded, in the words of Milton M. Gordon, in his book *Assimilation in American Life: The Role of Race, Religion and National Origins,* the "renunciation of the immigrant's ancestral culture in favor of the behavior and value of the Anglo-Saxon core group."

Although early America had almost as many settlers of German, Dutch and French descent as of Anglo-Saxon origin, the concurrent values and ethnic similarities shared by all West, Northwest and North European immigrants ensured that collaboration and harmony was attained with little if any friction. Indeed, there was a generally widespread acceptance of the English language and of the Anglo-Saxon character of the common law legal system and Constitution of the United States.

This attitude prevailed until the closing decade of the nineteenth century, when the immigration of numbers of immigrants from southern, central and eastern European countries stimulated people to begin to think consciously about a process of assimilation which they called the "melting pot." Because the immigrants were almost all of European origin, America did partially become a melting pot, but with the essential persistence of the "Old American" culture as the basis of "Americanism."

With this change of philosophy it has become popular to assume that the future of American society involves the preservation of distinctive immigrant cultures within a broadly overriding concept of American citizenship, and with only a steadily increasing integration of the immigrants into the American economic and political scene. The possibility that the immigrants might go so far as wishing to retain their own language was, at first, seldom considered as a serious question of any significance.

While America had acquired a small immigrant community of Asians, imported mainly as laborers in the nineteenth century, these were regarded with a tolerant nature as a rather amusing and quaint anachronism. The large black community, which had been a part of the fabric of America since colonial days, and the surviving American Indian element, were both likewise generally accepted as subgroups essentially subordinate to the truly "American" population of European provenance. In short, America was still a nation, albeit one with several relatively small, accepted, but definitely subordinate minorities.

The way in which America thinks it can absorb new immigrant minorities while still remaining a nation is important, since prevailing beliefs about assimilation may be more significant in determining public policy concerning immigration than the reality of assimilation. In daily life, moreover, relations between the "Old Americans" and the new Third World immigrants may be significantly affected by the ideal of assimilation which they do or do not hold in common; an ideal which may be perceived as inspiring, or threatening, depending upon the status of the individuals involved. Finally, the extent to which the "Old Americans" and the immigrants are able to identify with the nation—their implicit answer to the question whether they think of themselves and of others as being a part of "our nation"—is significantly influenced by the concept of assimilation and of national identity that they hold.

Assuming that elites do exist in a nation, and that these elites may or may not share the same views as the larger majority population, it becomes necessary also to ask whether the elite which dominates the political scene holds the same view on the question of how to absorb large immigrant minorities into the "American" culture, or indeed, whether such minorities should be absorbed at all. It is worth mentioning here that demands for "English only" in education have been attacked as "racist." This is nonsense, since a real racist would obviously prefer other stocks to remain separated by linguistic barriers, rather than risk the possibility of their children interbreeding with the original European stock.

During the 1920's the concept of Anglo-Saxon culture as constituting the root of American culture and of European stock as constituting the root base of the American ethnic type was still sufficiently strong among both the elite and the majority of the population of "Old Americans," to ensure a common desire to restrict immigration largely to people of European origin.

But the Anglo-Saxon cultural tradition and white America ideal has in recent decades found neither sufficient spokesmen in the governing elite and media nor sufficient grass roots support to constitute an effective mass movement. What feelings many of them had on this matter have been more recently weakened by the phenomenon of "neo-conservative" propagandists who continually portray every issue solely in economic terms, as though no other human goals or values existed. Although it could be argued that the elements of the "national" concept were still implicit in the Walter-McCarran Immigration Act of 1952, which reaffirmed the principle of quotas based on country of origin, the spirit of this ideal had died by the time John F. Kennedy, in 1963, came to publish his book, *A Nation of Immigrants.* This treatise expressed quite contrary views which were to become official policy with the Immigration Act of 1965 and all subsequent immigrant legislation—which effectively reversed the former policy of discrimination in favor of European immigrants to discrimination in favor of Third World immigrants. The official target now seems to be the reshaping of the American population into a miniature replica of the entire world.

Simply, the Kennedy viewpoint argued that America was traditionally a nation of immigrants, and that the "Old Americans" who had founded America, fought for its independence, given it its language, constitution and legal system, was no more "American" than any other immigrant group. The concept of the melting pot, with a subsidiary concession of the cultural pluralism view, has subsequently prevailed.

But the belief in the melting pot theory has come to be questioned as a result of the arrival of increasing numbers of non-European immigrants. Instead, the theory of America as a land of "cultural pluralism" has caught the official imagination—the idea of America as a multi-cultural and multi-racial microcosm of the entire world.

Since the legislation presently governing immigration gives preference not to the Northwest European countries that established the United States, but to the surplus populations of the overcrowded and teeming Third World—which are also entering the country in large numbers illegally, only to be given the legal right to remain and become American citizens after they have effected illegal entry successfully (not a difficult thing to do) and have managed to evade the law for a further period of time, again successfully. It is quite clear that it is no longer realistic to assume that this vast and growing number of immigrants, who also prove to be more prolific in child-bearing than the native white American population, are likely to comply with the cultural ideal of conformity to "Old American" ideals and institutions.

This has become particularly obvious in areas which have been heavily settled by Hispanics, where even the Spanish language has taken root, and political pressures by the immigrants have ensured that they receive permission to operate radio and T.V. stations dedicated to their own language and culture. Interestingly, this has sometimes caused tension amongst resident minorities, particularly the black minority, when a decision had to be made whether a new T.V. station should be allocated to the black minority or to the Hispanic minority.

Indeed, recent legislation has affirmed the right of illegal immigrants who have been permitted to stay in the U.S. under the amnesty provision to benefit from Affirmative Action programs, which is thus unfair to the American blacks and American Indians who were originally targeted to benefit from such programs in light of past disadvantages.

Surprisingly, one aspect of the "Old American" conformity concept does linger on as a phantom "residue," much like the whiff of scent which remains in a long-emptied bottle. Although realistically it seems apparent that this is currently a politically unrealizable ideal, the notion that the new immigrants will be absorbed into the historic Anglo-Saxon culture is allowed to survive as a perennial source of solace whenever anyone dares to suggest that future immigration might challenge the national premise of *e pluribus unum*.

This notion assures those who believe in it that, even if the "Old American" core group continues to dwindle in numbers and power to the point of becoming marginal, the political heritage of the Founding Fathers will survive. According to the most optimistic exponents of this belief, the republic will endure even if the descendants of its founders go into extinction, because it is based on an imperishable tradition going back to William Blackstone, John Locke, Magna Carta and Anglo-Saxon common law. Some even argue that these values will be better defended by Third World immigrants than by the "Old American" members of the nation which created that heritage.

This last "residue" of belief in the ability of the "Old American" institutions to survive simply because of their innate superiority would be simply an innocuous illusion were there not indications that official public policy is in fact moving in a direction directly contrary to those traditions. Today the government deliberately gives no recognition to race or ethnicity, except to advance the interests of minority ethnic and racial groups, which are thereby encouraged to maintain their own identity and to avoid being absorbed into the "Old American" tradition so readily accepted by most earlier immigrants of European origin.

But the reality is that there is no evidence that the European tradition can or will be transmitted to immigrants of African, Asian and Hispanic origin, or to any other of the millions of Third World immigrants who are now entering the country at an increasing rate.

Indeed, the social comforts of being among 'people of one's own kind,' and the political advantages of ethnic unity and ability to form pressure groups become significant forces now that the philosophy of cultural pluralism has gained broad acceptance in ruling circles.

As evidence that the new ethnic pluralism is becoming official public policy, author Gordon cites "recently introduced measures such as government-mandated affirmative action procedures in employment, education, and stipulated public programs, and court-ordered busing of school children across neighborhood district lines to effect racial integration. . . . As is widely known, the federal government has experienced difficulties implementing such measures with its present population. It is certainly not unreasonable, therefore, to expect that the present problems will only be exacerbated with the incorporation—one cannot call it assimilation—of masses of Third World immigrants."

There are optimists who still believe that the melting pot process will lead to the assimilation of today's immigrants into the "Old American" way of life—with all that means in respect of liberty, justice, democracy, and cultural tradition. They hope for an end result that will congeal in favor of the survival of the traditionally prized political and legal heritage of freedom and rational democracy.

Forecasting, it is to be admitted, is a hazardous enterprise, but major anomalies can be expected as the United States becomes the host country to truly massive numbers of Third World immigrants.

Asia, for example, has an enduring heritage of not simply feudalism, but of that Oriental Despotism, masterfully analyzed in Karl Wittfogel's thus named book, which has shown a capacity to overwhelm liberalizing Western tendencies. Japan, supposedly a parliamentary democracy, has given evidence—not limited to the widely-publicized statements of Prime Minister Nakasone—of being one of the most ethnocentric nations in the world. China remains a one-party state. The parliamentary democracy of India may not survive internecine warfare among the subcontinent's linguistic and religious power blocs. The future of democracy in the Philippines is very uncertain. The massacres in Cambodia are indistinguishable in enormity from the depredations of Tamerlane.

Latin America, with few exceptions, reveals a history of rotating authoritarian rule with failing democratic government, in which *el caudillo* follows *el golpe de estado*, and vice versa, in a succession without end. Mexico experienced a long period of what in effect has been corrupt one-party rule. The one notable exception to this pattern, Costa Rica, is virtually a European country, and possibly may not endure much longer. Democracy is, if anything, in even more disarray in Africa. The one African nation with any history of democratic forms, Liberia, fell to a military dictatorship several years ago which is now threatened by another military insurrection.

After even a cursory survey of the Third World, anyone can see that only a foolish ethnocentrism can account for the fond belief of many Americans that their political heritage—imperfectly received in the past by immigrants from nations having cultures closely related to that of the nation's founders—will in the future transform and overwhelm all that is alien. Such a universal constant cannot anywhere be found in the records of political history.

ISHMAEL REED

(1938-)

Ishmael Reed was born in Chattanooga, Tennessee, and grew up in Buffalo, New York, where he attended the University of Buffalo. Reed is one of the most original and prolific of the African-American writers who came of age during the civil rights movement. His satiric novels include Yellow Back Radio Broke Down *(1969),* Mumbo Jumbo *(1972),* Flight to Canada *(1976), and* Japanese by Spring *(1993). His essays are collected in* Shrovetide in Old New Orleans *(1978),* Writin' Is Fightin': Thirty-seven Years of Boxing on Paper *(1988), and* Airing Dirty Laundry *(1993). Reed has won numerous awards including nominations for the National Book Award in fiction and poetry for* Mumbo Jumbo *and* Conjure: Selected Poems, 1963-1970 *(1972). Reed was awarded a Guggenheim Foundation Award in fiction (1974) and won three National Endowment for the Arts grants. His poetry is collected in* Conjure, Chattanooga *(1976),* A Secretary of the Spirits *(1978), and* Poems: New and Collected Poems *(1988). Reed has taught for decades at the University of California, Berkeley. He has edited several journals, including* Y-bird, Quilt, *and* Konch, *and has edited both a collection of experimental fiction,* 19 Necromancers from Now *(1970), and a collection of social and political essays,*

MultiAmerica: Essays on Cultural Wars and Cultural Peace *(1997). In 1976, Reed cofounded the Before Columbus Foundation, an organization dedicated to supporting a multiethnic vision of America.*

"America: The Multinational Society" emphasizes that America is not an Anglo-Saxon sponge soaking up and assimilating outsiders but is rather a melange of changing, interrelating ethnic components.

America:
The Multinational Society

On the day before Memorial Day, 1983, a poet called me to describe a city he had just visited. He said that one section included mosques, built by the Islamic people who dwelled there. Attending his reading, he said, were large numbers of Hispanic people, forty thousand of whom lived in the same city. He was not talking about a fabled city located in some mysterious region of the world. The city he'd visited was Detroit.

A few months before, as I was leaving Houston, Texas, I heard it announced on the radio that Texas's largest minority was Mexican-American, and though a foundation recently issued a report critical of bilingual education, the taped voice used to guide the passengers on the air trams connecting terminals in Dallas Airport is in both Spanish and English. If the trend continues, a day will come when it will be difficult to travel through some sections of the country without hearing commands in both English and Spanish; after all, for some western states, Spanish was the first written language and the Spanish style lives on in the western way of life.

Shortly after my Texas trip, I sat in an auditorium located on the campus of the University of Wisconsin at Milwaukee as a Yale professor—whose original work on the influence of African cultures upon those of the Americas has led to his ostracism from some monocultural intellectual circles—walked up and down the aisle, like an old-time southern evangelist, dancing and drumming the top of the lectern, illustrating his points before some serious Afro-American intellectuals and artists who cheered and applauded his performance and his mastery of information. The professor was "white." After his lecture, he joined a group of Milwaukeeans in a conversation. All of the participants spoke Yoruban, though only the professor had ever traveled to Africa.

One of the artists told me that his paintings, which included African and Afro-American mythological symbols and imagery, were hanging in the local McDonald's restaurant. The next day I went to McDonald's and snapped pictures of smiling youngsters eating hamburgers below paintings that could grace the walls of any of the country's leading museums. The manager of the local McDonald's said, "I don't know what you boys are doing, but I like it," as he commissioned the local painters to exhibit in his restaurant.

Such blurring of cultural styles occurs in everyday life in the United States to a greater extent than anyone can imagine and is probably more prevalent than the sensational conflict between people of different backgrounds that is played up and often encouraged by the media. The result is what the Yale professor, Robert

Thompson, referred to as a cultural bouillabaisse, yet members of the nation's present educational and cultural Elect still cling to the notion that the United States belongs to some vaguely defined entity they refer to as "Western civilization," by which they mean, presumably, a civilization created by the people of Europe, as if Europe can be viewed in monolithic terms. Is Beethoven's Ninth Symphony, which includes Turkish marches, a part of Western civilization, or the late nineteenth- and twentieth-century French paintings, whose creators were influenced by Japanese art? And what of the cubists, through whom the influence of African art changed modern painting, or the surrealists, who were so impressed with the art of the Pacific Northwest Indians that, in their map of North America, Alaska dwarfs the lower forty-eight in size?

Are the Russians, who are often criticized for their adoption of "Western" ways by Tsarist dissidents in exile, members of Western civilization? And what of the millions of Europeans who have black African and Asian ancestry, black Africans having occupied several countries for hundreds of years? Are these "Europeans" members of Western civilization, or the Hungarians, who originated across the Urals in a place called Greater Hungary, or the Irish, who came from the Iberian Peninsula?

Even the notion that North America is part of Western civilization because our "system of government" is derived from Europe is being challenged by Native American historians who say that the founding fathers, Benjamin Franklin especially, were actually influenced by the system of government that had been adopted by the Iroquois hundreds of years prior to the arrival of large numbers of Europeans.

Western civilization, then, becomes another confusing category like Third World, or Judeo-Christian culture, as man attempts to impose his small-screen view of political and cultural reality upon a complex world. Our most publicized novelist recently said that Western civilization was the greatest achievement of mankind, an attitude that flourishes on the street level as scribbles in public restrooms: "White Power," "Niggers and Spics Suck," or "Hitler was a prophet," the latter being the most telling, for wasn't Adolph Hitler the archetypal monoculturalist who, in his pigheaded arrogance, believed that one way and one blood was so pure that it had to be protected from alien strains at all costs? Where did such an attitude, which has caused so much misery and depression in our national life, which has tainted even our noblest achievements, begin? An attitude that caused the incarceration of Japanese-American citizens during World War II, the persecution of Chicanos and Chinese-Americans, the near-extermination of the Indians, and the murder and lynchings of thousands of Afro-Americans.

Virtuous, hardworking, pious, even though they occasionally would wander off after some fancy clothes, or rendezvous in the woods with the town prostitute, the Puritans are idealized in our schoolbooks as "a hardy band" of no-nonsense patriarchs whose discipline razed the forest and brought order to the New World (a term that annoys Native American historians). Industrious, responsible, it was their "Yankee ingenuity" and practicality that created the work ethic. They were simple folk who produced a number of good poets, and they set the tone for the American writing style, of lean and spare lines, long before Hemingway. They worshiped in churches whose colors blended in with the New England snow, churches with simple structures and ornate lecterns.

The Puritans were a daring lot, but they had a mean streak. They hated the theater and banned Christmas. They punished people in a cruel and inhuman manner. They killed children who disobeyed their parents. When they came in contact with those whom they considered heathens or aliens, they behaved in such a bizarre and irrational manner that this chapter in the American history comes down to us as a late-movie horror film. They exterminated the Indians, who taught them how to survive in a world unknown to them, and their encounter with the calypso culture of Barbados resulted in what the tourist guide in Salem's Witches' House refers to as the Witchcraft Hysteria.

The Puritan legacy of hard work and meticulous accounting led to the establishment of a great industrial society; it is no wonder that the American industrial revolution began in Lowell, Massachusetts, but there was the other side, the strange and paranoid attitudes toward those different from the Elect.

The cultural attitudes of that early Elect continue to be voiced in everyday life in the United States: the president of a distinguished university, writing a letter to the *Times*, belittling the study of African civilizations; the television network that promoted its show on the Vatican art with the boast that this art represented "the finest achievements of the human spirit." A modern up-tempo state of complex rhythms that depends upon contacts with an international community can no longer behave as if it dwelled in a "Zion Wilderness" surrounded by beasts and pagans.

When I heard a schoolteacher warn the other night about the invasion of the American educational system by foreign curriculums, I wanted to yell at the television set, "Lady, they're already here." It has already begun because the world is here. The world has been arriving at these shores for at least ten thousand years from Europe, Africa, and Asia. In the late nineteenth and early twentieth centuries, large numbers of Europeans arrived, adding their cultures to those of the European, African, and Asian settlers who were already here, and recently millions have been entering the country from South America and the Caribbean, making Yale Professor Bob Thompson's bouillabaisse richer and thicker.

One of our most visionary politicians said that he envisioned a time when the United States could become the brain of the world, by which he meant the repository of all of the latest advanced information systems. I thought of that remark when an enterprising poet friend of mine called to say that he had just sold a poem to a computer magazine and that the editors were delighted to get it because they didn't carry fiction or poetry. Is that the kind of world we desire? A humdrum homogeneous world of all brains and no heart, no fiction, no poetry; a world of robots with human attendants bereft of imagination, of culture? Or does North America deserve a more exciting destiny? To become a place where the cultures of the world crisscross. This is possible because the United States is unique in the world: The world is here.

TREY ELLIS
(1962-)

Born in Washington, DC, Trey Ellis is noted for his works that challenge common stereotypes of African Americans. In his first novel, Platitudes *(1988), Ellis explores both middle-class black America and stereotypic images of African Americans. Other publications include two novels,* Home

Repairs *(1993) and* Right Here, Right Now *(1999), and* The Inkwell *(1994),*
a screenplay written under the name Tom Ricostranza. Ellis is also the
author of two teleplays produced by Home Box Office (HBO): Cosmic Slop
and Tuskegee. *He has contributed essays to* Interview *and* Playboy *and is*
presently at work on a screenplay based on Home Repairs.

   "Guess Who's Coming to Seder" plays not only with the title of the 1960s
film "Guess Who's Coming to Dinner" but also with expectations about ten-
sions betweens African Americans and Jewish Americans.

Guess Who's Coming to Seder

What?

   SHHHHH.

   So now you, my son, my only son, shush me? The one who took all your vicious
kicks. Like a Nazi bastard you goose-stepped in my belly and now with the shush?

   BUBA.

   So now with the Yiddish? I thought you'd forgotten in front of your pretty shiksa
wife and your goyim friends, call me Mammy or something?

   Mrs. Cohen's son, Alan, explodes his eyes overwide at his mother's bifocal
lenses. Hidden absolutely are her eyes, instead, the weighty glasses only televise the
two candle flames next to the two platefulls of matzah in front of her.

   It's getting late. Alan. Megan. Donnel Washington eyes first his wife Carlene, then
Vietta, his little girl. Their six palms push on the tablecloth, raising their asses off
the cane geometry of the Cohens' chairs' seat bottoms simultaneously.

   Donnel, please. My mother's from New York and she's lost almost all her hearing and her mind too. She doesn't mean anything by it. Carlene, I'm sorry.

   You call *this* wine? Does *she* think French is kosher now that she's an expert on
our religion or something?

   Heather, *please* pass your grandmother the Mogan David. Megan Cohen,
Heather's mother, starts to throw her hands at her mother-in-law's trachea but
snatches them back to wring her own blonde bun.

   Heather slides the now wet curl of brown hair from the soft crack between her
lips, latches it behind an ear. Pouring, her right nipple, through her bra and her
blouse, jostles a liver spot on her grandmother's bare triceps. The noise of a car's
wheels rolling, its engine screwing through missed gears to stop near the house,
pulls Heather's eyes, her head to the door.

   Such large, firm roses. I had such firm roses when I was young and sweet too,
back when grandfather was alive . . . but what use are they to anyone now that they
hang over the fat of my belly like dead things. Heatherchick, if you go a day in your
life without wearing a brassiere, so help me God I'll chop yours off.

   Drink the first cup of wine, and fill Elijah's cup. Pass around a basin to wash the
   hands. Take parsley or spring onion, dip them in vinegar or salt water, pass them
   around the table, and say:
   "Blessed are you YHWH our God, Ruler of the Universe who create the fruit of the
   earth."
   "Barukh atay YHWH elohenu melekh ha-olam boray p'ri ha a-da-mah."

It's a shame Derrick isn't here for this part of the ceremony. I think he would have liked it. Heather, you're sure you told him eight o'clock?

Yes, Dad. I told you already he has a big paper due. But I don't know where he is *all* the time. You *could* ask Mister and Miz Washington.

Carlene and Donnel Washington smile with Alan and Megan Cohen at the new pink on Heather's face.

We must apologize for him. I left a note on the kitchen table, but that boy's so willful no telling what mess he's into now. As she speaks about her son, Carlene reties the bow that her daughter has again untied in the burnt offering of her hot-combed hair.

Mah nishtanah ha-lai-lah? Mah nishtanah ha-lai-lah? Who's going to say it already? Billy, you're the baby, so tell me what is it that holds you so quiet?

Billy Cohen slurps the dangling lunger of saliva back through his lips but not before the last inch and three-quarters detaches, dives through the red surface of his Paschal wine, floats back white bubbles.

ACTUALLY BUBA, VIETTA WASHINGTON IS THE YOUNGEST. Vietta, could you please read from the top of page 72. Where it says, Why is this night . . .

Vietta looks hard at her mother. Ma, can't I just eat the crackers? I feel stupid.

Go on, baby. Don't be bashful. Carlene pets her neck.

Let Derrick do it, if he ever makes it. This is all his fault anyway.

Don't make me tell you twice.

[Huff] "Whyisthisnightdifferentfromallothernights? On all, other, nights we may—"

What? I'm sure she's not speaking Hebrew. Then let me help for God's sake: She-b'khol ha-le-lot a-nu okh-lin sh'ar y'ra-kot, ha-lai-lah ha-zeh ma-ror. She-b'khol ha-le-lot eyn anu mat-bilin a-fi-lu p-am a-chat, ha-lai-lah ha-zeh sh-tay f'a-mim. She-b'khol ha-le-lot a-nu okh-lin beyn yosh-vin u-veyn m'su-bin, ha-lai-lah ha-zeh ku-la-nu m'su-bin.

THANK YOU, BUBA. Continue reading, Vietta, please?

The teaching invites us to meet and to teach four children: one wise and one wicked, one innocent and one who does not relate by asking.
What does the wise one say? "What are the testimonies, and the statues, and the rules whic . . . ?"

. . . which Y-H-W . . . ?

Yahweh, Vietta. It's a sin for Jews to pronounce the real name of Him or Her.

You mean you can't say GOD-GOD-GOD-GOD-GOD!

I'll slap the black off you, girl, when we get home. Apologize.

That's OK, Carlene, my mother started it. Alan's eyes flick to their corners to watch his mother.

So now with the killer looks? At your own mother even? I wish I could've heard what terrible things you've all been spitting at me now that I'm deaf, more dead than alive, my last seder in all probability.

Invite and wait for discussion on these questions:
Who are the four children? Are they among us? Are they within each of us? Are these good answers?

It must be time to talk about the four children now and of course they are still with us, especially the wicked one who's lost the language, doesn't even get bat mitzvahed like my beautiful granddaughter next to me, or who marries out of the religion like my only son, so technically my two grandchildren here aren't even really Jewish. Back in olden times these would have been the ones saying, Freedom, shmeedom, I'd rather stay here with this bunch of greasy Arabs as their dirty slave . . . no offense.

Carlene crinkles the skin around her eyes, raising weakly her cheeks and upper lip from her teeth.

WHY SHOULD ANYONE BE OFFENDED, BUBA? All of us, blacks and Jews, have been enslaved, there's no hiding from it, right?

Come on, Alan, *our* emancipation was a tad more recent, don't you think? Were your great-grandparents born slaves? Hmmm? The knife in Donnel's left hand, coated in haroseth (ritualized mortar made of diced apples and nuts, wine and raisins), disintegrates the matzah (representing the brick), in his right hand. Haroseth and matzah flakes stucco his palm then the napkin.

Yes, but . . . Heather honey, what's your take on all this?

I don't know.

Come on now, sweetie, is tonight really that bad?

Heather handles the bottle of kosher French by its neck, jams its nose into the bottom of her glass until the rising choppy waves of wine redden her knuckles, then overflow and wound the white tablecloth.

Heatherchick! You know that it's not yet that we toast. I swear before your grandfather's ghost you even *sip* before the right time and PING! there again goes my blood clot and half of my face will die like your Aunt Estelle's in the home.

Lifting the glass to her mouth, Heather looks at no one. Noisily, gulp after gulp of wine bubbles back around her mouth's corners.

Young lady, that wasn't too nice. Megan turns a bit from her daughter, tilts her face into her hand, milks her rising smile from her cheeks into her palm.

Mrs. Cohen whistles "Dai Dai Eun" at the Hockney lithograph on the wall.

BUBA, WE'RE STILL TRYING TO DISCUSS THE FOUR CHILDREN AS THE B'NAI B'RAK RABBI'S INSTRUCTED.

Now it's getting very late Megan, Alan, and Vietta have school tomorrow.

So they're leaving in the middle of seder? They hate Jewish so that they want calamity to strike us all down?

Uh, Donnel, I'm so sorry. My mother thinks if anyone leaves, gets up from their chair before the last cup of wine is drunk, all the Jews in the house will be slain. See, in 1583, there was this thing in Istanbul.

Maybe they're Farrakhan mooslims.

I'll have you know that the Washington's son, Derrick, and our Megan, have been seeing each other all though U of M, so they might very soon be *family.*

Ma!

After discussion, all sing.
Go tell it on the mountain,
over the hills and everywhere.
Go tell it on the mountain—
Let my people go!
Who are the people dressed in white?
Let my people go!
Must be the children of the Israelite—
Let my people go!

Where did you get this hippie seder from anyhow?

Cousin Naomi found it at the Rainbow Reformed Temple in New York.

[A moment of silence. Then a reader says:]

"But let us also question the plagues: Can the winning of freedom be bloodless? It was not bloodless when Nat Turner proclaimed, I had a vision, and I saw white spirits and black spirits engaged in battle, and the sun was darkened—the thunder rolled in the heavens and blood flowed in streams—and I heard a voice saying, Such is your luck, such you are called to see, and let it come rough or smooth, you must surely bear it."

I-lu i-lu ho-tzi-a-nu, ho-tzi-a-nu mi-mitz-ra-yim, ho-tzi-a-nu- mi-mitz-ra-yim dai-ye-nu. DAI-DAI-YE-NU, DAI-DAI-YE-NU, DAI-DAI-YE-NU, dayenu, dayenu!

[All drink the third cup. Refill glasses, but not to the top.]

 [The door is opened]

 Alan returns Vietta's bow from the floor to her lap, slouches down to her as she confetties her paper napkin. It's almost over, sweetheart, then Billy can show you his Nintendo. He just got Donkey Kong. We're just waiting a little bit for the ghost of Elijah to come down and drink his cup of wine. If you leave milk and cookies out for Santa Clause, it's sort of like that. Alan stretches to pat Vietta's shoulder but she flinches.

 Miss Thing, I raised you better than acting up like this outside the house.

 Dingdingding-Dong.

 Billy's curtains of matzah-flaked lips pull back, reveal teeth behind braces. Heather's back straightens, red reclaims her face.

 Did I hear the doorbell go off? At least this you did right, my little Alan. Mrs. Cohen laughs. The messiah rings the doorbell! My uncle's half-brother, Arkady, the Shostakovich of indoor plumbing, used to rig a pump to Elijah's cup to make it look like the spirit was drinking it. Oh how I always fell for that as a girl.

 Dingdingding-Dong.

 Heather, get the door, it's okay.

 I miss any good fights? Sorry I'm late. I had to . . . finish a paper. Derrick shrugs out of his jean jacket, flies it to the coat rack. He peels off the black beret, jiggles the tiny dreadlocks on his head's top re-erect.

 Of one thing I'm sure, the Messiah, this is not.

 Shut up, mother.

 What?

 Derrick, you knew how much this meant to Heather. Your mother and I are very disappointed in you. . . . We'll talk about this at home. Go take your seat.

 You're just in time to read, Derrick.

 Uh, sorry, Mr. Cohen, but my eyes are watering so much from reading all day at the libr—His mother's eyes freeze his tongue.

Brothers and sisters, we have been remembering our slavery and our liberation. But just as it was we, not our forbearers only, who were liberated in Egypt, so it is we, not our forbearers only, who live in slavery. The task of liberation is long and it is work that we ourselves must do.

 [All sing]

We shall overcome,

We shall overcome,

We shall overcome some day!

Deep in my heart, I do believe,
We shall overcome some day.
We'll walk hand in hand . . . (Repeat as "We shall overcome")
We are not afraid . . . (Repeat . . .)
The people shall be free . . . (Repeat . . .)
Black and white together . . . (Repeat . . .)
We shall live in peace . . . (Repeat . . .)
We shall overcome!
[Dance Joyfully]

Now can I go play Donkey Kong? Please?

JOHN LEGUIZAMO
(1965-)

Born in Bogotá, Colombia, John Leguizamo is a writer, actor, and comedian.
Leguizamo states that he was inspired to write because of the absence of
interesting parts for Hispanics. He studied acting at the Strasberg Theater
Institute and H. B. Studio and also attended New York University. He has
been featured in many Hollywood films, including roles in Casualties of War
(1989), Die Hard 2: Die Harder *(1990),* William Shakespeare's Romeo and
Juliet *(1996), and* Summer of Sam *(1999).*

Leguizamo is best known, however, for his satiric plays and screenplays
involving New York City and Hispanic culture. His published plays include
Mambo Mouth: A Savage Comedy *(1993),* Spic-o-Rama: A Dysfunctional
Comedy *(1994), and* Freak: A Semi-Demi-Quasi-Pseudo Autobiography
(1997) with David Bar Katz. Two of Leguizamo's television screenplays, for
Mambo Mouth *(1991) and for* Spic-o-Rama *(1993) were produced by Home*
Box Office (HBO). Leguizamo was awarded the Obie Award for Perfor-
mance, the Outer Critics Circle Award for outstanding achievement, the
Cable Ace Award, and the Vanguard Award, all for the writing and per-
formance of Mambo Mouth.

"Crossover King" from Mambo Mouth *satirizes not only sterotypes*
about Hispanic Americans but stereotypes about the Japanese as well. It is
a two-edged sword that makes us laugh even as it cuts.

CROSSOVER KING

(Japanese gong sounds. Audience sees silhouette of a man doing a low bow. Lights
up as the Crossover King enters from behind the scrim. He wears a conservative gray
suit, white shirt, muted silk tie, silk hanky in breast pocket, wing tips, and thick black-
framed glasses, and he carries notes. His hair is slicked back and his movements are

controlled. He walks to the lectern, center stage, and places the notes on the stand, beside a full glass of water. When he speaks—in a Japanese accent—his gestures are stiff. He pushes the bridge of his glasses with his index finger.

CROSSOVER KING: Oh, yes, you in the right place. *(Arranges notes.)* The Crossover Seminar is about to begin, so hurry up and grab a seat. Hai! *(Violently bows head as he exclaims. Sips water.)*

Konichi-wa. Dozo ohairi kudusai. Hai! *(Jerks head.)* Welcome and welcome, Latino-sans, to the Crossover Seminar. Now, this could very well be the biggest investment of your entire life, so please hold your questions until the end. Hai! *(Jerks head, then sips water.)*

You too could be a crossover success. It's up to you *(points to an audience member)* and you *(points to another)*. This is purely a scientific method. There are no placebos or messy ointments.

Now, what exactly is a crossing over, you ask? That's a good question. Crossing over is the art of passing for someone that you are not in order to get something that you have not. Because there is no room in the corporate upscale world for flamboyant, fun-loving spicy people. So get used to it. I did.

Let's talk about the American mind made simple. Americans admire what? . . . Don't all volunteer at once. I have all day. . . . Am I speaking a foreign language? Americans admire what? I'll give you a hint: It's green, you used to be able to buy things with it. *(Answer from audience: "Money.")* Arrigato! She is ready for the advanced course, but the rest of you have to stay. Yes, Americans admire money, but they also admire the appearance of having money. The more money you have, the more respect you're going to get. But if you can't have the money, you sure better look like you have it. Because America keeps sending you the subliminal and not-so-subliminal signals that without money you are inadequate.

Stop. *(Hits himself on the head.)* Stop hitting yourselves in the head and think for a moment. Why settle for being Latin trash? Why even settle for being American trash, when you could be so much more? So much more—like Japanese! This is a rich market to be harvested, Latino-sans. You alone have the choice: American *(holds right hand low, by hip)* . . . Japanese *(holds left hand high in the air)* . . . Japanese . . . American . . . good . . . bad . . . bad . . . good. You choose. Hai! *(Jerks head.)*

I'm going to share a little secret with you. You won't believe this *(confessional)*, but I was a Latino-san myself. *(Visibly ashamed.)* Yes, it's true. But with this easy-to-follow program, I have evolved and become a Japanese warrior. Very repressed, but also very successful.

I used to be loud and obnoxious, full of street mannerisms. Constantly holding my crotch for self-assurance. *(Mimes awkwardly.)* I would yell all the time, "Hola, Ramón! I just had a girl with tetas to here and culo out to there!" *(Mimes.)* But now I zen-out and only speak when I have something really important to say.

I used to not even be able to walk down the street and hear rhythmic percussion without my hips beginning to gyrate wildly and uncontrollably. *(Hips gyrate beneath lectern.)* But now I listen to Lite FM. And I hardly move at all—even when I want to. *(Sips water.)*

I used to be full of Latino macho braggadocio, disrespecting my women and wanting to start fights all the time. *(Picks audience member.)* Watchoo looking at? Watchoo looking at? You talking to me? You talking to me? *(Steps out from behind lectern.)* I'll sucker-punch you, head-butt you, body-slam you, knock you to the ground, and spit in your eye. *(Suddenly all business again.)* Et cetera, et cetera, et cetera. *(Returns to lectern.)* Relax. It was just a dramatic re-creation. Hai! *(Jerks head.)*

But no more. Now all my aggression goes into beating up my business partners.

I know, a lot of you are thinking, "I don't need this. I don't see anything wrong with me. I like the way I am." Fine—but nobody cares what *you* think. It's what *they* think that counts.

(Sets up a projection screen.) Now, I'm going to accompany myself with some visual aids in order to more closely examine these cases of traditional stereotypicality. If you recognize yourself or loved ones, please do not panic. The Crossover King is here. Hai! *(Picks up projector remote from downstage.)* This is not for the squeamish, so be brave, Latino-sans, and face up.

Now, is your hair bleached to a color not found in nature? These are my cousins, the Henna sisters: Lizette, Annette, and Jeanette. They have a henna dependency from trying to be blonde sexy mamis. But I put them on a detox program, and I'm slowly easing them off the dyes and peroxides.

Do you wear Fourteenth Street doorknocker earrings, like my little sister, Yolanda? Those are dangerous! A big wind could come and knock her out and kill her. And you'd have another doorknocker-related death.

Do you make the streets your office?

Our photographer took this shot two weeks later and Miss Guzman was still there. Please get a life, Miss Guzman.

Oh, this is a special case. *(Ceremoniously takes collapsible pointer from breast pocket and unfolds it; uses to illustrate specific features on remaining slides.)* Are your clothes cutting off your circulation? Might you have the Aztec curse? *(To slide:)* Yes, Angela, you know what I'm talking about.

Guacamole hips.

Those arroz con pollo thighs.

Big ol' cuchifrito butt.

Look at that panty line.

The dreaded tortilla chins.

How many can you count? *(Uses pointer to count off at least four chins, then advances to black slide.)*

If you have developed any of these characteristics, you may have already become what Americans call, behind your back, the little, brown, roly-poly, Spanish, submissive, subservient, no-good Latina puta-bitch! Now let's not help perpetuate negative stereotypes. Only you can prevent this ugly misrepresentation.

I know some of you are thinking, "That's all very well and good, but what can that Crossover King really do for me? What is that little devil up to?" Stay with me.

Here we have my aunt, Rosa Herrera. She was a loud, gum-snapping, hairy-lipped, Bacardi-drinking, welfare-leeching, child-bearing, underachieving, no-good Latina puta-bitch. Oh, she was so loud! She would talk your head off all the time: "Did you see so-and-so? She's pregnant again. He'll never marry her now. Why buy the cow when you can get the milk for free? Blah, blah, blah. Yak, yak, yak."

But with our program, Rosa Herrera has become . . .

Rose Hara, the timid, self-disciplined, lonely, constipated workaholic. Her hair is a human color. No makeup to make her look like some exotic tropical fish. No American don't-push-me-I-get-paid-by-the-hour attitude. From head to toe she is a model of respectability. Why, she could attend a party at a Tokyo Hilton and not even be told that the servants' entrance is in back. She has crossed over nicely. Hai!

Now for you men—or homeys, as you like to be called—don't think I was going to forget you. I suggest you take special note. Awareness is the first step to self-improvement.

This is my cousin Hector, the drug dealer. Oh yes, he is hard and tough—but so are arithmetic and calculus!

Look at all that gold.

It is better invested in a money market account than hung around his nefarious neck.

This is Tito Testosterones. He beat me up in the seventh grade—because I knew who my father was. Tito is the typical greasy, catfish-mustachioed, fake-gold-chain-wearing, beeper-carrying, polyester-loving, untrustworthy, horny, uncircumcised spic specimen. He will never get anywhere, except in a lineup.

(Addresses slide.) Look at me, Tito. Look at this success story now. *(Uses pointer on himself.)* Savile Row worsted tweed, Sulka Sulka tie, Varnet frames, Gucci shoes, Fortune-500 Ivy Leaguer that I've become. *(Turns to slide again, agitated.)* Look at me, Tito. I said look at me. *(Loses control completely.)* Cabrón, idiota, medio-malparido, cagado, pedazo de mierda envuelto, baboso, bobo. . . . *(Struggles to regain composure.)* Shitsurei. *(Bows.)* Shitsurei. *(Bows.)* Excuse me. This never happened to me before. I had a little Latino relapse. *(Straightens clothes, smooths hair.)*

But our expert computer graphics team suggests that with only six months in our program, Tito could become . . .

Toshino, the quiet one! Well-dressed, manicured, somewhat anal retentive, but an overachiever who's ready to enter the job market at a drop of the value of the dollar. *(Clicks slides off and deposits remote downstage, then returns to lectern.)*

Once you have dulled your personality and have become lifeless and unimaginative, you are ready to reap the rewards of the corporate world. Don't wait for miracles. All it takes is a lot of restraint and a little bit of Japanese know-how.

(Incensed.) Now, I'm your Crossover King, and I'm going to help you to cross over. And if you don't like it, you can just kiss my yellow tail. Yes, I said it. Because we are going to own everything anyway. We are going to own your mother, your father, everybody, so you better cross over while you still can. It's nothing personal, just big business. And we're going to take all our competition, and we're going to sucker-punch them, head-butt them, body-slam them. . . . *(Shakes, sweats, and begins to fall apart.)* Ay coño, yo quiero perder control, ser lo que soy. . . . ayudame, mamacita, estoy jodido, quiero bailar y gozar . . . *(Becomes completely unhinged, conking, tearing open shirt, and spewing forth a torrent of Spanish profanity.)*

(Tries desperately to control himself, clinging to lectern, and is finally able to gulp down some water. Pants and sweats.) Just kidding. Just kidding, like you American people say, just kidding. Well, being Latino need not be a handicap. Don't settle for affirmative action and tokenism. *(His feet begin mambo dancing beneath the lectern, while the rest of his body tries to hold still.)* Purge yourself of all ethnicity. *(His dancing feet take him out from behind the lectern. His upper body is still stiff.)* Well, that's all the time we have for tonight. Thank you for attending. *(Tries to control his legs, slaps his thighs.)* Remember, all it takes is a lot of restraint and a little . . . *(Bursts.)* Go Loco! Go Loco! Go Loco! *(Grooves.)*

Sayonara. Hai! *(Deep bow to audience.)*

(Lights down.)

TATO LAVIERA
(1950-)

Jesús Abraham (Tato) Laviera, a poet and community activist, was born in Santurce, Puerto Rico. He moved to New York with his family in 1960. The family suffered a difficult period of adjustment in the Lower East Side ghetto where they took up residence, but Laviera's involvement with the church gave him a sense of pride and belonging.

Laviera's accomplishments include: directing the Association of Community Services; serving on the boards of Madison Neighbors in Action and Mobilization for Youth; working with the Jamaica Arts Center, the Puerto Rico Family Institute, and United Bronx Parents; producing the sixteenth Annual Puerto Rico Parade of Chicago; and organizing the First Latino Book Fair and Writers Festival in Chicago.

He has published a number of poetry collections, including La Carreta Made a U-Turn *(1979),* Enclave *(1981),* AmeRícan *(1985) and* Mainstream Ethics *(1988). The Henry Street Settlement New Federal Theater commissioned a play from him, and Jimmy Carter invited him to read his poetry at the White House in 1980.*

Laviera's poem "AmeRícan" from his 1985 collection characteristically celebrates Puerto Rican identity in a mix of Spanish and English words and rhythms.

AMERÍCAN

we gave birth to a new generation,
AmeRícan, broader than lost gold
never touched, hidden inside the
puerto rican mountains.

we gave birth to a new generation,
AmeRícan, it includes everything
imaginable you-name-it-we-got-it
society.

we gave birth to a new generation,
AmeRícan salutes all folklores,
european, indian, black, spanish,
and anything else compatible:

AmeRícan, singing to composer pedro flores' palm
    trees high up in the universal sky!

AmeRícan, sweet soft spanish danzas gypsies
    moving lyrics la espanola cascabelling
    presence always singing at our side!

AmeRícan, beating jíbaro modern troubadours*
　　crying guitars romantic continental
　　bolero† love songs!

AmeRícan, across forth and across back
　　back across and forth back
　　forth across and back and forth
　　our trips are walking bridges!

　　it all dissolved into itself, the attempt
　　was truly made, the attempt was truly
　　absorbed, digested, we spit out
　　the poison, we spit out the malice,
　　we stand, affirmative in action,
　　to reproduce a broader answer to the
　　marginality that gobbled us up abruptly!

AmeRícan, walking plena‡-rhythms in new york,
　　strutting beautifully alert, alive,
　　many turning eyes wondering,
　　admiring!

AmeRícan, defining myself my own way any way many
　　ways Am e Rican, with the big R and the
　　accent on the i!

AmeRícan, like the soul gliding talk of gospel
　　boogie music!

AmeRícan, speaking new words in spanglish tenements.
　　fast tongue moving street corner "que
　　corta"§ talk being invented at the insistence
　　of a smile!

AmeRícan, abounding inside so many ethnic english
　　people, and out of humanity, we blend
　　and mix all that is good!

AmeRícan, integrating in new york and defining our
　　own destino,¶ our own way of life.

AmeRícan, defining the new america, humane america,
　　admired america, loved america, harmonious
　　america, the world in peace, our energies
　　collectively invested to find other civili-

---

*Puerto Rican mountain folk　　†Slow tropical dance　　‡An Afro-Puerto Rican dance
§That cuts　¶Destiny

zations, to touch God, further and further,
to dwell in the spirit of divinity!

AmeRícan, yes, for now, for i love this, my second
land, and i dream to take the accent from
the altercation, and be proud to call
myself AmeRícan, in the U.S. sense of the
word, AmeRícan, America!

ARJUN APPADURAI
(1949-)

An immigrant to the United States from India, Arjun Appadurai is Professor of Anthropology at the University of Chicago and Director of the Chicago Humanities Institute. He is the author of several books, including Modernity at Large: Cultural Dimensions of Globalization *(1996), and the editor of several others, including* The Social Life of Things: Commodities in Cultural Perspective *(1986).*

"Heart of Whiteness" is excerpted from a somewhat longer essay that appeared in the journal Public Culture *in 1993. Appadurai addresses the changes in thinking about identity and ethnicity that result from the ability to maintain contact with a variety of cultural influences and to resist assimilation in ways that reconfigure the majority.*

FROM THE HEART OF WHITENESS

The Trope of the Tribe

In spite of all the evidence to the contrary, these are hard times for patriotism. Maimed bodies and barbed wire in Eastern Europe, xenophobic violence in France, flag-waving in the political rituals of the election year here in the United States, all seem to suggest that the willingness to die for one's country is still a global fashion. But patriotism is an unstable sentiment, which thrives only at the level of the nation-state. Below that level it is easily supplanted by more intimate loyalties; above that level, it gives way to empty slogans rarely backed by the will to sacrifice or to kill. So when thinking about the future of patriotism, it is necessary first to inquire into the health of the nation-state.

My doubts about patriotism are tied up with my father's biography, in which patriotism and nationalism were already diverging terms. As a war correspondent for Reuters in Bangkok in 1940, he met an expatriate Indian nationalist, Subhas Chandra Bose, who split with Gandhi and Nehru on the issue of violence. Bose had escaped from British surveillance in India, and with the active support of the Japanese, established a government-in-exile in South-East Asia. The army Bose formed from Indian officers and enlisted men whom the Japanese had taken prisoner called itself the Indian National Army. This Indian army was roundly defeated by the British Indian army in Assam (on Indian soil, as my father never tired of noting) in 1944, and the Provisional Government of Azad Hind (Free India), in which my father was Minister of Publicity and Propaganda, soon crumbled with the defeat of the Axis powers.

When my father returned to India in 1945, he and his comrades were unwelcome heroes, poor cousins in the story of the nationalist struggle for Indian independence. They were patriots, but Bose's anti-British sentiments and his links with the Axis made him an embarrassment both to Gandhi's non-violence and Nehru's Fabian anglophilia. To the end of his life, my father and his comrades remained pariah patriots, rogue nationalists. My brothers and I grew up in Bombay wedged beween ex-patriotism, Bose-style, and bourgeois nationalism, Nehru style. *Our* India, with its Japanese connections and anti-Western ways, carried the nameless aroma of treason, in respect to the cozy alliance of the Nehrus and the Mountbattens, and the bourgeois compact between Gandhian non-violence and Nehruvian socialism. My father's gut distrust of the Nehru dynasty (and his whispers of unholy affections between Nehru and Lady Mountbatten) predisposed us to imagine a strange, deterritorialized India, invented in Taiwan and Singapore, Bangkok and Kuala Lumpur, quite independent of New Delhi and the Nehrus, the Congress Party and mainstream nationalism.

So there is a special appeal for me in the possibility that the marriage between nations and states was always a marriage of convenience, and that patriotism needs to find new objects of desire. The many explosions of ethnicity, anti-government riots, refugee flows, and state-generated atrocity we see around the world are evidence that this is a marriage on the rocks. Our deep attachment, as Americans, to what we call our "country," has so far contained the tension between our deep fervor about the nation and our deep suspicions of the state. This attachment also has generated the widespread (and unthinkingly racist) image of *tribalism,* which dominates the media, in analyses of Los Angeles and New York, Sarajevo and Sri Lanka, Iraq and Miami.

It used to be that words like "tribe" and "tribalism" were parts of the technical vocabulary of anthropology, used in textbooks to refer to kin-based societies, contrasted equally with hunter-gatherer bands, peasant communities, monarchies, urban societies, nomadic groups and modern nation-states. But in the last year or two, tribalism has become the buzz word in much media coverage of urban riots in the United States, of ethnic violence in Eastern Europe and elsewhere, of separatist militance in Africa, Asia and Latin America. In analyzing the recent, ethnically based nationalisms, especially in Europe, we have found the misleading image of tribalism all too comforting. It allows us to see various minorities in our own society as well as all sorts of ethnic others around the world as still caught in a past which we have left behind. It indulges our tendency to distinguish *our* violence from *their* violence by seeing it as somehow more mindless, more mob-like, more bloody, less moral, less heroic, in a word, as *tribal.* Our violence, on the other hand, is always seen as more purposive, more organized, more skilled, more deliberate, and thus, implicitly somehow both more civil and more civilized, even when it is mercenary and massive. We need to revise our notion that ethnic and nationalist stirrings around the world, and in our urban backyards, are a throwback to something deep, biological, bloody and ancient (Comaroff).

This is not just a plea for politically correct anthropology, however. Recent letters to the editors of several prominent magazines, on both sides of the Atlantic, have pointed to the invidiousness of describing light-skinned groups as ethnic and dark-skinned ones as tribal, and there are signs that the Western media might clean up this obviously racist double standard. The loose use of the image of tribalism certainly revives our deepest racial images of black Africans and native Americans, of blind loyalties and arcane rituals, of cannibals and kings. Worse, the image of tribalism seduces us to focus on a few powerful images of violence, terror and displacement which surround ethnicity and the nation-state. But we have lost track of what may be going on less dramatically behind the mayhem on the front pages and our television screens, and that is a steady erosion of the values and commitments that guarantee the future of the nation-state.

One major fact which accounts for strains in the marriage of nation and state is that the nationalist genie, never perfectly contained in the bottle of the territorial state, is now itself a diasporic. Carried in the repertoires of increasingly mobile populations of refugees, tourists, guestworkers, transnational intellectuals, scientists, and illegal aliens, it is increasingly unrestrained by ideas of spatial boundary and territorial sovereignty. This massive revolution in the foundations of nationalism has crept up on us virtually unnoticed. Where soil and place were once the key to the linkage of territorial affiliation with state monopoly of the means of violence, key identities and identifications now only partially revolve around the realities and images of place. In the Sikh demand for Khalistan, in French-Canadian feelings about Quebec, in Palestinian demands for self-determination, images of a homeland are only part of the rhetoric of popular sovereignty and do not necessarily reflect a territorial bottom line. The considerable violence and terror surrounding the breakdown of many existing nation-states is not a sign of reversion to anything biological or innate, dark or primordial. What then are we to make of this renewed blood-lust in the name of the nation?

Modern nationalisms involve communities of citizens in the territorially defined nation-state who share the collective experience, not of face-to-face contact or common subordination to a royal person, but of reading books, pamphlets, newspapers, maps and other modern texts together (Calhoun; Habermas; Warner). In and through these collective experiences of what Benedict Anderson calls print capitalism (Anderson), citizens *imagine* themselves to belong to a national society. The modern nation-state, in this view, grows less out of natural facts—such as language, blood, soil and race—and more as a quintessential cultural product, a product of the collective imagination. This is very far from the views of the dominant theories of nationalism, from Herder to Mazzini and since then to all sorts of right-wing nationalists, who see nations as products of the natural destinies of peoples, whether rooted in language, race, soil or religion. It has recently been argued that historical conjunctures concerning reading and publicity, texts and their linguistic mediations, nations and their narratives, can usefully be considered together to understand the internationalization of mass-mediated public spheres (Lee).

The leaders of the new nations formed in Asia and Africa after World War II— Nasser, Nehru, Sukarno—would have been distressed to see the frequency with which the ideas of tribalism and nationalism are conflated in recent public discourse in the West. These leaders spent a great deal of their rhetorical energies in urging their subjects to give up what they saw as primordial loyalties—to family, tribe, caste and region—in the interests of the fragile abstractions they called India, Egypt and Indonesia. They understood that the new nations needed to subvert and annex the primary loyalties attached to more intimate collectivities. They rested their ideas of their new nations on the very edges of the paradox that modern nations were intended to be somehow open, universal, modern and emancipatory by virtue of their special commitment to citizenly virtue but that *their* nations were nonetheless, in some essential way, different from and even better than other nations. In many ways these leaders knew what we have tended to forget, namely that nations, especially in multi-ethnic settings, are tenuous collective projects, not eternal natural facts. This much seems uncontestable, even orthodox.

But the idea of the recent nationalisms as being the products of some long-standing ethnic ooze—as tribal—also distracts us from the extent to which the new ethnicities are direct products of and responses to the policies of various nation-states over the last century or more. Much of the force of and the sense of what it is to be Serbian or Kurdish, Tajik or Armenian, Sinhala or Samoan, are the products of *modern,* state-sponsored censuses and ethnologies, surveys and folklore, atlases and settlement policies. Slovak conflicts with Czechs, Croat conflict with Serbs, are impossible to imagine without the pecular state structures into which these peoples were placed after World War I, in the wake of the collapse of the Hapsburg, Ottoman and Russian empires. Much of the intensity of communal terror between Hindus and Muslims in India can be traced to the special ways in which religious communities were put into separate electorates by the British in the early part of the twentieth century. The divide between Sinhalas and Tamils in Sri Lanka owes at least as much to decisions about the Sinhala language as the exclusive medium of instruction in the post-colonial university system in Sri Lanka and to the exploitation of religious hatreds in the context of electoral politics there. As Eric Hobsbawm has recently noted (Hobsbawm), it was Stalin who gave Lithuania its capital city (it was previously in Poland) and Tito who created a bigger Serbia with a much larger Serbian minority in his effort to *contain* Serbian nationalism.

The modern nation-state, in its preoccupation with the control, classification and surveillance of its subjects, has often created, revitalized or fractured ethnic identities that were previously fluid, negotiable or nascent. Of course the terms used to mobilize ethnic violence today may have long histories. But the realities to which they refer—Serbo-Croatian language, Basque customs, Lithuanian cuisine—were most often crystallized in the nineteenth and early twentieth centuries. Constructed traditions for nascent nationhoods, rather than natural facts waiting for political expression. Nationalism and ethnicity thus feed each other, as nationalists construct ethnic categories which in turn drive others to construct counter-ethnicities, and then, in times of political crisis these others demand counter-states, based on newfound counter-nationalisms. For every nationalism that appears to be naturally destined, there is another that is a reactive by-product.

While violence in the name of Serbs and Mollucans, Khmer and Latvians, Germans and Jews, tempts us to think that all such identities run dark and deep, we need only turn to the recent riots in India occasioned by the report of a Government Commission which recommended reserving a large percentage of government jobs for certain castes defined by the census and the constitution as "backward." Much rioting and carnage, and not a few killings and suicides, took place in North India over such labels as OBC ("Other Backward Castes") which come out of the terminological distinctions of the Indian census and its specialized protocols and schedules. How astonishing it seems that anyone would die or kill for entitlements associated with being the member of an "Other Backward Caste." Yet this case is not an exception, but in its macabre bureaucratic banality shows how the tehnical needs of censuses and welfare legislation, combined with the cynical tactics of electoral politics, can draw groups into quasi-racial identifications and fears. The matter is not so different as it may appear for such apparently "natural" labels as Jew, Arab, German and Hindu, each of which involves people who choose these labels, others who are forced into them, yet others who through their philological scholarship shore up the histories of these labels or find them handy ways of tidying up messy problems of language and history, race and belief.

Thus, minorities in many parts of the world are as artificial as the majorities they are seen to threaten: "whites" in the United States, Hindus in India, Englishmen in Great Britain, all are examples of how the political and administrative designation of some groups as "minorities" (blacks and Hispanics in the United States, Celts and Pakistanis in the United Kingdom, Muslims and Christians in India) helps to pull majorities (silent or vocal) together under labels with short lives but long histories. The new ethnicities are often no older than the nation-states which they have come to resist. Ethnic nationalisms are frequently reactive and defensive rather than spontaneous or deep-rooted, as the tribalist model would have us believe. The Muslims of Bosnia are being reluctantly ghettoized though there is fear among both Serbians and Croats about the possibility of an Islamic state in Europe. Minorities are as often made as they are born.

Recent ethnic movements often involve thousands, often millions of people, spread across vast territories and often separated by vast distances. Whether we consider the linkage of Serbs separated by large chunks of Bosnia-Herzegovina; or Kurds spread across Iran, Iraq and Turkey; or Sikhs spread through London, Vancouver and California, as well as the Indian Punjab—the new ethno-nationalisms are complex, large-scale, highly coordinated acts of mobilization, reliant on news, logistical flows and propaganda across state borders. They can hardly be considered tribal, if by this we mean that they are spontaneous uprisings of closely bonded, spatially segregated, naturally allied groupings. In the case we find most frightening today, what we could call Serbian "tribalism" is hardly a simple thing since there are at least 2.8 million Yugoslav familes who have produced about 1.4 million mixed marriages between Serbs and Croats (Hobsbawm). To which tribe could these families be said to belong? In our horrified preoccupation with the shock-troops of ethno-nationalism, we have lost sight of the confused sentiments of civilians, the torn loyalties of families which have members of warring groups within the same household, and the urgings of those who hold to the view that Serbs, Muslims and Croats in Bosnia-Herzegovina have no fundamental enmity. What is harder to explain is how principles of ethnic affiliation, however dubious their provenience and fragile their pedigree, can mobilize large groups into violent action very rapidly.

What does seem clear is that the tribal model, insofar as it suggests pre-packaged passions waiting to explode, flies in the face of the contingencies that spark ethnic passion. The Sikhs, until recently the bulwark of the Indian army and historically the fighting arm of Hindu India against Muslim rule, today regard themselves as threatened by Hinduism and seem willing to accept aid and succor from Pakistan. The Muslims of Bosnia-Herzegovina have been forced, reluctantly, to revitalize their Islamic affiliations. Far from activating longstanding "tribal" sentiments, Bosnian Muslims are torn between their own conception of themselves as European Muslims (a term recently used by Ejub Ganic, vice-president of Bosnia) but transnational Islam is already actively involved in Bosnian warfare. Wealthy Bosnians who live abroad, in countries such as Turkey, are already buying weapons for the defense of Muslims in Bosnia.

The Heart of Whiteness

These global considerations have much to do with my own views about American-ness. Until a few years ago, I was content to live in that special space allotted to "for-eigners," especially Anglophone, educated ones like myself, with faint traces of a British accent. As a black women at a bus-stop in Chicago once said to me with approval, I was an *East* Indian. That was in 1972. But since that happy conversation two decades ago, it has become steadily less easy to see myself as somehow immune, armed with my Indian passport and my Anglophone ways, from the poli-tics of racial identity in the United States. Not only is it that after two decades of being a "Resident Alien" in the United States, married to an Anglo-Saxon American woman, the father of a bi-cultural teenager, my Indian passport seems like a rather slight badge of identity. The net of racial politics is now cast wider than ever before on the streets of the urban USA.

I knew that things had changed one day in downown Philadelphia in 1990, when my wife, my in-laws, my son and I were driving towards the Benjamin Franklin Bridge, in a posh part of the city called Society Hill. Driving in caravan, we stopped to pick up my son's Choir Director, who was joining us on a trip to New Jersey. Dou-ble-parked on a one-way street for a brief moment, we heard a scream behind us. We turned to see an enraged white male poking his head out of the sun-roof of the car behind us, purple-faced, ready for action, enraged that his car (driven by another man) should have been momentarily slowed down by ours. I stepped out, as did my father-in-law from his car, to greet a stream of invective, in which the punchline, directed to me was "Wipe that dot off your head, asshole" or words to that effect. The incident ended shortly thereafter, as we all walked up to the Rambo car, and with a few suitably middle-class expressions of shock and outrage, muted the screamer and shamed his companions. The fact that we were on a patrician street, rather than on, for example, a back street in Elizabeth, New Jersey, helped us to turn the moral tables.

The screamer was probably from New Jersey, and his reference to wiping the dot off my head was an allusion to a hate-group in and around Jersey City, which has seen it come into considerable prominence. It has attacked Indians in the area (even killed one) and calls itself the Dotbusters. Their name refers to the mark that Indian women often wear as a mark of beauty and auspiciousness on their foreheads. The Dotbusters clearly intend their epithet to be not only racist but feminizing as well, since they do not know that in traditional India men too wore this sort of mark. My wife and I talked about the incident and realized that something historic, even if small-scale, had happened to me. I, and my fellow migrants from India, had arrived. Someone out there hated me. The stakes of my own diasporic existence here had somehow changed: I was certainly American now. I have since been wondering about the ugly side of Americanness and the special status of diasporic groups.

I am now well advanced on the road to becoming a person of color. It's not exactly that I thought I was white before, but as an anglophone academic born in India and teaching in the Ivy League, I was certainly hanging out in the field of dreams, and had no cause to think myself black. As a child brought up with a profound sense of color in a Brahmin household in Bombay, I was always aware of the bad marriage prospects of my darker female relatives, of the glorious "milky" skin of my father's dead father, of the horrible "blue" blackness that my mother swore I acquired when I played in the mid-day sun in Bombay. So even though I was as hip as the next person to the fact that black was beautiful, I preferred to stay brown myself.

My own complexion and its role in "minority" politics, as well as in street encounters with racial hatred in Philadelphia, prompt me to re-open the links between America and the United States, between bi-culturalism and patriotism, between diasporic identities and the stabilities provided by passports and green cards. Postnational loyalties are not irrelevant to the problem of diversity in the United States. If indeed a post-national order is in the making, and Americanness changes its meanings, the whole problem of diversity in American life will have to be re-thought.

This brings us back to the pervasive idiom and image of tribalism. Applied to New York, Miami and Los Angeles (as opposed to Sarajevo, Soweto or Sri Lanka) it both conceals and indulges a diffuse racism about those others (Haitians, Hispanics, Iranians and African-Americans) who have insinuated themselves into the American body politic. It allows us to maintain the idea of an Americanness which precedes (and subsists in spite of) the hyphens that contribute to it, and to maintain a distinction between "tribal" Americans (the black, the brown and the yellow) and other Americans. It facilitates the fantasy that civil society in the United States has a special destiny in regard to peaceful multiculturalism. Intelligent multiculturalism for us, bloody ethnicity or mindless tribalism for them.

There has developed a special set of links between democracy, diversity and prosperity in American social thought. Built on a complex dialogue between political science (the only genuine made-in-America social science without obvious European counterparts or antecedents) and vernacular constitutionalism, a comfortable equilibrium was established between the ideas of cultural diversity and one or another version of the melting pot. Swinging between the *National Geographic* and the *Reader's Digest,* this anodyne polarity has proved remarkably durable and comforting. It accommodates, sometimes on the same page or in the same breath, a sense that plurality is the American genius and that there is an Americanness that somehow contains and transcends plurality. This second, post-Civil War accommodation with difference is now on its last legs, and the PC/multiculturalism debate is its peculiar, parochial Waterloo. Parochial because it insistently refuses to recognize that the challenge of diasporic pluralism is now global and that American solutions cannot be seen in isolation. Peculiar because there has been no systematic recognition that the politics of multiculturalism is now part and parcel of the extra-territorial nationalism of populations who love the United States but are not necesarily attached to America. More bluntly, neither popular nor academic thought in this country has come to terms with the difference between being a land of immigrants and being one node in a post-national network of diaporas.

In the post-national world we are seeing emerge, diaspora runs with, and not against, the grain of identity, movement and reproduction. Everyone has relatives working abroad. Many people—Muslims in Bosnia and Croats in Bosnia are only two recent examples—find themselves exiles without really having moved very far. Yet others find themselves in patterns of repeat migration—Indian indentured laborers who first went to East Africa in the nineteenth and early twentieth centuries and then found themselves pushed out of Uganda, Kenya and Tanzania to find fresh travails in England and the United States. Chinese from Hong Kong buying real estate in Vancouver, Gujarati traders from Uganda opening motels in New Jersey and newspaper kiosks in New York, Sikh cabdrivers in Chicago and Philadelphia, Turkish guestworkers in Germany—these are all examples of a new sort of world in which diaspora is the order of things and settled ways of life are increasingly hard to find. The United States, always in its self-perception a land of immigrants, finds itself awash in these global diasporas, no longer a closed space for the melting pot to work its magic but yet another diasporic switching point to which people come to seek their fortunes though no longer content to leave their homelands behind. Global democracy fever and the breakdown of the Soviet Empire have meant that most groups who wish to re-negotiate their links to their diasporic identities from their American vantage points are free to do so: thus, American Jews of Polish origin undertake Holocaust tours in Eastern Europe, Indian doctors from Michigan set up eye clinics in New Delhi, Palestinians in Detroit participate in the politics of the West Bank.

There is a widespread sense that the "mosiac," the "rainbow", the "quilt" and other images of complexity-in-diversity are growing rapidly threadbare. Whether in debates over immigration, bilingual education, the academic canon, or the "underclass," these liberal images have not come to terms with the tension between the centripetal pull of Americanness and the centrifugal pull of *diasporic diversity* in American life. The battles over affirmative action, quotas, welfare and abortion in America today suggest that the metaphor of the mosaic can no longer contain the contradiction between group identities, which Americans will tolerate (up to a point) in cultural life, and individual identities, which are still the non-negotiable principle behind American ideas of achievement, mobility and justice.

The Form of the Trans-Nation

The formula of hyphenation (Italian-Americans, Asian-Americans, and African-Americans) is reaching the point of saturation in the United States, and the right hand side of the hyphen can barely contain the unruliness of the left hand side. Even as the legitimacy of nation-states in their own territorial contexts is increasingly under threat, the idea of the nation flourishes transnationally. Safe from the depredations of their home-states, diasporic communities become doubly loyal to their nations of origin, thus ambivalent about their loyalties to America. The politics of ethnic identity in the United States is inseparably linked to the global spread of originally local national identities. For every nation-state that has exported significant numbers of its populations to the United States, as refugees, tourists or students, there is now a delocalized, *transnation,* which retains a special ideological link to a putative place of origin, but is otherwise a thoroughly diasporic collectivity. No existing conception of Americanness can contain this large variety of trans-nations.

In this scenario, the hyphenated American might have to be twice hyphenated (Asian-American-Japanese or Native-American-Seneca or African-American-Jamaican or Hispanic-American-Bolivian) as diasporic identities stay mobile and grow more protean. Or perhaps the sides of the hyphen will have to be reversed, and we become a federation of diasporas, American-Italians, American-Haitians, American-Irish, American-Africans. Dual citizenships might increase, if the societies from which we came stay or become more open. We might recognize that diasporic diversity actually puts loyalty to a non-territorial, trans-nation first, while recognizing that there is a specially American way to connect to these global diasporas. America, as a cultural space, will not need to compete with a host of global identities and diasporic loyalties. It might come to be seen as a model of how to arrange one territorial focus (among others) for a cross-hatching of diasporic communities.

The question is: can a post-national politics be built around this cultural fact? Many societies now face influxes of immigrants and refugees, wanted and unwanted. But America may be alone in having organized itself around a modern political ideology in which pluralism is central to the conduct of democratic life. Out of a different strand of its experience, this society has also generated a powerful fable of itself as a land of immigrants. In today's post-national, diasporic world, America is being invited to weld these two doctrines together, to confront the needs of pluralism *and* of immigration, to construct a society *around* diasporic diversity.

What is to be done? There could be a special place for America in the new, post-national order, and one which does not rely either on isolationism or global domination as its alternative bases. The United States is eminently suited to be a sort of cultural laboratory and a Free Trade Zone for the generation, circulation, importation and testing of the materials for a world organized around diasporic diversity. In a sense this experiment is already under way. The United States is already a huge, fascinating garage sale for the rest of the world. It provides golf vacations and real estate for the Japanese, business management ideologies and techniques for Europe and India, soap opera ideas for Brazil and the Middle East, Prime Ministers for Yugoslavia, supply-side economics for Poland, Russia and whoever else will buy, Christian fundamentalism for Korea, post-modern architecture for Hong Kong and so on. By also providing a set of images (Rambo in Afghanistan, We are the World, Bernard Shaw in Baghdad, Coke goes to Barcelona, Perot goes to Washington) which links human rights, consumer style, anti-statism and media glitz, it might be said that the United States is partly accountable for the idiosyncracies that attend struggles for self-determination in otherwise very different parts of the world. This is why a University of Iowa sweatshirt is not just a silly symbol in the jungles of Mozambique or on the barricades of Beirut. It captures the free-floating yearning for American style even in the most intense contexts of opposition to the United States. The rest is provided by authoritarian state policies, massive arms industries, the insistently hungry eye of the electronic media, and the despair of bankrupt economies.

Of course, these products and ideas are not the immaculate conceptions of some mysterious American know-how, but are precisely the product of a complex environment in which diasporic ideas and intellectuals meet in a variety of special settings (such as labs, libraries, classrooms, music studios, business seminars and political campaigns) to generate, re-formulate, and re-circulate cultural forms that are fundamentally post-national and diasporic. The role of American musicians, studios and record companies in the creation of "world beat" is an excellent example of this sort of down-home but off-shore entrepreneurial mentality. Americans are loathe to admit the piece-meal, pragmatic, haphazard, flexible and opportunistic ways in which these American products and re-products circulate around the world. We like to think that the Chinese have simply bought the virtues of free enterprise, the Poles of the supply-side, the Haitians and Filipinos of democracy, and everyone of human rights. We rarely pay attention to the complicated terms, traditions and cultural styles into which these ideas are folded, and thus transformed beyond our recognition. Thus, during the historic events of Tiananmen Square in 1989, when it seemed as if the Chinese people had become democratic overnight, there was considerable evidence that the ways in which different groups in China understood their problems was both internally varied and tied to various specificities of China's history and cultural style. Reflecting a venerable Chinese tradition of protest through expressions of supplication, a popular big character poster said "kneeling, we plead for democracy, crying we plead for freedom." Americans would find it difficult to associate this mixture of anger and pleading with their own sense of the naturalness of democratic rights. While the student leaders at Tienanmen Square used Chinese terms for "dialogue" which were egalitarian and colloquial, party leaders continued to use terms which implied asymmetry, appropriate to speech directed at inferiors. Thus, at the heart of the student movement in China lay debates about the meaning of democratic dialogue which were themselves products of semantic distinctions and linguistic ideologies alien to American usage.

When we see such transformations and cultural complications of vocabulary and style, if we notice them at all, we are annoyed and dismayed. In this misreading of how others handle what we still see as *our* national recipe for success, we perform a further act of narcissistic distortion: we imagine that these peculiarly American inventions (democracy, capitalism, free-enterprise, human rights, etc.) are automatically and inherently interconnected, and that our national saga holds the key to the combination. In the migration of our words, we see the victory of our myths. We are believers in terminal conversion.

The Western "victory" in the Cold War need not necessarily turn pyrrhic. The fact is that the United States is already, from a cultural point of view, a vast Free Trade Zone, full of ideas, technologies, styles and idioms (from McDonald's and the Harvard Business School to the Dream Team and Reverse Mortgages) that the rest of the world finds fascinating. This FTZ rests on a volatile economy, the major cities of the American borderland (Los Angeles, Miami, New York, Detroit) are now heavily militarized, and the American public shares a rather deep sense of despair about the candidates that the two major parties have offered to it. But these facts are of little relevance to those who come, either briefly or for more extended stays, to this Free Trade Zone. Some, fleeing vastly greater urban violence, state persecution and economic hardship, come as permanent migrants, legal or illegal. Others are short-term shoppers for clothes, entertainment, loans, armaments, or quick lessons in free-market economics or civil society politics. The very unruliness, the rank unpredictability, the quirky inventiveness, the sheer cultural vitality of this Free Trade Zone is what attracts all sorts of diasporas to the United States.

For the United States to play a major role in the cultural politics of a post-national world has very complex domestic entailments. It may mean making room for the legitimacy of cultural rights, rights to the pursuit of cultural difference under public protections and guarantees. It may mean a painful break from a fundamentally Fordist, manufacture-centered conception of the American economy, as we learn to be global information-brokers, service-providers, style-doctors. It may mean embracing as part of our livelihoods what we have so far confined to the world of Broadway, Hollywood and Disneyland: the import of experiments, the production of fantasies, the fabrication of identities, the export of styles, the hammering out of pluralities. It may mean distinguishing our attachment to America from our willingness to die for the United States. That is, it may mean rethinking mono-patriotism, patriotism directed exclusively to the hyphen between nation and state, and allowing the real problems we face—the deficit, the environment, abortion, race, drugs and jobs—to define those social groups and ideas for which we would be willing to live . . . and to die.

The queer nation may only be the first of a series of new patriotisms, in which others could be the retired, the unemployed and the disabled, as well as scientists, women and Hispanics. Some of us may still want to live—and die—for the United States. But many of these new sovereignties are inherently post-national. Surely they represent more humane motives for affiliation than statehood or party affiliation, the more interesting bases for debate and cross-cutting alliances. Ross Perot's volunteers gave us a brief, intense glimpse of the powers of patriotism totally divorced from party, government or state, during the election campaigns of 1992. Scary as many of us found the Perotistas, the way they came into being and their profound capability to mobilize very different sorts of voters should suggest that the American body politic is full of surprises and can bring together all sorts of coalitions, at large scales and short notice. America may yet construct another narrative of enduring significance, a narrative about the uses of loyalty after the end of the nation-state. In this narrative, bounded territories could give way to diasporic networks, nations to trans-nations, and patriotism itself could become plural, serial, contextual and mobile. Here lies one direction for the future of patriotism in a postcolonial world.

The nation form thus presents itself as a special site for work on post-colonial discourse, work which goes beyond the archaeology of this discourse. Such work cannot be confined to the colored and colorful sites and boundaries which mark the history of colonialism. Nor can it be confined to those social forms that invite the gaze of "theory" because of their sheer discursivity. In looking at human rights movements as well as new literatures, migration as well as third world cinema, refugee camps as well as nationalist speeches, we can begin to construct a set of theoretical practices that are not only post-colonial but also post-discursive. Such practices might shift the academic gaze beyond the discourses of nation, to the space where post-colonial (and post-national) social formations are being incubated.

Postcolonial discourse studies need to be alert to the ever present danger that they might become another way to contain the unruliness of the postcolony while satisfying the endless appetite of the Western academy for colorful topics. One way to avoid this danger is to ensure that the study of postcolonial discourse should include the United States, where debates about race, urban violence and affirmative action index more general anxieties about multiculturalism, about diasporic diversity and thus about new forms of transnationality. As to America, we need to explore and inhabit the elliptical space between it and the United States, so that the heart of whiteness can engage its true colors.

Works Cited

Anderson, B. *Imagined Communities: Reflections on the Origins and Spread of Nationalism.* 1983; London and New York: Verso, 1991.

Appadurai, A. "Disjuncture and Difference in the Global Cultural Economy." *Public Culture* 2.2 (Spring 1990): 1–24.

Balibar, E. "The Nation Form: History and Ideology." *Race, Nation, Class: Ambiguous Identities.* Ed. E. Balibar and I. Wallerstein. London and New York: Verso, 1991. 86–106.

Bhabha, H. K. ed. *Nation and Narration.* London and New York: Routledge, 1990.

Calhoun, C., ed. *Habermas and the Public Sphere.* Cambridge, Mass., and London: MIT Press, 1992.

Chatterjee, P. *Nationalist Thought and the Colonial World: A Derivative Discourse.* London: Zed Press, 1986.

Comaroff, J. and J. 1992. "Of Totemism and Ethnicity." *Ethnography and the Historical Imagination.* Boulder, Colorado: Westview Press, 1992. 49–67.

Habermas, J. *The Structural Transformation of the Public Sphere.* 1962 (German original); Cambridge, Mass.: MIT Press, 1989.

Hobsbawm, E. "Ethnicity and Nationalism in Europe Today." *Anthropology Today 8.1* (February 1992): 3–8.

Lee, B. "Going Public." *Public Culture* 5.2 (Winter 1993).

Mbembe, A., "The Banality of Power and the Aesthetics of Vulgarity in the Postcolony." *Public Culture* 4.2 (Spring 1992): 1–30

Mbembe, A., et al. "Belly Up: More on the Postcolony." Special Section. *Public Culture* 5.1 (Fall 1992): 46–145.

Warner, M. "The Mass Public and the Mass Subject." *Habermas and the Public Sphere,* 377–401.

BIBLIOGRAPHY

Anderson, Benedict. *Imagined Communities: Reflections on the Origin and Spread of Nationalism.* London: Verso, 1983.

Barth, Fredrik. *Ethnic Groups and Boundaries: The Social Organization of Cultural Difference.* Boston: Little, Brown, 1969.

Boas, Franz. *Anthropology and Modern Life.* 1928. New York: Norton, 1962.

Boelhower, William. *Through a Glass Darkly: Ethnic Semiosis in American Literature.* New York: Oxford UP, 1987.

Du Bois, W. E. B. *The Souls of Black Folk.* 1903. New York: Dodd, Mead, 1979.

Erikson, Erik H. *Identity: Youth and Crisis.* New York: Norton, 1968.

Gossett, Thomas. *Race: The History of an Idea in America.* Dallas, TX: Southern Methodist UP, 1963.

Hill, Mike, ed. *Whiteness: A Critical Reader.* New York: New York UP, 1997.

Jacobsen, Matthew Frye. *Whiteness of a Different Color: European Immigrants and the Alchemy of Race.* Cambridge: Harvard UP, 1998.

James, William. *Correspondence.* 2 vols. Ed. Ignas K. Skrupkelis and Elizabeth M. Berkeley. Charlottesville: UP of Virginia, 1992.

Locke, Alain. *The New Negro.* 1925. New York: Atheneum, 1969.

Morrison, Toni. *Playing in the Dark: Whiteness and the Literary Imagination.* Cambridge: Harvard UP, 1992.

———. "Unspeakable Things Unspoken: The Afro-American Presence in American Literature." *Michigan Quarterly Review,* 26.1 (Winter 1989): 1–34.

Renan, Ernest. "What Is a Nation?" 1882. *The Poetry of the Celtic Races and Other Essays.* Trans. by William Hutchinson. London: W. Scott, 1896.

Sollors, Werner. *Beyond Ethnicity: Consent and Descent in American Culture.* New York: Oxford UP, 1986.

Stocking, George W. *Victorian Anthropology.* New York: Free Press, 1987.

WRITING ABOUT LITERATURE AND CULTURE

This section of the book focuses on the relationship between critical thinking and effective writing. It provides an important linkage between the kinds of critical reading and interpretation skills and the necessary role that writing plays for thinking about literature and social issues.

It offers ideas, guidelines, strategies, and working principles for writing about literature. This appendix will accompany all the books in the Longman Literature and Culture series *(Popular Fiction: An Anthology; Literature and the Environment: A Reader on Nature and Culture; Literature, Class, and Culture: An Anthology; Literature, Race, and Ethnicity: Contesting American Identities; Literature and Gender: Thinking Critically Through Fiction, Poetry, and Drama),* a series devoted to reading and thinking critically in ways that promote exploration and discovery. Writing about literature furthers these goals of critical analysis.

I have attempted to focus on innovative approaches that will help you better analyze and understand the exciting and perhaps somewhat unfamiliar territory of writing about literature. I will begin by describing good writing—that is, writing that stays in the mind and positively influences readers. Next, I will offer some principles that underlie successful academic writing generally and critical work in literature classes more specifically. After that, I will discuss what it means to read for meaning, suggest how to get ready for class discussions, and then move to a consideration of the writing process with a particular focus on purpose, audience, drafting, and revising. Since one of the chief difficulties many writers face is "the blank page syndrome," I particularly address the problem of getting started on a writing project. The next section examines the various elements that comprise an essay, its various components. I then move to a brief consideration of the computer, with a particular focus on both word processing and electronic researching. Finally,

I offer a brief guide to research, with a listing of some of the most common bibliographic entries according to the Modern Language Association format.

What Is Good Writing?

Let's begin with some general principles that apply to all good academic writing. Many students equate academic writing with boredom, stuffiness, and abstraction. From their perspective, only academics write—and read—academic writing, which most others find dull, dry, and abstract. Now there is no doubt that writing of this kind exists, but most of it is not good writing, academic or otherwise.

Good writing has energy, clarity, and a liveliness of mind. It creates satisfaction by enlightening and persuading. It asks writers to place themselves at risk since they are making their ideas public. It changes minds because it illuminates its subject in a new light. It explores ideas thoughtfully, drawing upon research and other forms of evidence to persuade the reader.

Good writing has economy: it offers a thoughtful, efficient route toward increased understanding. No reader likes to read an essay that digresses or uses 35 words to state a 15-word idea. You may be assigned an essay with a required length, for example, "Write a 2500-word essay that argues for a specific environmental policy to preserve western wilderness." Such essays can be challenging since students sometimes think they have to pad them to get the necessary words. This procedure is ill advised; no essay profits from repetition or flabby style. In this situation, the only choice is to do more reading, researching, and analyzing—subjects I will consider shortly.

Good writing leaves the author with a sense of accomplishment and satisfaction. Writing a passing essay may be easy, but unless writers are engaged in the hard struggle with the text and with their writing process, they are unlikely to experience a meaningful sense of accomplishment. Take your internal pulse after you complete an essay. Do you like it? Do you feel that it succeeds? Are you glad to have written it? Are you aware of your struggles, frustrations, and accomplishments? If you can answer "yes" to these questions, you stand a good chance of success. Good writing reveals insights that are often as surprising to the writer as they are to the reader. Good writing packs a punch. It stays in the memory. It makes a difference.

Although there is no single formula for good writing, certain general truths apply. First, writers need to capture their excitement, passion, and intellectual commitment. If a writer lacks those qualities—that is, writes simply to get done or to fill blank pages—the writing almost always is lackluster. Many times, writers get stuck and cannot complete a good draft, or work for hours and then throw up their hands in despair. If they possess an emotional and intellectual desire to produce a good piece of work, however, half the battle is won. They will try again, revise, seek the help of a teacher or tutor, research the subject more extensively, experiment, and otherwise redouble their effort. Most writers do not produce good first drafts, but if they care about the writing, they find ways to make it into something worth reading.

Good writing thus requires both time and effort. Even a short assignment ("Write a 500-word essay that explores why you think America is—or is not—a classless society") makes significant demands on any writer: time and effort to think, read, reflect, procrastinate, get started and get nowhere, draft, revise, edit, proofread. Few writers, be they students or professionals, can dash off two or three quick pages and achieve satisfying results.

Good writing generally exhibits active and descriptive verbs that perform "work" for the writer. Thus, instead of stating "John McPhee is a good writer and is my favorite author," try "John McPhee writes well and remains my favorite author" or "John McPhee is my favorite author because he writes so well" or "John McPhee, my favorite author, writes so well that reading one of his books is like seeing a movie" or some other version. Note the differences among these sentences: the ways that verbs get changed, altering sentence structure and meaning as well. Lackluster writing can often be traced to overdependence on the verb "to be" in its various forms: "am," "is," "are," "was," "were," "be," "been." If your writing is flat, examine it for overuse of the various "to be" verbs and try to find meaningful, accurate replacements.

Good writing conveys new information to readers. At first glance, this seems to pose a problem: after all, how can you write something "new" about literature when your instructor knows so much more? Although instructors do possess considerable knowledge, they by no means know everything about an essay, story, poem, drama, author, or subject. In fact, their love of literature can make them easy to write for, since they enjoy learning more. The key is to convey new information: an interpretation supported by quotes, analysis, and research; a historical exploration of a work or author; an argument about the meaning or significance of a literary subject; a personal assessment of why or how a literary work affects you; a well-documented research paper; and so on. Instructors respond positively to student work that teaches them something, that changes their interpretations, adds to their knowledge, or improves their appreciation. When students accomplish one or more of those objectives, they produce "good writing."

READING FOR MEANING

To be able to write, you—like any good writer—must find something to say. Too often, students receive an assignment and produce a quick and visceral response (sometimes just before class). One important key to succeeding in a literature class is to learn how to engage in sustained inquiry—that is, learning how to read for meaning and asking questions that lead toward improved understanding. Most literary works are sufficiently complex that at first they often frustrate readers. Success in a literature class will depend on learning how to read well.

Typically, we read to gain information. That is why we read many textbooks, newspapers, magazines, instructions, and the like. The kind of reading required in an English literature or composition course, however, requires a different set of strategies. Although most of us first read a story, essay, poem, or drama to find out what happens—that is, to gain some information and knowledge of how the "story" will end—the primary intent of literature is not simply to provide readers with information or a plot. Rather, its purpose is to give pleasure, to offer multiple possibilities for interpretation, to surprise, to shock, to amaze, to alter the reader's thinking. Works such as the ones in this book offer *more* than information, and figuring out that "more" takes effort, time, and critical analysis.

Here are some practical strategies and suggestions for how to get the most out of the selections in this anthology:

Sound Reading Strategies

1. **Read when your concentration is at its peak.** Many people do their reading when they are tired or distracted. They read at work or during television commercials. This is fine if you are skimming for information or pleasure—reading a newspaper, magazine, or the comic page, for example—but the selections in this book demand concentration. You need to read when you are focused and full of energy, alert and clear eyed.

2. **Read for pleasure first.** During your first time through a text, read for enjoyment. Every author in this book intends to give you pleasure—to make you enjoy exploring and analyzing ideas, language, form, structure, style, arguments.

3. **Read actively, not passively.** As you read, stop occasionally and imagine what will happen on the next page or in the next section; such a process helps to involve you in the ebb and flow of the text. Stop, occasionally, to write down your prediction, your emerging interpretation, your view of why you think the author wrote this work, what its strengths and weaknesses are. Compare your responses to those of your classmates.

4. **Reread.** Read the first time for pleasure; read the second time for increased understanding. Most of the selections in this anthology present complicated ideas in complicated ways; the reader's job is to figure out what the selection means beyond the obvious. How does the writer make her/his points? What kinds of similes, metaphors, and other figurative language does the writer use? Are there contradictions and paradoxes? What choices does the writer make—and why? Are the writer's arguments convincing and well supported? These kinds of questions often can only be answered through rereading.

5. **Take notes.** Underline passages that are memorable, surprising, confusing, provocative—that provoke a personal response. Opposite each underlined passage, write a marginal comment explaining why you underlined the passage, such as:

   "What is she saying here?"
   "Why does he stumble—symbolic?"
   "Empty purse—are they also empty emotionally?"
   "This desert is real but it is also symbolic of her despair."
   "Who benefited from the slave trade?"
   "I can feel the author's love of his family here."

   These comments along with the underlinings point the way toward a good, critical essay. Most importantly, they provide a written record of thoughts and impressions, some of which you may otherwise lose.

6. **Discuss.** Although reading is a solitary activity, understanding improves when students share interpretations. All readers bring their own experiences

to a text, their own strengths, weaknesses, experiences, insights, and blind spots. Perhaps the most important aspect of discussion is learning how to listen, comprehend, and respond thoughtfully. Listening is a parallel activity to reading; it requires us to be attentive and to work hard at understanding someone else's point of view.

GETTING READY FOR CLASS DISCUSSION

Class discussion is almost always a crucial and fundamental element of a literature or composition class. Most of us both enjoy and learn better when we engage in focused, thoughtful discussion with our peers. Aside from reading and rereading the assignment, certain other habits and practices can improve the quality of class conversation. What follows are some suggestions and strategies for preparing yourself to discuss literature in this class and the others you might take.

- Bring your textbook and notes to class. This may seem like obvious common-sense advice, but surprisingly many students do not follow it. It is especially important to have the text handy when enrolled in a class that focuses on literature, because frequently in discussion students need to quote from the assigned text in order to provide support for a comment or clarify an interpretation. Since many students (and faculty, for that matter) write marginal notes in the text as they read, they have an additional reason for wanting the book handy—namely, for ready reference.
- Do not read any out-of-class assignments in class. One of the fastest ways to sour instructors is if they observe you reading the assignment at your desk rather than participating in class activities. Bring your text, have it ready, but use it only for reference or clarification, unless instructed otherwise.
- Take notes. Both lecture and class discussion often produce creative and surprising insights. They trigger important questions that can lead directly to an essay or term paper. When that happens, it is crucial to write them down so that they can be remembered and reconsidered. Some faculty have been known to stop discussion in the middle of class in order to take hurried notes on something that was said. Students should do the same. Aside from having a record of useful comments, taking notes has the added benefit of focusing one's attention more on the discussion, thus keeping the mind from wandering off while others speak.
- Listen carefully. One of the best ways to improve listening is to write down a brief, succinct summary of what someone has said once he or she has finished. This technique is, of course, a form of note-taking. As others in the class speak, good listeners work hard to understand what they are saying and how it improves understanding of the text.
- In a class that centers on literature, discussion usually does not center on factual material ("In what year did Frederick Douglass first publish his autobiography?" "Who was Mother Jones?"). That kind of information, which is very important in terms of knowledge and mastery, is usually presented in a short lecture by the instructor or is something you are expected to learn

through reading and outside research. Rather, most class discussions emphasize interpretation, analysis, and argumentation ("Consider the concept of family in Gwendolyn Brooks's poem, 'Mother.'" "What images and associations of the city does Tom Wolfe invoke in 'O Rotten Gotham'—and what effect do they have on you as a reader?"). Meaningful class discussion requires not only offering an interpretation or analysis but also providing support if others in the class disagree. When class discussion goes well, it is usually because reasonable and thoughtful readers express differing interpretations and explanations equally supported by careful textual analysis.

- Be ready to explain yourself. The key to illuminating discussions is not just offering an opinion about a work of literature; it is possessing the knowledge and information to explain it. To do this, a reader should constantly be asking "Why?" and then discovering the answer. For example, if a poem makes you feel exalted, it is important to know why and then pinpoint the language, ideas, and arguments that produce this result. Responses to literature are created through a combination of author intent, literary form and structure, social and historical contexts, the reader's personal history, and other factors. Thoughtful class participants learn how to explain themselves and their interpretations.

- Let others speak. When only the instructor or a few students dominate discussion, class soon becomes a bore. Although many instructors like to present short lectures in order to provide information efficiently, class discussion can only succeed if everyone limits his or her time and no one dominates. If you find yourself talking too much or too often, learn to love silence. Quite often, reticent students will begin to speak and participate if the "natural talkers" in the class restrain themselves.

- Be succinct. Students and teachers alike zone out when someone makes the same point repeatedly. Once you say it, don't repeat it. To say the same thing again and again is boring and repetitious—even redundant—even when there is slight variation. Like this paragraph.

- Focus. As you read an assignment, you may discover an interpretation or come up with questions. If so, write them out and bring them with you to class. Many instructors will welcome such written comments and provide class time for discussing them.

- Change the perspective from which you read and interpret the assignment. Put yourself in the place of the author: try to think why she wrote it, what she intended, why she made specific choices. Insert yourself in the role of a character or even that of a reviewer or critic. Write down your comments for use in class.

- Remember that not all interpretations or analyses are equally persuasive or insightful, but that does not mean they lack value, at least to the individual who offers them. This does not mean that anything goes; rather, that interpretation and analysis is a negotiation involving the reader, the author, the text, the class, historical circumstance, and the world of literary criticism. One of the major purposes of class discussion is to provide students and instructors with a rich and reasonable forum in which to test their hypotheses and participate in a collaborative give-and-take about meaning and understanding.

THE WRITING PROCESS

Preliminary Steps

Different writers write differently, and all writers must strive to find the composing process that best suits their needs. Professional writers demonstrate the diversity of composing processes. John McPhee, for example, plans extensively and creates an elaborate structure for his essays and books. This planning process can be extremely laborious, but once he develops the structure (which might take days, weeks, or longer), it provides a framework for the actual writing (and rewriting) that follows. When Jamaica Kincaid writes, she often spends a great deal of time deliberating and choosing. She might write down just one word in an hour, but once that word is on paper she knows it is the right one and seldom if ever changes it. Richard Selzer writes out of a sense almost of compulsion. He pours out many pages of prose every day longhand in his notebooks, only a small fraction of which ever makes its way to print. None of these writers would choose to follow the composing process of any other; what they do works for them.

The pages that follow offer a variety of approaches to writing, not all of which are likely to work for any one student. Even the order is somewhat arbitrary; my "Step One" might be someone else's "Step Four." What all writers must do is experiment, particularly if they are having trouble writing or are not achieving desired results. Although there is no one right way to write, there are wrong ways that can get someone stuck and frustrated. All writers, however, can alter their ways of composing and make the process more efficient and productive; it just takes time, practice, and the will to change.

Step One: Establish a Sense of Purpose

Frequently, instructors establish an outcome for their students in the assignment itself. For example:

> Analyze the metaphors that Barry Lopez uses to describe wilderness in his essay "The Stone Horse." In your essay, be sure to cite at least three metaphors and discuss their appropriateness to his themes of tenderness and fragility.

This instructor wants students to analyze Lopez's use of metaphors and offer reasons why they are—or are not—appropriate to two major themes in his work. Some students might prefer to write personal responses, but however satisfying to the writer, they are unlikely to fulfill the instructor's purpose (and will probably receive a poor grade).

Some instructors assign essays that allow more individual choice:

> Respond to Tillie Olsen's "I Stand Here Ironing." Can you relate your own experiences as either a parent or a child to this fictional monologue? In your essay, be sure to discuss who this speaker is—that is, describe in your own terms the speaker's values, feelings, and sense of self. Your essay should be at least 600 words, typed, and should include quotations from the story to support your interpretation.

This assignment asks students to present a written response, without specifying content. Students can write a personal reflection or an impersonal analysis, but they must analyze the speaker of the story in an essay of at least 600 typed words and include appropriate supporting quotations.

Whatever the assignment, students need to establish their own sense of purpose and commitment to their readers. Otherwise the writing becomes perfunctory.

Step Two: Analyze Your Audience's Expectations

Although audiences can vary, in most cases you will write essays that will be read by your instructor. My focus will thus be on writing for the teacher. Knowing that an essay is intended for an instructor does not necessarily help you successfully address this audience. What is more important is that your work satisfy the instructor's expectations. How can you accomplish this? Here are some suggestions.

- Study the assignment carefully and make sure that you understand what the instructor is asking you to do. Look for key words and phrases, especially those that are underlined or in boldface. Most assignments clearly state the instructor's expectations.
- Stuck? Then visit your instructor. A short conversation with an instructor can both clarify the situation and bolster confidence.
- Determine whether your instructor wants your essay to be a demonstration of knowledge (a synthesis of class discussion, an informed discussion of the ways a particular theory applies to a particular set of readings); a factual presentation (historical, biographical, a report); an interpretation (what a work means, why a student believes the meaning of the text to be "X"); an appreciation (why this work is so powerful and enduring); or something else. Asking detailed questions about expectations either in class or during an instructor's office hours is essential.
- Consider the assignment a form of conversation, of dialogue with the instructor. An essay offers each student an opportunity to have the instructor's exclusive attention. Successful essays engage readers because they bring a writer and reader together; they are a medium for the exchange of ideas.
- Try to state something new. Think of your audience as someone who is willing to try out your ideas and be surprised and informed by what you have to say. Instructors enjoy having their understanding and appreciation of a literary work enhanced because of something a student has written.
- Avoid plot summary. Because they want to learn something when they read student essays, most instructors do not like plot summary. When writing, assume that the reader already has read the work you are discussing. Plot summary is usually a surefire way to bore a reader—and write a pedestrian essay in the process.

Step Three: Draw On Your Resources

Student Resource List:

- conversations with other students in the class or others who have an interest in the topic

- the local Writing Center, where tutors can help you think through your subject, goals, possibilities, frustrations, structure, focus, and all the other aspects of writing
- the instructor, who is one of the best resources for getting comfortable with a topic and figuring out the best way to proceed
- the library research database, where you can look up primary material (that is, other works that the author has written, historical materials composed at the same time as the subject you are writing about) or secondary sources (books and articles written about your subject)
- electronic conversations over the Internet
- Web pages, which can be particularly helpful if you are researching a contemporary subject

Step Four: Start Early

The time to start writing an essay is immediately after an instructor hands out an assignment. The worst case scenario is to delay the writing until the day before it is due. To put it bluntly, this is a prescription for disaster.

Good ideas need to simmer. They need to be reflected upon, revised, researched, and explored. This takes time. Delay often results in ill-conceived work. Waiting too long to start can create a host of problems for writers, including: disliking what one has written but not having the time to change it; discovering that essential research materials are missing, stolen, or otherwise out of circulation; getting sick or stuck; or even deciding that one's argument no longer makes sense. There is no reason to have to create a panic situation every time a writing assignment is given.

Instead, good writers start early. That way, if something goes wrong, as it inevitably does in some situations, there is time to make adjustments.

Step Five: Share

Most professional writers share their work as they write: they produce a page or two, bring that work home, and read it to someone they trust to give an honest response. Students need to share their writing as well, and many instructors will create that possibility by setting up a rough draft workshop in the classroom or by reading drafts. Many times, an outside reader (not a roommate, spouse, or parent) can best tell a writer when an essay is making sense, where more support is needed, where the work is gaining or losing focus. Such readings can make a huge difference in the success of an essay; almost always, they provide a valuable road map for revision. Take advantage of this opportunity; it can make a world of difference.

Step Six: Revise

Virtually all successful writers spend the great majority of their time not drafting but revising, not writing but rewriting. In general, writing an essay is messy: It demands that writers explore a variety of ideas, go off on various tangents, explore various research sources, find appropriate examples and quotations, etc. As you write at this early stage, it is important not to spend much time editing and revising. Writing at this drafting stage should lead you forward; editing and revising are activities that require you constantly to look backward.

Only after you have finally produced a significant mass of words and ideas is it time to start pulling your essay together. This is revision: refocusing, deleting the unnecessary and repetitious, finding additional examples, cutting and pasting (using the computer, I hope), refining the essay so that it achieves its purpose. Sometimes revision means substantially changing the original; sometimes it means throwing out everything but two or three sentences! Whatever form it takes, revision is almost always the key to producing successful final essays.

Step Seven: Work Appropriately

At different points in the writing process, some kinds of attention are appropriate and others ill-advised. It is important to recognize that a first or second draft of an essay is just that: a draft. It is likely to have a variety of problems with focus, word usage, syntax, support, and other elements. Early in the composing process, writers need to concentrate on global issues: organization, development, finding examples, crafting the overall shape and scope of the essay. There is no sense editing and correcting sentences that may not make it into the final version. It makes no sense spell checking, correcting subject-verb agreement, or clarifying every phrase in the first draft. Instead, experienced writers focus on big ticket items such as building coherence or developing a cogent argument.

Only after a reasonably good draft has been achieved should you edit line by line for usage, correctness, and word choice. Correcting and editing are very important functions, but they should occur only when the writing is close to being finished.

GETTING STARTED

Many writers have trouble getting started; they defer the writing, often until too late. Then they do a poor job, excusing themselves because they ran out of time. Sometimes they sit down to write but run out of steam after a few paragraphs: the essay lacks focus; everything written down seems dumb or obvious; the essay is too general and vague; the room is too hot; the paper is too white; the pencils are too sharp or not sharp enough. Almost all writers, even professional authors who make their living selling what they produce, have trouble at times getting started. John McPhee, who has written over twenty nonfiction books on sports, geology, wilderness, and many other topics, had so much trouble getting started early in his career that he would go into his office and tie himself into his chair with his bathrobe sash to force himself to get words down on paper. Although tying yourself to your chair may be an excellent technique, here are some less drastic strategies that can help.

Keep a reading log. Marginal notation is an excellent strategy, but many students want their notes and commentary collected in one place rather than distributed in the white space of various textbooks. They use a reading log, which is a written record of their interpretations, questions, and concerns. Your instructor may assign you to keep such a log or journal because it has proven to be so helpful to many students. To be successful, a log must be used consistently, at least three entries per week. When an essay is assigned, a reading log can become a great resource, since it is a repository of ideas and personal responses.

A typical entry might look like the following:

"The Horse"

I loved this poem. The horse is described as being so fluid, so full of power. But I don't understand why its hooves flash "blood red" in the last stanza. Why blood? Nor am I clear as to why it is "eternally riderless." After all, it is the "horseman's desire."

Rhythm. There's a kind of klop/klop rhythm to the lines, especially the last line of each stanza. Or am I imagining it?

Is this in some kind of form—like a sonnet? It isn't 14 lines, so that's not right—but I wonder if this is some form I should know (ask instructor) . . .

I'd love to write about the ways that this horse stands for freedom. Am I reading that into the poem? I don't think so. Freedom is mentioned in line 4 and once again in lines 15 and 26. That has to mean something, I think. . . .

As you can see, this is mostly a response that describes the feelings of the writer—as well as her ideas, confusions, and maybe even a possible essay topic. Even if this student does not choose to write about "The Horse," she is engaging in the kind of close and active reading that will help her throughout this course and beyond.

Write a letter, not an essay. Most writers find it much easier to write a personal letter than an essay. The reasons are fairly obvious: they know and like their audience; the letter is informal; they are used to writing in this format; they can usually find a congenial style for themselves; etc. Some students write their essay as a letter addressed to a friend or close relative, explaining why it is important to write about this story or poem, or why they are uncomfortable and then what it is they would like to say about this topic in an essay. Even though the letter is a fiction, writing it can be a great way to make that initial leap into the topic.

Create writing rituals. Like any sustained activity, writing can be hard to start unless it becomes part of another set of actions. In order to wash the car, for example, a person might gather together clean cloths, fill a pail with soapy water, park the car at the curb, and bring out the garden hose. Washing the car becomes an inevitable result of those preparations.

Writing benefits from the same kinds of ritualized activities. One writer gathers her research materials, reads them over several times, cleans off her desk, turns on her computer, and makes some notes about how she will structure her writing for the day. Other writers have other actions they must perform to write: they make a fresh pot of coffee, put on a certain baseball cap, take a dessert out of the freezer and leave it as a reward for a certain amount of writing (of course, the latter ritual can produce both pages and pounds). A friend of mine takes his laptop every weekday morning to a local coffeehouse, finds a quiet table, and writes for two hours; somehow he finds that ritual more productive than coming into the office where he gets distracted by mail, phone calls, and personal visits from me.

Productive writers discover or create rituals that get them in the mood for writing, that lead them toward pen and paper or the computer. Once you have devised such rituals, they can lead you toward writing.

Use index cards or some easily organizable form of note-taking. Many writers keep track of different ideas, quotations, references, and other pertinent information by listing each as a single entry so that they all can be stored and rearranged. Copying quotations and taping them on cards is one handy technique; another is using the computer to create and organize files, which then can be easily printed out during the drafting process. Each card should include not only a quotation or idea but also source information about where it was found.

Write before writing. Professor Donald Murray, a well-known writer and teacher, advocated that students "write before writing"—and this is excellent advice. How do you do that? One of the best strategies is to purchase a small notebook that fits handily in purse or pocket. As you read, think, and research about your assignments, write down ideas, insights, fragments, potential topics, words, quotations, and snatches of relevant conversations. Use the material in that notebook to jump-start your essay.

Try freewriting. Other writers use the technique of freewriting or quick writing to get started. First, of course, they have to do the necessary reading, rereading, and research. Once they possess some knowledge and ideas, they write nonstop for 10 or more minutes, not worrying about spelling, correctness, transitions, or even coherence. The purpose is to get ideas and sentences on paper; once that is done, the writer organizes, cuts and pastes, develops some ideas and discards others. Freewriting is an excellent way to write before writing, especially since it is low stress and produces a lot of words. Some writers begin their writing process this way, and then use successive and more focused freewritings to create later and longer drafts of an essay. Freewriting usually cannot be used to write a final draft, but with practice, this technique can help a writer get quite far along in the drafting process.

THE ELEMENTS OF A SUCCESSFUL ESSAY

Although there are many different kinds of essays, most of the good ones share certain features.

1. **A main point.** Most successful essays drive toward a central conclusion or major insight. It really does not matter if the essay is an appreciation, a critique, an argument, or a close reading: it collects around a main point like iron filings around a magnet. For example, let's say I am writing about William Stafford's poem "Traveling Through the Dark." After multiple readings, two entries in my reading log, and one freewriting, I begin to glimpse what makes this poem moving and powerful to me. I write a "discovery" draft, toward the end of which I compose the following sentence that defines my main point and thus becomes my thesis:

   "Traveling Through the Dark" is therefore a powerful poem that holds a central contradiction: it is a celebration of life that describes the poet's act of destroying the life of an innocent fawn. I think it reveals the speaker as tender and compassionate, perhaps in contrast to the unnamed, unseen other driver who first hit the doe.

   This is enough of a start for an essay because it is making a significant point that I can now develop over the course of an essay.

Please note: Not every writer knows the main point when first starting an essay. Oftentimes, writers discover their main point during the composing process. Thus good writers do not worry if they begin to write without a main point; if they are completing the assignment and still do not know their main point, however, that usually means real trouble.

2. **Specificity.** A successful essay examines a work of literature by analyzing a particular theme, meaning, image, use of language, argument, or interpretation. Too often, beginning writers attempt general and grandiose themes or generalized statements; they try to write, for example, about "the genius of Edward Abbey" or "That Perfect Poetic Form: The Ballad." Although there is much that can be said about both topics, they are too vague as stated to be covered in a short essay; indeed, they are more appropriate for entire books. An essay needs to examine more specific topics: *What Edward Abbey means by "the Hoboken mystique" in his essay "Manhattan Twilight, Hoboken Night"* or *A Bittersweet Play of Voices in Langston Hughes's "Ballad of the Landlord."* An essay on either of these more focused topics is more likely to succeed.

3. **Complexity.** Good essays lock in on a complex subject and develop it thoughtfully. In general, this means that an essay must pursue a subject that is not superficially obvious to the most casual reader. To look for insights beyond the obvious, a writer must examine a work of literature for contradictions and paradox. Many literary authors use contradiction and paradox to put a spin on their creations. Theodore Roethke's "My Papa's Waltz," for example, is a poem that can be read simultaneously as a loving tribute and as a cry for help. Which interpretation is correct? Most critics would say that the poem can and should be read both ways at once, that it represents the complex and contradictory feelings a young boy has toward his father.

To achieve complexity, then, writers must be willing to explore seeming contradiction and not be afraid to take risks; they must be willing to explore questions that have no right answer. For example, to return to "Traveling Through the Dark," a student might at first compose the following focus sentence:

"Traveling Through the Dark" is a terrific poem because it is about a man in the wilderness.

This statement, though perhaps true, does not offer a writer any real purchase on a topic worth writing about. It is not very specific and does not offer a complex view of the poem. Why is the poem terrific? What is meant by "terrific"? Is every poem about a man and wilderness terrific? Other than finding a lot of different ways to repeat this main point, there is not much that can be said that would fill more than a page or so of text. This topic does not allow a very complicated or insightful essay to be written. After some struggle, this writer reformulates her main point as follows:

"Traveling Through the Dark" is about literal and figurative darkness, about the darkness of night and the darkness of death.

This statement is more specific, and it offers a thoughtful and complex interpretation of "darkness," an important image in this poem. The statement may need to be refined further, but it offers a useful starting point.

4. **Examples and illustrations.** Almost always, successful essays incorporate many examples, illustrative quotations, and statements that prove the point(s) that the writer is making. In English Studies, most successful essays put forward assertions that then have to be proven and supported. They move from the general to the specific and back again, weaving the particular constantly into the fabric of the overall argument. Clearly one of the most important ways to achieve this end is to use quotations, examples, and particular citations for support. Just as an economist uses statistics, a writer of essays about literature must nail down insights with an appropriate use of specific quotations. Quotes from the primary text (the actual work of literature being studied) or from secondary texts (criticism, history, biography, etc.) illustrate the points being made and persuade readers that the author knows what he or she is talking about. They also can inspire a writer to dig deeper into the meaning of a work of literature.

5. **Coherence.** All readers have formal expectations when they read. Although different in various cultures, these formal expectations guide readers and help them to understand what the writer is doing. They allow readers to anticipate where the writer is headed, a very important dimension to successful interaction between readers and writers. Typically, in United States higher education, successful essays have a beginning, middle, and end in some formal sense. They exhibit logical transitions between the various parts of the essay. They provide the reader with a sense of wholeness and completion. Typically, a formal essay will:

- articulate a main point
- illustrate and exemplify that main point through several pages that develop and explore the theme of the essay through the use of analysis, appropriate quotation, assertions, insights
- conclude by offering possibilities for additional exploration, returning to the image or argument presented at the beginning of the essay, summarizing and extending what has already been stated, or otherwise creating a sense of completion

6. **Style.** Instructors generally enjoy reading essays that express the voice, personal commitment, and investment of the writer—what we typically call "style." Style cannot be located in any one element; rather, it consists of a writer's individual perspective, phrasing, word choice, sentence construction, creation of paragraphs, organization, even formatting (font, type size, illustrations, spacing, etc.).

One of the most important aspects of style is word and sentence variety. Successful writing keeps readers interested not just because of ideas, examples, and coherence but also because of language use that pleases, surprises, and delights. Here is an example of a passage that has a lot of repetition and not much sentence variety:

Theodore Roethke's "My Papa's Waltz" is a powerful poem. It is a poem that draws its power from its theme of love and fear. The poem is written from the point of view of a young boy. The title of the poem . . .

This passage is likely to bore a reader because the sentences all have a similar subject-verb structure, use many of the same words, and express little sense of style. It is acceptable to write such sentences in a first draft, but once a writer starts moving toward the final draft, an improved version that achieves much more sentence variation is needed:

A powerful poem, Theodore Roethke's "My Papa's Waltz" expresses the love—and fear—that a young boy feels for his father. As is made clear from the title of the poem . . .

This revised version consolidates the sentences, cuts out the repetition of words ("is," "power," "of"), and expresses more vividly the stylistic personality of the writer. Successful writers create word and sentence variety in order to enhance their style.

Another key aspect to creating a successful style is not to overreach. That is, one of the worst decisions a writer can make is to refer constantly to a thesaurus while writing or to otherwise insert words and phrases that "sound good" because they are long, Latinate, or unfamiliar. A thesaurus is an excellent tool to rediscover a synonym that has slipped out of memory, but you should not use it to replace a familiar word with one you do not know. For example, a writer might state that he has "a great deal of empathy for a character's situation." But with the help of a thesaurus, he might revise that sentence to read that he has "a surfeit of vicarious emotion for a character's locale." Although brimming with excellent words, the second sentence makes little sense and sounds as though its author is living in the wrong century. It is far better to use words you know and can control.

7. **Correctness.** Correctness is easy to define but difficult to achieve: It consists of getting everything right. English instructors in particular urge their students to aim for correctness as part of what they do; after all, they are the educational caretakers of sentence structure, research format, spelling, grammar, and diction. Many writers have a difficult time achieving correctness on their own; they need the help of an outside reader (such as a tutor) to help them see error patterns or other areas where their essay needs to be edited and refashioned into standard academic English.

One of the best ways to get help with correctness is to go to the course instructor, who can provide professional help. Another good strategy is to buy a good handbook and then use it. Most handbooks have sections on grammar, usage, computers, footnoting, and other writing considerations. If a student possesses the motivation and knowledge to use such a handbook, it can be a great resource.

Here is a brief checklist that can help determine if an essay is ready to be handed in.

THE WRITER'S CHECKLIST

____ Essay has a title.

____ Writer's name is included on all the pages.

____ Spelling has been checked.

____ Footnotes are in proper form as determined by instructor.

____ Sentence structure has been checked, especially for fragments, run-on sentences, and comma splices (to obtain definitions of these terms, consult a handbook, or see instructor or Writing Center tutor).

____ Essay has been typed or completed on a word processor.

____ Pages are numbered.

____ Print is double-spaced with one-inch margins around all four borders.

____ Essay has been read carefully by a Writing Center tutor or some other informed and attentive reader.

____ Essay has been read carefully by the author at least one day after "finishing" it.

____ Quotation marks, semicolons, and colons are used properly and consistently (again, consult a handbook, or see instructor or Writing Center tutor).

____ Essay includes sufficient supporting material, such as quotations, examples, and narrative summaries.

A NOTE ABOUT USING COMPUTERS FOR WRITING AND RESEARCH

Another important resource is a computer. Students who know keyboarding and are familiar with word-processing programs (such as Microsoft Word or WordPerfect) have a strong advantage over those students who use less versatile technologies. Word processors allow writers to produce words relatively quickly and then revise them more easily. With the "copy" and "cut and paste" functions on a computer, basic revision becomes easy, as long as the writer has a good sense of the essay's structure, purpose, and overall organization. A good word-processing program can make a lot of editing easy, from spell-checking to formatting headers, footnotes, and page numbers.

Any writer who uses a computer to write an essay must *BACK THAT ESSAY UP CONTINUOUSLY* on a floppy disk during the entire writing process; too many tragedies occur when computers stall or otherwise eat up hours of work. Few events are more frustrating to a writer, especially one under deadline, than to write three or four effective paragraphs and then suddenly find that the computer has stalled or that the word-processing program has crashed. The only remedy is to SAVE the writing to a floppy disk continuously during composing.

Once an essay is on disk, a good word-processing program can make a lot of work easier, such as:

- adding and deleting sentences, paragraphs, ideas
- moving words and whole passages for improved focus and clarity
- revising passages until they are focused and coherent

- checking spelling (but be careful of misused words that are spelled correctly)
- making final copy look more presentable by formatting an essay in terms of margins, spacing, typeface, and related elements
- printing out rough drafts

Most writers who use computers agree that essays in progress should not just exist in virtual space, on screen. For one thing, a computer screen can hold only a small portion of the essay, even if it is single-spaced, making it hard to see how the different parts of the essay connect with one another. For another, many writers have a difficult time seeing errors or lapses on screen; somehow, the monitor display makes all writing look professionally presentable. Thus most writers find that they have to print out successive drafts of their essays; indeed, some of them revise the essay on paper the old-fashioned way, with pen, pencil, or scissors and paste, and then translate those revisions to the text via computer. Whatever revision method a writer chooses, printing drafts of the essay on paper is almost always a good idea.

Engaging in research on the World Wide Web via computer is much less beneficial, at least as of this writing, but it can be fun and it offers a dazzling array of images, texts, ideas, opinions, and information. To view material on the Web, users have to use a browser, the two chief competitors being Netscape's Navigator and Microsoft's Internet Explorer. The term "browser" is perfect for what these software programs do: They allow users to browse through an extraordinary array of verbal, audio, and visual presentations, from restaurant reviews and music CD catalogs to mapping programs and hobbyist bulletin boards. The materials available through the Web are seemingly infinite, but most of them are aimed toward the casual and commercial user.

The Web is much less useful to the student engaged in specific and narrow research on an author. Few long textual works have been scanned electronically, although there are sites that allow a user to access some classic works of literature, as well as dictionaries, thesauruses, handbooks, and the like. If a reader is looking for scholarly articles, however, the first and best resource is still the library. The library's electronic databases, including the Wilson Periodical Index, the PMLA Index, ERIC, and the Humanities Index, to name just a few, are extraordinarily rich electronic treasure-troves.

Starting one's research with the computer by accessing library databases, the Internet, or the Web is an excellent way to initiate a project. Using search engines and search commands, a writer can build a useful bibliography of names, articles, and periodicals; the next step is to make use of the library stacks and spend some time reading the scholarship the old-fashioned way, in books, magazines, and journals. The mode of doing scholarship may change, but it is unlikely that the print medium will be replaced by the digitized computer file, if only because it is easier both to read longer texts on paper and to write marginal notes about them. The other great advantage that books have is that they are not battery operated and do not have to be plugged in, a real plus when on the bus or at the beach.

REFERENCE AND CITATION

One of the most frustrating moments in writing a research essay is discovering that you cannot find where a crucial quotation comes from. Almost always, it seems, that quotation is the I-beam on which the entire essay hangs, and no matter where you look, it has totally disappeared from sight. You vaguely remember that it came from an article but that's all, and now you need to know author, title, periodical, year and date of publication, and page number. So you spend an hour searching desperately through books, note cards, legal pads, computer files, bookshelves, desktops, brief-cases, and wastebaskets while methodically beating your head against the nearest hard object.

There is no surefire way to prevent this from happening, other than careful researching. Each time you find a quotation or important item of source material, write it down, including essential information such as author, title, and page num-ber; that way, you will almost always be able to find it again if you need to cite it. Thus every note card or piece of paper with a quotation should have a brief refer-ence on it indicating where it came from. In addition, using either a copying machine, a word processor, or the old-fashioned pen and paper method, make sure you have all the necessary bibliographic material that you need to write a "Works Cited" page, something that I will discuss shortly. This means creating a separate file or folder where you keep full bibliographic information on all your sources. Researched essays require students to perform three related actions: to quote sources, to provide appropriate references for those sources, and then to indicate on a Works Cited page where those quotations can be found. Let's take these steps in order.

Quoting Sources

Whenever you are indebted to an author for a specific quotation, specific informa-tion, or a particular insight or idea, it is necessary to give that author credit through quotation and citation. This means that you have to know the difference between the knowledge gained through research and "common knowledge," which is what most people are expected to know. For example, if you were writing an essay about Amy Tan and you indicated that she is a popular contemporary author, such a state-ment would not need to be footnoted since it is common knowledge. If, however, you stated that she was born in 1952 in Oakland, California, and that both her par-ents are from China, you would need to indicate that you learned that information from, say, *Contemporary Authors*, since it is not general knowledge. Deciding what information you need to reference and what is common knowledge is a judgment call, one that your instructor can help you to determine. Remember, however, that if you are deeply indebted to an author for information or an interpretation, you need to state that in a footnote or a parenthetical citation.

The two primary ways of quoting material are through direct quotation and paraphrase. Direct quotation consists of putting specific words, phrases, or sen-tences within quotation marks followed by a parenthetical citation. For example:

In her autobiographical talk-story "White Tigers," Maxine Hong

Kingston writes: "My American life has been such a disappointment"

(45).

Note that the quotation from Kingston's essay/story appears in quotation marks and that it is followed by a parenthetical page citation so that the reader can turn to p. 45 in the cited book and find the quotation. The particular edition from which this quotation is taken will appear on the Works Cited page that appears at the end of every research essay. Whenever directly quoting an author or work, this kind of format is needed.

Indirect quotation is a bit trickier, in that it requires writers to decide whether the passage or idea that they are using is derived from a specific text or is common knowledge. If the idea or information is derived from a specific text, then it needs to be cited. For example:

> Many of us attribute great and even mystical powers to our mothers. This is certainly the case with Maxine Hong Kingston, who endows her mother with supernatural powers within a world of ghosts and dark spirits as illustrated in "Shaman" (The Woman Warrior 57-109).

Even though the writer is not quoting directly from the book, this statement is derived from a reading of Kingston's story "Shaman," and therefore a citation is required. Whether the writer paraphrases an interpretation, summarizes the writer's life, or condenses several articles into a two- or three-sentence review, if the idea derives from a book or article, parenthetical citation is required.

Using Footnotes and Parenthetical Citation

Many of the newer word processors have a footnote feature which will organize, number, and format your footnotes. This is a useful aid, especially since footnotes are often hard to format. Unfortunately, many contemporary research essays (at least in English classes) do not require formal footnoting. About the only occasion when students are required to use them is if they need to comment on a statement or source and do not wish to put that comment in the main body of the essay, or if the essay is quoting from just one source and thus it is easier to cite it in a footnote than on an entire page at the end of the essay. Check with your instructor to see if footnoting will be required.

The more common form of citation used today is parenthetical; that is, the citation is inserted between two parentheses as demonstrated in the quotations from *The Woman Warrior*. Parenthetical citation is advocated by the Modern Language Association, since it is efficient for both writers and readers. Footnotes drag a reader's eye down to the bottom of the page and break the flow of the text; parenthetical citations maintain the flow of the essay while providing necessary information about sources, page numbers, and research. Moreover, it is much easier for writers to use parenthetical citation since they do not have to worry about numbering their references in sequence and fitting them onto the page.

Parenthetical citation is formatted in slightly different ways, depending on whether the quotation appears within your sentence or as a block that is separated from your own writing. Note the differences below:

One of the more important genres that have recently received critical and popular attention are the narratives of slaves. One of the earliest and most influential collections of those narratives is <u>The Classic Slave Narratives</u> edited by Henry Louis Gates. Gates makes a good case for why these texts were created:

> The black slave narrators sought to indict both those who enslaved them and the metaphysical system drawn upon to justify their enslavement. They did so using the most enduring weapon at their disposal, the printing press. (ix)

Thus what we can see in the narratives is an account of the life they led as slaves, an account which by virtue of its own telling condemns the system of values that supports slavery for the sake of economic gain.

Note certain key conventions: Because the quotation is two or more sentences long, it gets set off in a block. Because it is set off, it does not need quotation marks around it. The page from which the quotation is taken appears at the very end within parentheses, after any end punctuation.

Here is a different version of the same student essay. In this case, the author is using only a part of the Gates quotation and is thus using internal parenthetical citation. It is called "internal" because the citation occurs within the student's own sentences:

One of the more important genres that have recently received critical and popular attention are the narratives of slaves. One of the earliest and most influential collections of those narratives is <u>The Classic Slave Narratives</u> edited by Henry Louis Gates. Gates makes a good case for why these texts were created, since he believes that the authors "sought to indict both those who enslaved them and the metaphysical system drawn upon to justify their enslavement" (ix). By that Gates means that what we can see in the narratives is an account of the life they led as slaves, an account which by virtue of its own telling condemns the system of values that supports slavery for the sake of economic gain.

Note the differences: Here the quotation is short, being less than a full sentence; thus it can be easily integrated into the student author's own paragraph. The page number still is cited, but now, since the citation occurs within the student's own sentence, it must be followed by a period since it ends a sentence.

Here is one more example of internal parenthetical citation:

> In his Introduction to <u>The Classic Slave Narratives</u>, Henry Louis Gates writes that the slaves wanted to be "free and literate" (ix) and that is why they told their powerful and terrible stories. I agree, but only in part: I think we have to be equally aware that the slaves told these stories as a profound way of coming to terms with an experience that virtually defies language.

This internal parenthetical citation immediately follows the quotation it references, and no punctuation marks surround it since they would interfere with the grammar of the sentence.

Internal parenthetical citation provides necessary reference information with as little obstruction as possible. Thus it does not include abbreviations such as "p." for page or "2nd ed." for second edition; all the necessary bibliographic information goes onto the "Works Cited" page so that the reader can locate your sources. If you are citing a poem, your instructor will likely want your parenthetical reference to include line numbers; if citing a play, you will need to include act, scene, and line so that your instructor can find the quotation easily. Such inclusions follow the rule of thumb for parenthetical references: Include only the information a reader will need to find the quotation easily, neither more nor less.

Providing Full References: The "Works Cited" Page

Once you have filled in all the appropriate parenthetical citations, it is time to complete the project by writing a "Works Cited" page. Just as its name suggests, the "Works Cited" page is a bibliographic list that allows the reader to track down the specific books, articles, magazines, films, and other resources you cite in your essay.

No short guide can provide a complete list of proper forms; indeed, the Modern Language Association, to name just one such group, publishes an entire book devoted to forms and formats for references and bibliographies (see Joseph Gibaldi and Walter S. Achtert, *MLA Handbook for Writers of Research Papers*, 4th ed. [New York: MLA, 1995]). What I will include here is a brief listing of the more common forms for books, articles, periodicals, short works of literature, film, TV, and newspapers. These forms should provide proper formatting for most of the research sources that you will use.

Titles on the "Works Cited" page should be arranged alphabetically according to the first letter of the author's or editor's last name. You need only include the texts you actually cite; if for some reason you want to include every book or article that you read while researching your essay, even if you did not use all of them, title your page "List of Works Consulted," but first check with your instructor. You can use the model entries in the pages that follow to put your entries in the correct format. The entries do not correspond to real authors or real books or articles (for the most part), but the form (and explanations) should prove useful.

One last suggestion: even when an essay has proper references and a full "Works Cited" page, it is often helpful to the reader if the author opens with an Acknowl-edgments page. You can find a model in many scholarly books: the author begins her or his book by thanking those people who have helped in the formation of ideas, the reading of drafts, the revision of sentences. If your instructor allows it, writing an Acknowledgments page that leads off your essay can help establish the context for the essay that you have produced, and it is an excellent way to say thank you to those students, staff members, and faculty who have helped you produce it, from conception to final draft.

SAMPLE CITATIONS FOR "WORKS CITED" FROM AN ESSAY ON LITERATURE AND CULTURE

A single book by a single author:

Auteur, Robin. Literature and Culture. New York: Knopf, 1997.

Note the order: author's name (last name first); then the title of the book, under-lined, except for the final period. Then the place of publication, followed by a colon (if the city is not well known, include the state abbreviation as well. If the title page lists several cities, give only the first, as in Portsmouth, N.H., or Fargo, N.D.). Then the name of the publisher, followed by a comma. And then the year of publication.

A single book by two or more authors:

Auteur, Robin, and Chang Lee. Literature and Culture. Columbus, Ohio:

   Ohio State UP, 1949.

The first author appears with last name first, then the second author follows with first name first. If the book has more than three authors, give the name of the first author only (last name first) and follow it with "et al." (Latin for "and others"). The phrase "University Press" is abbreviated as "UP" for the sake of efficiency.

A book in several volumes:

Auteur, Robin, et al., eds. Literature and Culture. 4th ed. 3 vols.

   Chicago: Gilead UP, 1998.

Note that "eds." here means "editors" and not "edited by." The abbreviation "eds." always means "editors," whereas "ed." can mean "edition," "editor," or "edited by," depending on its context.

Auteur, Robin. Literature and Culture. 11 vols. Ed. Chang Lee.

   Columbia, S.C.: Wellman, 1955.

You will need to indicate the total number of volumes after the title. If you have used more than one volume, you can indicate which one as follows: (3:30), which means you are referring to page 30 of volume 3. If you have used only one volume of a multivolume work, in your entry in Works Cited indicate the volume number right after the period following the date, e.g., "Wellman, 1955. Vol. 2." You need only include the page reference in your parenthetical citations since readers will know all examples come from volume 2 when they consult the "Works Cited" page.

A book with a separate title in a set of volumes:

Auteur, Robin. <u>Literature and Culture</u>. Vol. 1 of <u>Encyclopedia of</u>

    <u>Literature and Culture</u>. New York: Balloon, 1994.

Auteur, Robin. <u>Literature and Culture</u>. Ed. Chang Lee. Vol. 113 of <u>The</u>

    <u>Literature and Culture Reader</u>. Princeton: Princeton UP, 1988.

A revised edition of a book:

Auteur, Robin. <u>Literature and Culture</u>. Rev. ed. Hamburg, Germany:

    Berlin UP, 1974.

Auteur, Robin. <u>Literature and Culture</u>. Ed. Chang Lee. 5th ed. Norfolk:

    Harcourt, 1997.

A reprint of an earlier edition:

Auteur, Robin. <u>Literature and Culture</u>. 1911. Ellis, Iowa: Central UP,

    1993.

Note that the author is citing the original date (1911) but indicates that the writer is using the Iowa Central University Press reprint published in 1993.

An edited book other than an anthology:

Auteur, Robin. <u>Literature and Culture</u>. Ed. Chang Lee. 4 vols.

    Cambridge, MA: Harvard UP, 1969.

An anthology:

<u>Literature and Culture</u>. Ed. Robin Auteur. 12 vols. Monrovia, La.:

    Literature and Culture Books, 1918.

Or:

Auteur, Robin, ed. <u>Literature and Culture</u>. 12 vols. Monrovia, La.:

    Literature and Culture Books, 1918.

Note that you have two choices: You can list it either by title or by editor.

A work by one author in a multivolume anthology:

Auteur, Robin. "Critical Studies." <u>Literature and Culture</u>. Ed. Chang

    Lee. 5th ed. 3 vols. New York: Farrar, 1997. 3:145-98.

This entry indicates that you are citing Auteur's essay, entitled "Critical Studies," which appears in volume 3 of a three-volume anthology entitled *Literature and Culture,* edited by Chang Lee. Note that the page numbers of Auteur's complete essay are cited.

A work in an anthology that includes a number of authors:

Auteur, Robin. "Critical Studies." <u>Literature and Culture</u>. Ed. Chang

    Lee. Fargo, N.D.: Houghton, 1988. 243-76.

Start by listing the author and the title of the work you are citing, not the title of the anthology or the name of the editor. The entry ends by citing the pages of the selection you are citing. Note that the title of the short work you are citing is in quotation marks; if it is a long work (book length), the title is underlined. If the work is translated, after the period that follows the title, write "Trans." and give the name of the translator, followed by a period and then the name of the anthology.

Citing other works in the same anthology:

Auteur, Robin. <u>Literature and Culture</u>. Lee 301-46.

To avoid repetition, under each author's name (in the appropriate alphabetical order), list the author, the title of the work, then a period, one space, and the name of the editor of the anthology, followed by the page numbers for the selection.

Two or more works by the same author:

Auteur, Robin. <u>Critical Studies</u>. Boulder, Colo.: U of Harriman P,

    1948.

---. <u>Literature and Culture</u>. Seattle: Jacob H. Library, 1955.

Note that the works are given in alphabetical order on the "Works Cited" page, so that *Critical Studies* comes before *Literature and Culture.* In the second listing, the author's name is represented by three dashes followed by a period. If the author is the translator or editor of a volume, the three dashes are followed by a comma, then a space, then the appropriate abbreviation (trans. or ed.), then (one space after the period) the title.

The Bible:

<u>The HarperCollins Study Bible</u>. Wayne A. Meeks, Gen. ed. New York:

    HarperCollins, 1989.

Note: If using the King James version, do not list the Bible in your "Works Cited"

page, since it is familiar and available. In your essay, cite chapter and verse parenthetically as follows: (Isaiah 52.7-12 or Gen. 19.1-11).

A translated book:

```
Auteur, Robin. Literature and Culture. Trans. Chang Lee. New York:

    Culture Studies Press, 1990.
```

Note that "Trans." can mean "translated by" (just as "ed." can mean "edited by"). It
is also the abbreviation for "translator."

An introduction, foreword, afterword, or other editorial apparatus:

```
Auteur, Robin. Introduction. Literature and Culture. By Chang Lee. New

    York: Epicurean, 1990, vii-x.
```

Use this form if you are specifically referring to the Introduction, Foreword, Afterword, etc. Otherwise, list the work under the name of the book's author. Words such
as *Preface, Introduction, Afterword,* and *Conclusion* are capitalized in the entry but
are neither enclosed within quotation marks nor underlined.

A book review:

```
Auteur, Robin. Rev. of Literature and Culture. Ed. Chang Lee. Critical

    Studies 104 (1991): 1-48.
```

This is a citation for a review of a book entitled *Literature and Culture.* The review,
which does not have a title, was published in a journal entitled *Critical Studies.*

```
Auteur, Robin. "One Writer's View." Rev. of Literature and Culture.

    Ed. Chang Lee. Critical Studies 104 (1991): 1-48.
```

This is a citation for a review which has a title.

```
"One Writer's View." Rev. of Literature and Culture. Ed. Chang Lee.

    Critical Studies 104 (1991): 1-48.
```

This is an anonymous review of *Literature and Culture.* Place it on your "Works
Cited" page under the first word of the review's title; if the review lacks a title, begin
your entry with "Rev. of" and then alphabetize it under the title of the work being
reviewed.

An encyclopedia:

```
Auteur, Robin. "Literature and Culture." Encyclopaedia Britannica. 1984

    ed.
```

This is how you cite a signed article; note that the article is from the 1984 edition
of the *Encyclopaedia.*

"Literature and Culture." <u>Encyclopaedia Britannica</u>. 1984 ed.

This is how you would cite the same article if it were unsigned.

An article in a scholarly journal that numbers its pages consecutively from one issue to the other through the year:

Auteur, Robin. "Literature and Culture." <u>Critical Studies</u> 33 (1992):

   231-59.

Auteur's article appeared in the journal, *Critical Studies*, in 1992; the volume number was 33 and it appeared on pages 231 through 259. Even though each of the four issues of *Critical Studies* published in 1992 has a separate number, you do not need to indicate the issue number since the pages are numbered continuously throughout the year.

An article in a scholarly journal that begins each issue during the year with page one:

Auteur, Robin. "Literature and Culture." <u>Critical Studies</u> 12.2 (1993):

   9-21.

Note that you now must provide the volume number followed by a period and then the issue number, with no spaces in between.

An article in a weekly, biweekly, or monthly publication:

Auteur, Robin. "Literature and Culture." <u>Critical Studies</u> 30 Mar. 1945:

   1-12.

If you are citing from a very well known weekly, such as *Newsweek* or *The New Yorker*, you can omit the volume and issue numbers.

An article in a newspaper:

Auteur, Robin. "Literature and Culture." <u>Critical Studies Times</u> 17 Mar.

   1947, sec. 6: 9+.

Because newspapers often have a number of sections, you should include a section number before the page number so that your reader can find the article easily. Auteur's article begins on page 9 of section 6 and continues on to a later page.

A personal interview:

Lee, Chang. Personal interview. 26 Apr. 1974.

Auteur, Robin. Telephone interview. 14 Feb. 1983.

Note that the interviews are *with* Chang Lee and Robin Auteur, not *by* Chang Lee or Robin Auteur.

A lecture:

Lee, Chang. "Literature and Culture." University of Wisconsin-

Milwaukee. 31 Oct. 1995.

A television or radio program:

Literature and Culture. Public Television, Charlotte, N.C. 3 Feb. 1996.

A film or videotape:

Literature and Culture. Dir. Chang Lee. MGM, 1948.

A recording:

Auteur, Robin. "Literature and Culture." Chang Lee Reads Personal

Favorites from Around the World. Harmony, HAR 4853C, 1988.

A performance:

Literature. By Chang Lee. Dir. Robin Auteur. Urban Theatre of the

Arts, Urban, Wisconsin. 4 July 1912.

A file from the World Wide Web:

Auteur, Robin. "Literature and Culture." Critical Studies.

http://www.litcult.wor.vvv.ecp.tlc/text/rmudts/ittip.html (18 May

1995).

Note that the citation includes the author's name (if available), the name of the article, the name (underlined) of the entire text from which the article was taken (if available), and the URL (Uniform Resource Locator), followed immediately by the date that you visited the site.

At this point, you may have decided that you have had enough of citations. If the particular form you are looking for does not appear in this list, consult the *MLA Handbook for Writers of Research Papers* or some other more extensive reference book. The basic principle of citation is that you should be absolutely clear about essential research information in the most concise format possible.

FINAL WORDS

Much more could be said about writing essays about literature and culture, but perhaps the most important goal for such essays is that they provide a sense of satisfaction to both the writer and the reader. Writing an essay invites analysis, research, discovery, and satisfaction. The exciting and provocative reading selections in this book create many possible topics to engage writers on the voyage ahead.

CREDITS

FORUM 23.2 (Summer 1989). Reprinted by permission of the author.
"Can the United States Assimilate the Wave of New Immigrants?" by Robert Hopkins, *Conservative Review*, April 1990.
"About Men: Whites Without Money" by Lloyd Van Brunt, 3/27/94. Copyright © 1994 The New York Times.
Slave Auction Advertisement. Public Domain.

Photo Credits

Lucille Ball and Desi Arnaz: Reprinted by permission of the Neal Peters Collection.
Norman Rockwell, "The Problem We All Live With." Reprinted by permission of the Norman Rockwell Family Trust. Copyright © 1964 the Norman Rockwell Family Trust.
Cigar Store Indian. Reprinted by permission of Archive Photos, New York.
Sheet Music Cover—"The Phrenologist Coon." Bert Williams, Ernest Hogan, Will Accool. Reprinted with permission of the Brown University Library.
Photo of "Aunt Jemima." Reprinted by permission of the Corbis Collection.
Adrian Wong Shue, "Tropical Daydream." Gouache and Acrylic on Natsume Paper 38½ x 25¼, 1999. Reprinted by permission of Adrian Wong Shue.
Ralph Fasanella, "Subway Riders." Courtesy A.C.A. Galleries, New York City.
Charles Moore photo, 2 White Men Attack 2 Black Women/Alabama. Courtesy of Black Star, New York City.

INDEX OF AUTHORS AND TITLES